New Developments in Parsing Technology

T0225984

Text, Speech and Language Technology

VOLUME 23

The titles published in this series are listed on www.wkap.nl/prod/s/TLTB.

New Developments in Parsing Technology

Edited by

Harry Bunt
Tilburg University,
Tilburg, The Netherlands

John Carroll
University of Sussex,
Brighton, United Kingdom

and

Giorgio Satta
University of Padua,
Padua, Italy

KLUWER ACADEMIC PUBLISHERS
DORDRECHT / BOSTON / LONDON

A C.I.P. Catalogue record for this book is available from the Library of Congress.

ISBN 1-4020-2294-8 (PB)
ISBN 1-4020-2293-X (HB)
ISBN 1-4020-2295-6 (e-book)

Published by Kluwer Academic Publishers,
P.O. Box 17, 3300 AA Dordrecht, The Netherlands.

Sold and distributed in North, Central and South America
by Kluwer Academic Publishers,
101 Philip Drive, Norwell, MA 02061, U.S.A.

In all other countries, sold and distributed
by Kluwer Academic Publishers,
P.O. Box 322, 3300 AH Dordrecht, The Netherlands.

Printed on acid-free paper

Printed in the Netherlands

Contents

Preface   xi

1
Developments in Parsing Technology: From Theory to Application   1
Harry Bunt, John Carroll and *Giorgio Satta*
    1   Introduction   1
    2   About this book   6

2
Parameter Estimation for Statistical Parsing Models: Theory and Practice   19
    of Distribution-Free Methods
Michael Collins
    1   Introduction   19
    2   Linear Models   20
    3   Probabilistic Context-Free Grammars   23
    4   Statistical Learning Theory   26
    5   Convergence Bounds for Finite Sets of Hypotheses   29
    6   Convergence Bounds for Hyperplane Classifiers   34
    7   Application of Margin Analysis to Parsing   37
    8   Algorithms   39
    9   Discussion   46
    10   Conclusions   49

3
High Precision Extraction of Grammatical Relations   57
John Carroll and *Ted Briscoe*
    1   Introduction   57
    2   The Analysis System   59
    3   Empirical Results   61
    4   Conclusions and Further Work   68

4
Automated Extraction of TAGs from the Penn Treebank   73
John Chen and *K. Vijay Shanker*
    1   Introduction   73
    2   Tree Extraction Procedure   74

3	Evaluation	80
4	Extended Extracted Grammars	84
5	Related Work	86
6	Conclusions	87

5
Computing the Most Probable Parse for a Discontinuous Phrase-Structure
Grammar   91
Oliver Plaehn

1	Introduction	91
2	Discontinuous Phrase-Structure Grammar	92
3	The Parsing Algorithm	95
4	Computing the Most Probable Parse	98
5	Experiments	101
6	Conclusion and Future Work	103

6
A Neural Network Parser that Handles Sparse Data   107
James Henderson

1	Introduction	107
2	Simple Synchrony Networks	108
3	A Probabilistic Parser for SSNs	110
4	Estimating the Probabilities with a Simple Synchrony Network	113
5	Generalizing from Sparse Data	117
6	Conclusion	123

7
An Efficient LR Parser Generator for Tree-Adjoining Grammars   125
Carlos A. Prolo

1	Introduction	125
2	TAGS	127
3	On Some Degenerate LR Models for TAGS	129
4	Proposed Algorithm	133
5	Implementation	141
6	Example	146
7	Some Properties Of the Algorithms	146
8	Evaluation	151
9	Conclusions	151

8
Relating Tabular Parsing Algorithms for LIG and TAG   157
Miguel A. Alonso, Éric de la Clergerie, Víctor J. Díaz and *Manuel Vilares*

1	Introduction	158
2	Tree-Adjoining Grammars	158
3	Linear Indexed Grammars	160
4	Bottom-up Parsing Algorithms	162

5	Earley-like Parsing Algorithms	166
6	Earley-like Parsing Algorithms Preserving the Correct Prefix Property	171
7	Bidirectional Parsing	178
8	Specialized TAG parsers	180
9	Conclusion	182

9

Improved Left-Corner Chart Parsing for Large Context-Free Grammars   185
Robert C. Moore

1	Introduction	185
2	Evaluating Parsing Algorithms	186
3	Terminology and Notation	187
4	Test Grammars	187
5	Left-Corner Parsing Algorithms and Refinements	188
6	Grammar Transformations	193
7	Extracting Parses from the Chart	196
8	Comparison to Other Algorithms	197
9	Conclusions	199

10

On Two Classes of Feature Paths in Large-Scale Unification Grammars   203
Liviu Ciortuz

1	Introduction	203
2	Compiling the Quick Check Filter	205
3	Generalised Rule Reduction	215
4	Conclusion	224

11

A Context-Free Superset Approximation of Unification-Based Grammars   229
Bernd Kiefer and Hans-Ulrich Krieger

1	Introduction	229
2	Basic Inventory	231
3	Approximation as Fixpoint Construction	232
4	The Basic Algorithm	233
5	Implementation Issues and Optimizations	235
7	Revisiting the Fixpoint Construction	240
7	Three Grammars	241
8	Disambiguation of UBGs via Probabilistic Approximations	247

12

A Recognizer for Minimalist Languages   251
Henk Harkema

1	Introduction	251
2	Minimalist Grammars	252
3	Specification of the Recognizer	256

	4	Correctness	260
	5	Complexity Results	264
	6	Conclusions and Future Work	265

13
Range Concatenation Grammars 269
Pierre Boullier
	1	Introduction	269
	2	Positive Range Concatenation Grammars	270
	3	Negative Range Concatenation Grammars	276
	4	A Parsing Algorithm for RCGs	281
	5	Closure Properties and Modularity	284
	6	Conclusion	286

14
Grammar Induction by MDL-Based Distributional Classification 291
Yikun Guo, Fuliang Weng and *Lide Wu*
	1	Introduction	292
	2	Grammar Induction with the MDL Principle	293
	3	Induction Strategies	295
	4	MDL Induction by Dynamic Distributional Classification (DCC)	299
	5	Comparison and Conclusion	303
		Appendix	305

15
Optimal Ambiguity Packing in Context-Free Parsers with Interleaved Unification 307
Alon Lavie and *Carolyn Penstein Rosé*
	1	Introduction	307
	2	Ambiguity Packing in Context Free Parsing	309
	3	The Rule Prioritization Heuristic	311
	4	Empirical Evaluations and Discussion	315
	5	Conclusions and Future Directions	319

16
Robust Data Oriented Spoken Language Understanding 323
Khalil Sima'an
	1	Introduction	323
	2	Brief Overview of OVIS	324
	3	DOP vs. Tree-Gram	326
	4	Application to the OVIS Domain	332
	5	Conclusions	335

17
SOUP: A Parser for Real-World Spontaneous Speech 339
Marsal Gavaldà
| | 1 | Introduction | 339 |

2	Grammar Representation	340
3	Sketch of the Parsing Algorithm	341
4	Performance	343
5	Key Features	345
6	Conclusion	349

18
Parsing and Hypergraphs   351
Dan Klein and *Christopher D. Manning*

1	Introduction	351
2	Hypergraphs and Parsing	352
3	Viterbi Parsing Algorithm	359
4	Analysis	363
5	Conclusion	368
	Appendix	369

19
Measure for Measure: Towards Increased Component Comparability and   373
Exchange
Stephan Oepen and *Ulrich Callmeier*

1	Competence & Performance Profiling	375
2	Strong Empiricism: A Few Examples	378
3	PET – Synthesizing Current Best Practice	384
4	Quantifying Progress	385
5	Multi-Dimensional Performance Profiling	387
6	Conclusion – Recent Developments	391

Index   397

Preface

This book is based on contributions to two workshops in the series "International Workshop on Parsing Technology". IWPT2000, the 6th workshop in the series, was held in Trento, Italy, in February 2001, and was organized by John Carroll (Programme Chair), Harry Bunt (General Chair) and Alberto Lavelli (Local Chair). The 7th workshop, IWPT2001, took place in Beijing, China, in October 2001, and was organized by Giorgio Satta (Programme Chair), Harry Bunt (General Chair) and Shiwen Yu and Fuliang Weng (Local Co-Chairs). From each of these events the best papers were selected and re-reviewed, and subsequently revised, updated and extended by the authors, resulting in a chapter in this volume. The chapter by Alonso, De la Clergerie, Díaz and Vilares is based on material from two papers: the IWPT2000 paper by Alonso, De la Clergerie, Graña and Vilares, and the IWPT2001 paper by Alonso, Díaz and Vilares. The chapter by Michael Collins corresponds to the paper that he prepared for IWPT2001 as an invited speaker, but which he was unable to present at the workshop, due to travel restrictions relating to the events of September 11, 2001. The introductory chapter of this book was written by the editors in order to relate the individual chapters to recent issues and developments in the field of parsing technology.

We wish to acknowledge the important role of the programme committees of IWPT2000 and IWPT2001 in reviewing submitted papers; these reviews have been the basis for selecting the material published in this book. These committees consisted of Shuo Bai, Bob Berwick, Eric Brill, Harry Bunt, Bob Carpenter, John Carroll, Ken Church, Éric De la Clergerie, Mark Johnson, Aravind Joshi, Ron Kaplan, Martin Kay, Sadao Kurohashi, Bernard Lang, Alon Lavie, Yuji Matsumoto, Paola Merlo, Mark-Jan Nederhof, Anton Nijholt, Giorgio Satta, Christer Samuelsson, Satoshi Sekine, Virach Sornlertlamvanich, Mark Steedman, Oliviero Stock, Hozumi Tanaka, Masaru Tomita, Hans Uszkoreit, K. Vijay-Shanker, David Weir, Mats Wirén, Dekai Wu and Tiejun Zhao.

THE EDITORS

Chapter 1

DEVELOPMENTS IN PARSING TECHNOLOGY: FROM THEORY TO APPLICATION

Harry Bunt

Computational Linguistics and Artificial Intelligence, Tilburg University
PO Box 90153, 5000 LE Tilburg, The Netherlands
bunt@uvt.nl

John Carroll

Cognitive and Computing Sciences, University of Sussex
Falmer, Brighton BN1 9QH, UK
johnca@cogs.susx.ac.uk

Giorgio Satta

Department of Information Engineering, University of Padua
Via Gradenigo 6/A, 35131 Padua, Italy
satta@dei.unipd.it

1.   Introduction

Parsing can be defined as the decomposition of complex structures into their constituent parts, and parsing technology as the methods, the tools and the software to parse automatically. In this book, the complex structures under consideration are natural language sentences and constituent parts are the building blocks in a syntactic analysis, from clauses and phrases down to words and morphemes. Apart from when we speak of 'parsing technology' and 'parsing algorithm', the term 'parsing' in this book refers to the automatic parsing of natural language sentences.

Interest in parsing goes back to the first attempts to apply computers to natural language. This is not a coincidence: virtually any application of computers to linguistic material requires some process of decomposing the sentences in

H. Bunt et al. (eds.), New Technologies in Parsing Technology, 1-18.

the material into relevant parts. Machine translation, one of the oldest forms of natural language processing, has been and continues to be an area of inspiration and application of parsing technology. The earliest attempts at machine translation, in the 1950s and early '60s, capitalized on the use of large bilingual dictionaries where entries in the source language would give one or several equivalents in the target language, and processing consisted primarily of applying some rules for producing correct word order in the output; no significant results in parsing technology were obtained as part of this enterprise. This period ended with the notorious ALPAC report (ALPAC, 1966; see also Hutchins, 1986) which concluded that there was no immediate prospect of usable forms of machine translation. This marked the beginning of a dark period in computational linguistics.

In this period computer scientists put much effort into the development of new, higher-level programming languages (such as ALGOL68 and Pascal), and advanced parsing techniques were developed for the compilers and interpreters of these languages (see e.g. Aho and Ullman, 1972; 1977; Hopcroft and Ullman, 1979). Programming languages are in crucial ways simpler than natural languages, in particular in being syntactically unambiguous, and the first parsing techniques that were developed capitalized on these restrictions, leading to parsing algorithms that were not applicable to natural languages. For parsing natural language, the scene changed significantly when algorithms were developed for parsing general context-free languages, in particular the Earley algorithm (Earley, 1970) and other algorithms such as those described by Kasami (1965), Younger (1967), Lang (1974) and Graham *et al.* (1980). Natural languages were widely assumed by theoretical linguists to have a context-free backbone, and perhaps even to be describable entirely by context-free grammars (see Pullum and Gazdar, 1982; Pullum, 1984), so these algorithms were of great interest for natural language parsing. Parsing technology thus became of growing interest to linguists, and was no longer the domain of computer scientists only. (See Pullum, 1983 for a discussion of the implications for natural language processing of various claims and results concerning the formal properties of natural language.) With the introduction of chart parsing (Kay, 1973), various ways of dealing with the large amount of ambiguity inherent in grammars of natural language were made explicit, through a flexible control structure (the agenda), and different modes of invoking rules (bottom-up or top-down) or directions of scanning the input string (left-to-right or right-to-left).

Since then, although it has become clear that natural languages cannot be described in a satisfactory manner by context-free grammars (Huybregts, 1985; Shieber, 1985), context-free grammar parsing remains an important topic. There are two reasons for this. Firstly, more powerful grammar formalisms that are still based on phrase-structure rules can use versions of CFG parsing algorithms generalised such that the test for atomic category equality is replaced by, for instance, feature structure unification and subsumption operations (Alshawi, 1992; Oepen and Carroll, 2000). Secondly, assuming that we have a CFG that is more general than a particular grammatical description, for instance one in HPSG, then the CFG can be used as a cheap filter with worst-case performance $O(n^3)$, followed by the HPSG deterministically replaying and checking the CFG derivations. Kasper *et al.* (1996) describe such an approach for word graph parsing, employing only the context-free backbone of the original HPSG grammar. More generally, the approximation of languages by means of context-free grammars and other mathematically simple grammars, like regular grammars, remains important as it widens the application of efficient parsing algorithms (see e.g. Nederhof, 2000 and Moore, this volume).

In the 1980s, another wave of research in machine translation occurred, and inspired new work on natural language parsing. A highlight of this period was Tomita's GLR parsing algorithm, which generalized the LR parsing technique that had been developed for programming languages (Knuth, 1965; Aho and Ullman, 1972; Aho and Johnson, 1974) to make it applicable to natural language. Tomita introduced devices for dealing with syntactic ambiguity, his 'packed forest' technique for representing alternative partial parses being perhaps the most important innovation. Tomita's work was strongly inspired by practical applications, notably in machine translation, and was followed by further development of GLR-based techniques for use in speech-based systems and other applications (Rosé and Lavie, 2001; Langley *et al.*, 2002).

In the course of the 1980s, language technology started to broaden its reach, and new types of applications have been developing ever since. Areas of application include the following:

- *information and document retrieval,* where the recognition and parsing of noun phrases is of special relevance (Evans *et al.*, 1992; Grefenstette, 1993); more recently also the identification of specific types of information in web documents (see e.g. Maedche and Staab, 2001; Chakrabarti, 2002; Fensel *et al.*, 2002);

- *question answering,* where, in addition to 'classical' systems that rely on deep parsing and semantic interpretation, statistically-based approaches have been developed for using the web to find answers to queries by means of partial parsing and matching, possibly with the help of machine learning techniques. See e.g. Buchholz and Daelemans (2001); Buchholz (2002);

- *terminology extraction,* for example in support of cross-lingual information retrieval, applying either shallow parsing, as in the LIQUID project (Valderrábanos *et al.*, 2002) or full parsing, as used by Arppe (1995) and by Justeson and Katz (1995). See also Hull and Grefenstette (1996), and Jacquemin and Bourigault (2003);

- *lexicon induction,* in which lexical information such as collocations (Lin, 1999; Pearce, 2001) and the argument structures of predicates (Briscoe and Carroll, 1997; McCarthy, 2000) is acquired automatically from corpora;

- *text summarization,* where parsing is applied not only at the sentence level but also at discourse level. Marcu (1998) has shown that discourse-based summarization yields superior performance compared to other approaches; see also Teufel and Moens (2002) and Radev *et al.* (2002). Knight and Marcu (2000) train a system to compress the syntactic parse tree of a sentence in order to produce a shorter but grammatical version of the sentence, a technique that can perhaps be extended to compress several sentences into one;

- *knowledge and information extraction,* often using shallow parsing for the analysis of (non-recursive) NPs and verbal groups (e.g. Grishman, 1995; 1997; Aone *et al.*, 1998), but sometimes using full parsing (coupled with semantic analysis), as for example in the FACILE project (see Ciravegna and Lavelli, 1999), where full parsing is combined with the construction of Quasi-Logical Forms to extract stock market information from Italian, English, and Russian documents, or as in the KXDC project (Crouch *et al.*, 2002), that uses deep parsing and semantic interpretation for the detection of contradictions and redundancies in a large collection of documents containing photocopier repair tips;

- *high-accuracy OCR,* where morphological and syntactic parsing may be used to correct recognition errors. See Perez-Cortez *et al.* (2000) for a description of a stochastic approach to error correction for post-processing optical character recognition, both at word and sentence level. Some other approaches are described by Hisamatsu *et al.* (1995);

- *speech recognition,* often at the service of speech understanding (see below), where natural language syntactic structure is exploited for developing powerful language models for recognizing the words in spoken utterances (see e.g. Chelba and Jelinek, 1998; Charniak, 2001; Roark, 2001);

- *speech understanding,* typically used for interactive speech-based systems and thus requiring speech processing, robustness, and the ability to deal with speech disfluencies. Examples of parsers that were designed specifically for dealing with speech input include Ward's PHOENIX parser (Ward, 1991), the LCFlex parser (Rosé and Lavie, 2001), and the SOUP parser of the JANUS system (Gavaldà, this volume). It may be noted that speech parsing often involves the application of parsing techniques not to strings but to lattices or graphs of alternative word hypotheses; see e.g. Tomita (1986) and Amtrup (2000);

- *bilingual text alignment,* which supports a wide range of multilingual applications, such as bilingual lexicography (Langlais *et al.*, 1998; Klavans and Tzoukermann, 1995), cross-language information retrieval (Grefenstette, 1998; Hull and Grefenstette, 1996; Nie *et al.*, 1998), machine translation (Gildea, 2003; Och *et al.*, 1999), automatic translation verification (Macklovitch and Hannan, 1996), bilingual corpus construction (Gale and Church, 1991), and bilingual terminology research (Dagan *et al.*, 1993);

- *machine translation,* when interlingua- or transfer-based, relies heavily on deep parsing applied to the input sentences from the source language (e.g. Alshawi *et al.*, 1992). Stochastically-based machine translation approaches have used shallow parsing; although in general they produce relatively non-fluent translations they have the advantage of being robust to unexpected input (see e.g. Sawaf *et al.*, 2000; Vogel *et al.*, 2000; Yamada and Knight, 2001). The Verbmobil project uses a combination of transfer-based and stochastically-based translation, with deep and shallow processing (Wahlster, 2000a);

- *speech translation,* which is essentially the combination of speech recognition and machine translation, adding to the problems of translating text those of uncertain and disfluent input, plus the requirements of speed inherent in applications of on-line speech translation. See e.g. Amtrup (1999), and papers from projects at ATR in Japan (Takezawa *et al.*, 1998) and from the Verbmobil project (Wahlster, 2000b).

It may be noted that the applications of language processing mentioned above often involve either deep parsing in combination with semantic analysis, or 'shallow' or 'partial' parsing (also called 'chunking') combined with statistical and/or machine learning techniques. Very often, shallow techniques improve the robustness of the language processing, while 'deep' techniques are brittle but provide results of superior quality if they succeed. It might therefore be advantageous to combine the two approaches, using deep techniques wherever possible (and feasible in terms of processing time) and shallow techniques as a fall-back option to ensure robustness. The Verbmobil system has pioneered this approach not just as a system architecture feature, but in a flexible manner for within-sentence processing, using the results of several competing parsers and interpretation modules and allowing different parts of a sentence to be parsed and interpreted more or less 'deeply'. See Wahlster (2000a).

The chapters in this book form a collection of contributions that ranges from the theoretical to the purely empirical. This book is more about parsing technology than about its applications, although practical application or aspects of applicability, such as demands of robustness and speed, often motivate the technological developments described in these chapters.

2.   About this book

The first four chapters in this book are concerned with statistical parsing. In chapter 2, *Parameter Estimation for Statistical Parsing Models: Theory and Practice of Distribution-Free Methods*, Michael Collins addresses the fundamental problem in statistical parsing of choosing criteria and algorithms to estimate the parameters of a model. He introduces a framework including some fixed (but unknown) distribution over sentence/parse-tree pairs and some (possibly very simple) loss function, where the loss is 0 if the proposed parse is identical to the correct parse, and 1 otherwise. Under these assumptions, the quality of a parser is its expected loss on previously unseen test examples. The goal of learning is to use the training data as evidence for choosing a function with small expected loss. In the analysis of learning algorithms, a central idea is that of the margins on examples in training data. Collins describes theoretical bounds which motivate approaches that attempt to classify a large proportion of examples in training with a large margin, and describes several algorithms which can be used to achieve this goal for the parsing problem.

In chapter 3, *High-Precision Extraction of Grammatical Relations*, John Carroll and Ted Briscoe describe a parsing system that uses a manually constructed wide-coverage grammar of English to produce syntactic analyses in the form of sets of grammatical relations. They generalize this system to return statistically weighted relations from all possible analyses, and show that setting a probability threshold on the relations returned leads to an increase in precision from 75% to over 90% on a test corpus of naturally occurring text. This technique seems not only well suited for probabilistic parsing, but could benefit any parsing system, not necessarily statistical, that can represent ambiguity and return partial analyses.

In chapter 4, *Automated Extraction of TAGs from the Penn Treebank*, John Chen and K. Vijay-Shanker present new directions in both the extraction of a Lexicalized Tree Adjoining Grammar (LTAG) from a treebank, and in its application to statistical parsing models. Statistical parsing using LTAG is still relatively unexplored, partly due to the absence of large corpora that are accurately bracketed in terms of a perspicuous yet broad coverage LTAG. Chen and Vijay-Shanker's work alleviates this difficulty. They explore strategies for extracting LTAGs from the Penn Treebank that lead to improved compactness, coverage, and supertagging accuracy.

Oliver Plaehn presents in chapter 5, *Computing the Most Probable Parse for a Discontinuous Phrase Structure Grammar,* a probabilistic extension of Discontinuous Phrase Structure Grammar (DPSG) and an agenda-based chart parser that is capable of computing the most probable parse for a given input sentence for probabilistic versions of both DPSG and Context-Free Grammar. DPSG (Bunt 1991; 1996) is a natural and straightforward extension of CFG, designed to deal with discontinuous constituents by allowing trees with crossing branches. It is therefore to be expected that probabilistic approaches to CFG parsing can similarly be extended to deal with crossing branches. Experiments using the NEGRA corpus for Plaehn's PDPSG parser confirms this: although parsing with discontinuous trees is computationally much harder than context-free parsing, computing the most probable parse using probabilistic DPSG has the same accuracy as with probabilistic CFG. Plaehn also hints at directions for more efficient ways of parsing with discontinuous constituents.

The next six chapters are concerned with the development of new or improved parsing techniques for various extensions and variants of Context-Free Grammar, including Tree-Adjoining Grammar and Head-driven Phrase Structure Grammar. In many domains, neural networks are an effective alternative to statistical methods. James Henderson has identified a suitable neural network architecture for natural language parsing, called Simple Synchrony Networks (SSNs), which he discusses in chapter 6, *A Neural Network Parser that Handles Sparse Data.* In this chapter, Henderson presents performance results of his SSN parser, including comparisons on the same dataset with standard statistical parsing methods. He demonstrates an advantage of the SSN parser over PCFG parsers in the handling of sparse data and shows that the neural network parser performs best in terms of precision and recall. The strength of the SSN-based approach seems to be due to its ability to generalize across constituents as well as across sequence positions, together with the ability of neural networks in general to learn what input features are important as well as what they imply about the output. The resulting robustness makes SSNs appropriate for a wide range of parsing applications, particularly when a small amount of data is available or there is a large amount of variability in the output.

Carlos Prolo presents a variant of LR parsing applied to TAGs, in his chapter *An Efficient LR Parser Generator for Tree-Adjoining Grammars.* It has been claimed that LR parsing is inadequate for use with reasonably sized TAGs, since the size of the generated table becomes unmanageable (Nederhof, 1998), but Prolo proposes a new version of the algorithm that, by maintaining the degree of prediction while deferring over-eager reduction operations, dramatically reduces both the average number of conflicts per state and the size of the table (by a factor of about 75).

In chapter 8, *Relating Tabular Parsing Algorithms for LIG and TAG,* Miguel Alonso, Éric de la Clergerie, Victor Díaz and Manuel Villares define several parsing algorithms for Tree-Adjoining Grammars on the basis of their equivalent parsers for Linear Indexed Grammars (LIGs). TAG and LIG grammars are both extensions of Context Free Grammars (CFG), but instead of using trees rather than productions as the primary means of representing structure, LIG grammars associate a list of indices with each non-terminal symbol, with the restriction that the index list of the left hand side non-terminal of each production is inherited by exactly one right hand side non-terminal, while the other lists must have a bounded size. Although both TAGs and LIGs generate the class of Tree Adjoining Languages, LIG is more generic than TAG, with an easy encoding of TAG as LIG. Taking advantage of this property, and providing a method for translating a TAG into a LIG, this chapter also explores why some practical optimizations for TAG parsing cannot be applied to LIG, such as the *weak tabular interpretation* presented by de la Clergerie (2001).

In chapter 9, *Improved Left-corner Chart Parsing for Large Context-free Grammars,* Robert Moore presents an improved left-corner (LC) chart parser for large context-free grammars (for instance, a grammar with over 24,000 rules, compiled from a task-specific unification grammar for use as a speech recognition language model). He introduces improvements that result in significant speed-ups, compared to previously-known variants of LC parsing. Specifically, he shows that: (1) LC chart parsing with both a top-down left-corner check on the mother of a proposed incomplete edge and a bottom-up left-corner check on the symbol immediately to the right of the dot in the proposed incomplete edge is substantially faster if the bottom-up check is performed first; and (2) bottom-up prefix merging is a good match to LC chart parsing based on left-corner filtering, and outperforms left factoring combined with LC chart parsing. Moore compares his new method to several other major parsing approaches, and finds that his improved left-corner parser outperforms each of these other approaches across a range of grammars.

Liviu Ciortuz in his chapter *On Two Classes of Feature Paths in Large-scale Unification Grammars* studies two related techniques for speeding up parsing with large-scale typed unification grammars. Both techniques take advantage of the properties of two particular classes of feature paths. The Quick Check technique is concerned with the paths that most often lead to unification failure, whereas the Generalised Reduction technique takes advantage of paths that only seldom contribute to unification failure. Both sets of paths are obtained empirically by parsing a training corpus. Ciortuz reports on experiments using the two techniques and their combination, using a compilation-based parsing system on the HPSG grammar of English from the LinGO project (Flickinger *et al.*, 2000) showing an improvement in parsing speed of up to 56%.

In the chapter entitled *A Context-free Approximation of Head-Driven Phrase Structure Grammar*, Bernd Kiefer and Hans-Ulrich Krieger present a context-free approximation of unification-based grammars, such as HPSG and PATR-II. The theoretical underpinning of this approximation is established through a fixpoint construction over a certain monotonic function. The basic idea is to generalize first from the set of lexical entries, the resulting structures forming equivalence classes; the abstraction is specified by means of a 'lexicon restrictor' (Shieber, 1985). The grammar rules are then instantiated using the abstracted entries, resulting in derivation trees of depth one. A 'rule restrictor' is then applied to each resulting feature structure, removing all information contained only in the daughters of the rule. The restricted feature structures serve as a basis for the next instantiation step, which gives a feature structure encoding a derivation, to which the rule restrictor is again applied. The iteration continues until a fixpoint is reached. In parallel, annotated context-free rules are generated, leading to a set of CF productions. Kiefer and Krieger's implementation is parameterized to allow specifying a finite iteration depth, different restrictors, or different complexities of annotations of the CF rules. Methods are also presented for speeding up the approximation process and limiting the size of the resulting CF grammar. Applied to the English Verbmobil grammar, their method gives promising results.

The next three chapters are rather more theoretical in nature. Chapter 12, *A Recognizer for Minimalist Grammars* by Hans Harkema, is the only contribution in this book that draws strongly on linguistic theory. Harkema presents a recognizer for minimalist grammars, which are a rigorous formalization of the sort of grammars proposed in the framework of Chomsky's Minimalist Program (Chomsky, 1995). Formally, minimalist grammars are weakly equivalent to multiple context-free grammars (Seki *et al.*, 1991). One notable property of minimalist grammars is that they allow constituents to move during a derivation, thus creating discontinuous constituents (c.f. Bunt and van Horck, 1996). Harkema proves the completeness and soundness of the bottom-up recognizer that he describes, and shows that its time complexity is polynomial in the length of the input string.

In chapter 13, *Range Concatenation Grammars*, Pierre Boullier presents a new grammar formalism with a number of attractive features, particularly with respect to closure and generative power. For example, RCGs are more powerful formally than linear context-free rewriting systems, though this power is not at the cost of efficiency, since parsing is still polynomial time. Also, languages described by RCGs are closed both under intersection and complementation; these closure properties may lead to new ways of organizing linguistic processing. Boullier presents a parsing algorithm for RCGs which is the basis of a prototype implementation.

Yikun Guo, Fuliang Weng and Lide Wu introduce in their chapter *Grammar Induction by MDL-based Distributional Classification* a new learning algorithm, based on the Minimal Description Length principle, which can automatically induce high-quality parsing-oriented grammar rules from a tagged corpus without any structural annotation. This is aimed at addressing the risk of grammars, such as those extracted from manually annotated corpora like the Penn Treebank, being too tailored to the training data and not able to reliably process sentences from other domains. This ability is important for building NLP applications such as internet-based question answering and spoken dialogue systems. Preliminary experimental results show that the induction curve obtained is very close to its theoretical upper bound, and outperforms traditional MDL-based grammar induction.

Chapters 15–17 are concerned with parsers and parsing techniques motivated by the processing of spoken language. The first of these, by Alon Lavie and Carolyn Penstein Rosé, is concerned with the optimization of ambiguity packing for enhancing parser efficiency. In the case of parsing with a unification grammar, when rule application is interleaved with feature structure unification the propagation of feature values imposes difficulties for the parser to effectively perform ambiguity packing. Lavie and Rosé demonstrate that smart heuristics for prioritizing the execution order of grammar rules and parsing actions can lead to a high level of ambiguity packing that is provably optimal. They present empirical evaluations that demonstrate the effectiveness of this technique for several versions of both Lavie's GLR∗ parser (Lavie, 1996) and the LCFlex parser (Rosé and Lavie, 2001), a left-corner chart parser.

In chapter 16, *Robust Data-Oriented Parsing of Speech Utterances*, Khalil Sima'an addresses the issue of the robustness of the Data-Oriented Parsing (DOP) model within a Dutch speech-based dialogue system. He presents an extension of the DOP model into a head-driven variant, which allows Markovian generation of parse trees. The extension, called the Tree-gram model, generalizes the DOP model by assigning non-zero probability values to some utterances for which the DOP model assigns zero probability. The Tree-gram model is shown to improve over the original DOP model for two tasks: the task-based understanding of speech utterances, and the extraction of semantic concepts for word lattices output by a speech recognizer.

In chapter 17, Marsal Gavaldà describes the SOUP parser, a stochastic, chart-based, top-down parser especially engineered for real-time analysis of spoken language with large, multi-domain semantic grammars. The design of SOUP is inspired by the PHOENIX parser (Ward, 1991), and incorporates a variety of techniques in order to achieve the flexibility and robustness needed for the analysis of natural speech. Flexibility is provided by the lightweight formalism it supports (context-free grammars encoded as probabilistic recursive transition networks), which allows for dynamic modification of the grammar at runtime, and high speed. Robustness is achieved by the ability to find multiple parse trees and to skip words at any point, recovering in a graceful manner not only from false starts, hesitations, and other speech disfluencies, but also from insertions unforeseen in the grammar. Given its efficiency, robustness and support for emerging industry standards such as JSAPI, SOUP has the potential to become widely used in speech applications.

The final two chapters in this book are concerned with mathematical and engineering aspects of parsing technology. In the chapter *Parsing and Hypergraphs*, Dan Klein and Chris Manning present a new view on parsing, based on the observation that there is intuitively very little difference between (a) combining subtrees to form a tree; (b) combining hypotheses to form a conclusion; and (c) visiting all nodes of an arc in a directed hypergraph before traversing to a head node. The similarity of (a) and (b) underlies the view of parsing as deduction; Klein and Manning show that the similarity of (a) and (c) can be used to develop a view of parsing as graph traversal, which naturally covers both symbolic and probabilistic parsing. They illustrate this by using an extension of Dijkstra's algorithm for hypergraph traversal to construct an agenda-based probabilistic chart parser which can handle arbitrary PCFG grammars and can work with a variety of word and rule induction strategies, while maintaining cubic time complexity.

In the chapter 19, *Measure for Measure: Parser Cross-Fertilization*, Stephan Oepen and Ulrich Callmeier discuss impressive improvements that have been made in efficient processing of large HPSG-based grammars through the exchange of representational and algorithmic techniques, analytical insights, and software between a number of research groups worldwide. As a result of this cooperation, HPSG-based systems now exist that can process medium-complexity sentences in English and German in average parse times comparable to human reading time. In order to support collaborative grammar and system development and improvement, Oepen and Callmeier have developed an approach to grammar and system engineering that they call 'competence & performance profiling', following the profiling metaphor from software engineering. This approach enables grammar and parser developers to maintain an accurate record of system evolution, to identify grammar and system deficiencies quickly, and to compare to earlier versions or between different systems. They apply this approach to a detailed analysis of what was achieved over several years of collaborative development of HPSG-based grammars and systems.

References

Aho, A. and S.C. Johnson (1974). LR parsing. *Computing Surveys*, 6(2):99–124.

Aho, A. and J. Ullman (1972). *The Theory of Parsing, Translation and Compiling*. Englewood Cliffs, NJ: Prentice-Hall.

Aho, A. and J. Ullman (1977). *Principles of Compiler Design*. Reading, MA: Addison-Wesley.

ALPAC (1966). *Languages and Machines: Computers in Translation and Linguistics. A Report by the Automatic Language Processing Advisory Committee*. Washington, DC: National Academy of Sciences, National Research Council.

Alshawi, H. (ed.) (1992). *The Core Language Engine*. Cambridge, MA: MIT Press.

Alshawi, H., D. Carter, B. Gambäck, and M. Rayner (1992). Swedish-English QLF translation. In H. Alshawi (ed.), *The Core Language Engine*, pages 277–309. Cambridge, MA: MIT Press.

Amtrup, J. (1999). *Incremental Speech Translation. Lecture Notes in Computer Science 1735*. Berlin: Springer Verlag.

Amtrup, J. (2000). Hypergraph unification-based parsing for incremental speech processing. In *Proceedings of the Sixth International Workshop on Parsing Technologies (IWPT)*, pages 291–292, Trento, Italy.

Aone, C., L. Halverson, T. Hampton, and M. Ramos-Santacruz (1998). SRA: description of the IE^2 system used for MUC-7. In *Proceedings of the Seventh Message Understanding Conference MUC-7*, Menlo Park, CA: Morgan Kaufman.

Arppe, A. (1995). Term extraction from unrestricted text. Paper presented at the *10th Nordic Conference on Computational Linguistics*, Helsinki, Finland. `http://www.lingsoft.fi/doc/nptool/term-extraction.html`.

Briscoe, E. and J. Carroll (1997). Automatic extraction of subcategorization from corpora. In *Proceedings of the Fifth ACL Conference on Applied Natural Language Processing*, pages 356–363, Washington, DC.

Buchholz, S. (2002). *Memory-Based Grammatical Relation Finding*. Ph.D. Thesis, Tilburg University, The Netherlands.

Buchholz, S. and W. Daelemans (2001). SHAPAQA: shallow parsing for question answering on the world wide web. In *Proceedings of the EuroConference on Recent Advances in Natural Language Processing (RANLP)*, pages 47–51, Tzigov Chark, Bulgaria.

Bunt, H. (1991). Parsing with discontinuous phrase structure grammar. In M. Tomita (ed.), *Current Issues in Parsing Technology*, pages 49–63. Dordrecht: Kluwer Academic Publishers.

Bunt, H. (1996). Describing and processing discontinuous constituency structure. In H. Bunt and A. van Horck (ed.), *Discontinuous Constituency*, pages 63–83. Berlin: Mouton de Gruyter.

Bunt, H. and A. van Horck (ed.) (1996). *Discontinuous Constituency*. Berlin: Mouton de Gruyter.

Carroll, J. (1994). Relating complexity to practical performance in parsing with wide-coverage unification grammars. In *Proceedings of the 32nd Annual Meeting of the Association for Computational Linguistics*, pages 287–294, Las Cruces, NM.

Chakrabarti, S. (2002). *Mining the Web*. Menlo Park, CA: Morgan Kaufmann.

Charniak, E. (2001). Immediate-head parsing for language modeling. In *Proceedings of the 39th Annual Meeting of the Association for Computational Linguistics*, pages 116–123, Toulouse, France.

Chelba, C. and F. Jelinek (1998). Exploiting syntactic structure for language modeling. In *Proceedings of the 36th Annual Meeting of the ACL and the 19th Conference on Computational Linguistics (COLING-ACL)*, pages 225–231, Montreal, Canada.

Chomsky, N. (1995). *The Minimalist Program*. Cambridge, MA: MIT Press.

Ciravegna, F. and A. Lavelli (1999). Full text parsing using cascading of rules: an information extraction perspective. In *Proceedings of the Ninth Conference of the European Chapter of the ACL*, pages 102–109, Bergen, Norway.

Crouch, R., C. Condoravdi, R. Stolle, T. King, V. de Paiva, J. Everett, and D. Bobrow (2002). Scalability of redundancy detection in focused document collections. In *Proceedings of the First International Conference on Scalable Natural Language Understanding (ScaNaLu)*, Heidelberg, Germany.

Dagan, I., W. Gale, and K. Church (1993). Robust bilingual word alignment for machine aided translation. In *Proceedings of the Workshop on Very large Corpora: Academic and Industrial Perspectives*, pages 1–8, Columbus, OH.

de la Clergerie, E. (2001). Refining tabular parsers for TAGs. In *Proceedings of the Second Meeting of the North American Chapter of the ACL*, pages 167–174, Pittsburgh, PA.

Earley, J. (1970). An efficient context-free parsing algorithm. *Communications of the ACM*, 6:94–102.

Evans, D., R. Lefferts, G. Grefenstette, S. Henderson, W. Hersh, and A. Archbold (1992). CLARIT: TREC design, experiments, and results. In *Proceedings of the First Text Retrieval Conference, NIST Special Publication 500-207*, Gaithersburg, MD: National Institute of Standards and Technology.

Fensel, D., W. Wahlster, H. Lieberman, and J. Hendler (2002). *Spinning the Semantic Web*. Cambridge, MA: MIT Press.

Flickinger, D., A. Copestake, and I. Sag (2000). HPSG analysis of English. In W. Wahlster (ed.), *Verbmobil: Foundations of Speech-to-Speech Translation*, pages 254–263. Berlin: Springer Verlag.

Gale, W. and K. Church (1991). A program for aligning sentences in bilingual corpora. In *Proceedings of the 29th Annual Meeting of the Association for Computational Linguistics*, pages 177–184, Berkeley, CA.

Gavaldà, M. (2003) SOUP: A parser for real-world spontaneous speech. *This volume.*

Gildea, D. (2003). Loosely Tree-Based Alignment for Machine Translation. In *Proceedings of the 41th Annual Meeting of the Association for Computational Linguistics (ACL2003)*, pages 291–292, Sapporo, Japan.

Graham, S.L., M.A. Harrison and W.L. Ruzzo (1980). An Improved Context-free Recognizer. *ACM Transactions on Programming Languages and Systems*, 2(3):415–462.

Grefenstette, G. (1993). Evaluation techniques for automatic semantic extraction. Comparing syntactic and window based approaches. In *Proceedings of the ACL/SIGLEX Workshop on Acquisition of Lexical Knowledge from Text*, Columbus, OH.

Grefenstette, G. (1998). *Cross-language Information Retrieval.* Boston: Kluwer Academic Publishers.

Grishman, R. (1995). The NYU system for MUC-6 or where's the syntax?. In *Proceedings of the Sixth Message Understanding Conference MUC-6*, Menlo Park, CA: Morgan Kaufman.

Grishman, R. (1997). Information extraction: techniques and challenges. In M. Pazienza (ed.), *Information Extraction: a Multidisciplinary Approach to an Emerging Information Technology.* Berlin: Springer Verlag.

Hisamitsu, T., K. Marukawa, Y. Shima, H. Fujisawa, and Y. Nitta (1995). Optimal techniques for OCR error correction for Japanese texts. In *Proceedings of the Third International Conference on Document Analysis and Recognition (Vol. 2)*, pages 1014–1017, Montreal, Canada.

Hopcroft, J. and J. Ullman (1979). *Introduction To Automata Theory, Languages and Computation.* Reading, MA: Addison-Wesley.

Hull, D. and Grefenstette, G. (1996). Querying across languages: A dictionary-based approach to multilingual information retrieval. In *Proceedings of the 19th ACM SIGIR Conference on Research and Development in Information Retrieval*, pages 49–57, Zürich, Switzerland.

Hutchins, W. (1986). *Machine Translation: Past, Present, Future.* Chichester, UK: Ellis Horwood.

Huybregts, R. (1985). The weak inadequacy of context-free phrase structure grammars. In G. de Haan, M. Trommelen, and W. Zonneveld (ed.), *Van Periferie Naar Kern*, pages 81–99. Dordrecht: Foris.

Jacquemin, C. and D. Bourigault (2003). Term extraction and automatic indexing. In R. Mitkov (ed.), *Handbook of Computational Linguistics*, pages 599–615. Oxford, UK: Oxford University Press.

Justeson, J. and M. Katz (1995). Technical terminology: some linguistic properties and an algorithm for identification in text. *Natural Language Engineering*, 1(1):9–27.

Kasami, T. (1965). *An Efficient Recognition and Syntax Algorithm for Context-free Languages (Technical Report AFL-CRL-65-758)*. Bedford, MA: Air Force Cambridge Research Laboratory.

Kasper, W., H.-U. Krieger, J. Spilker, and H. Weber (1996). From word hypotheses to logical form: an efficient interleaved approach. In *Proceedings of the Natural Language Processing and Speech Technology: Results of the Third KONVENS Conference*, pages 77–88, Berlin: Mouton de Gruyter.

Kay, M. (1973). The MIND system. In R. Rustin (ed.), *Natural Language Processing*, pages 155–188. New York: Algorithmics Press.

Klavans, J. and E. Tzoukermann (1995). Combining corpus and machine-readable dictionary data for building bilingual lexicons. *Machine Translation*, 10(3):185–218.

Knight, K. and D. Marcu (2000). Statistics-based summarization – step one: sentence compression. In *Proceedings of the 17th National Conference on Artificial Intelligence (AAAI)*, pages 703–710, Austin, TX.

Knuth, D (1965). On the translation of languages from left to right. *Information and Control*, 8(6):607–639.

Lang, B. (1974). Deterministic techniques for efficient nondeterministic parsers. In J. Loeckx (ed.), *Automata, Languages and Programming, 2nd Colloquium. Lecture Notes in Computer Science 14*, pages 255–269. Berlin and Heidelberg: Springer Verlag.

Langlais, P., M. Simard, and J. Véronis (1998). Methods and practical issues in evaluating alignment techniques. In *Proceedings of the 36th Annual Meeting of the ACL and the 19th Conference on Computational Linguistics (COLING-ACL)*, pages 711–717, Montreal, Canada.

Langley, C., A. Lavie, L. Levin, D. Wallace, D. Gates, and K. Peterson (2002). Spoken language parsing using phrase-level grammars and trainable classifiers. In *Proceedings of the Speech-to-Speech Translation Workshop at the 40th Annual Meeting of the ACL*, Philadelphia, PA.

Lavie, A. (1996). *GLR*: A Robust Grammar-Focused Parser for Spontaneously Spoken Language*. Ph.D. Thesis, School of Computer Science, Carnegie Mellon University.

Lin, D. (1999). Automatic identification of non-compositional phrases. In *Proceedings of the 37th Annual Meeting of the Association for Computational Linguistics*, pages 317–324, College Park, MD.

Macklovitch, E. and M. Hannan (1996). Line'em up: advances in alignment technology and their impact on translation support tools. In *Proceedings of the Second Conference of the Association for Machine Translation in the Americas (AMTA-96)*, Montreal, Canada.

Maedche, A. and S. Staab (2001). Learning ontologies for the semantic web. *IEEE Intelligent Systems*, 16(2).

Marcu, D. (1998). *The Rhetorical Parsing, Summarization, and Generation of Natural Language Texts*. Ph.D. Thesis, Department of Computer Science, University of Toronto.

McCarthy, D. (2000). Using semantic preferences to identify verbal participation in role switching alternations. In *Proceedings of the First Meeting of the North American Chapter of the ACL*, pages 256–263, Seattle, WA.

Moore, R. (2003) Improved left-corner chart parsing for large context-free grammars. *This volume.*

Nederhof, M.-J. (1998). Context-free parsing through regular approximation. In *Proceedings of the First International Workshop on Finite State Methods in Natural Language Processing (FSMLNP)*, pages 13–24, Ankara, Turkey.

Nederhof, M.-J. (2000). Regular approximation of CFLs: a grammatical view. In H. Bunt and A. Nijholt (ed.), *Advances in Probabilistic and Other Parsing Technologies*. Dordrecht: Kluwer Academic Publishers, 221–241.

Nie, J., P. Isabelle, P. Plamondon, and G. Foster (1998). Using a probabilistic translation model for cross-language information retrieval. In *Proceedings of the Sixth Workshop on Very Large Corpora*, pages 18–27, Montreal, Canada.

Oepen, S. and J. Carroll (2000). Ambiguity packing in constraint-based parsing – practical results. In *Proceedings of the First Meeting of the North American Chapter of the ACL*, pages 162–169, Seattle, WA.

Och, F., C. Tillmann, and H. Ney (1999). Improved alignment models for statistical machine translation. In *Proceedings of the Joint Conference on Empirical Methods in Natural Language Processing and Very Large Corpora*, pages 20–28, College Park, MD.

Pearce, D. (2001). Synonymy in collocation extraction. In *Proceedings of the NAACL'01 Workshop on WordNet and Other Lexical Resources: Applications, Extensions and Customizations*, Pittsburgh, PA.

Perez-Cortez, J., J.-C. Amengual, J. Arlandis, and R. Llobet (2000). Stochastic error-correcting parsing for OCR. In *Proceedings of the 15th International Conference on Pattern Recognition*, pages 4402–4408, Barcelona, Spain.

Pullum, G. (1983). Context-freeness and the computer processing of human languages. In *Proceedings of the 21st Annual Meeting of the Association for Computational Linguisics*, pages 1–6, Cambridge, MA.

Pullum, G. (1984). On two recent attempts to show that English is not a context-free language. *Computational Linguistics*, 10(3–4):182–186.

Pullum, G. and G. Gazdar (1982). Natural languages and context-free languages. *Linguistics and Philosophy*, 4(4):471–504.

Radev, D., E. Hovy, and K. McKeown (ed.) (2002). Special issue on summarization. *Computational Linguistics*, 28(4).

Roark, B. (2001). Probabilistic top-down parsing and language modeling. *Computational Linguistics*, 27(2):249–285.

Rosé, C. and A. Lavie (2001). Balancing robustness and efficiency in unification-augmented context-free parsers for large practical applications. In G. van Noord and J.-C. Junqua (ed.), *Robustness in Language and Speech Technology*, pages 239–269. Dordrecht: Kluwer Academic Publishers.

Sawaf, H., K. Schütz, and H. Ney (2000). On the use of grammar based language models for statistical machine translation. In *Proceedings of the Sixth International Workshop on Parsing Technologies (IWPT)*, pages 231–241, Trento, Italy.

Seki, H., T. Matsumura, M. Fujii, and T. Kasami (1991). On multiple context-free grammars. *Theoretical Computer Science*, 88:191–229.

Shieber, S. (1985). Evidence against the context-freeness of natural language. *Linguistics and Philosophy*, 8:333–343.

Takezawa, T., T. Morimoto, Y. Sagisaka, N. Campbell, H. Iida, F. Sugaya, A. Yokoo, and S. Yamamoto (1998). A Japanese-to-English speech translation system: ATR-MATRIX. In *Proceedings of the Fifth International Conference on Spoken Language Processing (ICSLP)*, pages 957–960, Sydney, Australia.

Teufel, S. and M. Moens (2002). Summarizing scientific articles – experiments with relevance and rhetorical status. *Computational Linguistics*, 28(4):409–445.

Tomita, M. (1986). An efficient word lattice parsing algorithm for continuous speech recognition. In *Proceedings of the IEEE International Conference on Acoustics, Speech and Signal Processing (ICASSP)*, pages 1569–1572, Tokyo, Japan.

Valderrábanos, A., A. Belskis, and L. Moreno (2002). Terminology extraction and validation. In *Proceedings of the Third International Conference on Language Resources and Evaluation (LREC)*, pages 2163–2170, Las Palmas, Canary Islands.

Vogel, S., F. Och, C. Tilmann, S. Niessen, H. Sawaf, and H. Ney (2000). Statistical models for machine translation. In W. Wahlster (ed.), *Verbmobil: Foundations of Speech-to-Speech Translation*, pages 377–393. Berlin: Springer Verlag.

Wahlster, W. (2000a). Mobile speech-to-speech translation of spontaneous dialogs: an overview of the final Verbmobil system. In W. Wahlster (ed.), *Verbmobil: Foundations of Speech-to-Speech Translation*, pages 3–21. Berlin: Springer Verlag.

Wahlster, W. (2000b). *Verbmobil: Foundations of Speech-to-Speech Translation*. Berlin: Springer Verlag.

Ward, W. (1991). Understanding spontaneous speech: the Phoenix system. In *Proceedings of the IEEE International Conference on Acoustics, Speech and Signal Processing (ICASSP)*, pages 365–367, Toronto, Canada.

Yamada, K. and K. Knight (2001). A Syntax-based Statistical Translation Model. In *Proceedings of the 39th Annual Meeting of the Association for Computational Linguistics (ACL2001)*, pages 523–530, Toulouse, France.

Younger, D. (1967). Recognition and parsing of context-free languages in time n^3. *Information and Control*, 10(2):189–208.

Chapter 2

PARAMETER ESTIMATION
FOR STATISTICAL PARSING MODELS:
THEORY AND PRACTICE
OF DISTRIBUTION-FREE METHODS

Michael Collins

MIT Computer Science and Artificial Intelligence Laboratory
200 Technology Square, Cambridge, MA 02193, USA
mcollins@ai.mit.edu

Abstract   A fundamental problem in statistical parsing is the choice of criteria and algorithms used to estimate the parameters in a model. The predominant approach in
computational linguistics has been to use a parametric model with some variant
of maximum-likelihood estimation. The assumptions under which maximum-
likelihood estimation is justified are arguably quite strong. This chapter discusses the statistical theory underlying various parameter-estimation methods,
and gives algorithms which depend on alternatives to (smoothed) maximum-
likelihood estimation. We first give an overview of results from statistical learning theory. We then show how important concepts from the classification literature – specifically, generalization results based on margins on training data –
can be derived for parsing models. Finally, we describe parameter estimation
algorithms which are motivated by these generalization bounds.

1.   Introduction

A fundamental problem in statistical parsing is the choice of criteria and
algorithms used to estimate the parameters in a model. The predominant approach in computational linguistics has been to use a parametric model with
maximum-likelihood estimation, usually with some method for "smoothing"
parameter estimates to deal with sparse data problems. Methods falling into
this category include Probabilistic Context-Free Grammars and Hidden Markov
Models, Maximum Entropy models for tagging and parsing, and recent work
on Markov Random Fields.

H. Bunt et al. (eds.), New Technologies in Parsing Technology, 19-55.
© 2004 *Kluwer Academic Publishers. Printed in the Netherlands.*

This chapter discusses the statistical theory underlying various parameter-estimation methods, and gives algorithms which depend on alternatives to (smoothed) maximum-likelihood estimation. The assumptions under which maximum-likelihood estimation is justified are arguably quite strong – in particular, an assumption is made that the structure of the statistical process generating the data is known (for example, maximum–likelihood estimation for PCFGs is justified providing that the data was actually generated by a PCFG). In contrast, work in computational learning theory has concentrated on models with the weaker assumption that training and test examples are generated from the same distribution, but that the form of the distribution is unknown: in this sense the results hold across all distributions and are called "distribution-free". The result of this work – which goes back to results in statistical learning theory by Vapnik (1998) and colleagues, and to work within Valiant's PAC model of learning (Valiant, 1984) – has been the development of algorithms and theory which provide radical alternatives to parametric maximum-likelihood methods. These algorithms are appealing in both theoretical terms, and in their impressive results in many experimental studies.

In the first part of this chapter (sections 2 and 3) we describe linear models for parsing, and give an example of how the usual maximum-likelihood estimates for PCFGs can be sub-optimal. Sections 4, 5 and 6 describe the basic framework under which we will analyse parameter estimation methods. This is essentially the framework advocated by several books on learning theory (see Devroye et al., 1996; Vapnik, 1998; Cristianini and Shawe-Taylor, 2000). As a warm-up section 5 describes statistical theory for the simple case of finite hypothesis classes. Section 6 then goes on to the important case of hyperplane classifiers. Section 7 describes how concepts from the classification literature – specifically, generalization results based on margins on training data – can be derived for linear models for parsing. Section 8 describes parameter estimation algorithms motivated by these results. Section 9 gives pointers to results in the literature using the algorithms, and also discusses relationships to Markov Random Fields or maximum-entropy models (Ratnaparkhi et al., 1994; Johnson et al., 1999; Lafferty et al., 2001).

2.   Linear Models

In this section we introduce the framework for the learning problem that is studied in this chapter. The task is to learn a function $F : \mathcal{X} \to \mathcal{Y}$ where $\mathcal{X}$ is some set of possible inputs (for example a set of possible sentences), and $\mathcal{Y}$ is a domain of possible outputs (for example a set of parse trees). We assume:

- Training examples (x_i, y_i) for $i = 1, \ldots, m$, where $x_i \in \mathcal{X}, y_i \in \mathcal{Y}$.

- A function **GEN** which enumerates a set of candidates **GEN**(x) for an input x.

- A **representation** Φ mapping each $(x, y) \in \mathcal{X} \times \mathcal{Y}$ to a feature vector $\Phi(x, y) \in \Re^n$.

- A **parameter vector** $\Theta \in \Re^n$.

The components **GEN**, Φ and Θ define a mapping from an input x to an output $F(x)$ through

$$F(x) = \arg \max_{y \in \mathbf{GEN}(x)} \Phi(x, y) \cdot \Theta$$

where $\Phi(x, y) \cdot \Theta$ is the inner product $\sum_s \Theta_s \Phi_s(x, y)$. The learning task is to set the parameter values Θ using the training examples as evidence. (Note that the arg max may not be well defined in cases where two elements of **GEN**(x) get the same score $\Phi(x, y) \cdot \Theta$. In general we will assume that there is some fixed, deterministic way of choosing between elements with the same score – this can be achieved by fixing some arbitrary ordering on the set $\mathcal{Y}$.)

Several natural language problems can be seen to be special cases of this framework, through different definitions of **GEN** and Φ. In the next section we show how weighted context-free grammars are one special case. Tagging problems can also be framed in this way (e.g., Collins, 2002b): in this case **GEN**(x) is all possible tag sequences for an input sentence x. In (Johnson et al., 1999), **GEN**(x) is the set of parses for a sentence x under an LFG grammar, and the representation Φ can track arbitrary features of these parses. In (Ratnaparkhi et al., 1994; Collins, 2000; Collins and Duffy, 2002) **GEN**(x) is the top N parses from a first pass statistical model, and the representation Φ tracks the log-probability assigned by the first pass model together with arbitrary additional features of the parse trees. Walker et al. (2001) show how the approach can be applied to NLP generation: in this case x is a semantic representation, y is a surface string, and **GEN** is a deterministic system that maps x to a number of candidate surface realizations. The framework can also be considered to be a generalization of multi-class classification problems, where for all inputs x, **GEN**(x) is a fixed set of k labels $\{1, 2, \ldots, k\}$ (e.g., see Crammer and Singer, 2001; Elisseeff et al., 1999).

2.1 Weighted Context-Free Grammars

Say we have a context-free grammar $G = (N, \Sigma, R, S)$ where N is a set of non-terminal symbols, Σ is an alphabet, R is a set of rules of the form $X \to Y_1 Y_2 \cdots Y_n$ for $n \geq 0, X \in N, Y_i \in (N \cup \Sigma)$, and S is a distinguished start symbol in N. The grammar defines a set of possible strings, and possible string/tree pairs, in a language. We use **GEN**(x) for all $x \in \Sigma^*$ to denote the set of possible trees (parses) for the string x under the grammar (this set will be empty for strings not generated by the grammar).

For convenience we will take the rules in R to be placed in some arbitrary ordering $r_1, \ldots, r_n$. A weighted grammar $G = (N, \Sigma, R, S, \Theta)$ also includes a parameter vector $\Theta \in \Re^n$ which assigns a weight to each rule in R: the i-th component of Θ is the weight of rule r_i. Given a sentence x and a tree y spanning the sentence, we assume a function $\Phi(x, y)$ which tracks the counts of the rules in (x, y). Specifically, the i-th component of $\Phi(x, y)$ is the number of times rule r_i is seen in (x, y). Under these definitions, the weighted context-free grammar defines a function h_Θ from sentences to trees:

$$h_\Theta(x) = \arg \max_{y \in \mathbf{GEN}(x)} \Phi(x, y) \cdot \Theta \qquad (2.1)$$

Finding $h_\Theta(x)$, the parse with the largest weight, can be achieved in polynomial time using the CKY parsing algorithm (in spite of a possibly exponential number of members of $\mathbf{GEN}(x)$), assuming that the weighted CFG can be converted to an equivalent weighted CFG in Chomsky Normal Form.

In this chapter we consider the structure of the grammar to be fixed, the learning problem being reduced to setting the values of the parameters Θ. A basic question is as follows: given a "training sample" of sentence/tree pairs $\{(x_1, y_1), \ldots, (x_m, y_m)\}$, what criterion should be used to set the weights in the grammar? A very common method – that of Probabilistic Context-Free Grammars (PCFGs) – uses the parameters to define a distribution $P(x, y|\Theta)$ over possible sentence/tree pairs in the grammar. Maximum likelihood estimation is used to set the weights. We will consider the assumptions under which this method is justified, and argue that these assumptions are likely to be too strong. We will also give an example to show how PCFGs can be badly mislead when the assumptions are violated. As an alternative we will propose distribution-free methods for estimating the weights, which are justified under much weaker assumptions, and can give quite different estimates of the parameter values in some situations.

We would like to generalize weighted context-free grammars by allowing the representation $\Phi(x, y)$ to be essentially any feature-vector representation of the tree. There is still a grammar G, defining a set of candidates $\mathbf{GEN}(x)$ for each sentence. The parameters of the parser are a vector Θ. The parser's output is defined in the same way as equation (2.1). The important thing in this generalization is that the representation Φ is now not necessarily directly tied to the productions in the grammar. This is essentially the approach advocated by (Ratnaparkhi et al., 1994; Abney, 1997; Johnson et al., 1999), although the criteria that we will propose for setting the parameters Θ are quite different.

While superficially this might appear to be a minor change, it introduces two major challenges. The first problem is how to set the parameter values under these general representations. The PCFG method described in the next section, which results in simple relative frequency estimators of rule weights, is not applicable to more general representations. A generalization of PCFGs, Markov Random Fields (MRFs), has been proposed by several authors (Ratnaparkhi et al., 1994; Abney, 1997; Johnson et al., 1999; Della Pietra et al., 1997). In this chapter we give several alternatives to MRFs, and we describe the theory and assumptions which underly various models.

The second challenge is that now that the parameters are not tied to rules in the grammar the CKY algorithm is not applicable – in the worst case we may have to enumerate all members of $\mathbf{GEN}(x)$ explicitly to find the highest-scoring tree. One practical solution is to define the "grammar" G as a first pass statistical parser which allows dynamic programming to enumerate its top N candidates. A second pass uses the more complex representation Φ to choose the best of these parses. This is the approach used in several papers (e.g., Ratnaparkhi et al., 1994; Collins, 2000; Collins and Duffy, 2002).

3. Probabilistic Context-Free Grammars

This section reviews the basic theory underlying Probabilistic Context-Free Grammars (PCFGs). Say we have a context-free grammar $G = (N, \Sigma, R, S)$ as defined in section 2.1. We will use $\mathcal{T}$ to denote the set of all trees generated by G. Now say we assign a weight $p(r)$ in the range 0 to 1 to each rule r in R. Assuming some arbitrary ordering $r_1, \ldots, r_n$ of the n rules in R, we use Θ to denote a vector of parameters, $\Theta = \langle \log p(r_1), \log p(r_2), \ldots, \log p(r_n) \rangle$. If $c(T, r)$ is the number of times rule r is seen in a tree T, then the "probability" of a tree T can be written as

$$P(T|\Theta) = \prod_{r \in R} p(r)^{c(T,r)}$$

or equivalently

$$\log P(T|\Theta) = \sum_{r \in R} c(T, r) \log p(r) = \Phi(T) \cdot \Theta$$

where we define $\Phi(T)$ to be an n-dimensional vector whose i-th component is $c(T, r_i)$.

Booth and Thompson (1973) give conditions on the weights which ensure that $P(T|\Theta)$ is a valid probability distribution over the set $\mathcal{T}$, in other words that $\sum_{T \in \mathcal{T}} P(T|\Theta) = 1$, and $\forall T \in \mathcal{T}$, $P(T|\Theta) \geq 0$. The main condition is that the parameters define conditional distributions over the alternative ways of rewriting each non-terminal symbol in the grammar. Formally, if we use $R(\alpha)$ to denote the set of rules whose left hand side is some non-terminal α, then $\forall \alpha \in N$, $\sum_{r \in R(\alpha)} p(r) = 1$ and $\forall r \in R(\alpha)$, $p(r) \geq 0$. Thus the weight associated with a rule $\alpha \rightarrow \beta$ can be interpreted as a conditional probability $P(\beta|\alpha)$ of α rewriting as β (rather than any of the other alternatives in $R(\alpha)$).[1]

We can now study how to train the grammar from a training sample of trees. Say there is a training set of trees $\{T_1, T_2, \ldots, T_m\}$. The *log-likelihood* of the training set given parameters Θ is $L(\Theta) = \sum_j \log P(T_j|\Theta)$. The maximum-likelihood estimates are to take $\hat{\Theta} = \arg\max_{\Theta \in \Omega} L(\Theta)$, where Ω is the set of allowable parameter settings (i.e., the parameter settings which obey the constraints in Booth and Thompson, 1973). It can be proved using constrained optimization techniques (i.e., using Lagrange multipliers) that the maximum-likelihood estimate for the weight of a rule $r = \alpha \to \beta$ is $p(\alpha \to \beta) = \sum_j c(T_j, \alpha \to \beta) / \sum_j c(T_j, \alpha)$ (here we overload the notation c so that $c(T, \alpha)$ is the number of times non-terminal α is seen in T). So "learning" in this case involves taking a simple ratio of frequencies to calculate the weights on rules in the grammar.

So under what circumstances is maximum-likelihood estimation justified? Say there is a true set of weights Θ^*, which define an underlying distribution $P(T|\Theta^*)$, and that the training set is a sample of size m from this distribution. Then it can be shown that as m increases to infinity, then with probability 1 the parameter estimates $\hat{\Theta}$ converge to values which give the same distribution over trees as the "true" parameter values Θ^*.

To illustrate the deficiencies of PCFGs, we give a simple example. Say we have a random process which generates just 3 trees, with probabilities $\{p_1, p_2, p_3\}$, as shown in figure 2.1a. The training sample will consist of a set of trees drawn from this distribution. A test sample will be generated from the same distribution, but in this case the trees will be hidden, and only the surface strings will be seen (i.e., $\langle aaaa \rangle$, $\langle aaa \rangle$ and $\langle a \rangle$ with probabilities p_1, p_2, p_3 respectively). We would like to learn a weighted CFG with as small error as possible on a randomly drawn test sample.

As the size of the training sample goes to infinity, the relative frequencies of trees $\{T_1, T_2, T_3\}$ in the training sample will converge to $\{p_1, p_2, p_3\}$. This makes it easy to calculate the rule weights that maximum-likelihood estimation converges to – see figure 2.1b. We will call the PCFG with these asymptotic weights the *asymptotic PCFG*. Notice that the grammar generates trees never seen in training data, shown in figure 2.1c. The grammar is ambiguous for strings $\langle aaaa \rangle$ (both T_1 and T_4 are possible) and $\langle aaa \rangle$ (T_2 and T_5 are possible). In fact, under certain conditions T_4 and T_5 will get higher probabilities under the asymptotic PCFG than T_1 and T_2, and both strings $\langle aaaa \rangle$ and $\langle aaa \rangle$ will be mis-parsed. Figure 2.1d shows the distribution of the asymptotic PCFG over the 8 trees when $p_1 = 0.2, p_2 = 0.1$ and $p_3 = 0.7$. In this case both ambiguous strings are mis-parsed by the asymptotic PCFG, resulting in an expected error rate of $(p_1 + p_2) = 30\%$ on newly drawn test examples.

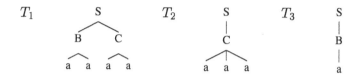

Figure 2.1a. Training and test data consists of trees T_1, T_2 and T_3 drawn with probabilities p_1, p_2 and p_3.

Rule Number	Rule	Asymptotic ML Estimate
1	S → B C	p_1
2	S → C	p_2
3	S → B	p_3
4	B → a a	$p_1/(p_1 + p_3)$
5	B → a	$p_3/(p_1 + p_3)$
6	C → a a	$p_1/(p_1 + p_2)$
7	C → a a a	$p_2/(p_1 + p_2)$

Figure 2.1b. The ML estimates of rule probabilities converge to simple functions of p_1, p_2, p_3 as the training size goes to infinity.

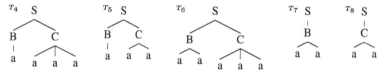

Figure 2.1c. The CFG also generates $T_4, \ldots, T_8$, which are unseen in training or test data.

Tree	Rules used	Asymptotic Estimate
T_1	1,4,6	0.0296
T_2	2,7	0.0333
T_3	3,5	0.544
T_4	1,5,7	0.0519
T_5	1,5,6	0.104
T_6	1,4,7	0.0148
T_7	3,4	0.156
T_8	2,6	0.0667

Figure 2.1d. The probabilities assigned to the trees as the training size goes to infinity, for $p_1 = 0.2, p_2 = 0.1, p_3 = 0.7$. Notice that $P(T_4) > P(T_1)$, and $P(T_5) > P(T_2)$, so the induced PCFG will incorrectly map ⟨aaaa⟩ to T_4 and ⟨aaa⟩ to T_2.

This is a striking failure of the PCFG when we consider that it is easy to derive weights on the grammar rules which parse both training and test examples with no errors.[2] On this example there exist weighted grammars which make no errors, but the maximum likelihood estimation method will fail to find these weights, even with unlimited amounts of training data.

4.   Statistical Learning Theory

The next 4 sections of this chapter describe theoretical results underlying the parameter estimation algorithms in section 8. In sections 4.1 to 4.3 we describe the basic framework under which we will analyse the various learning approaches. In section 5 we describe analysis for a simple case, finite hypothesis classes, which will be useful for illustrating ideas and intuition underlying the methods. In section 6 we describe analysis of hyperplane classifiers. In section 7 we describe how the results for hyperplane classifiers can be generalized to apply to the linear models introduced in section 2.

4.1   A General Framework for Supervised Learning

This section introduces a general framework for supervised learning problems. There are several books (Devroye et al., 1996; Vapnik, 1998; Cristianini and Shawe-Taylor, 2000) which cover the material in detail. We will use this framework to analyze both parametric methods (PCFGs, for example), and the distribution–free methods proposed in this chapter. We assume the following:

- An input domain $\mathcal{X}$ and an output domain $\mathcal{Y}$. The task will be to learn a function mapping each element of $\mathcal{X}$ to an element of $\mathcal{Y}$. In parsing, $\mathcal{X}$ is a set of possible sentences and $\mathcal{Y}$ is a set of possible trees.

- There is some underlying probability distribution $D(x, y)$ over $\mathcal{X} \times \mathcal{Y}$. The distribution is used to generate both training and test examples. It is an unknown distribution, but it is constant across training and test examples – both training and test examples are drawn independently, identically distributed from $D(x, y)$.

- There is a loss function $L(y, \hat{y})$ which measures the cost of proposing an output $\hat{y}$ when the "true" output is y. A commonly used cost is the 0-1 loss $L(y, \hat{y}) = 0$ if $y = \hat{y}$, and $L(y, \hat{y}) = 1$ otherwise. We will concentrate on this loss function in this chapter.

- Given a function h from $\mathcal{X}$ to $\mathcal{Y}$, its *expected loss* is

$$Er(h) = \sum_{x,y} D(x, y) L(y, h(x))$$

Under 0-1 loss this is the expected proportion of errors that the hypothesis makes on examples drawn from the distribution D. We would like to learn a function whose expected loss is as low as possible: $Er(h)$ is a measure of how successful a function h is. Unfortunately, because we do not have direct access to the distribution D, we cannot explicitly calculate the expected loss of a hypothesis.

- The training set is a sample of m pairs $\{(x_1, y_1), \ldots, (x_m, y_m)\}$ drawn from the distribution D. This is the only information we have about D. The *empirical loss* of a function h on the training sample is

$$\hat{E}r(h) = \frac{1}{m} \sum_i L(y_i, h(x_i))$$

Finally, a useful concept is the *Bayes Optimal* hypothesis, which we will denote as h_B. It is defined as $h_B(x) = \arg\max_{y \in \mathcal{Y}} D(x, y)$. The Bayes optimal hypothesis simply outputs the most likely y under the distribution D for each input x. It is easy to prove that this function minimizes the expected loss $Er(h)$ over the space of all possible functions – the Bayes optimal hypothesis cannot be improved upon. Unfortunately, in general we do not know $D(x, y)$, so the Bayes optimal hypothesis, while useful as a theoretical construct, cannot be obtained directly in practice. Given that the only access to the distribution $D(x, y)$ is indirect, through a training sample of finite size m, the learning problem is to find a hypothesis whose expected risk is low, using only the training sample as evidence.

4.2 Parametric Models

Parametric models attempt to solve the supervised learning problem by explicitly modeling either the joint distribution $D(x, y)$ or the conditional distributions $D(y|x)$ for all x.

In the joint distribution case, there is a parameterized probability distribution $P(x, y|\Theta)$. As the parameter values Θ are varied the distribution will also vary. The parameter space Ω is a set of possible parameter values for which $P(x, y|\Theta)$ is a well-defined distribution (i.e., for which $\sum_{x,y} P(x, y|\Theta) = 1$).

A crucial assumption in parametric approaches is that there is some $\Theta^* \in \Omega$ such that $D(x, y) = P(x, y|\Theta^*)$. In other words, we assume that D is a member of the set of distributions under consideration. Now say we have a training sample $\{(x_1, y_1), \ldots, (x_m, y_m)\}$ drawn from $D(x, y)$. A common estimation method is to set the parameters to the maximum-likelihood estimates, $\hat{\Theta} = \arg\max_{\Theta \in \Omega} \sum_i \log P(x_i, y_i|\Theta)$. Under the assumption that $D(x, y) = P(x, y|\Theta^*)$ for some $\Theta^* \in \Omega$, for a wide class of distributions it can be shown that $P(x, y|\hat{\Theta})$ converges to $D(x, y)$ in the limit as the training size m goes to infinity. Because of this, if we consider the function $\hat{h}(x) = \arg\max_{y \in \mathcal{Y}} P(x, y|\hat{\Theta})$, then in the limit $\hat{h}(x)$ will converge to the Bayes optimal function $h_B(x)$. So under the assumption that $D(x, y) = P(x, y|\Theta^*)$

for some $\Theta^* \in \Omega$, and with infinite amounts of training data, the maximum-likelihood method is provably optimal.

Methods which model the conditional distribution $D(y|x)$ are similar. The parameters now define a conditional distribution $P(y|x, \Theta)$. The assumption is that there is some Θ^* such that $\forall x,\ D(y|x) = P(y|x, \Theta^*)$. Maximum-likelihood estimates can be defined in a similar way, and in this case the function $\hat{h}(x) = \arg\max_{y \in \mathcal{Y}} P(y|x, \hat{\Theta})$ will converge to the Bayes optimal function $h_B(x)$ as the sample size goes to infinity.

4.3   An Overview of Distribution-Free Methods

From the arguments in the previous section, parametric methods are optimal provided that two assumptions hold:

1 The distribution generating the data is in the class of distributions being considered.

2 The training set is large enough for the distribution defined by the maximum-likelihood estimates to converge to the "true" distribution $D(x, y)$ (in general the guarantees of ML estimation are asymptotic, holding only in the limit as the training data size goes to infinity).

This chapter proposes alternatives to maximum-likelihood methods which give theoretical guarantees without making either of these assumptions. There is no assumption that the distribution generating the data comes from some predefined class – the only assumption is that the same, unknown distribution generates both training and test examples. The methods also provide bounds suggesting how many training samples are required for learning, dealing with the case where there is only a finite amount of training data.

A crucial idea in distribution-free learning is that of a *hypothesis space*. This is a set of functions under consideration, each member of the set being a function $h : \mathcal{X} \to \mathcal{Y}$. For example, in weighted context-free grammars the hypothesis space is

$$\mathcal{H} = \{h_\Theta : \Theta \in \Re^n\}$$

where

$$h_\Theta(x) = \arg \max_{y \in \mathbf{GEN}(x)} \Phi(x, y) \cdot \Theta$$

So each possible parameter setting defines a different function from sentences to trees, and $\mathcal{H}$ is the infinite set of all such functions as Θ ranges over the parameter space $\Re^n$.

Learning is then usually framed as the task of choosing a "good" function in $\mathcal{H}$ on the basis of a training sample as evidence. Recall the definition of the expected error of a hypothesis $Er(h) = \sum_{x,y} D(x, y) L(y, h(x))$. We will use

h^* to denote the "best" function in $\mathcal{H}$ by this measure,

$$h^* = \arg\min_{h \in \mathcal{H}} Er(h) = \arg\min_{h \in \mathcal{H}} \sum_{x,y} D(x,y) L(y, h(x))$$

As a starting point, consider the following approach. Given a training sample (x_i, y_i) for $i = 1, \ldots, m$, consider a method which simply chooses the hypothesis with minimum empirical error, that is

$$\hat{h} = \arg\min_{h \in \mathcal{H}} \hat{Er}(h) = \arg\min_{h \in \mathcal{H}} \frac{1}{m} \sum_i L(y_i, h(x_i))$$

This strategy is called "Empirical Risk Minimization" (ERM) by Vapnik (1998). Two questions which arise are:

- In the limit, as the training size goes to infinity, does the error of the ERM method $Er(\hat{h})$ approach the error of the best function in the set, $Er(h^*)$, regardless of the underlying distribution $D(x, y)$? In other words, is this method of choosing a hypothesis always consistent?

  The answer to this depends on the nature of the hypothesis space $\mathcal{H}$. For finite hypothesis spaces the ERM method is always consistent. For many infinite hypothesis spaces, such as the hyperplane classifiers described in section 6 of this chapter, the method is also consistent. However, some infinite hypothesis spaces can lead to the method being inconsistent – specifically, if a measure called the Vapnik-Chervonenkis (VC) dimension (Vapnik and Chervonenkis, 1971) of $\mathcal{H}$ is infinite, the ERM method may be inconsistent. Intuitively, the VC dimension can be thought of as a measure of the complexity of an infinite set of hypotheses.

- If the method is consistent, how quickly does $Er(\hat{h})$ converge to $Er(h^*)$? In other words, how much training data is needed to have a good chance of getting close to the best function in $\mathcal{H}$? We will see in the next section that the convergence rate depends on various measures of the "size" of the hypothesis space. For finite sets, the rate of convergence depends directly upon the size of $\mathcal{H}$. For infinite sets, several measures have been proposed – we will concentrate on rates of convergence based on a concept called the *margin* of a hypothesis on training examples.

5. Convergence Bounds for Finite Sets of Hypotheses

This section gives results and analysis for situations where the hypothesis space $\mathcal{H}$ is a finite set. This is in some ways an unrealistically simple situation – many hypothesis spaces used in practice are infinite sets – but we give the results and proofs because they can be useful in developing intuition for the nature of convergence bounds. In the following sections we consider infinite hypothesis spaces such as weighted context-free grammars.

A couple of basic results from probability theory will be very useful. The first results are the *Chernoff bounds*. Consider a binary random variable X (such as the result of a coin toss) which has probability p of being 1, and $(1 - p)$ of being 0. Now consider a sample of size m, $\{x_1, x_2, \ldots, x_m\}$ drawn from this process. Define the relative frequency of $x_i = 1$ (the coin coming up heads) in this sample to be $\hat{p} = \sum_i x_i/m$. The relative frequency $\hat{p}$ is a very natural estimate of the underlying probability p, and by the law of large numbers $\hat{p}$ will converge to p as the sample size m goes to infinity. Chernoff bounds give results concerning how quickly $\hat{p}$ converges to p. Thus Chernoff bounds go a step further than the law of large numbers, which is an asymptotic result (a result concerning what happens as the sample size goes to infinity). The bounds are:

Theorem 1 (Chernoff Bounds). *For all $p \in [0, 1], \epsilon > 0$, with the probability P being taken over the distribution of training samples of size m generated with underlying parameter p,*

$$P[p - \hat{p} > \epsilon] \leq e^{-2m\epsilon^2} \qquad (2.2)$$

$$P[\hat{p} - p > \epsilon] \leq e^{-2m\epsilon^2} \qquad (2.3)$$

$$P[\,|\hat{p} - p| > \epsilon] \leq 2e^{-2m\epsilon^2} \qquad (2.4)$$

The first bound states that for all values of p, and for all values of ϵ, if we repeatedly draw training samples of size m of a binary variable with underlying probability p, the relative proportion of training samples for which the value $(p-\hat{p})$ exceeds ϵ is at most[3] $e^{-2m\epsilon^2}$. The second and third bounds make similar statements. As an example, take $m = 1000$, and $\epsilon = 0.05$. Then $e^{-2m\epsilon^2} = e^{-5} \approx 1/148$. The first bound implies that if we repeatedly take samples of size 1000, and take the estimate $\hat{p}$ to be the relative number of heads in that sample, then for (roughly) 147 out of every 148 samples the value of $(p - \hat{p})$ will be less than 0.05. The second bound says that for roughly 147 out of every 148 samples the value of $(\hat{p} - p)$ will be less than 0.05, and the last bound says that for 146 out of every 148 samples the absolute value $|p - \hat{p}|$ will be less than 0.05. Roughly speaking, if we draw a sample of size 1000, we would be quite unlucky for the relative frequency estimate to diverge from the true probability p by more than 0.05. It is always *possible* for $\hat{p}$ to diverge substantially from p – it is possible to draw an extremely unrepresentative training sample, such as a sample of all heads when $p = 0.7$, for example – but as the sample size is increased the chances of us being this unlucky become increasingly unlikely.

A second useful result is the *Union Bound*:

Theorem 2 *(Union Bound)*. *For any n events $\{A_1, A_2, \ldots, A_n\}$, and for any distribution P whose sample space includes all A_i,*

$$P[A_1 \cup A_2 \cup \cdots \cup A_{n-1} \cup A_n] \leq \sum_i P[A_i] \qquad (2.5)$$

Here we use the notation $P[A \cup B]$ to mean the probability of A or B occurring. The Union Bound follows directly from the axioms of probability theory. For example, if $n = 2$, then $P[A_1 \cup A_2] = P[A_1] + P[A_2] - P[A_1 A_2] \leq P[A_1] + P[A_2]$, where $P[A_1 A_2]$ means the probability of both A_1 and A_2 occurring. The more general result for all n follows by induction on n.

We are now in a position to apply these results to learning problems. First, consider just a single member of $\mathcal{H}$, a function h. Say we draw a training sample $\{(x_1, y_1), \ldots, (x_m, y_m)\}$ from some unknown distribution $D(x, y)$. We can calculate the relative frequency of errors of h on this sample,

$$\hat{E}r(h) = \frac{1}{m} \sum_i [[h(x_i) \neq y_i]]$$

where $[[\pi]]$ is 1 if π is true, 0 otherwise. We are interested in how this quantity is related to the true error-rate of h on the distribution D, that is $Er(h) = \sum_{x,y} D(x, y)[[h(x) \neq y]]$. We can apply the first Chernoff bound directly to this problem to give for all $\epsilon > 0$

$$P[Er(h) > \hat{E}r(h) + \epsilon] \leq e^{-2m\epsilon^2} \qquad (2.6)$$

So for any single member of $\mathcal{H}$, the Chernoff bound describes how its observed error on the training set is related to its true probability of error. Now consider the entire set of hypotheses $\mathcal{H}$. Say we assign an arbitrary ordering to the $n = |\mathcal{H}|$ hypotheses, so that $\mathcal{H} = \{h_1, h_2, \ldots, h_n\}$. Consider the probability of *any one* of the hypotheses h_i having its estimated loss $\hat{E}r(h_i)$ diverge by more than ϵ from its expected loss $Er(h_i)$. This probability is

$$P\left[\left(Er(h_1) > \hat{E}r(h_1) + \epsilon\right) \cup \left(Er(h_2) > \hat{E}r(h_2) + \epsilon\right) \cup \cdots \cup \left(Er(h_n) > \hat{E}r(h_n) + \epsilon\right)\right]$$

By application of the union bound, and the result in equation (2.6), we get the following bound on this probability

$$P\left[\left(Er(h_1) > \hat{E}r(h_1) + \epsilon\right) \cup \left(Er(h_2) > \hat{E}r(h_2) + \epsilon\right) \cdots\right]$$

$$\leq \sum_{i=1}^{|\mathcal{H}|} P\left[Er(h_i) > \hat{E}r(h_i) + \epsilon\right]$$

$$\leq |\mathcal{H}| e^{-2m\epsilon^2}$$

It is useful to rephrase this result by introducing a variable $\delta = |\mathcal{H}|e^{-2m\epsilon^2}$, and solving in terms of ϵ, which gives $\epsilon = \sqrt{(\log|\mathcal{H}| + \log(1/\delta))/2m}$. We then have the following theorem:

Theorem 3 *For any distribution $D(x,y)$ generating training and test instances, with probability at least $1 - \delta$ over the choice of training set of size m drawn from D, for all $h \in \mathcal{H}$,*

$$Er(h) \leq \hat{E}r(h) + \sqrt{\frac{\log|\mathcal{H}| + \log\frac{1}{\delta}}{2m}}$$

Thus for all hypotheses h in the set $\mathcal{H}$, $\hat{E}r(h)$ converges to $Er(h)$ as the sample size m goes to infinity. This result is known as a *Uniform Convergence Result*, in that it describes how a whole set of empirical error rates converge to their respective expected errors. Note that this result holds for the hypothesis with minimum error on the training sample. It can be shown that this implies that the ERM method for finite hypothesis spaces – choosing the hypothesis $\hat{h}$ which has minimum error on the training sample – is consistent, in that in the limit as $m \to \infty$, the error of $\hat{h}$ converges to the error of the minimum error hypothesis.

Another important result is how the rate of convergence depends on the size of the hypothesis space. Qualitatively, the bound implies that to avoid overtraining the number of training samples should scale with $\log|\mathcal{H}|$.

5.1   Structural Risk Minimization over Finite Hypothesis Spaces

Ideally, we would like a learning method to have expected error that is close to the loss of the bayes-optimal hypothesis h_B. Now consider the ERM method. It is useful to write the difference from h_B in the form

$$Er(\hat{h}) - Er(h_B) = \left(Er(\hat{h}) - \min_{h \in \mathcal{H}} Er(h)\right) + \left(\min_{h \in \mathcal{H}} Er(h) - Er(h_B)\right)$$

Breaking the error down in this way suggests that there are two components to the difference from the optimal loss $Er(h_B)$. The first term captures the errors due to a finite sample size – if the hypothesis space is too large, then theorem 3 states that there is a good chance that the ERM method will pick a hypothesis that is far from the best in the hypothesis space, and the first term will be large. Thus the first term indicates a pressure to keep $\mathcal{H}$ small, so that there is a good chance of finding the best hypothesis in the set. In contrast, the second term reflects a pressure to make $\mathcal{H}$ large, so that there is a good chance that at least one of the hypotheses is close to the Bayes optimal hypothesis. The two terms can be thought of as being analogues to the familiar "bias–variance" trade-off, the first term being a variance term, the second being the bias.

In this section we describe a method which explicitly attempts to model the trade-off between these two types of errors. Rather than picking a single hypothesis class, Structural Risk Minimization (Vapnik, 1998) advocates picking a set of hypothesis classes $\mathcal{H}_1, \mathcal{H}_2, \ldots, \mathcal{H}_s$ of increasing size (i.e., such that $|\mathcal{H}_1| < |\mathcal{H}_2| < \cdots < |\mathcal{H}_s|$). The following theorem then applies (it is an extension of theorem 3, and is derived in a similar way through application of the Chernoff and Union bounds):

Theorem 4 *Assume a set of finite hypothesis classes* $\{\mathcal{H}_1, \mathcal{H}_2, \ldots, \mathcal{H}_s\}$, *and some distribution* $D(x, y)$. *For all* $i = 1, \ldots, s$, *for all hypotheses* $h \in \mathcal{H}_i$, *with probability at least* $1 - \delta$ *over the choice of training set of size* m *drawn from* D,

$$Er(h) \le \hat{E}r(h) + \sqrt{\frac{\log |\mathcal{H}_i| + \log \frac{1}{\delta} + \log s}{2m}}$$

This theorem is very similar to theorem 3, except that the second term in the bound now varies depending on which $\mathcal{H}_i$ a function h is drawn from. Note also that we pay an extra price of $\log(s)$ for our hedging over which of the hypothesis spaces the function is drawn from. The SRM principle is then as follows:

1 Pick a set of hypothesis classes, $\mathcal{H}_i$ for $i = 1, \ldots, s$, of increasing size. This must be done independently of the training data for the above bound to apply.

2 Choose the hypothesis h which minimizes the bound in theorem 4.

Thus rather than simply choosing the hypothesis with the lowest error on the training sample, there is now a trade-off between training error and the size of the hypothesis space of which h is a member. The SRM method advocates picking a compromise between keeping the number of training errors small versus keeping the size of the hypothesis class small.

Note that this approach has a somewhat similar flavour to Bayesian approaches. The Maximum A-Posteriori (MAP) estimates in a Bayesian approach involve choosing the parameters which maximize a combination of the data likelihood and a prior over the parameter values,

$$\Theta_{MAP} = \arg \max_{\Theta} \left(\log P(\text{data} \mid \Theta) + \log P(\Theta) \right)$$

The first term is a measure of how well the parameters Θ fit the data. The second term is a prior which can be interpreted as a term which penalizes more complex parameter settings. The SRM approach in our example implies choosing the hypothesis that minimizes the bound in theorem 4, i.e.,

$$h_{SRM} = \arg \min_{h} \left(\hat{E}r(h) + \sqrt{\frac{\log |\mathcal{H}_i| + \log \frac{1}{\delta} + \log s}{2m}} \right)$$

where $|\mathcal{H}_i|$ is the size of the hypothesis class containing h. The function indicating the "goodness" of a hypothesis h again has two terms, one measuring how well the hypothesis fits the data, the second penalizing hypotheses which are too "complex". Here complexity has a very specific meaning: it is a direct measure of how quickly the training data error $\hat{Er}(h)$ converges to its true value $Er(h)$.

6.   Convergence Bounds for Hyperplane Classifiers

This section describes analysis applied for binary classifiers, where the set $\mathcal{Y} = \{-1, +1\}$. We consider hyperplane classifiers, where a linear separator in some feature space is used to separate examples into the two classes. This section describes uniform convergence bounds for hyperplane classifiers. Algorithms which explicitly minimize these bounds – namely the Support Vector Machine and Boosting algorithms – are described in section 8.

There has been a large amount of research devoted to the analysis of hyperplane classifiers. They go back to one of the earliest learning algorithms, the Perceptron algorithm (Rosenblatt, 1958). They are similar to the linear models for parsing we proposed in section 2 (in fact the framework of section 2 can be viewed as a generalization of hyperplane classifiers). We will initially review some results applying to linear classifiers, and then discuss how various results may be applied to linear models for parsing.

We will discuss a hypothesis space of n-dimensional hyperplane classifiers, defined as follows:

- Each instance x is represented as a vector $\Phi(x)$ in $\Re^n$.

- For given parameter values $\Theta \in \Re^n$ and a bias parameter $b \in \Re$, the output of the classifier is

$$h_{\Theta,b}(x) = \text{sign}\left(\Phi(x) \cdot \Theta + b\right)$$

  where $\text{sign}(z)$ is $+1$ if $z \geq 0$, -1 otherwise. There is a clear geometric interpretation of this classifier. The points $\Phi(x)$ are in n-dimensional Euclidean space. The parameters Θ, b define a hyperplane through the space, the hyperplane being the set of points z such that $(z \cdot \Theta + b) = 0$. This is a hyperplane with normal Θ, at distance $b/||\Theta||$ from the origin, where $||\Theta||$ is the Euclidean norm, $\sqrt{\sum_j \Theta_j^2}$. This hyperplane is used to classify points: all points falling on one side of the hyperplane are classified as $+1$, points on the other side are classified as -1.

- The hypothesis space is the set of all hyperplanes,

$$\mathcal{H} = \{h_{\Theta,b} : \Theta \in \Re^n, b \in \Re\}$$

It can be shown that the ERM method is consistent for hyperplanes, through a method called VC analysis (Vapnik and Chervonenkis, 1971). We will not go into details here, but roughly speaking, the VC-dimension of a hypothesis space is a measure of its size or complexity. A set of hyperplanes in $\Re^n$ has VC dimension of $(n + 1)$. For any hypothesis space with finite VC dimension the ERM method is consistent.

An alternative to VC-analysis is to analyse hyperplanes through properties of "margins" on training examples. For any hyperplane defined by parameters (Θ, b), for a training sample $\{(x_1, y_1), \ldots, (x_m, y_m)\}$, the *margin* on the i-th training example is defined as

$$\gamma_{\Theta,b}^i = \frac{y_i \left(\Phi(x_i) \cdot \Theta + b\right)}{||\Theta||} \tag{2.7}$$

where $||\Theta||$ is again the Euclidean norm. Note that if $\gamma_{\Theta,b}^i$ is positive, then the i-th training example is classified correctly by $h_{\Theta,b}$ (i.e., y_i and $(\Phi(x_i) \cdot \Theta + b)$ agree in sign). It can be verified that the absolute value of $\gamma_{\Theta,b}^i$ has a simple geometric interpretation: it is the distance of the point $\Phi(x_i)$ from the hyperplane defined by (Θ, b). If $\gamma_{\Theta,b}^i$ is much greater than 0, then intuitively the i-th training example has been classified correctly and with *high confidence*.

Now consider the special case where the data is *separable* – there is at least one hyperplane which achieves 0 training errors. We define the margin of a hyperplane (Θ, b) on the training sample as

$$\gamma_{\Theta,b} = \min_i \gamma_{\Theta,b}^i \tag{2.8}$$

The margin $\gamma_{\Theta,b}$ has a simple geometric interpretation: it is the minimum distance of any training point to the hyperplane defined by Θ, b. The following theorem then holds:

Theorem 5 *(Shawe-Taylor et al. 1998). Assume the hypothesis class $\mathcal{H}$ is a set of hyperplanes, and that there is some distribution $D(x, y)$ generating examples. Define R to be a constant such that $\forall x, ||\Phi(x)|| \leq R$. For all $h_{\Theta,b} \in \mathcal{H}$ with zero error on the training sample, with probability at least $1 - \delta$ over the choice of training set of size m drawn from D,*

$$Er(h_{\Theta,b}) \leq \frac{c}{m} \left(\frac{R^2}{\gamma_{\Theta,b}^2} \log^2 m + \log \frac{1}{\delta} \right)$$

where c is a constant.

The bound is minimized for the hyperplane with maximum margin (i.e., maximum value for $\gamma_{\Theta,b}$) on the training sample. This bound suggests that if the training data is separable, the hyperplane with maximum margin should be chosen as the hypothesis with the best bound on its expected error. It can be shown that the maximum margin hyperplane is unique, and can be found efficiently using algorithms described in section 8.1. Search for the maximum-margin hyperplane is the basis of "Support Vector Machines" (hard-margin version; Vapnik, 1998).

The previous theorem does not apply when the training data cannot be classified with 0 errors by a hyperplane. There is, however, a similar theorem that can be applied in the non-separable case. First, define $\hat{L}(\Theta, b, \gamma)$ to be the proportion of examples on training data with margin less than γ for the hyperplane $h_{\Theta,b}$:

$$\hat{L}(\Theta, b, \gamma) = \frac{1}{m} \sum_i \left[\left[\gamma^i_{\Theta,b} < \gamma\right]\right] \tag{2.9}$$

The following theorem can now be stated:

Theorem 6 *Cristianini and Shawe-Taylor, 2000, theorem 4.19. Assume the hypothesis class $\mathcal{H}$ is a set of hyperplanes, and that there is some distribution $D(x, y)$ generating examples. Let R be a constant such that $\forall x, \|\Phi(x)\| \leq R$. For all $h_{\Theta,b} \in \mathcal{H}$, for all $\gamma > 0$, with probability at least $1 - \delta$ over the choice of training set of size m drawn from D,*

$$Er(h_{\Theta,b}) \leq \hat{L}(\Theta, b, \gamma) + \sqrt{\frac{c}{m}\left(\frac{R^2}{\gamma^2}\log^2 m + \log\frac{1}{\delta}\right)}$$

where c is a constant.

(The first result of the form of theorem 6 was given in (Bartlett 1998). This was a general result for large margin classifiers; the immediate corollary that implies the above theorem was given in (Anthony and Bartlett 1999). Note that Zhang (2002) proves a related theorem where the $\log^2 m$ factor is replaced by $\log m$. Note also that the square-root in the second term of theorem 6 means that this bound is in general a looser bound than the bound in theorem 5. This is one cost of moving to the case where some training samples are misclassified, or where some training samples are classified with a small margin.)

This result is important in cases where a large proportion of training samples can be classified with relatively large margin, but a relatively small number of outliers make the problem inseparable, or force a small margin. The result suggests that in some cases a few examples are worth "giving up on", resulting in the first term in the bound being larger than 0, but the second term being much smaller due to a larger value for γ. The *soft margin* version of Support Vector Machines (Cortes and Vapnik, 1995), described in section 8.1, attempts to explicitly manage the trade-off between the two terms in the bound.

A similar bound, due to (Schapire et al., 1998), involves a margin definition which depends on the 1-norm rather than the 2-norm of the parameters Θ

($||\Theta||_1$ is the 1-norm, $\sum_j |\Theta_j|$):

$$\hat{L}_1(\Theta, b, \gamma) = \frac{1}{m} \sum_i \left[\left[\frac{y_i\left(\Phi(x_i) \cdot \Theta + b\right)}{||\Theta||_1} < \gamma \right] \right] \qquad (2.10)$$

Theorem 7 *(Schapire et al., 1998). Assume the hypothesis class $\mathcal{H}$ is a set of hyperplanes in $\Re^n$, and that there is some distribution $D(x, y)$ generating examples. For all $h_{\Theta, b} \in \mathcal{H}$, for all $\gamma > 0$, with probability at least $1 - \delta$ over the choice of training set of size m drawn from D,*

$$Er(h_{\Theta, b}) \leq \hat{L}_1(\Theta, b, \gamma) + O\left(\sqrt{\frac{1}{m}\left(\frac{R_\infty^2 \log m \log n}{\gamma^2} + \log \frac{1}{\delta}\right)}\right)$$

where R_∞ is a constant such that $\forall x, ||\Phi(x)||_\infty \leq R_\infty$. ($||\Phi(x)||_\infty$ is the infinity norm, $||\Phi(x)||_\infty = \max_i |\Phi(x)_i|$.)

This bound suggests a strategy that keeps the 1-norm of the parameters low, while trying to classify as many of the training examples as possible with large margin. It can be shown that the AdaBoost algorithm (Freund and Schapire, 1997) is an effective way of achieving this goal; its application to parsing is described in section 8.2.

7. Application of Margin Analysis to Parsing

We now consider how the theory for hyperplane classifiers might apply to the linear models for parsing described in section 2. Recall that given parameters $\Theta \in \Re^n$, the hypothesis h_Θ is defined as

$$h_\Theta(x) = \arg \max_{y \in \mathbf{GEN}(x)} \Phi(x, y) \cdot \Theta \qquad (2.11)$$

and the hypothesis class $\mathcal{H}$ is the set of all such functions,

$$\mathcal{H} = \{h_\Theta \; : \; \Theta \in \Re^n\} \qquad (2.12)$$

The method for converting parsing to a margin-based problem is similar to the method for ranking problems described in (Freund et al., 1998), and to the approach to multi-class classification problems in (Schapire et al., 1998; Crammer and Singer, 2001; Elisseeff et al., 1999). As a first step, we give a definition of the margins on training examples. Assume we have a training sample $\{(x_1, y_1), \ldots, (x_m, y_m)\}$. We define the margin on the i-th training example with parameter values Θ as

$$\gamma_\Theta^i = \frac{1}{||\Theta||}\left(\Phi(x_i, y_i) \cdot \Theta - \max_{y \in \mathbf{GEN}(x_i), y \neq y_i} \Phi(x_i, y) \cdot \Theta\right) \qquad (2.13)$$

The margin on the i-th example is now the difference in scores between the correct tree for the i-th sentence and the highest scoring incorrect tree for that sentence. Notice that this has very similar properties to the value $\gamma^i_{\Theta,b}$ defined for hyperplanes in equation (2.7). If $\gamma^i_\Theta > 0$, then h_Θ gives the correct output on the i-th example. The larger the value of γ^i_Θ, the more "confident" we can take this prediction to be.

We can now make a very similar definition to that in equation (2.9):

$$\hat{L}(\Theta,\gamma) = \frac{1}{m}\sum_i \left[\left[\gamma^i_\Theta < \gamma\right]\right] \tag{2.14}$$

So $\hat{L}(\Theta,\gamma)$ tracks the proportion of training examples with margin less than γ. A similar theorem to theorem 6 can be stated:

Theorem 8 *Assume the hypothesis class $\mathcal{H}$ is a set of linear models as defined in equation (2.11) and equation (2.12), and that there is some distribution $D(x, y)$ generating examples. For all $h_\Theta \in \mathcal{H}$, for all $\gamma > 0$, with probability at least $1 - \delta$ over the choice of training set of size m drawn from D,*

$$Er(h_\Theta) \leq \hat{L}(\Theta,\gamma) + O\left(\sqrt{\frac{1}{m}\left(\frac{R^2}{\gamma^2}\left(\log m + \log N\right) + \log\frac{1}{\delta}\right)}\right)$$

where R is a constant such that $\forall x \in \mathcal{X}, \forall y \in \mathbf{GEN}(x), \forall z \in \mathbf{GEN}(x)$, $\|\Phi(x,y) - \Phi(x,z)\| \leq R$. The variable N is the smallest positive integer such that $\forall x \in \mathcal{X}, |\mathbf{GEN}(x)| - 1 \leq N$.

Proof: The proof follows from results in (Zhang, 2002). See the appendix of this chapter for the proof.

Note that this is similar to the bound in theorem 6. A difference, however, is the dependence on N, a bound on the number of candidates for any example. Even though this term is logarithmic, the dependence is problematic because the number of candidate parses for a sentence will usually have an exponential dependence on the length of the sentence, leading to $\log N$ having linear dependence on the maximum sentence length. (For example, the number of labeled binary-branching trees for a sentence of length n, with G non-terminals, is $\frac{G^n(2n)!}{(n+1)!n!}$, the log of this number is $O(n \log G + n \log n)$.) It is an open problem whether tighter bounds – in particular, bounds which do not depend on N – can be proved. Curiously, we show in section 8.3 that the perceptron algorithm leads to a margin-based learning bound that is independent of the value for N. This suggests that it may be possible to prove tighter bounds than those in theorem 8.

Not surprisingly, a theorem based on 1-norm margins, which is similar to theorem 7, also holds. We first give a definition based on 1-norm margins:

$$\hat{L}_1(\Theta, \gamma) = \frac{1}{m} \sum_i \left[\!\left[\gamma_\Theta^i < \gamma \right]\!\right]$$
(2.15)

where γ_Θ^i now depends on $\|\Theta\|_1$:

$$\gamma_\Theta^i = \frac{1}{\|\Theta\|_1} \left(\Phi(x_i, y_i) \cdot \Theta - \max_{y \in \mathbf{GEN}(x_i), y \neq y_i} \Phi(x_i, y) \cdot \Theta \right)$$
(2.16)

The following theorem then holds:

Theorem 9 *Assume the hypothesis class $\mathcal{H}$ is a set of linear models as defined in equation (2.11) and equation (2.12), and that there is some distribution $D(x, y)$ generating examples. For all $h_\Theta \in \mathcal{H}$, for all $\gamma > 0$, with probability at least $1 - \delta$ over the choice of training set of size m drawn from D,*

$$Er(h_\Theta) \leq \hat{L}_1(\Theta, \gamma) + O\left(\sqrt{\frac{1}{m} \left(\frac{R_\infty^2 (\log m + \log N) \log n}{\gamma^2} + \log \frac{1}{\delta} \right)} \right)$$

where R_∞ is a constant such that $\forall x \in \mathcal{X}, \forall y \in \mathbf{GEN}(x), \forall z \in \mathbf{GEN}(x)$, $\|\Phi(x, y) - \Phi(x, z)\|_\infty \leq R_\infty$. The variable N is the smallest positive integer such that $\forall x \in \mathcal{X}, |\mathbf{GEN}(x)| - 1 \leq N$.

Proof: The proof for the multi-class case, given in (Schapire et al., 1998), essentially implies this theorem. A different proof also follows from results in (Zhang, 2002) – see the appendix of this chapter for the proof.

The bounds in theorems 8 and 9 suggested a trade-off between keeping the values for $\hat{L}(\Theta, \gamma)$ and $\hat{L}_1(\Theta, \gamma)$ low and keeping the value of γ high. The algorithms described in section 8 attempt to find a hypothesis Θ which can achieve low values for these quantities with a high value for γ. The algorithms are direct modifications of algorithms for learning hyperplane classifiers for binary classification: these classification algorithms are motivated by the bounds in theorems 6 and 7.

8.   Algorithms

In this section we describe parameter estimation algorithms which are motivated by the generalization bounds for linear models in section 7 of this chapter. The first set of algorithms, support vector machines, use constrained optimization problems that are related to the bounds in theorems 8 and 9. The second algorithm we describe is a modification of AdaBoost (Freund and Schapire, 1997), which is motivated by the bound in theorem 9. Finally, we describe a variant of the perceptron algorithm applied to parsing. The perceptron algorithm does not explicitly attempt to optimize the generalization bounds in section 7, but its convergence and generalization properties can be shown to be dependent on the existence of parameter values which separate the training data with large margin under the 2-norm. In this sense they are a close relative to support vector machines.

8.1   Support Vector Machines

We now describe an algorithm which is motivated by the bound in theorem 8. First, recall the definition of the margin for the parameter values Θ on the i-th training example,

$$\gamma_{\Theta}^i = \frac{1}{||\Theta||} \left(\Phi(x_i, y_i) \cdot \Theta - \max_{y \in \mathbf{GEN}(x_i), y \neq y_i} \Phi(x_i, y) \cdot \Theta \right) \qquad (2.17)$$

We will also define the margin for parameter values Θ on the entire training sample as

$$\gamma_{\Theta} = \min_i \ \gamma_{\Theta}^i \qquad (2.18)$$

If the data is separable (i.e., there exists some Θ such that $\gamma_{\Theta} > 0$), then of all hyperplanes which have zero training errors, the "best" hyperplane by the bound of theorem 8 is the hyperplane Θ^* with maximum margin on the training sample,

$$\Theta^* = \arg \max_{\Theta \in \Re^n} \gamma_{\Theta} \qquad (2.19)$$

This hyperplane minimizes the bound in theorem 8 subject to the constraint that $\hat{L}(\Theta, \gamma)$ is 0.

Vapnik (1998) shows that the hyperplane Θ^* is unique[4], and gives a method for finding Θ^*. The method involves solving the following constrained optimization problem:

Minimize

$$||\Theta||^2$$

subject to the constraints

$$\forall i, \forall y \in \mathbf{GEN}(x_i), y \neq y_i, \quad \Theta \cdot \Phi(x_i, y_i) - \Theta \cdot \Phi(x_i, y) \geq 1$$

Any hyperplane Θ satisfying these constraints separates the data with margin $\gamma_{\Theta} = 1/||\Theta||$. By minimizing $||\Theta||^2$ (or equivalently $||\Theta||$) subject to the constraints, the method finds the parameters Θ with maximal value for γ_{Θ}.

Simply finding the maximum-margin hyperplane may not be optimal or even possible: the data may not be separable, or the data may be noisy. The bound in theorem 8 suggests giving up on some training examples which may be difficult or impossible to separate. (Cortes and Vapnik, 1995) suggest a refined optimization task for the classification case which addresses this problem; we suggest the following modified optimization problem as a natural analogue of this approach (our approach is similar to the method for multi-class classification problems in Crammer and Singer, 2001):

Minimize

$$\|\Theta\|^2 + C \sum \epsilon_i$$

with respect to Θ, ϵ_i for $i = 1, \ldots, m$,
subject to the constraints

$$\forall i, \forall y \in \mathbf{GEN}(x_i), y \neq y_i, \quad \Theta \cdot \Phi(x_i, y_i) - \Theta \cdot \Phi(x_i, y) \geq 1 - \epsilon_i$$

$$\forall i, \quad \epsilon_i \geq 0$$

Here we have introduced a "slack variable" ϵ_i for each training example. At the solution of the optimization problem, the margin on the i-th training example is at least $(1 - \epsilon_i)/\|\Theta\|$. On many examples the slack variable ϵ_i will be zero, and the margin γ_Θ^i will be at least $1/\|\Theta\|$. On some examples the slack variable ϵ_i will be positive, implying that the algorithm has "given up" on separating the example with margin $1/\|\Theta\|$. The constant C controls the cost for having non-zero values of ϵ_i. As $C \to \infty$, the problem becomes the same as the hard-margin SVM problem, and the method attempts to find a hyperplane which correctly separates all examples with margin at least $1/\|\Theta\|$ (i.e., all slack variables are 0). For smaller C, the training algorithm may "give up" on some examples (i.e., set $\epsilon_i > 0$) in order to keep $\|\Theta\|^2$ low. Thus by varying C, the method effectively modifies the trade-off between the two terms in the bound in theorem 8. In practice, a common approach is to train the model for several values of C, and then to pick the classifier which has best performance on some held-out set of development data.

Both kinds of SVM optimization problem outlined above have been studied extensively (e.g., see Joachims, 1998; Platt, 1998) and can be solved relatively efficiently. (A package for SVMs, written by Thorsten Joachims, is available from http://ais.gmd.de/~thorsten/svm_light/.)

A closely related approach which is based on 1-norm margins – the bound in theorem 9 – is as follows:

Minimize

$$\|\Theta\|_1 + C \sum \epsilon_i$$

with respect to Θ, ϵ_i for $i = 1, \ldots, m$,
subject to the constraints

$$\forall i, \forall y \in \mathbf{GEN}(x_i), y \neq y_i, \quad \Theta \cdot \Phi(x_i, y_i) - \Theta \cdot \Phi(x_i, y) \geq 1 - \epsilon_i$$

$$\forall i, \quad \epsilon_i \geq 0$$

Input: Examples $\{(x_1, y_1), \ldots, (x_m, y_m)\}$, Grammar G, representation $\Phi : \mathcal{X} \times \mathcal{Y} \to \Re^n$ such that $\forall(x, y_1, y_2) \in \mathcal{T}$, where $\mathcal{T}$ is defined below, for $s = 1, \ldots, n$, $-1 \leq (\Phi_s(x, y_1) - \Phi_s(x, y_2)) \leq 1$

Algorithm:

- Define the set of triples $\mathcal{T} = \{(x_i, y_i, y) : i = 1, \ldots, m, y \in \mathbf{GEN}(x_i) \text{ s.t. } y \neq y_i\}$
- Set initial parameter values $\Theta = 0$
- For $t = 1$ to T
  - Define a distribution over the training sample $\mathcal{T}$ as

$$\forall(x, y_1, y_2) \in \mathcal{T}, \quad D^t(x, y_1, y_2) = \frac{1}{Z^t} \frac{e^{-\Theta \cdot (\Phi(x,y_1) - \Phi(x,y_2))}}{|\mathbf{GEN}(x)| - 1}$$

  where $Z^t = \sum_{(x, y_1, y_2) \in \mathcal{T}} e^{-\Theta \cdot (\Phi(x,y_1) - \Phi(x,y_2))} / (|\mathbf{GEN}(x)| - 1)$.
  - For $s = 1$ to n calculate $r_s = \sum_{(x, y_1, y_2) \in \mathcal{T}} D^t(x, y_1, y_2) (\Phi_s(x, y_1) - \Phi_s(x, y_2))$
  - Choose $s_t = \arg\max_s |r_s|$
  - Update single parameter $\Theta_{s_t} = \Theta_{s_t} + \frac{1}{2} \log \left(\frac{1 + r_{s_t}}{1 - r_{s_t}} \right)$

Figure 2.2. The AdaBoost algorithm applied to parsing.

This can be framed as a linear programming problem. See (Demiriz et al., 2001) for details, and the relationships between linear programming approaches and the boosting algorithms described in the next section.

8.2 Boosting

The AdaBoost algorithm (Freund and Schapire, 1997) is one method for optimizing the bound for hyperplane classifiers in theorem 7 (Schapire et al., 1998). This section describes a modified version of AdaBoost, applied to the parsing problem. Figure 2.2 shows the modified algorithm. The algorithm converts the training set into a set of triples:

$$\mathcal{T} = \{(x_i, y_i, y) : i = 1, \ldots, m, y \in \mathbf{GEN}(x_i) \text{ s.t. } y \neq y_i\}$$

Each member (x, y_1, y_2) of $\mathcal{T}$ is a triple such that x is a sentence, y_1 is the correct tree for that sentence, and y_2 is an incorrect tree also proposed by $\mathbf{GEN}(x)$. AdaBoost maintains a distribution D^t over the training examples such that $D^t(x, y_1, y_2)$ is proportional to $\exp\{-\Theta \cdot (\Phi(x, y_1) - \Phi(x, y_2))\}$. Members of $\mathcal{T}$ which are well discriminated by the current parameter values Θ are given low weight by the distribution, whereas examples which are poorly discriminated are weighted more highly.

The value $r_s = \sum_{(x, y_1, y_2) \in \mathcal{T}} D^t(x, y_1, y_2) (\Phi_s(x, y_1) - \Phi_s(x, y_2))$ is a measure of how well correlated Φ_s is with the distribution D^t. The magnitude of

r_s can be taken as a measure of how correlated $(\Phi_s(x, y_1) - \Phi_s(x, y_2))$ is with the distribution D^t. If it is highly correlated, $|r_s|$ will be large, and the s-th parameter will be useful in driving down the margins on the more highly weighted members of $\mathcal{T}$.

In the classification case, Schapire et al. (1998) show that the AdaBoost algorithm has direct properties in terms of optimizing the value of $\hat{L}_1(\Theta, b, \gamma)$ defined in equation (2.10). Unfortunately it is not possible to show that the algorithm in figure 2.2 has a similar effect on the parsing quantity $\hat{L}_1(\Theta, \gamma)$ in equation (2.15). Instead, we show its effect on a similar quantity[5] $\hat{RL}_1$:

$$\hat{RL}_1(\Theta, \gamma) \;=\; \frac{1}{m} \sum_i \frac{1}{|\mathbf{GEN}(x_i)| - 1} \sum_{y \in \mathbf{GEN}(x_i), y \neq y_i} \left[\left[\gamma_\Theta^{i,y} < \gamma\right]\right]$$

$$(2.20)$$

where

$$\gamma_\Theta^{i,y} \;=\; \frac{1}{\|\Theta\|_1} \left(\Phi(x_i, y_i) \cdot \Theta - \Phi(x_i, y) \cdot \Theta\right)$$

In these definitions $\gamma_\Theta^{i,y}$ for $i = 1, \ldots, m, y \in \mathbf{GEN}(x_i), y \neq y_i$ is the degree to which the correct parse on the i-th sentence is separated from an incorrect parse y. The quantity $\hat{RL}_1(\Theta, \gamma)$ measures the proportion of margins $\gamma_\Theta^{i,y}$ that are at least γ, where the proportions are normalized for the number of candidates on each sentence (ensuring that sentences with very large numbers of candidates do not dominate). It is clear that $\hat{RL}_1$ is related to $\hat{L}_1$ – for example $\hat{RL}_1(\Theta, \gamma)$ is 0 if and only if $\hat{L}_1(\Theta, \gamma)$ is 0 – although they are somewhat different quantities.

There is a strong relation between the values of $|r_s|$, and the effect on the values of $\hat{RL}_1(\Theta, \gamma)$. If we define $\epsilon_t = (1 - |r_{s_t}|)/2$ then the following theorem holds:

Theorem 10 *(Slight modification of theorem 5 of Schapire et al., 1998). If we define $\hat{RL}_1(\Theta, \gamma)$ as in equation (2.20), and the Adaboost algorithm in figure 2.2 generates values $\epsilon_1, \epsilon_2, \ldots, \epsilon_T$, then for all $\gamma > 0$,*

$$\hat{RL}_1(\Theta, \gamma) \leq 2^T \prod_{t=1}^{T} \sqrt{\epsilon_t^{1-\gamma}(1 - \epsilon_t)^{1+\gamma}}$$

Schapire et al. (1998) point out that if for all $t = 1, \ldots, T$, $\epsilon_t \leq 1/2 - \delta$ (i.e., $|r_{s_t}| \geq 2\delta$) for some $\delta > 0$, then the theorem implies that

$$\hat{RL}_1(\Theta, \gamma) \leq \left(\sqrt{(1 - 2\delta)^{1-\gamma}(1 + 2\delta)^{1+\gamma}}\right)^T = f(\delta, \gamma)^T$$

It can be shown that $f(\delta, \gamma)$ is less than one providing that $\gamma < \delta$: the implication is that for all $\gamma < \delta$, $\hat{RL}_1(\Theta, \gamma)$ decreases exponentially in the number of

Input: Examples $\{(x_1, y_1), \ldots, (x_m, y_m)\}$, Grammar G, representation $\Phi : \mathcal{X} \times \mathcal{Y} \rightarrow \Re^n$
Algorithm: Initialise parameters Θ to be 0
         For $t = 1$ to T, For $i = 1$ to m,
            Calculate $y = h_\Theta(x_i) = \arg \max_{z \in \mathbf{GEN}(x_i)} \Phi(x_i, z) \cdot \Theta$
            If$(y = y_i)$ then do nothing; else if$(y \neq y_i)$ then $\Theta = \Theta + \Phi(x_i, y_i) - \Phi(x_i, y)$
Output: Parameter values Θ

Figure 2.3.   The perceptron algorithm for parsing. It takes T passes over the training set.

iterations, T. So if the AdaBoost algorithm can successfully maintain high values of $|r_{s_t}|$ for several iterations, it will be successful at minimizing $\hat{R}L_1(\Theta, \gamma)$ for a relatively large range of γ. Given that $\hat{R}L_1$ is related to $\hat{L}_1$, we can view this as an approximate method for optimizing the bound in theorem 9. In practice, a set of held-out data is usually used to optimize T, the number of rounds of boosting.

The algorithm states a restriction on the representation Φ. For all members (x, y_1, y_2) of $\mathcal{T}$, for $s = 1, \ldots, n$, $(\Phi_s(x, y_1) - \Phi_s(x, y_2))$ must be in the range -1 to $+1$. This is not as restrictive as it might seem. If Φ is always strictly positive, it can be rescaled so that its components are always between 0 and $+1$. If some components may be negative, it suffices to rescale the components so that they are always between -0.5 and $+0.5$. A common use of the algorithm, as applied in (Collins, 2000), is to have the n components of Φ to be the values of n indicator functions, in which case all values of Φ are either 0 or 1, and the condition is satisfied.

8.3   A Variant of the Perceptron Algorithm

The final parameter estimation algorithm which we will describe is a variant of the perceptron algorithm, as introduced by (Rosenblatt, 1958). Figure 2.3 shows the algorithm. Note that the main computational expense is in calculating $y = h_\Theta(x_i)$ for each example in turn. For weighted context-free grammars this step can be achieved in polynomial time using the CKY parsing algorithm. Other representations may have to rely on explicitly calculating $\Phi(x_i, z) \cdot \Theta$ for all $z \in \mathbf{GEN}(x_i)$, and hence depend computationally on the number of candidates $|\mathbf{GEN}(x_i)|$ for $i = 1, \ldots, m$.

It is useful to define the maximum-achievable margin γ on a separable training set as follows. Recall the definition of the maximum margin hyperplane in equation (2.19),

$$\Theta^* = \arg \max_{\Theta \in \Re^n} \gamma_\Theta$$

Then we define the maximum achievable margin as

$$\gamma = \gamma_{\Theta^*} = \max_\Theta \gamma_\Theta$$

It can then be shown that the number of mistakes made by the perceptron algorithm in figure 2.3 depends directly on the value of γ:

Theorem 11 *Let* $\{(x_1, y_1), \ldots, (x_m, y_m)\}$ *be a sequence of examples such that* $\forall i$, $\forall y \in$ **GEN**(x_i), $\|\Phi(x_i, y_i) - \Phi(x_i, y)\| \leq R$. *Assume the sequence is separable, and take* γ *to be the maximum achievable margin on the sequence. Then the number of mistakes made by the perceptron algorithm on this sequence is at most* $(R/\gamma)^2$.

Proof: See (Collins, 2002b) for a proof. The proof is a simple modification of the proof for hyperplane classifiers (Block, 1962; Novikoff, 1962, see also Freund and Schapire, 1999).

This theorem implies that if the training sample in figure 2.3 is separable, and we iterate the algorithm repeatedly over the training sample, then the algorithm converges to a parameter setting that classifies the training set with zero errors. (In particular, we need at most $(R/\gamma)^2$ passes over the training sample before convergence.) Thus we now have an algorithm for training weighted context-free grammars which will find a zero error hypothesis if it exists. For example, the algorithm would find a weighted grammar with zero expected error on the example problem in section 3.

Of course convergence to a zero-error hypothesis on training data says little about how well the method generalizes to new test examples. Fortunately a second theorem gives a bound on the generalization error of the perceptron method:

Theorem 12 *(Direct consequence of the sample compression bound in (Littlestone and Warmuth, 1986); see also theorem 4.25, page 70, Cristianini and Shawe-Taylor, 2000). Say the perceptron algorithm makes* d *mistakes when run to convergence over a training set of size* m. *Then for all distributions* $D(x, y)$, *with probability at least* $1 - \delta$ *over the choice of training set of size* m *drawn from* D, *if* h_Θ *is the hypothesis at convergence,*

$$Er(h_\Theta) \leq \frac{1}{m - d} \left(d \log \frac{em}{d} + \log m + \log \frac{1}{\delta} \right)$$

Given that $d \leq (R/\gamma)^2$, this bound states that if the problem is separable with large margin – i.e., the ratio R/γ is relatively small – then the perceptron will converge to a hypothesis with good expected error with a reasonable number of training examples.

The perceptron algorithm is remarkable in a few respects. First, the algorithm in figure 2.3 can be efficient even in cases where **GEN**(x) is of exponential size in terms of the input x, providing that the highest scoring structure can be found efficiently for each training example. For example, finding the arg max can be achieved in polynomial time for context-free grammars, so they can be trained efficiently using the algorithm. This is in contrast to the support vector machine and boosting algorithms, where we are not aware of algorithms whose computational complexity does not depend on the size of $\mathbf{GEN}(x_i)$ for $i = 1, \ldots, n$. Second, the convergence properties (number of updates) of the algorithm are also independent of the size of $\mathbf{GEN}(x_i)$ for $i = 1, \ldots, n$, depending on the maximum achievable margin γ on the training set. Third, the generalization theorem (theorem 12) shows that the generalization properties are again independent of the size of each $\mathbf{GEN}(x_i)$, depending only on γ. This is in contrast to the bounds in theorems 8 and 9, which depended on N, a bound on the number of candidates for any input.

The theorems quoted here do not treat the case where the data is not separable, but results for the perceptron algorithm can also be derived in this case. See (Freund and Schapire, 1999) for analysis of the classification case, and see (Collins, 2002b) for how these results can be carried over to problems such as parsing. Collins (2002b) shows how the perceptron algorithm can be applied to tagging problems, with improvements in accuracy over a maximum-entropy tagger on part-of-speech tagging and NP chunking; see this paper for more analysis of the perceptron algorithm, and some modifications to the basic algorithm.

9.   Discussion

In this section we give further discussion of the algorithms in this chapter. Section 9.1 describes experimental results using some of the algorithms. Section 9.2 describes relationships to Markov Random Field approaches.

9.1   Experimental Results

There are several papers describing experiments on NLP tasks using the algorithms described in this chapter. Collins (2000) describes a boosting method which is related to the algorithm in figure 2.2. In this case $\mathbf{GEN}(x)$ is the top N most likely parses from the parser of (Collins, 1999). The representation $\Phi(x, y)$ combines the log probability under the initial model, together with a large number of additional indicator functions which are various features of trees. The paper describes a boosting algorithm which is particularly efficient when the features are indicator (binary-valued) functions, and the features are relatively sparse. The method gives a 13% relative reduction in error over the original parser of (Collins, 1999). (See (Ratnaparkhi et al., 1994) for an approach which also uses a N-best output from a baseline model combined with "global" features, but a different algorithm for training the parameters of the model.)

Collins (2002a) describes a similar approach applied to named entity extraction. $\mathbf{GEN}(x)$ is the top 20 most likely hypotheses from a maximum-entropy tagger. The representation again includes the log probability under the original model, together with a large number of indicator functions. The boosting and perceptron algorithms give relative error reductions of 15.6% and 17.7% respectively.

Collins and Duffy (2002) and Collins and Duffy (2001) describe the perceptron algorithm applied to parsing and tagging problems. **GEN**(x) is again the top N most likely parses from a baseline model. The particular twist in these papers is that the representation $\Phi(x, y)$ for both the tagging and parsing problems is an extremely high-dimensional representation, which tracks all subtrees in the parsing case (in the same way as the DOP approach to parsing, see Bod, 1998), or all sub-fragments of a tagged sequence. The key to making the method computationally efficient (in spite of the high dimensionality of Φ) is that for any pair of structures (x_1, y_1) and (x_2, y_2) it can be shown that the inner product $\Phi(x_1, y_1) \cdot \Phi(x_2, y_2)$ can be calculated efficiently using dynamic programming. The perceptron algorithm has an efficient "dual" implementation which makes use of inner products between examples – see (Cristianini and Shawe-Taylor, 2000; Collins and Duffy, 2002). Collins and Duffy (2002) show a 5% relative error improvement for parsing, and a more significant 15% relative error improvement on the tagging task.

Collins (2002b) describes perceptron algorithms applied to the tagging task. **GEN**(x) for a sentence x of length n is the set of all possible tag sequences of length n (there are T^n such sequences if T is the number of tags). The representation used is similar to the feature-vector representations used in maximum-entropy taggers, as in (Ratnaparkhi, 1996). The highest scoring tagged sequence under this representation can be found efficiently using the perceptron algorithm, so the weights can be trained using the algorithm in figure 2.3 without having to exhaustively enumerate all tagged sequences. The method gives improvements over the maximum-entropy approach: a 12% relative error reduction for part-of-speech tagging, a 5% relative error reduction for noun-phrase chunking.

9.2 Relationship to Markov Random Fields

Another method for training the parameters Θ can be derived from log-linear models, or Markov Random Fields (otherwise known as maximum-entropy models). Several approaches (Ratnaparkhi et al., 1994; Johnson et al., 1999; Lafferty et al., 2001) use the parameters Θ to define a conditional probability distribution over the candidates $y \in$ **GEN**(x):

$$P(y \mid x, \Theta) = \frac{e^{\Phi(x,y)\cdot\Theta}}{\sum_{z \in \mathbf{GEN}(x)} e^{\Phi(x,z)\cdot\Theta}} = \frac{1}{1 + \sum_{z \in \mathbf{GEN}(x), z \neq y} e^{\Phi(x,z)\cdot\Theta - \Phi(x,y)\cdot\Theta}}$$

$$(2.21)$$

Once the model is trained, the output on a new sentence x is the highest probability parse, $\arg\max_{y \in \mathbf{GEN}(x)} P(y \mid x, \Theta) = \arg\max_{y \in \mathbf{GEN}(x)} \Phi(x, y) \cdot \Theta$. So the output under parameters Θ is identical to the method used throughout this chapter.

The differences between this method and the approaches advocated in this chapter are twofold. First, the statistical justification differs: the log-linear approach is a parametric approach (see section 4.2), explicitly attempting to model the conditional distribution $D(y \mid x)$, and potentially suffering from the problems described in section 4.3.

The second difference concerns the algorithms for training the parameters. In training log-linear models, a first crucial concept is the log-likelihood of the training data,

$$
\text{L-Loss}(\Theta) \;=\; \sum_i \log p(y_i \mid x_i, \Theta)
$$

$$
\;=\; -\sum_i \log \left(1 + \sum_{z \in \mathbf{GEN}(x_i), z \neq y_i} e^{(\Phi(x_i, z) \cdot \Theta - \Phi(x_i, y_i) \cdot \Theta)} \right)
$$

Parameter estimation methods in the MRF framework generally involve maximizing the log-likelihood while controlling for overfitting the training data. A first method for controlling the degree of overfitting, as used in (Ratnaparkhi et al., 1994), is to use feature selection. In this case a greedy method is used to minimize the log likelihood using only a small number of features. It can be shown that the boosting algorithms can be considered to be a feature selection method for minimizing the exponential loss

$$
\text{E-Loss}(\Theta) \;=\; \sum_i \sum_{z \in \mathbf{GEN}(x_i), z \neq y_i} e^{(\Phi(x_i, z) \cdot \Theta - \Phi(x_i, y_i) \cdot \Theta)} \tag{2.22}
$$

The two functions L-Loss and E-Loss look similar, and a number of papers (Friedman et al., 1998; Lafferty, 1999; Collins, Schapire and Singer, 2002; Lebanon and Lafferty, 2001) have drawn connections between the two objective functions, and algorithms for optimizing them. One result from (Collins, Schapire and Singer, 2002) shows that there is a trivial change to the algorithm in figure 2.2 which results in the method provably optimizing the objective function L-Loss. The change is to redefine D^t as $D^t(x, y_1, y_2) = p(y_2 \mid x, \Theta)/Z^t$ where Z^t is a normalization term, and $p(y_2 \mid x, \Theta)$ takes the form in equation (2.21).

A second method for controlling overfitting, used in (Johnson et al., 1999; Lafferty et al., 2001), is to use a gaussian prior over the parameters. The method then selects the MAP parameters – the parameters which maximize the objective function

$$
\text{L-Loss}(\Theta) - C||\Theta||^2
$$

for some constant C which is determined by the variance term in the gaussian prior. This method has at least a superficial similarity to the SVM algorithm in section 8.1 (2-norm case), which also attempts to balance the norm of the parameters versus a function measuring how well the parameters fit the data (i.e., the sum of the slack variable values).

We should stress again, however, that in spite of some similarities between the algorithms for MRFs and the boosting and SVM methods, the statistical justification for the methods differs considerably.

10.   Conclusions

This chapter has described a number of methods for learning statistical grammars. All of these methods have several components in common: the choice of a grammar which defines the set of candidates for a given sentence, and the choice of representation of parse trees. A score indicating the plausibility of competing parse trees is taken to be a linear model, the result of the inner product between a tree's feature vector and the vector of model parameters. The only respect in which the methods differ is in how the parameter values (the "weights" on different features) are calculated using a training sample as evidence.

Section 4 introduced a framework under which various parameter estimation methods could be studied. This framework included two main components. First, we assume some fixed but unknown distribution over sentence/parse-tree pairs. Both training and test examples are drawn from this distribution. Second, we assume some loss function, which dictates the penalty on test examples for proposing a parse which is incorrect. We focused on a simple loss function, where the loss is 0 if the proposed parse is identical to the correct parse, 1 otherwise. Under these assumptions, the "quality" of a parser is its expected loss (expected error rate) on newly drawn test examples. The goal of learning is to use the training data as evidence for choosing a function which has small expected loss.

A central idea in the analysis of learning algorithms is that of the margins on examples in training data. We described theoretical bounds which motivate approaches which attempt classify a large proportion of examples in training with a large margin. Finally, we described several algorithms which can be used to achieve this goal on the parsing problem.

There are several open problems highlighted in this chapter:

- The margin bounds for parsing (theorems 8 and 9) both depend on N, a bound on the number of candidates for any input sentence. It is an open question whether bounds which are independent of N can be proved. The perceptron algorithm in section 8.3 has generalization bounds which are independent of N, suggesting that this might also be possible for the margin bounds.

- The Boosting and Support Vector Machine methods both require enumerating all members of $\mathbf{GEN}(x_i)$ for each training example x_i. The perceptron algorithm avoided this in the case where the highest scoring hypothesis could be calculated efficiently, for example using the CKY algorithm. It would be very useful to derive SVM and boosting algorithms whose computational complexity can be shown to depend on the separation γ rather than the size of $\mathbf{GEN}(x_i)$ for each training example x_i.

- The boosting algorithm in section 8.2 optimized the quantity $\hat{R}\hat{L}_1$, rather than the desired quantity $\hat{L}_1$. It would be useful to derive a boosting algorithm which provably optimized $\hat{L}_1$.

Acknowledgments

I would like to thank Sanjoy Dasgupta, Yoav Freund, John Langford, David McAllester, Rob Schapire and Yoram Singer for answering many of the questions I have had about the learning theory and algorithms in this chapter. Fernando Pereira pointed out several issues concerning analysis of the perceptron algorithm. Thanks also to Nigel Duffy, for many useful discussions while we were collaborating on the use of kernels for parsing problems. I would like to thank Tong Zhang for several useful insights concerning margin-based generalization bounds for multi-class problems. Thanks to Brian Roark for helpful comments on an initial draft of this chapter, and to Patrick Haffner for many useful suggestions. Thanks also to Peter Bartlett, for feedback on the chapter, and some useful pointers to references.

Appendix: Proof of theorems 8 and 9

The proofs in this section closely follow the framework and results of (Zhang, 2002). The basic idea is to show that the covering number results of (Zhang, 2002) apply to the parsing problem, with the modification that any dependence on m (the sample size) is replaced by a dependence on mN (where N is the smallest integer such that $\forall x$, $|\mathbf{GEN}(x)| \leq (N + 1)$).

Zhang (2002) takes each sample (x, y) where $x \in \Re^n$, $y \in \{-1, +1\}$ and "folds" the label into the example to create a new sample point $z = xy$. The new point z is therefore also in $\Re^n$. He then gives covering numbers for linear function classes

$$\mathcal{L}(\Theta, z) = \Theta \cdot z$$

under various restrictions, for example restrictions on the norms of the vectors Θ and z.

In the problems in this chapter we again assume that sample points are (x, y) pairs, where $x \in \mathcal{X}$ is an input, and $y \in \mathcal{Y}$ is the correct structure for that input. There is some function $\mathbf{GEN}(x)$ which maps any $x \in \mathcal{X}$ to a set of candidates. There is also a function $\Phi : \mathcal{X} \times \mathcal{Y} \to \Re^n$ that maps each (x, y) pair to a feature vector. We will transform any sample point

(x, y) to a matrix $Z \in \Re^{N \times n}$ in the following way. Take N to be a positive integer such that $\forall x \in \mathcal{X}$, $|\mathbf{GEN}(x)| - 1 \leq N$. First, for simplicity assume that $\forall x$, $|\mathbf{GEN}(x)| = (N+1)$. Assume that there is some fixed, arbitrary ordering on the members of $\mathcal{Y}$, implying an ordering $y_1, y_2, \ldots, y_N$ on the members of $\mathbf{GEN}(x)$ which are not equal to the correct output y. Then we will take the j-th row of the matrix Z to be

$$Z_j = \Phi(x, y) - \Phi(x, y_j)$$

In the case that $|\mathbf{GEN}(x)| = N'$ is strictly less than $N - 1$, we will simply define $Z_j = Z_{N'}$ for $j > N'$, thereby "padding" the final rows of Z with $\Phi(x, y) - \Phi(x, y_{N'})$. Under this transformation, the distribution $D(x, y)$ over $(x, y) \in \mathcal{X} \times \mathcal{Y}$ is mapped to a distribution $D(Z)$ which generates training and test examples that are in $\Re^{N \times n}$.

The next step is to replace $\mathcal{L}$ with a new function, $\mathcal{M}(\Theta, Z)$ where $Z \in \Re^{N \times n}$. We define

$$\mathcal{M}(\Theta, Z) = \min_{j=1,\ldots,N} \Theta \cdot Z_j$$

It can be seen that if Z is created from a pair (x, y) then

$$\mathcal{M}(\Theta, Z) = \Theta \cdot \Phi(x, y) - \max_{z \in \mathbf{GEN}(x), z \neq y} \Theta \cdot \Phi(x, z)$$

Because of this there are some other useful relationships:

$$Er(h_\Theta) = \sum_{x,y} D(x, y)[[h_\Theta(x) \neq y]] = \sum_{Z} D(Z)[[\mathcal{M}(\Theta, Z) \leq 0]]$$

and for a sample $\{(x_1, y_1), \ldots, (x_m, y_m)\}$ creating a transformed sample $\{Z^1, \ldots, Z^m\}$

$$\frac{1}{m} \sum_{i=1}^{m} [[\Theta \cdot \Phi(x, y) - \max_{z \in \mathbf{GEN}(x), z \neq y} \Theta \cdot \Phi(x, z) < \gamma]] = \frac{1}{m} \sum_{i=1}^{m} [[\mathcal{M}(\Theta, Z^i) < \gamma]]$$

Zhang (2002) shows how bounds on the covering numbers of $\mathcal{L}$ lead to the theorems 6 and 8 of (Zhang, 2002), which are similar but tighter bounds than the bounds given in theorems 6 and 7 in section 6 of the current chapter. Theorem A1 below states a relationship between the covering numbers for $\mathcal{L}$ and $\mathcal{M}$. Under this result, theorems 8 and 9 in the current chapter follow from the covering bounds on $\mathcal{M}$ in exactly the same way that theorems 6 and 8 of (Zhang, 2002) are derived from the covering numbers of $\mathcal{L}$, and theorem 2 of (Zhang, 2002). So theorem A1 leads almost directly to theorems 8 and 9 in the current chapter.

Theorem A1 *Let $\mathcal{N}_\infty(\mathcal{L}, \epsilon, m)$ be the covering number, as defined in definition 1 of (Zhang, 2002), for $\mathcal{L}(\Theta, z)$ under restrictions R_1 on Θ and R_2 on each sample point $z \in \Re^n$. Let $\mathcal{N}_\infty(\mathcal{M}, \epsilon, m)$ be the covering number for the function class $\mathcal{M}(\Theta, Z)$ where Θ also satisfies restriction R_1, and any row Z_j of a sample matrix $Z \in \Re^{N \times n}$ satisfies restriction R_2. Then*

$$\mathcal{N}_\infty(\mathcal{M}, \epsilon, m) \leq \mathcal{N}_\infty(\mathcal{L}, \epsilon, mN)$$

Proof: The proof rests on the following result. Take any sample $\mathcal{S}^m = \{Z^1, Z^2, \ldots, Z^m\}$ where $\forall i$, $Z^i \in \Re^{N \times n}$. Construct another sample $\bar{\mathcal{S}}^{mN}$ of length $m \times N$, of elements Z_j^i for $i = 1, \ldots, m, j = 1, \ldots, N$, where $Z_j^i \in \Re^n$:

$$\bar{\mathcal{S}}^{mN} = \{Z_1^1, Z_2^1, \ldots, Z_N^1, Z_1^2, Z_2^2, \ldots, Z_N^2, \ldots, Z_1^m, Z_2^m, \ldots, Z_N^m\}$$

We will show that

$$\mathcal{N}_\infty(\mathcal{M}, \epsilon, \mathcal{S}^m) \leq \mathcal{N}_\infty(\mathcal{L}, \epsilon, \bar{\mathcal{S}}^{mN}) \tag{2.A.1}$$

This implies the result in the theorem, because $\mathcal{N}_\infty(\mathcal{L}, \epsilon, \bar{\mathcal{S}}^{mN}) \leq \mathcal{N}_\infty(\mathcal{L}, \epsilon, mN)$ by definition, and therefore for all samples $\mathcal{S}^m$, $\mathcal{N}_\infty(\mathcal{M}, \epsilon, \mathcal{S}^m) \leq \mathcal{N}_\infty(\mathcal{L}, \epsilon, mN)$, which implies that $\mathcal{N}_\infty(\mathcal{M}, \epsilon, m) = \max_{\mathcal{S}^m} \mathcal{N}_\infty(\mathcal{M}, \epsilon, \mathcal{S}^m) \leq \mathcal{N}_\infty(\mathcal{L}, \epsilon, mN)$.

To prove equation (2.A.1), we introduce the definitions

$$
\begin{aligned}
v_\mathcal{L}(\Theta) &= \langle \mathcal{L}(\Theta, Z_1^1), \mathcal{L}(\Theta, Z_2^1), \ldots, \mathcal{L}(\Theta, Z_1^m), \ldots, \mathcal{L}(\Theta, Z_N^m) \rangle \\
\mathcal{V}_\mathcal{L} &= \{ v_\mathcal{L}(\Theta) : \Theta \in \Re^n \} \\
v_\mathcal{M}(\Theta) &= \langle \mathcal{M}(\Theta, Z^1), \ldots, \mathcal{M}(\Theta, Z^m) \rangle \\
\mathcal{V}_\mathcal{M} &= \{ v_\mathcal{M}(\Theta) : \Theta \in \Re^n \}
\end{aligned}
$$

So $v_\mathcal{L}$ and $v_\mathcal{M}$ are functions which map Θ to vectors in $\Re^{mN}$ and $\Re^m$ respectively. Let $\mathcal{A}$ be a set of vectors which form an ϵ–cover of the set $\mathcal{V}_\mathcal{L}$, and for which $|\mathcal{A}| \leq \mathcal{N}_\infty(\mathcal{L}, \epsilon, \bar{\mathcal{S}}^{mN})$. Each member of $\mathcal{A}$ is a vector $\langle a_1^1, a_2^1, \ldots, a_N^m \rangle \in \Re^{mN}$. Because $\mathcal{A}$ forms an ϵ–cover of $\mathcal{V}_\mathcal{L}$,

$$\forall v \in \mathcal{V}_\mathcal{L}, \; \exists \bar{a} \in \mathcal{A} \; \text{s.t.} \; \forall i, j \; |v_j^i - a_j^i| \leq \epsilon$$

We define a new set $\mathcal{B}$ of vectors in $\Re^m$ as

$$\mathcal{B} = \{ \langle b^1, \ldots, b^m \rangle \; : \; \langle a_1^1, a_2^1, \ldots, a_N^m \rangle \in \mathcal{A}, \forall i = 1, \ldots, n, b^i = \min_{j=1,\ldots,N} a_j^i \}$$

Thus $|\mathcal{B}| \leq |\mathcal{A}|$, because each member of $\mathcal{B}$ is formed by a deterministic mapping from an element of $\mathcal{A}$. We will show that $\mathcal{B}$ forms an ϵ–cover of $\mathcal{V}_\mathcal{M}$. Consider any vector $v_\mathcal{M}(\Theta)$ in $\mathcal{V}_\mathcal{M}$. Consider a "parallel" vector $v_\mathcal{L}(\Theta)$. There is some $\bar{a} \in \mathcal{A}$ such that $\forall i, j \; |a_j^i - (v_\mathcal{L}(\Theta))_j^i| \leq \epsilon$. Next consider the vector $\bar{b} \in \Re^m$ such that $b^i = \min_j a_j^i$. Then clearly $\bar{b} \in \mathcal{B}$. It can also be shown that $\forall i, \; |b^i - (v_\mathcal{M}(\Theta))^i| \leq \epsilon$. This is because

$$
\begin{aligned}
& \forall i, j \; |a_j^i - \Theta \cdot Z_j^i| \leq \epsilon \\
\Rightarrow \; & \forall i \; |\min_j a_j^i - \min_j \Theta \cdot Z_j^i| \leq \epsilon \\
\Rightarrow \; & \forall i \; |b^i - \mathcal{M}(\Theta, Z^i)| \leq \epsilon
\end{aligned}
$$

Thus we have constructed a set $\mathcal{B}$ which forms an ϵ–cover of $\mathcal{V}_\mathcal{M}$, and also has $|\mathcal{B}| \leq |\mathcal{A}|$. Because $|\mathcal{A}| \leq \mathcal{N}_\infty(\mathcal{L}, \epsilon, \bar{\mathcal{S}}^{mN})$ we have $|\mathcal{B}| \leq \mathcal{N}_\infty(\mathcal{L}, \epsilon, \bar{\mathcal{S}}^{mN})$, and the theorem follows.

Notes

1. Booth and Thompson (1973) also give a second, technical condition on the probabilities $p(r)$, which ensures that the probability of a derivation halting in a finite number of steps is 1.

2. Given any finite weights on the rules other than B $\rightarrow$ a, it is possible to set the weight B $\rightarrow$ a sufficiently low for T_1 and T_2 to get higher scores than T_4 and T_5.

3. By "at most" we mean in the worst case under the choice of p. For some values of p convergence may be substantially quicker.

4. In our formulation this is not quite accurate: the values γ_Θ^i and γ_Θ remain constant when Θ is scaled by a constant $\beta > 0$ (i.e., $\gamma_\Theta^i = \gamma_{\beta\Theta}^i$ and $\gamma_\Theta = \gamma_{\beta\Theta}$ for any $\beta > 0$). To be more precise, the optimal hyperplane is unique up to arbitrary scalings by some value $\beta > 0$.

5. We are implicitly assuming that there are at least two candidates for each training sentence – sentences with only one candidate can be discarded from the training set.

References

Abney, S. (1997). Stochastic attribute-value grammars. *Computational Linguistics, 23*, 597-618.

Anthony, M. and P. L. Bartlett. (1999). *Neural Network Learning: Theoretical Foundations*. Cambridge University Press.

Bartlett, P. L. (1998). The sample complexity of pattern classification with neural networks: the size of the weights is more important than the size of the network. *IEEE Transactions on Information Theory*, 44(2): 525-536, 1998.

Block, H. D. (1962). The perceptron: A model for brain functioning. *Reviews of Modern Physics*, 34, 123–135.

Bod, R. (1998). *Beyond Grammar: An Experience-Based Theory of Language*. CSLI Publications/Cambridge University Press.

Booth, T. L., and Thompson, R. A. (1973). Applying probability measures to abstract languages. *IEEE Transactions on Computers*, C-22(5), 442–450.

Collins, M. (1999). Head-Driven Statistical Models for Natural Language Parsing. PhD Dissertation, University of Pennsylvania.

Collins, M. (2000). Discriminative reranking for natural language parsing. In *Proceedings of the Seventeenth International Conference on Machine Learning (ICML 2000)*, pages 175–182. San Francisco: Morgan Kaufmann.

Collins, M., and Duffy, N. (2001). Convolution kernels for natural language. In Dietterich, T. G., Becker, S., and Ghahramani, Z., (eds.) *Advances in Neural Information Processing Systems 14 (NIPS 14)*. MIT Press, Cambridge, MA.

Collins, M., Schapire, R. E., and Singer, Y. (2002). Logistic regression, AdaBoost and Bregman distances. In *Machine Learning*, 48(1–3):253–285.

Collins, M., and Duffy, N. (2002). New ranking algorithms for parsing and tagging: Kernels over discrete structures, and the voted perceptron. In *Proceedings of the 40th Annual Meeting of the Association for Computational Linguistics (ACL 2002)*, pages 263–270. San Francisco: Morgan Kaufmann.

Collins, M. (2002a). Ranking algorithms for named–entity extraction: Boosting and the voted perceptron. In *Proceedings of the 40th Annual Meeting of the Association for Computational Linguistics (ACL 2002)*, pages 489–496. San Francisco: Morgan Kaufmann.

Collins, M. (2002b). Discriminative training methods for hidden markov models: Theory and experiments with the perceptron algorithm. In *Proceedings of the 2002 Conference on Empirical Methods in Natural Language Processing (EMNLP 2002)*, pages 1–8.

Cortes, C. and Vapnik, V. (1995). Support–vector networks. In *Machine Learning*, 20(3):273-297.

Crammer, K., and Singer, Y. (2001). On the algorithmic implementation of multiclass kernel-based vector machines. In *Journal of Machine Learning Research*, 2(Dec):265-292.

Cristianini, N. and Shawe-Taylor, J. (2000). *An Introduction to Support Vector Machines (and other Kernel-Based Learning Methods)*. Cambridge University Press.

Della Pietra, S., Della Pietra, V., & Lafferty, J. (1997). Inducing features of random fields. *IEEE Transactions on Pattern Analysis and Machine Intelligence, 19*, 380–393.

Devroye, L., Gyorfi, L., and Lugosi, G. (1996). *A Probabilistic Theory of Pattern Recognition*. Springer.

Demiriz, A., Bennett, K. P., and Shawe-Taylor, J. (2001). Linear programming boosting via column generation. In *Machine Learning*, 46(1):225–254.

Elisseeff, A., Guermeur, Y., and Paugam-Moisy, H. (1999). Margin error and generalization capabilities of multiclass discriminant systems. *Technical Report NeuroCOLT2*, 1999-051.

Freund, Y. and Schapire, R. (1997). A decision-theoretic generalization of online learning and an application to boosting. *Journal of Computer and System Sciences*, 55(1):119–139.

Freund, Y. and Schapire, R. (1999). Large margin classification using the perceptron algorithm. In *Machine Learning*, 37(3):277–296.

Freund, Y., Iyer, R.,Schapire, R.E., & Singer, Y. (1998). An efficient boosting algorithm for combining preferences. In *Proceedings of the Fifteenth International Conference on Machine Learning (ICML 1998)*, pages 170–178. Morgan Kaufmann.

Friedman, J. H., Hastie, T. and Tibshirani, R. (1998). Additive logistic regression: A statistical view of boosting. *Annals of Statistics*, 38(2), 337-374.

Joachims, T. (1998). Making large-scale SVM learning practical. In (Scholkopf et al., 1998), pages 169–184.

Johnson, M., Geman, S., Canon, S., Chi, S., & Riezler, S. (1999). Estimators for stochastic "unification-based" grammars. In *Proceedings of the 37th Annual Meeting of the Association for Computational Linguistics (ACL 99)*, pages 535–541. San Francisco: Morgan Kaufmann.

Lafferty, J. (1999). Additive models, boosting, and inference for generalized divergences. In *Proceedings of the Twelfth Annual Conference on Computational Learning Theory (COLT'99)*, pages 125–133.

Lafferty, J., McCallum, A., and Pereira, F. (2001). Conditional random fields: Probabilistic models for segmenting and labeling sequence data. In *Proceedings of the Eighteenth International Conference on Machine Learning (ICML 2001)*, pages 282–289. Morgan Kaufmann.

Lebanon, G., and Lafferty, J. (2001). Boosting and maximum likelihood for exponential models. In Dieterich, T. G., Becker, S., and Ghahramani, Z., (eds.) *Advances in Neural Information Processing Systems 14 (NIPS 14)*. MIT Press, Cambridge, MA.

Littlestone, N., and Warmuth, M. (1986). Relating data compression and learnability. *Technical report, University of California, Santa Cruz.*

Novikoff, A. B. J. (1962). On convergence proofs on perceptrons. In *Proceedings of the Symposium on the Mathematical Theory of Automata*, Vol XII, 615–622.

Platt, J. (1998). Fast training of support vector machines using sequential minimal optimization. In (Scholkopf et al., 1998), pages 185–208.

Ratnaparkhi, A., Roukos, S., and Ward, R. T. (1994). A maximum entropy model for parsing. In *Proceedings of the International Conference on Spoken Language Processing (ICSLP 1994)*, pages 803-806. Yokohama, Japan.

Ratnaparkhi, A. (1996). A maximum entropy part-of-speech tagger. In *Proceedings of the 1996 Conference on Empirical Methods in Natural Language Processing (EMNLP 1996)*, pages 133–142.

Rosenblatt, F. (1958). The Perceptron: A probabilistic model for information storage and organization in the brain. *Psychological Review*, 65, 386–408.

Schapire R., Freund Y., Bartlett P. and Lee W. S. (1998). Boosting the margin: A new explanation for the effectiveness of voting methods. *The Annals of Statistics*, 26(5):1651-1686.

Scholkopf, B., Burges, C., and Smola, A. (eds.). (1998). *Advances in Kernel Methods – Support Vector Learning*, MIT Press.

Shawe-Taylor, J., Bartlett, P. L., Williamson, R. C., and Anthony, M. (1998). Structural Risk Minimization over Data-Dependent Hierarchies. *IEEE Transactions on Information Theory*, 44(5): 1926-1940.

Valiant, L. G. (1984). A theory of the learnable. In *Communications of the ACM*, 27(11):1134–1142.

Vapnik, V. N., and Chervonenkis, A. (1971). On the uniform convergence of relative frequencies of events to their probabilities. *Theory of probability and its applications*, 16(2):264–280.

Vapnik, V. N. (1998). *Statistical Learning Theory*. New York: Wiley.

Walker, M., Rambow, O., and Rogati, M. (2001). SPoT: A trainable sentence planner. In *Proceedings of the 2nd Meeting of the North American Chapter of the Association for Computational Linguistics (NAACL 2001)*, pages 17–24.

Zhang, T. (2002). Covering Number Bounds of Certain Regularized Linear Function Classes. In *Journal of Machine Learning Research*, 2(Mar):527-550, 2002.

Chapter 3

HIGH PRECISION EXTRACTION OF GRAMMATICAL RELATIONS

John Carroll
Cognitive and Computing Sciences, University of Sussex
Falmer, Brighton BN1 9QH, UK
johnca@cogs.susx.ac.uk

Ted Briscoe
Computer Laboratory, University of Cambridge
JJ Thomson Avenue, Cambridge CB3 0FD, UK
ejb@cl.cam.ac.uk

Abstract   A parsing system returning analyses in the form of sets of grammatical relations can obtain high precision if it hypothesises a particular grammatical relation only when it is certain that the relation is correct. We operationalise this technique – in a statistical parser using a manually-developed wide-coverage grammar of English – by only returning relations that form part of all analyses licensed by the grammar. We observe an increase in precision from 75% to over 90% (at the cost of a reduction in recall) on a test corpus of naturally-occurring text.

1.   Introduction

Head-dependent grammatical relationships (possibly labelled with a relation type) have been advocated as a useful level of representation for grammatical structure in a number of different large-scale language-processing tasks. For instance, in recent work on statistical treebank grammar parsing (e.g. Collins, 1999) high levels of accuracy have been reached using lexicalised probabilistic models over head-dependent relations. Bouma *et al.* (2001) create dependency treebanks semi-automatically in order to induce dependency-based statistical models for parse selection. Lin (1998), Srinivas (2000) and others have evaluated the accuracy of both phrase structure and dependency parsers by matching head-dependent relations against 'gold standard' relations, rather than matching

H. Bunt et al. (eds.), New Technologies in Parsing Technology, 57-72.

(labelled) phrase structure bracketings. Research on unsupervised acquisition of lexical information from corpora, such as argument structure of predicates (Briscoe and Carroll, 1997; McCarthy, 2000), word classes for disambiguation (Clark and Weir, 2001), and collocations (Lin, 2000), has used grammatical or head-dependent relations. Such relations also constitute a convenient intermediate representation in applications such as information extraction (Palmer *et al.*, 1993; Yeh, 2000), and document retrieval on the Web (Grefenstette,1997).

A variety of different approaches have been taken for robust extraction of relations from unrestricted text. Dependency parsing is a natural technique to use, and there has been some work in that area on robust analysis and disambiguation (e.g. Lafferty *et al.*, 1992; Srinivas, 2000). Finite-state approaches (e.g. Karlsson *et al.*, 1995; Aït-Mokhtar and Chanod, 1997; Grefenstette, 1999) have used hand-coded transducers to recognise linear configurations of words and to assign labels to words associated with, for example, subject/object-verb relationships. An intermediate step may be to mark nominal, verbal etc. 'chunks' in the text and to identify the head word of each of the chunks. Statistical finite-state approaches have also been used: Brants *et al.* (1997) train a cascade of hidden Markov models to tag words with their grammatical functions. Approaches based on memory based learning have also used chunking as a first stage, before assigning grammatical relation labels to heads of chunks (Argamon *et al.*, 1998; Buchholz *et al.*, 1999). Blaheta and Charniak (2000) assume a richer input representation consisting of labelled trees produced by a treebank grammar parser, and use the treebank again to train a further procedure that assigns grammatical function tags to syntactic constituents in the trees. Alternatively, a hand-written grammar can be used that produces similar phrase structure analyses and perhaps partial analyses from which grammatical relations are extracted (e.g. Carroll *et al.*, 1998b; Lin, 1998).

Recently, Schmid and Rooth (2001) have described an algorithm for computing expected *governor labels* for terminal words in labelled headed parse trees produced by a probabilistic context-free grammar. A governor label (implicitly) encodes a grammatical relation type (such as subject or object) and a governing lexical head. The labels are *expected* in the sense that each is weighted by the sum of the probabilities of the trees giving rise to it, and are computed efficiently by processing the entire parse forest rather than individual trees. The resulting set of governing-head tuples will not typically constitute a globally coherent analysis, but may be useful for interfacing to applications that primarily accumulate fragments of grammatical information from text (such as for instance information extraction, or systems that acquire lexical data from corpora). The approach is not so suitable for applications that need to interpret complete and consistent sentence structures (such as the analysis phase of transfer-based machine translation). Schmid and Rooth have implemented the algorithm for parsing with a lexicalised probabilistic context-free grammar of

English and applied it in an open domain question answering system, but they do not give any practical results or an evaluation.

In this paper we investigate empirically Schmid and Rooth's proposals, using a wide-coverage parsing system applied to a test corpus of naturally-occurring text, extend it with various thresholding techniques, and observe the trade-off between precision and recall in grammatical relations returned. Using the most conservative threshold results in a parser that returns only grammatical relations that form part of all analyses licensed by the grammar. In this case, precision rises to over 90%, as compared with a baseline of 75%.

2.   The Analysis System

In this work, our starting point is an existing statistical shallow parsing system for English (Briscoe and Carroll, 2002). Briefly, the system works as follows: input text is tokenised and then labelled with part-of-speech (PoS) tags by a tagger, and these are parsed using a wide-coverage unification-based grammar of English PoS tags and punctuation. For disambiguation, the parser uses a probabilistic LR model derived from parse tree structures in a treebank, augmented with a set of lexical entries for verbs, acquired automatically from a 10 million word sample of the British National Corpus (Leech, 1992), each entry containing subcategorisation frame information and an associated probability. The parser is therefore 'semi-lexicalised' in that verbal argument structure is disambiguated lexically, but the rest of the disambiguation is purely structural.

The coverage of the grammar (the proportion of sentences for which at least one complete spanning analysis is found) is around 80% when applied to the SUSANNE corpus (Sampson, 2001). In addition, the system is able to perform parse failure recovery, finding the highest scoring sequence of phrasal fragments (following the approach of Kiefer *et al.*, 1999), and the system has produced at least partial analyses for over 98% of the sentences in the 90M word written part of the British National Corpus.

The parsing system reads off grammatical relation tuples (GRs) from the constituent structure tree that is returned from the disambiguation phase. Information is used about which grammar rules introduce subjects, complements, and modifiers, and which daughter(s) is/are the head(s), and which the dependents. In the evaluation reported in Carroll *et al.*, 1998b, the system achieves GR accuracy that is comparable to published results for other systems: extraction of non-clausal subject relations with 83% precision, compared with a figure of 80% (Grefenstette, 1999); and overall F_1-score[1] of unlabelled head-dependent pairs of 80, as opposed to 83 (Lin, 1998)[2] and 84 (Srinivas, 2000 – this with respect only to binary relations, and omitting the analysis of control relationships). Blaheta and Charniak (2000) report an F_1-score of 87 for

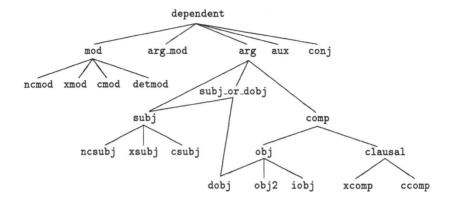

Figure 3.1. Grammatical relation hierarchy.

assigning grammatical function tags to constituents, but the task, and therefore the scoring method, is rather different.

For the work reported in this paper we have extended the basic system, implementing a version of Schmid and Rooth's expected governor technique (see Section 1 above) but adapted for unification-based grammar and GR-based analyses. Each sentence is analysed as a set of weighted GRs where the weight associated with each grammatical relation is computed as the sum of the probabilities of the parses that relation was derived from, divided by the sum of the probabilities of all parses. So, if we assume that Schmid and Rooth's example sentence *Peter reads every paper on markup* has 2 parses, one where *on markup* attaches to the preceding noun having overall probability 0.007 and the other where it has verbal attachment with probability 0.003, then some of the weighted GRs would be:

    1.0   ncsubj(reads, Peter, _)
    0.7   ncmod(on, paper, markup)
    0.3   ncmod(on, reads, markup)

The GR scheme is described in detail by Carroll *et al.* (1998a). Figure 3.1 gives the full set of named relation types represented as a subsumption hierarchy. The most generic relation between a head and a dependent is *dependent*. Where the relationship between the two is known more precisely, relations further down the hierarchy can be used, for example *mod*ifier or *arg*ument. Relations *mod*, *arg_mod*, *aux*, *clausal*, and their descendants have slots filled by a type, a head, and its dependent; *arg_mod* has an additional fourth slot initial_gr. Descendants of *subj* and also *dobj* have the three slots head, dependent, and initial_gr. Relation *conj* has a type slot and one or more head slots. The *nc*, *x* and *c* prefixes to relation names differentiate non-clausal, clausal and externally-controlled clausal dependents, respectively. Figure 3.2 contains a

1.0	aux(_, continue, will)	0.4490	iobj(on, place, tax-payers)
1.0	detmod(_, burden, a)	0.3276	ncmod(on, burden, tax-payers)
1.0	dobj(do, this, _)	0.2138	ncmod(on, place, tax-payers)
1.0	dobj(place, burden, _)	0.0250	xmod(to, continue, place)
1.0	ncmod(_, burden, disproportionate)	0.0242	ncmod(_, Fulton, tax-payers)
1.0	ncsubj(continue, Failure, _)	0.0086	obj2(place, tax-payers)
1.0	ncsubj(place, Failure, _)	0.0086	ncmod(on, burden, Fulton)
1.0	xcomp(to, Failure, do)	0.0020	mod(_, continue, place)
0.9730	clausal(continue, place)	0.0010	ncmod(on, continue, tax-payers)
0.9673	ncmod(_, tax-payers, Fulton)		

Figure 3.2. Weighted GRs for the sentence *Failure to do this will continue to place a dispro-portionate burden on Fulton taxpayers.*

more extended example of a weighted GR analysis for a short sentence from the SUSANNE corpus.

3. Empirical Results

3.1 Weight Thresholding

Our first experiment compared the accuracy of the parser when extracting GRs from the highest ranked analysis (the standard probabilistic parsing setup) against extracting weighted GRs from all parses in the forest. To measure accuracy we use the precision, recall and F_1-score measures of parser GRs against 'gold standard' GR annotations in a 10,000-word test corpus of in-coverage sentences derived from the SUSANNE corpus and covering a range of written genres.[3] GRs are, in general, compared using an equality test, except that in a specific, limited number of cases the parser is allowed to return *mod*, *subj* and *clausal* relations rather than the more specific ones they subsume, and to leave unspecified the filler for the type slot in the *mod*, *iobj* and *clausal* relations.[4] The head and dependent slot fillers are in all cases the base forms of a single (head) word.

When a parser GR has a weight of less than one, we proportionally discount its contribution to the precision and recall scores. Thus, given a set T of GRs with associated weights produced by the parser, i.e.

$$T = \{(w_i, t_i) \mid w_i \text{ is the weight associated with GR } t_i, \text{ where } 0 < w_i \le 1\}$$

and a set S of gold-standard (unweighted) GRs, we compute the weighted match between S and the elements of T as

$$m = \sum_{(w_i, t_i) \in T} w_i \, \delta(t_i \in S)$$

Table 3.1.   GR accuracy comparing extraction from just the highest-ranked parse compared to weighted GR extraction from all parses.

	Precision (%)	*Recall (%)*	F_1-score
Best parse	76.25	76.77	76.51
All parses	74.63	75.33	74.98

where $\delta(x) = 1$ if x is true and 0 otherwise. The weighted precision and recall are then

$$\frac{m}{\sum\limits_{(w_i,t_i) \in T} w_i} \quad \text{and} \quad \frac{m}{|S|}$$

respectively, expressed as percentages. We are not aware of any previous published work using weighted precision and recall measures, although there is an option for associating weights with complete parses in the distributed software implementing the PARSEVAL scheme (Harrison *et al.*, 1991) for evaluating parser accuracy with respect to phrase structure bracketings. The weighted measures make sense for application tasks that can utilise potentially incomplete sets of potentially mutually-inconsistent GRs.

In this initial experiment, precision and recall when extracting weighted GRs from all parses were both one and a half percentage points lower than when GRs were extracted from just the highest ranked analysis (see Table 3.1).[5] This decrease in accuracy might be expected, though, given that a true positive GR may be returned with weight less than one, and so will not receive full credit from the weighted precision and recall measures.

However, these results only tell part of the story. An application might only utilise GRs which the parser is fairly confident are correct. For instance, in unsupervised acquisition of lexical information (such as subcategorisation frames for verbs), the usual methodology is to (partially) analyse the text, retaining only reliable hypotheses which are then filtered based on the amount of evidence for them over the corpus as a whole. Thus, Brent (1993) only creates hypotheses on the basis of instances of verb frames that are reliably and unambiguously cued by closed class items (such as pronouns) so there can be no other attachment possibilities. In recent work on unsupervised learning of prepositional phrase disambiguation, Pantel and Lin (2000) derive training instances only from relevant data appearing in syntactic contexts that are guaranteed to be unambiguous. In our system, the weights on GRs indicate how certain the parser is of the associated relations being correct. We therefore investigated whether more highly weighted GRs are in fact more likely to be correct than ones with

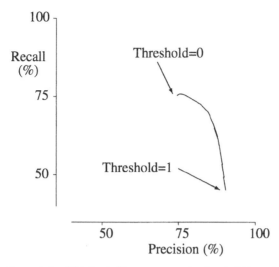

Figure 3.3.   Weighted GR accuracy as the threshold is varied.

lower weights. We did this by setting a *threshold* on the output, such that any GR with weight lower than the threshold is discarded.

Figure 3.3 plots weighted recall and precision as the threshold is varied between zero and one The results are intriguing. Precision increases monotonically from 74.6% at a threshold of zero (the situation as in the previous experiment where all GRs extracted from all parses in the forest are returned) to 90.4% at a threshold of 1.0. (The latter threshold has the effect of allowing only those GRs that form part of every single analysis to be returned). The influence of the threshold on recall is equally dramatic, although, since we have not escaped the usual trade-off with precision, the results are somewhat less positive. Recall decreases from 75.3% to 45.2%, initially rising slightly, then falling at a gradually increasing rate. At about the same point, precision shows a sharp rise, although smaller in magnitude. Table 3.2 shows in detail what is happening in this region. Between thresholds 0.99 and 1.0 there is only a two percentage point difference in precision, but recall differs by almost fourteen percentage points.[6] Over the whole range, as the threshold is increased from zero, precision rises faster than recall falls until the threshold reaches 0.65; here the F_1-score attains its overall maximum of 77.

It turns out that the eventual figure of over 90% precision is not due to 'easier' GR types (such as the that between a determiner and a noun) being returned and more difficult ones (for example, that between a verb and a clausal complement) being ignored. Table 3.3 shows that the majority of relation types are produced with frequency consistent with the overall 45% recall figure. Exceptions are *arg_mod* (encoding the English passive 'by-phrase') and *iobj* (indirect object),

Table 3.2.   Weighted GR accuracy as the threshold approaches 1.0.

GR Weight Threshold	Precision (%)	Recall (%)	F_1-score
1.0	90.40	45.21	60.27
0.99999999	90.27	46.28	61.19
0.9999999	90.17	46.87	61.68
0.999999	90.08	47.64	62.32
0.99999	90.03	48.91	63.38
0.9999	89.68	51.15	65.15
0.999	89.11	54.06	67.29
0.99	88.43	59.13	70.87
0.9	86.39	66.27	75.00
⋮	⋮	⋮	⋮
0.0	74.63	75.33	74.98

Table 3.3.   Total numbers of parser and test corpus GRs by type, using a threshold of 1.0.

Relation Type	Parser GRs	Test Corpus GRs
mod	1915	2710
ncmod	979	2377
xmod	14	170
cmod	51	163
detmod	840	1124
arg_mod	0	39
arg	1058	1941
subj	664	993
ncsubj	659	984
xsubj	0	5
csubj	2	4
subj_or_dobj	852	1339
comp	394	948
obj	205	559
dobj	188	396
obj2	17	19
iobj	0	144
clausal	189	389
xcomp	161	323
ccomp	26	66
aux	237	379
conj	60	164

for which no GRs at all are produced. The reason for this is that both types of relation originate from an occurrence of a prepositional phrase in contexts where it could be either a modifier or a complement of a predicate. This pervasive ambiguity means that there will always be disagreement between analyses over the relation type (but not necessarily over the identity of the head and dependent themselves).

3.2   Parse Unpacking

Schmid and Rooth's algorithm computes expected governors efficiently by using dynamic programming and processing the entire parse forest rather than individual trees. In contrast, we unpack the whole parse forest and then extract weighted GRs from each tree individually. Our implementation is certainly less elegant, but in practical terms for sentences where there are relatively small numbers of parses the speed is still acceptable. However, throughput goes down linearly with the number of parses, and when there are many thousands of parses – and particularly also when the sentence is long and so each tree is large – the system becomes unacceptably slow.

One possibility to improve the situation would be to extract GRs directly from forests. At first glance this looks viable: although our parse forests are produced by a probabilistic LR parser using a unification-based grammar, they are similar in content to those computed by a context-free grammar, probabilistic, as assumed by Schmid and Rooth's algorithm. However, there are problems. If the test for being able to pack local ambiguities in the unification grammar parse forest is feature structure subsumption, unpacking a parse apparently encoded in the forest can fail due to non-local inconsistency in feature values (Oepen and Carroll, 2000),[7] so every GR hypothesis would have to be checked to ensure that the parse it came from was globally valid. It is likely that this verification step would cancel out the efficiency gained from using an algorithm based on dynamic programming. This problem could be side-stepped (but at the cost of less compact parse forests) by instead testing for feature structure equivalence rather than subsumption. A second, more serious problem is that some of our relation types encode more information than is present in a single governing-head tuple (the non-clausal subject relation, for instance, encoding whether the surface subject is the 'deep' object in a passive construction); this information can again be less local and violate the conditions required for the dynamic programming approach.

Another possibility is to compute only the n highest ranked parses and extract weighted GRs from just those. The basic case where $n = 1$ is equivalent to the standard approach of computing GRs from the highest probability parse. Table 3.4 shows the effect on accuracy as n is increased in stages to 1000, using a threshold for GR extraction of 1.0; also shown is the previous setup (labelled

Table 3.4. Weighted GR accuracy using a threshold of 1.0, with respect to the maximum number of ranked parses considered.

Maximum Parses	Precision (%)	Recall (%)	F_1-score
1	76.25	76.77	76.51
2	80.15	73.30	76.57
5	84.94	67.03	74.93
10	86.73	62.47	72.63
100	89.59	51.45	65.36
1000	90.24	46.08	61.00
unlimited	90.40	45.21	60.27

'unlimited') in which all parses in the forest are considered.[8] (All differences in precision in the Table are significant to at least the 95% level, except between 1000 parses and an unlimited number). The results demonstrate that limiting processing to a relatively small, fixed number of parses – even as low as 100 – comes within a small margin of the accuracy achieved using the full parse forest. These results are striking, in view of the fact that the grammar assigns more than 300 parses to over a third of the sentences in the test corpus, and more than 1000 parses to a fifth of them. Another interesting observation is that the relationship between precision and recall is very close to that seen when the threshold is varied (as in the previous section); there appears to be no loss in recall at a given level of precision. We therefore feel confident in unpacking a limited number of parses from the forest and extracting weighted GRs from them, rather than trying to process all parses. We have tentatively set the limit to be 1000, as a reasonable compromise in our system between throughput and accuracy.

3.3   Parse Weighting

The way in which the GR weighting is carried out does not matter when the weight threshold is equal to 1.0 (since then only GRs that are part of every analysis are returned, each with a weight of 1). However, we wanted to see whether the precise method for assigning weights to GRs has an effect on accuracy, and if so, to what extent. We therefore tried an alternative approach where each GR receives a contribution of 1 from every parse, no matter what the probability of the parse is, normalising in this case by the number of parses considered. This tends to increase the numbers of GRs returned for any given threshold, so when comparing the two methods we found thresholds such that each method obtained the same precision figure (of roughly 83.38%). We then compared the recall figures (see Table 3.5). The recall for the probabilistic

Table 3.5. Accuracy at the same level of precision using different weighting methods, with a 1000-parse tree limit.

Weighting Method	Precision (%)	Recall (%)	F_1-score
Probabilistic (at threshold 0.99)	88.38	59.19	70.90
Equally (at threshold 0.768)	88.39	55.17	67.94

weighting scheme is 4% higher (statistically significant at the 99.95% level) as expected, given the loss of information entailed by ignoring parse probabilities.

It could be that an application has a preference for GRs that arise from less ambiguous sentences. In this case the parser could re-weight GRs such that the new weight is proportional to the inverse of the number of parses for the sentence: for instance changing weight w to

$$\left(\frac{1}{|P|}\right)^{(w-1)^2}$$

where $|P|$ is the number of parses. A weight of 1 would then be retained; however with this formula most values end up being either within a small region of 1, or extremely small. Using the absolute value of $w - 1$ instead of $(w - 1)^2$ seems to improve matters, but, in general, the best re-weighting method is likely to be application-specific and can only be determined empirically.

3.4   Maximal Consistent Relation Sets

Rather than returning all weighted GRs for a sentence, we could instead produce the maximal *consistent set* of weighted GRs. We might want to do this if we want complete and coherent sentence analyses, interpreting the weights as confidence measures over sub-analysis segments. To compute consistent relation sets we use a 'greedy' approximation, taking GRs sorted in order of decreasing weight and adding a GR to the set if and only if there is not already a GR in the set with the same dependent. (But note that the correct analysis may in fact contain more than one GR with the same dependent, such as the *ncsubj ... Failure* GRs in Figure 3.2, and in these cases this method will introduce errors). The weighted precision, recall and F_1-score at threshold zero are 79.31%, 73.56% and 76.33 respectively. Precision and F_1-score are significantly better (at the 95.95% level) than the baseline of all parses in Table 3.1. Improvement in the algorithm used to compute consistent sets of GRs should increase this margin. This technique provides a way of building a complete analysis in terms of GRs which do not necessarily derive from a single syntactic phrase structure tree.

4.   Conclusions and Further Work

We have extended a parsing system for English that returns analyses in the form of sets of grammatical relations, reporting an investigation into the extraction of *weighted* relations from probabilistic parses. We observed that setting a threshold on the output, such that any relation with weight lower than the threshold is discarded, allows a trade-off to be made between recall and precision. We found that by setting the threshold at 1.0 the precision of the system was boosted dramatically – from a baseline of 75% to over 90%. With this setting, the system returns only relations that form part of all analyses licensed by the grammar: the system can have no greater certainty that these relations are correct, given the knowledge that is available to it.

The technique is most appropriate for applications where a complete and consistent analysis is not required. However, the preliminary experiment reported in Section 3.4 suggests that the technique can be extended to yield a high confidence consistent set of relations drawn from the set of *n*-best phrase structure analyses. Although we believe this technique to be especially well suited to statistical parsers, it could also potentially benefit any parsing system that can represent ambiguity and return analyses that are composed of a collection of elementary units. Such a system need not necessarily be statistical, since parse probabilities are not required when checking that a given sub-analysis segment forms part of all possible global analyses. Moreover, a statistical parsing system could use the technique to construct a reliable partially-annotated corpus automatically, which it could then be trained on.

One of our primary research goals is to explore unsupervised acquisition of lexical knowledge. The parser we use in this work is 'semi-lexicalised', using subcategorisation probabilities for verbs acquired automatically from (unlexicalised) parses. In the future we intend to acquire other types of lexico-statistical information (for example on PP attachment) which we will feed back into the parser's disambiguation procedure, bootstrapping successively more accurate versions of the parsing system. There is still plenty of scope for improvement in accuracy, since compared with the number of correct GRs in top-ranked parses there are roughly a further 20% that are correct but present only in lower-ranked parses. Table 3.6 gives the actual figures, broken down by relation type. There appears to be less room for improvement with argument relations (*ncsubj, dobj* etc.) than with modifier relations (*ncmod* and similar). This indicates that our next efforts in improving parser accuracy should be directed to collecting information on modification.

Acknowledgments

We are grateful to Mats Rooth for early discussions about the expected governor label work. This research was supported by UK EPSRC projects

Relation Type	In Parse Ranked 1	Not in Parse Ranked 1 but in Parses 2–1000
ncmod	1691	538
xmod	56	36
cmod	99	65
detmod	1026	31
arg_mod	20	6
ncsubj	872	54
xsubj	4	1
csubj	1	1
dobj	337	31
obj2	16	1
iobj	109	34
xcomp	270	36
ccomp	65	6
aux	330	21
conj	114	24
Total	5010	885

Table 3.6. Number of correct GRs in top-ranked parse, and number not in top-ranked parse but in others.

GR/N36462/93 'Robust Accurate Statistical Parsing (RASP)' and by EU FP5 project IST-2001-34460 'MEANING: Developing Multilingual Web-scale Language Technologies'.

Notes

1. The F_1-score is defined as $2 \times precision \times recall/(precision + recall)$.

2. Our calculation is based on Table 2 of Lin, 1998.

3. The annotated test corpus is available from http://www.cogs.susx.ac.uk/lab/nlp/carroll/greval.html

4. We are currently refining the implementation of the extraction of GRs from parse trees, and will soon be able to remove these minor relaxations.

5. Ignoring the weights on GRs, standard (unweighted) evaluation results for all parses are: precision 36.65%, recall 89.42% and F_1-score 51.99.

6. Roughly, each percentage point increase or decrease in precision and recall is statistically significant at the 95% level. In this and all significance tests reported in this paper we use a one-tailed paired *t-test* (with 499 degrees of freedom).

7. The forest therefore also 'leaks' probability mass since it contains derivations that are in fact not legal.

8. At $n = 1000$ parses, the (unlabelled) weighted precision of head-dependent pairs is 91.0%.

References

Aït-Mokhtar, S. and J-P. Chanod (1997). Subject and object dependency extraction using finite-state transducers. In *Proceedings of the ACL/EACL Workshop on Automatic Information Extraction and Building of Lexical Semantic Resources*, 71–77. Madrid, Spain.

Argamon, S., I. Dagan and Y. Krymolowski (1998). A memory-based approach to learning shallow natural language patterns. In *Proceedings of the 36th Annual Meeting of the Association for Computational Linguistics*, 67–73. Montreal.

Blaheta, D. and E. Charniak (2000). Assigning function tags to parsed text. In *Proceedings of the 1st Conference of the North American Chapter of the Association for Computational Linguistics*, 234–240. Seattle, WA.

Bouma, G., G. van Noord and R. Malouf (2001). Alpino: wide-coverage computational analysis of Dutch. *Computational Linguistics in the Netherlands 2000. Selected Papers from the 11th CLIN Meeting.*

Brants, T., W. Skut and B. Krenn (1997). Tagging grammatical functions. In *Proceedings of the 2nd Conference on Empirical Methods in Natural Language Processing*, 64–74. Providence, RI.

Brent, M. (1993). From grammar to lexicon: unsupervised learning of lexical syntax. *Computational Linguistics*, 19(3):243–262.

Briscoe, E. and J. Carroll (1997). Automatic extraction of subcategorization from corpora. In *Proceedings of the 5th Association for Computational Linguistics Conference on Applied Natural Language Processing*, 356–363. Washington, DC.

Briscoe, E. and J. Carroll (2002). Robust Accurate Statistical Annotation of General Text. In *Proceedings of the 3rd International Conference on Language Resources and Evaluation*, Las Palmas, Gran Canaria. 1499–1504.

Buchholz, S., J. Veenstra and W. Daelemans (1999). Cascaded grammatical relation assignment. In *Proceedings of the Joint SIGDAT Conference on Empirical Methods in Natural Language Processing and Very Large Corpora*, College Park, MD. 239–246.

Carroll, J., E. Briscoe and A. Sanfilippo (1998). Parser evaluation: a survey and a new proposal. In *Proceedings of the 1st International Conference on Language Resources and Evaluation*, 447–454. Granada, Spain.

Carroll, J., G. Minnen and E. Briscoe (1998). Can subcategorisation probabilities help a statistical parser?. In *Proceedings of the 6th ACL/SIGDAT Workshop on Very Large Corpora*, 118–126. Montreal, Canada.

Clark, S. and D. Weir (2001). Class-based probability estimation using a semantic hierarchy. In *Proceedings of the 2nd Conference of the North American Chapter of the Association for Computational Linguistics*, 95–102. Pittsburgh, PA.

Collins, M. (1999). *Head-driven statistical models for natural language parsing*. PhD thesis, University of Pennsylvania.

Grefenstette, G. (1997). SQLET: short query linguistic expansion techniques, palliating one-word queries by providing intermediate structure to text. In *Proceedings of the RIAO'97*, 500–509. Montreal, Canada.

Grefenstette, G. (1999). Light parsing as finite-state filtering. In A. Kornai (Ed.), *Extended Finite State Models of Language*, Cambridge University Press. 86–94.

Harrison, P., S. Abney, E. Black, D. Flickinger, C. Gdaniec, R. Grishman, D. Hindle, B. Ingria, M. Marcus, B. Santorini and T. Strzalkowski (1991). Evaluating syntax performance of parser/grammars of English. In *Proceedings of the ACL Workshop on Evaluating Natural Language Processing Systems*, 71–78. Berkeley, CA.

Karlsson, F., A. Voutilainen, J. Heikkilä and A. Anttila (1995). *Constraint Grammar: a Language-Independent System for Parsing Unrestricted Text*. Berlin, Germany: de Gruyter.

Kiefer, B., H-U. Krieger, J. Carroll and R. Malouf (1999). A bag of useful techniques for efficient and robust parsing. In *Proceedings of the 37th Annual Meeting of the Association for Computational Linguistics*, 473–480. University of Maryland.

Lafferty, J., D. Sleator and D. Temperley (1992). Grammatical trigrams: a probabilistic model of link grammar. In *Proceedings of the AAAI Fall Symposium on Probabilistic Approaches to Natural Language*, 89–97. Cambridge, MA.

Leech, G. (1992). 100 million words of English: the British National Corpus. *Language Research*, 28(1):1–13.

Lin, D. (1998). Dependency-based evaluation of MINIPAR. In *Proceedings of the Evaluation of Parsing Systems: Workshop at the 1st International Conference on Language Resources and Evaluation*. Granada, Spain (also available as University of Sussex technical report CSRP-489).

Lin, D. (1999). Automatic identification of non-compositional phrases. In *Proceedings of the 37th Annual Meeting of the Association for Computational Linguistics*, 317–324. College Park, MD.

McCarthy, D. (2000). Using semantic preferences to identify verbal participation in role switching alternations. In *Proceedings of the 1st Conference of the North American Chapter of the Association for Computational Linguistics*, 256–263. Seattle, WA.

Oepen, S. and J. Carroll (2000). Ambiguity packing in constraint-based parsing – practical results. In *Proceedings of the 1st Conference of the North American Chapter of the Association for Computational Linguistics*, 162–169. Seattle, WA.

Palmer, M., R. Passonneau, C. Weir and T. Finin (1993). The KERNEL text understanding system. *Artificial Intelligence*, 63:17–68.

Pantel, P. and D. Lin (2000). An unsupervised approach to prepositional phrase attachment using contextually similar words. In *Proceedings of the 38th Annual Meeting of the Association for Computational Linguistics*, 101–108. Hong Kong.

Sampson, G. (1995). *English for the Computer*. Oxford University Press.

Schmid, H. and M. Rooth (2001). Parse forest computation of expected governors. In *Proceedings of the 39th Annual Meeting of the Association for Computational Linguistics*, 458–465. Toulouse, France.

Srinivas, B. (2000). A lightweight dependency analyzer for partial parsing. *Natural Language Engineering*, 6(2):113–138.

Yeh, A. (2000). Using existing systems to supplement small amounts of annotated grammatical relations training data. In *Proceedings of the 38th Annual Meeting of the Association for Computational Linguistics*, 126–132. Hong Kong.

Chapter 4

AUTOMATED EXTRACTION OF TAGS FROM THE PENN TREEBANK

John Chen

Department of Computer Science, Columbia University
11214 Amsterdam Avenue, New York, NY 10027-7003
jchen@cs.columbia.edu

Vijay K. Shanker

Department of Computer and Information Sciences, University of Delaware
103 Smith Hall, Newark, DE 19716
vijay@cis.udel.edu

Abstract   The accuracy of statistical parsing models can be improved with the use of lexical information. Statistical parsing using Lexicalized tree adjoining grammar (LTAG), a kind of lexicalized grammar, has remained relatively unexplored. We believe that is largely in part due to the absence of large corpora accurately bracketed in terms of a perspicuous yet broad coverage LTAG. Our work attempts to alleviate this difficulty. We extract different LTAGs from the Penn Treebank. We show that certain strategies yield an improved extracted LTAG in terms of compactness, broad coverage, and supertagging accuracy. Furthermore, we perform a preliminary investigation in smoothing these grammars by means of an external linguistic resource, namely, the tree families of the XTAG grammar, a hand built grammar of English.

1.   Introduction

Not only have lexicalized grammars been shown to be linguistically appealing, but they have also been shown to be desirable for parsing disambiguation as well. Among others, for example, Charniak (1996) and Collins (1996) have found that lexicalizing a probabilistic model substantially increases parsing accuracy. As introduced in Schabes et al. (1988), lexicalized tree adjoining grammar (LTAG) is a lexicalized grammar formalism in which lexical items

73

H. Bunt et al. (eds.), New Technologies in Parsing Technology, 73-89.
© 2004 *Kluwer Academic Publishers. Printed in the Netherlands.*

are associated with sets of grammatical structures. Resnik (1992) shows that parsing disambiguation can be aided by statistical knowledge of cooccurrence relationships between LTAG structures. Srinivas (1997) and Chen et al. (1999) show that considerable parsing disambiguation is accomplished by assigning LTAG structures to words in the sentence using part of speech tagging techniques (supertagging).

An LTAG grammar G and a means of estimating parameters associated with G are prerequisites for probabilistic LTAG. Schabes (1992) shows how this may be done through grammar induction from an unbracketed corpus. The number of parameters that must be estimated, however, is prohibitively large for all but the most simple grammars. In contrast, the XTAG group has developed XTAG, a complex, relatively broad coverage grammar for English (XTAG-Group, 2001) . It is difficult, however, to estimate parameters with XTAG because it has been verified to accurately parse only relatively small corpora, such as the ATIS corpus. Marcus et al. (1993) describes the Penn Treebank, a corpus of parsed sentences that is large enough to estimate statistical parameters. From the treebank, Srinivas (1997) heuristically derives a corpus of sentences where each word is annotated with an XTAG tree, thus allowing statistical estimation of an LTAG. This method entails certain drawbacks: the heuristics make several mistakes, some unavoidable because of discrepancies between how XTAG and the Penn Treebank annotate the same grammatical constructions, or because XTAG does not cover all of the grammatical phenomena found in the Penn Treebank. Furthermore, these corpus mistakes usually propagate to the statistical model.

In this work, we explore extraction of an LTAG from the Penn Treebank. This allows us not only to obtain a wide coverage LTAG but also one for which statistical parameters can be reliably estimated. First, we develop various methods for extracting an LTAG from the treebank with the aim of being consistent with current principles for developing LTAG grammars such as XTAG. Second, we evaluate each grammar resulting from these methods in terms of its size, its coverage on unseen data, and its supertagging performance. Third, we introduce a preliminary method to extend an extracted grammar in order to improve coverage. Fourth, we situate our current work with respect to other approaches to tree extraction. Lastly, we present our conclusions and suggestions for future work.

2.   Tree Extraction Procedure

In this section, we first describe the goals behind a tree extraction procedure and then describe the tree extraction procedure and its variations.

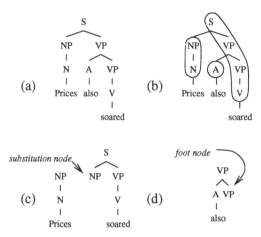

Figure 4.1. (a) Sentential structure. (b) Sentential structure where nonterminals belonging to the same trunk have been circled. (c) Localizing argument dependencies in the same elementary tree. (d) Each instance of recursion is factored into a separate elementary tree.

An LTAG G is defined as a set of *elementary trees* T which are partitioned into a set I of *initial trees* and a set A of *auxiliary trees*. The frontier of each elementary tree is composed of a lexical *anchor*; the other nodes on the frontier are *substitution nodes*, and, in the case of an auxiliary tree, one node on the frontier will be a *foot node*. The foot node of a tree β is labeled identically with the root node of β. The *spine* of an auxiliary tree is the path from its root to its foot node. This is distinct from the *trunk* of an elementary tree which is the path from its root node to the lexical anchor.

Although the formalism of LTAG allows wide latitude in how trees in T may be defined, several linguistic principles generally guide their formation. First, dependencies, including long distance dependencies, are typically localized in the same elementary tree by appropriate grouping of syntactically or semantically related elements; i.e., complements of a lexical item are included in the same tree as shown in Figure 4.1(c). Second, recursion is factored into separate auxiliary trees as shown in Figure 4.1(d).

The genesis of a tree γ lexicalized by a word $w \in S$, where S is a bracketed sentence in the Penn Treebank, using our tree extraction procedure proceeds as follows. First, a *head percolation table* is used to determine the trunk of γ. Introduced by Magerman (1995), a head percolation table assigns to each node in S a *headword* using local structural information. The trunk of γ is defined to be that path through S whose nodes are labeled with the headword w, examples of which are shown in Figure 4.1(b). Each node η' that is immediately dominated by a node η on the trunk may either be itself on the trunk, a complement of the trunk's headword – in which case it belongs to γ, or an adjunct of the trunk's headword – in which case it belongs to another (auxiliary) tree β which modifies γ.

It is therefore necessary to determine a node's status as a complement or adjunct. Collins (1997) introduces a procedure which determines just this from the treebank according to the node's label, its semantic tags, and local structural information. As described in Marcus et al. (1994), a node's semantic tags provide useful information in determining the node's status, such as grammatical function and semantic role. Our procedure for identifying complements or adjuncts closely follows Collins's method. The main differences lie in our attempt to treat those nodes as complements which are typically localized in LTAG trees. A critical departure from Collins is in the treatment of landing site of wh-movement. Collins's procedure treats the NP landing site as the head and its sibling (typically labelled S) as a complement. In our procedure for extracting LTAG trees, we project from a lexical item up a path of heads. Then, by adopting Collins's treatment, the landing site would be on the path of projection and from our extraction procedure, the wh-movement would not be localized. Hence, we treat the sibling (S node) of the landing site as the head child and the NP landing site as a complement. Figure 4.4(c) shows an example of a lexicalized tree we extract that localizes long-distance movement.

We have conducted experiments on two procedures for determining a node's status as complement or adjunct. The first procedure that we consider, "CA1," uses the label and semantic tags of node η and η's parent in a two step procedure. In the first step, exactly this information is used as an index into a manually constructed table, a *complement adjunct table*, which determines complement or adjunct status. "IF current node is PP-DIR AND parent node is VP THEN assign adjunct to current node" is an example of an entry in this table. The table is sparse; should the index not be found in the table then the second step of the procedure is invoked:

1. Nonterminal PRN is an adjunct.

2. Nonterminals with semantic tags NOM, DTV, LGS, PRD, PUT, SBJ are complements.

3. Nonterminals with semantic tags ADV, VOC, LOC, PRP are adjuncts.

4. If none of the other conditions apply, the nonterminal is an adjunct.

Whereas CA1 uses the label and semantic tags of a node η and its parent η', the procedure described in Xia (1999), "CA2," uses the label and semantic tags of a node η, its *head sibling* η_h, and *distance* between η and η_h in order to determine the complement or adjunct status of node η. CA2 relies on two manually constructed tables: an argument table and a tagset table. The argument table votes for η being a complement given the label and semantic tags of η and η_h and the distance between them. For example, if η is marked as NP,

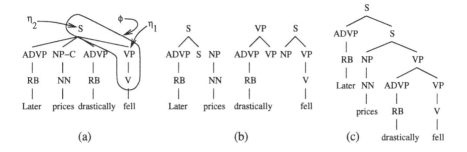

Figure 4.2. (a) Original Treebank bracketing with head sibling η_1 and its parent η_2 both on trunk of headword "fell," and siblings of η_1 marked "-C" for complement or no annotation for adjunct. (b) Extracted trees. (c) Bracketing as defined from extracted trees.

then the argument table votes for η if η_h is labeled VB and if there is a less than four node separation between η and η_h. The tagset table votes for η being a complement based on the semantic tags of η alone. If both the argument table and the tagset table vote that η should be a complement, it is labeled as such. Otherwise, it is labeled as an adjunct.

A recursive procedure is used to extract trees bottom up given a particular treebank bracketing. Figure 4.2(a) shows one step in this process. Among all of the children of node η_2, one child η_1 is selected using the head percolation table so that the trunk ϕ associated with η_1 is extended to η_2. η_1's siblings are subsequently marked as either complement or adjunct. Complement nodes are attached to trunk ϕ and the trees that they dominate become initial trees. Adjuncts are factored into auxiliary trees such that those farthest from η_1 adjoin to η_2 and those closest to η_1 adjoin to η_1, as seen in Figure 4.2(b). These are *modifier* auxiliary trees, not *predicative* auxiliary trees, which will be discussed later. Although the structure that is defined by the resulting grammar may differ from the original bracketing (see Figure 4.2(c)), none of the modified bracketings contradicts those in the original Treebank structure, unlike the heuristically derived corpus used by Srinivas (1999). This is important for our goal of ultimately comparing a parser based on this grammar to others' parsers trained on the Penn Treebank. This factoring tends to reduce the number of trees in the resulting grammar. For example, the extracted trees in Figure 4.2(b) can be used to represent not only "Later prices drastically fell" but other sentences such as "Prices fell" and "Later prices fell."

Our tree extraction procedure also factors the recursion that is found in conjunction. Conjunction in the Treebank is represented as a flat structure such as Figure 4.3(a). We define an *instance of conjunction* to be a sequence of siblings in the tree $\langle \langle X \rangle_1 \langle , \rangle_2 \langle X \rangle_2 \dots \langle CC \rangle_k \langle X \rangle_k \rangle$ where $\langle , \rangle_i$, $\langle X \rangle_i$, and $\langle CC \rangle_i$ are labels of the siblings, and there are k conjuncts. This follows from a

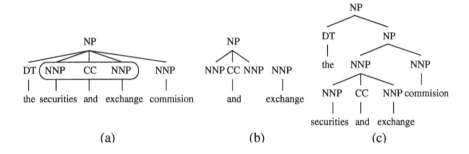

Figure 4.3. (a) Treebank bracketing of conjunction where instance of conjunction is circled. (b) Trees extracted from conjunct. (c) Bracketing as defined from extracted trees.

basic linguistic notion which states that only like categories can be conjoined. When this configuration occurs in a Treebank bracketing, each pair $\langle \langle , \rangle_i \langle X \rangle_i \rangle$ (or $\langle \langle CC \rangle_k \langle X \rangle_k \rangle$) is factored into elementary trees as follows. The $\langle , \rangle_i$th (or $\langle CC \rangle_k$th) sibling anchors an auxiliary tree β representing the ith (kth) conjunct. The $\langle X \rangle_i$th (or $\langle X \rangle_k$th) sibling anchors an elementary tree that substitutes into β. See Figure 4.3(b) for an example where $k = 1$. After factoring of recursion found in the conjunction and in the adjuncts of Figure 4.3(a), the tree extraction procedure returns a grammar that licenses the structure in Figure 4.3(c).

The technique described above only considers the conjunction of like categories. Although most conjunction is of this nature, it sometimes occurs that constituents with unlike categories are conjoined. In the Penn Treebank, these are annotated with the nonterminal label UCP. Although our current tree extraction procedure does not treat these cases specially as conjunction, a similar strategy may be employed that does so, and in any case they are quite rare.

The commas that were found in instances of conjunction were only one example of numerous cases of punctuation that are found in the treebank. Punctuation symbols are treated as adjuncts. On the other hand, we found it difficult to form a coherent strategy for dealing with quotes. Many times, an open quote would be found in one sentence and the closed quote would be found in an entirely different sentence. Therefore, we chose the simple strategy that quotes would anchor auxiliary trees that would adjoin to a neighboring sibling, namely, that sibling that was closer to the head sibling.

The Penn Treebank has an extensive list of empty elements which are used to define phenomena that are not usually expressed in LTAG. Among these are *U*, expressing a currency value, and *ICH*, indicating constituency relationships between discontinuous constituents. This observation led us to try two different strategies to cope with empty elements. The first strategy "ALL" is to include all empty elements in the grammar. The second strategy "SOME"

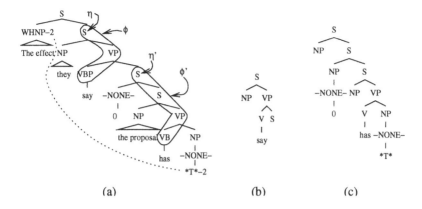

(a)   (b)   (c)

Figure 4.4. (a) Predicative auxiliary tree associated with ϕ is factored out because nodes η and η' have the same label, leaving trunk ϕ' to be extended to capture long distance movement. (b) The extracted predictive auxiliary tree. (c) The tree showing long distance movement.

is to only include empty elements demarcating empty subjects (0), empty PRO and passive NP trace (*), and traces (*T*) of syntactic movement; these are usually found in LTAG grammars of English.

The set of nonterminal and terminal labels in the Penn Treebank is extensive. A large set generally means that a greater number of trees are extracted from the Treebank; these trees could miss some generalizations and exacerbate the sparse data problem faced by any statistical model based on them. Also, some nonterminal labels are superfluous because they indicate structural configurations. For example, NX is used to label nodes in the internal structure of multi-word NP conjuncts inside an encompassing NP. If NX were replaced by NP, the tree extraction procedure can still determine that an instance of conjunction exists and take appropriate action. Conversely, distinctions that are made in a larger set of labels may aid the statistical model. For these reasons, we evaluated two different strategies. One strategy, "FULL," uses the original Penn Treebank label set. Another strategy, "MERGED," uses a reduced set of labels. In the latter approach, the original set is mapped onto a label set similar to that used in the XTAG grammar (XTAG-Group, 2001). In our approach, headedness and status as complement or adjunct was first determined according to the full set of labels before the trees were relabeled to the reduced set of labels.

Besides modifier auxiliary trees, there are predicative auxiliary trees which are generated as follows. During the bottom up extraction of trees, suppose trunk ϕ has a node η that shares the same label as another node η', where η' is a complement, not on ϕ, but is immediately dominated by a node on ϕ. In this case, a predicative auxiliary tree is extracted where η is its root, η' is its foot and with ϕ serving as its trunk. Subsequently, the path ϕ' dominated by η' becomes a candidate for being extended further. See Figure 4.4(a). This mechanism works in concert with other parts of our tree extraction procedure (notably complement and adjunct identification, merging of nonterminal labels – from SBAR to S, and policy of handling empty elements) in order to produce trees that localize long distance movement as shown in Figure 4.4(c).

Figure 4.4 also shows that the foot nodes of predicative auxiliary trees in LTAG typically correspond to sentential complements out of which extraction has occurred (XTAG-Group, 2001). In many cases, these are exactly the kinds of predicative auxiliary trees that the tree extraction procedure produces. On the other hand, there do exist anomalous cases. For example, it is possible for the procedure to produce a predicative auxiliary tree where the foot node corresponds to a sentential subject, even though in English it is not possible for extraction to occur from that position. One solution is to modify the tree extraction procedure to keep track explicitly of where extraction has occurred as trees are being constructed. Details of this solution are given in Chen (2001).

3.   Evaluation

Each variation of tree extraction procedure was used to extract a grammar from Sections 02-21 of the Penn Treebank. These grammars were evaluated according to size, well formedness of trees, their coverage on Section 22, and their performance in supertagging Section 22. We subsequently evaluated truncated forms of these grammars which we term *cutoff* grammars.

Table 4.1.   Size of various extracted grammars in number of tree frames and number of lexicalized trees

Comp Adjunct	Empty Elements	Label Set	Grammar Size	
			Frames	Lexicalized Trees
CA1	ALL	FULL	8996	118333
CA1	ALL	MERGED	5165	111220
CA1	SOME	FULL	8623	117527
CA1	SOME	MERGED	4911	110428
CA2	ALL	FULL	5354	116326
CA2	ALL	MERGED	2632	108370
CA2	SOME	FULL	4936	115335
CA2	SOME	MERGED	2366	107387

The grammars' sizes in terms of number of lexicalized trees and *tree frames* are shown in Table 4.1. Removing the anchor from a lexicalized tree yields a tree frame. In terms of different tree extraction strategies, MERGED yields more compact grammars than FULL, SOME more than ALL, and CA2 more

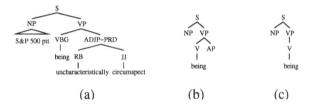

Figure 4.5. (a) Bracketed sentence S. (b) Lexicalized tree extracted from S using strategy CA1. (c) Lexicalized tree extracted from S using strategy CA2.

than CA1. Perhaps the last dichotomy requires more of an explanation. Basically, CA2 factors more nodes into auxiliary trees, with the result being that there are fewer trees because each one is structurally simpler.

We may also qualitatively judge grammars according to how well they satisfy our goal of extracting well formed trees in the sense of selecting the appropriate domain of locality and factoring recursion when necessary. There is not much difference between SOME and ALL because the empty elements that SOME ignores are the ones that are not usually captured by any LTAG grammar. Likewise, there is little difference between MERGED and FULL because most of MERGE's label simplification does not occur until after completion of tree extraction. The main difference lies between CA1 and CA2, strategies for labeling complements and adjuncts.

Nodes detected as complements of a particular lexical item belong in the same elementary tree, thus satisfying the criterion of localizing dependencies. We believe that CA1 labels nodes closer to what is traditionally found in LTAG grammars such as XTAG than does CA2, in that use of CA2 will generate less appropriate subcategorization frames because it tends to factor what might be considered as complements into separate auxiliary trees. It is difficult, however, to quantify the degree to which strategies CA1 and CA2 are successful in distinguishing complements from adjuncts because there are no precise definitions of these terms. Here we resign ourselves to a qualitative comparison of an example of a lexicalized tree extracted from the same sentence by a CA1 derived grammar G_1 (CA1-SOME-MERGED) and a CA2 derived grammar G_2 (CA2-SOME-MERGED). First, a tree frame F is selected from G_1 that is absent from G_2. A bracketed sentence S out of which the CA1 approach extracts F is then randomly culled from the training corpus. Figure 4.5(a) shows S, (b) shows the tree corresponding to the main verb extracted to G_1, (c) shows the analogous tree extracted to G_2. It is typical of the examples of divergence between CA1 and CA2 derived grammars: the CA1 approach leads to a verb subcategorization that is more complicated, yet more appropriate.

Table 4.2.   Coverage of various extracted grammars and their corresponding supertagging performance. Coverage is in terms of percentage of tree frames and lexicalized trees in the test corpus. Missed coverage is divided into *in dict* – word seen in training corpus and *out dict* – word not seen in training corpus. Supertagging performance is based on either the full grammar or cutoff grammar, cutoff value $k = 3$.

Comp Adj	*Empty Elemt*	*Label Set*	*% found*		*% miss*		*Supertag Acc*	*Cutoff Acc*
			frames	*lex trees*	*in dict*	*out dict*		
CA1	ALL	FULL	99.56	91.57	5.67	2.76	77.79	77.85
CA1	ALL	MERGED	99.82	92.18	5.06	2.76	78.70	78.57
CA1	SOME	FULL	99.60	91.66	5.58	2.76	78.00	78.07
CA1	SOME	MERGED	99.83	92.27	4.98	2.76	78.90	78.78
CA2	ALL	FULL	99.80	92.05	5.19	2.76	77.85	77.79
CA2	ALL	MERGED	99.94	92.71	4.53	2.76	78.25	78.25
CA2	SOME	FULL	99.83	92.14	5.10	2.76	78.07	78.08
CA2	SOME	MERGED	99.96	92.80	4.44	2.76	78.55	78.50

The various extracted grammars may also be evaluated according to breadth of coverage. In order to evaluate coverage of a particular grammar G, the strategy used to produce G was used to produce trees from held out data. We subsequently determined the degree of coverage of that strategy by the overlap in terms of tree frames and lexicalized trees as shown in Table 4.2. For lexicalized trees t extracted from held-out data such that $t \notin G$, we also show the percentage of cases where the *lexical anchors* of such trees t were or were not found in the training corpus (column *in dict* and *out dict* respectively). For example, the first row of Table 4.2 reports that use of strategy CA1-ALL-FULL resulted in a grammar such that 99.56% of instances of tree frames in held out data were available in the grammar, and 91.57% of instances of lexicalized trees in held out data were found in the grammar. Of the remaining 8.43%, 2.76% (*out dict*) of the lexicalized trees in the held out data involved words not seen in the training corpus. The remaining 5.67% therefore are anchored by words in the training corpus but the corresponding associations of tree frames and lexical items were not made in the training corpus. The table shows that strategies that reduce the number of extracted trees (SOME, CA2, MERGED) tend also to increase coverage.

We also measure the accuracies of supertagging models which are based on the various grammars that we are evaluating. Supertagging is the task of assigning the most appropriate lexicalized tree, or *supertag*, to each word of the input sentence (Bangalore and Joshi, 1999). In our experiments, we use the basic trigram model for supertagging, a linear time model that is quite akin to hidden Markov models for part of speech tagging. Results are shown in Table 4.2. Curiously, the grammars whose associated models achieved the highest ac-

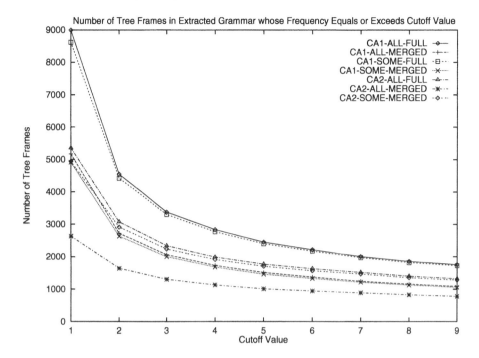

Figure 4.6. Number of tree frames occurring k times or more in the training corpus

curacies did not also have the highest coverage. For example, CA1-SOME-MERGED beat CA2-SOME-MERGED in terms of accuracy of supertagging model although the latter achieved higher coverage. This could possibly be caused by the fact that a high coverage grammar might have been obtained because it doesn't distinguish between contexts on which a statistical model can make distinctions. Alternatively, the cause may lie in the fact that a particular grammar makes better (linguistic) generalizations on which a statistical model can base more accurate predictions.

A large grammar may lead to a statistical model that is prohibitively expensive to run in terms of space and time resources. Furthermore, it is difficult to obtain accurate estimates of statistical parameters of trees with low counts. And, in any case, trees that only infrequently appear in the training corpus are also unlikely to appear in the test corpus. For these reasons, we considered the effect on a grammar if we removed those tree frames that occurred less than k times, for some cutoff value k. We call these *cutoff grammars*. As shown in Figure 4.6, even low values for k yield substantial decreases in grammar size.

Even though a cutoff grammar may be small in size, perhaps a statistical model based on such a grammar would degrade unacceptably in its accuracy.

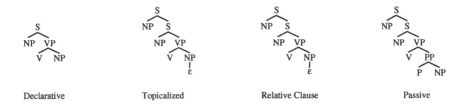

| Declarative | Topicalized | Relative Clause | Passive |

Figure 4.7. Some trees that are found in an XTAG tree family corresponding to transitive verbs

In order to see if this could indeed be the case, we trained and tested the supertagging model on various cutoff grammars. In the training data for these supertagging models, if a particular full grammar suggested a certain tree t_i for word w_i, but the cutoff grammar did not include t_i then word w_i was tagged as *miss*. The cutoff value of $k = 3$ was chosen in order to reduce the size of all of the original grammars at least in half. By the results shown in Table 4.2, it can be seen that use of a cutoff grammar instead of a full extracted grammar makes essentially no difference in the accuracy of the resulting supertagging model.

4.   Extended Extracted Grammars

The grammars that have been produced with the tree extraction procedure suffer from sparse data problems as shown in Table 4.2 by the less than perfect coverage that these grammars achieve on the test corpus. This is perhaps one reason for the relatively low accuracies that supertagging models based on these grammars achieve compared to, for example, Srinivas (1997) and Chen et al. (1999). Many approaches may be investigated in order to improve the coverage. For example, although XTAG may be inadequate to entirely cover the Penn Treebank, it may be sufficient to ameliorate sparse data. Here we discuss how linguistic information as encoded in XTAG tree families may be used for this purpose. In particular, we use this information in order to augment an extracted grammar to obtain an *extended extracted grammar* and also deliver some preliminary results.

(XTAG-Group, 2001) explains that the tree frames anchored by verbs in the XTAG grammar are divided into tree families. Each tree family corresponds to a particular subcategorization frame. The trees in a given tree family correspond to various syntactic transformations as shown in Figure 4.7. Hence, if a word w_i is seen in the training corpus with a particular tree frame t_i, then it is likely for word w_i to appear with other tree frames $t \in T$ where T is the tree family to which t_i belongs.

This observation forms the basis of our experiment. The extracted grammar G_0 derived from CA1-SOME-MERGED was selected for this experiment. Call the extended grammar G_1. Initially, all of the trees $t \in G_0$ are inserted into G_1. Subsequently, for each lexicalized tree $t \in G_0$, lexicalized trees t' are added to G_1 such that t and t' share the same lexical anchor and the tree frames of t and t' belong to the same tree family. Out of approximately 60 XTAG tree families, those tree families that were considered in this experiment were those corresponding to relatively common subcategorization frames including intransitive, NP, PP, S, NP-NP, NP-PP and NP-S.

We achieved the following results. Recall that in Table 4.2 we divided the lapses in coverage of a particular extracted grammar into two categories: those cases where a word in the test corpus was not seen in the training corpus (*out dict*), and those cases where the word in the test corpus was seen in training, but not with the appropriate tree frame (*in dict*). Because our procedure deals only with reducing the latter kind of error, we report results from the latter's frame of reference. Using grammar G_0, the *in dict* lapse in coverage occurs 4.98% of the time whereas using grammar G_1, such lapses occur 4.61% of the time, an improvement of about 7.4%. This improvement must be balanced against the increase in grammar size. Grammar G_0 has 4900 tree frames and 114850 lexicalized trees. In comparison, grammar G_1 has 4999 tree frames and 372262 lexicalized trees.

The results are quite encouraging and there exist avenues for improvement. For example, the number of lexicalized trees in the extended extracted grammar can be reduced if we account for morphological information. Note for instance that "drove," the simple past tense form of the verb "to drive," does not license passive structures. Instead of capitalizing on this distinction, our current procedure simply associates all of the tree frames in the transitive tree family with "drove." Also, in order to use these extended extracted grammars in statistical models, there needs to be a way to estimate parameters for lexicalized trees that are unseen in the training corpus.

In related work, we have conducted experiments to quantitatively extract a measure of similarity between pairs of supertags (tree frames) by taking into account the distribution of the supertags with words that anchor them Chen (2001). When a particular supertag-word combination is absent from the training corpus, instead of assigning it a zero probability, we assign a probability that is obtained by considering similar supertags and their probability of being assigned with this word. This method seems to give promising results, circumventing the need for manually designed heuristics such as those found in the supertagging work of Srinivas (1997) and Chen et al. (1999). In applying this strategy to our extracted grammar, we show that significant improvements in supertagging accuracy can be obtained.

5.   Related Work

Neumann (1998) presents a method for extracting an LTAG from a treebank. Like our work, that method determines the trunks of elementary trees by finding paths in the tree with the same headword, headwords being determined by a head percolation table. Unlike our work, that method factors neither adjuncts nor instances of conjunction into auxiliary trees. As a result, it generates many more trees than we do. Using only Sections 02 through 04 of the Penn Treebank, it produces about 12000 tree frames. Our approaches produces about 2000 to 9000 tree frames using Sections 02-21 of the Penn Treebank.

Xia (1999) also presents work in extracting an LTAG from a treebank, work that was done in parallel with our own work. Like our work, that method determines the trunk of elementary trees by finding paths in the tree with the same headword. Furthermore, it factors adjuncts (according to CA2 only) into separate auxiliary trees. Also, following our suggestion it factors instances of conjunction into separate auxiliary trees. Xia's approach yields either 3000 or 6000 tree frames using Sections 02-21 of the Penn Treebank, depending on the preterminal tagset used. Our work explores a wider variety of parameters in the extraction of trees, yielding grammars that have between about 2000 to 9000 tree frames on the same training data. Unlike our work in the extraction of an LTAG, Xia's method extracts a multi-component LTAG through coindexation of traces in the Penn Treebank. Another difference is that it is more concerned with extraction of grammar for the purpose of grammar development (for which it for example makes the distinction between extracted tree frames that are grammatically correct and those that are incorrect), whereas our current work in extraction of grammar betrays our ultimate interest in developing statistical models for parsing (for which we perform an investigation of coverage, supertagging accuracy, effect of cutoff frequency, as well as explore the issue of extending extracted grammars using XTAG tree families for eventual use in statistical smoothing).

Chiang (2000) presents an alternative method for extracting a lexicalized grammar from a treebank. Like our work, that method uses a head percolation table in order to find the trunks of elementary trees, factors adjuncts into separate auxiliary trees, and factors conjuncts into separate auxiliary trees. There also exist various differences. Instead of extracting an LTAG, that method extracts a lexicalized tree insertion grammar (LTIG) (Schabes, 1993). Certain configurations of dependencies that are legal in LTAG are not easily represented in LTIG. Another difference is the extracted LTIG of Chiang (2000) does not represent any empty elements. Insofar as empty elements are linguistically merited, the extracted LTIG may be said to be linguistically impoverished. On the other hand, not including empty elements is one reason why the extracted LTIG is so compact (3600 tree frames), using the label set FULL, when compared to the our smallest comparable grammar, CA2-SOME-FULL (4936 tree frames). Another difference is that work documents the extraction of only one kind of grammar whereas we experiment with different parameterizations of extracted grammar. However, it does include results of the additional task of experimenting with statistical parsing using the extracted LTIG, showing that its performance is quite close to parsing models based on a lexicalized context free formalism (Collins, 1997; Charniak, 2000). That work also experiments with smoothing probability distributions based on the extracted LTIG, similar to our motivation behind extended extracted grammars, but only by backing off from tree frames to their corresponding preterminals (parts of speech).

6. Conclusions

Our work presents new directions in both the extraction of an LTAG from the Penn Treebank as well as its application to statistical models. In the extraction of an LTAG from the Penn Treebank, we have extended Neumann's procedure to produce less unwieldy grammars by factoring recursion that is found in adjuncts as well as in instances of conjunction. We have explored the effects that different definitions of complement and adjunct, whether or not to ignore empty elements, and the amount of detail in label sets have on the quality and size of the extracted grammar, as well as ability to cover an unseen test corpus. We have also evaluated those grammars according to supertagging accuracy. We have experimented with the notion of cutoff grammar, and seen that these grammars are more compact and yet yield little in the way of supertagging accuracy. We have introduced the notion of an extended extracted grammar, which enriches an extracted grammar by use of an external resource, namely, the tree families of XTAG. We have seen that this technique expands an extracted grammar's coverage, and discussed how this technique may be developed in order to achieve better results.

There are a number of ways to extend this work of extracting an LTAG from the Penn Treebank. Because our primary goal is to develop a grammar around which to base statistical models of parsing, we are in particular interested in better procedures for coping with the sparse data problems engendered by the relatively large sizes of extracted grammars. Extended extracted grammars provide one means of doing this, albeit it is an incomplete solution because for it to be used in a statistical framework, there also needs to be a method for estimating parameters for those lexicalized trees that are unseen in the training corpus, but are part of the extended extracted grammar. More complete solutions can be found in Chen (2001), which provides a comparative study of several different approaches for smoothing an extracted grammar. Subsequently, we would like to see how the extracted grammar could be used as a basis for probabilistic models for LTAG, as delineated in Schabes (1992) and Resnik (1992). These models can then be applied to parsing, as in Chiang (2000). The work of Chiang (2000) may be extended to determine how different parameterizations of extracted grammars affect parsing accuracy, as well as to rate different approaches to creating extended extracted grammars. Models that are based on extracted grammars can also be potentially useful in applications other than parsing, such as stochastic natural language generation, as in Bangalore et al. (2001) and Chen et al. (2002).

Acknowledgments

This work was supported by NSF grants #SBR-9710411 and #GER-9354869.

References

Bangalore, S., Chen, J., and Rambow, O. (2001). Impact of quality and quantity of corpora on stochastic generation. In *Proceedings of the 2001 Conference on Empirical Methods in Natural Language Processing*, Pittsburgh, PA.

Bangalore, S. and Joshi, A. K. (1999). Supertagging: An approach to almost parsing. *Computational Linguistics*, 25(2).

Charniak, E. (1996). Tree-bank grammars. Technical Report CS-96-02, Brown University, Providence, RI.

Charniak, E. (2000). A maximum-entropy-inspired parser. In *Proceedings of First Annual Meeting of the North American Chapter of the Association for Computational Linguistics*, Seattle, WA.

Chen, J. (2001). *Towards Efficient Statistical Parsing Using Lexicalized Grammatical Information*. PhD thesis, University of Delaware.

Chen, J., Bangalore, S., Rambow, O., and Walker, M. (2002). Towards automatic generation of natural language generation systems. In *Proceedings of the 19th International Conference on Computational Linguistics (COLING 2002)*, Taipei, Taiwan.

Chen, J., Bangalore, S., and Vijay-Shanker, K. (1999). New models for improving supertag disambiguation. In *Proceedings of the 9th Conference of the European Chapter of the Association for Computational Linguistics*, Bergen, Norway.

Chiang, D. (2000). Statistical parsing with an automatically-extracted tree adjoining grammar. In *Proceedings of the the 38th Annual Meeting of the Association for Computational Linguistics*, pages 456–463, Hong Kong.

Collins, M. (1996). A new statistical parser based on bigram lexical dependencies. In *Proceedings of the 34th Annual Meeting of the Association for Computational Linguistics*.

Collins, M. (1997). Three generative lexicalized models for statistical parsing. In *Proceedings of the 35th Annual Meeting of the Association for Computational Linguistics*.

Magerman, D. M. (1995). Statistical decision-tree models for parsing. In *Proceedings of the 33th Annual Meeting of the Association for Computational Linguistics*.

Marcus, M., Kim, G., Mary, Marcinkiewicz, MacIntyre, R., Bies, A., Ferguson, M., Katz, K., and Schasberger, B. (1994). The Penn treebank: Annotating predicate argument structure. In *Proceedings of the 1994 Human Language Technology Workshop*, pages 110–115.

Marcus, M., Santorini, B., and Marcinkiewicz, M. A. (1993). Building a large annotated corpus of english: the penn treebank. *Computational Linguistics*, 19(2):313–330.

Neumann, G. (1998). Automatic extraction of stochastic lexicalized tree grammars from treebanks. In *Proceedings of the Fourth International Workshop on Tree Adjoining Grammars and Related Frameworks*, pages 120–123.

Resnik, P. (1992). Probabilistic tree-adjoining grammar as a framework for statistical natural language processing. In *Proceedings of the 15th International Conference on Computational Linguistics (COLING 92)*, pages 418–424, Copenhagen, Denmark.

Schabes, Y. (1992). Stochastic lexicalized tree-adjoining grammars. In *Proceedings of the 15th International Conference on Computational Linguistics (COLING 92)*, pages 426–432, Copenhagen, Denmark.

Schabes, Y. (1993). Lexicalized context-free grammars. Technical Report 93-01, Mitsubishi Electric Research Laboratories, Cambridge, MA.

Schabes, Y., Abeillé, A., and Joshi, A. K. (1988). Parsing strategies with 'lexicalized' grammars: Application to tree adjoining grammars. In *Proceedings of the 12th International Conference on Computational Linguistics*, Budapest, Hungary.

Srinivas, B. (1997). Performance evaluation of supertagging for partial parsing. In *Proceedings of the Fifth International Workshop on Parsing Technologies*, pages 187–198, Cambridge, MA.

Xia, F. (1999). Extracting tree adjoining grammars from bracketed corpora. In *Fifth Natural Language Processing Pacific Rim Symposium (NLPRS-99)*, Beijing, China.

XTAG-Group, T. (2001). A Lexicalized Tree Adjoining Grammar for English. Technical report, University of Pennsylvania. Updated version available at http://www.cis.upenn.edu/~xtag.

Chapter 5

COMPUTING THE MOST PROBABLE PARSE FOR A DISCONTINUOUS PHRASE STRUCTURE GRAMMAR

Oliver Plaehn

XtraMind Technologies

Stuhlsatzenhausweg 3, 66123 Saarbrücken, Germany

oliver.plaehn@web.de

Abstract   This chapter presents a probabilistic extension of Discontinuous Phrase Structure Grammar (DPSG), a formalism designed to describe discontinuous constituency phenomena adequately and perspicuously by means of trees with crossing branches. We outline an implementation of an agenda-based chart parsing algorithm that is capable of computing the Most Probable Parse for a given input sentence for probabilistic versions of both DPSG and Context-Free Grammar. Experiments were conducted with both types of grammars extracted from the NEGRA corpus. In spite of the much greater complexity of DPSG parsing in terms of the number of (partial) analyses that can be constructed for an input sentence, accuracy results from both experiments are comparable. We also briefly hint at possible future lines of research aimed at more efficient ways of probabilistic parsing with discontinuous constituents.

1.   Introduction

Natural languages exhibit a good deal of discontinuous constituency phenomena, especially with regard to languages with a relatively free word order like German or Dutch. These phenomena cannot be described adequately by context-free phrase structure trees alone. Arguments from linguistics motivate the representation of structures containing discontinuous constituents by means of trees with crossing branches (McCawley, 1982; Blevins, 1990; Bunt, 1996). Bunt (1991, 1996) proposed a formalism called *Discontinuous Phrase Structure Grammar* (DPSG) for use in generation of and parsing with discontinuous trees and outlined an active chart parsing algorithm for DPSGs.

H. Bunt et al. (eds.), New Technologies in Parsing Technology, 91-106.
© 2004 *Kluwer Academic Publishers. Printed in the Netherlands.*

As will become clear in the next section, DPSG is quite a natural and straightforward extension of the common formalism of Context-Free Grammar (CFG). Hence, it is reasonable to assume that *probabilistic* approaches to parsing with CFGs might also be extended with similar ease to deal with crossing branches. In order to test this hypothesis, we adapted the well-known algorithm for computing the Most Probable Parse (MPP) for a sentence given a probabilistic CFG (PCFG) to perform the same task for a DPSG enhanced with rule probabilities (PDPSG). We conducted experiments with this algorithm based on grammars extracted from the NEGRA corpus (Skut et al., 1997). It turned out that accuracy results from PDPSG experiments are comparable to those obtained in PCFG experiments on the same corpus.

In Sections 2 and 3, we define precisely what we mean by a discontinuous tree and a DPSG and present our chart parser for DPSGs. The theoretical foundations of our MPP algorithm for DPSG are discussed in Section 4, in which we also explain how the MPP is computed by a slightly modified version of our parser. Section 5 reports on experiments conducted with grammars extracted from a corpus of discontinuous trees and discusses the results we obtained. The chapter concludes with a brief summary and an outline of possible future lines of research.

2.   Discontinuous Phrase Structure Grammar

The formalism of Discontinuous Phrase Structure Grammar (DPSG) is originally due to Bunt (1991, 1996). In the presentation of DPSG below, we slightly deviate from Bunt's notation in order to have a suitable basis for defining the notion of Most Probable Parse (MPP), which is central to our parsing algorithm.

We start with a recursive definition of discontinuous trees (or discotrees for short). Discotrees consist of substructures which themselves are not necessarily valid discotrees. Consider, for instance, the discotree (a) in Figure 5.1 that contains the two substructures in (b) and (c). These substructures do not constitute valid discotrees, since they contain motherless nodes.

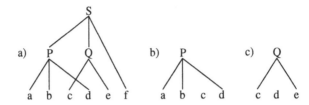

Figure 5.1. The discotree in (a) contains substructures (b) and (c), which are not valid discotrees.

A definition of these substructures is thus needed first.

Definition 1 (Subdiscotree)
Let N be a non-empty set of nodes. A subdiscotree is recursively defined as follows.

> *1 If $x \in N$, then the pair $\langle x, [\ ] \rangle$ is a subdiscotree; such a subdiscotree is called* atomic.

> *2 If $x \in N$ and $X_1, \ldots, X_n$ ($n \geq 1$) are subdiscotrees that do not share any subdiscotrees[1], and $c_i \in \{0, 1\}$ for $1 < i < n$, then the pair $\langle x, [X_1, X_2^{c_2}, \ldots, X_{n-1}^{c_{n-1}}, X_n] \rangle$ is a subdiscotree.*

> *3 No other structures than those defined by (1) and (2) are subdiscotrees.*

∎

In a subdiscotree $\langle x, [X_1, X_2^{c_2}, \ldots, X_{n-1}^{c_{n-1}}, X_n] \rangle$, the node x *immediately dominates* the top nodes of X_1, X_n, and of every $X_i^{c_i}$ such that $c_i = 0$. In other words, subdiscotrees consist of a top node x and a sequence of daughter constituents whose top nodes are immediately dominated by x, possibly interrupted by constituents whose top nodes are not dominated by x. These latter nodes are called *internal context* of x or *context daughters* of x (as opposed to the 'direct daughters' of x). As shorthand notation for $\langle x, [X_1, \ldots, X_n] \rangle$, we use $x(X_1, \ldots, X_n)$ and mark context daughters by enclosing them in square brackets instead of using superscripts for this purpose. For example, the structure in Figure 5.1a is a graphical representation of the subdiscotree $S(P(a, b, [c], d), Q(c, [d], e), f)$.

Let I denote the immediate dominance relation. *Dominance* (D) is defined as the reflexive and transitive closure of I, as usual. A *discotree* is now simply a subdiscotree T in which every node except the root node is immediately dominated by some other node in T.

Next, we introduce the DPSG notion of linear precedence in discotrees. To this end, we first need two auxiliary definitions. The *leftmost daughter* of a subdiscotree $T = x(X_1, \ldots, X_n)$, $Lm(T)$, is the top node of X_1; if $T = \langle x, [\ ] \rangle$ is atomic, then $Lm(T) = x$. The *leaf sequence* of a discotree T, *LeafSeq*(T), is the sequence of terminal nodes in T's formal representation in left to right order; if a leaf appears more than once, only its leftmost appearance is included in the sequence. The leaf sequence of $S(P(a, b, [c], d), Q(c, [d], e), f)$ is thus $\langle a, b, c, d, e, f \rangle$.

Definition 2 (Linear precedence ($<$))
Linear precedence ($<$) in a discotree A with LeafSeq(A) $= \langle x_1, \ldots, x_n \rangle$ is defined as follows.

> *1 For two leaves x_i and x_j in LeafSeq(A), $x_i < x_j$ if and only if $i < j$.*

2 For two arbitrary nodes x and y in A, $x < y$ if and only if

   (a) $Lm(x) < Lm(y)$ and

   (b) $\exists$ node z: $Lm(x) < z \leq Lm(y) \wedge \neg(xDz)$. ∎

Informally, the leaves of a discotree are totally ordered according to $<$. For two arbitrary nodes x and y, x precedes y if and only if the leftmost daughter of x precedes the leftmost daughter of y and there exists a node z in between $Lm(x)$ and $Lm(y)$ or identical to the latter, such that x does not dominate z. In the discotree in Figure 5.1a, we thus have a<b, a<c, a<d, a<e, a<f, b<c, b<d, b<e, b<f, c<d, c<e, c<f, d<e, d<f, e<f, P<c, P<d, P<e, P<f, a<Q, b<Q, Q<d, Q<e, Q<f, P<Q. Note that both P<d and PId holds; that is, there is no "Exclusivity Condition" in discotrees. This is necessary because we want a node n to precede its first context daughter (and $<$ to be a strict partial order) since the latter might be the leftmost daughter of a different constituent that is preceded by n. Two nodes x and y are said to be *adjacent* (denoted by $x + y$) if x precedes y and there is no node z such that $x < z < y$. In our example discotree, the following adjacency relations hold: a+b, b+c, c+d, d+e, e+f, P+c, b+Q, P+Q, Q+d.

A CFG rule is used to rewrite its left-hand side category as a sequence of pairwise adjacent constituents. If we directly apply this concept to the generation of discotrees, we encounter a problem, as Bunt (1991) noticed. To see this, consider again the discotree in Figure 5.1a which we would like to be generated by the rules in (1).

   (1) S → P Q f   (2) S → P Q [d] [e] f
        P → a b [c] d   P → a b [c] d
        Q → c [d] e   Q → c [d] e

But the first rule is not applicable, since Q and f are not adjacent. We would thus be forced to use the rules in (2) which are quite awkward and counter-intuitive. In order to eliminate this problem, DPSG relaxes the condition that the symbols on the right-hand side of a rule have to be pairwise adjacent and instead requires them to form an *adjacency sequence,* as defined below.

Definition 3 (Adjacency sequence)
A sequence of nodes $\langle x_1, x_2, \ldots, x_n \rangle$ in a subdiscotree A is an adjacency sequence if and only if the following two conditions hold:

   1 $\forall 1 \leq i < n$: $(x_i + x_{i+1} \vee (\exists$ nodes $y_1, \ldots, y_m$ in A: $x_i + y_1 \wedge y_1 + y_2 \wedge \ldots \wedge y_{m-1} + y_m \wedge y_m + x_{i+1} \wedge \forall 1 \leq j \leq m$: $\exists 1 \leq k \leq i$: $x_k D y_j))$

   2 $\forall 1 \leq i < j \leq n$: $\neg (\exists$ node z in A: $x_i D z \wedge x_j D z)$. ∎

Informally, we require in clause (1) that every pair $\langle x_i, x_{i+1} \rangle$ in the sequence is either an adjacency pair or is connected by a sequence of adjacency pairs of which all members are dominated by some element in the subsequence $\langle x_1, \ldots, x_i \rangle$ and in clause (2) that the elements of the sequence do not share any constituents. Thus, in our example, $\langle P, Q, f \rangle$ constitutes an adjacency sequence since P and Q are adjacent, Q and f are connected by the sequence of adjacency pairs Q+d, d+e, e+f, and d and e are dominated by P and Q, respectively. Furthermore, P, Q and f do not share any constituents. We can therefore use the rules in (1) to generate the discotree in Figure 5.1a.

A Discontinuous Phrase Structure Grammar then essentially consists of a set of rules which can be used in generating a discotree such that the nodes corresponding to the symbols on the right-hand sides of rules form adjacency sequences.

Definition 4 (Discontinuous Phrase Structure Grammar)
A Discontinuous Phrase Structure Grammar (DPSG) *is a quadruple* $\langle V_N, V_T, S, R \rangle$, *where*

- V_N *is a finite set of* nonterminal symbols;

- V_T *is a finite set of* terminal symbols; *let* V *denote* $V_N \cup V_T$;

- $S \in V_N$ *is the distinguished* start symbol *of the grammar;*

- R *is a finite set of* rules $X \to Y^{1,c_1} Y^{2,c_2} \ldots Y^{n,c_n}$, *where* $X \in V_N$, $Y^1, \ldots, Y^n \in V$, *and* $c_i \in \{0, 1\}$ $(1 \le i \le n)$ *indicates whether* Y^i *is a* context daughter *in the rule. Since neither the first nor the last daughter may be marked as internal context,* $c_1 = c_n = 0$. ∎

This definition makes apparent the close similarity between CFG and DPSG. In fact, a DPSG not containing rules with context daughters degenerates to a CFG.

3. The Parsing Algorithm

Bunt (1991) outlined an active chart parsing algorithm for DPSG that constructs discotrees bottom-up (see also van der Sloot, 1990 and Bunt & van der Sloot, 1996). Here, we present an agenda-based chart parser that provides us with greater flexibility with respect to the order in which edges are to be processed.

The algorithm makes use of three data structures. *Edges* correspond to (partial) parse trees (subdiscotrees, that is) and an *agenda* stores edges considered for combination with other edges already residing on the *chart*. An edge consists of the starting and ending positions of its corresponding subparse, a pointer to the DPSG rule which has been used to construct the edge, and the number of its right-hand side symbols for which constituents have already been found (fields `start`, `end`, `rule` and `dot_pos`, resp.). This information

alone, though, is not sufficient to uniquely describe a possibly discontinuous
constituent. We also need to know which terminal symbols are dominated by
direct daughters of the edge and which by context daughters. To this end,
each edge is additionally associated with two bit-strings (fields `covers` and
`ctxt_covers`)[2].

For instance, during the construction of the discotree in Figure 5.1a given
the DPSG in (1), our parser creates the *inactive* (or *completed*) edge $[0, 4, P \rightarrow$
a b [c] d •, 110100, 001000] for the subparse in Figure 5.1b. Later on,
it also builds the edge $[0, 4, S \rightarrow P • Q f, 110100, 000000]$, which
is called *active* since it still needs to be combined with constituents for Q and
f. Notice that the input symbol c is not yet dominated by a direct or a context
daughter of the edge. Therefore, the third bit in both `covers` (110100) and
`ctxt_covers` (000000) is unset (equals 0).

The core of the parsing algorithm works as follows.

> /* Initialization */
> for $i = 0$ to $n - 1$ do
> $edge \leftarrow$ new edge $[i, i + 1, t_i \rightarrow •, 0^i 1 0^{n-i-1}, 0^n]$;
>   agenda.add($edge$);
>
> /* Parsing */
> while not agenda.is_empty() do
> $edge \leftarrow$ agenda.get_next();
>   chart.add($edge$);
>
> /* Termination */
> if chart.success($goal$) then output parse(s);

During initialization, edges corresponding to the terminal symbols
$t_0, \ldots, t_{n-1}$ of the input sentence are added to the agenda. Edges are then
popped off the agenda and added to the chart, one after the other. In the process of adding an active edge to the chart, it is combined with all matching
inactive edges already on the chart, thus giving rise to new edges, which are
added to the agenda. Likewise, an inactive edge popped from the agenda is
combined with suitable active ones on the chart and, in addition, gives rise to
new edges based on matching DPSG rules. This is repeated until the agenda is
empty. If the chart then contains an inactive edge that is headed by the goal category and spans the entire input (that is, if $edge.covers = 1^n$), it corresponds
to one or more complete parse trees for the input sentence.

Let us make the pecularities due to dealing with discotrees instead of ordinary context-free trees more precise. Firstly, what conditions must hold so that
an active edge ae and an inactive edge ie can be combined? The left-hand side
category of ie (ie.lhs) must match the symbol to the right of the dot on ae's

right-hand side (ae.**next_cat**). Furthermore, in order to ensure that the constituents corresponding to the right-hand side symbols of ae form an adjacency sequence, the next edge to be combined with ae has to start at the position of the first terminal symbol within ae's span that is neither dominated by a direct nor by a context daughter of ae. We therefore compute the bit-wise 'or' ($\lor$) of ae.**covers** and ae.**ctxt_covers** restricted to the interval $[ae.\mathbf{start}, ae.\mathbf{end}]$, set ae.**next_pos** to the position of the first unset bit in this bit-string, and require that $ie.\mathbf{start} = ae.\mathbf{next\_pos}$ holds. Additionally, we need to check that the two edges do not share any constituents. This is the case, if the bit-wise 'and' of ae.**covers** and ie.**covers** and of ae.**ctxt_covers** and ie.**covers** is zero. To summarise,

$$(3) \quad ae.\mathbf{next\_pos} = ie.\mathbf{start}, \qquad ae.\mathbf{next\_cat} = ie.\mathbf{lhs},$$
$$ae.\mathbf{covers} \land ie.\mathbf{covers} = 0, \quad \text{and} \quad ae.\mathbf{ctxt\_covers} \land ie.\mathbf{covers} = 0$$

must hold so that ae and ie can be combined, resulting in a new edge n with

$$(4) \quad \begin{aligned}
n.\mathbf{start} \quad &\leftarrow \ ae.\mathbf{start} \\
n.\mathbf{end} \quad &\leftarrow \ \max\{ae.\mathbf{end}, ie.\mathbf{end}\} \\
n.\mathbf{rule} \quad &\leftarrow \ ae.\mathbf{rule} \\
n.\mathbf{dot\_pos} \quad &\leftarrow \ ae.\mathbf{dot\_pos} + 1
\end{aligned}$$

$$n.\mathbf{covers} \quad \leftarrow \begin{cases} ae.\mathbf{covers} & \text{if } ie \text{ is context daughter} \\ ae.\mathbf{covers} \lor ie.\mathbf{covers} & \text{otherwise} \end{cases}$$

$$n.\mathbf{ctxt\_covers} \leftarrow \begin{cases} ae.\mathbf{ctxt\_covers} \lor ie.\mathbf{covers} & \text{if } ie \text{ is context d.} \\ ae.\mathbf{ctxt\_covers} & \text{otherwise.} \end{cases}$$

Suppose, for example, that the inactive edge $ie = [2, 5, Q \rightarrow c \ [d] \ e \ \bullet, 001010, 000100]$ has just been popped from the agenda and added to the chart, and that the active edge $ae = [0, 4, S \rightarrow P \ \bullet \ Q \ f, 110100, 000000]$ is already contained in the chart. We thus check whether these two edges can be combined. ae.**next_pos** is 2 (we start counting at 0) and equals ie.**start**. The left-hand side category of ie and the symbol to the right of the dot in ae are both Q.

Furthermore, ae.**covers** $\land$ ie.**covers** $= 110100 \land 001010 = 0$ and ae.**ctxt_covers** $\land$ ie.**covers** $= 000000 \land 001010 = 0$. All necessary conditions are fulfilled, so ae and ie are combined, yielding the new edge $[0, 5, S \rightarrow P \ Q \ \bullet \ f, 111110, 000000]$, which is added to the agenda. Additionally, the new inactive edge ie is combined with each rule in the given DPSG whose left-corner category equals the left-hand side category of ie. Suppose that the input DPSG contains a rule $X \rightarrow Q \ R$. This would result in a new edge $[2, 2, X \rightarrow \bullet \ Q \ R, 000000, 000000]$ to be added to the agenda[3].

The mechanisms described above are sufficient to ensure that constituents corresponding to right-hand side symbols of edges constructed by our parser form adjacency sequences, as is required by the DPSG formalism. One problem remains, though. Consider the DPSG in Figure 5.2a.

a) S → a P X
    P → b [Y] e
    X → c d
    Y → c d

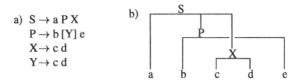

Figure 5.2.   The discotree in (b) should not be constructed from the DPSG in (a).

The parser would construct the discotree shown in Figure 5.2b, even though the P constituent assumes a context daughter Y dominating the input symbols c and d, whereas the direct daughter corresponding to Y in span is headed by an X. In other words, the X constituent is not licensed as a context daughter of P according to rule P → b [Y] e. In order to prevent the construction of such ill-formed structures, our algorithm additionally checks that context daughters and corresponding direct daughters match in category[4].

In order to be able to reconstruct all (partial) parse trees corresponding to an edge e, we associate with e a list of pairs of edge pointers (field `children`), each pair representing one possible way in which e has been constructed from an active and an inactive edge. When a new edge n is to be added to the chart, we check whether an edge e corresponding to an equivalent subparse already exists. If yes, the `children` list of n is appended to e's list, and n is discarded. Two edges correspond to equivalent subparses if they would behave in the same way would parsing proceed without them being merged. It turns out that e and n can only be merged safely if they both correspond to a continuous constituent[5]. Additionally, if e and n are inactive, they have to agree in the values of their fields `start`, `end` and `lhs`. If the two edges are active, their fields `start`, `end`, `rule` and `dot_pos` have to contain the same values.

Note, finally, that the parsing algorithm described above constructs context-free trees when presented with a Context-Free Grammar as input. The additional mechanisms for dealing with discotrees come into play only if at least one input rule contains context daughters.

4.   Computing the Most Probable Parse

As in the CFG/PCFG case, we can extend a DPSG with a probability distribution on its rule set, yielding a *Probabilistic Discontinuous Phrase Structure Grammar* (PDPSG).

Definition 5 (Probabilistic DPSG)
A Probabilistic Discontinuous Phrase Structure Grammar (PDPSG) *is a quintuple* $\langle V_N, V_T, S, R, P \rangle$, *where* $\langle V_N, V_T, S, R \rangle$ *is a DPSG and P is a func-*

tion $R \mapsto [0,1]$ that assigns a probability to each rule such that $\forall X \in V_N$:
$$\sum_{\Delta} P(X \to \Delta) = 1. \quad \blacksquare$$

Informally, we assign a probability to each rule such that the probabilities of all rules with the same left-hand side category sum to 1. Note that Δ denotes right-hand sides of DPSG rules and as such contains information about which symbols are marked as context daughters. We define the probability of a string of terminal symbols as the sum of the probabilities of all parse trees that yield this string. The probability of a parse tree is the product of the probabilities of all rule instances used in constructing this tree.

We adapted the algorithm for computing the MPP given a PCFG (see e.g. Brants, 1999 for a nice presentation) to perform the same task for PDPSGs. The algorithm maintains a set of accumulators $\delta_n(Y)$ for each symbol $Y \in V$ and each node n in the parse tree. Contrary to the context-free case, a node in a discontinuous tree cannot uniquely be described by the starting and ending position of its corresponding subparse. We instead use two bit-strings for this purpose, as explained in the previous section, which we shall below denote by $b (= \texttt{covers})$ and $\hat{b} (= \texttt{ctxt\_covers})$ for the sake of brevity. A node n dominates all terminal symbols for which the corresponding bit in b is set (equals 1); $\hat{b}$ indicates which input symbols are dominated by context daughters of n. That is to say, given a DPSG $G = \langle V_N = \{X^1, \ldots, X^N\}, V_T, X^1, R, P \rangle$ and an input string $w_{0,T} = w_0, \ldots, w_{T-1}$, we define the accumulators as variables $\delta_{b,\hat{b}}(Y)$, where $Y \in V$ and $b, \hat{b} \in \{0,1\}^T$, and compute their values bottom-up as follows.

Initialization:

$$\delta_{b,\hat{b}}(Z) = \begin{cases} 1 & \text{if } Z = w_{t-1} \\ 0 & \text{if } Z \neq w_{t-1} \end{cases} \qquad \begin{array}{l} 1 \leq t \leq T, \ Z \in V_T, \\ b = 0^{t-1} 1 0^{T-t}, \ \hat{b} = 0^T \end{array} \quad (5.5)$$

Recursion:

$$\delta_{b,\hat{b}}(X^i) = \max_{\substack{(X^i \to \Delta) \in R, \\ \Delta = Y^{1,c_1}_{b_1,\hat{b}_1} \ldots Y^{k,c_k}_{b_k,\hat{b}_k}, \\ \text{AdjSeq}\left(Y^{1,o_1}_{b_1,\hat{b}_1} \ldots Y^{k,c_k}_{b_k,\hat{b}_k}\right), \\ b = \bigvee_{\substack{1 \leq j \leq k \\ c_j = 0}} b_j, \ \hat{b} = \bigvee_{\substack{1 \leq j \leq k \\ c_j = 1}} b_j}} P(X^i \to \Delta) \prod_{\substack{1 \leq j \leq k \\ c_j = 0}} \delta_{b_j,\hat{b}_j}(Y^j) \qquad \begin{array}{l} 1 \leq i \leq N, \\ b, \hat{b} \in \{0,1\}^T \end{array}$$

$$(5.6)$$

Termination:

$$P_{\text{MPP}}(w_{0,T} \mid G) = \delta_{b,\hat{b}}(X^1) \qquad b = 1^T, \ \hat{b} = 0^T \qquad (5.7)$$

We initialize the algorithm by assigning a value of 1 to $\delta_{b,\hat{b}}(Z)$ for each terminal symbol $w_{t-1} = Z$ $(1 \leq t \leq T)$ in the input, such that b is a bit-string in which only the t-th bit is set and $\hat{b}$ is an all-zero bit-string. Next, we recursively compute the values of accumulators for larger and larger subparses. For each $\delta_{b,\hat{b}}(X^i)$, the algorithm explores all ways in which the subparse $X^i_{b,\hat{b}}$ can be constructed[6] from smaller parts and maximises over the respective probabilities. The basic idea behind the algorithm is thus the same as in the PCFG case. The PDPSG version of the algorithm differs from the PCFG one only with respect to how partial parses are combined to yield larger constituents. Each alternative for $X^i_{b,\hat{b}}$ is based on a DPSG rule $X^i \rightarrow Y^{1,c_1}_{b_1,\hat{b}_1} \ldots Y^{k,c_k}_{b_k,\hat{b}_k}$, where $Y^j_{b_j,\hat{b}_j}$ denotes the subparse corresponding to the j-th right-hand side symbol of the rule and $c_j \in \{0,1\}$ indicates whether this symbol is marked as a context daughter. A (partial) parse $X^i_{b,\hat{b}}$ can be constructed from the smaller parts corresponding to the $Y^j_{b_j,\hat{b}_j}$'s if the latter form an adjacency sequence, as indicated by the term $\text{AdjSeq}\left(Y^{1,c_1}_{b_1,\hat{b}_1} \ldots Y^{k,c_k}_{b_k,\hat{b}_k}\right)$ in the recursion formula (5.6). Given the two bit-strings of each subconstituent, we can perform the checks described in the previous section to ensure that the subconstituents form an adjacency sequence.

The probability of each alternative is computed as the product of the probability of the rule used to construct it and the accumulators for all right-hand side symbols corresponding to its direct daughters, and $\delta_{b,\hat{b}}(X^i)$ is set to the maximum of the probabilities of all alternatives. After the values for all $\delta_{b,\hat{b}}(X^i)$ have been computed, the probability of the MPP is that of the accumulator for parse trees headed by the start symbol of the input grammar (X^1) that dominate all terminal symbols in the input $(b = 1^T, \hat{b} = 0^T)$.

The computation of these accumulators can easily be incorporated within a slightly modified version of our DPSG parser. To this end, we associate each edge with an additional field **prob** that stores the accumulator value for the subparse the edge corresponds to. Edges for the terminal symbols in the input added to the agenda during initialization are assigned a **prob** value of 1, mirroring Equation 5.5. A new active edge that results from a DPSG rule matching an inactive edge that has been added to the chart inherits its probability from the underlying rule. When an active edge ae and an inactive edge ie are combined, the probability of the new edge is computed as the product of ae's and ie's probabilities, if ie is a direct daughter in the new edge, and is set to ae's probability otherwise (cf. Equation 5.6). Furthermore, we do not store more than one subparse with each edge, but only the most probable one found so far. In other words, if we encounter a new edge that would be merged with an already existing one, we instead discard the edge with the lower probability value. This implies that the discarded edge must not already be contained in a higher subparse, because if this were the case, the probability of the higher subparse would have been computed incorrectly. In order to prevent this, we organise the agenda in such a way that parsing proceeds strictly bottom-up.

Finally, when the agenda is empty, the edge that is headed by the start symbol of the grammar and that spans the entire input represents the Most Probable Parse for the given input sentence. The probability of the MPP is contained in the `prob` field of this edge (cf. Equation 5.7).

Again, this algorithm can be used to find the Most Probable Parse for either a probabilistic Context-Free Grammar or a probabilistic Discontinuous Phrase Structure Grammar, depending on whether the input grammar contains rules with context daughters.

5.   Experiments

All experiments we conducted were based on grammars extracted from the NEGRA corpus (Skut et al., 1997), which consists of German newspaper text. The version we used contains 20 571 sentences and constitutes an early version of the second release of the corpus[7].

All sentences are part-of-speech tagged, and their syntactic structures are represented as discontinuous trees. In a preprocessing step, we removed sentences without syntactic structure, attached punctuation marks to suitable nodes in the discotree, and removed unbound tokens. The corpus of discotrees thus obtained consists of 19 445 sentences with an average length of 17 tokens. In order to have some sort of baseline against which we could compare our results from PDPSG parsing, we additionally transformed the discotrees in this corpus to context-free trees by re-attaching all continuous parts of discontinuous constituents to higher nodes. We kept 1 005 sentences from each corpus to be used in case of unforeseen events and split the remaining corpus into a training set of 16 596 sentences (90%) and a test set of 1 844 sentences (10%), such that both test sets (and both training sets) contained the same sentences, albeit with different structures.

Next, we extracted rule instances from both training sets. For context-free trees, we extracted rules in the usual way. For each nonterminal n in the tree, a rule is generated in which n's label constitutes the left-hand side and the labels of n's direct daughters form the right-hand side. Given a discotree, we also need to determine context daughters of discontinuous constituents, such that right-hand sides form adjacency sequences. This is done as follows. For each terminal t between two direct daughters d_1 and d_2 of a nonterminal n such that n does not dominate t, we determine the highest node dominating t that does not dominate n and whose yield is contained within the bounds of n. These nodes are the context daughters of n between d_1 and d_2 (with duplicates removed). For instance, we extract the rules in (a) from the discotree given in (b). We then compute the probability of each rule as the ratio of its frequency to the frequency of all rules with the same left-hand side category, thus obtaining a PCFG and a PDPSG[8].

(a) S → X Z e
     X → b [Z] [e] g
     Z → Y [e] f
     Y → c d

Figure 5.3.   The rules in (a) are extracted from the discotree in (b).

Due to limited computational resources, we restricted the two test sets to sentences with a maximum length of 15 tokens. We ran our parser on the part-of-speech tag sequences of these 959 sentences, once with the PCFG as input, and once using the PDPSG. The parse trees from the PCFG (PDPSG) experiment were then compared against the correct context-free trees (discotrees) in the test set. We determined average CPU time[9] per sentence and various accuracy measures for both experiments, which are summarised in Table 5.1.

Table 5.1.   Accuracy and average CPU time per sentence for both experiments.

	PCFG	PDPSG
Precision	79.24%	77.75%
Recall	78.09%	76.81%
F-score	78.66%	77.28%
Labeled precision	75.12%	73.61%
Labeled recall	74.03%	72.72%
Labeled F-score	74.57%	73.16%
Coverage	96.35%	96.04%
Exact matches	39.83%	39.00%
Structural matches	43.07%	42.23%
CPU time per sentence	0.53 secs	24.78 secs

Precision is defined as the percentage of constituents proposed by our parser which are actually correct according to the tree in the corpus. "Correct" means that the two constituents dominate the same terminals; for the different "labeled" measures, the node labels must match in addition. Recall is the percentage of constituents in the test set trees which are found by our parser. We define F-score as the harmonic mean of recall R and precision P, that is, as $F = \frac{2PR}{P+R}$. Coverage denotes the percentage of sentences for which a complete parse has been found by our parser. A proposed parse tree with an F-score of 100% is a structural match; if the *labeled* F-score is 100%, the tree is called an exact match.

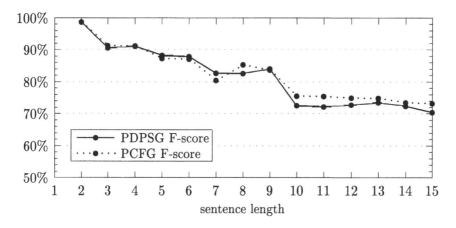

Figure 5.4. F-scores from both experiments plotted against sentence length.

In comparing the results from the PDPSG experiment against the PCFG results, it is important to keep in mind that parsing with discotrees is a much harder task than parsing with context-free trees. The complexity of the latter is cubic in sentence length, whereas our parsing algorithm for PDPSG takes, in the worst case, exponential time (see also Reape, 1991). Therefore, unsurprisingly, the average CPU time per sentence in the PDPSG experiment is almost 50 times larger than in the PCFG case. To make things worse, the difference in running time would be even larger for longer sentences.

The good news, on the other hand, is that accuracy drops only slightly (see Figure 5.4) when we accommodate within our parser the possibility of constituents to be discontinuous.

6. Conclusion and Future Work

We have presented a probabilistic extension of Discontinuous Phrase Structure Grammar, a formalism suitable for describing restricted discontinuities in a perspicuous single-level representation. Furthermore, we have developed a parser that can be used with probabilistic and non-probabilistic versions of both Context-Free Grammar and Discontinuous Phrase Structure Grammar, constructing context-free or discontinuous trees, respectively.

Although the probabilistic method applied is rather simplistic, the accuracy results obtained in the PDPSG experiment are comparable to the PCFG results. A severe drawback of our approach is its worst-case exponential running time. Future work should thus be primarily aimed at reducing this complexity (and additionally at increasing accuracy). There are at least two avenues towards this goal.

Firstly, we could try to restrict the formalism of DPSG further with respect to the kinds of discontinuities it is capable of representing. Vogel and Erjavec (1994) presented a restricted version of DPSG, called $DPSG^R$, and claimed that this formalism is properly contained in the class of mildly context-sensitive languages and that consequently a polynomial time recognition procedure exists for it. Note, however, that $DPSG^R$ does not allow for the description of cross-serial dependencies; it is therefore too restricted to represent the discontinuity phenomena occuring in the NEGRA corpus[10]. A similar account, although within a different grammatical framework, was provided by Müller (1999) who presented an HPSG system in which linguistically motivated constraints on (dis)continuity were imposed, which led to a notable decrease in running time.

An alternative, orthogonal approach towards faster mechanisms for probabilistic parsing with discontinuous constituents is to stick to DPSG and try to find suitable approximation algorithms that reduce the *observed* running time. Several such approaches exist in the literature on probabilistic parsing, mostly based on (P)CFGs. Since DPSG is a straightforward extension of CFG, we expect that at least some of these can be extended with reasonable effort to also deal with discontinuous trees. In fact, the work presented in this chapter serves as a first indication confirming this intuition. A more sophisticated approach could, for instance, be based on the statistical parser devised by Ratnaparkhi (1997). He utilized a set of procedures implementing certain actions to incrementally construct (context-free) parse trees. The probabilities of these actions were computed by Maximum Entropy models based on certain syntactic characteristics (features) of the current context, and effectively rank different parse trees. A beam search heuristic was used that attempts to find the highest scoring parse tree. In order to extend this approach to DPSG, we would need a different set of procedures capable of constructing discontinuous trees and a suitable set of features.

Edge-based best-first chart parsing (Charniak et al., 1998; Charniak and Caraballo, 1998) is another very promising approach. Charniak et al. (1998) proposed to judge edges according to some probabilistic figure of merit that is meant to approximate the likelihood that an edge will ultimately appear in a correct parse. Edges are processed in decreasing order of this value until a complete parse has been found (or perhaps several ones), leaving edges on the agenda. They reported results comparable to the best previous ones using only one twentieth the number of edges.

The edge-based best-first parsing approach could easily be applied to DPSG and our chart parsing algorithm as well. To this end, we would need to organise the agenda as a priority queue, so that edges are processed in decreasing order of their respective figure of merit values. We are confident that suitable figures of merit can be found for DPSG chart parsing that would lead to a significant decrease in running time.

Acknowledgments

The author is grateful to Hans Uszkoreit who supervised the Diplom thesis from which this work emerged (Plaehn, 1999). Thanks are also due to Thorsten Brants and Alexander Koller for valuable comments and discussion.

Notes

1. Two subdiscotrees X and Y share a subdiscotree Z, if both X and Y contain a node dominating the top node of Z. The inclusion of this condition ensures that subdiscotrees do not contain multidominated nodes.

2. The use of bit-strings for representing locations of discontinuous constituents is motivated by Johnson (1985).

3. In order to improve efficiency, we perform a lookahead test for each new active edge n to check whether the remaining symbols on n's right-hand side can be "satisfied" at all with the input symbols not already dominated by n. If not, we discard n. The details of this test are beyond the scope of this chapter, but can be found in Plaehn (1999).

4. The parser described in Bunt (1991) and van der Sloot (1990) performs a check that every daughter (direct or context) is dominated by the top node, in order to avoid constructing the discotree in Figure 5.2b when presented with the DPSG in Figure 5.2a. This check is quite expensive.

5. We say that an edge e is *continuous*, if and only if $\prod_{i=e.\mathtt{start}}^{e.\mathtt{end}-1} b_i = 1$ where b_i is the i-th bit in $e.\mathtt{covers}$.

6. We use $X^i_{b,\hat{b}}$ to denote a subparse headed by the nonterminal symbol X^i whose direct daughters dominate the input symbols for which the corresponding bits in b are set and whose context daughters dominate the symbols for which the bits in $\hat{b}$ are set.

7. Please consult `http://www.coli.uni-sb.de/sfb378/negra-corpus` for information on how to obtain the corpus.

8. The PCFG training corpus gave rise to 120 831 rule instances and 18 709 rules, of which 13 419 appear only once in the corpus. The PDPSG consists of 21 965 rules (generated from 123 528 rule instances); 16 317 of these appear only once in the training corpus.

9. On a Sun Ultra Sparc 300 MHz with 1 GB main memory running Solaris 2.6.

10. Bresnan (1982) provided additional evidence that formalisms capable of representing cross-serial dependencies are desirable.

References

Blevins, J. P. (1990). *Syntactic Complexity: Evidence for Discontinuity and Multidomination*. PhD thesis, University of Massachusetts, Amherst, MA.

Brants, T. (1999). *Tagging and Parsing with Cascaded Markov Models — Automation of Corpus Annotation*. PhD thesis, University of the Saarland, Saarbrücken, Germany.

Bresnan, J., Kaplan, R. M., Peters, S., and Zaenen, A. (1982). Cross-serial dependencies in Dutch. *Linguistic Inquiry*, 13(4):613–635.

Bunt, H. (1991). Parsing with Discontinuous Phrase Structure Grammar. In Tomita, M., editor, *Current Issues in Parsing Technology*, pages 49–63. Kluwer Academic Publishers, Dordrecht, Boston, London.

Bunt, H. (1996). Formal tools for describing and processing discontinuous constituency structure. In Bunt, H. and van Horck, A., editors, *Discontinuous Constituency*, Natural Language Processing 6, pages 63–83. Mouton de Gruyter, Berlin, New York.

Bunt, H. and van der Sloot, K. (1996). Parsing as dynamic interpretation of feature structures. In Bunt, H. and Tomita, M., editors, *Recent Advances in Parsing Technology*, Text, Speech and Language Technology 1, pages 91–114. Kluwer Academic Publishers, Dordrecht, Boston, London.

Charniak, E. and Caraballo, S. (1998). New figures of merit for best-first probabilistic chart parsing. *Computational Linguistics*, 24(2):275–298.

Charniak, E., Goldwater, S., and Johnson, M. (1998). Edge-based best-first chart parsing. In *Proceedings of the Sixth Workshop on Very Large Corpora*, Montreal, Canada.

Johnson, M. (1985). Parsing with discontinuous constituents. In *Proceedings of the 23rd ACL meeting*, pages 127–132, Chicago. Association for Computational Linguistics.

McCawley, J. D. (1982). Parentheticals and discontinuous constituent structure. *Linguistic Inquiry*, 13(1):91–106.

Müller, S. (1999). Restricting discontinuity. In *Proceedings of the 5th Natural Language Processing Pacific Rim Symposium 1999 (NLPRS '99)*, Peking.

Plaehn, O. (1999). Probabilistic parsing with Discontinuous Phrase Structure Grammar. Diplom thesis, University of the Saarland, Saarbrücken. http://www.coli.uni-sb.de/~plaehn/papers/dt.html.

Ratnaparkhi, A. (1997). A linear observed time statistical parser based on maximum entropy models. In *Proceedings of the Conference on Empirical Methods in Natural Language Processing EMNLP-97*, Providence, RI.

Reape, M. (1991). Parsing bounded discontinuous constituents: Generalisations of some common algorithms. In van der Wouden, T. and Sijtsma, W., editors, *Computational Linguistics in the Netherlands. Papers from the First CLIN-meeting*, Utrecht. Utrecht University-OTS.

Skut, W., Krenn, B., Brants, T., and Uszkoreit, H. (1997). An annotation scheme for free word order languages. In *Proceedings of the Fifth Conference on Applied Natural Language Processing ANLP-97*, Washington, DC.

van der Sloot, K. (1990). The TENDUM 2.7 parsing algorithm for DPSG. ITK research memo, ITK, Tilburg.

Vogel, C. and Erjavec, T. (1994). Restricted Discontinuous Phrase Structure Grammar and its ramifications. In Martin-Vide, C., editor, *Current Issues in Mathematical Linguistics*, pages 131–140. Elsevier, Amsterdam.

Chapter 6

A NEURAL NETWORK PARSER THAT HANDLES SPARSE DATA

James Henderson

Dept of Computer Science, University of Geneva
24, rue du Général Dufour, 1211 Genève 4, Switzerland
henderson@cui.unige.ch

Abstract   Simple Synchrony Networks (SSNs) have previously been shown to be a viable
alternative method for syntactic parsing. Here we use an SSN to estimate the
parameters of a probabilistic parsing model, and compare this parser's performance against a standard statistical parsing method, a Probabilistic Context Free
Grammar. We focus these experiments on demonstrating one of the main advantages of SSNs, handling sparse data. We use smaller datasets than are typically
used with statistical methods, resulting in the PCFG finding parses for only half
of the test sentences, while the SSN parser finds parses for all sentences. Even
on the PCFG's parsed half, the SSN parser performs better than the PCFG.

1.   Introduction

In many domains neural networks are an effective alternative to statistical
methods for estimating probabilities. This has not been the case for syntactic
parsing, but work on using neural networks for structure processing has developed a viable architecture for this problem, called Simple Synchrony Networks (SSNs) (Henderson and Lane, 1998; Lane, 2001). This alternative parsing technology is potentially of interest because neural networks have different
strengths from statistical methods, and thus may be more applicable to some
tasks. Like statistical methods, neural networks are robust against noise in
the input and errors in the data. But unlike statistical methods, neural networks are particularly good at handling sparse data. In order to compensate
for the necessarily limited amount of data available, statistical methods must
make strong independence assumptions. These assumptions lead to undesir-
able biases in the model generated, and may still not guarantee coverage of
less frequent cases. Neural networks also require independence assumptions

H. Bunt et al. (eds.), New Technologies in Parsing Technology, 107-124.

in order to define their input-output format, but these assumptions can be much weaker. Because neural networks learn their own internal representations, neural networks can decide automatically what features to count and how reliable they are for estimating the desired probabilities.[1]

In this chapter we empirically investigate the ability of SSNs to handle sparse data. We present a probabilistic parser which uses an SSN to estimate its parameters, and compare it to two models which use statistical methods to estimate their parameters, a Probabilistic Context Free Grammar (PCFG) and a parser which uses the same probability model as the SSN. We use a small dataset relative to those typically used with statistical methods, which results in sparse data. We train all the models on the same dataset and compare their results, both in terms of coverage and performance on the covered portion. The statistical version of the SSN parser has good coverage, but its performance is worse than both the other two models. The PCFG covers under half of the test sentences. The SSN parser produces a parse for all of the sentences, while still achieving better performance than that of the PCFG on the PCFG's parsed sentences, as measure by recall and precision on both constituents and a dependency-like measure.

2.   Simple Synchrony Networks

The neural network architecture used in this chapter has previously been shown to be a viable parsing technology based on both initial empirical results (Henderson and Lane, 1998) and the linguistic characteristics of the basic computational model (Henderson, 1994). Their appropriateness for application to syntactic parsing is a result of their ability to learn generalizations over structural constituents. This generalization ability is a result of using a neural network method for representing sets of objects, called Temporal Synchrony Variable Binding (TSVB) (Shastri and Ajjanagadde, 1993). In Simple Synchrony Networks (SSNs) this method is used to extend a standard neural network architecture for processing sequences, Simple Recurrent Networks (SRNs) (Elman, 1991). SRNs can learn generalizations over positions in an input sequence (and thus can handle unbounded input sequences), which has made them of interest in natural language processing. By using TSVB to represent the constituents in a syntactic structure, SSNs also learn generalizations over structural constituents. The linguistic relevance of this class of generalizations is what accounts for the fact that SSNs generalize from training set to testing set in an appropriate way, as demonstrated in Section 4. In this section we briefly outline the SSN architecture and how it can be used to estimate the parameters of a probability model.

2.1   Representing Constituents

Standard pattern-recognition neural networks such as Multi-Layered Perceptrons (MLPs) take a vector of real values as input, compute hidden internal representation which is also a vector of real values, and output a third vector of real values. If trained properly, each output value can be interpreted as the probability that the true output should be 1 given the input (Bishop, 1995). Simple Recurrent Networks extend MLPs to sequences by using the hidden representations as representations of the network's state at a given point in the sequence. As with Hidden Markov Models, the state for one sequence position is computed from the state for the previous sequence position plus the new inputs, and the output is computed from this new state. Because the state representation is learned during training, the SRN can induce its own internal representation of the previous input history. Simple Synchrony Networks extend SRNs by computing one of these sequences for each object in a set of objects. For our purposes these objects are the constituents on the sentence's phrase structure tree. This means that there is one hidden state representation for each constituent at each position in the sentence. There is also one input vector and one output vector for each constituent at each position in the sentence.

2.2   Learning Generalizations over Constituents

The most important feature of any learning architecture is how it generalizes from training data to testing data. SRNs are popular for sequence processing because they inherently generalize over sequence positions. Because inputs are fed to an SRN one at a time, and the same trained parameters (called link weights) apply at every time, information learned at one sequence position will inherently be generalized to other sequence positions. This generalization ability manifests itself in the fact that SRNs can handle arbitrarily long sequences. The same argument applies to SSNs and constituents. Using TSVB to represent constituents amounts to cycling through the set of constituents and processing them one at a time. Because the same trained parameters are applied every time, information learned for one constituent will inherently be generalized to other constituents. This generalization ability manifests itself in the fact that these networks can handle arbitrarily many constituents, and therefore unbounded phrase structure trees.

2.3   Estimating Probabilities over Constituents

Standard neural network methods for estimating probability distributions can be applied to SSNs, provided the probability distributions are over a finite number of alternatives. This is the case, for example, when choosing the label of a given constituent, since there are a finite number of labels. Under these circumstances the neural network methods are equivalent to a log-linear probability model (sometimes known as a maximum entropy model), except that the features which form the input to the model are the induced hidden representations rather than pre-defined features (Bishop, 1995).

For the parsing model used in this work we also need to be able to estimate probability distributions over an unbounded number of alternatives. For example, if we have the sentence *John said Mary left yesterday*, we need to estimate a probability distribution over the possible attachment sites for *yesterday*. In this case there are only two possibilities, *said* and *left*, but in general there is no bound on the number of possible attachment sites, so the probability distribution which we need to estimate is unbounded. A variety of solutions to this problem have been proposed (Henderson, 2002). Here we use the solution which extends the standard normalized-exponential output function to include normalization over an unbounded number of outputs. As in the finite case, this output function ensures that training will converge to an estimate of the desired probability (in the limit as the number of training examples, amount of training time, and number of hidden units grow, and given weak assumptions about the probability distributions) (Henderson, 2002).[2]

3.   A Probabilistic Parser for SSNs

Because we are using SSNs as a statistical estimation method, and not directly as a parser, we first need to define the probability model whose parameters the SSN estimates. The model defines the probability of a labeled syntactic tree structure given its list of terminals. Each tree is represented in terms of a list of terminals, a set of labeled nonterminals, and a set of structural relationships between nonterminals and terminals. In this work the terminals are part-of-speech tags, and the nonterminals are labeled as sentences, noun phrases, verb phrases, etc. Each tree's set of structural relationships is sufficient to fully specify the tree. After the SSN has estimated the parameters of this model, a separate procedure searches for the most probable parse.

3.1   The Probabilistic Model of Syntactic Structure

Two structural relationships are sufficient to fully specify the structures in the corpus used in this chapter, *parent*, and *grand*parent. *Parent* is the relationship between a terminal and the nonterminal that immediately dominates it in the tree. *Grand*parent is the relationship between a terminal and the nonterminal which immediately dominates the terminal's parent nonterminal. These structural relationships are illustrated in Figure 6.1. For the corpus used in this chapter these *grand*parent relationships are sufficient to specify all immediate dominance relationships between two nonterminals, because all nonterminals have at least one terminal of which they are the *parent*. To prevent redundancy, we only specify the *grand*parent relationship for the first such terminal child for each nonterminal. In our notation we will always use the same index for a nonterminal as for its first terminal child. Thus in our notation we specify *grand*parent relationships for w_j when *parent*(c_j, w_j) is true, and $grand(c_i, w_j)$ means there is an immediate dominance relationship between c_i and c_j. As an example, the structure of the sentence depicted in Figure 6.1 would be represented as

$$parent(c_1, w_1), parent(c_2, w_2), N(c_1), S(c_2), grand(c_2, w_1), grand(c_0, w_2)$$

where c_0 is a special root nonterminal, c_1, c_2 are the other nonterminals, w_1, w_2 are the terminals, and N, S are labels.

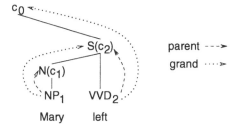

Figure 6.1. A structure illustrating the parameters of the probability model.

To allow the probability of a given structure to be calculated, we decompose the probability into one probability for each of the labels or structural relationships in the structure. We do this by applying the chain rule for conditional probabilities in a bottom-up, left-to-right order. We then apply the independence assumptions of the probability model to simplify the conditioning in these probabilities. The first assumption is that labeling nonterminals is sufficiently simple (for our label set) that knowing a label doesn't tell us anything the we don't already know from the part-of-speech tags for the terminals. This allows us to determine labels and structural relationships independently of each other. The second assumption is that nonterminals can be labeled incrementally, as soon as we see the first terminal which is an immediate child of the nonterminal. This assumption is motivated by the idea that the first terminal child of a nonterminal is a reasonable approximation to the syntactic head of the nonterminal (the functional head, if not the semantic head). Similarly, the model assumes that the probability of a structural relationship can be estimated as soon as both the terminal involved in the relationship and the first terminal child of the nonterminal involved in the relationship have been seen. Latter terminals are assumed to be independent of these labels and relationships.

The number of such probabilities for a given sentence is still exponential in the sentence's length, due to the large amount of information in the conditional. This is a problem both for efficiency and because we need to estimate these probabilities with a SSN. The SSN architecture we are using can only output $O(n^2)$ probability estimates. One approach would be to incrementally disambiguate some of the parsing decisions, so as to eliminate some of the theoretically required probabilities. We take this approach for some of the parent decisions, as discussed in Section 2.2. However in other cases we take the approach of simplifying the probability estimates further through additional independence assumptions.

The idea behind these additional independence assumptions is that if all the previous terminals are known, then each nonterminal can model its relationship to the next terminal without needing to know information about other nonterminals. If information about other nonterminals is necessary (such as for nested constituents), then this information needs to be modeled implicitly by the nonterminal itself. To allow a nonterminal to model its own relationships to the terminals, the conditional of the probabilities involving that nonterminal include all its own *parent* relationships to terminals. If a probability involves more than one nonterminal, which is only the case for *grand*parent probabilities, then the *parent* relationships for both nonterminals are included in the conditional. However, because it is assumed that a nonterminal does not need to know about relationships to other nonterminals, the conditionals of its probabilities do not include any *grand*parent relationships, and do not include *parent* relationships for other nonterminals.

Given this full set of independence assumptions, the probability of the structure shown in Figure 6.1 is the following:

$$
\begin{aligned}
P(parent&(c_1, w_1), parent(c_2, w_2), N(c_1), S(c_2), grand(c_2, w_1), \\
&grand(c_0, w_2) \mid w_1, w_2) \\
= \ &P(parent(c_1, w_1) \mid w_1) \\
&\times P(parent(c_2, w_2) \mid parent(c_1, w_1), w_1, w_2) \\
&\times P(N(c_1) \mid parent(c_1, w_1), w_1) \\
&\times P(S(c_2) \mid parent(c_2, w_2), w_1, w_2) \\
&\times P(grand(c_2, w_1) \mid parent(c_2, w_2), parent(c_1, w_1), w_1, w_2) \\
&\times P(grand(c_0, w_2) \mid parent(c_2, w_2), w_1, w_2)
\end{aligned}
$$

These probabilities are the parameters of the probability model, which need to be estimated by the SSN.

Unfortunately, the last set of independence assumptions have the effect of creating a "leaky" probability model, in that probability is being assigned to impossible structures. In particular, this model does not enforce the constraint that links in the syntactic structure do not cross. Under some syntactic theories, and for some languages, it might be reasonable to allow crossing links, but not for the English treebank we are using, and thus the probability model is deficient in this respect. As an example, consider the probabilities which would need to be estimated if a third terminal was input at the end of the above example. We would want to know the probability of this terminal w_3 attaching to the first nonterminal c_1. This should have a value of 0, because the attachment is incompatible with $grand(c_0, w_2)$ due to crossing links. But with the above independence assumptions it is reduced to $P(parent(c_1, w_3) \mid parent(c_1, w_1), w_1, w_2, w_3)$, which could have a nonzero value. Fortunately, because the main verb w_2 remains in the conditional, this probability is likely to be given a very small value by the SSN estimation method.

3.2 Searching for the Most Probable Parse

Given the probability model and estimates for the parameters of that model, the output of the parser should be the most probable parse of the given sentence according to those estimates. Searching for this most probable parse is complicated by the fact that latter parsing decisions are governed by parameters which depend on earlier parsing decisions. In particular, they depend on the *parent* choices made earlier in the sentence. To simplify this search, first the *parent* of each terminal is chosen based on the maximum *parent* probability estimates. After the *parent* of a terminal is chosen it is used by the SSN to estimate the parameters for latter portions of the sentence, including latter *parent* estimates. This disambiguation chooses which nonterminals c_i are parents of their terminal w_i, and thus which nonterminals are actually included in the output structure. Then a best-first chart parser uses the total set of parameter estimates to compute the optimal parse, given the set of nonterminals included in the output structure. If this resulted in a structure which did not include all the disambiguated *parent* decisions, then the SSN was run again using the new set of *parent* choices instead of the incrementally disambiguated choices, and a new optimal structure was computed from the resulting estimates. If necessary the process was repeated until a consistent set of *parent* choices was found, but this never took more than four runs.

4. Estimating the Probabilities with a Simple Synchrony Network

To estimate the parameters of the probability model with an SSN, we need to define an output format which has a separate output value for each parameter, and then define the input format and the training method so that these outputs do indeed estimate the desired probabilities. The training methods which are required are a straightforward application of those discussed in Section 1. Once a SSN has been trained, it is used to compute the estimates for the given sentence, and these estimates are used in the search procedure to find the most probable parse for that sentence.

4.1   The Set of Nonterminals

The main challenge in defining an input-output format is that a syntactic structure consists of a set of relationships between constituents, whereas SSNs only provide us with outputs about individual constituents. More precisely, there are $O(n^2)$ possible relationships between constituents and only $O(n)$ outputs at any given time. The solution is simply to output the syntactic structure incrementally. By making use of the $O(n)$ positions in the input sentence to produce output, the network can produce the necessary $O(n^2)$ outputs over the course of the parse.

The SSN architecture can produce $O(n)$ outputs at any given time because the number of nonterminals in its set grows with the length of the sentence. This growth is achieved by incrementally adding nonterminals to its set of nonterminals as it proceeds through the sentence. For the corpus we use here, introducing only one nonterminal at each terminal is sufficient to ensure that at the end of the sentence there are enough nonterminals to fully specify the desired structure. This is due to the fact that every nonterminal has at least one terminal as an immediate child. As discussed in Section 2.1, we take the first such terminal child to be a reasonable approximation of the syntactic head of that nonterminal, and we index the nonterminals with the position of this head terminal. At every position i in the sentence, we have the terminal w_i as the input and we introduce a new nonterminal c_i to the set of nonterminals being stored in the SSN. Whether this nonterminal c_i actually plays a part in the final output structure depends on whether it is chosen to be the immediate parent of w_i, in other words whether *parent*(c_i, w_i) is chosen. Because the nonterminals are introduced incrementally, the SSN only produces outputs for a nonterminal c_i at a terminal w_j if $i \leq j$. This influences the design of the output format, as discussed next.

4.2   The Output Format

Each output unit produces a different output for each nonterminal c_i at each terminal w_j. The outputs for a given pair c_i, w_j are all estimates of probabilities of predications involving c_i, w_i, c_j and/or w_j, where $i \leq j$. The different structural relations or labels predicated of these nonterminals and terminals are estimated by different output units. The information specified by each of these output units is illustrated in Figure 6.2.

The probabilities for the *parent* predications can be estimated with a single output unit. The *parent* output for nonterminal c_i at terminal w_j is the estimate of $P(parent(c_i, w_j) \mid parent(c_i, w_i), \ldots, w_1, \ldots, w_j),$[3] or if $i = j$ it is the estimate of $P(parent(c_i, w_i) \mid w_1, \ldots, w_i)$. In Figure 6.2 the latter case applies to the *parent* output for NP_1 and VVD_2, and the former case applies to the *parent* output for RR_3. Because of the incremental introduction of

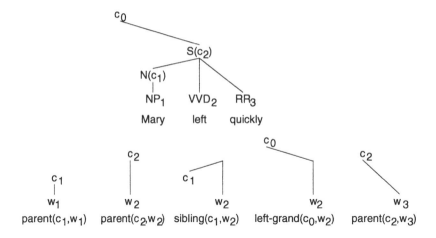

Figure 6.2.   An example of the SSN's output format, depicted graphically.

nonterminals, two output units are needed to estimate the probabilities for the *grand*parent predications, one for right branching cases and one for left branching cases. The *left-grand*parent output for nonterminal c_i at terminal w_j is the estimate of $P(grand(c_i, w_j) \mid parent(c_i, w_i), \ldots, parent(c_j, w_j), w_1, \ldots, w_j)$. The *sibling* output for nonterminal c_i during time step w_j is the estimate of $P(grand(c_j, w_i) \mid parent(c_i, w_i), \ldots, parent(c_j, w_j), w_1, \ldots, w_j)$. In addition to these structural outputs, there is also one output unit for each possible nonterminal label. Although these outputs could calculate different values for each pair c_i, w_j, we only use the outputs for the pair c_i, w_i. The output for label L_k for nonterminal c_i at terminal w_i is the estimate of $P(L_k(c_i) \mid parent(c_i, w_i), w_1, \ldots, w_i)$.

4.3   Implementing the Conditioning

Ensuring that the SSN's probability estimates are conditioned on the information required by the probability model is mostly achieved by defining an appropriate input format. The training method then ensures that the SSN's outputs are estimates of probabilities conditioned on the information provided in the inputs. The outputs specified at terminal w_j are all estimates of probabilities conditioned on w_j and all the previous terminals $w_1, \ldots, w_{j-1}$. To achieve this, when computing the outputs for terminal w_j, a set of input units specify the part-of-speech tag of the jth word of the sentence. This terminal input is received by all nonterminals at time w_j. Because the SSN is proceeding left to right through the sentence, information about all the previous terminal inputs $w_1, \ldots, w_{j-1}$ can be stored in each nonterminal's state vector.[4] Thus when computing the outputs for w_j, every nonterminal has received input specifying the terminals $w_1, \ldots, w_j$. Therefore all the probabilities output at w_j are conditioned on $w_1, \ldots, w_j$, as required by the probability model.

The probability model also requires that the outputs for nonterminal c_i at terminal w_j estimate probabilities which are conditioned on all c_i's *parent* relationships to previous terminals. This is achieved through a *last-parent* input unit, which specifies which nonterminal was chosen as the *parent* of the previous terminal w_{j-1}. This nonterminal input can be used for computing the nonterminal's output and can also be stored in the nonterminal's state vector, thereby making c_i's outputs at w_j conditional on any relationships $parent(c_i, w_k)$ such that $k < j$.

The only other information which the probability model requires to be in the conditionals of some output probabilities at w_j is $parent(c_j, w_j)$, but because this information is not included for all the outputs at w_j (namely not for the *parent* outputs), this requirement cannot be accommodated through the input format. Instead we provide this conditioning using the training method. To provide this conditioning, we use a mixture model approach (Bishop, 1995), where the $parent(c_j, w_j)$ outputs are used as the mixing coefficients. The effect of this technique is simply that we only train the conditioned outputs in cases where $parent(c_j, w_j)$ is true in the correct structure. We also apply this training technique to enforce the conditioning on $parent(c_i, w_i)$ for the outputs for $grand(c_i, w_j)$, even though this information is already available in the input. This enforces the discrete requirement that the probability of a *grand*parent relationships is exactly zero if the nonterminal is not included in the output structure.

Given enough data and enough training time, a network with the above input pattern can accurately estimate the probabilities in the grammar model. However, given that we always have limited amounts of data it is important to bias the network towards solutions which we have some prior reason to believe will be good. We can do this with the SSN parser by adding inputs which will emphasize the importance of certain information, plus making use of the timing of the computation.

In theory any earlier input can affect a later output, and thus these inputs are included in the conditioning. However, in practice a recurrent network such as a SSN will learn more about the dependencies between an input and an output if they are close together in time. The immediate effect of this is a form of recency bias; the most recent input terminals will affect an output more than earlier input terminals. We can also make use of this property by adding input units which express information that the network should already have, but that may need emphasizing at different times during the parse. For example, we bias the network to pay particular attention to the head terminal (the first terminal child) of each nonterminal by providing the head terminal as an input at every position. Thus the input for nonterminal c_i at terminal

w_j includes w_i as the nonterminal's head, as well as w_j as the current input terminal. This results in the network paying particular attention to the terminals that are directly related to the outputs being produced for nonterminal c_i at terminal w_j, with previous input terminals providing an influence proportional to their recency.

We also bias the network training by providing a *new-nonterminal* input unit which is only active for c_i at terminal w_i. This helps the *parent* output unit distinguish between making w_i the head of a new nonterminal (c_i) and attaching w_i to an old nonterminal. In addition this input helps the network produce other outputs because the short period after this input is when most of the outputs involving c_i will be required. Similarly, the *last-parent* input unit, discussed above, also helps the SSN produce outputs because it is also correlated with nonzero outputs being required for a short time afterwards. These additional inputs have been devised in part on the basis of the author's linguistic knowledge and in part on the basis of experimental results using a validation set.

5.   Generalizing from Sparse Data

To test the ability of Simple Synchrony Networks to handle sparse data we train the SSN parser described in the previous section on a relatively small set of sentences and then test how well it generalizes to a set of previously unseen sentences. Because the training set is small, the testing sentences will contain many constituents and constituent contexts which the network has never seen before. Thus the network cannot simply choose the constituents which it has seen the most times in the training set, because in most cases it will have never seen any of the constituents which it needs to choose between. To handle this sparseness of training data the network must learn which of the inputs about a constituent are important, as well as how they correlate with the outputs. The advantage of SSNs is that they automatically learn the relative importance of different inputs as part of their training process.

To provide a comparison with the SSN parser we also apply a standard statistical method to the same data sets. We use the relative frequencies of CFG rules in the SSN's training and validation sets to estimate the probabilities for a Probabilistic Context Free Grammar, and we test this PCFG on the network's testing set. PCFGs deal with the problem of sparse data by ignoring everything about a constituent other than its nonterminal label. The strength of this independence assumption depends on how many nonterminal labels the corpus has, and thus how much information the labels convey. Because we are dealing with small training sets, we only use a small number of labels (only 15). Even so, the PCFG has only seen enough CFG rules in the training sets to produce parses for about half of the test sentences. A smoothing method such as deleted interpolation could be applied, but this would require backing off to a less informative specification of CFG rules, and with only 15 labels and no lexicalization we are already using a much less informative specification than that used in other work.

Because the PCFG uses a very different probability model from the SSN parser, as well as using a different method for estimating the parameters of the model, we also used frequency counts to estimate the parameters of a probability model very similar to the one used for the SSN parser. We will call this alternative the Probabilistic Structural Relationships (PSR) model. In addition to all the independence assumptions discussed in Section 2.1, the PSR model assumes every structural relationship is dependent on the terminal involved in the relationship and the head terminal of the nonterminal involved in the relationship (and whether they are the same), but they are independent of all other terminals. This independence assumption is strong enough to provide us with sufficient statistics given our training data, but still captures to the extent possible the relevant information for estimating the same parameters used in the SSN parser's probability model. The only difference is that the PSR model makes a hard independence assumption in the cases where the SSN's model imposes only a soft bias, namely the recency preferences discussed in Section 3.3. Given this assumption, all the parameters of the SSN's model can be estimated by counting the pairs of terminals and head terminals involved in each type of relationship. The PSR model is closely related to dependency-based statistical models, such as that in Collins (1999).

5.1   A Small Corpus

Work on statistical parsing typically uses very large corpora of preparsed sentences (for example, more than a million words in the Penn Treebank Wall Street Journal corpus; Marcus, 1993). Such corpora are very expensive to produce, and are currently only available for English. In addition, using a very large training corpus helps hide inadequacies in the parser's ability to generalize, because the larger the training corpus the better results can be obtained by simply memorizing the common cases. Here we use a training set of only 26,480 words, plus a validation set of 4365 words (30,845 words total). By using a small training set we are placing greater emphasis on the ability of the parser to generalize to novel cases in a linguistically appropriate way, and to do so robustly. In other words, we are testing the parser on its ability to deal with sparse data.

We use the Susanne[5] corpus as our source of preparsed sentences. The Susanne corpus consists of a subset of the Brown corpus, preparsed according to the Susanne classification scheme described in (Sampson, 1995), and we make use of the "press reportage" subset of this. These parses have been converted to a format appropriate for this investigation, as described in the rest of this section.[6]

We do not use words as the input to the parser, but instead use part-of-speech tags. The tags in the Susanne scheme are a detailed extension of the tags used in the Lancaster-Leeds Treebank (see Garside et al., 1987), but we use the simpler Lancaster-Leeds scheme. Each tag is a two or three letter sequence, for example 'John' would be encoded 'NP', the articles 'a' and 'the' are encoded 'AT', and verbs such as 'is' encoded 'VBZ'. There are 105 tags in total.

The syntactic structure in the Susanne scheme is also more complicated than is needed for our purposes. Firstly, the meta-sentence level structure has been discarded, leaving only the structures of individual sentences. Secondly, the 'ghost' markers have been removed. These elements are used to represent long distance dependencies, but they are not needed here because they do not affect any of the evaluation measures used below. Third, as was discussed above, we simplify the nonterminal labels so as to help the PCFG deal with the small training set. We only use the first letter of each nonterminal label, resulting in 15 nonterminal labels (including a new start symbol). Finally, we simplified the structures in the corpus slightly so that they could be expressed in terms of only *parent* and *grand*parent relationships. In particular, some pairs of nonterminals are conflated so that every nonterminal has at least one terminal as an immediate child, since otherwise great-grandparent relationships would be necessary. There are very few constructions in the Susanne corpus that violate this constraint, but one of them is very common, namely the S-VP division. The head terminal of the S (the verb) is within the VP, and thus the S often occurs without any terminals as immediate children. In these cases, we collapse the S and VP into a single nonterminal, giving it the label S. The same is done for other such constructions, conflating nonterminals based on syntactic head relationships. This is a local modification which does not change the recursive nature of the structures or the ability to extract predicate-argument information from them. Also, we should emphasize that it would be possible to define a different input-output format for a SSN parser which could use any corpus' definition of constituency.

The total set of converted sentences was divided into three disjoint subsets, one for training, one for validation, and one for testing. The division was done at random, with the objective of producing validation and testing sets which are each about an eighth of the total set. No restrictions were placed on sentence length in any set. The training set has 26480 words, 15411 constituents, and 1079 sentences, the validation set has 4365 words, 2523 constituents, and 186 sentences, and the testing set has 4304 words, 2500 constituents, and 181 sentences.

5.2   Training the Models

The SSN parser was trained using standard training techniques extended for SSNs (Henderson, 2002). Neural network training is an iterative process, in which the network is run on training examples and then modified so as to make less error the next time it sees those examples. This process can be continued until no more changes are made, but to avoid over-fitting it is better to check the performance of the network on a validation set and stop training when the performance on the validation set reaches a maximum. This is why we have split the corpus into three datasets, one for training, one for validation, and one for testing. This technique also allows multiple versions of the network to be trained and then evaluated using the validation set, without ever using the testing set until a single network has been chosen. A variety of hidden layer sizes and random initial weight seeds were used in the different networks. Larger hidden layers result in the network being able to fit the training data more precisely, but can lead to over-fitting and therefore bad performance on the validation set. Various standard neural network training techniques were used.[7] From the multiple networks trained, the best network was chosen on the basis of its performance on the validation set, and this one network was used in testing. The best network had 100 hidden units and trained for a total of 145 passes through the training set.

We estimate the parameters of a PCFG using relative frequency. All the sequences of child labels that occur in the corpus for each parent label need to be extracted, counted, and normalized in accordance with the conditional probabilities required by the model. Because this process does not require a validation set, we estimate these parameters using the combination of the training set and the validation set.

We also estimate the parameters of the PSR model using relative frequency. All the head tag bigrams associated with each structural relationship (or label-head tag bigrams) are extracted, counted, and normalized in accordance with the probability model. As with the PCFG, we use the network's training set plus its validation set to estimate the probabilities.

In addition to embodying the same linguistic assumptions as the SSN parser, the PSR model has the advantage that it has a finite space of possible parameters (namely one probability per tag bigram for each relationship). Because a PCFG places no bound on the number of children that a parent nonterminal can have, a PCFG has an infinite space of possible parameters (namely one probability for each of the infinite number of possible rules). This makes it difficult to apply smoothing to a PCFG to avoid the problem of assigning zero probability to rules that did not occur in the training set. Thus we have not applied smoothing to the PCFG, contributing to the bad test set coverage discussed in the next section. However the PSR's finite space of parameters makes it simple to apply smoothing to the PSR model. Before normalizing we add half to all the counts so that none of them are zero.

5.3 Testing Results

Once all development and training had been completed, the SSN parser, the PCFG, and the two PSRs were tested on the data in the testing set. For the PCFG and the PSRs the most probable parse according to the model was taken as the output of the parser.[8] The results of this testing are shown in Table 6.1, where "PSR" is the unsmoothed PSR, and "PSR Sm" is the smoothed PSR.

The first thing to notice about the testing results is that the PCFG only finds parses for about half of the sentences. For the unparsed sentences the PCFG had not found enough rules in its training set to construct a tree that spans the entire sentence, and thus there is no straightforward way to choose the most probable parse.[9] In contrast, the SSN parser is able to make a guess for every sentence. This is a result of the definition of the SSN parser, as with the smoothed PSR, but unlike both PSR models the SSN parser produces good guesses. The first evidence of the quality of the SSN parser's guesses is that they are exactly correct nearly five times as often as for the PCFG and PSRs, as shown in the second column of Table 6.1.

The remaining six columns in Table 6.1 give the performance of each parser on both constituents and parent-child relationships. An output constituent is the same as a desired constituent if they contain the same terminals and have the same label. The constituent measures are the most common ones used for comparing parsers. Parent-child relationships are the result of interpreting the parse tree as a form of dependency structure. Each parent-child relationship in the parse tree is interpreted as a dependency from the head word of the child to the head word of the parent. Two such relationships are the same if their words are the same and they are of the same type. This criteria is more closely related to the output of the SSN network and the PSR model, and may be more appropriate for some applications. For both criteria, performance is measured in terms of recall (percentage of desired which are output), precision (percentage of output which are desired), and F-measure (an equally weighted combination of recall and precision).

Given that the PCFG produces no parse for about half of the sentences, it is no surprise that the SSN parser achieves about twice the recall of the PCFG on both constituents and parent-child relationships. Thus we also compute these performance figures for the subset of sentences which are parsed by the PCFG, as discussed below. However, restricting attention to the parsed subset will not change the PCFG's precision figures. Just as the recall figures are particularly low, the precision figures are improved due to the fact that the PCFG is not outputting anything for those sentences which are particularly hard for it (i.e.

	Sentences		Constituents			Parent-child		
	Parsed	Correct	Rec	Prec	$F_{\beta=1}$	Rec	Prec	$F_{\beta=1}$
SSN	100%	16.0%	64.8%	65.9%	65.4%	81.9%	82.4%	82.2%
PCFG	50.8%	3.3%	29.2%	53.7%	37.8%	39.3%	75.5%	51.7%
PSR	93.4%	3.3%	38.8%	40.7%	39.7%	64.9%	66.0%	65.5%
PSR Sm	100%	2.8%	35.9%	36.8%	36.3%	58.8%	59.4%	59.1%

Table 6.1.   Testing results.

	Sentences		Constituents			Parent-child		
	Parsed	Correct	Rec	Prec	$F_{\beta=1}$	Rec	Prec	$F_{\beta=1}$
SSN	100%	17.4%	63.3%	65.1%	64.2%	82.1%	82.9%	82.5%
PCFG		6.5%	57.5%	53.7%	55.5%	77.4%	75.5%	76.4%

Table 6.2.   Testing results on the sentences parsed by the PCFG.

the sentences it cannot parse). Even so, the SSN does about 10% better than the PCFG on both constituent precision and parent-child precision.

Table 6.2 shows the performance of the PCFG and SSN on the subset of test sentences parsed by the PCFG. Note that these figures are biased in favor of the PCFG, since we are excluding only those sentences which are difficult for the PCFG, as determined by the results on the testing set itself. Even so, the SSN outperforms the PCFG under every measure. In fact, under every measure the SSN's performance on the entire testing set is better than the PCFG's performance on the subset of sentences which they parse.

Given the large difference between the linguistic assumptions embodied in the PCFG and the SSN parser, we need to address the possibility that the better performance of the SSN parser on this corpus is due to its linguistic assumptions and not due to the SSN architecture. The poor performance of both PSR models clearly demonstrates this. The PSR model was designed to follow the linguistic assumptions embodied in the SSN parser as closely as possible, only imposing additional independence assumptions to the extent that they were required to get sufficient counts for estimating the model's probabilities. Nonetheless, both PSR models do much worse than the PCFG, even on the parent-child relationships, which are directly related to the parameters of the PSR model. The only exception is comparing against the recall results of the PCFG models including their unparsed sentences, but the recall results of the PCFG models on the parsed subsets indicates that this is simple an artifact of the low coverage of the PCFG. Thus the better performance of the SSN parser cannot be due to its linguistic assumptions alone. It must be due to the SSN architecture's ability to handle sparse data without the need to impose strong independence assumptions.

One final thing to notice about these results is that there is not a big difference between the results of the SSN parser on the full testing set and the results on the subsets which are parsed by the PCFG. The lack of any improvement is a further demonstration that the SSN is not simply returning parses for every sentence because it is defined in such a way that it must do so. The SSN is making good guesses, even on the difficult sentences. This demonstrates the robustness of the SSN parser in the face of sparse training data and the resulting novelty of testing cases.

6.   Conclusion

The relatively good performance of the Simple Synchrony Network parser despite being trained on a very small training set demonstrates that SSN parsers are good at handling sparse data. In comparison with Probabilistic Context Free Grammars trained on the same data, the SSN parser not only returns parses for twice as many sentences, its performance on the full testing set is even better than the performance of the PCFG on the subset of sentences which it parses.

By demonstrating SSNs' ability to handle sparse data we have in fact shown that SSNs generalize from training data to testing data in a linguistically appropriate way. The poor performance of the PSR model shows that this is not simply due to clever linguistic assumptions embodied in the particular parser used. This generalization performance is due to SSNs' ability to generalize across constituents as well as across sequence positions, plus the ability of neural networks in general to learn what input features are important as well as what they imply about the output. The resulting robustness makes SSNs appropriate for a wide variety of parsing applications, particularly when a small amount of data is available or there is a large amount of variability in the input.

Notes

1. It should be noted that we are using the term "statistical method" here in a rather narrow sense, intending to reflect common practice in parsing technology. Indeed, neural networks themselves are a statistical method in the broader sense.

2. Note that this solution was found to be superior to the approach used in other approaches to parsing, where the unbounded distribution is decomposed into an unbounded sequence of finite distributions, where each probability in the sequence is conditioned on none of the alternatives earlier in the sequence being correct (Henderson, 2002).

3. In this notation we are using "$parent(c_i, w_i), \ldots,$" to denote all the *parent* predications involving c_i, and specifically that it must be included in the output structure.

4. When a nonterminal is introduced, its state vector is initialized with a memory of all previous terminal inputs. It is as if the new nonterminal had existed in the set of nonterminals during the whole previous computation, but had received no nonterminal inputs.

5. We acknowledge the roles of the Economic and Social Research Council (UK) as sponsor and the University of Sussex as grant holder in providing the Susanne corpus used in the experiments described in this chapter. A major motivation for originally adopting the Susanne corpus over the larger Penn Treebank corpus is that it is available for free.

6. We would like to thank Peter Lane for performing most of this conversion.

7. In particular, we used a momentum of 0.9 and weight decay regularization of between 0.1 and 0.0. Both the learning rate and the weight decay were decreased as the learning proceeded, based on training error and validation error, respectively.

8. We would like to thank Jean-Cedric Chappelier and the LIA-DI at EPFL, Lausanne, Switzerland for providing the tools used to train and test the PCFG.

9. It would be possible to use methods for choosing partial parses, and thus improve the recall results in Table 6.1 (at the cost of precision). Instead we choose to report results on the parsed subset, since this is sufficient to make our point.

References

Bishop, C. M. (1995). *Neural Networks for Pattern Recognition*. Oxford University Press, Oxford, UK.

Collins, M. (1999). *Head-Driven Statistical Models for Natural Language Parsing*. PhD thesis, University of Pennsylvania, Philadelphia, PA.

Elman, J. L. (1991). Distributed representations, simple recurrent networks, and grammatical structure. *Machine Learning*, 7:195–225.

Garside, R., Leech, G., and (eds), G. S. (1987). *The Computational Analysis of English: a corpus-based approach*. Longman Group UK Limited.

Henderson, J. (1994). *Description Based Parsing in a Connectionist Network*. PhD thesis, University of Pennsylvania, Philadelphia, PA. Technical Report MS-CIS-94-46.

Henderson, J. (2002). Estimating probabilities for unbounded categorization problems. In *Proceedings of the Tenth European Symposium on Artificial Neural Networks*, pages 383–388.

Henderson, J. and Lane, P. (1998). A connectionist architecture for learning to parse. In *Proceedings of COLING-ACL*, pages 531–537, Montreal, Quebec, Canada.

Lane, P. and Henderson, J. (2001). Incremental syntactic parsing of natural language corpora with simple synchrony networks. *IEEE Transactions on Knowledge and Data Engineering*, 13(2):219–231.

Marcus, M. P., Santorini, B., and Marcinkiewicz, M. A. (1993). Building a large annotated corpus of English: The Penn Treebank. *Computational Linguistics*, 19(2):313–330.

Sampson, G. (1995). *English for the Computer*. Oxford University Press, Oxford, UK.

Shastri, L. and Ajjanagadde, V. (1993). From simple associations to systematic reasoning: A connectionist representation of rules, variables, and dynamic bindings using temporal synchrony. *Behavioral and Brain Sciences*, 16:417–451.

Chapter 7

AN EFFICIENT LR PARSER GENERATOR FOR TREE-ADJOINING GRAMMARS

Carlos A. Prolo

Department of Computer and Information Science, University of Pennsylvania

200 S. 33rd Street, Philadelphia, PA, 19104, USA

prolo@linc.cis.upenn.edu

Abstract   In this chapter we discuss practical LR-like parser generator models for Tree Adjoining Grammars (TAGs) and propose a new algorithm. The algorithm has been implemented and applied to two large coverage TAGs for English: the XTAG English grammar, and a grammar automatically extracted from the Penn Treebank. The generated tables have very favorable characteristics compared to an existing approach by Nederhof, undermining earlier beliefs that LR parsing for TAGs would be inadequate for parsing natural language. Indeed, our parser generator has been used to build fast accurate best-parse parsers for natural language, as reported in (Prolo, 2002a).

1.   Introduction

The LR approach for parsing (Knuth, 1965) has long been considered for natural language parsing due to its high capacity of postponement of structural decisions, therefore allowing for much of the spurious local ambiguity to be automatically discarded (e.g., Lang, 1974; Tomita, 1985; Wright and Wrigley, 1991; Shieber, 1983; Pereira, 1985; Merlo, 1996; Briscoe and Carroll, 1993). The aforementioned work has concentrated on LR parsing for CFGs which has a clear deficiency in making available sufficient context in the LR states for parsing natural language. Shieber and Johnson (1993) hint at the relevance of Tree Adjoining Grammars (TAGs) (Joshi and Schabes, 1997; Joshi et al., 1975) on this respect. They use TAGs to defend the possibility of granular incremental computations in LR parsing. Incidentally or not, they make use

H. Bunt et al. (eds.), New Technologies in Parsing Technology, 125-155.

of disambiguation contexts that are only possible in a state of a conceptual LR parser for a rich grammar formalism such as TAG, but not for a CFG.

A fundamental characteristic of "true" LR parsing is that decisions concerning structural commitments should be postponed by the parser until full evidence of the commitment is shifted from the input to the control memory. This is a highly desirable property in left-to-right parsing, that reduces the amount of local ambiguity (e.g., compared to predictive parsers). In (Prolo, 2002b) we show that if we want to maintain this characteristic, the LR driver has to significantly deviate from the simplicity of the traditional Knuth implementation (Aho and Ullman, 1972, Section 5.2.3), where the available actions can be obtained by just traversing a finite-state automaton (with traversal "resyncronization" in constant time each time an action is executed). This fact does not come as a big surprise (see the discussion about the valid prefix property[1] in Section 7). So, research in LR parsing for TAGs has concentrated in what we call in this chapter "degenerate" or "LR-like" algorithms, which maintain the practical desirable characteristic of having an underlying finite-state automaton, giving up some (as little as possible) of the capacity of postponing structural commitments.

The first published LR algorithm for TAGs was due to Schabes and Vijay-Shanker (1990). Nederhof (1998) showed that it was incorrect (after (Kinyon, 1997)), and proposed a new one. Experimenting with his new algorithm over the XTAG English Grammar (XTAG Research Group, 1998), Nederhof concluded that LR parsing was inadequate for use with reasonably sized grammars for natural language because the size of the generated table was unmanageable. Also the ammount of conflicts was too high.

In this chapter we discuss degenerate models for LR parser generators for TAGs and propose a new algorithm that, compared to Nederhof's, dramatically reduces both the average number of conflicts per state and the size of the parser. We do not deal here with conflict resolution and final parsing evaluation, which is the subject of (Prolo, 2002a), where we show that our algorithm can be effectively used to obtain fast and reasonably accurate best-parse parsers.

In Section 2 we provide a brief introduction to TAGs. In Section 3 we discuss degenerate LR models for TAGs. We develop our algorithm from Section 4 to 7, including an example and a summary of its properties. Evaluation of the generated tables and comparison to Nederhof's proposal is the subject of Section 8. We conclude in Section 9.

2. TAGS

A TAG is a set of ***elementary trees*** as in Figure 7.1. Leaf nodes marked with a down arrow (↓) are called ***substitution nodes***. A leaf node marked with a star(*) is called a ***foot node***. Remaining leaves are called ***anchors***, constituting the nodes where the lexical items attach. An elementary tree may have at most one foot node, whose label must match the root, in which case the tree is called an ***auxiliary tree***. Otherwise the elementary tree is called an ***initial tree***. A derivation is accomplished as tree grafting process, starting with an initial tree, followed by the recursive application of two operations: (1) ***tree substitution***, where a substitution node is replaced with an initial tree whose root has a matching label; and (2) ***tree adjunction***, where a node (that is not a foot or a substitution node) is replaced by an entire auxiliary tree, which connects through its root and foot nodes, whose labels must match that of the one being replaced. After the derivation process is completed, the resulting tree (which should have no remaining substitution nodes) is called a ***derived tree***. The sequence of leaves of a derived tree from left to right is the ***derived sentence***. A derived tree for the sentence *John saw Mary from the window* is shown in Figure 7.2. The corresponding ***derivation tree*** describes the history of the tree grafting process, being usually regarded as the most important description of the derivation. In the figure, it shows that the derivation starts with the tree *vt* for *saw* (the root of the derivation tree), onto which the *np* trees for *John* and *Mary* have substituted in (solid lines) and the tree for the *pp* tree (*from*) has adjoined in (dashed lines). Technically each arc should contain the Gorn address[2] of the node where the substitution or adjunction took place, which we omitted for simplicity. For a more comprehensive introduction to TAGs and LTAGs we refer the reader to (Joshi and Schabes, 1997). We will base our exposition in this chapter in a ***normal form*** for TAGs in which all nodes are marked either ***OA*** for ***obligatory adjunction***, meaning that, once the tree is used in a derivation, there has to be an adjunction at that node for the derivation to be valid; or ***NA*** for ***null adjunction***, meaning that there cannot be adjunction at that node for the derivation to be valid. Any TAG can be converted to this normal form, preserving the set of derivations (see Section 4.3). The conventional form where nodes are usually unmarked (i.e., allowing though not requiring adjunction), will be referred to as a ***shorthand notation***.

The linguistic relevance of TAGs comes from its suitability to a certain kind of grammar design methodology, used in the example above, that has the following properties:

1 **Extended Domain of Locality:** The backbone structure of lexical projections can be fully represented in a single rule (the elementary tree). In the grammar above we can see that the anchor for the transitive verb and the place-holders for its arguments are kept together in one tree. Long

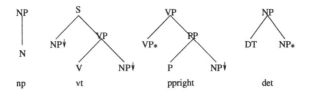

Figure 7.1. An example of Tree Adjoining Grammar

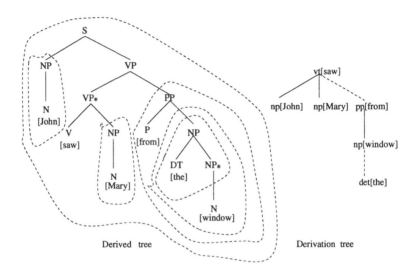

Figure 7.2. The derivation of *John saw Mary from the window*

distance dependencies, as wh-movement and topicalization, can also be represented locally in an elementary tree.

2 **Factoring of Recursion:** The complement to the property above is that non-grammatical relations are introduced by recursively adjoining them to the trees they modify, while still causing the desired effect of discontinuity in the surface structures (both derived trees and strings).

3 **Rich Descriptions:** The elementary trees can be associated with full predicate descriptions on the semantic side; and the derivation tree – not the derived tree – with the natural hierarchical structure of application of this predicates according to the dependency relations in the sentence allowing for immediate semantic processing.

The very same properties that argue for their linguistic relevance also suit TAGs as a target for the application of LR parsing techniques. The rational is that whenever a reduction is called for, the corresponding rule is a full tree with all the hierarchical argument relations, which is impossible to get with CFGs. Therefore the parser can make sound choices having seen the whole structure of what is being generated, as opposed to, e.g., a lower VP with a trace that later will have to be confirmed with the existence of the wh-word.

3.   On Some Degenerate LR Models For TAGS

For Context Free Grammars, the traditional LR parser implementation of (Knuth, 1965; Aho and Ullman, 1972)) can be viewed as follows. If at a certain state q_0 of the LR automaton, during the parsing of a sentence, we expect to see the expansion of a certain nonterminal A, and there is a production $A \rightarrow X_1 X_2 X_3 ... X_n$ in the grammar, then the automaton must have a path labeled $X_1 X_2 X_3 ... X_n$ starting at q_0. This is usually represented by saying that each state in the path contains a *"dotted item"* for the production, starting with $A \rightarrow \bullet X_1 X_2 X_3 ... X_n$ at q_0, with the dot moving one symbol ahead at each state in the path. We will refer to the last state of such paths as *final*. A dot in front of a symbol X_i represents the fact that we expect to see the expansion of X_i in the string. If X_i is a nonterminal, then, before advancing to the next state, we have to check that some expansion of X_i is actually next in the input.

The situation is depicted in Figure 7.3, where paths are represented as winding lines and single arcs as straight lines. At a certain state q_1, where some possible yield of the prefix α_1 of a production $A \rightarrow \alpha_1 B \alpha_2$ has just been scanned, the corresponding dotted item is at a nonterminal B. This state turns out to be itself the beginning of other paths, such as β in the picture, that lead to the recognition of some match for B through some of its rules. The machine, guided by the input string, could traverse this sub-path until reaching q_4. At this final state, some sort of memory is needed to get back to the previous path for A, in order to then cross from q_1 to q_2 (i.e. B has just been seen). In LR parsing this procedure is traditionally realized by a stack that stores the sequence of states traversed during recognition. At each final state, the recognized production is unwound from the stack, in an operation called a *reduction*, leaving the state q_1 exposed and making a transition over the nonterminal B to q_2 (a *goto* transition).

A reduction means a commitment to a certain substructure in the attempt to find a parse for the sentence. Whenever the parser reaches a state that contains a reduction (a final state), and there are also additional reduce actions or a shift, it has to decide whether to perform that reduction or an alternative action. This is certainly a limitation of the method, but at least the decision needs to be

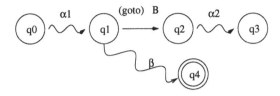

Figure 7.3. LR parsing for Context Free Grammars

taken only after witnessing that the input contains a complete yield for the production. This is exactly what is hard to guarantee in the TAG case.

The problem with LR parsing for TAGs is adjunction, as illustrated in Figure 7.4. Figure 7.4.a sketches the adjunction of a tree β at a node labeled B of a tree α. α:l(B) is the part of α that appears before (to the left of) node B. Similarly, α:b(B) and α:r(B) are the parts below and to the right of B, respectively. β:l(foot) and β:r(foot) are the two halves of β split by its spine.

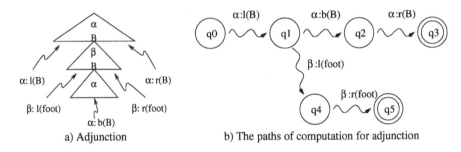

a) Adjunction

b) The paths of computation for adjunction

Figure 7.4. The problem of adjunction

There are two natural paths the LR parsing nature would induce the machine to have (Figure 7.4.b). One traverses α: state q_1 is the natural candidate to predict what comes below B (even after having recognized the left side of the adjoined tree); and state q_2 similarly is the natural state to start the prediction of what comes after B. As for the other path, state q_1 predicts the adjunction of β, more specifically its left side; and the right side (i.e., past the foot node) is naturally predicted at q_4. Now let us look at the dynamic path of computation, corresponding to the projection of each segment in the sentence. This is:

$$q_0 \xrightarrow{\alpha:l(B)} q_1 \xrightarrow{\beta:l(foot)} q_4 \Rightarrow q_1 \xrightarrow{\alpha:b(B)} q_2 \Rightarrow q_4 \xrightarrow{\beta:r(foot)} q_5 \Rightarrow q_2 \xrightarrow{\alpha:r(B)} q_3$$

Although we have marked only q_3 and q_5 as final (as we would like it to be, since they mark the end of the recognition of each tree), there are two other points of disruption at states q_4 and q_2. In the LR computation model for CFGs these points would correspond to reduction-like operations with goto transitions to jump to the resuming state. Two problems immediately arise: one that we call *"early reduction"*; the other is the unsuitability of the standard stack model.

Figure 7.5 shows an intuitive but rather naive first attempt to solve the problem. At state q_4 a reduction would be triggered sending the machine to state q_6 via a *"goto-below"* transition. But notice that this operation would pop out all the states after q_1, including q_4. Later, at q_2, when a new reduction would be required, we no longer know how to get back to the state that contains the *"goto-foot"* transition (the popped-out q_4), unless we change the underlying storage model to something other than a stack. But we are not finished: even if we could get to q_8, we have to keep q_2 alive somehow, because when reaching q_5 we need q_2 in order to access the *"goto-right"* transition to state q_7. It is important to note that we do not know in advance (i.e., at compilation time) which states those are. They are dependent on the actual runtime computation. Although we could look for another storage model, the more serious problem is the early reduction: the need to commit to tree β before seeing its right side in the input.

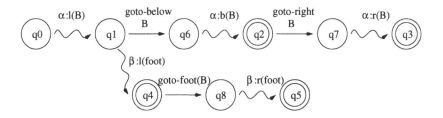

Figure 7.5. A naive solution for adjunction

A second model, used by Nederhof (1998), shown in Figure 7.6, is clearly an improvement over the naive one, as it increases the prediction capacity. The prediction of α:b(B) is made at q_4, instead of q_1. Hence we lose the need for the first reduction mentioned above. The reduction in q_2 does not cause any trouble since the state from which we want to take the goto transition, q_4, will be in the stack at that moment and therefore is easy to recover. At q_5 the reduction takes its goto-right transition to q_7 from q_1, which is recoverable from the stack, instead of q_2 as in the previous approach, which has been popped out. Alas, things are not that simple.

The problem of "early reduction" is still significant, although not as much as in the first model. When the parser is in a state where (as one of the alternatives) it has just finished recognizing the subtree below a node where something has adjoined, as in state q_2 in Figure 7.6, somehow it has to get back to

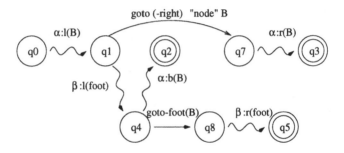

Figure 7.6. Nederhof's solution for adjunction

state q_4, and with a goto transition (goto-foot) to resume the recognition of the adjoined tree at state q_8. In Nederhof's approach this is done by performing a reduction, that is, choosing one of the items in q_2 that signifies that a subtree below an adjunction node has been recognized (e.g., the subtree corresponding to α:b(B)), and performing a reduction of that subtree. This means committing to tree α too early, before seeing whether the rest of the input matches α:r(B). In the example in Figure 7.7, immediately after seeing a prefix "N", as in (1) below, that could be anchoring any of the innumerably many α_i trees generating continuations such as those in (2), the parser would have to commit in advance to one of them, due to the need to go back to the right side of the relative clause tree β.[3] The most visible consequence of this problem is the huge rate of conflicts in the table involving this kind of reduction, which we drastically reduce with our approach, as shown in Section 8.

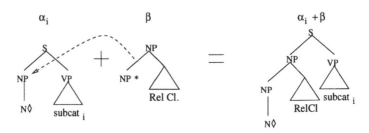

Figure 7.7. Example of early reduction

(1) (the) cat/N ...

(2) ... [that John saw] died.
    ... [that John saw] ate an apple.

... [that John saw] asked for Meow Mix.

The second problem is an immediate consequence of the first. Goto transitions are traditionally made as functions whose domain is the set of symbols. In Nederhof's approach, however, because we have already committed to (a certain node of) a tree at state q_2, a strategy of having one goto transition per node is adopted. In addition to increasing the number of states, it simultaneously causes an explosion in the number of goto transitions per state, making the size of the table unmanageable. What we had in mind when looking for a new algorithm was precisely to solve those two problems.

There is still a third problem, related to the lack of the valid prefix property. Predicting the path α:b(B), below a node where adjunction is supposed to take place after the left part of the adjoined tree, is difficult. Actually, we show in Section 7 that this is impossible with Nederhof's approach as well as our own (although it would not be a problem for the "naive" solution: recall the natural candidate for such prediction would be q_1). An attempt to do that in the algorithm for table generation would lead to nontermination for some grammars. Hence, at state q_4 all items corresponding to adjunction nodes labeled B in some tree are inserted with the dot past the node, even if many of those nodes were not possible at that state, for a particular input prefix. Although in our approach the effects of misprediction and overgeneration are less harmful, it decisively affects the design of the algorithm as we see below.

Figure 7.8 sketches our proposed solution. The goto transition now depends on both q_1 and q_2. At state q_2, the items that correspond to the end of the recognition of bottom subtrees labeled B, such as α:b(B), are grouped into subsets of the same size, size being the number of leaves of the subtree. Hence goto-adj(q_1, q_2, B, l) has the set of possibilities of continuations like α:r(B) that were predicted at q_1 and confirmed at q_2, that have l leaves under B. The dependency on q_1 has the sole purpose of fixing the overprediction we mentioned above, originating at q_4, and propagated to q_2. When q_2 is reached, an action called *bpack(B,l)* extracts from the stack the l nodes under B (α:b(B), uncovering q_4 and the goto-foot), and puts them back in the stack as a single embedded stack element. The material is unpacked during β reduction before moving to q_7.[4] The details of the algorithm are in the next section.

4. Proposed Algorithm

4.1 Table Generation for the NA/OA Case

In this section, we describe an algorithm for TAGs in which all nodes are marked either NA (for Null Adjunction) or OA (for Obligatory Adjunction). Later we deal with the general case. We do not consider selective adjunction (SA).

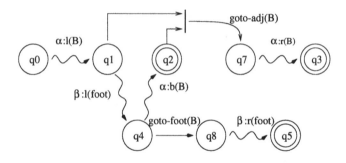

Figure 7.8. Proposed solution for adjunction

To refer to the symbol (label) of a node n, we use $symb(n)$. ϵ is used to label anchors to represent the absence of a terminal symbol (the "empty" label).

A *dotted node* is a pair (n, pos) where n is a tree node and pos, as in (Schabes, 1990), can be la (at the left and above the node), lb (left and below), rb (right and below), or ra (right and above). We represent the dotted nodes pictorially as $^\bullet n$, $_\bullet n$, $n_\bullet$, and $n^\bullet$. A *dotted item* (*item*, for short) is a pair (t, dn), where t is an elementary tree, and dn a dotted node whose node component belongs to t.

We define a congruence relation $\cong$ as the least symmetric and transitive relation such that, for any pair of items $i_1 = (t, dn_1)$ and $i_2 = (t, dn_2)$ of the same tree t, $i_1 \cong i_2$ if any of the following conditions apply:

1 $dn_1 = {}^\bullet n$, $dn_2 = {}_\bullet n$, and n is marked for null adjunction (NA).

2 $dn_1 = {}_\bullet n$, $dn_2 = n_\bullet$, and n is an anchor labeled ϵ.

3 $dn_1 = {}_\bullet n$, $dn_2 = {}^\bullet m$, and m is the leftmost child of n.

4 $dn_1 = n_\bullet$, $dn_2 = n^\bullet$, and n is marked for null adjunction (NA).

5 $dn_1 = n_\bullet$, $dn_2 = m^\bullet$, and m is the rightmost child of n,

6 $dn_1 = n^\bullet$, $dn_2 = {}^\bullet m$, and m is the right sibling of n.

Congruent items are indistinguishable for the purpose of our algorithm and its underlying theory. Hence instead of dealing with separate items, we use equivalence classes under $\cong$. If i is a term, $[i]$ is the congruence class to which i belongs. Each congruence class has one and only one *active* item, where an active item has one of the following forms:

- $(t, {}^\bullet n)$, where n is marked OA: this item triggers adjunction on n.

- $(t, {}_\bullet n)$, where n can be: a substitution node (triggers substitution), a non-ϵ anchor (triggers a shift action), or a foot node (triggers the return to the tree where adjunction occurred).

- $(t, n_\bullet)$, where n is marked OA: this item triggers a bpack action, that we will define later.

- $(t, n^\bullet)$, where n is the root of t: triggers a reduce tree (α or β) operation.

Figure 7.9 shows an example elementary tree with the four dot positions at each node. The dots are grouped according to the equivalence classes determined by $\cong$. The arrows mark the active positions, at the end of each chain. In order to further clarify the meaning of $\cong$, in Figure 7.10 we draw an analogy with one possible view of the dotted positions for CFGs, in which there would be the positions *before* and *after* each symbol occurrence in the productions. For CFGs there is a well-known elegant way of avoiding that presentation. That unfortunately is not the case for TAGs.

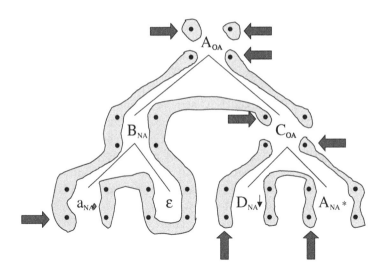

Figure 7.9. The congruence relation and the active items

Given a set S of dotted items (under $\cong$) of a TAG, we define $closure(S)$ as the minimal set that satisfies the following conditions:

1 If $[i] \in S$, then $[i] \in closure(S)$.

2 If $[(t, {}_\bullet n)] \in closure(S)$, and n is a substitution node, then for every initial tree t_1 with root node r labeled $symb(n)$, $[(t_1, {}^\bullet r)] \in closure(S)$.

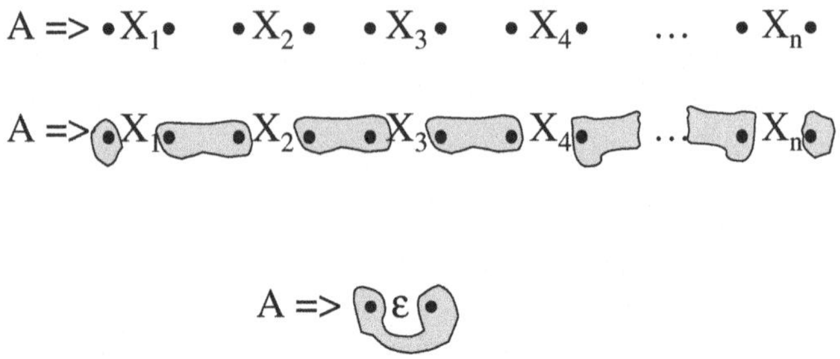

$$A => \bullet X_1 \bullet \quad \bullet X_2 \bullet \quad \bullet X_3 \bullet \quad \bullet X_4 \bullet \quad \ldots \quad \bullet X_n \bullet$$

Figure 7.10.   An analogy to the congruence relation for CFGs

3 If $[(t, {}^\bullet n)] \in closure(S)$ and n is a node marked OA, then for every auxiliary tree t_1 with root node r labeled $symb(n)$, $[(t_1, {}^\bullet r)] \in closure(S)$.

4 If $[(t, {}_\bullet n)] \in closure(S)$, where n is a foot node, then for every OA node m of the grammar such that $symb(m) = symb(n)$, $[(t_1, {}_\bullet m)] \in closure(S)$, where t_1 is the elementary tree that contains m. We point out that it is at this closure operation that the valid prefix property is lost.

To define a parsing table for a grammar G with goal symbol S, we first extend G by adding one new tree called *start*, with two nodes: the root, labeled with a fresh symbol ST, marked NA; and ST's single child, a substitution node labeled S.[5] Then, let I be the set of all equivalence classes of items of G under $\cong$. Let N be the set of symbols, $T \subseteq N$ be the set of symbols that appear in some anchor, and $\mathbb{N}$ the set of non-negative integers. We define the *"parsing table"* as a set $Q \subseteq 2^I$ of states with initial state $q_0 = closure(\{[(start, {}^\bullet ST)]\}) \in Q$, together with the functions $GOTO_{subst} : Q \times N \to Q$, $GOTO_{foot} : Q \times N \to Q$, $GOTO_{adj} : Q \times Q \times N \times \mathbb{N} \to Q$, and $ACTIONS : Q \times T \to 2^A$, where $A = \{\text{shift } q \,|\, q \in Q\} \cup \{\alpha\text{-reduce } t | t \text{ is an alpha tree }\} \cup \{\beta\text{-reduce } t | t \text{ is a beta tree }\} \cup \{\text{bpack } (A, l) | A \in N, l \in \mathbb{N}\} \cup \{\text{accept}\}$. Q, $GOTO_{subst}$, $GOTO_{foot}$, $GOTO_{adj}$, and $ACTIONS$ are the minimal set and functions that satisfy the following inductive definition:

1 $q_0 \in Q$.

2 If $q \in Q$ and $p = \{[(t, n_\bullet)] \,|\, [(t, {}_\bullet n)] \in q$ and n is an anchor $\}$, then $p' = closure(p) \in Q$, and $(\text{shift } p') \in ACTIONS(q, symb(n))$. See Figure 7.11.

3 If $q \in Q$ and $[(t, n^\bullet)] \in Q$, where n is the root of t, then, for every $a \in T$: if t is an initial tree, then $(\alpha\text{-reduce } t) \in ACTIONS(q, a)$, else $(\beta\text{-reduce } t) \in ACTIONS(q, a)$. See Figures 7.12 and 7.17.

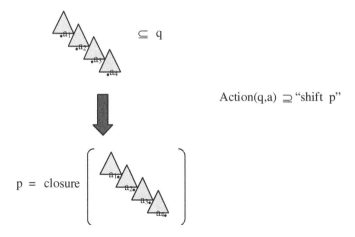

$\subseteq q$

Action(q,a) $\supseteq$ "shift p"

p = closure

Figure 7.11. Shift

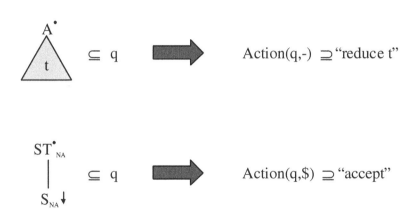

$\subseteq q$ Action(q,-) $\supseteq$ "reduce t"

$\subseteq q$ Action(q,$) $\supseteq$ "accept"

Figure 7.12. Reductions and accept

4 If $q \in Q$ and $[(start, ST^\bullet)] \in Q$, then accept $\in ACTIONS(q, \$)$. See Figure 7.12.

5 If $q \in Q$ and $[(t, n_\bullet)] \in Q$, where n is marked OA, then, for every $a \in T$, (bpack($symb(n), l$)) $\in ACTIONS(q, a)$, where l is the number of non-ϵ leaves under n. See Figures 7.13 and 7.16.

6 If $q \in Q$ and $p = \{[(t, n_\bullet)] \mid [(t, _\bullet n)] \in q$ and n is a substitution node, then $p' = closure(p) \in Q$, and $GOTO_{subst}(q, symb(n)) = p'$.

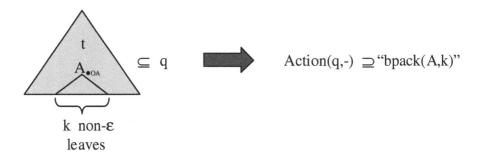

Figure 7.13.   Bpack

7 If $q \in Q$ and $p = \{[(t, n_\bullet)] \mid [(t, {}_\bullet n)] \in q$ and n is a foot node, then $p' = closure(p) \in Q$, and $GOTO_{foot}(q, symb(n)) = p'$. See Figures 7.14 and 7.16.

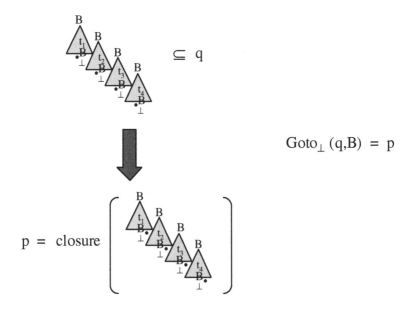

Figure 7.14.   Goto$_{foot}$ transition ($\perp$ indicates the position of the foot)

8 If $q_1, q_2 \in Q$, and for some $k \in \mathbb{N}$, $p = \{[(t, n^\bullet)]) \mid [(t, {}^\bullet n)] \in q_1, [(t, n_\bullet)] \in q_2$, n is marked OA, and the number of leaves under n in t equals $k\}$, then $p' = closure(p) \in Q$, and $GOTO_{adj}(q_1, q_2, symb(n), k) = p'$. See Figures 7.15 and 7.17.

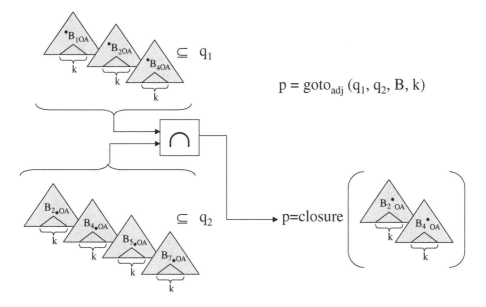

$$p = goto_{adj} (q_1, q_2, B, k)$$

Figure 7.15. Goto_{adj} transition

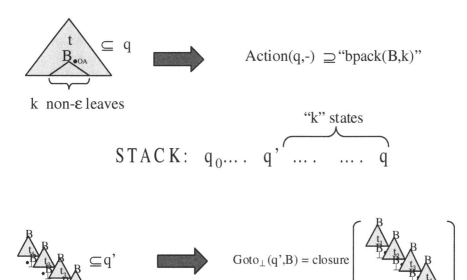

Figure 7.16. Interaction between bpack and goto_{foot}

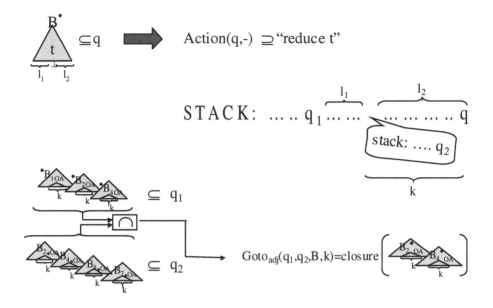

Figure 7.17.   Interaction between β-reduce and goto$_{adj}$

The state corresponding to the empty set is called *error*. The domain of k, in practice, is bounded by the grammar: the maximum number of leaves of any node. As usual, if an entry contains more than one action, we say that there is a *conflict* in the entry. As expected, two shift actions are never in conflict. Although reduce and bpack actions do not actually depend on a terminal symbol in the current algorithm, in practice the table could be constrained in this way, either by extending the algorithm to an LR(1) version or by using empirical evidence to resolve or reduce conflicts. In our inductive definition, each state was associated with the closure of a (usually much smaller) set of items. This set prior to the closure is generally known as its *kernel*. It is a property of our framework that an alternative definition whose states are associated with kernels would produce an automaton isomorphic to the one we defined above.

4.2   The Driver

The algorithm for the driver shown in Figure 7.18 uses a stack. Let st, st_1 be stacks and el be a stack element. **PUSH** (el,st), **TOP** (st) and **POP** (st) have the usual meanings. **POP** (st, k) pops out the top k elements from st. **EXTRACT** (st, k) pops out the top k elements returning another stack with the k elements in the same order they were in st. Its counterpart, **INSERT** (st_1, st), pushes onto st all elements in st_1, again preserving the order. null is the empty stack. size(st) is the number of elements in the stack st. The stack is a sort of higher order structure, in the sense that an element of the stack may contain an embedded stack. More precisely, an element of the stack is a pair (X, q), where q is a state of the parsing table, and X is either a grammar symbol or another stack.

The algorithm for the driver also uses *input*, the sequence of symbols to be recognized. Two operations are defined over it: **look**, which returns the leftmost symbol of *input* (or $ if *input* is the null sequence); and **advance**, which removes the leftmost symbol from *input*.

Let $ACTIONS$, $GOTO_{subst}$, $GOTO_{foot}$, and $GOTO_{adj}$ be the four tables/functions for a grammar G. Let q_0 be the initial state of the corresponding machine. Let *input* and the stacks *stack*, *emb-stack* be as defined above. The algorithm for the driver is then as shown in Figure 7.18.

4.3 The General Case

The obvious way to handle the general case is to transform the arbitrary input grammar (shorthand notation) into an equivalent one with all nodes marked NA/OA (normal form) prior to the application of the algorithm of Section 4.1. For every TAG G, there is a grammar G' equivalent to G with respect to the possible derivations, whose nodes are all OA/NA marked. For instance, given the grammar G in Figure 7.19,[6] we can construct G' in Figure 7.20 by replacing each tree t of G by 2^n new trees, where n is the number of unmarked nodes of t. Each new tree corresponds to one of the possible assignments of marks NA/OA to each of the unmarked nodes. In fact, in a TAG derivation, a tree instance together with the Gorn addresses at which other trees have adjoined defines exactly one of these G' component trees.

5. Implementation

This section describes two details of the implementation that may be relevant for one seeking a better understanding of our algorithm. The first topic describes how we avoid the growth in the number of items that comes with the NA/OA decomposition of the trees. The second shows how we deal with the $GOTO_{adj}$ matrix, so that it does not use $|Q|^2 * |N| * ml$ cells (where $|Q|$ is the number of states, $|N|$ the number of symbols that allow adjunction, and ml the maximum number of leaves in a tree in the grammar), what could be prohibitive. The details of this section which follow may be skipped in a first reading without preventing further comprehension.

Our implementation does not actually rely on the NA/OA decomposition of Section 4.3. Instead it takes advantage of the original compact shorthand representation, avoiding exploding the number of trees, and hence items and item sets. In principle, an OA/NA tree originated from the decomposition of Section 4.3 can be represented in the items as the original unmarked one plus

stack = null
PUSH (<null,q_0 >, *stack*)
forever
  let <−, *state*> = **TOP** (*stack*)
  let *lookahead* = **look** (*input*)
  if *ACTIONS* (*state*, *lookahead*) = error **then return** failure
  else let *action* be in *ACTIONS* (*state*, *lookahead*)
                        /* (a nondeterministic choice) */
      case *action* **of**:
       shift p:
         PUSH (< *lookahead,p* >, *stack*)
         advance (*input*)
       α-reduce t:
         let k be the number of non-empty leaves of t
         let A be the symbol at the root of t
         POP (*stack*, k)
         let <−, *state1*> = **TOP** (*stack*)
         PUSH (<A,$GOTO_{subst}$(*state1,A*)>, *stack*)
       β-reduce t:
         let kl and kr be the number of non-empty leaves of t
             respectively to the left and to the right of the foot of t
         POP (*stack*, kr)
         let < *aux-stack,-*> = **TOP** (*stack*)
         POP (*stack*)
         let k = size (*aux-stack*)
         let <-, *state2*> = **TOP** (if $k > 0$ then *aux-stack* else *stack*)
         POP (*stack*, kl)
         let <-, *state1*> = **TOP** (*stack*)
         INSERT (*aux-stack*, *stack*)
         let A be the symbol at the root of t
         let *state* = $GOTO_{adj}$ (*state1, state2,A,k*)
         if *state* = error **then return** failure
         /* (a consequence of the lack of the prefix property) */
         let < *el,-* > = **TOP** (*stack*)
         POP (*stack*)
         PUSH (< *el*, *state*>, *stack*)
       bpack (A,k):
         emb-stack = **EXTRACT** (*stack*, k)
         let <-, *state1*>= **TOP** (*stack*)
         PUSH (< *emb-stack*, $GOTO_{foot}$ (*state1,A*)>, *stack*)
       accept:
         return success

Figure 7.18.   LR parser driver algorithm

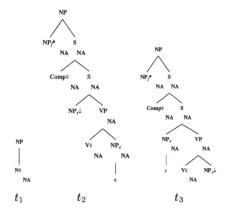

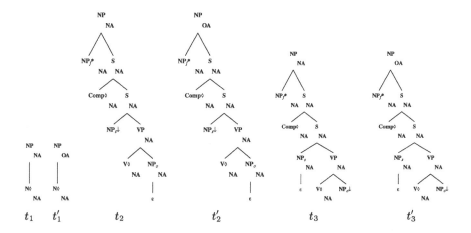

Figure 7.19. TAG G for relative clauses

Figure 7.20. TAG G', equivalent to G, with only OA/NA nodes

a list of the OA nodes, much like the Gorn addresses in derivations. If t is a tree in the original grammar, U_t is the set of unmarked nodes of t, s_i is any of the $2^{|U_t|}$ subsets of U_t, and t_i is the OA/NA tree generated from t by marking OA the nodes in s_i and NA the nodes in $U_t - s_i$, then we can represent t_i by the pair, $< t, s_i >$. Hence an item (t_i, dn) for the NA/OA grammar can be represented as $(< t, s_i >, dn)$. It turns out that certain distinctions in s_i are irrelevant for the algorithm. For instance, it is not relevant to identify in an item whether or not tree nodes to the right of the dotted node allow for adjunction. In fact markings at nodes that come "after" the dotted node according to the usual dot traversal order defined in (Schabes, 1990, p.58;Joshi and Schabes,

1997, p.104) are indistinguishable. On the other hand there are nodes which are distinguishable but still not crucial to the functionality of the algorithm. The relevant cases are depicted in the tree in Figure 7.21. We assume we are representing an item $(< t, s_i >, dn)$ where t is the tree in the figure, the dotted node dn is n with the dot at one of the four positions), and we want to discuss whether it is relevant or not to include in s_i the information on adjunction for each of the relevant cases, i.e., nodes n_1 to n_4 and n itself.

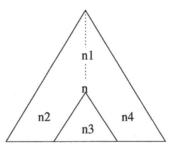

Figure 7.21.   Possible positions for unmarked nodes relative to the dotted node

n_4: a node to the right of the dotted node.   As said before the OA/NA marking at this node is indistinguishable to the parser, in items with the dotted node at n. That is, for any state generated by our algorithm, the state will contain the item in focus for a particular tree with n_4 marked OA if and only if it also contains the item for a tree with n_4 marked NA. Hence we may reformulate our initial definition of s_i so that it will not include these kind of nodes. We may think of this as a compact representation of the items for the NA/OA form.

n_2: a node to the left of the dotted node.   The OA/NA character of this kind of node is distinguishable by our algorithm but not crucial. We explain. It is quite possible for one state to have the item $(< t, s_i >, dn)$ with n_2 marked OA in t, but not the item with n_2 marked NA in t. The first item records an earlier commitment to the fact that some tree adjoined at n_2, and it has already been reduced. The second item denies that. The question is whether this distinction affects the parsing possibilities when resuming parsing from those states. The obvious answer is that it does not. In particular, if the only difference between two states is those two items, then, for any input suffix, whatever sequence of actions can be attained from one state can also be achieved from the other. Hence, if we ignore this distinction we will have a generated parsing table which is equivalent to the one presented in Section 4.3 but is more compact, i.e. it has fewer states. The only caveat is that if we assign "weights" for the conflicting actions, for instance, based on corpus evidence (e.g., as we do in (Prolo, 2002a)), the effect of the compaction may alter the final numbers, and therefore the behavior of the parser. That is, the preferred behavior to continue parsing conditioned to the fact that something has adjoined at n_2 may be different from when no adjunction has occurred. An independence assumption is clearly being posed here.

n_3: a node properly dominated by the dotted node.   There are two cases: If dn is $^\bullet n$ or $_\bullet n$, then the OA/NA marking at n_3 is indistinguishable, as n_4. If dn is $n_\bullet$ or $n^\bullet$, then marking at n_3 is distinguishable but not crucial, as n_2.

n.   We have to consider n itself, when it is unmarked in the original tree t. There are three cases: If dn is $^\bullet n$, then the OA/NA marking at n is indistinguishable, as n_4. If dn is $n^\bullet$, then the marking at n is distinguishable but not crucial, as n_2. If dn is $_\bullet n$ or $n_\bullet$, then the marking at n is crucial, that is, we have to represent it (but see item for n_1 below).

n_1: a node properly dominating n.   The analysis of this kind of node is more complex and actually includes the crucial cases for n just seen above. Let dom be the set of nodes dominating n with $\{n\}$ included only if dn is $_\bullet n$ or $n_\bullet$. Let $s_i|dom = s_i \cap dom$. Let $OA|dom$ be the set of nodes in dom that are marked OA in the original tree t. Let $adj_i|dom = s_i|dom \cup OA|dom$. Let $deep_i$ be the deepest node in $adj_i|dom$. We claim that the OA/NA marking at any node that properly dominates $deep_i$ is not distinguishable by the algorithm. This is a consequence of our abandon of the valid prefix property at closure rule 4 in Section 4.1. The dotted item we are focusing on is derived from an item generated by closure rule 4, to start scanning the subtree below $deep_i$. Since we consider there all possible trees to scan below the node with a certain symbol (the symbol at $deep_i$), all possible combinations of OA/NA marking of nodes above $deep_i$ are included and preserved together since then by the algorithm. Hence either all of them are present at a certain state, in items with the dot as in dn, or none of them are. Notice that here the notion of distinguishability is dependent on s_i. In summary, the only information we need regarding $s_i|dom$ is $deep_i$, or, equivalently, either we need to know that $deep_i$ is not in s_i, or else, in case $deep_i$ is in s_i, we need to know which node is $deep_i$.

According to the case analysis above, the only information from s_i we actually need to keep track is $deep_i$. Notice that even the information about n is included here since, when the marking at n is crucial, n happens to be $deep_i$. The algorithm we implemented therefore represents the items as $(< t, deep_i >, dn)$, losing the distinctions regarding the nodes which are distinguishable but not crucial. Finally we observe that if the original grammar is already in the NA/OA normal form (for instance, obtained with a preprocessing option), the algorithm produces a table which is exactly the same as in Section 4.3. Therefore, at the end we have only gains with the adopted strategy.

The second implementation aspect we discuss now is of a rather different nature than the first. It does not have any influence in the formal properties of the model we propose. The only reason why we discuss it here is to avoid the reader's perplexity when in the evaluation section (Section 8), we show that the size of the generated table is much smaller than the expected $|Q|^2 * |N| * ml$ value (where $|Q|$ is the number of states, $|N|$ the number of symbols that allow adjunction, and ml the maximum number of leaves in a tree in the grammar).

As seen before the $GOTO_{adj}$ function is drawn from a domain $Q \times Q \times N \times \mathbb{N}$. The trick is to evaluate $GOTO_{adj}$ as

$$GOTO_{adj}(q_1, q_2, X, k) = GOTO'_{adj}(proj_1(q_1, X), proj_2(q_2, X), k),$$

where $proj_1(q_1, X) = \{[(t, {}^\bullet n)] \in q_1 | n \text{ is marked OA and } symb(n) = X\}$, and $proj_2(q_2, X) = \{[(t, n_\bullet)] \in q_2 | n \text{ is marked OA and } symb(n) = X\}$. The ranges of both $proj_1(., X)$ and $proj_2(., X)$ are significantly smaller than Q, and so is the matrix for $GOTO'_{adj}$ compared to $GOTO_{adj}$. The overhead from the two auxiliary tables for $proj_1$ and $proj_2$ is of small size, since they depend only linearly on Q. Notice that we strongly use the fact that $GOTO_{adj}$ distinguishes the states by using only a fraction of their content consisting of the items whose node is labeled with the argument symbol X at certain positions.

6.   Example

The set of states and the $GOTO_{adj}$ function produced by the OA/NA algorithm for grammar G' of Figure 7.20 are shown in Figure 7.22. Non-shift actions were defined together with the states. $GOTO_{foot}$, $GOTO_{subst}$, and shift actions are better viewed as a graph in Figure 7.23. Figure 7.25 shows the parsing sequence for "pets/N that/Comp Mary/N likes/V" (Figure 7.24).

7.   Some Properties of the Algorithms

We state in this section how our algorithm behaves with respect to some important properties of LR parsers for CFG.

1 Whenever a reduction for a tree t is available during the parsing of a sentence, the appropriate sequence of leaves is present in the top of the stack, and similarly for a bpack. That is, for every instantaneous description reachable during the parsing of a sentence:

(a) If an action α-reduce t is available and the sequence of non-empty leaves of t read from left to right is $X_1, X_2, \ldots, X_l$, then the top

S_0 : { [(*start*, $^\bullet$NP)], [(t_1, $_\bullet$N)], [(t'_1, $^\bullet$NP)], [(t_2, $_\bullet$NP$_f$)], [(t'_2, $^\bullet$NP)], [(t_3, $_\bullet$NP$_f$)], [(t'_3,
$^\bullet$NP)], [(t'_1, $_\bullet$N)], [(t'_2, $_\bullet$NP$_f$)], [(t'_3, $_\bullet$NP$_f$)] }

S_1 : { [(*start*, ST$^\bullet$)] }; $ACTIONS(S_1,\$) = \{$ accept $\}$

S_2 : { [(t_1, NP$^\bullet$)], [(t'_1, NP$_\bullet$)] }; $ACTIONS(S_2,-) = \{$ α-reduce t_1, bpack(NP,1) $\}$

S_3 : { [(t_2, $_\bullet$Comp)], [(t_3, $_\bullet$Comp)], [(t'_2, $_\bullet$Comp)], [(t'_3, $_\bullet$Comp)] }

S_4 : { [(t_2, $_\bullet$NP$_s$)], [(t_3, $_\bullet$V)], [(t'_2, $_\bullet$NP$_s$)],[(t'_3, $_\bullet$V)], [(t_1, $_\bullet$N)], [(t'_1, $^\bullet$NP)], [(t_2,
$_\bullet$NP$_f$)], [(t'_2, $^\bullet$NP)], [(t_3, $_\bullet$NP$_f$)], [(t'_3, $^\bullet$NP)], [(t'_1, $_\bullet$N)], [(t'_2, $_\bullet$NP$_f$)], [(t'_3, $_\bullet$NP$_f$)]
}

S_5 : { [(t_2, $_\bullet$V)], [(t'_2, $_\bullet$V)] }

S_6 : { [(t_3, $_\bullet$NP$_o$)], [(t'_3, $_\bullet$NP$_o$)], [(t_1, $_\bullet$N)], [(t'_1, $^\bullet$NP)], [(t_2, $_\bullet$NP$_f$)], [(t'_2, $^\bullet$NP)], [(t_3,
$_\bullet$NP$_f$)], [(t'_3, $^\bullet$NP)], [(t'_1, $_\bullet$N)], [(t'_2, $_\bullet$NP$_f$)], [(t'_3, $_\bullet$NP$_f$)] }

S_7 : { [(t_2, NP$^\bullet$)], [(t'_2, NP$_\bullet$)] }; $ACTIONS(S_7,-) = \{$ β-reduce t_2, bpack(NP,4) $\}$

S_8 : { [(t_3, NP$^\bullet$)], [(t'_3, NP$_\bullet$)] }; $ACTIONS(S_8,-) = \{$ β-reduce t_3, bpack(NP,4) $\}$

S_9 : { [(t'_1, NP$^\bullet$)] } ; $ACTIONS(S_9,-) = \{$ β-reduce t'_1 $\}$

S_{10} : { [(t'_2, NP$^\bullet$)] } ; $ACTIONS(S_{10},-) = \{$ β-reduce t'_2 $\}$

S_{11} : { [(t'_3, NP$^\bullet$)] } ; $ACTIONS(S_{11},-) = \{$ β-reduce t'_3 $\}$

$$GOTO_{adj}(S_0, S_2, NP, 1) = S_9$$
$$GOTO_{adj}(S_4, S_2, NP, 1) = S_9$$
$$GOTO_{adj}(S_0, S_7, NP, 4) = S_{10}$$
$$GOTO_{adj}(S_4, S_7, NP, 4) = S_{10}$$
$$GOTO_{adj}(S_0, S_8, NP, 4) = S_{11}$$
$$GOTO_{adj}(S_4, S_8, NP, 4) = S_{11}$$

Figure 7.22. Sets of states, actions, and $GOTO_{adj}$ function for G'

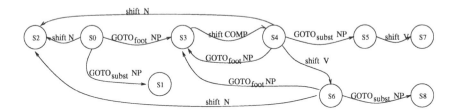

Figure 7.23. shift actions and functions $GOTO_{subst}$, $GOTO_{foot}$ for G'

l positions in the stack of the instantaneous description will contain that sequence of symbols, that is, the stack is of the form
$[(-, q_0) \ldots, (?, q_{k-l}), (X_1, q_{k-l+1}), \ldots, (X_{l-1}, q_{k-1}), (X_l, q_k)]$.

(b) If an action β-reduce t is available and the sequence of non-empty leaves of t read from left to right is $X_1, X_2, \ldots, X_f, \ldots, X_l$, where $X_f, 1 \leq f \leq l$ is at the foot node, then the top l positions in the

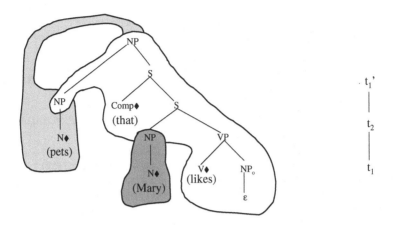

Figure 7.24.   Derived and derivation trees for "pets/N that/Comp Mary/N likes/V"

Stack	Input	Sel. action
$[(-,S_0)]$	pets/N ...	shift S_2
$[(-,S_0)$ (pets/N, S_2)]	that/Comp ...	bpack (NP,1)
$[(-,S_0)$ ([(pets/N, S_2)], S_3)]	that/Comp ...	shift S_4
$[(-,S_0)$ ([(pets/N, S_2)], S_3) (that/Comp, S_4)]	Mary/N ...	shift S_2
$[(-,S_0)$ ([(pets/N, S_2)], S_3) (that/Comp, S_4) (Mary/N, S_2)]	likes/V \$	α-reduce t_1
$[(-,S_0)$ ([(pets/N, S_2)], S_3) (that/Comp, S_4) (NP, S_5)]	likes/V \$	shift S_7
$[(-,S_0)$ ([(pets/N, S_2)], S_3) (that/Comp, S_4) (NP, S_5) (likes/V, S_7)]	\$	β-reduce t_2
$[(-,S_0)$ (pets/N, S_9)]	\$	α-reduce t_1'
$[(-,S_0)$ (NP, S_1)]	\$	accept

Figure 7.25.   Parsing of "*pets/N that/Comp Mary/N likes/V*"

stack of the instantaneous description will contain that sequence of symbols except that at the position corresponding to X_f there will be an embedded stack. That is, the stack will have the form

$$[(-, q_0) \ldots (?, q_{k-l}), (X_1, q_{k-l+1}) \ldots (stk, q_{k-l+f}) \ldots (X_l, q_k)],$$

where stk is an (embedded) stack.

2 The following statements, which are counterparts of some valid properties in the CFG case, do – NOT – hold for TAGs, in general:

   (a) If either an action α-reduce t or β-reduce t is available and l is the number of non-empty leaves of t, than the pair of states (q_{k-l}, q_k)

uniquely determine the sequence of $l+1$ topmost states in the stack, where k is the index of the top of the stack.

(b) If an action bpack(X,l) is available, then the pair of states (q_{k-l}, q_k) uniquely determine the sequence of $l+1$ topmost states in the stack, where k is the index of the top of the stack.

(c) Let ml be the maximum integer such that either there is an action bpack(X,ml) available or a (α or β) reduce t, where the number of non-empty leaves in t is ml. The pair of states (q_{k-ml}, q_k) uniquely determine the sequence of $ml+1$ topmost states in the stack, where k is the index of the top of the stack.

Properties 2(a) and 2(b) above are false (therefore implying that 2(c) is false as well) when an instance of adjunction has been predicted in the range of the currently proposed reduction or bpack. Suppose a reduction operation has already been performed, call it r_p, in the range considered now for the current reduce/bpack operations. Say, the reduced tree had its left material between the current q_i and q_{i+1} and its right material between q_j and q_{j+1} for some i, j in the stack range covered by the currently proposed operation (in 2(a) or 2(b) above). The claim is that the particular sequence currently in the stack from q_{i+1} to q_j was influenced by the material consumed in the reduction, and hence is not uniquely determinable now from the state q_{q-l} above and the sequence X_1 to X_l. In fact the state q_j, which is even outside the scope dominated by the reduced node, was obtained via a $GOTO_{adj}(q_1, q_2, \ldots)$, where q_2 was dependent on the material consumed from the stack by r_p.

The reason we are stating this negative result is because in (Prolo, 2002a) we make an independence assumption based on the "truth" of statement 2(c) above. We argue there that the statement is "approximately" correct in a probabilistic sense. We use a probabilistic model on which the likelihood of actions depend only on (q_{k-ml}, q_k). Here, however, it is important to make clear that the statement fails to be a theorem.

3 The parser does not have the valid prefix property[1]. Consider the TAG in Figure 7.26 for the language $a^n b^n e c^n d^n$, $n \geq 0$. Following our algorithm, we can check that only shift actions are executed until the symbol e is shifted into the stack. So, in order to have the valid prefix property, for this particular case, the driver would have to be able to recognize the prefix language $a^n b^n e$, i.e., the driver has to know if at a certain point it finds a b that exceds the number of a symbols previously shifted. But such language is not a regular language, and therefore cannot be regonized by the underlying pre-compiled finite-state automaton.

In fact the example also shows that any LR parsing model with an underlying finite-state model to decide the available actions cannot have the valid prefix property, unless it substantially relaxes the LR requirement that any structural commitment for a grammar rule (reduction for a tree, and also in our case the partial bpack commitment) cannot be made until all of the yield of such rule has been shifted to the control memory.

Finally that also shows that "true" LR parsers cannot be implemented with a finite-state model to decide the available actions. A more complete analysis of true LR parsing can be found in (Prolo, 2002b).

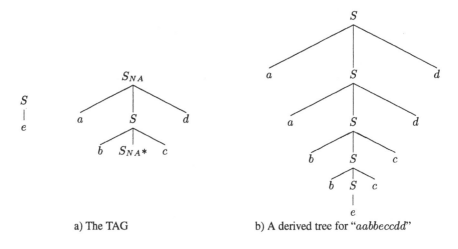

a) The TAG   b) A derived tree for "*aabbeccdd*"

Figure 7.26.   TAG for $a^n b^n e c^n d^n$

4 Minimization: the automata have minimum number of states. This is largely due to the congruence relation in Section 4.1, Figure 7.9.[7]

5 The automata built according to the algorithm of Section 4.3 (NA/OA decomposition) may use only the state kernel to uniquely identify itself.

6 In the automata generated by our implemented compact version, built according to the algorithm of Section 5, the state kernel may not uniquely identify itself. Under that algorithm, it is possible to obtain two different kernels that after closure turn out to be the same. However, it is very unlikely for that to happen in a large scale, real grammar (the pathological counterexamples need a combination of circumstances involving empty leaves under nodes free for adjunction, and a special kind of recursion among the trees). We generate our automata using the kernel set as the criterion for state identity. Then, although absolute minimality is not a

crucial issue for us, we perform a minimization step after the automaton is built (this step most commonly keep the automaton unchanged).

8. Evaluation

In this section we evaluate the algorithm with regards to the characteristics of the tables produced. In (Prolo, 2002a) we focus in its use in parsing. We show in Table 7.1 the results of the application of our algorithm as well as Nederhof's[8] to two large wide-coverage grammars: the first is a 1999 version of the XTAG English grammar with 1,009 trees and 11,490 nodes (XTAG Research Group, 1998); the second is a grammar with 3,161 trees and 22,641 nodes extracted from the Penn Treebank (Marcus et al., 1994) with the help of Xia's extractor (Xia, 1999). *Conflicts* is the average number (arithmetic mean) of actions per (state,terminal) pair. *Reductions* and *Bpacks* are respectively the average number of reduce and bottom pack (bpack) actions in a state (for Nederhof's approach reduction stands for "reduce tree" and bpack stands for "reduce subtree"). *Transitions* is the total number of transition entries, including shifts and goto transitions. The number of conflicts is drastically reduced with our algorithm. In particular the problematic early reduction (bpack) conflicts are decreased, improving the general quality of the conflicts (shifting part of it to full tree reductions). The size of the table, roughly evaluated as the sum of the number of transitions and the number of action entries, is reduced by a factor of about 75 (from unmanageable 75M to 1M) for the XTAG grammar.

ALGORITHM	Grammar	States	Transitions	Conflicts	Reductions	Bpacks
Nederhof's	XTAG	17490	40 M	113	0.9	112
Ours	XTAG	5861	202 K	7.6	2.8	4.3
Nederhof's	Treebank	22101	60 M	635	2.0	633
Ours	Treebank	13058	844 K	15.6	4.7	10.3

Table 7.1. Summary of the parsing tables generated by the algorithms

9. Conclusions

We aim at using LR parsing techniques associated with TAGs to generate practical parsers that read sentences from left to right, and are able to take sound incremental decisions towards reaching their correct analysis. In this chapter we analyze possible models for such LR parser generators and propose a novel algorithm which is largely superior in all accounts to the others currently known (Schabes and Vijay-Shanker, 1990; Nederhof, 1998): first, it works; second, the tables produced are much smaller; and third, conflicts are far fewer and of better quality. The algorithm has the desirable property of finding and executing actions in constant time with the length of the sentence, and therefore making the process of non-deterministically following a path of decisions toward computing a parse linear with the size of the sentence.[9]

One could ask whether the effort we have gone through will give us any reward towards our main goal of building good parsers for natural language. In fact there is even some evidence hinting to the contrary: the amount of conflict in our tables is still high enough to raise a lot of skepticism. In answer to that, in (Prolo, 2002a) we show that the algorithm proposed here, jointly with a set of corpus-based heuristics for conflict resolution, allows for the construction of fast and accurate best-parse parsers for naturally occuring natural language sentences.

We have sacrificed some desirable properties of the formal model: the bpack action violates the rule that a commitment for a structural restriction should be made only when full evidence of that structure has been witnessed in a sentence prefix (and we have lost the valid prefix property). From the work in (Prolo, 2002a) we have indications that the early partial adjunction commitments (bpacks) hurt the parser's ability to correctly solve conflicts. We are currently working on the use of certain subclasses of TAGs, in particular Tree Insertion Grammars(TIGs) (Schabes and Waters, 1995), for which we can reconcile the desirable fundamental properties of true LR algorithms with he desirable characteristic of having characteristic languages to be regular languages.

Finally, the algorithm could be extended to have reductions dependent on lookaheads (e.g., an LALR(1) version), what is reasonably easy to do, that would not increase the number of states or transitions and would reduce the ammount of conflicts. The reason we did not do it is because we want to use empirical evidence from annotated corpora to rank the conflict alternatives, conditioned to the lookahead, as we in fact did in (Prolo, 2002a). This subsumes the effect of the LR(1) version.

Acknowledgments

I am grateful: to Aravind Joshi that made this work possible; to Erwin Chan, Alessandra Kinyon, Joseph Rozentzweig, Anoop Sarkar and Giorgio Satta for comments on earlier versions of this work; to Fei Xia for the help with the grammar extraction; to the reviewers of the original IWPT 2000 version of this chapter; and to the XTAG group at the University of Pennsylvania for the numerous discussions that in one way or another contributed to this work.

Notes

1. A parser has the *valid prefix property* (also *correct prefix property* or *error-detecting property*) if it is able to detect errors "as soon as possible", which for an LR parser means that no prefix w of an input sentence would be shifted to the stack unless there is a sentence in the recognized language of which w is a prefix. If w is not a prefix of any sentence in the language, the parser should reject the input before the last symbol in w is shifted to the stack.

2. The Gorn address of a tree node (Gorn, 1967) is a sequence of integers: the root has the empty sequence ϵ as its address, and the k_{th} child of a node with address a has address $a.k$.

3. The example given is for explanatory purposes, and one could claim that the subjects of the α_i trees should be substitution nodes, for instance, which is true. The problem of early reduction described, however, largely appears in more subtle contexts.

4. This is quite similar to how stacks of stacks are used in the theories of automata for TAGs. Also the model resembles the one used in Schabes and Vijay-Shanker, 1990 in their attempt.

5. For a set of goal symbols, we create as many new trees as the number of symbols, replacing only the symbol at the child node.

6. Substitution nodes are always assumed to be NA, even if not explicitly marked as such in the trees. Nodes are represented by their label, e.g. NP, plus an optional subscript for identification purposes, as in NP, NP_s, and NP_o. Subscripts are ignored by the algorithm.

7. This statement does not contradict Section 5 and should be understood in the light of the distinguishability discussion at the end of the paragraph for n_2 in Section 5.

8. We re-implemented the algorithm in Nederhof, 1998.

9. More precisely the time to follow the single non-deterministic sequence of decisions that results in a certain parse tree is $O(n + m)$ where n is the length of the input and m is the number of elementary trees in the parse. This is the same as in the CFG case.

References

Aho, A. V. and Ullman, J. D. (1972). *The Theory of Parsing, Translation, and Compiling*, volume I: Parsing. Prentice-Hall, Englewood Cliffs, NJ, USA.

Briscoe, T. and Carroll, J. (1993). Generalized probabilistic LR parsing of natural language (corpora) with unification-based grammars. *Computational Linguistics*, 19(1):25–59.

Gorn, S. (1967). Explicit definitions and linguistic dominoes. In *Proceedings of the Conference on Systems and Computer Science*, pages 77–115, London,Ontario,Canada. University of Toronto Press.

Joshi, A. K., Levy, L., and Takahashi, M. (1975). Tree Adjunct Grammars. *Journal of Computer and System Sciences*, 10(1).

Joshi, A. K. and Schabes, Y. (1997). Tree-Adjoining Grammars. In *Handbook of Formal Languages*, volume 3, pages 69–123. Springer-Verlag, Berlin.

Kinyon, A. (1997). Un algorithme d'analyse LR(0) pour les grammaires d'arbres adjoints lexicaliseées. In Genthial, D., editor, *Quatrième conférence annuelle sur Le Traitement Automatique du Langage Naturel, Actes*, pages 93–102, Grenoble, France.

Knuth, D. E. (1965). On the translation of languages from left to right. *Information and Control*, 8(6):607–639.

Lang, B. (1974) Deterministic techniques for efficient non-deterministic parsers. In *Automata, Languages and Programming, 2nd Colloquium*, volume 14 of

Lecture Notes in Computer Science, pages 255–269, Saarbrücken. Springer-Verlag, Berlin.

Marcus, M., Kim, G., Marcinkiewicz, M. A., MacIntyre, R., Bies, A., Ferguson, M., Katz, K., and Schasberger, B. (1994). The Penn Treebank: Annotating predicate argument structure. In *Proceedings of the 1994 Human Language Technology Workshop*.

Merlo, P. (1996). *Parsing with Principles and Classes of Information*. Kluwer Academic Publishers, Boston, MA, USA.

Nederhof, M.-J. (1998). An alternative LR algorithm for TAGs. In *Proceedings of the 36th Annual Meeting of the Association for Computational Linguistics and 16th International Conference on Computational Linguistics*, Montreal, Canada.

Pereira, F. (1985). A new characterization of attachment preferences. In Dowty, D. R., Kartunen, L., and Zwicky, A. M., editors, *Natural Language Parsing: Psychological, computational, and theoretical perspectives*, pages 307–319. Cambridge University Press, New York, NY, USA.

Prolo, C. A. (2002a). Fast lr parsing using rich (tree adjoining) grammars. In *Proceedings of Seventh Conference on Empirical Methods in Natural Language Processing*, pages 103–110, Philadelphia, PA, USA.

Prolo, C. A. (Feb., 2002b). LR parsing for Tree Adjoining Grammars and its application to corpus-based natural language parsing. Ph.D. Dissertation Proposal, Department of Computer and Information Science, University of Pennsylvania.

Schabes, Y. (1990). *Mathematical and Computational Aspects of Lexicalized Grammars*. PhD thesis, Department of Computer and Information Science, University of Pennsylvania.

Schabes, Y. and Vijay-Shanker, K. (1990). Deterministic left to right parsing of tree adjoining languages. In *Proceedings of 28th Annual Meeting of the Association for Computational Linguistics*, pages 276–283, Pittsburgh, Pennsylvania, USA.

Schabes, Y. and Waters, R. C. (1995). Tree Insertion Grammar: a cubic-time, parsable formalism that lexicalizes Context-Free Grammar without changing the trees produced. *Computational Linguistics*, 21(4):479–513.

Shieber, S. and Johnson, M. (1993). Variations on incremental interpretation. *Journal of Psycholinguistic Research*, 22(2):287–318.

Shieber, S. M. (1983). Sentence disambiguation by a Shift-Reduce parsing technique. In *Proceedings of the 21st Annual Meeting of the Association for Computational Linguistics*, pages 119–122, Cambridge, MA, USA.

Tomita, M. (1985). *Efficient Parsing for Natural Language*. Kluwer Academic Publishers, Boston, MA, USA.

Wright, J. H. and Wrigley, E. N. (1991). GLR parsing with probability. In Tomita, M., editor, *Generalized LR Parsing*, pages 113–128. Kluwer Academic Publishers, Boston, MA, USA.

Xia, F. (1999). Extracting tree adjoining grammars from bracketed corpora. In *Proceedings of the 5th Natural Language Processing Pacific Rim Symposium (NLPRS-99)*, Beijing, China.

XTAG Research Group, T. (1998). A Lexicalized Tree Adjoining Grammar for English. Technical Report IRCS 98-18, University of Pennsylvania.

Chapter 8

RELATING TABULAR PARSING ALGORITHMS FOR LIG AND TAG

Miguel A. Alonso
Departamento de Computación, Facultad de Informática, Universidad de La Coruña
Campus de Elviña s/n, 15071 La Coruña, Spain
alonso@udc.es

Éric de la Clergerie
INRIA, Domaine de Voluceau, Rocquencourt, B.P. 105
78153 Le Chesnay, France
Eric.De_La_Clergerie@inria.fr

Víctor J. Díaz
Departamento de Lenguajes y Sistemas Informáticos, E.T.S. de Ingeniería Informática
Universidad de Sevilla, Av. Reina Mercedes s/n, 41012 Sevilla, Spain
vjdiaz@lsi.us.es

Manuel Vilares
Departamento de Informática, Escuela Superior de Ingeniería Informática, Universidad de Vigo
Campus As Lagoas s/n, 32004 Orense, Spain
vilares@ei.uvigo.es

Abstract   Tree Adjoining Grammars (TAG) and Linear Indexed Grammars (LIG) are extensions of Context Free Grammars that generate the class of Tree Adjoining Languages. Taking advantage of this property, and providing a method for translating a TAG into a LIG, we define several parsing algorithms for TAG on the basis of their equivalent LIG parsers. We also explore why some practical optimizations for TAG parsing cannot be applied to the case of LIG.

H. Bunt et al. (eds.), New Technologies in Parsing Technology, 157-184.

1.   Introduction

Tree Adjoining Grammars (TAG; Joshi and Schabes, 1997) and Linear Indexed Grammars (LIG; Gazdar, 1987) are extensions of Context Free Grammars (CFG). Tree adjoining grammars use trees instead of productions as the primary means of representing structure and seem to be adequate for describing syntactic phenomena occurring in natural language, due to their extended domain of locality and to their ability to factor recursion from the domain of dependencies. Linear indexed grammars associate a list of indices with each non-terminal symbol, with the restriction that the index list of the left hand side non-terminal of each production (the *mother*) can be inherited by at most one right hand side non-terminal (the *dependent child*) while the other lists must have a bounded size.

Several parsing algorithms have been proposed for TAG, ranging from simple bottom-up algorithms to sophisticated extensions of the Earley's algorithm (Vijay-Shanker and Weir, 1993; Joshi and Schabes, 1997; Nederhof, 1999). In (Alonso et al., 1999) we have shown the relationships among them, creating a continuum of parsing algorithms and showing what transformations must be applied to each one in order to obtain the next one in the continuum. For this purpose, we have selected Parsing Schemata (Sikkel, 1997) as the framework for describing parsing algorithms.

In order to improve efficiency, it is usual to translate the source tree adjoining grammar into a linear indexed grammar (Vijay-Shanker and Weir, 1991; Schabes and Shieber, 1994; Vijay-Shanker and Weir, 1993). We have presented in (Alonso et al., 2000a) a set of parsing algorithms for LIG that mimic the parsing strategies for TAG shown in (Alonso et al., 1999), including a strategy that preserves the correct prefix property. However, in (Alonso et al., 2000a) we did not present the relations, for each parsing strategy, between the algorithm for TAG and the algorithm for LIG implementing that strategy. In this chapter we study the relations among the way TAG parsers recognize adjunction and the way LIG parsers transmit information from one index list to another.

2.   Tree Adjoining Grammars

Formally, a TAG is a tuple $\mathcal{G} = (V_N, V_T, S, \boldsymbol{I}, \boldsymbol{A})$, where V_N is a finite set of non-terminal symbols, V_T is a finite set of terminal symbols, S is the axiom of the grammar, $\boldsymbol{I}$ is a finite set of *initial trees* and $\boldsymbol{A}$ is a finite set of *auxiliary trees*. $\boldsymbol{I} \cup \boldsymbol{A}$ is the set of *elementary trees*. Internal nodes are labeled by non-terminals and leaf nodes by terminals or the empty string ε, except for just one leaf per auxiliary tree (the *foot*) which is labeled by the same non-terminal used as the label of its root node. The path in an elementary tree from the root node to the foot node is called the *spine* of the tree. We write $N^\gamma \in \mathrm{spine}(\gamma)$ to denote that a node N^γ belongs to the spine of γ.

New trees are derived by *adjunction*: let γ be a tree containing a node N^γ labeled by A and let β be an auxiliary tree whose root and foot nodes are also labeled by A. Then, the adjunction of β at the *adjunction node* N^γ is obtained by excising the subtree of γ with root N^γ, attaching β to N^γ and attaching the excised subtree to the foot of β. We write $\beta \in \mathrm{adj}(N^\gamma)$ to denote that a tree β may be adjoined at node N^γ of the elementary tree γ. If adjunction is not mandatory at N^γ then $\mathbf{nil} \in \mathrm{adj}(N^\gamma)$ where $\mathbf{nil} \notin I \cup A$ is a dummy symbol. If adjunction is not allowed at N^γ then $\{\mathbf{nil}\} = \mathrm{adj}(N^\gamma)$.

In order to describe the parsing algorithms for TAG, we must be able to represent the partial recognition of elementary trees. Parsing algorithms for context-free grammars usually denote partial recognition of productions by dotted productions. We can extend this approach to the case of tree-based grammars by considering each elementary tree γ as formed by a set of context-free productions $\mathcal{P}(\gamma)$: a node N^γ and its children $N_1^\gamma, \ldots, N_g^\gamma$ are represented by a production $N^\gamma \rightarrow N_1^\gamma \cdots N_g^\gamma$. Thus, the position of the dot in the tree is indicated by the position of the dot in a production in $\mathcal{P}(\gamma)$. The elements of the productions are the nodes of the tree, with $\mathbf{R}^\gamma$ denoting its root and $\mathbf{F}^\gamma$ its possible foot. To simplify the description of parsing algorithms we add a production $\top \rightarrow \mathbf{R}^\gamma$ for each $\gamma \in I \cup A$, and the production $\mathbf{F}^\beta \rightarrow \perp$ for each $\beta \in A$.

Let $\mathcal{P}(\mathcal{G})$ be the union of all $\mathcal{P}(\gamma)$, $\gamma \in I \cup A$. The relation $\overset{*}{\Rightarrow}$ of derivation on $\mathcal{P}(\mathcal{G})$ is defined as the smallest reflexive and transitive relation including the following base cases:

- $\delta' M^\gamma \delta'' \overset{*}{\Rightarrow} \delta' v \delta''$ if $M^\gamma \rightarrow v \in \mathcal{P}(\gamma)$ and $\mathbf{nil} \in \mathrm{adj}(M^\gamma)$.

- $\delta' M^\gamma \delta'' \overset{*}{\Rightarrow} \delta' v_1 v v_2 \delta''$ if $M^\gamma \rightarrow v \in \mathcal{P}(\gamma)$, $\beta \in \mathrm{adj}(M^\gamma)$, and $\mathbf{R}^\beta \overset{*}{\Rightarrow} v_1 \mathbf{F}^\beta v_2$.

The language defined by a TAG is the set of strings $w \in V_T$ such that $\mathbf{R}^\alpha \overset{*}{\Rightarrow} w$ with $S = \mathrm{label}(\mathbf{R}^\alpha)$.

We also define additional forms of derivations for TAG. The first two, used to distinguish derivations with and without adjunction at a node M^γ such that $M^\gamma \rightarrow v$, are defined by $M^\gamma \overset{*}{\Rightarrow}_t \delta$ (resp. $M^\gamma \overset{*}{\Rightarrow}_b \delta$) if $M^\gamma \overset{*}{\Rightarrow} \delta$ (resp. $v \overset{*}{\Rightarrow} \delta$). The other two are used to denote derivations crossing root nodes of auxiliary trees and derivations crossing foot nodes. They are defined respectively as $\overset{*}{\Rightarrow}_r =_{\mathrm{def}} (\Rightarrow_r \cup \overset{*}{\Rightarrow})^*$ and $\overset{*}{\Rightarrow}_f =_{\mathrm{def}} (\Rightarrow_f \cup \overset{*}{\Rightarrow})^*$ with the base cases $\delta_1 M^\gamma \delta_2 \Rightarrow_r \delta_1 \mathbf{R}^\beta \delta_2$ and $\delta_1 \mathbf{F}^\beta \delta_2 \Rightarrow_f \delta_1 v \delta_2$ if $\beta \in \mathrm{adj}(M^\gamma)$ and $M^\gamma \rightarrow v \in \mathcal{P}(\gamma)$.

3.   Linear Indexed Grammars

A linear indexed grammar is a tuple (V_T, V_N, V_I, P, S), where V_T is a finite set of terminals, V_N is a finite set of non-terminals, V_I is a finite set of indices, $S \in V_N$ is the start symbol and P is a finite set of productions. Following (Gazdar, 1987) we consider productions in which at most one index can be pushed on or popped from a list of indices:

$$A_0[\circ\circ\eta] \rightarrow A_1[\,] \cdots A_{d-1}[\,] \, A_d[\circ\circ\eta'] \, A_{d+1}[\,] \, \cdots A_m[\,]$$

$$A_0[\,] \rightarrow a$$

where m is the length of the production, $A_j \in V_N$ for each $0 \leq j \leq m$, A_d is the dependent child, $\circ\circ$ is the part of the index list transmitted from the mother to the dependent child, $\eta, \eta' \in V_I \cup \{\varepsilon\}$ and for each production either η or η' or both must be ε, and $a \in V_T \cup \{\varepsilon\}$.

The derivation relation $\Rightarrow$ is defined for LIG by the following cases:

- $\Upsilon A[\zeta\eta]\Upsilon' \Rightarrow \Upsilon \Upsilon_1 A'[\zeta\eta']\Upsilon_2 \Upsilon'$ if there exists a production $A[\circ\circ\eta] \rightarrow \Upsilon_1 A'[\circ\circ\eta'] \, \Upsilon_2$.

- $\Upsilon A[\,]\Upsilon' \Rightarrow \Upsilon a \Upsilon'$ if there exists a production $A[\,] \rightarrow a$

where $A \in V_N$, $\zeta \in V_I^*$ and $\eta, \eta' \in V_I \cup \{\varepsilon\}$. The reflexive and transitive closure of $\Rightarrow$ is denoted by $\overset{*}{\Rightarrow}$. The language defined by a LIG is the set of strings $w \in V_T^*$ such that $S[\,] \overset{*}{\Rightarrow} w$.

In a derivation step $\Upsilon A[\zeta\eta]\Upsilon' \Rightarrow \Upsilon \Upsilon_1 A'[\zeta\eta']\Upsilon_2 \Upsilon'$, we say that $A'[\zeta\eta']$ is the dependent successor of $A[\zeta\eta]$. We define the notion of dependent descendent as the reflexive and transitive closure of dependent successor.

To parse this type of grammars, tabulation techniques with polynomial complexity can be designed based on a property defined in (Vijay-Shanker and Weir, 1993), that we call the *context-freeness property of LIG*, such that if $A[\eta] \overset{*}{\Rightarrow} uB[\,]w$ where $u, w \in V_T^*$, $A, B \in V_N$, $\eta \in V_I \cup \{\varepsilon\}$ and $B[\,]$ is a dependent descendent of $A[\eta]$, then for each $\Upsilon_1, \Upsilon_2 \in (V_N[V_I^*] \cup V_T)^*$ and $\zeta \in V_I^*$ we have $\Upsilon_1 A[\zeta\eta]\Upsilon_2 \overset{*}{\Rightarrow} \Upsilon_1 uB[\zeta]w\Upsilon_2$ Conversely, if $B[\eta]$ is a dependent descendent of $A[\,]$ and $A[\,] \overset{*}{\Rightarrow} uB[\eta]w$ then $\Upsilon_1 A[\zeta]\Upsilon_2 \overset{*}{\Rightarrow} \Upsilon_1 uB[\zeta\eta]w\Upsilon_2$.

3.1   Compiling TAG to LIG

LIG is often used as an intermediate formalism for TAG parsing. Given a TAG (V_T, V_N, S, I, A) we can obtain a strongly equivalent LIG (V_T, V_N', V_I, S', P), where $V_N' = \{M^{\gamma t}|M^\gamma \in \mathcal{N}\} \cup \{M^{\gamma b}|M^\gamma \in \mathcal{N}\}$ and $V_I = \{M^\gamma | M^\gamma \in \mathcal{N}\}$, $\mathcal{N}$ denoting the set of every node M^γ of every elementary tree $\gamma \in I \cup A$ (Vijay-Shanker and Weir, 1991). The set P is constructed applying the following rules:

1 A production $S'[\infty] \to \mathbf{R}^{\alpha \mathbf{t}}[\infty]$ is generated for each initial tree α having its root labeled by S.

2 A production $M_0^{\gamma \mathbf{b}}[\infty] \to M_1^{\gamma \mathbf{t}}[\infty]\ M_2^{\gamma \mathbf{t}}[\ ] \cdots M_m^{\gamma \mathbf{t}}[\ ]$ is generated for each $M_0^\gamma \to M_1^\gamma \cdots M_m^\gamma \in \mathcal{P}(\gamma)$ such that $\gamma \in \boldsymbol{I}$ or $\gamma \in \boldsymbol{A}$ and $\forall_{1 \le i \le m} M_i \notin \mathrm{spine}(\gamma)$.

3 A production $M_0^{\beta \mathbf{b}}[\infty] \to M_1^{\beta \mathbf{t}}[\ ] \cdots M_d^{\beta \mathbf{t}}[\infty] \cdots M_m^{\beta \mathbf{t}}[\ ]$ is generated for each $M_0^\beta \to M_1^\beta \cdots M_d^\beta \cdots M_m^\beta \in \mathcal{P}(\beta)$ such that $\beta \in \boldsymbol{A}$ and $M_0^\beta, M_d^\beta \in \mathrm{spine}(\beta)$.

4 A production $M^{\gamma \mathbf{t}}[\infty] \to M^{\gamma \mathbf{b}}[\infty]$ is generated for each node M^γ such that $\mathbf{nil} \in \mathrm{adj}(M^\gamma)$.

5 A production $M^{\gamma \mathbf{t}}[\infty] \to \mathbf{R}^{\beta \mathbf{t}}[\infty M^\gamma]$ is generated for each adjunction node M^γ such that $\beta \in \boldsymbol{A}$ and $\beta \in \mathrm{adj}(M^\gamma)$.

6 A production $\mathbf{F}^{\beta \mathbf{b}}[\infty M^\gamma] \to M^{\gamma \mathbf{b}}[\infty]$ is generated for each node M^γ such that $\beta \in \boldsymbol{A}$ and $\beta \in \mathrm{adj}(M^\gamma)$.

7 A production $M^{\gamma \mathbf{t}}[\ ] \to a$ is generated for each node M^γ labeled by $a \in V_T \cup \{\varepsilon\}$.

Considering a top-down traversal of trees and adjunctions, the productions generated by rule 1 start the traversal from the root node of initial trees labeled by the axiom of the grammar. Rule 2 productions are slightly artificial productions used to traverse nodes not on the spine of auxiliary trees; indeed, to respect the kind of expected LIG productions, we have chosen the first child as dependent child when there is actually none, as every indices list should be empty. A more natural LIG production (if allowed) would be (2') $M_0^{\gamma \mathbf{b}}[\ ] \to M_1^{\gamma \mathbf{t}}[\ ]\ M_2^{\gamma \mathbf{t}}[\ ] \cdots M_m^{\gamma \mathbf{t}}[\ ]$. Rule 3 productions are used to traverse nodes on the spine of auxiliary trees. By means of the set of productions generated by rule 4, we can continue regular traversal when adjunction is not mandatory at a given node, while rule 5 productions suspend the traversal of an elementary tree γ to start the traversal of the auxiliary tree that can be adjoined at node M^γ; the fact that we will have to return to M^γ is recorded by pushing this node on the index list. When the auxiliary tree has been completely traversed, a rule 6 production pops M^γ from the index list to resume the traversal of γ at this node. Productions generated by rule 7 are in charge of recognizing terminal symbols and the empty string.

Superscripts $\mathbf{t}$ and $\mathbf{b}$ are used to guarantee that at most one auxiliary tree is adjoined at each node. Given an adjunction node M^γ, in a top-down view of adjunction, $M^{\gamma \mathbf{t}}$ corresponds to reaching the node M^γ before adjunction and

$M^{\gamma \mathbf{b}}$ corresponds to reaching this node after adjunction. In a bottom-up view of adjunction, $M^{\gamma \mathbf{b}}$ corresponds to reaching the node M^{γ} before adjunction and $M^{\gamma \mathbf{t}}$ corresponds to reaching this node after adjunction.

4.   Bottom-up Parsing Algorithms

The basic bottom-up parsing algorithm for context-free grammars is the one defined by Cocke, Younger and Kasami (Kasami, 1965; Younger, 1967). Extensions have been defined for TAG (Vijay-Shanker and Weir, 1991; Alonso et al., 1999) and LIG (Vijay-Shanker and Weir, 1991; Alonso et al., 2000a). In the case of LIG, grammars are restricted to have at most two non-terminal elements, or one element which must be a terminal, in the right-hand side of each production. This restriction could be considered as the transposition of Chomsky Normal Form to linear indexed grammars. In the case of TAG, nodes in elementary trees can have at most two children.

We will describe parsing algorithms using *Parsing Schemata*, a framework for high-level descriptions of parsers (Sikkel, 1997). A *parsing system* for a grammar G and string $a_1 \cdots a_n$ is a triple $\langle \mathcal{I}, \mathcal{H}, \mathcal{D} \rangle$, with $\mathcal{I}$ a set of *items* which represent intermediate parse results, $\mathcal{H}$ an initial set of items $[a_{j+1}, j, j+1]$, with $0 \leq j < n$, called the *hypothesis* that encodes the sentence $a_1 \cdots a_n$ to be parsed, and $\mathcal{D}$ a set of *deduction steps* that allow new items to be derived from already known items. Deduction steps are of the form $\frac{\eta_1, \ldots, \eta_k}{\xi}$ *cond*, meaning that if all antecedents η_i of a deduction step are present and the conditions *cond* are satisfied, then the consequent ξ should be generated by the parser. A set $\mathcal{F} \subseteq \mathcal{I}$ of *final items* represents the recognition of a sentence. A *parsing schema* is a parsing system parameterized by a grammar and a sentence.

4.1   Items

Items used in the tabular interpretation of the CYK-like algorithm for LIG are of the form

$$[A, \eta, i, j \mid B, p, q]$$

where, in general, $A, B \in V_N$, $\eta \in V_I$, $0 \leq i \leq j$ and $i \leq p \leq q \leq j$ denoted $(p, q) \leq (i, j)$. Elements B, η, p and q may be unbound in some cases and represented by $-$.

Each item represents one of the following kinds of derivations:

- $A[\eta] \overset{*}{\Rightarrow} a_{i+1} \cdots a_p \, B[\,] \, a_{q+1} \cdots a_j$ iff $(B, p, q) \neq (-, -, -)$, $B[\,]$ is a dependent descendent of $A[\eta]$ and $(p, q) \leq (i, j)$.

- $A[\,] \overset{*}{\Rightarrow} a_{i+1} \cdots a_j$ iff $\eta = -$ and $(B, p, q) = (-, -, -)$.

If the index list associated with A is empty then $\eta = -$ and $(B, p, q) = (-, -, -)$, otherwise η is the topmost element of the index list and the part (B, p, q) acts as a logical pointer to other items of the form $[B, \eta', p, q \mid B', p', q']$ from which we can retrieve the second element η' of that list. By following the chains of pointers, we can retrieve the entire index list associated to A. The string $a_1 \cdots a_n$ to be parsed has been successfully recognized if a final item in the set $\mathcal{F} = \{ [S, -, 0, n \mid -, -, -] \}$ has been generated.

These items are like those proposed for the tabulation of right-oriented linear indexed automata (Alonso et al., 2000b; Nederhof, 1998) and for the tabulation of bottom-up 2–stack automata (De la Clergerie et al., 1998). They are slightly different from the items of the form $[A, \eta, i, j \mid B, \eta', p, q]$ proposed by (Vijay-Shanker and Weir, 1991) for their CYK-like algorithm, where the element $\eta' \in V_I$ is useless: the context-freeness property of LIG implies that if $A[\eta] \overset{*}{\Rightarrow} a_{i+1} \cdots a_p B[\;] a_{q+1} \cdots a_j$ then for any η' we have that $A[\eta'\eta] \overset{*}{\Rightarrow} a_{i+1} \cdots a_p B[\eta'] a_{q+1} \cdots a_j$.

In the case of TAG parsing, if we translate the grammar to LIG following the mechanism shown in section 3.1, we obtain items of the form:

$$[N^{\gamma \mathbf{x}}, M^{\gamma'}, i, j \mid M^{\gamma'}, p, q]$$

where $\mathbf{x} \in \{\mathbf{t}, \mathbf{b}\}$, representing one of the following two situations:

- $N^\gamma \overset{*}{\Rightarrow}_{\mathbf{x}} a_{i+1} \cdots a_p \, \mathbf{F}^\gamma \, a_{q+1} \cdots a_j \Rightarrow_f a_{i+1} \cdots a_p \, v \, a_{q+1} \cdots a_j \overset{*}{\Rightarrow}_f a_{i+1} \cdots a_j$, $M^{\gamma'} \to v$, and $\gamma \in \mathrm{adj}(M^{\gamma'})$ iff $(M^{\gamma'}, p, q) \neq (-, -, -)$.

- $N^\gamma \overset{*}{\Rightarrow}_{\mathbf{x}} a_{i+1} \cdots a_j$ iff $(M^{\gamma'}, p, q) = (-, -, -)$.

We can observe that each item represents a state in the parsing process, storing information about the node that we are currently visiting, the part of the input string spanned by this node, and the list of nested adjunctions that have been started but not yet finished. The topmost element $M^{\gamma'}$ of this list is explicitly stored in the item. However, the element $M^{\gamma'}$ is redundant, as an item is valid for any node $M^{\gamma'}$ of an elementary tree such that γ can be adjoined at $M^{\gamma'}$. Therefore, by discarding redundant information, we can obtain a more compact form of items for TAG parsing:

$$[N^{\gamma \mathbf{x}}, i, j \mid p, q]$$

Final items are those belonging to the set $\mathcal{F} = \{ [\mathbf{R}^{\alpha \mathbf{t}}, 0, n \mid -, -] \}$, with $\alpha \in \boldsymbol{I}$ and $S = \mathrm{label}(\mathbf{R}^\alpha)$.

4.2   Deduction Steps

The bottom-up parsing process is started by steps recognizing terminal symbols and the empty string:

$$\mathcal{D}_{\text{CYK-LIG}}^{\text{Scan}} = \frac{[a, j, j+1]}{[A, -, j, j+1 \mid -, -, -]} \quad A[\,] \to a \in P$$

$$\mathcal{D}_{\text{CYK-LIG}}^{\varepsilon} = \frac{}{[A, -, j, j \mid -, -, -]} \quad A[\,] \to \varepsilon \in P$$

The other steps are in charge of combining the items corresponding to the body elements in the right-hand side of a production in order to generate the item corresponding to the left-hand side element, propagating bottom-up the information about the index list:

$$\mathcal{D}_{\text{CYK-LIG}}^{[\infty][\,][\infty]} = \frac{\begin{array}{c}[B, -, i, k \mid -, -, -], \\ [C, \eta, k, j \mid D, p, q]\end{array}}{[A, \eta, i, j \mid D, p, q]} \quad A[\infty] \to B[\,] \, C[\infty] \in P$$

$$\mathcal{D}_{\text{CYK-LIG}}^{[\infty][\infty][\,]} = \frac{\begin{array}{c}[B, \eta, i, k \mid D, p, q], \\ [C, -, k, j \mid -, -, -]\end{array}}{[A, \eta, i, j \mid D, p, q]} \quad A[\infty] \to B[\infty] \, C[\,] \in P$$

$$\mathcal{D}_{\text{CYK-LIG}}^{[\infty][\infty]} = \frac{[B, \eta, i, j \mid D, p, q],}{[A, \eta, i, j \mid D, p, q]} \quad A[\infty] \to B[\infty] \in P$$

$$\mathcal{D}_{\text{CYK-LIG}}^{[\infty\eta][\,][\infty]} = \frac{\begin{array}{c}[B, -, i, k \mid -, -, -], \\ [C, \eta', k, j \mid D, p, q]\end{array}}{[A, \eta, i, j \mid C, k, j]} \quad A[\infty\eta] \to B[\,] \, C[\infty] \in P$$

$$\mathcal{D}_{\text{CYK-LIG}}^{[\infty\eta][\infty][\,]} = \frac{\begin{array}{c}[B, \eta', i, k \mid D, p, q], \\ [C, -, k, j \mid -, -, -]\end{array}}{[A, \eta, i, j \mid B, i, k]} \quad A[\infty\eta] \to B[\infty] \, C[\,] \in P$$

$$\mathcal{D}_{\text{CYK-LIG}}^{[\infty\eta][\infty]} = \frac{[B, \eta', i, j \mid D, p, q],}{[A, \eta, i, j \mid B, i, j]} \quad A[\infty\eta] \to B[\infty] \in P$$

$$\mathcal{D}_{\text{CYK-LIG}}^{[\infty][\,][\infty\eta]} = \frac{\begin{array}{c}[B, -, i, k \mid -, -, -], \\ [C, \eta, k, j \mid D, p, q], \\ [D, \eta', p, q \mid E, r, s]\end{array}}{[A, \eta', i, j \mid E, r, s]} \quad A[\infty] \to B[\,] \, C[\infty\eta] \in P$$

$$\mathcal{D}_{\text{CYK-LIG}}^{[\infty][\infty\eta][\,]} = \frac{\begin{array}{c}[B, \eta, i, k \mid D, p, q], \\ [C, -, k, j \mid -, -, -], \\ [D, \eta', p, q \mid E, r, s]\end{array}}{[A, \eta', i, j \mid E, r, s]} \quad A[\infty] \to B[\infty\eta] \, C[\,] \in P$$

$$\mathcal{D}_{\text{CYK-LIG}}^{[oo][oo\eta]} = \frac{\begin{array}{c}[B,\eta,i,j \mid D,p,q],\\ [D,\eta',p,q \mid E,r,s]\end{array}}{[A,\eta',i,j \mid E,r,s]} \quad A[oo] \to B[oo\eta] \in P$$

These steps have counterparts in TAG parsing. The steps in charge of starting the TAG parser are the following:

$$\mathcal{D}_{\text{CYK-TAG}}^{\text{Scan}} = \frac{[a,j,j+1]}{[N^{\gamma\mathbf{b}},j,j+1 \mid -,-]} \quad a = \text{label}(N^\gamma)$$

$$\mathcal{D}_{\text{CYK-TAG}}^{\varepsilon} = \frac{}{[N^{\gamma\mathbf{b}},j,j \mid -,-]} \quad \varepsilon = \text{label}(N^\gamma)$$

The sets $\mathcal{D}_{\text{CYK-LIG}}^{[oo][\ ][oo]}$ and $\mathcal{D}_{\text{CYK-LIG}}^{[oo][oo][\ ]}$ correspond to the bottom-up propagation of information through the spine of an auxiliary tree when the right child and the left child, respectively, is placed on the spine:

$$\mathcal{D}_{\text{CYK-TAG}}^{\text{RightDom}} = \frac{\begin{array}{c}[M^{\gamma\mathbf{t}},i,k \mid -,-],\\ [P^{\gamma\mathbf{t}},k,j \mid p,q]\end{array}}{[N^{\gamma\mathbf{b}},i,j \mid p,q]} \quad \begin{array}{c}N^\gamma \to M^\gamma P^\gamma \in \mathcal{P}(\gamma),\\ P^\gamma \in \text{spine}(\gamma)\end{array}$$

$$\mathcal{D}_{\text{CYK-TAG}}^{\text{LeftDom}} = \frac{\begin{array}{c}[M^{\gamma\mathbf{t}},i,k \mid p,q],\\ [P^{\gamma\mathbf{t}},k,j \mid -,-]\end{array}}{[N^{\gamma\mathbf{b}},i,j \mid p,q]} \quad \begin{array}{c}N^\gamma \to M^\gamma P^\gamma \in \mathcal{P}(\gamma),\\ M^\gamma \in \text{spine}(\gamma)\end{array}$$

The set $\mathcal{D}_{\text{CYK-LIG}}^{[oo][oo][\ ]}$ also corresponds to the bottom-up propagation of information, in this case for productions not covering the spine of an auxiliary tree:

$$\mathcal{D}_{\text{CYK-TAG}}^{\text{NoDom}} = \frac{\begin{array}{c}[M^{\gamma\mathbf{t}},i,k \mid -,-],\\ [P^{\gamma\mathbf{t}},k,j \mid -,-]\end{array}}{[N^{\gamma\mathbf{b}},i,j \mid -,-]} \quad \begin{array}{c}N^\gamma \to M^\gamma P^\gamma \in \mathcal{P}(\gamma),\\ N^\gamma \notin \text{spine}(\gamma)\end{array}$$

The set $\mathcal{D}_{\text{CYK-LIG}}^{[oo][oo]}$ corresponds to the bottom-up propagation of information for nodes with only one child and to the bottom-up traversal of nodes at which adjunction is not mandatory:

$$\mathcal{D}_{\text{CYK-TAG}}^{\text{Unary}} = \frac{[M^{\gamma\mathbf{t}},i,j \mid p,q]}{[N^{\gamma\mathbf{b}},i,j \mid p,q]} \quad N^\gamma \to M^\gamma \in \mathcal{P}(\gamma)$$

$$\mathcal{D}_{\text{CYK-TAG}}^{\text{NoAdj}} = \frac{[N^{\gamma\mathbf{b}},i,j \mid p,q]}{[N^{\gamma\mathbf{t}},i,j \mid p,q]} \quad \text{nil} \in \text{adj}(N^\gamma)$$

The set $\mathcal{D}_{\text{CYK-LIG}}^{[oo\eta][oo]}$ corresponds to the bottom-up starting of an adjunction operation from the foot node of an auxiliary tree:

$$\mathcal{D}_{\text{CYK-TAG}}^{\text{Foot}} = \frac{[N^{\gamma\mathbf{b}},i,j \mid p,q]}{[\mathbf{F}^{\beta\mathbf{b}},i,j \mid i,j]} \quad \beta \in \text{adj}(N^\gamma)$$

The set $\mathcal{D}_{\text{CYK-LIG}}^{[oo][oo\eta]}$ corresponds to the bottom-up ending of an adjunction operation when the root node of an auxiliary tree is reached:

$$\mathcal{D}_{\text{CYK-TAG}}^{\text{Adj}} = \frac{[\mathbf{R}^{\beta^{\mathbf{t}}}, i, j \mid p, q], \ [N^{\gamma \mathbf{b}}, p, q \mid r, s]}{[N^{\gamma \mathbf{t}}, i, j \mid r, s]} \quad \beta \in \text{adj}(N^{\gamma})$$

The space complexity of these bottom-up parsers with respect to the length n of the input string is $\mathcal{O}(n^4)$, as each item stores four positions of the input string. The time complexity is $\mathcal{O}(n^6)$ and is given by the deduction steps in $\mathcal{D}_{\text{CYK-LIG}}^{[oo][\ ][oo\eta]}$ and $\mathcal{D}_{\text{CYK-LIG}}^{[oo][oo\eta][\ ]}$. Although these steps involve 7 positions of the input string, each step can be decomposed, by partial application, into a set of deduction steps involving at most 6 positions. As an example, the application of a step in $\mathcal{D}_{\text{CYK-LIG}}^{[oo][\ ][oo\eta]}$ can be performed by combining its second and third items in $\mathcal{O}(n^6)$ complexity:

$$\frac{[C, \eta, k, j \mid D, p, q], \ [D, \eta', p, q \mid E, r, s]}{\langle C, \eta', k, j, E, r, s \rangle}$$

At this point, positions p and q are discarded, being only useful when combining the second and third items. The resulting element $\langle C, \eta', k, j, E, r, s \rangle$ may be combined with the first item, in $\mathcal{O}(n^5)$ complexity, in order to obtain the consequent item of the original step:

$$\frac{\langle C, \eta', k, j, E, r, s \rangle, \ [B, -, i, k \mid -, -, -]}{[A, \eta', i, j \mid E, r, s]} \quad A[oo] \rightarrow B[\ ] \ C[oo\eta] \in P$$

It is worth noting that this rule transformation may be related to the grammar transformation of production $A[oo] \rightarrow B[\ ] \ C[oo\eta]$ into the two equivalent productions $A[oo] \rightarrow B[\ ] \ C'[oo]$ and $C'[oo] \rightarrow C[oo\eta]$, where C' is some fresh non-terminal.

5. Earley-like Parsing Algorithms

Earley-like parsers overcome the limitation of binary branching imposed by CYK-like parsing algorithms and incorporate top-down prediction in order to reduce the number of deduced items.

5.1 Items

To overcome the limitation imposed by CYK-like algorithms, we introduce dotted productions into items. Thus, we can distinguish the part of a production already processed from the unprocessed part. In the case of LIG, we write $\underline{A}$

as a shorthand for $A[\circ\circ\eta]$, $A[\circ\circ]$ and $A[\ ]$ when the specification of the list of indices is not relevant in the context. Therefore, LIG items are now of the form:

$$[\underline{A} \to \Upsilon_1 \bullet \Upsilon_2, \eta, i, j \mid B, p, q]$$

and they represent one of the following two cases:

- $A[\eta] \Rightarrow \Upsilon_1 \Upsilon_2 \overset{*}{\Rightarrow} a_{i+1} \cdots a_p \, B[\ ] \, a_{q+1} \cdots a_j \, \Upsilon_2$ iff $(B, p, q) \neq (-, -, -)$, $B[\ ]$ is a dependent descendant of $A[\eta]$ and $(p, q) \leq (i, j)$.

- $\Upsilon_1 \overset{*}{\Rightarrow} a_{i+1} \cdots a_j$ iff $\eta = -$ and $(B, p, q) = (-, -, -)$. If the dependent child is in Υ_1 then the list of indices associated with $\underline{A}$ and with the dependent child must be empty.

The recognition of the input string is indicated by the presence of final items in the set $\mathcal{F} = \{\, [\underline{S} \to \Upsilon\bullet, -, 0, n \mid -, -, -]\,\}$.

In the case of TAG parsing, if we translate the grammar to LIG following the mechanism shown in section 3.1, we obtain items of the form:

$$[N^\gamma \to \delta \bullet \nu, M^{\gamma'}, i, j \mid M^{\gamma'}, p, q]$$

representing the following cases:

- $\delta \overset{*}{\Rightarrow} a_{i+1} \cdots a_p \, F^\gamma \, a_{q+1} \cdots a_j \Rightarrow_f a_{i+1} \cdots a_p \, \nu \, a_{q+1} \cdots a_j \overset{*}{\Rightarrow}_f$ $a_{i+1} \cdots a_j$, $M^{\gamma'} \to \nu$, and $\gamma \in \mathrm{adj}(M^{\gamma'})$ iff $(M^{\gamma'}, p, q) \neq (-, -, -)$.

- $\delta \overset{*}{\Rightarrow} a_{i+1} \cdots a_j$ iff $(M^{\gamma'}, p, q) = (-, -, -)$.

As mentioned for the CYK-like algorithm, the element $M^{\gamma'}$ is redundant, allowing a more compact form of items for TAG parsing:

$$[N^\gamma \to \delta \bullet \nu, i, j \mid p, q]$$

The set of final items is $\mathcal{F} = \{\, [\mathbf{R}^\alpha \to \delta\bullet, 0, n \mid -, -]\,\}$, with $\alpha \in I$ and $S = \mathrm{label}(\mathbf{R}^\alpha)$.

5.2 Deduction Steps

The CYK-like parsing algorithm for LIG does not take into account whether the part of the input string recognized by each grammar element can be derived from S, the axiom of the grammar. Earley-like algorithms limit the number of deduction steps that can be applied at each point by predicting productions which are candidates to be part of a derivation starting from the grammar axiom. As a first approach, we consider that prediction is performed by taking into account only the context-free skeleton. The resulting parsing system has the following characteristics:

- A set of Init deduction steps is in charge of starting the top-down prediction by considering only the productions with S as left-hand side.

- In any state of the parsing process, a set of Pred deduction steps generates only those items involving productions with a relevant context-free skeleton.

The following list specifies the sets of deduction steps for an Earley-like parsing algorithm for linear indexed grammars:

$$\mathcal{D}^{\text{Init}}_{\text{E-LIG}} = \frac{}{[\underline{S} \to \bullet\Upsilon, -, 0, 0 \mid -, -, -]}$$

$$\mathcal{D}^{\text{Scan}}_{\text{E-LIG}} = \frac{[A[\,] \to \bullet a, -, j, j \mid -, -, -],\ [a, j, j+1]}{[A[\,] \to a\bullet, -, j, j+1 \mid -, -, -]}$$

$$\mathcal{D}^{\varepsilon}_{\text{E-LIG}} = \frac{[A[\,] \to \bullet\varepsilon, -, j, j \mid -, -, -]}{[A[\,] \to \varepsilon\bullet, -, j, j \mid -, -, -]}$$

$$\mathcal{D}^{\text{Pred}}_{\text{E-LIG}} = \frac{[\underline{A} \to \Upsilon_1 \bullet \underline{B}\ \Upsilon_2, \gamma, i, j \mid C, p, q]}{[\underline{B} \to \bullet\Upsilon_3, -, j, j \mid -, -, -]}$$

$$\mathcal{D}^{\text{Comp}[\,]}_{\text{E-LIG}} = \frac{[\underline{A} \to \Upsilon_1 \bullet B[\,]\ \Upsilon_2, \gamma, i, k \mid C, p, q],\ [\underline{B} \to \Upsilon_3\bullet, -, k, j \mid -, -, -]}{[\underline{A} \to \Upsilon_1 B[\,] \bullet \Upsilon_2, \gamma, i, j \mid C, p, q]}$$

$$\mathcal{D}^{\text{Comp}[\circ\circ\eta][\circ\circ]}_{\text{E-LIG}} = \frac{[A[\circ\circ\eta] \to \Upsilon_1 \bullet B[\circ\circ]\ \Upsilon_2, -, i, k \mid -, -, -],\ [\underline{B} \to \Upsilon_3\bullet, \eta', k, j \mid C, p, q]}{[A[\circ\circ\eta] \to \Upsilon_1 B[\circ\circ] \bullet \Upsilon_2, \eta, i, j \mid B, k, j]}$$

$$\mathcal{D}^{\text{Comp}[\circ\circ][\circ\circ]}_{\text{E-LIG}} = \frac{[A[\circ\circ] \to \Upsilon_1 \bullet B[\circ\circ]\ \Upsilon_2, -, i, k \mid -, -, -],\ [\underline{B} \to \Upsilon_3\bullet, \eta', k, j \mid C, p, q]}{[A[\circ\circ] \to \Upsilon_1 B[\circ\circ] \bullet \Upsilon_2, \eta', i, j \mid C, p, q]}$$

$$\mathcal{D}^{\text{Comp}[\circ\circ][\circ\circ\eta]}_{\text{E-LIG}} = \frac{[A[\circ\circ] \to \Upsilon_1 \bullet B[\circ\circ\eta]\ \Upsilon_2, -, i, k \mid -, -, -],\ [\underline{B} \to \Upsilon_3\bullet, \eta, k, j \mid C, p, q],\ [\underline{C} \to \Upsilon_4\bullet, \eta', p, q \mid D, r, s]}{[A[\circ\circ] \to \Upsilon_1 B[\circ\circ\eta] \bullet \Upsilon_2, \eta', i, j \mid D, r, s]}$$

The resulting algorithm, which has a space complexity $\mathcal{O}(n^4)$ and a time complexity $\mathcal{O}(n^6)$, is very close to the Earley-like algorithm described in (Schabes and Shieber, 1994) although the latter can only be applied to a specific class of linear indexed grammars obtained from tree adjoining grammars. However, both algorithms share an important feature: they are weakly predictive as they do not consider the contents of the index lists when predictive steps are applied. At first glance, the algorithm proposed in (Schabes and

Table 8.1.   Productions proposed by Schabes and Shieber

Schabes & Shieber Production	Equivalent Production
$\mathbf{b}[\infty N^\gamma] \to \mathbf{t}[N_1^\gamma] \cdots \mathbf{t}[\infty N_s^\gamma] \cdots \mathbf{t}[N_m^\gamma]$	$N^{\gamma\,\mathbf{b}}[\infty] \to N_1^{\gamma\,\mathbf{t}}[\,] \cdots N_s^{\gamma\,\mathbf{t}}[\infty] \cdots N_m^{\gamma\,\mathbf{t}}[\,]$
$\mathbf{b}[N^\gamma] \to \mathbf{t}[N_1^\gamma] \cdots \mathbf{t}[N_m^\gamma]$	$N^{\gamma\,\mathbf{b}}[\,] \to N_1^{\gamma\,\mathbf{t}}[\,] \cdots N_m^{\gamma\,\mathbf{t}}[\,]$
$\mathbf{t}[\infty N^\gamma] \to \mathbf{b}[\infty N^\gamma]$	$N^{\gamma\,\mathbf{t}}[\infty] \to N^{\gamma\,\mathbf{b}}[\infty]$
$\mathbf{t}[\infty N^\gamma] \to \mathbf{t}[\infty N^\gamma \mathbf{R}^\beta]$	$N^{\gamma\,\mathbf{t}}[\infty] \to \mathbf{R}^{\beta\,\mathbf{t}}[\infty N^\gamma]$
$\mathbf{b}[\infty N^\gamma] \to \mathbf{t}[\infty N^\gamma \mathbf{R}^\beta]$	$N^{\gamma\,\mathbf{b}}[\infty] \to \mathbf{R}^{\beta\,\mathbf{t}}[\infty N^\gamma]$
$\mathbf{b}[\infty N^\gamma \mathbf{F}^\beta] \to \mathbf{b}[\infty N^\gamma]$	$\mathbf{F}^{\beta\,\mathbf{b}}[\infty N^\gamma] \to N^{\gamma\,\mathbf{b}}[\infty]$
$\mathbf{t}[N^\gamma] \to \mathbf{t}[\mathbf{R}^\alpha]$	$N^{\gamma\,\mathbf{t}}[\,] \to \mathbf{R}^{\alpha\,\mathbf{t}}[\,]$

Shieber, 1994) consults the element on the top of the index list during prediction, but a deeper study of the behavior of the algorithm makes it clear that this is not true, due to the fact that the context-free skeleton of the elementary trees of a TAG is stored in the index lists, reducing the non-terminal set of the resulting LIG to $\{\mathbf{t}, \mathbf{b}\}$. In table 8.1, an equivalent set of productions with a richer non-terminal set is given. If we consider these productions, there is no consultation of the top of the index lists in the application of predictive steps.

From this parsing algorithm for LIG, we can derive an Earley-like parsing algorithm for TAG, similar to the one described in (Schabes, 1991), that applies prediction with respect to the structure of elementary trees, but not with respect to the lists of pending adjunctions. In the case of TAG, parsing begins by creating the item corresponding to a production that has the root of an initial tree as left-hand side and the dot in the leftmost position of the right-hand side:

$$\mathcal{D}_{\text{E−TAG}}^{\text{Init}} = \frac{}{[\top \to \bullet \mathbf{R}^\alpha, 0, 0 \mid -, -]} \quad \alpha \in \mathbf{I}, \; S = \text{label}(\gamma)$$

Terminal symbols and the empty string are recognized by the following deduction steps:

$$\mathcal{D}_{\text{E−TAG}}^{\text{Scan}} = \frac{[N^\gamma \to \delta \bullet M^\gamma \nu, i, j \mid p, q], \quad [a, j, j+1]}{[N^\gamma \to \delta M^\gamma \bullet \nu, i, j+1 \mid p, q]} \quad a = \text{label}(M^\gamma)$$

$$\mathcal{D}_{\text{E−TAG}}^{\varepsilon} = \frac{[N^\gamma \to \delta \bullet M^\gamma \nu, i, j \mid p, q],}{[N^\gamma \to \delta M^\gamma \bullet \nu, i, j \mid p, q]} \quad \varepsilon = \text{label}(M^\gamma)$$

The set $\mathcal{D}_{\text{E−LIG}}^{\text{Pred}}$ of deduction steps has its counterpart in several different steps, one for each kind of predictions that we can perform on TAG parsing, namely:

- Prediction of a child node:

$$\mathcal{D}_{\text{E−TAG}}^{\text{Pred}} = \frac{[N^\gamma \to \delta \bullet M^\gamma \nu, i, j \mid p, q]}{[M^\gamma \to \bullet \nu, j, j \mid -, -]} \quad \mathbf{nil} \in \text{adj}(M^\gamma)$$

- Prediction of the adjunction on a node of an elementary tree γ, starting the traversal of an auxiliary tree β:

$$\mathcal{D}_{\text{E}-\text{TAG}}^{\text{AdjPred}} = \frac{[N^\gamma \rightarrow \delta \bullet M^\gamma \nu, i, j \mid p, q]}{[\top \rightarrow \bullet \mathbf{R}^\beta, j, j \mid -, -]} \quad \beta \in \text{adj}(M^\gamma)$$

- Prediction, when the foot node of β is reached, of some subtree of γ to be attached to this foot node and traversed (after suspension of the traversal of β). At this point, no information is available about the adjunction node, so all possible nodes are predicted:

$$\mathcal{D}_{\text{E}-\text{TAG}}^{\text{FootPred}} = \frac{[\mathbf{F}^\beta \rightarrow \bullet \bot, k, k \mid -, -]}{[M^\gamma \rightarrow \bullet v, k, k \mid -, -]} \quad \beta \in \text{adj}(M^\gamma)$$

The counterpart of $\mathcal{D}_{\text{E}-\text{LIG}}^{\text{Comp}[\,]}$ corresponds to a bottom-up traversal of nodes not on the spine of an auxiliary tree:

$$\mathcal{D}_{\text{E}-\text{TAG}}^{\text{CompNoSpine}} = \frac{\begin{array}{c}[N^\gamma \rightarrow \delta \bullet M^\gamma \nu, i, k \mid p, q],\\ [M^\gamma \rightarrow v\bullet, k, j \mid -, -]\end{array}}{[N^\gamma \rightarrow \delta M^\gamma \bullet \nu, i, j \mid p, q]} \quad \begin{array}{l} M^\gamma \notin \text{spine}(\gamma)\\ \mathbf{nil} \in \text{adj}(M^\gamma)\end{array}$$

whereas the counterpart of $\mathcal{D}_{\text{E}-\text{LIG}}^{\text{Comp}[\infty][\infty]}$ is in charge of the bottom-up traversal of nodes on the spine of an auxiliary tree:

$$\mathcal{D}_{\text{E}-\text{TAG}}^{\text{CompSpine}} = \frac{\begin{array}{c}[N^\gamma \rightarrow \delta \bullet M^\gamma \nu, i, k \mid -, -],\\ [M^\gamma \rightarrow v\bullet, k, j \mid p, q]\end{array}}{[N^\gamma \rightarrow \delta M^\gamma \bullet \nu, i, j \mid p, q]} \quad \begin{array}{l} M^\gamma \in \text{spine}(\gamma)\\ \mathbf{nil} \in \text{adj}(M^\gamma)\end{array}$$

Upon completion of the traversal of a subtree predicted at the foot node $\mathbf{F}^\beta$, a step in the counterpart of $\mathcal{D}_{\text{E}-\text{LIG}}^{\text{Comp}[\infty\eta][\infty]}$ resumes the traversal of auxiliary tree β at $\mathbf{F}^\beta$:

$$\mathcal{D}_{\text{E}-\text{TAG}}^{\text{FootComp}} = \frac{\begin{array}{c}[\mathbf{F}^\beta \rightarrow \bullet \bot, k, k \mid -, -],\\ [M^\gamma \rightarrow v\bullet, k, j \mid p, q]\end{array}}{[\mathbf{F}^\beta \rightarrow \bot\bullet, k, j \mid k, j]} \quad \beta \in \text{adj}(M^\gamma)$$

Upon completion of the traversal of β, a deduction step in the counterpart of $\mathcal{D}_{\text{E}-\text{LIG}}^{\text{Comp}[\infty][\infty\eta]}$ checks if the subtree attached to the foot of β corresponds to the one rooted at the adjunction node M^γ, when M^γ is placed on a spine:

$$\mathcal{D}_{\text{E}-\text{TAG}}^{\text{AdjCompSpine}} = \frac{\begin{array}{c}[N^\gamma \rightarrow \delta \bullet M^\gamma \nu, i, k \mid -, -],\\ [\top \rightarrow \mathbf{R}^\beta \bullet, k, j \mid p, q],\\ [M^\gamma \rightarrow v\bullet, p, q \mid r, s]\end{array}}{[N^\gamma \rightarrow \delta M^\gamma \bullet \nu, i, j \mid r, s]} \quad \begin{array}{l} \beta \in \text{adj}(M^\gamma)\\ M^\gamma \in \text{spine}(\gamma)\end{array}$$

If the adjunction node M^γ is not placed on a spine, then the completion of an adjunction is equivalent to the consecutive application of the counterparts of $\mathcal{D}_{E-LIG}^{Comp[\circ\circ][\circ\circ\eta]}$ and $\mathcal{D}_{E-LIG}^{Comp[\ ]}$:

$$\mathcal{D}_{E-TAG}^{AdjCompNoSpine} = \frac{\begin{array}{l}[N^\gamma \rightarrow \delta \bullet M^\gamma \nu, i, k \mid p', q'],\\ [\top \rightarrow \mathbf{R}^\beta \bullet, k, j \mid p, q],\\ [M^\gamma \rightarrow \upsilon \bullet, p, q \mid -, -]\end{array}}{[N^\gamma \rightarrow \delta M^\gamma \bullet \nu, i, j \mid p', q']} \quad \begin{array}{l}\beta \in adj(M^\gamma)\\ M^\gamma \notin spine(\gamma)\end{array}$$

The space complexity of these parsing algorithms for LIG and TAG remains $\mathcal{O}(n^4)$ and the time complexity remains $\mathcal{O}(n^6)$.

6. Earley-like Parsing Algorithms Preserving the Correct Prefix Property

Parsers satisfying the *correct prefix property* (CPP) guarantee that, as they read the input string from left to right, the substrings read so far are valid prefixes of the language defined by the grammar. More formally, a parser satisfies the correct prefix property if, for any substring $a_1 \cdots a_k$ read from the input string $a_1 \cdots a_k a_{k+1} \cdots a_n$, it guarantees that there exists a string of tokens $b_1 \cdots b_m$, where b_i need not be part of the input string, such that $a_1 \cdots a_k b_1 \cdots b_m$ is a valid string of the language.

To maintain the correct prefix property, a parser must recognize all possible derived trees in prefix form. In order to do that, two different phases must work coordinately: a top-down phase that expands the children of each node visited and a bottom-up phase grouping the children nodes to indicate the recognition of the parent node (Schabes, 1991).

6.1 Items

A parser for LIG that preserves the correct prefix property must check that each predicted element $A[\zeta]$ satisfies $S[\ ] \overset{*}{\Rightarrow} w' A[\zeta] \Upsilon$ where w' is a prefix of the input string w. To obtain a CPP Earley-like parser, we need to modify the Pred steps in order to predict information about the index lists. As a consequence, items must be also modified, introducing a new element that allows us to track the contents of the predicted index lists. The items are now of the form

$$[E, h \mid \underline{A} \rightarrow \Upsilon_1 \bullet \Upsilon_2, \eta, i, j \mid B, p, q]$$

and they represent one of the following kinds of derivations:

- $S[\ ] \overset{*}{\Rightarrow} a_1 \cdots a_h E[\zeta] \Upsilon_4 \overset{*}{\Rightarrow} a_1 \cdots a_h \cdots a_i A[\zeta\eta] \Upsilon_3 \Upsilon_4 \overset{*}{\Rightarrow} a_1 \cdots a_h \cdots a_i \cdots a_p B[\zeta] a_{q+1} \cdots a_j \Upsilon_2 \Upsilon_3 \Upsilon_4$ if and only if $(B, p, q) \neq (-, -, -)$, $A[\zeta\eta]$ is a dependent descendent of $E[\zeta]$, and $B[\zeta]$ is a dependent descendent of $A[\zeta\eta]$. Such a derivation corresponds to the completion of the dependent child of a production having the non-terminal A with a non empty index list as left-hand side.

- $S[\,] \overset{*}{\Rightarrow} a_1 \cdots a_h E[\zeta]\Upsilon_4 \overset{*}{\Rightarrow} a_1 \cdots a_h \cdots a_i\ A[\zeta\eta]\ \Upsilon_3\Upsilon_4 \overset{*}{\Rightarrow} a_1 \cdots a_h \cdots a_i \cdots a_j\ \Upsilon_2\Upsilon_3\Upsilon_4$ iff $(E, h) \neq (-,-)$, $(B, p, q) = (-,-,-)$, $A[\zeta\eta]$ is a dependent descendent of $E[\zeta]$, Υ_1 does not contain the descendent child of $A[\zeta\eta]$, and $(p, q) \leq (i, j)$. Such a derivation corresponds to prediction of the non-terminal A with a non-empty index list.

- $S[\,] \overset{*}{\Rightarrow} a_1 \cdots a_i A[\,]\Upsilon_4 \overset{*}{\Rightarrow} a_1 \cdots a_i \cdots a_j \Upsilon_2\Upsilon_4$ iff $(E, h) = (-,-)$, $\eta = -$, and $(B, p, q) = (-,-,-)$. If Υ_1 includes the dependent child of $A[\,]$ then the index list associated with that dependent child is empty. Such a derivation corresponds to the prediction or completion of an element $A[\,]$.

The new items are refinements of the items in the Earley-like parser without the CPP: the element η is used to store the top of the predicted index list and the pair (E, h) allows us to track the item involved in the prediction. At first glance, we could suppose that, in order to track this item, it would be necessary to store (E, η', h, k). However, due to the context-freeness property of LIG, the index η' may be discarded as the derivation must be valid independently of the rest of the index list. The position k may be discarded because every predicted item in the parsing system is of the form $[\underline{A} \to \bullet\Upsilon, h, h \mid B, p, q]$ and therefore $h = k$.

The recognition of the input string is indicated by the generation of items in the set of final items $\mathcal{F} = \{ [-, - \mid \underline{S} \to \Upsilon\bullet, -, 0, n \mid -, -, -] \}$.

In the case of TAG parsing, if we translate the grammar to LIG as shown in section 3.1, we obtain items of the form:

$$[M^{\gamma'}, h \mid N^\gamma \to \delta \bullet \nu, M^{\gamma'}, i, j \mid M^{\gamma'}, p, q]$$

representing the following cases, where α denotes an initial tree with label$(\mathbf{R}^\alpha) = S$:

- $\mathbf{R}^\alpha \overset{*}{\Rightarrow}_r a_1 \cdots a_h M^{\gamma'}\nu'$, $\mathbf{R}^\gamma \overset{*}{\Rightarrow} a_{h+1} \cdots a_i \delta\nu\nu'$, $\delta \overset{*}{\Rightarrow} a_{i+1} \cdots a_p\ \mathbf{F}^\gamma\ a_{q+1} \cdots a_j \Rightarrow_f a_{i+1} \cdots a_p\ \nu\ a_{q+1} \cdots a_j \overset{*}{\Rightarrow}_f a_{i+1} \cdots a_j$, $M^{\gamma'} \to \nu$, and $\gamma \in$ adj$(M^{\gamma'})$ iff $(M^{\gamma'}, h) \neq (-,-)$ and $(p, q) \neq (-,-)$.

- $\mathbf{R}^\alpha \overset{*}{\Rightarrow}_r a_1 \cdots a_h M^{\gamma'}\nu'$, $\mathbf{R}^\gamma \overset{*}{\Rightarrow} a_{h+1} \cdots a_i \delta\nu\nu$, $\delta \overset{*}{\Rightarrow} a_{i+1} \cdots a_j$, and $\gamma \in$ adj$(M^{\gamma'})$ iff if $(M^{\gamma'}, h) \neq (-,-)$ and $(p, q) = (-,-)$.

- $\mathbf{R}^\alpha \overset{*}{\Rightarrow}_r a_1 \cdots a_i \delta \nu \nu'$, $\delta \overset{*}{\Rightarrow} a_{i+1} \cdots a_j$, and N^γ not on a spine iff $(M^{\gamma'}, h) = (-, -)$ and $(p, q) = (-, -)$.

When bound, $M^{\gamma'}$ and h indicate, respectively, the node at which γ has been adjoined and the position of the input string where this adjunction was started. Note that h is also the left-most position of the frontier of γ. Once again, the element $M^{\gamma'}$ is redundant, allowing a more compact form of items for TAG parsing:

$$[h \mid N^\gamma \to \delta \bullet \nu, i, j \mid p, q]$$

The set of final items is $\mathcal{F} = \{ [- \mid \mathbf{R}^\alpha \to \delta\bullet, 0, n \mid -, -] \}$, with $\alpha \in I$ and $S = \mathrm{label}(\mathbf{R}^\alpha)$.

6.2 Deduction Steps

With respect to deduction steps for LIG, the completion steps must be adapted to the new form of the items in order to manipulate the new components E and h, and the prediction steps must be refined to take into account the different kinds of productions:

$$\mathcal{D}_{\mathrm{Earley-LIG}}^{\mathrm{Init}} = \frac{}{[-, - \mid \underline{S} \to \bullet\Upsilon, -, 0, 0 \mid -, -, -]}$$

$$\mathcal{D}_{\mathrm{Earley-LIG}}^{\mathrm{Scan}} = \frac{[-, - \mid A[\ ] \to \bullet a, -, j, j \mid -, -, -],\ [a, j, j+1]}{[-, - \mid A[\ ] \to a\bullet, -, j, j+1 \mid -, -, -]}$$

$$\mathcal{D}_{\mathrm{Earley-LIG}}^{\varepsilon} = \frac{[-, - \mid A[\ ] \to \bullet\varepsilon, -, j, j \mid -, -, -]}{[-, - \mid A[\ ] \to \varepsilon\bullet, -, j, j \mid -, -, -]}$$

$$\mathcal{D}_{\mathrm{Earley-LIG}}^{\mathrm{Pred}[\ ]} = \frac{[E, h \mid \underline{A} \to \Upsilon_1 \bullet B[\ ]\ \Upsilon_2, \eta, i, j \mid C, p, q]}{[-, - \mid \underline{B} \to \bullet\Upsilon_3, -, j, j \mid -, -, -]} \quad \begin{array}{l} \underline{B} = B[\mathrm{oo}] \\ \text{or } \underline{B} = B[\ ] \end{array}$$

$$\mathcal{D}_{\mathrm{Earley-LIG}}^{\mathrm{Pred}[\mathrm{oo}\eta][\mathrm{oo}]} = \frac{\begin{array}{l}[E, h \mid A[\mathrm{oo}\eta] \to \Upsilon_1 \bullet B[\mathrm{oo}]\ \Upsilon_2, \eta, i, j \mid -, -, -],\\ [M, m \mid \underline{E} \to \bullet\Upsilon_3, \eta', h, h \mid -, -, -]\end{array}}{[M, m \mid \underline{B} \to \bullet\Upsilon_4, \eta', j, j \mid -, -, -]}$$

such that $\underline{B} = B[\ ]$ iff $\eta' = -$, while $\underline{B} = B[\mathrm{oo}]$ or $\underline{B} = B[\mathrm{oo}\eta']$ iff $\eta' \neq -$.

$$\mathcal{D}_{\mathrm{Earley-LIG}}^{\mathrm{Pred}[\mathrm{oo}][\mathrm{oo}]} = \frac{[E, h \mid A[\mathrm{oo}] \to \Upsilon_1 \bullet B[\mathrm{oo}]\ \Upsilon_2, \eta, i, j \mid -, -, -]}{[E, h \mid \underline{B} \to \bullet\Upsilon_3, \eta, j, j \mid -, -, -]}$$

such that $\underline{B} = B[\ ]$ iff $\eta = -$, while $\underline{B} = B[\mathrm{oo}]$ or $\underline{B} = B[\mathrm{oo}\eta]$ iff $\eta \neq -$.

$$\mathcal{D}_{\mathrm{Earley-LIG}}^{\mathrm{Pred}[\mathrm{oo}][\mathrm{oo}\eta]} = \frac{[E, h \mid A[\mathrm{oo}] \to \Upsilon_1 \bullet B[\mathrm{oo}\eta]\ \Upsilon_2, \eta', i, j \mid -, -, -]}{[A, i \mid \underline{B} \to \bullet\Upsilon_3, \eta, j, j \mid -, -, -]}$$

such that $\underline{B} = B[\circ\circ]$ or $\underline{B} = B[\circ\circ\eta]$.

$$\mathcal{D}_{\text{Earley-LIG}}^{\text{Comp}[\,]} = \frac{\begin{array}{l}[E,h \mid \underline{A} \to \Upsilon_1 \bullet B[\,] \, \Upsilon_2, \eta, i, j \mid C, p, q], \\ [-,- \mid \underline{B} \to \Upsilon_3\bullet, -, j, k \mid -,-,-]\end{array}}{[E,h \mid \underline{A} \to \Upsilon_1 B[\,] \bullet \Upsilon_2, \eta, i, k \mid C, p, q]}$$

$$\mathcal{D}_{\text{Earley-LIG}}^{\text{Comp}[\circ\circ\eta][\circ\circ]} = \frac{\begin{array}{l}[E,h \mid A[\circ\circ\eta] \to \Upsilon_1 \bullet B[\circ\circ] \, \Upsilon_2, \eta, i, j \mid -,-,-], \\ [M,m \mid \underline{E} \to \bullet\Upsilon_3, \eta', h, h \mid -,-,-], \\ [M,m \mid \underline{B} \to \Upsilon_4\bullet, \eta', j, k \mid C, p, q]\end{array}}{[E,h \mid A[\circ\circ\eta] \to \Upsilon_1 B[\circ\circ] \bullet \Upsilon_2, \eta, i, k \mid B, j, k]}$$

$$\mathcal{D}_{\text{Earley-LIG}}^{\text{Comp}[\circ\circ][\circ\circ]} = \frac{\begin{array}{l}[E,h \mid A[\circ\circ] \to \Upsilon_1 \bullet B[\circ\circ] \, \Upsilon_2, \eta, i, j \mid -,-,-], \\ [E,h \mid \underline{B} \to \Upsilon_3\bullet, \eta, j, k \mid C, p, q]\end{array}}{[E,h \mid A[\circ\circ] \to \Upsilon_1 B[\circ\circ] \bullet \Upsilon_2, \eta, i, k \mid C, p, q]}$$

$$\mathcal{D}_{\text{Earley-LIG}}^{\text{Comp}[\circ\circ][\circ\circ\eta]} = \frac{\begin{array}{l}[E,h \mid A[\circ\circ] \to \Upsilon_1 \bullet B[\circ\circ\eta] \, \Upsilon_2, \eta', i, j \mid -,-,-], \\ [A,i \mid \underline{B} \to \Upsilon_3\bullet, \eta, j, k \mid C, p, q], \\ [E,h \mid \underline{C} \to \Upsilon_4\bullet, \eta', p, q \mid D, r, s]\end{array}}{[E,h \mid A[\circ\circ] \to \Upsilon_1 B[\circ\circ\eta] \bullet \Upsilon_2, \eta', i, k \mid D, r, s]}$$

The space complexity of this algorithm with respect to the length n of the input string is $\mathcal{O}(n^5)$, as each item stores five positions of the input string. The time complexity is $\mathcal{O}(n^8)$ due to steps in the set $\mathcal{D}_{\text{Earley}}^{\text{Comp}[\circ\circ][\circ\circ\eta]}$. To reduce the time complexity, we use a technique, inspired by the work of (Nederhof, 1999), and similar to the one used in (De la Clergerie and Alonso, 1998; Alonso et al., 2000b) to reduce the complexity of the tabular interpretations of automata for tree adjoining languages. The idea is to split each deduction step in $\mathcal{D}_{\text{Earley}}^{\text{Comp}[\circ\circ][\circ\circ\eta]}$ into two different steps such that their final complexity is at most $\mathcal{O}(n^6)$:

$$\mathcal{D}_{\text{Earley-LIG}}^{\text{Comp}[\circ\circ][\circ\circ\eta]^0} = \frac{\begin{array}{l}[A,j \mid \underline{B} \to \Upsilon_3\bullet, \eta, j, k \mid C, p, q], \\ [E,h \mid \underline{C} \to \Upsilon_4\bullet, \eta', p, q \mid D, r, s]\end{array}}{[[\underline{B} \to \Upsilon_3\bullet, \eta, j, k \mid D, r, s]]}$$

$$\mathcal{D}_{\text{Earley-LIG}}^{\text{Comp}[\circ\circ][\circ\circ\eta]^1} = \frac{\begin{array}{l}[[\underline{B} \to \Upsilon_3\bullet, \eta, j, k \mid D, r, s]], \\ [E,h \mid A[\circ\circ] \to \Upsilon_1 \bullet B[\circ\circ\eta] \, \Upsilon_2, \eta', i, j \mid -,-,-], \\ [E,h \mid \underline{C} \to \Upsilon_4\bullet, \eta', p, q \mid D, r, s]\end{array}}{[E,h \mid A[\circ\circ] \to \Upsilon_1 B[\circ\circ\eta] \bullet \Upsilon_2, \eta', i, k \mid D, r, s]}$$

Deduction steps in $\mathcal{D}_{\text{Earley}}^{\text{Comp}[\circ\circ][\circ\circ\eta]^0}$ generate an intermediate item of the form $[[\underline{B} \to \Upsilon_3\bullet, \eta, j, k \mid D, r, s]]$ that will be taken as antecedent for steps in $\mathcal{D}_{\text{Earley}}^{\text{Comp}[\circ\circ][\circ\circ\eta]^1}$ and that represents a derivation

$$\begin{aligned}B[\eta'\eta] &\overset{*}{\Rightarrow} a_{j+1} \cdots a_p \, C[\eta'] \, a_{q+1} \cdots a_k \\ &\overset{*}{\Rightarrow} a_{j+1} \cdots a_p \cdots a_r \, D[\,] \, a_{s+1} \cdots a_q \cdots a_k\end{aligned}$$

for some η', p and q. Deduction steps $\mathrm{Comp}[\circ\circ][\circ\circ\eta]^1$ combine this pseudo-item with an item $[E, h \mid A[\circ\circ] \to \Upsilon_1 \bullet B[\circ\circ\eta] \Upsilon_2 , \eta', i, j \mid -, -, -]$ that represents a derivation

$$S[\,] \overset{*}{\Rightarrow} a_1 \cdots a_h E[\zeta] \Upsilon_5$$
$$\overset{*}{\Rightarrow} a_1 \cdots a_h \cdots a_i A[\zeta\eta'] \Upsilon_3 \Upsilon_5$$
$$\overset{*}{\Rightarrow} a_1 \cdots a_h \cdots a_i \cdots a_j B[\zeta\eta'\eta] \Upsilon_2 \Upsilon_3 \Upsilon_5$$

and with an item $[E, h \mid \underline{C} \to \Upsilon_4 \bullet, \gamma', p, q \mid D, r, s]$ representing a derivation

$$S[\,] \overset{*}{\Rightarrow} a_1 \cdots a_h E[\zeta] \Upsilon_5$$
$$\overset{*}{\Rightarrow} a_1 \cdots a_h \cdots a_p C[\zeta\eta''] \Upsilon_4 \Upsilon_5$$
$$\overset{*}{\Rightarrow} a_1 \cdots a_h \cdots a_p \cdots a_r D[\zeta] a_{s+1} \cdots a_q \Upsilon_4 \Upsilon_5$$

As a result, a new item of the form $[E, h \mid A[\circ\circ] \to \Upsilon_1 B[\circ\circ\eta] \bullet \Upsilon_2, \eta', i, k \mid D, r, s]$ is generated. This last item represents the existence of a derivation

$$S[\,] \overset{*}{\Rightarrow} a_1 \cdots a_h E[\zeta] \Upsilon_5$$
$$\overset{*}{\Rightarrow} a_1 \cdots a_h \cdots a_i A[\zeta\eta'] \Upsilon_3 \Upsilon_5$$
$$\overset{*}{\Rightarrow} a_1 \cdots a_h \cdots a_i \cdots a_j B[\zeta\eta'\eta] \Upsilon_2 \Upsilon_3 \Upsilon_5$$
$$\overset{*}{\Rightarrow} a_1 \cdots a_h \cdots a_i \cdots a_j \cdots a_p C[\zeta\eta'] a_{q+1} \cdots a_k \Upsilon_2 \Upsilon_3 \Upsilon_5$$
$$\overset{*}{\Rightarrow} a_1 \cdots a_h \cdots a_i \cdots a_j \cdots a_p \cdots a_r D[\zeta] a_{s+1} \cdots a_{q+1} \cdots a_k \Upsilon_2 \Upsilon_3 \Upsilon_5$$

In the case of TAG, the CYK-like and Earley-like parsing algorithms described in the previous sections do not preserve the correct prefix property because foot-prediction (a top-down operation) is not restrictive enough to guarantee that the subtree attached to the foot node is really a subtree of the tree involved in the adjunction. The following is the list of deduction steps for TAG obtained from the list of deduction steps for LIG:

$$\mathcal{D}_{\mathrm{Earley-TAG}}^{\mathrm{Init}} = \frac{}{[- \mid \top \to \bullet \mathbf{R}^\alpha, 0, 0 \mid -, -]} \quad \alpha \in I, \ S = \mathrm{label}(\alpha)$$

$$\mathcal{D}_{\mathrm{Earley-TAG}}^{\mathrm{Scan}} = \frac{\begin{array}{c}[h \mid N^\gamma \to \delta \bullet M^\gamma \nu, i, j \mid p, q], \\ [a, j, j+1]\end{array}}{[h, N^\gamma \to \delta M^\gamma \bullet \nu, i, j+1 \mid p, q]} \quad a = \mathrm{label}(M^\gamma)$$

$$\mathcal{D}_{\mathrm{Earley-TAG}}^{\mathcal{E}} = \frac{[h \mid N^\gamma \to \delta \bullet M^\gamma \nu, i, j \mid p, q],}{[h \mid N^\gamma \to \delta M^\gamma \bullet \nu, i, j \mid p, q]} \quad \varepsilon = \mathrm{label}(M^\gamma)$$

The set $\mathcal{D}_{\mathrm{E-LIG}}^{\mathrm{Pred}[\,]}$ has its counterparts in the set of steps in charge of predicting a node not placed on the spine:

$$\mathcal{D}_{\mathrm{Earley-TAG}}^{\mathrm{PredNoSpine}} = \frac{[h \mid N^\gamma \to \delta \bullet M^\gamma \nu, i, j \mid p, q]}{[- \mid M^\gamma \to \bullet \nu, j, j \mid -, -]} \quad \begin{array}{l} M^\gamma \notin \mathrm{spine}(\gamma), \\ \mathbf{nil} \in \mathrm{adj}(M^\gamma) \end{array}$$

Items related to a node M^γ not on a spine need not keep trace of h (corresponding to the input position when starting the traversal of γ), as done for LIG for non descendant children.

The counterpart of $\mathcal{D}_{\text{Earley-LIG}}^{\text{Pred}[\infty][\infty]}$ is the set of steps in charge of predicting children nodes of a node placed on the spine:

$$\mathcal{D}_{\text{Earley-TAG}}^{\text{PredSpine}} = \frac{[h \mid N^\gamma \to \delta \bullet M^\gamma \nu, i, j \mid -, -]}{[h \mid M^\gamma \to \bullet v, j, j \mid -, -]} \quad \begin{array}{l} M^\gamma \in \text{spine}(\gamma), \\ \textbf{nil} \in \text{adj}(M^\gamma) \end{array}$$

Prediction of adjunction is performed by steps equivalent to the consecutive application of two steps in $\mathcal{D}_{\text{Earley-LIG}}^{\text{Pred}[\infty][\infty]}$ and $\mathcal{D}_{\text{Earley-LIG}}^{\text{Pred}[\infty][\infty\eta]}$:

$$\mathcal{D}_{\text{Earley-TAG}}^{\text{AdjPred}} = \frac{[h \mid N^\gamma \to \delta \bullet M^\gamma \nu, i, j \mid p, q]}{[j \mid \top \to \bullet \mathbf{R}^\beta, j, j \mid -, -]} \quad \beta \in \text{adj}(M^\gamma)$$

Each step performing the prediction at a foot node of the excised subtree rooted by M^γ corresponds to the consecutive application of the counterparts of a step in $\mathcal{D}_{\text{Earley-LIG}}^{\text{Pred}[\infty\eta][\infty]}$ and a step in $\mathcal{D}_{\text{Earley-LIG}}^{\text{Pred}[\,]}$ if M^γ is not on a spine:

$$\mathcal{D}_{\text{Earley-TAG}}^{\text{FootPredNoSpine}} = \frac{\begin{array}{c}[h \mid \mathbf{F}^\beta \to \bullet \bot, j, j \mid -, -], \\ [m \mid N^\gamma \to \delta \bullet M^\gamma \nu, i, h \mid p, q]\end{array}}{[- \mid M^\gamma \to \bullet v, j, j \mid -, -]} \quad \begin{array}{l} \beta \in \text{adj}(M^\gamma), \\ M^\gamma \notin \text{spine}(\gamma) \end{array}$$

but if M^γ is placed on the spine of γ then the resulting step corresponds to the consecutive application of the counterparts of a step in $\mathcal{D}_{\text{Earley-LIG}}^{\text{Pred}[\infty\eta][\infty]}$ and a step in $\mathcal{D}_{\text{Earley-LIG}}^{\text{Pred}[\infty][\infty]}$:

$$\mathcal{D}_{\text{Earley-TAG}}^{\text{FootPredSpine}} = \frac{\begin{array}{c}[h \mid \mathbf{F}^\beta \to \bullet \bot, j, j \mid -, -], \\ [m \mid N^\gamma \to \delta \bullet M^\gamma \nu, i, h \mid -, -]\end{array}}{[m \mid M^\gamma \to \bullet v, j, j \mid -, -]} \quad \begin{array}{l} \beta \in \text{adj}(M^\gamma), \\ M^\gamma \in \text{spine}(\gamma) \end{array}$$

The counterparts of $\mathcal{D}_{\text{E-LIG}}^{\text{Comp}[\,]}$ and $\mathcal{D}_{\text{E-TAG}}^{\text{Comp}[\infty][\infty]}$ corresponds to steps traversing elementary trees bottom-up:

$$\mathcal{D}_{\text{Earley-TAG}}^{\text{CompNoSpine}} = \frac{\begin{array}{c}[h \mid N^\gamma \to \delta \bullet M^\gamma \nu, i, j \mid p, q], \\ [- \mid M^\gamma \to v \bullet, j, k \mid -, -]\end{array}}{[h \mid N^\gamma \to \delta M^\gamma \bullet \nu, i, k \mid p, q]} \quad \begin{array}{l} M^\gamma \notin \text{spine}(\gamma) \\ \textbf{nil} \in \text{adj}(M^\gamma) \end{array}$$

$$\mathcal{D}_{\text{Earley-TAG}}^{\text{CompSpine}} = \frac{\begin{array}{c}[h \mid N^\gamma \to \delta \bullet M^\gamma \nu, i, j \mid -, -], \\ [h \mid M^\gamma \to v \bullet, j, k \mid p, q]\end{array}}{[h \mid N^\gamma \to \delta M^\gamma \bullet \nu, i, k \mid p, q]} \quad \begin{array}{l} M^\gamma \in \text{spine}(\gamma) \\ \textbf{nil} \in \text{adj}(M^\gamma) \end{array}$$

Upon completion of the traversal of the subtree rooted at a node M^γ, not on the spine, and predicted at a foot node $\mathbf{F}^\beta$, the traversal of β is resumed by the following step which is the result of the consecutive application of the counterparts of $\mathcal{D}_{\text{Earley}-\text{LIG}}^{\text{Comp}[\infty\eta][\infty]}$ and $\mathcal{D}_{\text{Earley}-\text{LIG}}^{\text{Comp}[\ ]}$:

$$\mathcal{D}_{\text{Earley}-\text{TAG}}^{\text{FootCompNoSpine}} = \frac{\begin{array}{l}[h \mid \mathbf{F}^\beta \to \bullet\bot, j, j \mid -, -], \\ [m \mid N^\gamma \to \delta \bullet M^\gamma\nu, i, h \mid p, q], \\ [- \mid M^\gamma \to v\bullet, j, k \mid -, -]\end{array}}{[h \mid \mathbf{F}^\beta \to \bot\bullet, j, k \mid j, k]} \quad \begin{array}{l}\beta \in \text{adj}(M^\gamma), \\ M^\gamma \notin \text{spine}(\gamma)\end{array}$$

If M^γ is not in the spine of γ then the set of deduction steps for the completion of foot is the counterpart of $\mathcal{D}_{\text{E}-\text{LIG}}^{\text{Comp}[\infty\eta][\infty]}$:

$$\mathcal{D}_{\text{Earley}-\text{TAG}}^{\text{FootCompSpine}} = \frac{\begin{array}{l}[h \mid \mathbf{F}^\beta \to \bullet\bot, j, j \mid -, -], \\ [m \mid N^\gamma \to \delta \bullet M^\gamma\nu, i, h \mid -, -], \\ [m \mid M^\gamma \to v\bullet, j, k \mid p, q]\end{array}}{[h \mid \mathbf{F}^\beta \to \bot\bullet, j, k \mid j, k]} \quad \begin{array}{l}\beta \in \text{adj}(M^\gamma), \\ M^\gamma \in \text{spine}(\gamma)\end{array}$$

Upon completion of the traversal of β, a deduction step in the counterpart of $\mathcal{D}_{\text{Earley}-\text{LIG}}^{\text{Comp}[\infty][\infty\eta]}$ checks if the subtree attached to the foot of β corresponds to the one rooted at the adjunction node M^γ. When M^γ is on a spine, each step works in coordination with a $\mathcal{D}_{\text{Earley}-\text{LIG}}^{\text{Comp}[\infty][\infty]}$ step:

$$\mathcal{D}_{\text{Earley}-\text{TAG}}^{\text{AdjCompSpine}} = \frac{\begin{array}{l}[h \mid N^\gamma \to \delta \bullet M^\gamma\nu, i, j \mid -, -], \\ [j \mid \top \to \mathbf{R}^\beta\bullet, j, k \mid p, q], \\ [h \mid M^\gamma \to v\bullet, p, q \mid r, s]\end{array}}{[h \mid N^\gamma \to \delta M^\gamma \bullet \nu, i, k \mid r, s]} \quad \begin{array}{l}\beta \in \text{adj}(M^\gamma), \\ M^\gamma \in \text{spine}(\gamma)\end{array}$$

If the adjunction node is not on a spine, then deduction steps for the completion of adjunction are equivalent to the consecutive application of two steps in the counterparts of $\mathcal{D}_{\text{Earley}-\text{LIG}}^{\text{Comp}[\infty][\infty\eta]}$ and $\mathcal{D}_{\text{Earley}-\text{LIG}}^{\text{Comp}[\ ]}$:

$$\mathcal{D}_{\text{Earley}-\text{TAG}}^{\text{AdjCompNoSpine}} = \frac{\begin{array}{l}[h \mid N^\gamma \to \delta \bullet M^\gamma\nu, i, j \mid p', q'], \\ [j \mid \top \to \mathbf{R}^\beta\bullet, j, k \mid p, q], \\ [- \mid M^\gamma \to v\bullet, p, q \mid -, -]\end{array}}{[h \mid N^\gamma \to \delta M^\gamma \bullet \nu, i, k \mid p', q']} \quad \begin{array}{l}\beta \in \text{adj}(M^\gamma), \\ M^\gamma \notin \text{spine}(\gamma)\end{array}$$

The time complexity of this algorithm, with respect to the length n of the input string, is $\mathcal{O}(n^7)$, and is given by the adjunction completion steps. To reduce it to the standard $\mathcal{O}(n^6)$ time complexity, we must apply the same technique used in the case of LIG parsing, splitting $\mathcal{D}_{\text{Earley}-\text{TAG}}^{\text{AdjCompSpine}}$ into $\mathcal{D}_{\text{Earley}-\text{TAG}}^{\text{AdjComp}^0}$ and $\mathcal{D}_{\text{Earley}-\text{TAG}}^{\text{AdjCompSpine}^1}$, whereas $\mathcal{D}_{\text{Earley}-\text{TAG}}^{\text{AdjCompNOSpine}}$ is split into $\mathcal{D}_{\text{Earley}-\text{TAG}}^{\text{AdjComp}^0}$ and $\mathcal{D}_{\text{Earley}-\text{TAG}}^{\text{AdjCompNoSpine}^1}$:

$$\mathcal{D}_{\text{Earley-TAG}}^{\text{AdjComp}^0} = \frac{\begin{array}{c}[j \mid \top \to \mathbf{R}^\beta\bullet, j, k \mid p, q], \\ [h \mid M^\gamma \to \delta\bullet, p, q \mid r, s]\end{array}}{[[M^\gamma \to \delta\bullet, j, k \mid r, s]]} \quad \beta \in \text{adj}(M^\gamma)$$

$$\mathcal{D}_{\text{Earley-TAG}}^{\text{AdjCompSpine}^1} = \frac{\begin{array}{c}[[M^\gamma \to v\bullet, j, k \mid r, s]], \\ [h \mid N^\gamma \to \delta \bullet M^\gamma v, i, j \mid -, -], \\ [h \mid M^\gamma \to v\bullet, p, q \mid r, s]\end{array}}{[h \mid N^\gamma \to \delta M^\gamma \bullet v, i, k \mid r, s]} \quad \begin{array}{c}\beta \in \text{adj}(M^\gamma), \\ M^\gamma \in \text{spine}(\gamma)\end{array}$$

$$\mathcal{D}_{\text{Earley-TAG}}^{\text{AdjCompNoSpine}^1} = \frac{\begin{array}{c}[[M^\gamma \to v\bullet, j, k \mid r, s]], \\ [h \mid N^\gamma \to \delta \bullet M^\gamma v, i, j \mid p', q'], \\ [- \mid M^\gamma \to v\bullet, p, q \mid -, -]\end{array}}{[h \mid N^\gamma \to \delta M^\gamma \bullet v, i, k \mid p', q']} \quad \begin{array}{c}\beta \in \text{adj}(M^\gamma), \\ M^\gamma \notin \text{spine}(\gamma)\end{array}$$

7. Bidirectional Parsing

Bidirectional parsing strategies can start computations at any position of the input string and can span to the right and to the left to include substrings which were scanned in a bidirectional manner by subcomputations. Although these kinds of strategies seems to be naturally adapted for TAG, only a few bidirectional parsing algorithms have been proposed (Lavelli and Satta, 1991; van Noord, 1994; Díaz et al., 2000). In the case of LIG, to the best of our knowledge, only a bottom-up head-corner parser has been defined (Schneider, 2000).

In this section we propose a new bidirectional bottom-up parser for LIG derived from the context-free parser defined by De Vreught and Honig (Sikkel, 1997). Intermediate results of the parsing process are stored as items of the form

$$[\underline{A} \to \Upsilon_1 \bullet \Upsilon_2 \bullet \Upsilon_3, \eta, i, j \mid B, p, q]$$

with double-dotted productions. Each item represents one of the following kinds of derivation:

- $\Upsilon_2 \overset{*}{\Rightarrow} \Upsilon_{2'} E[\eta] \Upsilon_{2''} \overset{*}{\Rightarrow} a_{i+1} \cdots a_p B[\ ] a_{q+1} \cdots a_j$ iff $(B, p, q) \neq (-, -, -)$, where $B[\ ]$ is a dependent descendent of $E[\eta]$ and $(p, q) \leq (i, j)$.

- $\Upsilon_2 \overset{*}{\Rightarrow} a_{i+1} \cdots a_j$ iff $\eta = -$ and $(B, p, q) = (-, -, -)$.

The input string $a_1 \cdots a_n$ is recognized if an item in $\mathcal{F} = \{[\underline{S} \to \bullet \Upsilon \bullet, -, 0, n \mid -, -, -]\}$ is generated.

The parsing process starts by recognizing a terminal symbol or the empty string:

$$\mathcal{D}_{\text{dVH-LIG}}^{\text{Scan}} = \frac{[a, j, j+1]}{[A[\ ] \to \bullet a\bullet, -, j, j+1 \mid -, -, -]}$$

$$\mathcal{D}_{\text{dVH-LIG}}^{\varepsilon} = \frac{}{[A[\,] \to \bullet\varepsilon\bullet, -, j, j \mid -, -, -]}$$

Upon recognition of a production defining non-terminal B, the bottom-up recognition of productions having B in their body is triggered:

$$\mathcal{D}_{\text{dVH-LIG}}^{\text{Inc}[\,]} = \frac{[B \to \bullet\Upsilon_3\bullet, -, i, j \mid -, -, -]}{[A \to \Upsilon_1 \bullet B[\,] \bullet \Upsilon_2, -, i, j \mid -, -, -]}$$

$$\mathcal{D}_{\text{dVH-LIG}}^{\text{Inc}[\infty][\infty]} = \frac{[B \to \bullet\Upsilon_3\bullet, \eta, i, j \mid C, p, q]}{[A[\infty] \to \Upsilon_1 \bullet B[\infty] \bullet \Upsilon_2, \eta, i, j \mid C, p, q]}$$

$$\mathcal{D}_{\text{dVH-LIG}}^{\text{Inc}[\infty\eta][\infty]} = \frac{[B \to \bullet\Upsilon_3\bullet, \eta', i, j \mid C, p, q]}{[A[\infty\eta] \to \Upsilon_1 \bullet B[\infty] \bullet \Upsilon_2, \eta, i, j \mid B, i, j]}$$

$$\mathcal{D}_{\text{dVH-LIG}}^{\text{Inc}[\infty][\infty\eta]} = \frac{\begin{array}{c}[B \to \bullet\Upsilon_3\bullet, \eta, i, j \mid C, p, q], \\ [C \to \bullet\Upsilon_4\bullet, \eta', p, q \mid D, r, s]\end{array}}{[A[\infty\eta] \to \Upsilon_1 \bullet B[\infty] \bullet \Upsilon_2, \eta', i, j \mid D, r, s]}$$

When two consecutive parts of the right-hand side of a rule have been recognized, they are concatenated:

$$\mathcal{D}_{\text{dVH-LIG}}^{\text{Conc}[\,]} = \frac{\begin{array}{c}[A \to \Upsilon_1 \bullet \Upsilon_2 \bullet \Upsilon_3\Upsilon_4, \eta, i, j \mid C, p, q], \\ [A \to \Upsilon_1\Upsilon_2 \bullet \Upsilon_3 \bullet \Upsilon_4, \eta', j, k \mid C', p', q'],\end{array}}{[A \to \Upsilon_1 \bullet \Upsilon_2\Upsilon_3 \bullet \Upsilon_4, \eta \cup \eta', i, k \mid C \cup C', p \cup p', q \cup q']}$$

where, given X and Y, we define $X \cup Y$ as X if Y is unbound, as Y if X is unbound, and being undefined otherwise.

The translation of this algorithm to TAG uses items of the form

$$[N^\gamma \to \nu \bullet \delta \bullet \omega, M^{\gamma'}, i, j \mid M^{\gamma'}, p, q]$$

representing one of the following two situations:

- $\delta \overset{*}{\Rightarrow} a_{i+1} \cdots a_p \; \mathbf{F}^\gamma \; a_{q+1} \cdots a_j \Rightarrow_f a_{i+1} \cdots a_p \; \nu \; a_{q+1} \cdots a_j \overset{*}{\Rightarrow}_f$
  $a_{i+1} \cdots a_j$, $M^{\gamma'} \to \nu$, and $\gamma \in \text{adj}(M^{\gamma'})$ iff $(p, q) \neq (-, -)$.

- $\delta \overset{*}{\Rightarrow} a_{i+1} \cdots a_j$ iff $(p, q) = (-, -)$.

As already mentioned for other TAG parsing algorithms, the element M^γ is redundant, allowing more compact items (Díaz et al., 2000) of the form:

$$[N^\gamma \to \nu \bullet \delta \bullet \omega, i, j \mid p, q]$$

As before, the parsing process is started bottom-up by means of the recognition of terminal symbols or the empty string:

$$\mathcal{D}_{\text{dVH-TAG}}^{\text{Scan}} = \frac{[a, j, j+1]}{[N^\gamma \to \nu \bullet M^\gamma \bullet \omega, j, j+1 \mid -, -]} \quad a = \text{label}(M^\gamma)$$

$$\mathcal{D}_{\mathrm{dVH-TAG}}^{\varepsilon} = \frac{}{[N^{\gamma} \to \nu \bullet M^{\gamma} \bullet \omega, j, j \mid -, -]} \quad \varepsilon = \mathrm{label}(M^{\gamma})$$

Steps in $\mathcal{D}_{\mathrm{dVH-LIG}}^{\mathrm{Inc[\,]}}$ correspond to the bottom-up traversal of nodes not placed on the spine:

$$\mathcal{D}_{\mathrm{dVH-TAG}}^{\mathrm{IncNoSpine}} = \frac{[M^{\gamma} \to \bullet\delta\bullet, i, j \mid -, -]}{[N^{\gamma} \to \nu \bullet M^{\gamma} \bullet \omega, i, j \mid -, -]} \quad M^{\gamma} \notin \mathrm{spine}(\gamma), \ \mathbf{nil} \in \mathrm{adj}(M^{\gamma})$$

whereas steps in $\mathcal{D}_{\mathrm{dVH-LIG}}^{\mathrm{Inc[oo][oo]}}$ correspond to the bottom-up traversal of nodes in the spine of an auxiliary tree, propagating the list of pending adjunctions:

$$\mathcal{D}_{\mathrm{dVH-TAG}}^{\mathrm{IncNoSpine}} = \frac{[M^{\gamma} \to \bullet\delta\bullet, i, j \mid p, q]}{[N^{\gamma} \to \nu \bullet M^{\gamma} \bullet \omega, i, j \mid p, q]} \quad M^{\gamma} \in \mathrm{spine}(\gamma), \ \mathbf{nil} \in \mathrm{adj}(M^{\gamma})$$

Steps in $\mathcal{D}_{\mathrm{dVH-LIG}}^{\mathrm{Inc[oo\eta][oo]}}$ correspond to the bottom-up starting of an a adjunction operation at the foot node of an auxiliary tree:

$$\mathcal{D}_{\mathrm{dVH-TAG}}^{\mathrm{Foot}} = \frac{[M^{\gamma} \to \bullet\delta\bullet, i, j \mid p, q]}{[\mathbf{F}^{\beta} \to \bullet\bot\bullet, i, j \mid i, j]} \quad \beta \in \mathrm{adj}(M^{\gamma})$$

whereas steps in $\mathcal{D}_{\mathrm{dVH-LIG}}^{\mathrm{Inc[oo][oo\eta]}}$ correspond to finishing the adjunction operation once the auxiliary tree has been completely traversed:

$$\mathcal{D}_{\mathrm{dVH-TAG}}^{\mathrm{Adj}} = \frac{[\top \to \bullet\mathbf{R}^{\beta}\bullet, i, j \mid p, q] \quad [M^{\gamma} \to \bullet\delta\bullet, p, q \mid r, s]}{[N^{\gamma} \to \nu \bullet M^{\gamma} \bullet \omega, i, j \mid r, s]} \quad \beta \in \mathrm{adj}(M^{\gamma})$$

Steps in $\mathcal{D}_{\mathrm{dVH-LIG}}^{\mathrm{Conc}}$ correspond to the combination of two partial analyses spanning consecutive parts of the input string:

$$\mathcal{D}_{\mathrm{dVH-TAG}}^{\mathrm{Conc}} = \frac{[N^{\gamma} \to \nu \bullet \delta_1 \bullet \delta_2 \omega, i, j \mid p, q] \quad [N^{\gamma} \to \nu\delta_1 \bullet \delta_2 \bullet \omega, j, k \mid p', q']}{[N^{\gamma} \to \nu \bullet \delta_1\delta_2 \bullet \omega, i, j \mid p \cup p', q \cup q']}$$

The same relations between dVH-LIG and dVH-TAG can be found between the bottom-up head-corner parser defined by (Schneider, 2000) and a bottom-up head-corner parser for TAG. It is also possible to define bidirectional parsing algorithms for LIG that mimic the head-corner algorithm for TAG defined by (van Noord, 1994) or the algorithm proposed by (Lavelli and Satta, 1991).

8.   Specialized TAG parsers

We have shown in the previous sections that TAG and LIG are very closely related and that a parsing schema for one formalism may easily be transposed to the other formalism. However, LIG is more generic than TAG (with an easy encoding of TAG as LIG) which means that more specialized and efficient schemata are possible for TAG. Actually, this fact has been used in previous schemata to simplify the items for TAG by deleting redundant or useless information. These simplifications exploited the facts that (a) the traversal of an auxiliary tree does not need any information about the adjunction node, and that (b) the foot node of an auxiliary tree resumes the traversal of the subtree rooted at the adjunction node and attached to the foot node.

There is another particularity that may help us to design specialized parsing algorithms for TAG, namely that elementary trees represent domains of locality that are lost when converting to LIG clauses. A simple algorithm based on this notion of domain of locality has been presented in (De la Clergerie, 2001). An item of the form $[h \mid N^\gamma \rightarrow \delta \bullet M^\gamma \nu, j \mid p, q \mid S]$ retraces the history of the traversal of some elementary tree γ, from the point h where it was started up to the current point j, with (possibly) some hole p, q covered by a foot node, and a (possibly empty) stack S of pairs (u, v) denoting adjunctions which have been predicted but not yet completed. In such a pair, u denotes the point where the traversal was suspended because of an adjunction and v denotes the point where the traversal was resumed after leaving the foot node of an auxiliary tree. We note $(u, v) = (-, -)$ in case of null adjunction. Parsing succeeds if a final item belonging to $\mathcal{F} = \{ [0 \mid \mathbf{R}^\alpha \rightarrow v\bullet, n \mid -, - \mid \emptyset] \mid \alpha \in \mathbf{I}$ and $S = \text{label}(\mathbf{R}^\alpha) \}$ is derivable.

$$\mathcal{D}_{\text{Weak-TAG}}^{\text{Init}} = \frac{}{[0 \mid \top \rightarrow \bullet \mathbf{R}^\alpha, 0 \mid -, - \mid \emptyset]} \quad \alpha \in \mathbf{I}, \ S = \text{label}(\alpha)$$

$$\mathcal{D}_{\text{Weak-TAG}}^{\text{Scan}} = \frac{[h \mid N^\gamma \rightarrow \delta \bullet M^\gamma \nu, j \mid p, q \mid S],\ [a, j, j+1]}{[h, N^\gamma \rightarrow \delta M^\gamma \bullet \nu, j+1 \mid p, q \mid S]} \quad a = \text{label}(M^\gamma)$$

$$\mathcal{D}_{\text{Weak-TAG}}^{\varepsilon} = \frac{[h \mid N^\gamma \rightarrow \delta \bullet M^\gamma \nu, j \mid p, q \mid S]}{[h, N^\gamma \rightarrow \delta M^\gamma \bullet \nu, j \mid p, q \mid S]} \quad \varepsilon = \text{label}(M^\gamma)$$

$$\mathcal{D}_{\text{Weak-TAG}}^{\text{Pred}} = \frac{[h \mid N^\gamma \rightarrow \delta \bullet M^\gamma \nu, j \mid p, q \mid S]}{[h \mid M^\gamma \rightarrow \bullet v, j \mid p, q \mid S, (-, -)]} \quad \text{nil} \in \text{adj}(M^\gamma)$$

$$\mathcal{D}_{\text{Weak-TAG}}^{\text{Comp}} = \frac{[h \mid M^\gamma \rightarrow v\bullet, j \mid p, q \mid S, (-, -)]}{[h \mid N^\gamma \rightarrow \delta M^\gamma \bullet \nu, j \mid p, q \mid S]} \quad \text{nil} \in \text{adj}(M^\gamma)$$

$$\mathcal{D}_{\text{Weak-TAG}}^{\text{AdjPred}} = \frac{[h \mid N^\gamma \rightarrow \delta \bullet M^\gamma \nu, j \mid p, q \mid S]}{[j \mid \top \rightarrow \bullet \mathbf{R}^\beta, j \mid -, - \mid \emptyset]} \quad \beta \in \text{adj}(M^\gamma)$$

$$\mathcal{D}_{\text{Weak-TAG}}^{\text{FootPred}} = \frac{[h \mid \mathbf{F}^\beta \rightarrow \bullet \perp, i \mid -, - \mid S'],\ [m \mid N^\gamma \rightarrow v \bullet M^\gamma \nu, h \mid p, q \mid S]}{[m \mid M^\gamma \rightarrow \bullet v, i \mid p, q \mid S, (h, i)]} \quad \beta \in \text{adj}(M^\gamma)$$

$$\mathcal{D}_{\text{Weak-TAG}}^{\text{FootComp}} = \frac{\begin{array}{c}[h \mid \mathbf{F}^\beta \to \bullet\bot, i \mid -, - \mid \mathcal{S}'], \\ [m \mid M^\gamma \to v\bullet, j \mid p, q \mid \mathcal{S}, (h, i)]\end{array}}{[h \mid \mathbf{F}^\beta \to \bot\bullet, j \mid i, j \mid \mathcal{S}']} \quad \beta \in \text{adj}(M^\gamma)$$

$$\mathcal{D}_{\text{Weak-TAG}}^{\text{AdjComp}} = \frac{\begin{array}{c}[h \mid \top \to \mathbf{R}^\beta\bullet, k \mid i, j \mid \emptyset], \\ [m \mid M^\gamma \to v\bullet, j \mid p, q \mid \mathcal{S}, (h, i)]\end{array}}{[m \mid N^\gamma \to \delta M^\gamma \bullet \nu, k \mid p, q \mid \mathcal{S}]} \quad \beta \in \text{adj}(M^\gamma)$$

The resulting algorithm corresponds to a left-to-right top-down parsing strategy preserving the correct prefix property and is simpler than many other algorithms. Its worst-case complexity is $\mathcal{O}(n^{4+2d})$ in space and $\mathcal{O}(n^{5+2d})$ in time where d denotes the maximal depth of elementary trees, and hence the maximal number of uncompleted adjunctions at some point in an elementary tree. These complexities are not optimal but experiments performed with linguistic grammars have nevertheless shown that this algorithm can be efficient (De la Clergerie, 2001).

9.   Conclusion

We have presented a set of algorithms for LIG and TAG parsing, including pure bottom-up algorithms, Earley-like algorithms with weak prediction, Earley-like algorithms with strong prediction that preserves the correct prefix property and bidirectional algorithms. Other algorithms could also have been included, but for reasons of space we have chosen to show only the algorithms we consider milestones in the development of parsers for LIG and TAG.

We have also studied the relations among the steps in charge of recognizing the adjunction operation in a TAG and the steps in charge of transmitting information through the spine in a LIG, obtaining fruitful results. For example, the TAG formalism restricts combination of items by means of (explicit or implicit) adjoining constraints. These constraints are not present in LIG, and so LIG parsing algorithms must take into account phenomena that never occur in TAG parsing. As a result, items in TAG parsers are more compact than their counterparts in LIG parsers. In addition, some practical optimizations for TAG parsing algorithms (e.g., the *weak tabular interpretation* presented by De la Clergerie, 2001) are not valid for LIG parsers.

Acknowledgments

The research reported in this chapter has been partially supported by Plan Nacional de Investigación Científica, Desarrollo e Innovación Tecnológica (TIC2000-0370-C02-01), by Ministerio de Ciencia y Tecnología (HP2001-0044), by Xunta de Galicia (PGIDT01PXI10506PN, PGIDIT02PXIB30501PR, PGIDIT02SIN01E), and by Universidade da Coruña.

References

Alonso, M. A., Cabrero, D., De la Clergerie, É., and Vilares, M. (1999). Tabular algorithms for TAG parsing. In *Proc. of EACL'99, Ninth Conference of the European Chapter of the Association for Computational Linguistics*, pages 150–157, Bergen, Norway. ACL.

Alonso, M. A., De la Clergerie, É., Graña, J., and Vilares, M. (2000a). New tabular algorithms for LIG parsing. In *Proc. of the Sixth International Workshop on Parsing Technologies (IWPT 2000)*, pages 29–40, Trento, Italy.

Alonso, M. A., Nederhof, M.-J., and De la Clergerie, É. (2000b). Tabulation of automata for tree adjoining languages. *Grammars*, 3(2/3):89–110.

De la Clergerie, É. (2001). Refining tabular parsers for TAGs. In *Proceedings of Language Technologies 2001: The Second Meeting of the North American Chapter of the Association for Computational Linguistics (NAACL'01)*, pages 167–174, CMU, Pittsburgh, PA, USA.

De la Clergerie, É. and Alonso, M. A. (1998). A tabular interpretation of a class of 2-Stack Automata. In *COLING-ACL'98, 36th Annual Meeting of the Association for Computational Linguistics and 17th International Conference on Computational Linguistics, Proceedings of the Conference*, volume II, pages 1333–1339, Montreal, Quebec, Canada. ACL.

De la Clergerie, É., Alonso, M. A., and Cabrero, D. (1998). A tabular interpretation of bottom-up automata for TAG. In *Proc. of Fourth International Workshop on Tree-Adjoining Grammars and Related Frameworks (TAG+4)*, pages 42–45, Philadelphia, PA, USA.

Díaz, V. J., Carrillo, V. and Alonso, M. A. (2000). A bidirectional bottom-up parser for TAG. In *Proc. of the Sixth International Workshop on Parsing Technologies (IWPT 2000)*, pages 299–300, Trento, Italy.

Gazdar, G. (1987). Applicability of indexed grammars to natural languages. In Reyle, U. and Rohrer, C., editors, *Natural Language Parsing and Linguistic Theories*, pages 69–94. D. Reidel Publishing Company.

Joshi, A. K. and Schabes, Y. (1997). Tree-adjoining grammars. In Rozenberg, G. and Salomaa, A., editors, *Handbook of Formal Languages. Vol 3: Beyond Words*, chapter 2, pages 69–123. Springer-Verlag, Berlin/Heidelberg/New York.

Kasami, T. (1965). An efficient recognition and syntax algorithm for context-free languages. Scientific Report AFCRL-65-758, Air Force Cambridge Research Lab., Bedford, Massachussetts.

Lavelli, A. and Satta, G. (1991) Bidirectional parsing of lexicalized tree adjoining grammars. In *Proceedings of the 5th Conference of the European Chapter of the Association for Computational Linguistics (EACL'91)*, pages 27–32, Berlin, Germany.

Nederhof, M.-J. (1998). Linear indexed automata and tabulation of TAG parsing. In *Proc. of First Workshop on Tabulation in Parsing and Deduction (TAPD'98)*, pages 1–9, Paris, France.

Nederhof, M.-J. (1999). The computational complexity of the correct-prefix property for TAGs. *Computational Linguistics*, 25(3):345–360.

Van Noord, G. (1994). Head-corner parsing for TAG. *Computational Intelligence*, 10(4):525–534, 1994.

Schabes, Y. (1991). The valid prefix property and left to right parsing of tree-adjoining grammar. In *Proc. of II International Workshop on Parsing Technologies, IWPT'91*, pages 21–30, Cancún, Mexico.

Schabes, Y. and Shieber, S. M. (1994). An alternative conception of tree-adjoining derivation. *Computational Linguistics*, 20(1):91–124.

Schneider, K.-M. (2000). Algebraic construction of parsing schemata. In *Proc. of the Sixth International Workshop on Parsing Technologies (IWPT 2000)*, pages 242–253, Trento, Italy.

Sikkel, K. (1997). *Parsing Schemata – A Framework for Specification and Analysis of Parsing Algorithms*. Texts in Theoretical Computer Science – An EATCS Series. Springer-Verlag, Berlin/Heidelberg/New York.

Vijay-Shanker, K. and Weir, D. J. (1991). Polynomial parsing of extensions of context-free grammars. In Tomita, M., editor, *Current Issues in Parsing Technology*, chapter 13, pages 191–206. Kluwer Academic Publishers, Norwell, MA, USA.

Vijay-Shanker, K. and Weir, D. J. (1993). Parsing some constrained grammar formalisms. *Computational Linguistics*, 19(4):591–636.

Younger, D. H. (1967). Recognition and parsing of context-free languages in time n^3. *Information and Control*, 10(2):189–208.

Chapter 9

IMPROVED LEFT-CORNER CHART PARSING FOR LARGE CONTEXT-FREE GRAMMARS

Robert C. Moore
Microsoft Research
One Microsoft Way, Redmond, Washington 98052, USA
bobmoore@microsoft.com

Abstract   We develop an improved form of left-corner chart parsing for large context-free grammars, introducing improvements that result in significant speed-ups compared to previously-known variants of left-corner parsing. We also compare our method to several other major parsing approaches, and find that our improved left-corner parsing method outperforms each of these across a range of grammars. In addition, we describe a new technique for minimizing the extra information needed to efficiently recover parses from the data structures built in the course of parsing.

1.   Introduction

Parsing algorithms for contex-free grammars (CFGs) are generally recognized as the backbone of virtually all approaches to parsing natural-language. Even in systems that use a grammar formalism more complex than CFGs (e.g., unification grammar), the parsing method is usually an extension of one of the well-known CFG parsing algorithms. Moreover, recent developments have once again made direct parsing of CFGs more relevant to natural-language processing, including the recent explosion of interest in parsing with stochastic CFGs or related formalisms, and the fact that commercial speech recognition systems are now available (from Nuance Communications and Microsoft) that accept CFGs as language models for constraining recognition.

These applications of context-free parsing share the common trait that the grammars involved can be expected to be very large. A "treebank grammar" extracted from the sections of the Penn Treebank commonly used for training stochastic parsers contains over 15,000 rules, and we also have a CFG containing over 24,000 rules, compiled from a task-specific unification grammar for

H. Bunt et al. (eds.), New Technologies in Parsing Technology, 185-201.

use as a speech-recognition language model. Grammars such as these stress established approaches to context-free parsing in ways and to an extent not encountered with smaller grammars.

In this work we develop an improved form of left-corner chart parsing for large context-free grammars. We introduce improvements that result in speed-ups averaging 38% or more compared to previously-known variants of left-corner parsing. We also compare our method to several other major parsing approaches: Cocke-Kasami-Younger (CKY), Earley/Graham-Harrison-Ruzzo (E/GHR), and generalized LR (GLR) parsing. Our improved left-corner parsing method outperforms each of these by an average of at least 50%. Finally, we also describe a new technique for minimizing the extra information needed to efficiently recover parses from the data structures built in the course of parsing.

2.   Evaluating Parsing Algorithms

In this work we are interested in algorithms for finding all possible parses for a given input. We measure the efficiency of the algorithms in building a complete chart (or comparable structure) for the input, where the chart includes information sufficient to recover every parse without additional searching.[1] We take CPU time to be the primary measure of performance. Implementation-independent measures, such as number of chart edges generated, are sometimes preferred in order to factor out the effects of different platforms and implementation methods, but only time measurement provides a practical way of evaluating some algorithmic details. For example, one of our major improvements to left-corner parsing simply transposes the order of performing two independent filtering checks, resulting in speed ups of up to 67%, while producing exactly the same chart edges as the previous method. To ensure comparability of time measurements, we have re-implemented all the algorithms considered, in Perl 5,[2] on as similar a basis as possible.

One caveat about this evaluation should be noted. None of the algorithms were implemented with general support for empty categories (i.e., nonterminals that can derive the empty string), due to the fact that none of the large, independently motivated grammars we had access to contained empty categories. We did, however make use of a grammar transformation (left factoring) that can produce empty categories, but only as the right-most daughter of a rule with at least two daughters. For the algorithms we wanted to test with this form of grammar, we added limited support for empty categories specifically in this position.

3. Terminology and Notation

Nonterminals, which we will sometimes refer to as categories, will be designated by "low order" upper-case letters (A, B, etc.); and terminals will be designated by lower-case letters. We will use the notation a_i to indicate the ith terminal symbol in the input string. We will use "high order" upper-case letters (X, Y, Z) to denote single symbols that could be either terminals or nonterminals, and Greek letters to denote (possibly empty) sequences of terminals and/or nonterminals. For a grammar rule $A \rightarrow B_1 \cdots B_n$ we will refer to A as the mother of the rule and to $B_1 \cdots B_n$ as the daughters of the rule. We will assume that there is a single nonterminal category S that subsumes all sentences allowed by the grammar.

All the algorithms considered here build a collection of data structures representing segments of the input partially or completely analyzed as a phrase of some category in the grammar, which we will refer to as a "chart". We will use the term "item" to mean an instance of a grammar rule with an indication of how many of the daughters have been recognized in the input. Items will be represented as dotted rules, such as $A \rightarrow B_1.B_2$. An "incomplete item" will be an item with at least one daughter to the right of the dot, indicating that at least one more daughter remains to be recognized before the entire rule is matched; and a "complete item" will be an item with no daughters to the right of the dot, indicating that the entire rule has been matched.

We will use the terms "incomplete edge" or "complete edge" to mean an incomplete item or complete item, plus two input positions indicating the segment of the input covered by the daughters that have already been recognized. These will be written as (e.g.) $\langle A \rightarrow B_1B_2.B_3, i, j \rangle$, which would mean that the sequence B_1B_2 has been recognized starting at position i and ending at position j, and has been hypothesized as part of a longer sequence ending in B_3, which is classified as a phrase of category A. Positions in the input will be numbered starting at 0, so the ith terminal of an input string spans position $i - 1$ to i. We will refer to items and edges none of whose daughters have yet been recognized as "initial".

4. Test Grammars

For testing context-free parsing algorithms, we have selected three CFGs that are independently motivated by analyses of natural-language corpora or actual applications of natural language processing. The CT grammar[3] was compiled into a CFG from a task-specific unification grammar written for CommandTalk (Moore et al., 1997), a spoken-language interface to a military simulation system. The ATIS grammar was extracted from an internally generated treebank of the DARPA ATIS3 training sentences. The PT grammar was extracted from the Penn Treebank.[4] We employ a standard test set for each of the three grammars. The test set for the CT grammar is a set of sentences made up by the system designers to test the functionality of the system, and the test set for the ATIS grammar is a randomly selected subset of the DARPA ATIS3 development test set. The test set for the PT grammar is a set of sentences randomly generated from a probabilistic version of the grammar, with the probabilities based on the frequency of the bracketings occuring in the training data, and then filtered for length to make it possible to conduct experiments in a reasonable amount of time, given the high degree of ambiguity of the grammar.

The terminals of the grammars are preterminal lexical categories rather than words. Preterminals were generated automatically, by grouping together all the words that could occur in exactly the same contexts in all grammar rules, to eliminate lexical ambiguity.

Table 9.1.   Grammars and test sets for parser evaluations

	CT Grammar	*ATIS Grammar*	*PT Grammar*
Rules	24,456	4,592	15,039
Nonterminals	3,946	192	38
Terminals	1,032	357	47
# Test Sentences	162	98	30
Average Length	8.3	11.4	5.7
# Grammatical	150	70	30
Average # Parses	5.4	940	7.2×10^{27}

Some statistics on the grammars and test sets are contained in Table 9.1. Note that for the CT and ATIS sets, not all sentences are within the corresponding grammars. The most striking difference among the three grammars is the degree of ambiguity. The CT grammar has relatively low ambiguity, the ATIS grammar may be considered highly ambiguous, and the PT grammar can only be called massively ambiguous.

5.   Left-Corner Parsing Algorithms and Refinements

Left-corner (LC) parsing – more specifically, left-corner parsing with top-down filtering – originated as a method for deterministically parsing a restricted class of CFGs. It is often attributed to Rosenkrantz and Lewis (1970), who may have first used the term "left-corner parsing" in print. Griffiths and Petrick (1965), however, previously described an LC parsing algorithm under the name "selective bottom-to-top" (SBT) parsing, which they assert to be an abstraction of previously described algorithms.

The origins of LC parsing for general CFGs (other than by naive backtracking) are even murkier. Pratt's (1975) algorithm is sometimes considered to be a generalized LC method, but it is perhaps better described as CKY parsing with top-down filtering added. Kay's (1980) method for undirected bottom-up chart parsing is clearly left-corner parsing without top-down filtering, but in adding top-down filtering to obtain directed bottom-up chart parsing, he changed the method significantly. The BUP parser of Matsumoto et al. (1983) appears to be the first clearly described LC parser capable of parsing general CFGs in polynomial time.[5]

LC parsing depends on the left-corner relation for the grammar, where X is recursively defined to be a left corner of A if $X = A$, or the grammar contains a rule of the form $B \rightarrow X\alpha$, where B is a left corner of A. This relation is normally precompiled and indexed so that any pair of symbols can be checked in essentially constant time.

Although LC parsing was originally defined as a stack-based method, implementing it in terms of a chart enables polynomial time complexity to be achieved by the use of dynamic programming; which simply means that if the same chart edge is derived in more than one way, only one copy is retained for further processing. A chart-based LC parsing algorithm can be defined by the following set of rules for populating the chart:

1 For every grammar rule with S as its mother, $S \rightarrow \alpha$, add $\langle S \rightarrow .\alpha, 0, 0 \rangle$ to the chart.

2 For every pair of edges of the form $\langle A \rightarrow \alpha.X\beta, i, k \rangle$ and $\langle X \rightarrow \gamma., k, j \rangle$ in the chart, add $\langle A \rightarrow \alpha X.\beta, i, j \rangle$ to the chart.

3 For every edge of the form $\langle A \rightarrow \alpha.a_j\beta, i, j - 1 \rangle$ in the chart, where a_j is the jth terminal in the input, add $\langle A \rightarrow \alpha a_j.\beta, i, j \rangle$ to the chart.

4 For every pair of edges of the form $\langle A \rightarrow \alpha.C\beta, i, k \rangle$ and $\langle X \rightarrow \gamma., k, j \rangle$ in the chart and every grammar rule with X as its left-most daughter, of the form $B \rightarrow X\delta$, if B is a left corner of C, add $\langle B \rightarrow X.\delta, k, j \rangle$ to the chart.

5 For every edge of the form $\langle A \rightarrow \alpha.C\beta, i, j - 1 \rangle$, and every grammar rule with a_j as its left-most daughter, of the form $B \rightarrow a_j\delta$, where a_j is the jth terminal in the input, if B is a left corner of C, add $\langle B \rightarrow a_j.\delta, j - 1, j \rangle$ to the chart.

An input string is successfully parsed as a sentence if the chart contains an edge of the form $\langle S \rightarrow \alpha., 0, n \rangle$ when the algorithm terminates.

Rules 1–3 are shared with other parsing algorithms, notably E/GHR, but rules 4 and 5 are distinctive to LC parsing. If naively implemented, however, they can lead to unnecessary duplication of work. Rules 4 and 5 state that for every triple consisting of an incomplete edge, a complete edge or input terminal, and a grammar rule, meeting certain conditions, a new edge should be added to the chart. Inspection reveals, however, that the form of the edge to be added depends on only the complete edge or input terminal and the grammar rule, not the incomplete edge. Thus if this parsing rule is applied separately for each triple, the same new edge may be proposed repeatedly if several incomplete edges combine with a given complete edge or input terminal and grammar rule to form triples satisfying the required conditions. A number of implementations of generalized LC parsing have suffered from this problem, including the BUP parser, the left-corner parser of the SRI Core Language Engine (Moore and Alshawi, 1991), and Schabes's (1991) table-driven predictive shift-reduce parser.

However, if parsing is performed strictly left-to-right, so that every incomplete edge ending at k has already been computed before any top-down left-corner checks are performed for new edges proposed from complete edges or input terminals starting at k, there is a solution that can be seen by rephrasing rules 4 and 5 follows:

4a For every edge of the form $\langle X \to \gamma., k, j \rangle$ in the chart and every grammar rule with X as its left-most daughter, of the form $B \to X\delta$, if there is an incomplete edge in the chart ending at k, $\langle A \to \alpha.C\beta, i, k \rangle$, such that B is a left corner of C, add $\langle B \to X.\delta, k, j \rangle$ to the chart.

5a For every input terminal a_j and every grammar rule with a_j as its left-most daughter, of the form $B \to a_j\delta$, if there is an incomplete edge in the chart ending at $j - 1$, $\langle A \to \alpha.C\beta, i, j - 1 \rangle$, such that B is a left corner of C, add $\langle B \to a_j.\delta, j - 1, j \rangle$ to the chart.

This formulation suggests driving the parser by proposing a new edge from every grammar rule exactly once for each complete edge or input terminal corresponding to the rule's left-most daughter, and then checking whether some previous incomplete edge licenses it via top-down filtering. If implemented by nested iteration, this still requires as many nested loops as the naive method; but the inner-most loop does much less work, and it can be aborted as soon as one previous incomplete edge has been found to satisfy the left-corner check. Wirén (1987) seems to have been the first to explicitly propose performing top-down filtering in an LC parser in this way. Nederhof (1993) proposes essentially the same solution, but formulated in terms of a graph-structured stack of the sort generally associated with GLR parsing.

Several additional optimizations can be added to this basic schema. Wirén adds bottom-up filtering (Wirén uses the term "selectivity", following Griffiths and Petrick, 1965) of incomplete edges based on the next terminal in the input. That is, no incomplete edge of the form $\langle A \to \alpha.X\beta, i, j \rangle$ is added to the chart unless a_{j+1} is a left corner of X. Nederhof proposes that, rather than iterate over all the incomplete edges ending at a given input position each time a left-corner check is performed, compute just once for each input position a set of nonterminal predictions, consisting of the symbols immediately to the right of the dot in the incomplete edges ending at that position, and iterate over that set for each left-corner check at the position.[6] With this optimization, it is no longer necessary to add initial edges to the chart at position 0 for rules of the form $S \rightarrow \alpha$. If P_i denotes the set of predictions for position i, we simply let $P_0 = \{S\}$.

Another optimization from the recent literature is due to Leermakers (1992), who observes that in Earley's algorithm the daughters to the *left* of the dot in an item play no role in the parsing algorithm; thus the representation of items can ignore the daughters to the left of the dot, resulting in fewer distinct edges to be considered. This observation is equally true for LC parsing. Thus, instead of $A \rightarrow B_1 B_2.B_3$, we will write simply $A \rightarrow .B_3$. Note that with this optimization, $A \rightarrow .$ becomes the notation for an item all of whose daughters have been recognized; the only information it contains being just the mother of the rule. We will therefore write complete edges simply as $\langle A, i, j \rangle$, rather than $\langle A \rightarrow ., i, j \rangle$. We can also unify the treatment of terminal symbols in the input with complete edges in the chart by adding a complete edge $\langle a_i, i - 1, i \rangle$ to the chart for every input terminal a_i.[7]

Taking all these optimizations together, we can define an optimized LC parsing algorithm by the following set of parsing rules:

1 Let $P_0 = \{S\}$.

2 For every input position $j > 0$, let $P_j = \{B \mid$ there is an incomplete edge in the chart ending at j, of the form $\langle A \rightarrow .B\alpha, i, j \rangle\}$.

3 For every input terminal a_i, add $\langle a_i, i - 1, i \rangle$ to the chart.

4 For every pair of edges $\langle A \rightarrow .XY\alpha, i, k \rangle$ and $\langle X, k, j \rangle$ in the chart, if a_{j+1} is a left corner of Y, add $\langle A \rightarrow .Y\alpha, i, j \rangle$ to the chart.

5 For every pair of edges $\langle A \rightarrow .X, i, k \rangle$ and $\langle X, k, j \rangle$ in the chart, add $\langle A, i, j \rangle$ to the chart.

6 For every edge $\langle X, k, j \rangle$ in the chart and every grammar rule with X as its left-most daughter, of the form $A \rightarrow XY\alpha$, if there is a $B \in P_k$ such that A is a left corner of B, and a_{j+1} is a left corner of Y, add $\langle A \rightarrow .Y\alpha, k, j \rangle$ to the chart.

7 For every edge $\langle X, k, j \rangle$ in the chart and every grammar rule with X as its only daughter, of the form $A \rightarrow X$, if there is a $B \in P_k$ such that A is a left corner of B, add $\langle A, k, j \rangle$ to the chart.

Note that in Rule 6, the top-down left-corner check on the mother of the proposed incomplete edge and the bottom-up left-corner check on the symbol immediately to the right of the dot in the proposed incomplete edge are independent of each other, and therefore could be performed in either order. Wirén, the only author we have found who includes both, is vague on the ordering of these checks. For each proposed edge, however, the top-down check requires examining an entry in the left-corner table for each of the elements of the prediction list, until a check succeeds or the list is exhausted; while the bottom-up check requires examining only a single entry in the left-corner table for the next terminal of the input. It therefore seems likely to be more efficient to do the bottom-up check before the top-down check, since the top-down check need not be performed if the bottom-up check fails. To test this hypothesis, we have done two implementations of the algorithm: LC_1, which performs the top-down check first, and LC_2, which performs the bottom-up check first.

Shann (1991) uses a different method of top-down filtering in an LC parser. Shann expands the list of predictions created by rules 1 and 2 to include all the left-corners of the predictions. He does this by precomputing the proper left corners of all nonterminal categories and adding to the list of predictions all the left-corners of the original members of the list. Then top-down filtering consists of simply checking whether the mother of a proposed incomplete edge is on the corresponding prediction list. Graham, Harrison, and Ruzzo (1980) attribute this type of top-down filtering to Cocke and Schwartz, so we will refer to it as "Cocke-Schwartz filtering". Since our original form of filtering uses the left-corner relation directly, we will call it "left-corner filtering".

We have implemented Cocke-Schwartz filtering as described by Shann, except that for efficiency in both forming and checking the sets of predictions, we use hash tables rather than lists. The resulting algorithm, which we will call LC_3, can be stated as follows:

1 Let $P_0 = \{$all left corners of $S\}$.[8]

2 For every input position $j > 0$, let $P_j = \{$all left corners of $B \mid$ there is an incomplete edge in the chart ending at j, of the form $\langle A \rightarrow .B\alpha, i, j\rangle\}$.

3 For every input terminal a_i, add $\langle a_i, i - 1, i\rangle$ to the chart.

4 For every pair of edges $\langle A \rightarrow .XY\alpha, i, k\rangle$ and $\langle X, k, j\rangle$ in the chart, if a_{j+1} is a left corner of Y, add $\langle A \rightarrow .Y\alpha, i, j\rangle$ to the chart.

5 For every pair of edges $\langle A \rightarrow .X, i, k\rangle$ and $\langle X, k, j\rangle$ in the chart, add $\langle A, i, j\rangle$ to the chart.

6 For every edge $\langle X, k, j\rangle$ in the chart and every grammar rule with X as its left-most daughter, of the form $A \rightarrow XY\alpha$, if $A \in P_k$, and a_{j+1} is a left corner of Y, add $\langle A \rightarrow .Y\alpha, k, j\rangle$ to the chart.

7 For every edge $\langle X, k, j \rangle$ in the chart and every grammar rule with X as its only daughter, of the form $A \to X$, if $A \in P_k$, add $\langle A, k, j \rangle$ to the chart.

There is one simple refinement, not mentioned by Shann, that we can add to this algorithm. Since we already have the information needed to perform bottom-up filtering, we can apply bottom-up filtering to building the prediction sets, omitting any left-corner of an existing prediction that is incompatible with the next terminal of the input. This will certainly save space, and may save time as well, depending on the relative costs of adding a nonterminal to the prediction set compared to performing the bottom-up left-corner check. Our modification of LC parsing with Cocke-Schwartz filtering to include this refinement is implemented as LC_4.

Table 9.2. LC parsing algorithm performance comparisons

	CT Grammar	ATIS Grammar	PT Grammar
LC_1	4.3	15.6	45.0
LC_2	3.4	11.9	43.0
LC_3	3.1	11.6	41.8
LC_4	2.7	11.8	42.3

The results of running algorithms LC_1–LC_4 appear in Table 9.2. The numbers are CPU time in seconds required by the parser to completely process the standard test set associated with each grammar.[9] LC_2, which performs the bottom-up left-corner check on proposed incomplete edges before top-down left-corner check, is faster on all three grammars than LC_1, which performs the checks in the reverse order – substantially so on the CT and ATIS grammars. Comparing LC_3 with LC_4 – which both use Cocke-Schwartz filtering, but differ as to whether the prediction sets are bottom-up filtered – the results are less clear. LC_4, which does filter the predictions, is noticably faster on the CT grammar, while LC_3 which does not filter predictions is slightly faster, but not significanly so, on the ATIS grammar and PT grammar. Finally, both parsers that use Cocke-Schwartz filtering are faster on all grammars than either of the parsers that use left-corner filtering.

6.   Grammar Transformations

One other issue remains to be addressed in our examination of LC parsing. It is a common observation about left-to-right parsing, that if two grammar rules share a common left prefix, e.g., $A \to BC$ and $A \to BD$, many parsing algorithms will duplicate work for the two rules until reaching the point where they differ. A simple solution often proposed to address the problem is to "left factor" the grammar. Left factoring applies the following grammar transformation repeatedly, until it is no longer applicable:

> For each nonterminal A, let α be a maximal nonempty sequence such that there is more than one grammar rule of the form $A \rightarrow \alpha\beta$. Replace the set of rules $A \rightarrow \alpha\beta_1, \cdots, A \rightarrow \alpha\beta_n$ with $A \rightarrow \alpha A', A' \rightarrow \beta_1, \cdots, A' \rightarrow \beta_n$, where A' is a new nonterminal symbol.

Left factoring has been explored in the context of generalized LC parsing by Nederhof (1994), who refers to LC parsing with left factoring as PLR parsing. Shann (1991) also applies left factoring directly in the representation of the rules he uses in his LC parser, e.g. $A \rightarrow B(C, D)$.

One complication associated with left factoring is that if the daughters of one rule are a proper prefix of the daughters of another rule, then empty categories will be introduced into the grammar, even if there were none originally. For example $A \rightarrow BC$ and $A \rightarrow BCD$ will be replaced by $A \rightarrow BCA', A' \rightarrow D, A' \rightarrow \epsilon$. To explore the cost of this additional complication we compare full left factoring with the following restricted form of left factoring;

> For each nonterminal A, let α be a maximal nonempty sequence such that there is more than one grammar rule of the form $A \rightarrow \alpha\beta$, for some nonempty string β. Replace the set of rules $A \rightarrow \alpha\beta_1, \cdots, A \rightarrow \alpha\beta_n$ with $A \rightarrow \alpha A', A' \rightarrow \beta_1, \cdots, A' \rightarrow \beta_n$, where A' is a new nonterminal symbol.

The requirement that β always be nonempty blocks the introduction of empty categories, so with this transformation $A \rightarrow BC$ and $A \rightarrow BCD$ will be replaced by $A \rightarrow BA', A' \rightarrow CD, A' \rightarrow C$.

Left factoring is not the only transformation that can be used to address the problem of common rule prefixes. Left factoring applies only to sets of rules with a common mother category, but as an essentially bottom-up method, generalized LC parsing does most of its work before the mother of a sequence of daughters is completely determined. There is another grammar transformation that seems better suited to LC parsing, introduced by Griffiths and Petrick (1965), but apparently neglected since:

> Let α be a maximal sequence of two or more symbols such that there is more than one grammar rule of the form $A \rightarrow \alpha\beta$. Replace the set of rules $A_1 \rightarrow \alpha\beta_1, \cdots, A_n \rightarrow \alpha\beta_n$ with $A' \rightarrow \alpha, A_1 \rightarrow A'\beta_1, \cdots, A_n \rightarrow A'\beta_n$, where A' is a new nonterminal symbol.

Like left factoring, this transformation is repeated until it is no longer applicable. Griffiths and Petrick do not give this transformation a name, so we will call it "bottom-up prefix merging".

It should be noted that all of these grammar transformations simply add additional levels of nonterminals to the grammar, without otherwise disturbing the structure of the analyses produced by the grammar. Thus, when parsing with a grammar produced by one of these transformations, the original analyses can be recovered simply by ignoring the newly introduced nonterminals, and treating their subconstituents as subconstituents of the next higher original nonterminal of the grammar.

Before we apply our LC parsers to our test grammars transformed in these three ways, we make a few small adjustments to the implementations. First, as noted above, full left factoring requires the ability to handle empty categories, at least as the right-most daughter of a rule. We have created modified versions of LC_1–LC_4 specifically to use with the fully left-factored grammar. Second we note that with a left-factored grammar,[10] the non-unary rules have the property that, given the mother and the left-most daughter, there is only one possibility for the rest of the rule. With a bottom-up prefix-merged grammar, the non-unary rules have the property that, given the two left-most daughters, there is only one possibility for the rest of the rule. We take advantage of these facts to store the indexed forms of the rules more compactly and simplify the logic of the implementations of variants of our parsers specialized to these grammar forms.

Table 9.3. LC parsing grammar transformation performance comparisons.

		CT Grammar	*ATIS Grammar*	*PT Grammar*
LC_1	UTF	4.3	15.6	45.0
LC_1	FLF	7.4	63.5	timed out
LC_1	PLF	6.2	66.2	timed out
LC_1	BUPM	3.6	11.7	34.1
LC_2	UTF	3.4	11.9	43.0
LC_2	FLF	5.1	38.2	timed out
LC_2	PLF	4.2	37.7	timed out
LC_2	BUPM	3.1	7.0	27.0
LC_3	UTF	3.1	11.6	41.8
LC_3	FLF	4.2	12.3	45.4
LC_3	PLF	3.8	12.1	43.6
LC_3	BUPM	5.0	17.1	64.6
LC_4	UTF	2.7	11.8	42.3
LC_4	FLF	3.6	11.9	46.6
LC_4	PLF	3.2	11.7	44.4
LC_4	BUPM	3.2	14.7	63.6

The results of applying our four LC parsing algorithms with these three grammar transformations are displayed in Table 9.3, along with results for the untransformed grammars presented previously. The grammar transformations are designated by the symbols UTF (untransformed), FLF (fully left-factored), PLF (partially left-factored), and BUPM (bottom-up prefix-merged). We set a time-out of 10 minutes on some experiments, since that was already an order of magnitude longer than any of the other parse times. Several observations stand out from these results. First, in every case but one, partial left factoring out-performed full left factoring. Much more surprising is that, in every case but one, either form of left factoring degraded parsing performance relative to the untransformed grammar. For LC_1 and LC_2, the algorithms that use left-corner filtering, the degradation is dramatic, while for LC_3 and LC_4, which use Cocke-Schwartz filtering, the degradation is very slight in the case of the ATIS and PT grammars, but more pronounced in the case of the CT grammar. On the other hand, bottom-up prefix merging significantly – in some cases dramatically – speeds up parsing for LC_1 and LC_2, while significantly degrading the performance of LC_3 and LC_4.

Looking at the overall results of these experiments, we see that bottom-up prefix merging reverses the previous advantage of Cocke-Schwartz filtering over left-corner filtering. With bottom-up prefix merging, LC_2 is at least 66% faster on the ATIS grammar and 55% faster on the PT grammar than either LC_3 or LC_4; and it is only 15% slower than LC_4 on the CT grammar, and the same speed as LC_3. Averaging over the three test grammars, LC_2 is 40% faster than LC_3 and 38% faster than LC_4.

7.   Extracting Parses from the Chart

The Leermakers optimization of omitting recognized daughters from items raises the question of how parses are to be extracted from the chart. The daughters to the left of the dot in an item are often used for this purpose in item-based methods, including Earley's original algorithm. Graham, Harrison, and Ruzzo (1980), however, suggest storing with each noninitial edge in the chart a list that includes, for each derivation of the edge, a pair of pointers to the preceding edges that caused it to be derived. This provides sufficient information to extract the parses without additional searching, even without the daughters to the left of the dot.

In fact, we can do even better than this. For each derivation of a noninitial edge, even in the Leermakers representation, it is sufficient to attach to the edge only the mother category and starting position of the complete edge that was used in the last step of the derivation. Every noninitial edge is derived by combining a complete edge with an incomplete edge or a grammar rule. Suppose $\langle A \rightarrow .\beta, k, j \rangle$ is a derived edge, and we know that the complete edge used in the derivation had category X and start position i. We then know that the complete edge must have been $\langle X, i, j \rangle$, since the complete edge and the derived edge must have the same end position. We further know that the incomplete edge (or grammar rule) used in the derivation must have been $\langle A \rightarrow .X\beta, k, i \rangle$, since that is the only item that could have combined with the complete edge to produce the derived edge. In this way, for any complete edge, we can trace back through the chart until we have found all the complete edges for the daughters that derived it. The back-trace terminates when we reach a derived edge that has the same start point as the complete edge it was derived from.

8. Comparison to Other Algorithms

We have compared our LC parsers to efficient implementations of three other important approaches to context-free parsing: Cocke-Kasami-Younger (CKY), Earley/Graham-Harrison-Ruzzo (E/GHR), and generalized LR (GLR) parsing. We include CKY, not because we think it may be the fastest parsing algorithm, but because it provides a baseline of how well one can do with no top-down filtering. Our implementation of E/GHR includes many optimizations not found in the original descriptions of this approach, including the techniques used to optimize our LC parsers, where applicable. In our GLR parser we used the same reduction method as Tomita's (1985) original parser, which results in greater-than-cubic worst-case time complexity, after verifying that a cubic-time version was, in fact, slower in practice, as Tomita has asserted.

Table 9.4. Alternative parsing algorithm performance comparisons.

	CT Grammar	*ATIS Grammar*	*PT Grammar*
LC$_2$+BUPM	3.1	7.0	27.0
CKY	25.0	7.7	50.9
E/GHR	7.3	8.6	27.7
GLR(0)	3.2	14.0	timed out
LC+follow	2.4	6.6	29.6
GLR(0)+follow	2.3	14.1	timed out
GLALR(1)	3.8	14.7	—

Table 9.4 shows the comparison between these three algorithms, and our best overall LC algorithm. As the table shows, LC$_2$+BUPM outperforms all of the other algorithms with all three grammars. While each of the other algorithms approaches our LC parser in at least one of the tests, the LC parser outperforms each of the others by at least a factor of 2 with at least one of the grammars.

The comparison between LC$_2$+BUPM and GLR is instructive in view of the claims that have been made for GLR. While GLR(0) was essentially equal in performance to LC$_2$+BUPM on the least ambiguous grammar, it appears to scale very badly with increasing ambiguity. Moreover, the parsing tables required by the GLR parser are far larger than for LC$_2$+BUPM. For the CT grammar, LC$_2$+BUPM requires 27,783 rules in the transformed grammar, plus

210,701 entries in the left-corner table. For the (original) CT grammar, GLR requires 1,455,918 entries in the LR(0) parsing tables.

The second part of Table 9.4 shows comparisons of LC_2+BUPM and two versions of GLR with look ahead. The "LC+follow" line is for LC_2+BUPM plus an additional filter on complete edges using a "follow check" equivalent to the look ahead used by SLR(1) parsing. The "GLR(0)+follow" line adds the same follow check to the GLR(0) parser. This builds exactly the same edges as a GSLR(1) parser would, but allows smaller parsing tables at the expense of more table look ups.[11] With the follow check, the parse times for the CT grammar are substantially reduced, but LC_2+BUPM and GLR remain essentially equivalent, while only small changes are produced for the ATIS and PT grammars.

The final line gives results for GLALR(1) parsing with the CT and ATIS grammars.[12] These results are not directly comparable to the others because the LALR(1) reduce tables for the CT and ATIS grammars contained more than 6.1 million and 1.8 million entries, respectively, and they would not fit in the memory of the test machine along with the other LR tables. Various methods were investigated to obtain timing results by loading only a subset of the reduce tables sufficient to handle the test set. These gave inconsistent results, but in all cases times were longer than for either GLR(0) or GLR(0)+follow, presumably due to additional overhead caused by the large tables, with relatively little additional filtering (5–6% fewer edges). The numbers in the table represent the best results obtained for each grammar.

Table 9.5.   Results with longer sentences.

	CT Grammar	ATIS Grammar
LC_2+BUPM	1.8	11.7
CKY	15.4	13.7
E/GHR	3.2	12.1
GLR(0)	1.8	17.8
LC+follow	1.4	10.9
GLR(0)+follow	1.3	18.1

A final set of experiments was performed to address possible concerns that the test sentences in our other experiments were too short, and that our results would not generalize to longer sentences. We selected two modified test sets of CT and ATIS sentences. The CT sentences were the 50 longest sentences covered by our CT grammar in the original CT test set, with an average length of 13.5 words, and an average number of parses of 4.2. The ATIS sentences were the 50 longest sentences covered by our ATIS grammar in the DARPA

ATIS3 development test set, with an average length of 20.5 words, and an average number of parses of 4516. The results for the principal methods compared in our original cross-algorithm experiments are given in Table 9.5. When compared to the results in Table 9.4, the relative performance of the algorithms remains virtually unchanged.

9.   Conclusions

Probably the two most significant results of this investigation are the discoveries that:

- LC chart parsing incorporating both a top-down left-corner check on the mother of a proposed incomplete edge and a bottom-up left-corner check on the symbol immediately to the right of the dot in the proposed incomplete edge is substantially faster if the bottom-up check is performed before the top-down check.

- Bottom-up prefix merging is a particularly good match to LC chart parsing based on left-corner filtering, and in fact substantially outperforms left factoring combined with LC chart parsing in most circumstances.

Moreover we have shown that with these enhancements, LC parsing outperforms several other major approaches to context-free parsing, including some previously claimed to be the best general context-free parsing method. We conclude that our improved form of LC parsing may now be the leading contender for that title.

Notes

1. Formally, we require that for any m up to the total number of parses of the input, we can extract from the chart m parses of a string of length n in time proportional to $m \cdot n$.

2. We take advantage of Perl 5's ability to arbitrarily nest hash tables and linked lists to produce efficient implementations of the data structures required by the algorithms. In particular, the multi-dimensional arrays required by many of the algorithms are given a sparse-matrix implementation in terms of multiply-nested Perl hash tables.

3. Courtesy of John Dowding, SRI International.

4. Courtesy of Eugene Charniak, Brown University.

5. Cyclic grammars and empty categories were not supported, however.

6. Nederhof proposes several other optimizations, which we evaluated and found not to repay their overhead.

7. Many chart parsers unify the treatment of input terminals and complete edges in this way, by ignoring daughters to the left of the dot, but only for complete edges. The Leermakers optimization permits a unified treatment of incomplete edges, complete edges, and input terminals.

8. Recall that by our definition, the left-corner relation is reflexive so S will be included.

9. All timings in this report are for execution on a Dell 610 workstation with Pentium III Xeon 550 MHz processors running Windows 2000.

10. Either fully left-factored, or partially left-factored using our restricted transformation.

11. A GSLR(1) reduce table is just the composition of a GLR(0) reduce table and a follow-check table.

12. No experiments were done for the PT grammar due to the excessively long time required to compute LALR(1) parsing tables for that grammar, given the expectation that the parser would still time out.

References

Graham, S.L., M.A. Harrison, and W.L. Ruzzo (1980) An Improved Context-Free Recognizer, *ACM Transactions on Programming Languages and Systems*, Vol. 2, No. 3, pages 415–462.

Griffiths, T.V., and S.R. Petrick (1965) On the Relative Efficiencies of Context-Free Grammar Recognizers, *Communications of the ACM*, Vol. 8, No. 5, pages 289–300.

Kay, M. (1980) Algorithm Schemata and Data Structures in Syntactic Processing, Report CSL–80–12, Xerox PARC, Palo Alto, California. Also in: B.J. Gross, K. Sparck Jones and B.L. Webber, editors, *Natural Language Processing*, pages 35-70, Kaufmann, Los Altos, CA., 1986.

Leermakers, R. (1992) A Recursive Ascent Earley Parser, *Information Processing Letters*, Vol. 41, No. 2, pages 87–91.

Matsumoto, Y., et al. (1983) BUP: A Bottom-Up Parser Embedded in Prolog, *New Generation Computing*, Vol. 1, pages 145–158.

Moore, R., et al. (1997) CommandTalk: A Spoken-Language Interface for Battlefield Simulations, in *Proceedings of the Fifth Conference on Applied Natural Language Processing*, Association for Computational Linguistics, Washington, DC, pages 1–7.

Moore, R., and H. Alshawi (1991) Syntactic and Semantic Processing, in *The Core Language Engine*, H. Alshawi (ed.), The MIT Press, Cambridge, Massachusetts, pages 129–148.

Nederhof, M.J. (1993) Generalized Left-Corner Parsing, in *Proceedings of the Sixth Conference of the European Chapter of the Association for Computational Linguistics*, Utrecht, The Netherlands, pages 305–314.

Nederhof, M.J. (1994) An Optimal Tabular Parsing Algorithm, in *Proceedings of the 32nd Annual Meeting of the Association for Computational Linguistics*, Las Cruces, New Mexico, pages 117–124.

Pratt, V.R. (1975) LINGOL – A Progress Report, in *Advance Papers of the Fourth International Joint Conference on Artificial Intelligence*, Tbilisi, Georgia, USSR, pages 422–428.

Rosenkrantz, D.J., and P.M. Lewis (1970) Deterministic Left Corner Parsing, in *IEEE Conference Record of the 11th Annual Symposium on Switching and Automata Theory*, pages 139–152.

Shann, P. (1991) Experiments with GLR and Chart Parsing, in *Generalized LR Parsing*, M. Tomita (ed.), Kluwer Academic Publishers, Boston, Massachusetts, pages 17–34.

Schabes, Y. (1991) Polynomial Time and Space Shift-Reduce Parsing of Arbitrary Context-free Grammars, in *Proceedings of the 29th Annual Meeting of the Association for Computational Linguistics*, Berkeley, California, pages 106–113.

Tomita, M. (1985) *Efficient Parsing for Natural Language*, Kluwer Academic Publishers, Boston, Massachusetts.

Wirén, M. (1987) A Comparison of Rule-Invocation Strategies in Context-Free Chart Parsing, in *Proceedings of the Third Conference of the European Chapter of the Association for Computational Linguistics*, Copenhagen, Denmark, pages 226–233.

Chapter 10

ON TWO CLASSES OF FEATURE PATHS IN LARGE-SCALE UNIFICATION GRAMMARS

Liviu Ciortuz

Computer Science Department, University of York

York Yo10 5DD, UK

ciortuz@cs.york.ac.uk

Abstract   We investigate two related techniques, Quick Check and Generalised Reduction, that contribute significantly to speeding up parsing with large-scale typed-unification grammars. The techniques take advantage of the properties of two particular classes of feature paths. Quick check is concerned with paths that most often lead to unification failure, whereas generalised reduction takes advantage of paths that do not (or only seldom) contribute to unification failure. Both sets of paths are obtained empirically by parsing a training corpus. We experiment with the two techniques, using a compilation-based parsing system on a large-scale grammar of English. The combined improvement in parsing speed we obtained is 56%.

1.   Introduction

Interest in unification grammars in Natural Language Processing can be traced back to the seminal work on the PATR-II system (Shieber et al., 1983). Since then, a number of different unification-based grammar formalisms have been developed in the computational linguistics community: for example Lexical Functional Grammar (LFG; Kaplan and Bresnan, 1983), Head-driven Phrase Structure Grammar (HPSG; Pollard and Sag, 1994), and Categorial Unification Grammar (Uszkoreit, 1986). In the past few years, a number of wide-coverage unification grammars have been implemented: the HPSG of English developed by the LinGO project at Stanford (Flickinger et al., 2000), two HPSGs of Japanese developed at Tokyo University and at DFKI, Saarbrücken, Germany (Mitsuishi et al., 1998; Siegel, 2000), and an HPSG for German also

H. Bunt et al. (eds.), New Technologies in Parsing Technology, 203-228.

developed at DFKI (Müller, 1999). Large-scale LFG grammars have been developed in a consortium led by Xerox Corporation, but these are not publicly available.

Feature structure (FS) unification is by far the most time-consuming task during parsing with large-scale typed-unification grammars. Therefore making it more efficient is of great interest. Several solutions for speeding up FS unification have been proposed, for instance FS sharing (Pereira, 1985; Tomabechi, 1992), FS unfilling (Gerdemann, 1995), FS restriction (Kiefer et al., 1999) and the quick check pre-unification filter (Malouf et al., 2000). Grammar compilation is another approach to speeding up FS unification (Aït-Kaci and Di Cosmo, 1993; Wintner and Francez, 1999; Ciortuz, 2001a).

The *quick check* (QC) pre-unification filter, one of the most effective speed-up techniques for FS unification, is conceptually very simple. It considers the set of feature paths most likely to lead to unification failure, and then compares the corresponding values of these paths inside two FSs to be unified. If any such pair of values is incompatible, then it must be the case that the two FSs do not unify. The quick check filter reduces FS unification time by a significant amount on all large-scale grammars on which it has been tested (Callmeier, 2000; Oepen and Callmeier, 2000). On the LinGO wide-coverage HPSG of English, the QC filter speeds up parsing by around 63% for the PET system (Callmeier, 2000), and 42% for the LIGHT compiler (Ciortuz, 2002b).[1]

The effectiveness of the QC pre-unification technique is based on the fact that the proportion of failure paths inside rule FSs is relatively small. Using the LIGHT system, we identified 148 failure paths in LinGO on the CSLI test suite (Oepen and Carroll, 2000), out of a total of 494 rule FS paths. Among these paths, only a small number is responsible for most of the unification failures: for the LinGO grammar, in the LIGHT system, we used a maximum of 43 QC-paths. The quick check filter must be compiled in a setup where rule argument FS creation is avoided through a Specialised Rule Compilation scheme like the one developed in the LIGHT system (Ciortuz, 2001a). Recently, a version of quick check on dynamically determined QC-paths was proposed by Ninomiya et al. (2002), for use in information retrieval and database query answering.

In contrast to the quick check, the *generalised reduction* (GR) technique works on paths inside rule FSs, eliminating those that that do not contribute (or only seldom contribute) to unification failure. We refer to the set of paths retained by the GR technique as *GR-paths*. We present an efficient algorithm for generalised reduction of rule FSs in large-scale typed-unification grammars. Measurements done on the LinGO grammar and CSLI test suite show that almost 60% of the feature constraints in the expanded rule FSs can be eliminated without affecting the parsing results. As a consequence, the LIGHT system registered a reduction in unification time that sped parsing up to 22%. It turns out that most QC-paths are also GR-paths – the few exceptions are extensions of maximal GR-paths – so the quick check and the generalised reduction techniques are orthogonal: they can be applied at the same time leading to significant improvements in parsing speed.

The fact that – despite their declarative/logic un-differentiated status – feature constraints inside rule FSs can be preferentially treated in order to speed up parsing was the subject of some early work on unification-based grammars. In the context of bottom-up parsing, Shieber (1985) selected certain features for enabling top-down (predictive) operations. Nagata (1992) studied empirically the effect of interleaving parsing with two versions of FS unification: early unification and late unification. Maxwell and Kaplan (1993) report experiments in which a small LFG grammar was tuned by changing the status of certain constraints (from 'functional' into 'phrasal') and compared the effect these changes had on parsing performance.

Generalised reduction performs feature constraint selection in an automatic way, based on a learning procedure using as parameter the parsing result. Unlike Nagata (1992) and Maxwell and Kaplan (1993), our strategy for feature constraint selection does not propose new rules. It simply proposes for each rule a new FS version to be used in early unification. The active bottom-up chart-based parsing strategy in LIGHT, when using (early unification on) the GR-restricted form of rules, is extended with a consistency-check phase, which is performed by either type-checking or late unification. In this way, a parsing algorithm which may slightly over-generate when using early unification may in the end perform better than one which does not differentiate between classes of feature constraints/paths. This fact, which is true for LinGO, is similar to the effect noted by Maxwell and Kaplan (1993) following experiments with a small LFG grammar: with that grammar, a parser which does not prune may behave better than one that prunes.

Although the quick check and generalised reduction were developed independently, they complement each other in the sense that both are concerned with classes of feature paths that warrant specialised processing in large-scale typed-unification grammars. We first concentrate on the two techniques separately: Section 2 describes compilation of the quick check, and Section 3 describes generalised reduction of rule feature structures. We use as our experimental setup the LIGHT compiler and the LinGO English grammar. We bring the two strands of work together at the end of Section 3 and in the Conclusions.

2.   Compiling the Quick Check Filter

This section describes how to obtain a compiled form of the QC filter, such that it can be elegantly and efficiently combined with compilers for unification-based grammars. In Section 2.1 we outline the problems we encountered when trying to accommodate the simple (interpreted-like) QC filter into the LIGHT compiler setup, in particular its co-existence with another optimisation technique, the specialised compiled form of rules (Ciortuz, 2001a). Section 2.2 describes the compiled, pre-computed form of the QC-vectors, and Section 2.3 details the computation of their run-time, completed form. Section 2.4 reports measurements for running the LIGHT system with the LinGO grammar on the CSLI test suite, both with and without QC filtering, and makes suggestions for further improvements.

The main idea behind the pre-unification QC test is the following: having acquired the knowledge about the most probable failure paths $\pi_1, \pi_2, ..., \pi_n$ in the application of parsing rules, before doing the unification of a certain feature structure ψ_1 (representing a phrase) with another feature structure ψ_2 (representing a syntactic rule argument), one can check for every path π_i whether its values in ψ_1 and respectively ψ_2 are compatible, i.e., $root(\psi_1.\pi_i) \wedge root(\psi_2.\pi_i)$ $\neq \perp$. (The function *root* designates the root sort of its argument FS, $\psi.\pi$ is the usual notation for the sub-structure identified inside ψ by the feature path π, and $\perp$ is the bottom/inconsistent sort in the grammar's sort hierarchy.) The sort hierarchy is assumed to be an inferior semi-lattice, with $s \wedge t$ designating the unique greatest lower bound (glb) of the sorts s and t. If the sort compatibility test is not passed for a path π, then it follows immediately that the feature structures ψ_1 and ψ_2 do not unify. This simple technique eliminates much of the unnecessary work performed during unification in case of unification failure.

Introducing the QC technique in the compilation approach as used in the LIGHT system was not immediately effective. Even at first sight, one can see that the QC filter might not be so effective in the compilation approach, since compiled unification is significantly faster than interpreted unification. Of course, performing the QC has a cost. Measurements made on the LKB, TDL/PAGE (Krieger and Schäfer, 1994), and PET systems revealed that with interpreted parsing with LinGO-like grammars it is worthwhile paying for the QC test, since most unifications fail even after the rules' combinatorial filter was applied. But in the case of compiled parsing, the trade-off to be made between the time required by the QC test (expressed as a function of the number of failure paths to be checked) on the one hand, and the speed of the unification procedure on the other hand is dramatically narrowed. A compiled form of the QC filter as will be presented here is proven able to 'enlarge' again this trade-off area to speed up parsing.

Basically, we show how QC-vectors $\{root(\psi.\pi_1), root(\psi.\pi_2), ..., root(\psi.\pi_n)\}$ can be computed in two stages. The first stage (QC pre-computation) is done once for all at compilation time, and is completed at run-time by the second-stage computation, according to specific circumstances. The basis for this two-stage computation of QC-vectors resides in the facts that (a) the order in which one rule's arguments will be processed is known at grammar preprocessing/compilation time, and (b) for any (in general not known in advance) feature structure ψ which will be involved in the QC test, we know that ψ will be an instance of (i.e., subsumed by) a certain feature structure Ψ fully known at compilation time ($\psi \sqsubseteq \Psi$). Formally, for any QC feature-path π, the $QC_\pi(\psi)$ = $root(\psi.\pi)$ value will be computed by applying at run-time a function ρ to a certain argument $preComp(\Psi, \pi)$, computed at compilation time:

$$QC_\pi(\psi) = \rho(preComp(\Psi, \pi)).$$

2.1   Integrating Interpreted QC with Compiled Parsing

We first analyse the way the QC was conceived in the interpreted setup of the LKB and PAGE systems for parsing with HPSG-like grammars:

- As soon as a phrase is parsed, a 'passive' QC-*vector* is computed for its associated feature structure ψ. This QC-vector is defined as $\{root(\psi.\pi_1), root(\psi.\pi_2), ..., root(\psi.\pi_n)\}$. If one of the paths π_i is not defined for ψ, then the i-th component in the computed QC-vector is taken as $\top$, the top element in the grammar's sort hierarchy.

- Every m-ary rule is associated with m 'active' QC-vectors; in the case of a binary rule φ, we have first a 'key' QC-vector $\{root(\varphi'.\pi_1), root(\varphi'.\pi_2), ..., root(\varphi'.\pi_n)\}$, where $\varphi' = \varphi$.KEY-ARG, namely the sub-structure corresponding to the key/head argument in the FS representing the rule.

- Before trying to apply the rule φ to a candidate key argument ψ (i.e., before unifying ψ with φ'), the QC pre-unification test computes the conjunction of the corresponding components of the two QC-vectors, $root(\psi.\pi_i) \wedge root(\varphi'.\pi_i)$ for $i = \overline{1, n}$. If every result is consistent (i.e., not $\perp$), the system unifies ψ with φ', and if this unification succeeds, then the system produces a new, 'active' QC-vector, corresponding to the next argument to be parsed. If the current rule is a binary one, this new active QC-vector is what we call the 'complete' QC-vector, corresponding to $\varphi'' = \phi$.NON-KEY-ARG: $\{root(\varphi''.\pi_1), root(\varphi''.\pi_2), ..., root(\varphi''.\pi_n)\}$, where ϕ is what φ has become after $\varphi' = \varphi$.KEY-ARG has been unified with ψ.

As mentioned above, the main problem that arose when we tried to integrate the QC pre-unification test with the **LIGHT** compiler was its integration with the previously included main optimisation: specialised compilation of rules. While the 'key' QC-vector φ' can be completely computed at grammar compilation/loading time, computing the QC-vector for $\varphi'' = \phi$.NON-KEY-ARG is not immediately possible simply because the ϕ.NON-KEY-ARG structure does not effectively exist on the heap. This happens because in the

LIGHT system grammar rules are represented as feature structures, and their application is done in a bottom-up manner. In order to eliminate unnecessary copying, when dealing with LinGO-like grammars (working with only binary and unary rules), we have specialised each rule's execution into (i) key/head-corner mode application, and (ii) complete mode application. This distinction between two different modes for one (binary) rule application – together with the FS environment-based sharing facility – allows for an incremental construction of the feature structure representing a phrase, in such a way that, if completion is ultimately impossible, then no space (otherwise needed in an interpreter framework) for constructing the FS corresponding to the rule's non-key argument is wasted. This strategy of incremental parsing in LIGHT is simple and elegant, due to the use of open FSs as in the OSF constraint theory (Aït-Kaci and Podelski, 1993), in contrast with closed records used in the appropriateness-based approach (Carpenter, 1992) underlying other recent HPSG parsing systems. Specialised rule computation gave LIGHT a factor of 2.75 speed-up on the CSLI test suite.

Note that even in the hyper-active head-corner parsing approach described by Oepen and Carroll (2000), in which an indexing scheme is used to minimise the copying of possibly unnecessary parts of a rule's FS (notably the non-key argument and the LHS of the rule), one initial full representation of a rule's FS must be constructed before applying the rule in order to fill its key argument. In LIGHT a full FS representation of a rule is obtained only after the rule arguments have been successfully unified with FSs already present on the heap.

In order to solve the problem that the computation of the 'complete' QC-vector is prevented by the missing representation of the non-key argument, we initially proposed a rather naive solution: we relaxed the QC test for the complete/non-key argument by checking the QC-vector of the candidate argument ϕ against the QC-vector computed for $\varphi.\text{NON-KEY-ARG}$. As this latter QC-vector is more general than the one computed for φ'' – in the sense that if both $\varphi.\text{NON-KEY-ARG}.\pi$ and $\varphi''.\pi$ exist, then $root(\varphi.\text{NON-KEY-ARG}.\pi) \preceq root(\varphi''.\pi)$ in the sort hierarchy – we were entitled to use it for QC.[2] However, using this method, the speed-up from using the QC test on parsing the CSLI test suite with LIGHT was not significant.

The method we actually adopted was to compile (the computation of) the QC-vectors. For instance, in the interpreted approach for a binary rule one has to compute three QC-vectors: one 'key' QC-vector at loading/pre-processing time, a 'complete', and finally a 'passive' one at run-time. (These QC-vectors are shown on the bottom line of Table 10.1). Instead, in the compilation approach we compute five QC-vectors, three of which are computed at compilation time and two at run-time (Table 10.1), the latter two building on the pre-computed ones. QC-vector compilation is presented in detail in the next two sections.

Table 10.1. The QC-vectors computed for a rule φ in the compilation approach. ϕ is what φ becomes after the key argument (φ') is unified with ψ, the FS of a passive item. ϕ' is what ϕ becomes after the non-key argument (φ'') is unified with ψ', the FS of another passive item.

QC test	'key' QC-vector	'complete' QC-vector	'passive' QC-vector
compilation time:	$preComp(\varphi') =$	$preComp(\varphi'')$	$preComp(\varphi)$
run time:	$= QC(\varphi')$	$QC(\phi)$	$QC(\phi')$

2.2   Pre-computing QC-Vectors

So far we have shown that

- the QC test acts as a pre-unification filter for rule application; in an interpreted approach to parsing with LinGO-like grammars, rules are represented as FSs, and therefore computing whether a given FS will match the argument of a rule is straightforward; and

- what makes pre-computation of QC necessary is that specialised compilation of rules in **LIGHT** eliminates the presence (of the full representation) of rule FSs in the heap.

Note that – assuming as in key/head-corner parsing (Kay, 1989) that the key argument is always parsed before the non-key arguments – the 'key' QC-vector, as introduced in the previous subsection for a certain rule φ is unique for all key-mode applications of that rule. All the other computed QC-vectors depend on the actual application of φ, i.e., on the already parsed/filled arguments. However, one can see all these QC-vectors as computable in two stages/components: (i) a pre-computed/preliminary form of QC-vectors, which can be computed at compilation time independently of the FS that will be eventually unified with the arguments; and (ii) the actual, form/content of QC-vectors, which will be filled at run time starting from the pre-computed forms and which depends on the already parsed arguments.

The main idea of the QC test as introduced in the previous subsection is easy to formalise: given a finite set of feature paths $\Pi = \{\pi_1, ..., \pi_m\}$, and the feature structures ψ_1, ψ_2, check whether

$$root(\psi_1.\pi_i) \wedge root(\psi_2.\pi_i) \neq \bot, \text{ for } i = 1, ..., m.$$

It will be assumed by definition that $root(\psi.\pi) = \top$ if the feature path π is undefined for ψ (this fact will be denoted as $\psi.\pi\uparrow$).

It turns out that if $\pi' = f_1. ... .f_j$ is the longest prefix of $\pi = f_1. ... .f_n$ such that $\psi.\pi'$ is defined ($\psi.\pi' \downarrow$), and $root(\psi.\pi') = s_j$, then we can improve our definition of QC-values and take $root(\psi.\pi) = s_n$, where $s_{j+1} = \Psi(s_j).f_{j+1}$,

$$preComp(\psi, \pi) = \begin{cases} s : \text{sort} & \text{if } root(\psi.\pi) = s, \text{ and} \\ & \psi.\pi' \not\subseteq \mathcal{X}, \text{ for any prefix } \pi' \text{ of } \pi; \\ & \text{at the run time } QC_\pi(\psi) = s; \\ i : \text{int} & \text{if } \psi.\pi \downarrow, \ \psi.\pi = X_i, \text{ and} \\ & \psi.\pi' \in \mathcal{X}, \text{ for a prefix } \pi' \text{ of } \pi; \\ & \text{at the run time } QC_\pi(\psi) = \underline{\text{heap}[X_i].\text{SORT}}; \\ -j : \text{int} & \text{if } \psi.\pi \uparrow, \\ & \psi.\pi' \in \mathcal{X}, \text{ for a prefix } \pi' \text{ of } \pi, \\ & \pi' = f_1. \ldots .f_j \text{ is the longest prefix of } \pi \text{ such that} \\ & \psi.\pi' \downarrow, \text{ and } \psi.\pi = X_j; \\ & \text{at the run time } QC_\pi(\psi) = \underline{\text{heap}[X_j.f_{j+1}. \ldots .f_n].\text{SORT}}. \end{cases}$$

Figure 10.1. $QC_\pi(\psi)$ as function of $preComp(\psi, \pi)$.

$s_{j+2} = \Psi(s_{j+1}).f_{j+2}, \ldots, s_n = \Psi(s_{n-1}).f_n$, where $\Psi(s)$ is the type associated with the sort s in the input grammar. Of course, $\Psi(s).f$ has to be considered $\top$ if f is not defined at the root level in $\Psi(s)$. Alternatively, we could try to expand ψ by local unfolding, i.e., unifying $\psi.\pi'$ with (a copy of) the type $\Psi(s_j)$ provided by the grammar. If necessary, further local expansion/unfolding can be performed. Note that local expansion/unfolding provides more refined constraints, so it is good to use this information for the the pre-computation of QC-vectors. But it is not a good idea to involve these refined constraints in the computation of QC-vectors at run time, since it would consume additional time and space. At run time, the previous solution, based on appropriateness constraints is preferable.

We distinguish the following three cases in (pre-)computing the QC-vectors:

1. If ψ is a rule argument without containing references to preceding[3] arguments – this is the case of the head-corner argument in head-corner chart-based parsing – then we define

$$preComp(\psi, \pi) = s : \text{sort, where } s = root(\psi.\pi).$$

2. If ψ is a rule argument with references to substructures of the preceding arguments, $\mathcal{X}$ is the set of all variables/tags in ψ which refer to preceding arguments (according to the parsing order), and $\pi = f_1 f_2 \ldots f_n$ is a feature path, then assuming that the **heap** is the (main) data structure used for the internal representation of FSs, we define the values of QC-vectors starting from their pre-computed form (*preComp*) as in Figure 10.1. (The underlined expressions in Figure 10.1 are in fact thought of as extended to $QC_\pi(\varphi) = \ldots$, for any feature structure φ subsumed by ψ.) If, as in the current implementation of **LIGHT**, the computation of certain QC-vectors is delayed until really needed, then the actual values of the variables X_i, X_j representing addresses/indices of heap cells will

```
sentence
[ ARGS      < vp
                [ HEAD      #1:verb
                              [ AGREEMENT #3:agr ],
                    OBJECT  np ],
                #2:np
                    [ HEAD     noun
                              [ AGREEMENT #3 ] ] >,
         HEAD     #1,
         SUBJECT #2 ]
```

Figure 10.2.   The OSF-term associated with a sentence rule.

have to be saved (together with those in the set $\mathcal{X}$) in the environment associated with the preceding argument (which is saved after it has been parsed), in order to make them available to the current argument.

3. If ψ is the feature structure corresponding to a non-unary rule instance, the 'passive' QC-vector corresponding to that instance is defined in a similar way to the one detailed above, with the only one difference that $\mathcal{X}$ is taken as the set of all variables/coreferences shared between the rule's *LHS* and its arguments (*RHS*).

We mention that in the **LIGHT** system, a pre-computed QC-vector is stored as an array of tuples of the form (s, sort), (i, int), $(-j, \text{int})$, with $i \geq 0$, and $j > 0$, while at run-time a QC-vector is represented simply as an array of sorts.

2.2.1   Example.

Consider a rule consisting of a context-free backbone $s \rightarrow np \,*vp$ (where $*$ marks the rule's key/head argument), augmented with feature constraints as in Figure 10.2 (example adapted from Sikkel, 1997). Suppose that we want to consider the failure paths $\pi_1 = \text{HEAD}$, $\pi_2 = \text{OBJECT}$, $\pi_3 = \text{HEAD.AGREEMENT}$. The 'key', the *preComp*, and the final QC-vectors are shown in Table 10.2. The *preComp* QC-vector is presented in a more intuitive form than in the formalisation given in Section 2.2 above. The final, complete QC-vector corresponds to the (expected) analysis of the sentence *The cat catches a mouse*. Note that in the complete QC-vector, the value for π_2 is $\top$ since the FS corresponding to the noun phrase *a mouse* does not have the OBJECT feature defined.

One can see that the vp feature structure corresponding to the verb phrase *catches a mouse*, as shown in Figure 10.3, passes the QC test with the key QC-vector shown in Table 10.2. Then the np FS shown in Figure 10.3 for the noun phrase *the cat* passes the QC test in conjunction with the complete QC-vector in Table 10.2, but the (slightly different) FS for *the cats* would not, due

Table 10.2.   The active ('key' and 'complete') QC-vectors for the `sentence` rule.

QC-paths	'key' QC-vector	preComp	'complete' QC-vector
π_1 = HEAD	*verb*	*noun*	*noun*
π_2 = OBJECT	*np*	#2.OBJECT	⊤
π_3 = HEAD.AGREEMENT	*agr*	#3	*3sg*

```
vp
[ ARGS  < catches
            [ HEAD      #7:verb
                        [ AGREEMENT #5:3sg ],
                OBJECT  #6:np
                        [ ARGS < a
                                   [ HEAD det ],
                                 mouse
                                   [ HEAD #4:noun
                                          [ AGREEMENT 3sg ] ]
                                 HEAD #4 ],
                SUBJECT #8:sign
                        [ HEAD top
                                [ AGREEMENT #5 ] ] ],
          #6 >,
  HEAD      #7,
  SUBJECT #8 ]
```

paths	QC-vector
π_1	*verb*
π_2,	⊤
π_3	*3sg*

```
np
[ ARGS < the
           [ HEAD det ],
         cat
           [ HEAD #9:noun
                  [ AGREEMENT 3sg ] ] >,
  HEAD #9 ]
```

paths	QC-vector
π_1	*noun*
π_2	⊤
π_3	*3sg*

Figure 10.3.   The parses corresponding to the vp *catches a mouse* and the np *the cat*, and the computed 'passive' QC-vectors.

to an (AGREEMENT) inconsistency on the path π_3 (*non-3sg* vs. *3sg*). The sorts *non-3sg* and *3sg* are both assumed to be subsorts of *agr*.

2.3   From Pre-computed QC to Compiled QC

After getting the *preComp* vectors at compilation time, we must find the right place to put together (i) the QC-vector computation, and (ii) the QC test within the compiled rule's code or, alternatively, into the sequence containing a call to the rule's application.

Consider ψ, the FS corresponding to a rule, and φ, the FS (corresponding to a passive item) to be unified with the next-to-be-parsed argument. For the LinGO grammar, which contains only unary and binary rules,

1. For the rule's key/head-corner argument, (i) its associated QC vector is computed at compile time, and (ii) the QC test is compiled as a sequence of conditional statements of the form

   if (glb(s_π, QC$_\pi(\varphi)$ = $\bot$) return FALSE;

   where s_π = $\mathbf{QC}_\pi(\psi.\text{KEY-ARG})$ = $preComp(\psi.\text{KEY-ARG}, \pi)$ is known at compile time.

2'. If ψ is binary rule, and (after the QC test) φ unifies successfully with the rule's key argument, then before building (and saving) the corresponding environment, we have to compute the QC-vector for the non-key argument:[4]

   set QC$_\pi(\psi')$, t_π

   where $\psi' = \psi.\text{NON-KEY-ARG}$, and

   $$t_\pi = \rho(preComp(\psi', \pi)) = \begin{cases} s & \text{if } preComp(\psi', \pi) = s : \text{sort;} \\ \text{heap}[X_i].\text{SORT} & \text{if } preComp(\psi', \pi) = i : \text{int}, i \geq 0; \\ & i \geq 0; \\ \text{heap}[path(\pi, j, X_j)].\text{SORT} & \text{if } preComp(\psi', \pi) = -j : \text{int}, j > 0 \\ & j > 0 \end{cases}$$

   and $path(\pi, j, \psi')$ computes the value for the path $f_{j+1}. \ \ldots \ .f_n$ inside the FS ψ', starting from the node X_j. (As in the previous subsection, $\pi = f_1. \ \ldots \ .f_n$.)

2''. If ψ is a binary rule, and φ is a candidate for its non-key argument, before restoring the environment for the item corresponding to φ, we have to perform the QC test, which is in fact a sequence of conditional statements of the following form, one for each QC path π:

   if (glb(QC$_\pi(\psi.\text{NON-KEY-ARG})$, QC$_\pi(\varphi)$ = $\bot$) return FALSE;

   Note that $\mathbf{QC}_\pi(\psi.\text{NON-KEY-ARG})$ has already been computed (see 2').

3. If the rule ψ was successfully completed, then we have to compute the 'passive' QC-vector for the newly created item/FS: we proceed as above (2''), with the single difference that instead of $preComp(\psi', \pi)$ we have to consider $preComp'(\psi, \pi)$, where $preComp'$ is computed similarly to $preComp$, but taking $\mathcal{X}$ as the set of all variables used in the rule's arguments. (See case 3 in Section 2.2 above).

2.4   Compiled QC: Evaluation and Improvements

When running the LinGO grammar on the CSLI test suite without the QC filter, the **LIGHT** system took 0.07 sec/sentence.[5] With QC turned on, **LIGHT** took only 0.04 sec/sentence. The compiled QC filter in **LIGHT** thus gave a speed-up of a factor of 42%. The optimal set of failure paths contained 43 paths, with lengths of between 2 and 14 features. As expected the speed-up is lower than for interpreted QC (the speed-up is 63% for PET) because compiled unification is already significantly faster than interpreted unification. In other words, one has to keep in mind that in **LIGHT** the specialised compiled form of rules already significantly speeds up parsing, before applying the QC filter. However this factor can be further increased by implementing the improvements outlined below. (Some of these improvements also apply to interpreted parsing systems.)

The run-time QC test can be incorporated into the functions 'encapsulating' the compiled code of rules as a sequence of **if** statements. This would have the following advantages, which further improve QC filter efficiency:

- tests like $\top \wedge \mathit{root}(\phi)$, which in fact correspond to paths that are not fully defined in the argument being currently checked, may be eliminated since they always succeed;

- when using appropriateness constraints (Carpenter, 1992), tests on $s \wedge \mathit{root}(\phi.f)$ may be eliminated if s is the maximal appropriate sort for the feature f;

- certain parts in the *preComp* vectors overlap; subject to the failure paths' order, the definition of these vectors can be improved so to eliminate duplicate work:

  > if $QC_\pi(\psi) = \mathsf{heap}[X_j.f_{j+1}.\ \dots\ .f_k.f_{k+1}.\ \dots\ .f_n].\mathsf{SORT}$, and $QC_{\pi'}(\psi)$ $= \mathsf{heap}[X_j.f_{j+1}.\ \dots\ .f_k.f'_{k+1}\ \dots\ .f'_m].\mathsf{SORT}$, then $QC_{\pi'}(\psi)$ can be computed as $\mathsf{heap}[Y_l.f_{j+l}.\ \dots\ .f_k.f'_{k+1}\ \dots\ .f'_m].\mathsf{SORT}$, where Y_l is the last Y definable variable in the sequence $Y_1 = X_j.f_1, ..., Y_k = Y_{k-1}.f_k$ is the sequence used to compute $QC_\pi(\psi)$;[6]

- the sort *glb* tests (represented by the **if** statements) can be reordered, depending on the applied rule and the type of the filtered argument, because the most probable failure paths at the grammar-level are not necessarily the most probable failure paths for each rule and argument.

Indeed, one of the main criticisms that can be made of the QC filter technique in the form presented in the beginning of this subsection – and used as such in the LKB, PAGE and PET systems – is that it is a grammar-level technique, in the sense that the QC-paths to be tested are grammar- and corpus-derived, and not 'personalised' at the rule and argument level. However, one can compute such QC-vectors so to be rule and argument dependent. A disadvantage still remaining is that the QC-vectors associated with a passive item (completed rule) must contain all the paths addressed by those rules and arguments for which that completed rule/passive item is a potential candidate. Therefore it is unlikely that the dimensionality of 'personalised' QC-vectors would be significantly reduced.

To our knowledge, the compilation scheme we presented here for quick check is the first attempt to incorporate this pre-unification speed-up technique in a compiler system dealing with large-scale unification grammars. The QC compilation is by no means HPSG-dependent; it is basically independent of the variant of (order-sorted) feature constraint logics that supports parsing (which in turn calls unification). In LIGHT we used as the background logic the order- and type-consistent OSF-theories (Ciortuz, 2002b) for which OSF-theory unification is equivalent to unification of typed FSs as defined by Carpenter (1992). Therefore, the technique here presented can be applied to other systems dealing with typed-unification grammars like $\mathcal{A}$MALIA (Wintner and Francez, 1999) and LiLFeS (Miyao et al., 2000).

3. Generalised Rule Reduction

This section presents Generalised Reduction (GR), a learning technique for speeding up parsing typed-unification grammars, based on generalising feature values. GR eliminates as many as possible of the feature constraints (FCs) from typed feature structures (FSs) while applying the criterion of preserving the original parsing results on a given, training corpus. For parsing with GR-restricted rule FSs, and for checking the correctness of obtained parses on other corpora, we use a form of FS unification which we call two-step unification. We will report results of GR application on the LinGO English grammar.

Below we formally define generalised reduction and present the idea of two-step unification. Then Section 3.1 presents our GR algorithms, and Section 3.2 reports performance measurements for GR-versions of the LinGO grammar. Section 3.3 outlines proposals for further work, on quick check over generalised reduction paths.

From a logical point of view, FSs can be viewed as positive OSF-clauses, which are finite sets of atomic OSF-constraints (Aït-Kaci and Podelski, 1993), namely sort constraints, feature constraints and equation constraints. Therefore the generalisation of FSs can be logically achieved through elimination of some atomic constraints from the FS. The approach we followed in developing both the generalisation and specialisation procedures for learning feature values in typed-unification grammars is basically the one proposed by Inductive Logic Programming (ILP; Muggleton and Raedt, 1994). We have adapted/applied the main ILP ideas to OSF-logic, the feature constraint (subset of the first-order) logic underlying such grammars (Aït-Kaci and Podelski, 1993; Carpenter, 1992; Aït-Kaci et al., 1997). Ciortuz (2002d) shows how one can improve the linguistic competence – i.e., enhance the coverage – of a given typed-unification grammar by guided generalisation, using parsing failures.

Generalised reduction is a restricted form of FS generalisation that eliminates as many as possible of the feature constraints from a typed FS of a given unification grammar while applying an *evaluation criterion* for maintaining the parsing results on a large corpus/test suite. Note that although GR explicitly eliminates only feature constraints, it may be the case that sort and/or equation constraints associated with the value of an eliminated feature constraint get implicitly eliminated through FS normalisation (Aït-Kaci and Podelski, 1993).

We make the observation that the notion of restriction in the HPSG literature designates the elimination of particular features following the application of a parsing rule. Generalised reduction extends this operation on arbitrary chosen features (of course, ensuring parsing correctness on the given training corpus). We prefer the term 'reduction' for this operation, since from the logical point of view, eliminating one feature constraint from a FS logically generalises that FS, while its set of feature paths indeed gets restricted. However, we will denote the result of applying GR to a FS as the 'GR-restricted form' or the 'GR-learnt form' of that FS. Alternatively, one may think of generalised reduction as 'relative unfilling'. Indeed, expansion for typed-unification grammars – the procedure that propagates both top-down in the type hierarchy and locally in the typed FS the constraints associated with types in the grammar – is often followed by unfilling (Gerdemann, 1995), a feature constraint removal technique which is corpus-independent. Generalised reduction may be thought as a corpus/test-suite-relative unfilling technique.

GR is shown not only to improve the performance of the given grammar, since it maximally reduces the size of the (rule) FSs in grammar, but also adds an interesting improvement to the parsing system design. As measurements on parsing the CSLI test suite have shown that on average only 8% of the items added to the chart during parsing form part of a full parse, one can reformulate unification as a two-step operation. Parsing with *two-step unification* will (i) use the GR-learnt form of the grammar rules to produce full parses, and (ii) eventually complete/check the final parses using the full (or, rather complementary) form of rule FSs.

The second/late unification step in fact performs 'consistency checking' with respect to the full form of rule FSs. From this point of view it plays a symmetric role to the quick check pre-unification filter presented in Section 2. From an implementation point of view, we can first emulate the second/late unification step as type-checking, via FS unfolding. As further work, we suggest that different techniques may be used to apply the second phase of unification more efficiently.

3.1 Generalised Reduction of Rule FSs: Algorithms

We present two algorithms for generalised reduction of types in unification grammars. The first one, called A below is a simple, non-incremental one. From it we derived a second, incremental algorithm (B) that we have optimised. Both algorithms have roughly the same kinds of inputs and outputs:

> *Input:* G, a typed-unification grammar, and Θ a test suite, i.e., a set of sentences annotated by a 'parsing evaluation' function; and

> *Output:* a more general grammar than G obtained by generalised reduction of FSs that produces the same parsing evaluation results as G on Θ.

The measurements given below use the following parsing evaluation criterion: the number of full parses, the number of attempted unifications and the number of successful unifications must be preserved for each sentence in the test suite, after the elimination of a (selected) feature constraint. Due to the large size of both the LinGO grammar and the test suite used for running GR, this parsing evaluation criterion is a good approximation of the following 'tough' criterion: the set of actual parses (up to the associated FSs) delivered for each sentence by the two versions of the grammar must be exactly the same. We make the remark that after applying GR on the LinGO using the CSLI test suite, this 'tough' criterion was satisfied. The parsing evaluation criteria to be used in getting the GR-restricted form of a grammar must in practice be combined with one regarding exhaustion of memory/space resources: if for a given sentence, after elimination of a feature constraint the resources initially allocated for parsing are exhausted, then that feature constraint is kept in the grammar.

Although in our experiments only the rule types in G were subject to generalised reduction, the formulation of the two GR algorithms can be extended to any FS in the input grammar. Applying GR to the type FSs used in type-checking is easy, but if parsing correctness must be ensured – i.e., elimination of over-generalised parses is required in the end – then things get more complicated than for rule FSs. Extending GR to lexical entries is even more demanding if lexical rules are used.

3.1.1 A Simple Generalised Reduction Procedure.

A simple procedure for deriving the generalised reduction of a grammar is given in Figure 10.4. Basically, each feature constraint (FC) in the grammar's rule FSs is tested for elimination. If removing a constraint φ does not change the parsing (evaluation) results on the test suite Θ, then φ is eliminated from G for the purpose of constructing the grammar's GR-restricted form. The algorithm constructs monotonic generalisations of the grammar G. From the logical point of view, $G_n \models G_{n+1} \models \dots \models \dots \models G_1 \models G = G_0$.

Procedure A:

> **for** each rule $\Psi(r)$ in the grammar $\mathcal{G}$
>   **for** each feature constraint φ in $\Psi(r)$
>   **if** removing φ from $\Psi(r)$
>   preserves the parsing (evaluation) results
>   for each sentence in the test suite Θ
>   **then** $\Psi(r) := \Psi(r) - \{\varphi\}$;

Figure 10.4. A simple, non-incremental Generalised Reduction procedure.

Obviously, the GR result is dependent on the order in which feature constraints are processed: elimination of the constraint φ can block the elimination of the constraint φ' if φ is tried first, and vice-versa. Therefore usually there is no unique most general GR form for a given grammar. In the actual implementation of the GR algorithms we first worked on the elimination of feature constraints from key arguments (in decreasing order of their 'usage' frequency on the given test suite), then from non-key arguments (according to the same kind of frequency), and finally from rule LHS sub-structures. Inside a 'reduction partition' (key argument, non-key argument, LHS structure), feature constraints were tested for elimination following the bottom-up traversal order of the acyclic rooted graph representing the rule FS.

Note that the first two **for**'s in the procedure A can be combined into a single **for** iterating over the set of all feature constraints $< r, \varphi >$ in the grammar's rules ($\varphi \in \Psi(r)$).

3.1.2   An Improved, Incremental GR Procedure.
The simple GR algorithm presented in Figure 10.4 can be substantially improved in two ways.

- The order of the **for** loops iterating over the set of all feature constraints and iterating over the sentences in the test suite can be reversed. The advantage of this is that those sentences which are correctly parsed by $\mathcal{G}_i$ – an intermediate generalised form of $\mathcal{G}$ – need not to be tried again when computing $\mathcal{G}_{i+1}$;

- A first GR version of the input grammar can be obtained by running the simple procedure A on one or more sentences, and subsequently improving it iteratively.

The improved procedure is shown in Figure 10.5.

It should be noted that the set of FCs to be tried for elimination in Procedure A (called from step 1 of Procedure B) is $\mathcal{G} - \mathcal{G}_i$, so it decreases in size each time around the loop. Indeed, from the logical point of view, $\mathcal{G} =$

Procedure B:

> **do** 0. $\mathcal{G}_0 = \mathcal{G}$, $i = 0$;
>   1. Apply Procedure A to a sentence s from Θ;
>   let $\mathcal{G}_{i+1}$ be the result
>   2. eliminate from Θ the sentences for which $\mathcal{G}_{i+1}$
>   provides the same parsing results as $\mathcal{G}$
> **until** $\Theta = \emptyset$.

Figure 10.5. An improved, incremental Generalised Reduction procedure.

$\mathcal{G}_0 \models \ \dots\ \models \mathcal{G}_{n+1} \models \mathcal{G}_n \ \dots\ \models \mathcal{G}_2 \models \mathcal{G}_1$. Viewed as set of constraints, $\mathcal{G} = \mathcal{G}_0 \supset \ \dots\ \supset \mathcal{G}_{i+1} \supset \mathcal{G}_i \ \dots\ \supset \mathcal{G}_2 \supset \mathcal{G}_1$ therefore $\mathcal{G} - \mathcal{G}_{n+1} \subset \mathcal{G} - \mathcal{G}_n$.

We have made a number of further improvements to the algorithm in our implementation:

- At step 2, the elimination of sentences from Θ is done in a lazy manner: initially Θ is sorted according to the number of failed unifications per sentence when using $\mathcal{G}$, – so the sentence s chosen at step 1 may be considered the first sentence in Θ_i – and subsequently only the first sentences from Θ_i which are correctly parsed by $\mathcal{G}_{i+1}$ are eliminated. (Θ_{i+1} starts with the first sentence in Θ_i which causes over-parsing with $\mathcal{G}_{i+1}$. Obviously, we take $\Theta_0 = \Theta$.) The reason for lazy elimination of sentences from Θ is the significant time consumption caused by over-parsing and/or exhaustion of allocated resources that may occur – very frequently, in the beginning – for some of the the the remaining sentences in Θ due to the (premature) elimination of certain constraints in preceding loops in Procedure B.

- Only FCs from rules involved in the parsing of sentence s at step 1 must be checked for elimination. If the sentence exhausted the allocated resources for parsing, this optimisation does not apply, because it is not possible to tell in advance which rules might have been used if exhaustion had not occurred.

- A 'preview' test which decides whether a whole rule partition is immediately learnable is highly effective in improving the running time of the GR procedure with the LinGO grammar. This test means eliminating from $\mathcal{G} - \mathcal{G}_i$ in a single step all the constraints in a partition (either an argument or the LHS substructure) for the rules previously identified as contributing to parsing the sentence s. At the rule level, identifying the FCs that must be retained in $\mathcal{G}_{i+1}$ may be further sped up through halving the FC search space.

- As the feature constraints in a rule FS are implicitly ordered by their position in the rooted acyclic graph representing the rule, another optimisation is possible: if all ancestors of a FC have been approved for elimination then that FC may be eliminated immediately, assuming that its value is not coreferenced in a subsequent partition (argument of LHS substructure), and this property can be determined in the preparation of the GR application.

In our current implementation of Procedure B, exhaustion of resources allocated for parsing is controlled by a sentence-independent criterion. Currently, the allocated resources allow for the complete parsing of all sentences in the test suite. But using such a criterion has the following drawback: if Procedure A causes strong over-parsing (possibly looping) for a sentence, then this fact is detected eventually only after *all* resources are exhausted. We suggest a better, more punctual criterion for evaluating the consumption of allocated resources for parsing: (i) initially, for each sentence in the given test suite register the parsing time using $\mathcal{G}$; (ii) if during the generalised reduction, parsing a sentence using the current generalised form of rules consumes more than n times the initially registered parsing time without finishing, then consider that sentence as a resource exhausting one.

Incorporating all but the last improvement mentioned above, Procedure B required 61 minutes on a Pentium III PC at 933MHz running Red Hat Linux 7.1. (All measurements reported in the next section were also done on that PC.) We expect that this amount of time will be approximately halved by using a parser which incorporates quick check; our GR procedure cannot use rules in Specialised Rule Compilation (SRC) format, and the non-SRC parser in LIGHT currently does not use QC.

Because the test suite for training is processed incrementally only by Procedure B, we refer to it as the 'incremental' GR algorithm, while Procedure A is called the 'non-incremental' algorithm.

3.2 Generalised Reduction: Measurements and Comparisons

When running GR Procedure A on the LinGO grammar and the CSLI test suite, the reduction in the number of FCs in rule argument sub-structures was impressive: 61.38% for key/head arguments and 61.85% for non-key arguments (see Table 10.3). The number of feature paths in rule argument substructures was reduced from 494 to 234, revealing that the main contribution to unification failures is restricted to less than half of the feature paths in the arguments. We will call those feature paths 'GR-paths'.

This result complements the view provided by the QC technique: only 8.5% of all feature paths in the arguments are responsible for most of the unification

Table 10.3. Comparison between the results of applying the two GR procedures on the LinGO grammar and the CSLI test suite.

GR procedure	Procedure A		Procedure B	
FC reduction rate: average	58.92%		56.64%	
GR vs. total feature paths in rule arguments	234/494	(47.36%)	318/494	(64.38%)
Average parse time, in msec.				
using full-form rule FSs		21.617		
1st-step unification (reduction %)	16.662	(22.24%)	16.736	(22.07%)
emulated 2-step unification (reduction %)	18.657	(13.12%)	18.427	(14.20%)

Table 10.4. A snapshot view of reduction in memory usage when parsing the CSLI test suite with the GR-restricted form of LinGO.

	full-form rules	GR-restricted rules			
		first-step unification		emulated 2-step unification	
heap cells	101614	38320	(62.29%)	76998	(24.23%)
feature frames	60303	30370	(49.64%)	58963	(2.22%)

failures during parsing with LinGO. As expected, most of the (43) QC-paths we are using in LIGHT for LinGO are among the GR-paths identified by Procedure A; the QC-paths which are not GR-paths are extensions of maximal GR-paths.

While the average number of FCs eliminated from LinGO by GR Procedure B, and the parsing performance of the resulting grammar are only slightly different than those provided by Procedure A, the number of GR-paths retained in rule arguments is significantly higher in the former case than in the latter. This difference is explained by the fact that Procedure B fragments the test suite.

Table 10.4 presents a snapshot of the most used memory resources (and the corresponding percentage reduction) when parsing with full-form rule FSs compared with GR-restricted rule FSs. The graph in Figure 10.6 presents the change in the average rule reduction rate for obtaining the GR version of LinGO using Procedure B. Figure 10.7 illustrates the reduction in parsing time for the CSLI test suite when running the LinGO grammar with the GR-restricted rules. One can see in this last figure – especially for the sentences requiring many unifications – that although the number of unifications is increased, the total parsing time is reduced.

Procedure B may be generalised so as to provide the inner loop (the call to A) with not only one but several (n) sentences which are incorrectly parsed

Table 10.5. Results of running the parameterised GR Procedure B on the CSLI test suite; n designates the number of sentences used in the inner (A) loop.

n	running time	FCs reduction rate	GR-paths
1	1h 27min	56.64	318
2	1h 36min	59.38	200
4	2h 27min	59.42	187
8	4h 03min	59.39	187

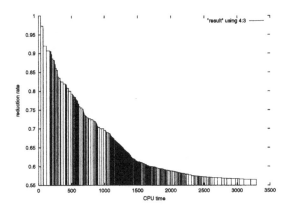

Figure 10.6. Procedure B: rule reduction rate vs. CPU time consumption on LinGO/CSLI.

by $\mathcal{G}_{i+1}$. If so, the processing time for getting the GR-version of the given grammar will increase. However, as Table 10.5 shows, this is a convenient way to get empirically a smaller number of computed GR-paths.[7]

We tested a GR-version of LinGO (produced using the CSLI test suite) on the *aged* test suite also provided with LinGO. This test suite requires on average 4.65 times more unifications per sentence than the CSLI test suite. The CSLI test suite has 1348 sentences with an average length of 6.38 tokens and ambiguity 1.5 readings. For the *aged* test suite, the average length is 8.5 and the ambiguity 14.14. Of the 96 sentences in the *aged* test suite, 59 were correctly parsed, 3 exhausted the allocated resources, and 34 were over-parsed. The average parsing precision for the sentences that did not exhaust the allocated resources was 83.79%. In order to produce a GR-version of LinGO using the *aged* test suite for training, procedure B needed 4h 44min, and the reduction rate was 65.60%. However, it took only 38min to further improve

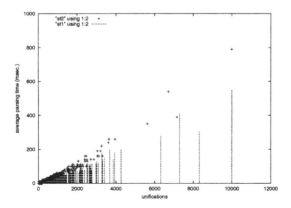

Figure 10.7. Comparisons: unifications vs. parsing time on the CSLI test suite using LIGHT on LinGO: the full version vs. the GR-restricted version using 1st-step unification.

the previously obtained GR-version of LinGO (on the CSLI test suite), using the *aged* test suite, and the rule FS reduction rate went down by only 3.1%.

We investigated the effect of changing the ordering of the test suite Θ for the GR algorithms. Applying Procedure A only to the most complicated sentence in the CSLI test suite resulted in a 18% reduction in the number of FCs inside rule FSs. We obtained the same reduction rate running 30 iterations using the simplest sentences in the CSLI test suite. Further generalising with the next (slightly less) complicated sentences in Θ would also take a lot of time, but may not significantly improve the FC reduction rate.

3.3 Further Work: Quick Check on GR-paths

As an alternative to 'personalising' the QC test for each rule as we proposed in Section 2.3, we could consider doing pre-unification filtering on GR-paths (instead of QC-paths). This would require the construction of GR-vectors associated with rules and their arguments. For LinGO, the size of GR-vectors is several times larger than that of QC-vectors (187 vs. 43). We estimate however that the number of actual sort intersections during pre-unification tests would be significantly lower than currently done by the quick check, as the size of rule argument FSs is greatly reduced by GR. The immediate advantage in doing pre-unification filtering on GR-paths would be that the sort compatibility checks would fully 'cover' the rule argument FSs. Moreover, the (compiled) computation of GR-vectors could be done directly by the abstract machine for

FS unification (Ciortuz, 2002c), by augmentation of abstract instructions. Note that the few QC-paths which extend maximal GR-paths could be 'injected' into the GR-restricted form of rules.

4. Conclusion

This paper presented a study of two interesting classes of feature paths inside rule feature structures of LinGO, a large-scale HPSG grammar of English.

The first class of feature paths consists of those which most probably lead to unification failure when parsing a given corpus. The fact that there are only a relatively small number of such paths responsible for most of the unification failures during parsing enables the use of the quick check pre-unification filter; hence these paths are called QC-paths (Malouf et al., 2000). Usually, prior to the application of the QC test, the values of QC-paths in a given FS are stored in a (QC-)vector. Our contribution consists of the adaptation of this technique to a situation in which the computation of QC-vectors must precede the construction of the FS itself. Such a situation appears in parsing with compiled typed-unification grammars using the specialised rule compilation technique (Ciortuz, 2001a), as is the case with the LIGHT system (Ciortuz, 2002b). We show that a two-stage computation of QC-vectors is both feasible and effective, firstly getting a pre-computed/off-line form of the QC-vectors, and secondly computing their final/on-line form.

The second class of feature paths we have explored are generalised reduction paths in rule arguments. These are paths which contribute to unification failure. In the early stage of a rule application (via FS unification) in bottom-up parsing, checking constraints which are not on GR-paths may be delayed. Eventually the constraints are checked only on full, successful parses. For a grammar like LinGO in which the percentage of GR-paths among all feature paths in rule arguments is high, applying generalised reduction and eventually two-step unification leads to a significant speed-up (supplementing the one provided by quick check), and an impressive reduction of memory usage. In the LIGHT system, to the 42% speed-up factor provided by QC on the LinGO grammar, GR may add a subsequent 22%. We described two GR algorithms for rule FSs, firstly a simple, non-incremental one, and then an optimised, incremental one. A procedure for automatic detection of cycles in parsing with generalised forms of the input typed-unification grammar would further improve the GR algorithms. Integrating linguistic knowledge, and testing GR on other grammars and test suites would provide additional insights into the use of this learning method.

We found that most QC-paths are GR-paths; the exceptions are extensions of maximal GR-paths. Generalised reduction limits the early unification step to just the GR-paths, delaying the completion of unification and only applying it (eventually) to full parses. The quick check is a pre-unification filter; more exactly, in our design it operates in connection with the early/first unification step. Therefore the quick check and generalised reduction techniques are orthogonal. The second/late unification step acts as a post-parsing filter, and so it is symmetric (with respect to parsing) to the quick check pre-unification filter.

Acknowledgments

The conception and implementation of the work on compilation of quick check was done while the author was employed at the Language Technology Lab of the German Research Center for Artificial Intelligence (DFKI) in Saarbrücken, Germany. Investigation of the generalised reduction technique and the two papers (Ciortuz, 2001b; Ciortuz, 2002a) on which this chapter is based were supported by an EPSRC ROPA grant at the Computer Science Department of the University of York.

Thanks go to Ulrich Callmeier who implemented the interpreted form of the QC filter for CHIC/ago,[8] the development prototype of the **LIGHT** compiler. Thanks to Dr. Stephan Oepen who pointed me to the precursor work of Maxwell and Kaplan. I wish to express special thanks to Professor Hans Uszkoreit for the support I received in order to get **LIGHT** designed and implemented during my employment at DFKI. I am grateful also to Professor Steven Muggleton, Dr. Dimitar Kazakov, Dr. Suresh Manandhar, Dr. James Cussens and Dr. John Carroll who, in different ways, made possible my work on generalised reduction.

Notes

1. The LIGHT acronym stands Logic, Inheritance, Grammars, Heads, and Types. The analogy with the name of LIFE – Logic, Inheritance, Functions and Equalities – a well-known constraint logic language based on the OSF constraint system Aït-Kaci and Podelski, 1993 is evident.

2. We use here the notation established above: φ is the FS associated with the rule which is being applied, and φ'' is obtained from φ after $\varphi' = \varphi$.KEY-ARG was unified with ψ, the FS corresponding to a passive item.

3. Here the term 'preceding' is used in the sense of the parsing order.

4. This QC-vector will be stored within the active item corresponding to the key/head-corner argument and will be used for the QC test at the rule's completion attempt.

5. The tests were run on a 400MHz SUN Sparc server.

6. The $Y_1 = X_j.f_1, ..., Y_k = Y_{k-1}.f_k$ sequence might not be entirely computed.

7. The running time of all GR algorithms can be significantly improved if, in the beginning of the GR application, all feature constraints not used when parsing the training test suite are eliminated from the initial grammar. (Unfortunately, the current version of the LIGHT system cannot identify these unused FCs.) However, eliminating these FCs from the start will bias the set of GR-paths to be computed. In general, FCs initially not used in parsing the training test suite may however appear in the GR-restricted grammar version.

8. CHIC stands for Compiling Hpsg Into C. 'CHIC/ago' is pronounced exactly like the city Chicago.

References

Aït-Kaci, H. and Di Cosmo, R. (1993). Compiling order-sorted feature term unification. Technical report, Digital Paris Research Laboratory. PRL Technical Note 7, downloadable from http://www.isg.sfu.ca/life/.

Aït-Kaci, H. and Podelski, A. (1993). Towards a meaning of LIFE. *Journal of Logic Programming*, 16:195–234.

Aït-Kaci, H., Podelski, A., and Goldstein, S. (1997). Order-sorted feature theory unification. *Journal of Logic, Language and Information*, 30:99–124.

Callmeier, U. (2000). PET — a platform for experimentation with efficient HPSG processing techniques. *Natural Language Engineering*, 6 (1) (Special Issue on Efficient Processing with HPSG):99–108.

Carpenter, B. (1992). *The Logic of Typed Feature Structures – with applications to unification grammars, logic programs and constraint resolution.* Cambridge University Press.

Ciortuz, L. (2001a). Compilation of head-corner bottom-up chart-based parsing with unification grammars. In *Proceedings of the IWPT 2001 International Workshop on Parsing Technologies*, pages 209–212, Beijing, China.

Ciortuz, L. (2001b). On compilation of the Quick-Check filter for feature structure unification. In *Proceedings of the IWPT 2001 International Workshop on Parsing Technologies*, pages 90–100, Beijing, China.

Ciortuz, L. (2002a). Learning attribute values in typed-unification grammars: On generalised rule reduction. In *Proceedings of the 6th Conference on Natural Language Learning (CoNLL–2002)*, Taipei, Taiwan. Morgan Kaufmann Publishers and ACL.

Ciortuz, L. (2002b). LIGHT — a constraint language and compiler system for typed-unification grammars. In *Proceedings of the 25th German Conference on Artificial Intelligence (KI-2002)*, Aachen, Germany. Springer-Verlag.

Ciortuz, L. (2002c). LIGHT — another abstract machine for feature structure unification. In Flickinger, D., Oepen, S., Tsujii, J., and Uszkoreit, H., editors, *Collaborative Language Engineering*. CSLI Publications, The Center for studies of Language, Logic and Information, Stanford University.

Ciortuz, L. (2002d). Towards inductive learning of typed-unification grammars. In *Proceedings of the 17th Workshop on Logic Programming*. Dresden Technical University.

Flickinger, D. P., Copestake, A., and Sag, I. A. (2000). HPSG analysis of English. In Wahlster, W., editor, *Verbmobil: Foundations of Speech-to-Speech Translation*, Artificial Intelligence, pages 254–263. Springer-Verlag, Berlin Heidelberg New York.

Gerdemann, D. (1995). Term encoding of typed feature structures. In *Proceedings of the 4th International Workshop on Parsing Technologies*, pages 89–97, Prague, Czech Republik.

Kaplan, R. M. and Bresnan, J. (1983). Lexical-functional grammar: A formal system for grammatical representation. In Bresnan, J., editor, *The Mental Representation of Grammatical Relations*, pages 173–381. MIT Press.

Kay, M. (1989). Head driven parsing. In *Proceedings of the 1st Workshop on Parsing Technologies*, pages 52–62, Pittsburg.

Kiefer, B., Krieger, H.-U., Carroll, J., and Malouf, R. (1999). A bag of useful techniques for efficient and robust parsing. In *Proceedings of the 37th Annual Meeting of the Association for Computational Linguistics*, pages 473–480.

Krieger, H.-U. and Schäfer, U. (1994). TDL – A Type Description Language for HPSG. Research Report RR-94-37, German Research Center for Artificial Intelligence (DFKI).

Malouf, R., Carroll, J., and Copestake, A. (2000). Efficient feature structure operations without compilation. *Natural Language Engineering*, 6 (1) (Special Issue on Efficient Processing with HPSG):29–46.

Maxwell III, J. and Kaplan, R. (1993). The interface between phrasal and functional constraints. *Computational Linguistics*, 19, Number 4:571–590.

Mitsuishi, Y., Torisawa, K., and Tsujii, J. (1998). HPSG-Style Underspecified Japanese Grammar with Wide Coverage. In *Proceedings of the 17th International Conference on Computational Linguistics (COLING)*, pages 867–880.

Miyao, Y., Makino, T., Torisawa, K., and Tsujii, J. (2000). The LiLFeS abstract machine and its evaluation with the LinGO grammar. *Natural Language Engineering*, 6 (1) (Special Issue on Efficient Processing with HPSG):47–61.

Muggleton, S. and Raedt, L. D. (1994). Inductive logic programming: Theory and methods. *Journal of Logic Programming*, 19,20:629–679.

Müller, S. (1999). *Deutsche Syntax deklarativ. Head-Driven Phrase Structure Grammar für das Deutsche.* Number 394 in Linguistische Arbeiten. Max Niemeyer Verlag, Tübingen.

Nagata, M. (1992). An empirical study on rule granularity and unification interleaving: toward an efficient unification-based parsing system. In *Proceedings of COLING-92*, pages 177–183.

Ninomiya, T., Makino, T., and Tsujii, J. (2002). An indexing scheme for typed feature structures. In *Proceedings of the 19th International Conference on Computational Linguistics: COLING-2002*.

Oepen, S. and Callmeier, U. (2000). Measure for measure: Parser cross-fertilization. Towards increased component comparability and exchange. In *Proceedings of the International Workshop on Parsing Technologies IWPT-2000*, pages 183–194, Trento, Italy.

Oepen, S. and Carroll, J. (2000). Performance profiling for parser engineering. *Natural Language Engineering*, 6 (1) (Special Issue on Efficient Processing with HPSG: Methods, Systems, Evaluation):81–97.

Pereira, F. (1985). A structure-sharing representation for unification-based grammar formalisms. In *Proceedings of the 23rd meeting of the Association for Computational Linguistics*, pages 137–144, Chicago, Illinois.

Pollard, C. and Sag, I. (1994). *Head-driven Phrase Structure Grammar*. CSLI Publications, Stanford.

Shieber, S. (1985). Using restriction to extend parsing algorithms for complex feature-based formalisms. In *Proceedings of the 23rd Annual Meeting of the ACL*, pages 145–152, Chicago, Illinois.

Shieber, S. M., Uszkoreit, H., Pereira, F. C., Robinson, J., and Tyson, M. (1983). The formalism and implementation of PATR-II. In Bresnan, J., editor, *Research on Interactive Acquisition and Use of Knowledge*. SRI International, Menlo Park, Calif.

Siegel, M. (2000). HPSG analysis of Japanese. In *Verbmobil: Foundations of Speech-to-Speech Translation*, pages 264–279. Springer Verlag.

Sikkel, N. (1997). *Parsing Schemata*. Springer Verlag.

Tomabechi, H. (1992). Quasi-destructive graph unification with structure sharing. In *Proceedings of COLING-92*, pages 440–446, Nantes, France.

Uszkoreit, H. (1986). Categorial Unification Grammar. In *International Conference on Computational Linguistics (COLING'92)*, pages 498–504, Nancy, France.

Wintner, S. and Francez, N. (1999). Efficient implementation of unification-based grammars. *Journal of Language and Computation*, 1(1):53–92.

Chapter 11

A CONTEXT-FREE SUPERSET APPROXIMATION OF UNIFICATION-BASED GRAMMARS

Bernd Kiefer and Hans-Ulrich Krieger

German Research Center for Artificial Intelligence (DFKI)
Stuhlsatzenhausweg 3, D-66123 Saarbrücken, Germany
{ kiefer|krieger } @dfki.de

Abstract   We present a simple and intuitive approximation method for turning unification-based grammars into context-free grammars. We apply our method to several grammars and report on the quality of the approximation. We also present several methods that speed up the approximation process and that might be interesting to other areas of unification-based processing. Finally, we introduce a novel disambiguation method for unification grammars which is based on probabilistic context-free approximations.

1.   Introduction

In this chapter we present a simple and intuitive approximation method for turning unification-based grammars (UBG), such as HPSG (Pollard and Sag, 1994), PATR-II (Shieber, 1985) or CLE (Alshawi, 1992), into context-free grammars (CFG).[1] The approximation method can be seen as the construction of the least fixpoint of a certain monotonic function and shares similarities with the instantiation of rules in a bottom-up passive chart parser or with partial evaluation in logic programming. One of the interesting properties of our method is that the language generated by the CFG is always a true superset of the language represented by the UBG.

The basic idea of our approach is as follows. In a first step, we generalize the set of all lexicon entries. The resulting structures form equivalence classes, since they abstract from word-specific information, such as FORM or STEM. The abstraction is specified by means of a restrictor, the so-called *lexicon restrictor*. After that, the grammar rules are instantiated by unification, using the abstracted lexicon entries and resulting in derivation trees of depth 1. We apply the *rule restrictor* to each resulting feature structure, removing all infor-

H. Bunt et al. (eds.), New Technologies in Parsing Technology, 229-250.

mation contained only in the daughters of a rule. Additionally, the restriction gets rid of information that will either lead to infinite growth of the feature structures or that does not constrain the search space. Why this is crucial is explained in sections 4 and 5.6. The restricted feature structures (together with older ones) then serve as the basis for the next instantiation step. Again, this gives us feature structures encoding a derivation, and again we are applying the rule restrictor. We proceed with the iteration, until we reach a fixpoint, meaning that further iteration steps will not add (or remove) new (or old) feature structures. Given the feature structures from the fixpoint, it is then easy to generate context-free productions, using the full feature structures as symbols of the CFG (see section 5.5).

Approximating a UBG through a CFG is exciting for several reasons. From a more theoretical point of view, it is interesting to see how close a concrete UBG can be approximated by the CFG in terms of chart edges, readings, etc., given a large corpus of positive and negative sentences. There are also very practical interests. *Firstly*, assuming that we have a CFG $\mathcal{G}$ that comes close to a UBG, we can use the CFG as a cheap filter, having a running time of $O(|\mathcal{G}|^2 \cdot n^3)$. The main idea is to use the CFG first and then let the UBG deterministically replay the derivations of the CFG, resulting in less failing *and* less successful unifications. The important point here is that (i) the CFG encodes a superset language of the UBG and (ii) one can correlate every CF production with a UBG rule (but not the other way round). *Secondly*, given a UBG, it would be nice to have an automated method that yields a CFG for the purpose of a context-free language model, as is possible in the Nuance speech recognizer (Dowding et al., 2001). Given such a CFG, one might then eventually produce a weaker language model for other speech recognizers by means of a regular approximation (Nederhof, 2000). *Thirdly*, an approximated CFG can be a starting point for a (finite) stochastic parsing model, even though the UBG usually encodes an infinite number of categories; cf. section 8. This model would then allow a deterministic reconstruction of the 'best' UBG analysis for a given utterance, without having to fully explore the search space, together with an estimation of the parsing results. *Finally*, we believe that the result of the approximation (i.e., the feature structures in the fixpoint) reveals weak points in the given grammar, thus helping us to improve the quality of the UBG (see section 5.6). Indeed, this happened during our enterprise.

The structure of the chapter is as follows. We first recapitulate some basic UBG terminology in section 2. After that, section 3 presents the theoretical foundation of our method: successive approximation as least fixpoint construction over a certain monotonic function T. Section 4 presents the basic algorithm which exactly implements T. In order to overcome some running time deficiencies of the basic algorithm, we describe useful optimizations in section 5. We also elaborate on how the context-free productions are obtained.

As a consequence of these optimizations, the mathematics for T is no longer valid. Section 6 investigates the slightly different setting. In order to see how the method proceeds, we present three grammars and discuss the outcome of the approximation process in section 7. We end by introducing an improved disambiguation method for unification grammars that is based on unsupervised learning of a probabilistic model for the approximated CFG.

2.   Basic Inventory

Unification-based theories of grammar allow for an elegant integration of different levels of linguistic descriptions in the common framework of typed feature structures; see, e.g., Carpenter (1992) for an introduction. Interaction between these levels is specified by means of coreferences, indicating the sharing of information. Such coreferences also describe how the linguistic strata constrain each other mutually.

A crucial property of many unification-based grammar theories is that they are *lexicalized*, meaning that the rules (often called rule schemata or ID schemata) are very general (and there are only a few of them) and that the lexicon entries (actually the lexical types) are relatively specific. Due to this fact, one can not translate a UBG rule directly into a single context-free production. Furthermore, UBG rules (and lexicon entries) contain coreference constraints that are not allowed as a descriptive means in CFGs. Finally, rules and lexicon entries in UBGs must be interpreted w.r.t. a type hierarchy, a feature unavailable to CFGs.

In this chapter, we make a distinction between grammar rules and lexicon entries, but uniformly represent them as typed feature structures, as, e.g., HPSG does. (Section 7.1 shows how PATR-II rules can be translated into typed feature structures, using a specialized ARGS feature). The set of all *rules* is depicted by $\mathcal{R}$. An example of a rule is the head-complement schema in HPSG (Pollard and Sag, 1994, p. 38). $ar(r)$ denotes the number of daughters of a given rule $r \in \mathcal{R}$ and is called the *arity* of r. The collection of all *lexicon entries* constitutes the lexicon $\mathcal{L}$.

We also need the notion of a *restrictor*, as originally introduced by Shieber (1985). A restrictor can be seen as an automaton or alternatively as a function (and specified as a feature structure in our system), describing the paths in a feature structure that will remain after *restriction*, that is, after applying the deletion operation. The result of this operation is again a feature structure that always subsumes (is more general than) the input structure. Let us give an example. Since HPSG requires all relevant information to be contained in the SYNSEM feature of the mother structure, the unnecessary daughters, encoding the derivation, only increase the size of the overall structure without constraining the search space. Due to the Locality Principle of HPSG, they can therefore be legally removed in fully instantiated items (Pollard and Sag, 1987, pp. 143–144). Other portions of a feature structure will also be deleted during the iteration process. In section 5.6, we will describe why this is necessary. We employ two different restrictors in our approach: the *lexicon restrictor L* and the *rule restrictor R*.

3. Approximation as Fixpoint Construction

The basic inventory from the last section now comes into play in order to formalize our idea. Assuming a finite set of features $\mathcal{F}$ (often called attributes), a finite set of atoms $\mathcal{A}$ (often called constants), and a finite set of types $\mathcal{T}$ (often called sorts), let $\mathcal{FS}$ be the countably infinite domain of typed feature structures (also called f-structures, attribute-value matrices, DAGs, or categories) which can inductively be defined as the least solution of the recursive domain equation $\mathcal{FS} = \mathcal{T} \times (\mathcal{F} \to \mathcal{FS}) + \mathcal{A}$; see Pereira and Shieber (1984) for the untyped treatment.[2]

We can then view a rule $r \in \mathcal{R}$, with $ar(r) = n$, as an n-ary function, mapping n-tuples of feature structures into a single feature structure:

$$r : \mathcal{FS}^n \longmapsto \mathcal{FS} \tag{11.1}$$

Similarly, we can view the lexicon restrictor and the rule restrictor as a (unary) function:

$$L, R : \mathcal{FS} \longmapsto \mathcal{FS} \tag{11.2}$$

During each iteration step i, we obtain the following sets T_i of feature structures:

$$T_0 := \bigcup_{l \in \mathcal{L}} L(l) \tag{11.3}$$

$$T_{i+1} := \bigcup_{k=0}^{i} \bigcup_{r \in \mathcal{R}} \bigcup_{t \in (T_k)^{ar(r)}} R(r(t)) \tag{11.4}$$

(11.3) corresponds to the generalization process of the lexicon, whereas (11.4) exactly describes the $i + 1$ step of the iteration, taking into account feature structures from the previous steps $0, \ldots, i$.[3]

More formally in terms of the (upward) ordinal power of a monotonic mapping T (Lloyd, 1987, pp. 26–31), we define

$$T(S) := S \cup \bigcup_{r \in \mathcal{R}} \bigcup_{s \in S^{ar(r)}} R(r(s)) \tag{11.5}$$

Mathematically speaking, T itself operates on the *powerset* of our domain of feature structures $\mathcal{FS}$, mapping approximations into approximations, i.e.,

$$T : 2^{\mathcal{FS}} \longmapsto 2^{\mathcal{FS}} \tag{11.6}$$

The idea behind T is that it will exactly enumerate those feature structures which are legal instantiations of underspecified rule schemata and which have undergone the application of the rule restrictor R. In the end, we are interested in sets of feature structures $S \in 2^{\mathcal{FS}}$, where

$$T(S) = S \tag{11.7}$$

since in this case, S has been saturated, hence we can stop the iteration process. If so, we call S a *fixpoint* of T. We say that S is the *least* fixpoint of T iff S is a fixpoint and for all other fixpoints S' of T, we have $S \subseteq S'$. Clearly, T is *monotonic*, since for all $S, S' \in 2^{\mathcal{FS}}$ with $S \subseteq S'$, we have $T(S) \subseteq T(S')$. This is due to the fact that set union employed in the definition of T is a monotonic operation (and does not delete any other information). Furthermore, the argument S of T occurs on the right side of definition (11.5), thus $S \subseteq T(S)$ is always true.

We then define the approximated context-free grammar $\mathcal{G}$ as the *least fixpoint* of T which is well-defined, since T is monotonic and operates on a complete lattice, viz., $2^{\mathcal{FS}}$ (the famous Knaster-Tarski fixpoint theorem):

$$\mathcal{G} := lfp(T) \tag{11.8}$$

It should now be clear that a *finite* fixpoint can only be reached if features, leading to an infinite growth of the overall structure, are deleted by the restrictor. Clearly, the more features are removed, the more general the CFG will be and the sooner the fixpoint will be reached.

4.   The Basic Algorithm

We will now describe the naïve approximation algorithm which can be seen as a direct implementation of the definitional equations (11.3) and (11.4), together with the fixpoint termination criterion given by (11.7). Several optimizations are discussed later in section 5 that improve the efficiency of the algorithm, but are uninteresting at this stage of presentation.

We start with the description of the top-level function *UBG2CFG* which initiates the approximation process. We begin the approximation by first abstracting from the lexicon entries $\mathcal{L}$ with the help of the lexicon restrictor L (line 5 of the algorithm). This constitutes our initial set T_0 (line 6). We note here that an abstracted lexicon entry is not merely added using set union but instead through a more complex operation, depicted by $\sqcup_\sqsubseteq$. We will describe this operation in section 5. At this stage of presentation, it suffices to assume that $\sqcup_\sqsubseteq$ simply denotes set union. Finally, we start the true iteration calling *Iterate* with the necessary parameters.

1   *UBG2CFG*$(\mathcal{R}, \mathcal{L}, R, L) :\Longleftrightarrow$
2   **var** T_0;
3   $T_0 := \emptyset$;
4   **for each** $l \in \mathcal{L}$ **do**
5    $l := L(l)$;
6    $T_0 := T_0 \sqcup_\sqsubseteq \{l\}$;
7   *Iterate*$(\mathcal{R}, R, T_0)$.

After that, the instantiation of the rule schemata with rule-/lexicon-restricted elements from the previous iteration T_i begins (lines 10–13). The instantiation is performed in *Iterate* by *Fill-Daughters* which takes into account a single rule r and T_i, returning successfully instantiated feature structures t to which we apply the rule restrictor. *Fill-Daughters* is explained in section 5. We then add the restricted t to T_{i+1}, employing $\sqcup_\sqsubseteq$ (line 13).

It should be noted that the rule restrictor should be carefully tuned to get rid of those paths whose values would otherwise grow infinitely during the approximation. Now, to guarantee a fixpoint that can be reached in *finitely* many steps (and we are clearly interested in this), such information must be deleted in order to enforce a convergence of $\langle T_i \rangle_{i \geq 0}$. This issue is discussed in more detail in section 5.6.

We finally come to the point where we compare the (restricted) feature structures from the previous iteration T_i with the new ones from T_{i+1}. If both sets contain the same elements, we clearly have reached a fixpoint. In this case we immediately terminate with T_i; otherwise, we proceed with the iteration (lines 14–16).

8   *Iterate*$(\mathcal{R}, R, T_i) :\Longleftrightarrow$
9   **var** $T_{i+1} := T_i$;
10 **for each** $r \in \mathcal{R}$ **do**
11   **for each** $t \in$ *Fill-Daughters*(r, T_i) **do**
12    $t := R(t)$;
13    $T_{i+1} := T_{i+1} \sqcup_\sqsubseteq \{t\}$;
14 **if** $T_i = T_{i+1}$

15   **then return** T_i
16   **else** *Iterate*$(\mathcal{R}, R, T_{i+1})$.

5.   Implementation Issues and Optimizations

In order to make the basic algorithm work for large-size grammars, we modified it in several ways. Without these optimizations, the method would *not* be tractable.

5.1   Avoiding Recomputations of Rule Instantiations

The most obvious optimization applies to the function *Fill-Daughters*, where the number of unifications is reduced by avoiding recomputation of combinations of daughters and rules that have already been checked. To do this in a simple way, we split the set T_i into $T_i \setminus T_{i-1}$ and T_{i-1} during step $i + 1$ and fill a rule with only those permutations of daughters which contain at least one element from $T_i \setminus T_{i-1}$. This guarantees checking of only those configurations which were enabled by the last iteration. Given T_i and T_{i+1}, the termination criterion in line 14 then becomes much easier: $T_{i+1} \setminus T_i = \emptyset$, thus we have only to remember (by using a flag) whether at least one structure has been added to T_{i+1} or not.

5.2   Detecting Unification Failures Quickly

We also use techniques developed in Kiefer *et al.* (1999), namely the so-called *rule filter* and the *quick-check method*. The rule filter precomputes the applicability of rules into each other and thus is able to predict a failing unification using a simple and fast table lookup in a three-dimensional Boolean array. The quick-check method exploits the fact that unification fails more often at certain points in feature structures than at others. In an off-line stage, we parse a large test corpus, using a special unifier that records all failures instead of bailing out after the first one in order to determine the most prominent failure points. These points constitute the *quick-check vector* (qc-vector). Given a feature structure $t \in \mathcal{FS}$, let $q(t) \in \mathcal{T}^n$ denote the qc-vector for t of length n and $q^i(t) \in \mathcal{T}$ the i-th projection of $q(t)$ ($1 \leq i \leq n$).

When executing a unification during approximation, those points are efficiently accessed and checked using type unification prior to the rest of the structure. During our experiments (see section 7.3), more than 94% of all failing unifications in *Fill-Daughters* (line 15) could be quickly detected using the above techniques. The last filter heavily relies on type unification being very fast, which in fact is the case, as it can be precompiled; see Kiefer *et al.* (2000a).

5.3   Detecting Subsumption Failures Quickly

As it was mentioned in section 4, instead of applying set union (under feature structure equivalence) we use the more elaborate operation $\cup_{\sqsubseteq}$ when adding new feature structures to T_{i+1}. In fact, we add a new structure only if it is not subsumed by some structure already in the set. If this is the case, we remove all those structures in T_{i+1} that are subsumed by the new structure. Both tests are very expensive since every new feature structure has to be tested against the whole set T_i.

The qc-vectors from above can also be used to accelerate these tests. T_i can be partitioned exhaustively by constructing a tree whose nodes of depth $j - 1$ correspond to the j-th position in the vector and the outgoing edges to the possible types at that position (the j-th projection) (see figure 11.1).

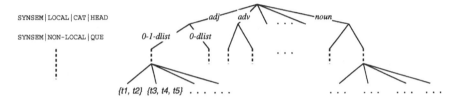

Figure 11.1.   A partition tree based on quick-check vectors. The feature paths on the left side point to the substructure corresponding to the position in the qc-vector. Node labels such as *adj* or *0-1-dlist* are types, whereas t1, t2,... are feature structures.

In this tree, a path from the root to a leaf corresponds to an instance of a qc-vector. The leaves form a disjoint partition of T_i, in that each leaf contains all feature structures whose qc-vector content equals the types collected at the tree path. During traversal of the tree, we can eventually rule out whole subtrees (and consequently subsets of T_i) by checking a single type subsumption $\leq$.[4] Hereby, we exploit the following property ($s, t \in \mathcal{FS}$):

$$\exists i \in \{1, \dots, |q(s)|\} . q^i(t) \not\leq q^i(s) \Rightarrow t \not\sqsubseteq s \tag{11.9}$$

If the i-th type in the qc-vector of the new feature structure t is not subsumed by the type of the corresponding tree edge, no feature structure in the subtree the edge points to can subsume t.

To draw full benefit of this method, two points have to be considered. Firstly, if all positions of the qc-vectors are used, the tree gets extremely large and its traversal becomes a significant overhead. Secondly, several positions in a qc-vector are often filled with the most unspecific type (e.g., because the corresponding path does not exist in the feature structure). Those positions have a low potential to differentiate the feature structures of T_i but increase the tree size drastically. To account for these problems, only a small subset of the qc-vector positions is used, namely those that contain specific types most of the time.

This means that when a leaf is reached, still a lot of feature structures need to be checked. Here, the rest of the qc-vector can be employed to check if subsumption is possible according to (11.9) before applying the expensive feature structure subsumption. Using the qc-vectors for subsumption too definitely pays off: nearly 97% of all failing subsumptions could thus be detected early.

By exchanging the role of t and s, the same tree can also be used to speed up the search for elements of T_i that are subsumed by a newly created feature structure as well as during the production of the CF grammar (see section 5.5).

The application of $\cup_{\sqsubseteq}$ will usually change the language of the resulting CF grammar. As we already said, large-scale grammars (as the one from section 7.3) are at the moment no longer tractable if we use $\cup$ to gather the feature structures during the iteration. In the worst case, there might be exponentially more structures in the fixpoint when using $\cup$ instead of $\cup_{\sqsubseteq}$. We believe, however, that by choosing proper restrictors, the resulting context-free languages are still useful. The overall strategy thus must be to use $\cup$ as long as possible, and only if the iteration will exceed certain time/space limitations, to change to $\cup_{\sqsubseteq}$. Due to space requirements, we can only glimpse at a third, more complex operation $\cup_{\sim}$ that 'lies between' $\cup$ and $\cup_{\sqsubseteq}$, and which retains most of the good properties of both operations. The idea here is to compare (a number of) the quick-check paths under feature structure equivalence (as in $\cup$) and the rest of the feature structure under feature structure subsumption.

5.4   Conflation by Folding/Unfilling Structures

Finally, we also implemented a mechanism which has helped us to shrink the number of feature structures in T_i (we obtain a reduction of 20–30% in the number of structures). The idea is to conflate those feature structures into a single structure which only differ in features whose types are maximally unspecific, as is the case for, e.g., [SUBCAT list] or [MOOD mood]. We like to dub this technique as *folding* or *unfilling*, since it reminds us of the fold/unfold transformations in term rewriting systems/functional programming (Courcelle, 1990) and unfilling in the TROLL system (Götz, 1994). Notice that the process of folding a feature structure is not as easy as it may seem to be, since is started recursively from the leaves of the feature structure. Consider, for instance,

$$\begin{bmatrix} A & 1 \\ B & \begin{bmatrix} C & \top \\ D & \top \end{bmatrix} \end{bmatrix} \text{ and } \begin{bmatrix} A & 1 \\ E & \top \end{bmatrix}$$

which can both be folded into $\begin{bmatrix} A & 1 \end{bmatrix}$, whereas

$$\begin{bmatrix} A\ \boxed{1}\ \top \\ B\ \boxed{1} \end{bmatrix} \text{ and } \begin{bmatrix} A\ \top \\ C\ \top \end{bmatrix}$$

can *not* be conflated into [ ], due to the coreference constraint (indicated by $\boxed{1}$). The implementation works as follows. At the end of each iteration step i, we map over $T_i \setminus T_{i-1}$, looking for feature structures that can be folded/unfilled. Using the fast subsumption check from above, we finally sort out those structures that are subsumed by already existing structures in T_i.

5.5 Computing Context-Free Productions

There is still one piece missing, viz., how the context-free productions are actually obtained. Although they can be generated in parallel with the instantiation of the UBG rules, it seems to be more efficient (and theoretically cleaner) to generate them after the fixpoint was reached. This is due to the fact that many feature structures are removed during the iteration (and are replaced by more general ones), hence the corresponding productions then have to be removed too. In order to avoid this useless work, we produce the CFG at the end of the fixpoint iteration. The *theoretical* basis of this strategy comes from the properties of the fixpoint under the usage of $\cup$.[5] Since (11.5) tells us that elements from iteration step i are always present in step j, $j \geq i$ (remember, T is monotonic under $\cup$), it suffices to generate a CF production simply by instantiating an n-ary rule schema r a final time with feature structures $t_1, \ldots, t_n$ from the last iteration step. After applying the rule restrictor R, we must obtain a feature structure t from the fixpoint. Hence, we are allowed to generate the following CF production: $t \to t_1 \ldots t_n$.

Clearly, a context-free parser cannot work with feature structures as terminal or nonterminal symbols and furthermore, since we use $\cup_{\sqsubseteq}$ instead of $\cup$ in the implementation, $R(r(t_1, \ldots, t_n))$ might not be in the fixpoint, but however a more general feature structure. In order to make the above theoretical idea feasible in our system, we map in a first step each feature structure from the fixpoint onto a unique integer (we write $t.i$ to indicate that feature structure t is associated with integer i). After the instantiation of r with $t.1, \ldots, t.n$ takes place, we have to classify the result $t = R(r(t.1, \ldots, t.n))$ against the fixpoint by using feature structure subsumption – remember that the feature structures from the fixpoint are pairwise incomparable, due to the use of the $\cup_{\sqsubseteq}$ operation as explained above (cf. section 5.3). Assuming that $t.l_1, \ldots, t.l_m$ are the feature structures from the fixpoint with $t \sqsubseteq t.l_i$ $(1 \leq i \leq m)$, we get the following set of CF productions: $\{l_i \to 1 \ldots n \mid 1 \leq i \leq m\}$. Notice that the $t.l_i$ $(1 \leq i \leq m)$ are pairwise incompatible and that there will be *no* other feature structures in the fixpoint that are more general than one of the $t.l_i$, due to the special nature of $\cup_{\sqsubseteq}$; see section 6 for an explanation.

Since the lexicon abstraction process (lines 4–6 in the algorithm) collapses lexicon entries into classes, the context-free parser must also remember to which classes a single terminal string form belongs. Since this information is encoded under the feature PHONOLOGY (or perhaps MORPH or FORM), we must remember this mapping during the iteration of the lexicon (lines 4–6). Of course, when using $\sqcup_\sqsubseteq$ (instead of $\sqcup$), this mapping needs to be updated. Note that the lexicon abstraction classes (or generalizations of them) form exactly the terminal symbols of the CF grammar.

It is worth noting that there might be several feature structures $t.s_1, \ldots, t.s_k$ from the fixpoint which can serve as start symbols for the CFG, hence we introduce a unique synthetic symbol 0 that does the job and add the following CF productions: $\{0 \rightarrow s_j \mid 1 \leq j \leq k\}$. The question remains how to obtain the $t.s_j$ $(1 \leq j \leq k)$. This is usually achieved by specifying in advance well-formedness constraints for other feature structures to be legal utterances/phrases (e.g., empty SUBCAT list). These constraints, which we call *root nodes*, are represented as feature structures and checking well-formedness then is achieved via unification. Note that there might exist several such root nodes.[6]

One might be confused that we use the full feature structures as context-free symbols. This is due to the fact that we have already reached a fixpoint and that we want to take all the information embodied in the feature structures into account, not merely parts of them. If we would limit ourselves to certain pieces only, mimicking annotated CF symbols à la GPSG (Gazdar et al., 1985), a lot of feature structures from the fixpoint would certainly collapse, hence in the end the resulting CFG would be less specific (however, consisting of fewer CF rules).

5.6 Tuning the Approximation Process

To be able to reach a finite fixpoint and to compute a good approximation from a large-scale grammar, it is crucial to delete exactly the right information from the feature structures: keeping parts of the feature structures that only collect information and seldom or never constrain derivations will lead to lots of new feature structures, maybe even infinitely many. Examples in HPSG include the (already discussed) DTRS feature, which only encodes the immediate dominance structure of the derivation so far. Additionally, big parts of the semantics (roughly speaking: information under feature CONTENT in HPSG) do not constrain the search space. The quick-check vectors already mentioned in section 5.2 are a good starting point for finding the right paths that need to be deleted by the restrictor during the fixpoint iteration. Clearly, we let only those paths survive which are the most prominent ones, e.g., which correspond to the highest failure counts. However, the more paths we take into account, the more feature structures we obtain during the iteration.

Usually, deleting information only in these parts does not suffice. The amount of different feature/value configurations is still too big to be handled in practice. The methods and problems in tuning the process, such that the fixpoint construction is completed in acceptable time and closely approximates the original grammar, are described in Kiefer and Krieger (2002).

6.   Revisiting the Fixpoint Construction

As we noted in the last section, new feature structures are not added by simply using set union, but instead through a more sophisticated operation (depicted by $\sqcup_{\sqsubseteq}$) which takes feature structure subsumption $\sqsubseteq$ into account (cf. lines 6 and 13 in the above algorithm). This operation might even delete elements from T_{i+1} in case that a new feature structure t subsumes (several) older elements. Hence for arbitrary sets S and $T(S)$, it could be that $S \subseteq T(S)$ is *no* longer valid and even $card(S) > card(T(S))$ might be the case (we often found this behavior in our experiments after a few iteration steps), i.e., T itself is no longer monotonic according to $\subseteq$.

In order to address these facts, we must accommodate the mathematical apparatus introduced in section 3. This can be easily achieved by slightly changing the domain/range and the definition of T. First of all, we move from the powerset $2^{\mathcal{FS}}$ to the *complete restricted powerset* $2^{[\mathcal{FS}]}$ of $\mathcal{FS}$. Elements of $2^{[\mathcal{FS}]}$ are no longer arbitrary sets, but instead sets of pairwise incomparable feature structures, usually called *cochains* or *crowns* (Aït-Kaci et al., 1989). These sets are ordered by employing the so-called *Hoare ordering* (Rounds, 1988; Gunter and Scott, 1990) which we will also denote by $\sqsubseteq$ (thus overloading this symbol):

$$S \sqsubseteq S' :\Longleftrightarrow \forall s \in S, \exists s' \in S' . s \sqsubseteq s' \tag{11.10}$$

Monotonicity of T in $2^{[\mathcal{FS}]}$ is obviously defined as follows:

$$T \text{ is monotonic} :\Longleftrightarrow \forall S, S' \in 2^{[\mathcal{FS}]} . S \sqsubseteq S' \Rightarrow T(S) \sqsubseteq T(S') \tag{11.11}$$

The new definition of T reflects these changes:

$$T(S) := S \cup_{\sqsubseteq} \bigcup_{\sqsubseteq}_{r \in \mathcal{R}} \bigcup_{\sqsubseteq}_{s \in S^{ar(r)}} R(r(s)) \tag{11.12}$$

Now, the interesting point here is that since $\langle 2^{[\mathcal{FS}]}, \sqsubseteq \rangle$ is a *complete* lattice, the *least upper bound* $\sqcup$ (as well as the greatest lower bound) is well-defined for *arbitrary* sets $S, S' \in 2^{[\mathcal{FS}]}$. Since $S \sqcup S'$ results in the least general set of incomparable feature structures under the Hoare order, $\sqcup$ is exactly the operation $\cup_{\sqsubseteq}$ which we have already used in the algorithm and informally described in section 5:

$$T(S) := S \sqcup \bigsqcup_{r \in \mathcal{R}} \bigsqcup_{s \in S^{ar(r)}} R(r(s)) \tag{11.13}$$

To show that the new definition of T is also monotonic, we must prove $T(S) \sqsubseteq T(S')$, i.e.,

$$S \sqcup \bigsqcup_{r \in \mathcal{R}} \bigsqcup_{s \in S^{ar(r)}} R(r(s)) \sqsubseteq S' \sqcup \bigsqcup_{r \in \mathcal{R}} \bigsqcup_{s' \in S'^{ar(r)}} R(r(s'))$$

Since $S \sqsubseteq S'$ (assumption), we have

$$\bigsqcup_{r \in \mathcal{R}} \bigsqcup_{s \in S^{ar(r)}} R(r(s)) \sqsubseteq \bigsqcup_{r \in \mathcal{R}} \bigsqcup_{s' \in S'^{ar(r)}} R(r(s'))$$

Because $S \sqsubseteq S'$, there must exist an S'' s.t. $S \sqcup S'' = S'$ (recall that $2^{[\mathcal{FS}]}$ is complete), hence we finally have for *every* $r \in \mathcal{R}$

$$\bigsqcup_{s \in S^{ar(r)}} R(r(s)) \sqsubseteq \bigsqcup_{s \in S^{ar(r)}} R(r(s)) \sqcup \bigsqcup_{s'' \in S''^{ar(r)}} R(r(s''))$$

$$\sqsubseteq \bigsqcup_{t \in (S \sqcup S'')^{ar(r)}} R(r(t)) = \bigsqcup_{s' \in S'^{ar(r)}} R(r(s')) \quad \blacksquare$$

Having proved that T is monotonic, we can guarantee that T has a (unique) *least* fixpoint (but not several smallest, incomparable ones).

7. Three Grammars

As mentioned before, we encode grammar rules as pure feature structures, using a special list-valued feature ARGS to define the right-hand side (the daughters), while the other top-level features belong to the left-hand side (the mother).[7]

This section describes the results of applying our method to a small-size PATR-II grammar, a mid-size CLE grammar, and a large-size HPSG grammar.

7.1 Shieber's Toy Grammar

The first example is the feature structure encoding of Stuart Shieber's second sample PATR-II grammar (Shieber, 1986, pp. 71–76). This grammar uses two underspecified rules for verb phrase construction. Overall, the grammar consists of three rules, together with 13 lexicon entries. Two of the lexicon entries can be collapsed into a single category.

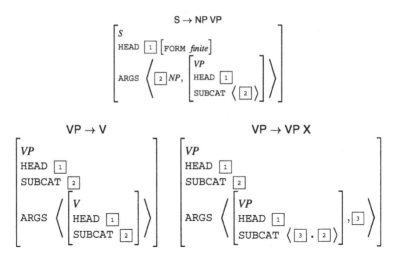

We made two tests with different restrictors, one allowing only agreement, the other containing also subcategorization information (the ARGS feature was deleted in both cases). After four iterations, both processes stopped with 31 feature structures. Without subcategorization information, we got 20 context-free productions. However by using also the type and agreement information of subcategorized elements, we obtained 33 productions. It should be noted that only the second set of productions correctly distinguishes VP non-terminals subcategorizing for NPs with specific agreement values, such as [HEAD | FORM *finite*]. Clearly, a more specific CF grammar results in more productions, together with more nonterminal symbols. We also made an experiment using ∪ instead of ∪⊑, but also obtained the same 31 feature structures and the same 33 CF productions.

It is worth noting that the resulting CFGs even contain *useless* productions, e.g., productions that will never contribute to a reading. There exist fast decidable algorithms that, given a grammar, produce a weakly equivalent one which does not contain useless productions at all; see e.g., Hopcroft and Ullman (1979), pp. 87–92. In our case, 8 of the 33 productions of the second CF grammar were useless. This observation could have a repercussion on the PATR grammar in that it might show pieces of redundant information. We also chose (by mistake) an empty restrictor, not even deleting the growing ARGS feature. It turned out that the above PATR-II grammar is not only context-free, but even describes a finite language: in the end, we obtained 85 FSs and 85 productions, from which 30 turned out to be useless.

7.2   Dowding's Gemini Grammar

Dowding *et al.* (2001) compared the approach of Moore (1999) to grammar approximation to that of Kiefer and Krieger (2000), a forerunner of this chapter. As a basis for the comparison, he chose a command-and-control grammar written in the Gemini/CLE formalism. The motivation for this enterprise comes from the use of the resulting CFG as a context-free language model for the Nuance speech recognizer. John Dowding kindly provided the Gemini grammar and a test corpus of 500 sentences, allowing us to measure the quality of our approximation method for a realistic mid-size grammar, both under $\cup$ and $\cup_{\sqsubseteq}$.

The Gemini grammar consisted of 57 unification rules and a small lexicon of 216 entries which expanded into 425 full forms. Since the grammar allows for atomic disjunctions (and makes heavy use of them), we ended in 1,886 type definitions overall. Given the 500 test sentences, the Gemini grammar licensed 720 readings. We only deleted the ARGS feature (the daughters) during the iteration and found that the grammar encodes a context-free language, due to the fact that the iteration terminates under $\cup$ – this means that we have even obtained a correct approximation of the Gemini grammar.

To measure the quality of the CF approximation, we implemented a very simple bottom-up passive chart parser that uses the CFG alone, followed by a second unification stage that replays derivations proposed by the CFG. The second stage uses a chart to avoid the recomputation of derivations which are licensed by more than one CF derivation. At the moment, the CF parser is not optimized by using techniques such as top-down prediction or head-driven parsing, since we focused, at first, on the quality of the approximation in terms of the number of readings and the reduction of successful and failing unifications. Despite this fact, we nevertheless present the running time of the two-stage system.

Table 11.1 presents the relevant numbers for the test corpus, both under $\cup$ and $\cup_{\sqsubseteq}$, and shows that the ambiguity rate for $\cup_{\sqsubseteq}$ goes up only mildly, whereas parsing time and grammar size drastically decrease.

Note that although the CFG obtained under $\cup_{\sqsubseteq}$ encodes a true superset of the language licensed by the Gemini grammar, the two-step parsing approach described above guarantees that the right readings will be definitely found on the unification side, going hand in hand with a reduction in running time (see table) and a reduction in space of more than 65% (even for this preliminary implementation).

We note that the measurements in Dowding *et al.* (2001) differ from those presented here. It is not clear at the moment why their implementation of our method comes off so badly and we are currently investigating what has gone wrong here. Dowding *et al.* (2001) argued that the worse behavior is due to the use of $\cup_{\sqsubseteq}$ – however, our measurements above show that this is not true, at least not for this grammar. Of course, the fixpoint iteration under $\cup$ will always yield a better approximation than under $\cup_{\sqsubseteq}$ and the generated CFGs might drastically differ, but as we explained in section 5.3, when attacking

Table 11.1. A comparison of the approximated CFGs derived under ∪ and ∪⊑, followed by a deterministic second unification stage. We compare these numbers, in part, with those obtained by pure unification-based parsing. The fixpoint for ∪ (∪⊑) was reached after 9 (8) iteration steps and took 5 minutes (34 seconds) to be computed, including post-processing time to compute the CF productions. The numbers are derived w.r.t. a test corpus of 500 sentences. The measurements were conducted on a 833 MHz Linux workstation.

	Gemini	∪	∪⊑
# readings	720	720	747
ambiguity rate	1.44	1.44	1.49
#terminals	—	152	109
#nonterminals	—	3,158	998
#rules	57	24,101	5,269
#useful rules	57	19,618	4,842
#successful unifications	65,472	8,001	8,004
#failing unifications	456,857	0	0
#quick-check failures	1,805,336	9	36
running time (secs)	32.9	14.6	9.5
run time speed-up (%)	0	55.6	71.1
total space (MBytes)	250	191	87

really huge complex grammars (see next section), ∪⊑ is – at the moment – the only way to go, since otherwise the approximation process would no longer be tractable in time and space.

7.3 CSLI's LinGO Grammar

We also applied our method to the large English LinGO grammar, developed at CSLI Stanford. The grammar consists of 61 rule schemata, 8,082 types, and a lexicon of 6,930 stems. We used the *aged* test suite (Oepen and Callmeier, 2000), consisting of approx. 100 syntactically highly diverse sentences, to measure the quality of our approximation (average sentence length: 8.4; maximal length: 19). *aged* consists of 202 stems that cover a great deal of morphological and lexical variation. 719 full forms were computed from these stems. The lexicon restrictor for the English grammar, as shown in figure 11.2, maps these forms onto 321 lexical abstractions/feature structures. This restrictor tells us which parts of a feature structure have to be deleted – it is the kind of restrictor we are usually going to use. According to Harrison and Ellison (1992), we call this a *negative* restrictor, contrary to the *positive* restrictors used in the PATR-II system that only specify those parts of a feature structure which will survive after restricting it. Since a feature structure could have reentrance points, we extend the notion of a restrictor in that one can even define a *recursive* (or *cyclic*) restrictor to foresee recursive embeddings as is the case in HPSG. I.e., multiple occurrences of the same feature (e.g., CONTENT) in a given feature structure at an arbitrary depth can be deleted this way. The rule restrictor looks quite similar, cutting off additional feature-value pairs, such as DTRS and ARGS.

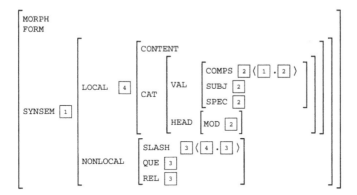

Figure 11.2. The simplified lexicon restrictor used in our experiments. This negative restrictor essentially only cuts off the CONTENT feature in local and nonlocal objects, together with MORPH and FORM. In addition, ARGS and DTRS are deleted by the rule restrictor.

The fixpoint for the full English grammar was reached after 9 iteration steps, resulting in 3,623 feature structures. The computation of the fixpoint (incl. the generation of the CF productions) took about 4 CPU hours on a 833 MHz Linux workstation under Allegro Common Lisp 6.0.1. During the iteration, 3,221,899 full top-level unification and 708,472,337 full subsumption operations were performed. The quick-check method, used both during unification and subsumption, leads to a filter rate of 92.9% and 99.8%, resp. This translates into an enormous number of 27,482,882 and 704,904,258 quickly failing unification and subsumption operations. The smart lookup determines more than 99.99% of the right feature structures. It is worth noting that without the smart lookup and the quick-check method used during unification and subsumption, the above approach would (at the moment) no longer be tractable.

The full grammar consists of 61 rules (31 unary and 30 binary rules). As we indicated in section 5, we compute the CF productions after reaching the fixpoint, viewing full feature structures from the fixpoint as complex CF symbols. We did this and obtained the following results: given the feature structures from the fixpoint which are exactly the terminal and nonterminal symbols of the CF grammar, the 61 rules might lead to $31 \times 3,623 + 30 \times 3,623 \times 3,623 = 393,896,183$ CF productions in the worst case. Our method produces 623,199 productions, only 0.16% of all possible ones. Given these productions, we detected that 8,831 of them were useless, i.e., will never contribute to a reading.

Overall, the final CFG consists of 3,302 nonterminal symbols, 321 terminal symbols, and 614,368 (useful) productions.

We also made a similar experiment, choosing the same grammar, but a different test suite called *eng2000* of 1,238 sentences with an average length of 7.8 (maximal sentence length: 37). Given the words from the test suite, we found 805 stems which expanded into 3,007 lexical entries. By applying the lexicon restrictor, we started the fixpoint iteration with 827 feature structure abstractions. The fixpoint was reached again after 9 iteration steps, consisting of 6,364 feature structures, taking 17 CPU hours. In the end, 1,551,897 CF productions were computed, thereof 1,531,754 useful (= 0.13% of possible combinations).

Using the HPSG parser alone, *aged* resulted in 1,366 readings and 49,292 passive chart edges. The system performed 73,535 successful and 305,327 failing unifications; 3,109,215 failing unifications were avoided using the filtering technique, described in section 5.2.

The CFG parser produces 1,099 packed readings and 41,608 packed passive edges. The replay stage finds the same number of readings as the pure HPSG parser (of course), but only needs 19,539 successful, 24,309 failing and 28,703 filtered unifications (= 73.4%, 92.0%, and 99.1% reduction).

Considering the above numbers, the interesting point here is that the numbers of successful, failing as well as filtered unifications have been reduced dramatically. Especially, parts of the extremely time- and space-consuming successful unifications have been avoided. Exactly these unifications never contribute to a reading, representing dead derivation branches, and are, in a way, the analogue to useless context-free productions. However, useless CF productions can be predicted offline, whereas all unsuccessful rule configurations can *not* be computed beforehand, due to the infinite number of 'categories' in a unification-based grammar.

For the *aged* test suite, the two-stage system consisting of the CF parser together with the deterministic HPSG replay stage needs 1:24 minute for exhaustive parsing, whereas pure HPSG parsing explores the whole search space in 2:23 minutes. This translates into a preliminary runtime speedup of 41%. We guess that a solid reimplementation of the CF parser that will incorporate standard CF optimization techniques will lead to a much bigger speedup.

Let us finally report the results for the large *eng2000* test suite for which the pure HPSG parser (as well as the two-stage system) found 14,678 readings. We measured pure HPSG parsing and the two-stage approach as follows: 883,714 vs. 520,570 passive edges, 1,247,812 vs. 279,329 successful unifications (77.6% reduction), 7,389,117 vs. 325,513 failing unifications (95.6%), 58,578,467 vs. 591,511 filtered unifications (99.0%). Compared to the *aged* suite the runtime speedup is even better: 1:55 hour vs. 0:43 hour (= 62% speedup).

8.   Disambiguation of UBGs via Probabilistic Approximations

This chapter suggested that, given a UBG, the approximated CFG can be used as a cheap filter during a two-stage parsing approach. The idea was to let the CFG explore the search space, whereas the UBG deterministically replays the derivations, proposed by the CFG. To be able to carry out the replay, during the creation of the CF grammar, each CF production is correlated with the UBG rules it was produced from.

The above mentioned two-stage parsing approach not only speeds up parsing, but can also be a starting point for an efficient stochastic parsing model, even though the UBG might encode an infinite number of categories. Given a training corpus, the idea is to move from the approximated CFG to a PCFG which predicts probabilities for the CFG trees. Clearly, the probabilities can be used for disambiguation, and more important, for ranking of CFG trees. The idea is, that the ranked parsing trees can be replayed one after another by the UBG (processing the most probable CFG trees first), establishing an order of best UBG parsing trees. Since the approximation always yields a CFG that is a superset of the UBG, it might be possible that derivation trees proposed by the PCFG can *not* be replayed by the UBG. Nevertheless, this behavior does not alter the ranking of reconstructed UBG parsing trees.

As a nice side effect, our proposed stochastic parsing model should usually *not* explore the full search space, nor should it statically estimate the parsing results afterwards, assuming we are interested in the most probable parse (or say, the n most probable results) – the disambiguation of UBG results is simply established by the dynamic ordering of most probable CFG trees during the first parsing stage.

For a first experiment, of which big parts were contributed by our colleague Detlef Prescher, we used the mid-size CLE grammar from section 7.2 and a corpus of 500 sentences. A sample of the sentences served as the input to the inside-outside algorithm, the standard algorithm for unsupervised training of PCFGs (Lari and Young, 1990). Our statistical ambiguation model was tested on an exact match task, where exact correspondence of the manually annotated correct parse and the most probable UBG parse was checked. Considering a random baseline of ca. 72% precision, our model showed an increase of about 16% (= 88%). The exact details, plus additional information are presented in Kiefer *et al.* (2002).

Acknowledgments

We would like to thank our colleagues Dan Flickinger, Stephan Oepen, John Dowding, and Jason Baldridge for fruitful discussions and helping us with the grammars. Special thanks to Detlef Prescher for conducting the experiments to build a stochastic model for the approximated CFG. The research described here was supported by the German Federal Ministry for Education, Science, Research, and Technology under grant nos. 01 IV 701 V0 (Verbmobil) and 01 IW 002 (Whiteboard).

Notes

1. This chapter combines and updates work originally presented in (Kiefer and Krieger, 2000), (Kiefer et al., 2000b), (Kiefer and Krieger, 2002), and (Kiefer et al., 2002).

2. The solution of this domain equation can be seen as the set of all typed rational feature trees; see Krieger (2001) .

3. $(T_k)^{ar(r)}$ represents the $ar(r)$-times cartesian product of T_k, i.e., vectors (or tuples) of length $ar(r)$ with elements from T_k (i.e., from previous iterations).

4. We implemented type subsumption $\leq$ by using the fast type unification operation $\wedge$, mentioned above: $s \leq t : \Longleftrightarrow s \wedge t = s$.

5. A slightly revised fixpoint construction that mirrors the properties of $\sqcup_{\sqsubseteq}$ is described in section 6.

6. Grammar systems that employ a bottom-up chart parser need to have such root node conditions in order to let the parser know that a reading has been obtained.

7. We used the PAGE grammar development system throughout our experiments (Uszkoreit et al., 1994).

References

Aït-Kaci, H., Boyer, R., Lincoln, P., and Nasr, R. (1989). Efficient implementation of lattice operations. *ACM Transactions on Programming Languages and Systems*, 11(1):115–146.

Alshawi, H., editor (1992). *The Core Language Engine*. ACL-MIT Press Series in Natural Language Processing. MIT Press.

Carpenter, B. (1992). *The Logic of Typed Feature Structures*. Tracts in Theoretical Computer Science. Cambridge University Press, Cambridge.

Courcelle, B. (1990). Recursive applicative program schemes. In van Leeuwen, J., editor, *Handbook of Theoretical Computer Science, Vol. B*, chapter 9. Elsevier.

Dowding, J., Hockey, B. A., Gawron, J. M., and Culy, C. (2001). Practical issues in compiling typed unification grammars for speech recognition. In *Proceedings of the 39th Annual Meeting of the Association for Computational Linguistics, ACL-2001*, pages 164–171.

Gazdar, G., Klein, E., Pullum, G., and Sag, I. (1985). *Generalized Phrase Structure Grammar*. Harvard University Press, Cambridge, MA.

Götz, T. (1994). A normal form for typed feature structures. Technical Report 40-1994, Sonderforschungsbereich 340, IBM Germany, Heidelberg.

Gunter, C. A. and Scott, D. S. (1990). Semantic domains. In van Leeuwen, J., editor, *Handbook of Theoretical Computer Science, Volume B*, chapter 12, pages 633–674. Elsevier, Amsterdam.

Harrison, S. and Ellison, T. (1992). Restriction and termination in parsing with feature-theoretic grammars. *Computational Linguistics*, 18(4):519–530.

Hopcroft, J. E. and Ullman, J. D. (1979). *Introduction to Automata Theory, Languages, and Computation*. Addison-Wesley, Reading, MA.

Kiefer, B. and Krieger, H.-U. (2000). A context-free approximation of Head-Driven Phrase Structure Grammar. In *Proceedings of the 6th International Workshop on Parsing Technologies, IWPT2000*, pages 135–146.

Kiefer, B. and Krieger, H.-U. (2002). A context-free approximation of head-driven phrase structure grammar. In *Collaborative Language Engineering. A Case Study in Efficient Grammar-based Processing*, pages 69–100. CSLI Publications, Stanford.

Kiefer, B., Krieger, H.-U., Carroll, J., and Malouf, R. (1999). A bag of useful techniques for efficient and robust parsing. In *Proceedings of the 37th Annual Meeting of the Association for Computational Linguistics, ACL-99*, pages 473–480.

Kiefer, B., Krieger, H.-U., and Nederhof, M.-J. (2000a). Efficient and robust parsing of word hypotheses graphs. In Wahlster, W., editor, *Verbmobil: Foundations of Speech-to-Speech Translation*, pages 280–295. Springer, Berlin.

Kiefer, B., Krieger, H.-U., and Prescher, D. (2002). A novel disambiguation method for unification-based grammars using probabilistic context-free approximations. In *Proceedings of the 19th International Conference on Computational Linguistics, COLING2002*.

Kiefer, B., Krieger, H.-U., and Siegel, M. (2000b). An HPSG-to-CFG approximation of Japanese. In *Proceedings of the 18th International Conference on Computational Linguistics, COLING2000*, pages 1046–1050.

Krieger, H.-U. (2001). Greatest model semantics for typed feature structures. *Grammars*, 4(2):139–165. Kluwer.

Lari, K. and Young, S. J. (1990). The estimation of stochastic context-free grammars using the inside-outside algorithm. *Computer Speech and Language*, 4:35–56.

Lloyd, J. (1987). *Foundations of Logic Programming*, 2nd edition. Springer, Berlin.

Moore, R. C. (1999). Using natural-language knowledge sources in speech recognition. In Ponting, K., editor, *Computational Models of Speech Pattern Processing*. Springer.

Nederhof, M.-J. (2000). Practical experiments with regular approximation of context-free languages. *Computational Linguistics*, 26(1):17–44.

Oepen, S. and Callmeier, U. (2000). Measure for measure: Parser cross-fertilization. In *Proceedings of the 6th International Workshop on Parsing Technologies, IWPT 2000*, pages 183–194.

Pereira, F. C. and Shieber, S. M. (1984). The semantics of grammar formalisms seen as computer languages. In *Proceedings of the 10th International Conference on Computational Linguistics*, pages 123–129.

Pollard, C. and Sag, I. A. (1987). *Information-Based Syntax and Semantics. Vol. I: Fundamentals*. CSLI Lecture Notes, Number 13. Center for the Study of Language and Information, Stanford.

Pollard, C. and Sag, I. A. (1994). *Head-Driven Phrase Structure Grammar*. Studies in Contemporary Linguistics. University of Chicago Press, Chicago.

Rounds, W. C. (1988). Set values for unification-based grammar formalisms and logic programming. Technical Report CSLI-88-129, Center for the Study of Language and Information, Stanford.

Shieber, S. M. (1985). Using restriction to extend parsing algorithms for complex-feature-based formalisms. In *Proceedings of the 23rd Annual Meeting of the Association for Computational Linguistics, ACL-85*, pages 145–152.

Shieber, S. M. (1986). *An Introduction to Unification-Based Approaches to Grammar*. CSLI Lecture Notes, Number 4. Center for the Study of Language and Information, Stanford.

Uszkoreit, H., Backofen, R., Busemann, S., Diagne, A. K., Hinkelman, E. A., Kasper, W., Kiefer, B., Krieger, H.-U., Netter, K., Neumann, G., Oepen, S., and Spackman, S. P. (1994). DISCO—an HPSG-based NLP system and its application for appointment scheduling. In *Proceedings of COLING-94*, pages 436–440. A version of this paper is available as DFKI Research Report RR-94-38.

Chapter 12

A RECOGNIZER FOR MINIMALIST LANGUAGES

Henk Harkema

Department of Computer Science, University of Sheffield
Regent Court, 211 Portobello Street, Sheffield S1 4DP, UK
harkema@dcs.shef.ac.uk

Abstract   Minimalist Grammars are a rigorous formalization of the kind of grammars proposed in the linguistic framework of Chomsky's Minimalist Program. One notable property of Minimalist Grammars is that they allow constituents to move
during the derivation of a sentence, thus creating discontinuous dependencies.
In this chapter we will present a bottom-up recognition method for languages
generated by Minimalist Grammars, prove its correctness, and discuss its complexity.

1.   Introduction

It seems to be a general feature of natural language that the elements of a
sentence can be pronounced in one position, while at the same time serving
a function in another part of the structure of the sentence. Linguistic theories
in the transformational tradition try to capture this observation by proposing
analyses that involve movement of constituents. In this chapter we will present
a bottom-up recognition algorithm for a grammar formalism with movement.
The recognizer will recognize languages generated by Minimalist Grammars
as defined in (Stabler, 1997). Minimalist Grammars are formal grammars that
are based on the minimalist approach to linguistic theory (Chomsky, 1995).
Minimalist Grammars are derivational and feature-driven: phrase structure
trees are derived by applying structure building functions to lexical items and
intermediate structures, and the applicability of these functions is determined
by the syntactic features of the trees involved.

The recognizer described in this chapter is similar to the CYK algorithm for
Context-Free Languages (Younger, 1967). Following the 'parsing as deduction' paradigm advocated by Shieber et al. (1995), the recognizer is a deductive
system in which items representing trees generated by Minimalist Grammars

H. Bunt et al. (eds.), New Technologies in Parsing Technology, 251-268.

are closed under a set of rules of inference. If the set thus generated contains
a distinguished goal item representing a complete tree, the input sentence is
grammatical, otherwise it is not. The specification of the items follows from a
formal result established in (Michaelis, 1998), which implies that the geometry
of the trees generated by Minimalist Grammars is largely irrelevant. Consequently, the items of the recognizer are expressions that are much simpler than
the trees they represent.

The important insight contained in (Michaelis, 1998) is that Minimalist
Grammars are non-concatenative in the same way that Multiple Context-Free
Grammars are. Multiple Context-Free Grammars (Seki et al., 1991) are non-
concatenative in the sense that a non-terminal symbol in this grammar can
dominate a sequence of strings of terminal symbols, rather than just one string
as in the case of ordinary Context-Free Grammars. Each of the strings dominated by a non-terminal symbol in a Multiple Context-Free Grammar will be
a substring of a sentence whose derivation includes this non-terminal, but in
the eventual sentence these strings are not necessarily adjacent. In Minimalist
Grammars, non-concatenation arises as the result of movement. Thus, in these
grammars a constituent can dominate non-adjacent substrings of a sentence.

The rest of this chapter is structured as follows. Section 2 provides a definition of Minimalist Grammars. Section 3 contains the specification of the
recognizer. Section 4 presents proofs of soundness and completeness, and section 5 describes some complexity results. The chapter concludes with some
directions for future work.

2.   Minimalist Grammars

In this section we will give a definition of Minimalist Grammars, following
(Stabler, 1997).

Definition 1. *A tree over a feature set F is a quintuple* $\tau = (N_\tau, \triangleleft_\tau, \prec_\tau, <_\tau, Label_\tau)$ *which meets the following three conditions:*

> *1 Triple $(N_\tau, \triangleleft_\tau, \prec_\tau)$ is a finite, binary ordered tree: N_τ is a non-empty set
> of nodes, $\triangleleft_\tau \subseteq N_\tau \times N_\tau$ denotes the relation of immediate dominance,
> $\prec_\tau \subseteq N_\tau \times N_\tau$ denotes the relation of immediate precedence.*

> *2 $<_\tau \subseteq N_\tau \times N_\tau$ denotes the relation of immediate projection: for any
> two nodes $\nu_1, \nu_2 \in N_\tau$ which are sisters in τ, either ν_1 projects over ν_2,
> $\nu_1 <_\tau \nu_2$, or ν_2 projects over ν_1, $\nu_2 <_\tau \nu_1$.*

> *3 $Label_\tau$ is a function from N_τ to F^*, assigning to each leaf of τ a finite
> sequence of features from F.*

Let $\tau = (N_\tau, \lhd_\tau, \prec_\tau, <_\tau, Label_\tau)$ be tree over a feature set F. Tree τ is a simple tree if it consists of just one node, otherwise it is a complex tree. If τ is a complex tree, then there are proper subtrees τ_0 and τ_1 of τ such that $\tau = [_{<}\tau_0, \tau_1]$ or $\tau = [_{>}\tau_0, \tau_1]$, where $[_{<}\tau_0, \tau_1]$ denotes a tree whose root immediately dominates subtrees τ_0 and τ_1 and in which the root of τ_0 immediately projects over and precedes the root of τ_1, and $[_{>}\tau_0, \tau_1]$ denotes a tree whose root immediately dominates subtrees τ_0 and τ_1 and in which the root of τ_0 immediately precedes the root of τ_1 and the root of τ_1 immediately projects over τ_0.

If τ is a simple tree, then its head is the single node making up τ. If τ is a complex tree $[_{<}\tau_0, \tau_1]$, then the head of τ is the head of τ_0; if τ is a complex tree $[_{>}\tau_0, \tau_1]$, then the head of τ is the head of τ_1. Tree τ is a projection of node $\nu \in N_\tau$, if, and only if, τ is a tree whose head is ν. A subtree τ_0 of τ is maximal if it is τ or if the smallest subtree of τ properly including τ_0 has a head other than the head of τ_0.

Tree τ is said to have a feature $f \in F$ if the left-most feature of the sequence that labels the head of τ is f.

Definition 2. *A Minimalist Grammar G is a quadruple G = (V, Cat, Lex, $\mathcal{F}$), which satisfies the following four conditions.*

1 *V = P $\cup$ I is a finite set of non-syntactic features, consisting of a set of phonetic features P and a set of semantic features I.*

2 *Cat = base $\cup$ select $\cup$ licensors $\cup$ licensees is a finite set of syntactic features, such that for each feature x $\in$ base there is a feature =x $\in$ select, and for each feature +y $\in$ licensors there is a feature –y $\in$ licensees. The set base minimally contains the distinguished feature c.*

3 *Lex is a finite set of trees over V $\cup$ Cat such that for each $\tau = (N_\tau, \lhd_\tau, \prec_\tau,$ $<_\tau, Label_\tau) \in Lex$, the function $Label_\tau$ assigns a string from Cat* P* I* to each leaf of τ.*

4 *The set $\mathcal{F}$ consists of the structure building functions merge and move, which are defined as follows:*

(a) *A pair of trees (τ, υ) is in the domain of merge if τ has feature =x $\in$ select and υ has feature x $\in$ base. Then,*

$$\text{merge}(\tau, \upsilon) = [_{<}\tau', \upsilon'] \text{ if } \tau \text{ is simple, and}$$
$$\text{merge}(\tau, \upsilon) = [_{>}\upsilon', \tau'] \text{ if } \tau \text{ is complex,}$$

where τ' is like τ except that feature =x is deleted, and υ' is like υ except that feature x is deleted.

> *(b) A tree τ is in the domain of move if τ has feature $+y \in$ licensors and τ has exactly one maximal subtree τ_0 that has feature $-y \in$ licensees. Then,*
>
> $$\text{move}(\tau) = [_{>}\tau_0', \tau'],$$
>
> *where τ_0' is like τ_0 except that feature $-y$ is deleted, and τ' is like τ except that feature $+y$ is deleted and subtree τ_0 is replaced by a single node without any features.[1]*

Note that the structure building function *move* does not apply to a tree τ which has feature $+y \in$ *licensors* if τ has more than one maximal subtree that has feature $-y \in$ *licensees*; in that case tree τ is said to violate the Shortest Movement Constraint.[2]

Let $G = (V, Cat, Lex, \mathcal{F})$ be a Minimalist Grammar. Then $CL(G) = \cup_{k \in \mathbb{N}}$ $CL^k(G)$ is the closure of the lexicon under the structure building functions in $\mathcal{F}$, where $CL^k(G)$, $k \in \mathbb{N}$, are inductively defined by:

1 $CL^0(G) = \text{Lex}$

2 $CL^{k+1}(G) = CL^k(G) \cup \{merge(\tau, \upsilon) \mid (\tau, \upsilon) \in \text{Dom}(merge) \cap (CL^k(G) \times CL^k(G))\} \cup \{move(\tau) \mid \tau \in \text{Dom}(move) \cap CL^k(G)\}$,

where $\text{Dom}(merge)$ and $\text{Dom}(move)$ are the domains of the functions *merge*, *move* $\in \mathcal{F}$.

Let τ be a tree in $CL(G)$. Tree τ is a tree of category a if the head of τ does not contain any syntactic features except for the feature a $\in$ *base*. Tree τ is a complete tree if it is a tree of distinguished category c and no node other than the head of τ contains any syntactic features. The yield $Y(\tau)$ of τ is the concatenation of the phonetic features in the labels of the leaves of τ, ordered according to the precedence relation on the nodes of τ. The language derivable by G consists of the yields of the complete trees in $CL(G)$: $L(G) = \{Y(\tau) \mid \tau \in CL(G), \tau \text{ is complete}\}$. With regard to their generative capacity, Minimalist Grammars are mildly context-sensitive.[3]

To simplify the presentation, we will assume that Lex is a set of simple trees.[4] Furthermore, we will assume without loss of generality that the sequence of syntactic features of any lexical item contains one and only one category feature from the set *base* and that all syntactic features to the right of this feature are drawn from the set *licensees*. Lexical items that do not meet these conditions are useless in the sense that they are not complete trees by themselves and cannot participate in the generation of a complete tree, because no combination of the structure building functions *merge* and *move* will be able to remove all the syntactic features of these items.

Example 1 The Minimalist Grammar whose lexicon contains the six simple trees given in 1 through 6 below generates simple English sentences, including *Titus praise s Lavinia*.[5]

1 d -k *Lavinia*

2 d -k *Titus*

3 =d vt -v *praise*

4 =pred +v +k i *s*

5 =i c *ε*

6 =vt +k =d pred *ε*

The first three steps of the derivation of the sentence *Titus praise s Lavinia* are given in 7, 8, and 9 below.

7 τ_1 = *merge*(=d vt -v *praise*, d -k *Lavinia*) =

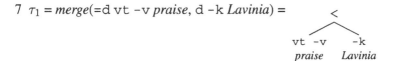

8 τ_2 = *merge*(=vt +k =d pred, τ_1) =

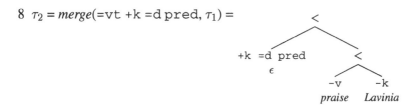

9 τ_3 = *move*(τ_2) =

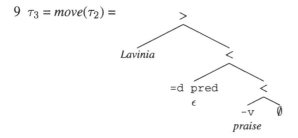

After 5 more steps, the derivation arrives at the tree given in 10. This is a complete tree with yield *Titus praise s Lavinia*.

10 $\tau_3 =$

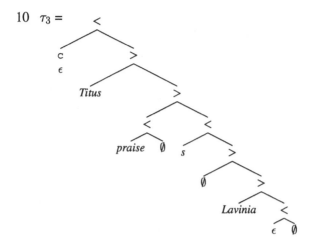

3. Specification of the Recognizer

This section contains a formal definition of an agenda-driven, chart-based recognizer for languages generated by Minimalist Grammars. Taking a logical perspective on parsing as presented in (Shieber et al., 1995), the definition of the recognizer includes a specification of a grammatical deductive system and a specification of a deduction procedure. The formulae of the deductive system, which are commonly called items, express claims about grammatical properties of strings. Under a given interpretation, these claims are either true or false. For a given grammar and input string, there is a set of items that, without proof, are taken to represent true grammatical claims. These are the axioms of the deductive system. Goal items represent the claim that the input string is in the language defined by the grammar. Since our objective is to recognize a string, the truth of the goal items is of particular interest. The deductive system is completed with a set of inference rules, for deriving new items from old ones. The other component of the definition of the recognizer is the specification of a deduction procedure. This is a procedure for finding all items that are true for a given grammar and input string.

3.1 Deduction Procedure

The deduction procedure used in the recognizer presented in this chapter is taken from (Shieber et al., 1995). It uses a chart holding unique items in order to avoid applying a rule of inference to items to which the rule of inference has already applied before. Furthermore, there is an agenda for temporarily keeping items whose consequences under the inference rules have not been generated yet. The procedure is defined as follows:

1 Initialize the chart to the empty set of items and the agenda to the axioms of the deduction system.

2 Repeat the following steps until the agenda is exhausted:

(a) Select an item from the agenda, called the trigger item, and remove it.

(b) Add the trigger item to the chart, if the item is not already in the chart.

(c) If the trigger item was added to the chart, generate all items that can be derived from the trigger item and any items in the chart by one application of a rule of inference,[6] and add these generated items to the agenda.

3 If a goal item is in the chart, the goal is proved, i.e., the string is recognized, otherwise it is not.

Shieber et al. (1995) prove that the deductive procedure is sound – it generates only items that are derivable from the axioms – and complete – it generates all the items that are derivable from the axioms.

3.2   Deductive System

The recognizer presented here is based on the proof in (Michaelis, 1998) showing that for every Minimalist Grammar there is a Multiple Context-Free Grammar which generates the same language. It follows from the particular construction used in this proof that the behavior with regard to the structure building functions *merge* and *move* of any tree generated by a Minimalist Grammar is completely determined by the syntactic features appearing in the tree and whether the tree is simple or complex. The geometry of the tree is a derivational artifact of no relevance, except for the fact that the syntactic features of the head of the tree should be distinguished from syntactic features appearing at other nodes of the tree. Hence, for the purpose of recognition, a tree may be collapsed into a sequence of sequences of features, associated with a tuple of position vectors representing the yield of the tree and an indication whether the tree is simple or complex. Expressions of this kind will be the items of the deductive system.

The proper interpretation of the items of the recognizer requires the notion of narrow yield of a tree. The narrow yield $Y_n(\phi)$ of a tree ϕ generated by a Minimalist Grammar is defined in the following way. If ϕ is a complex tree, then either $\phi = [_> \tau, v]$, or $\phi = [_< \tau, v]$. If $\phi = [_> \tau, v]$, then:

$Y_n(\phi) = Y_n(\tau) \cdot Y_n(v)$ if τ does not have a feature $-f \in licensees$[7]

$Y_n(\phi) = Y_n(v)$ otherwise.

If $\phi = [_{<}\tau, v]$, then:

$Y_n(\phi) = Y_n(\tau) \cdot Y_n(v)$ if v does not have a feature $-f \in licensees$

$Y_n(\phi) = Y_n(\tau)$ otherwise.

If ϕ is not a complex tree, it must be a simple tree. In that case:

$$Y_n(\phi) = Y(\phi)$$

where $Y(\phi)$ denotes the yield of ϕ. Informally, the narrow yield of a tree is that part of its yield that will not move out of the tree by some application of the structure building function *move*. For example, for the trees from example 1, $Y_n(\tau_1) = praise$, $Y_n(\tau_2) = \epsilon$, $Y_n(\tau_3) = Lavinia$, and $Y_n(\tau_4) = Titus\ praise\ s$ *Lavinia*.

3.2.1   Items.   Given an input string $w = w_1 \ldots w_n$ and a Minimalist Grammar G = (V, Cat, Lex, $\mathcal{F}$), the items of the deductive system will be of the form $[\alpha_0, \alpha_1, \ldots, \alpha_m]_t$, where $m \leq |licensees|$, $t \in \{s, c\}$. For $0 \leq i \leq m$, α_i is of the form $(x_i, y_i){:}\gamma_i$, where $0 \leq x_i \leq y_i \leq n$, and $\gamma_i \in Cat^*$.

An item $[(x_0, y_0){:}\gamma_0, (x_1, y_1){:}\gamma_1, \ldots, (x_m, y_m){:}\gamma_m]_t$ is understood to assert the existence of a tree $\tau \in CL(G)$ with the following properties:

1 If $t = s$, τ is a simple tree; if $t = c$, τ is a complex tree.

2 The head of τ is labeled $\gamma_0 \pi \iota$, for some $\pi \in P^*$ and $\iota \in I^*$.

3 For every $(x_i, y_i){:}\gamma_i$, $1 \leq i \leq m$, there is a leaf in τ labeled $\gamma_i \pi \iota$, for some $\pi \in P^*$ and $\iota \in I^*$.

4 The narrow yield of the maximal subtree projected by the node labeled $\gamma_i \pi \iota$ is $w_{x_i+1} \ldots w_{y_i}$, $0 \leq i \leq m$.

5 Besides the nodes labeled $\gamma_i \pi \iota$, $0 \leq i \leq m$, no other nodes in τ are labeled with syntactic features.

3.2.2   Axioms and Goals.   The set of axioms of the deductive system is specified in the following way. For each lexical item in Lex with syntactic features $\gamma \in Cat^*$ and phonetic features covering $w_{i+1} \ldots w_j$ of the input string, there will be an axiom $[(i, j){:}\gamma]_s$ in the deductive system.

There are two goal items: $[(0, n){:}c]_s$ and $[(0, n){:}c]_c$, $c \in base$ being the distinguished category feature. These are appropriate goal items for a recognizer, since their truth under the interpretation provided above requires the existence of a complete tree $\tau \in CL(G)$, either simple or complex, with narrow yield $Y_n(\tau) = w_1 \ldots w_n = w$. Since τ is complete, $Y_n(\tau) = Y(\tau)$. Therefore, $w \in L(G) = \{Y(\tau) \mid \tau \in CL(G), \tau$ is complete$\}$.

3.2.3 Rules of Inference.
The deductive system has five rules of inference, grouped into Merge rules and Move rules:

$$\frac{[(p, q){:}{=}x\gamma]_s \qquad [(q, v){:}x, \alpha_1, \ldots, \alpha_k]_t}{[(p, v){:}\gamma, \alpha_1, \ldots, \alpha_k]_c} \quad \text{Merge-1}$$

$$\frac{[(p, q){:}{=}x\gamma, \alpha_1, \ldots, \alpha_k]_c \qquad [(v, p){:}x, \iota_1, \ldots, \iota_l]_t}{[(v, q){:}\gamma, \alpha_1, \ldots, \alpha_k, \iota_1, \ldots, \iota_l]_c} \quad \text{Merge-2}$$

$$\frac{[(p, q){:}{=}x\gamma, \alpha_1, \ldots, \alpha_k]_{t_1} \qquad [(v, w){:}x\delta, \iota_1, \ldots, \iota_l]_{t_2}}{[(p, q){:}\gamma, \alpha_1, \ldots, \alpha_k, (v, w){:}\delta, \iota_1, \ldots, \iota_l]_c} \quad \text{Merge-3}$$

$$\frac{[(p, q){:}{+}y\gamma, \alpha_1, \ldots, \alpha_{i-1}, (v, p){:}{-}y, \alpha_{i+1}, \ldots, \alpha_k]_c}{[(v, q){:}\gamma, \alpha_1, \ldots, \alpha_{i-1}, \alpha_{i+1}, \ldots, \alpha_k]_c} \quad \text{Move-1}$$

$$\frac{[(p, q){:}{+}y\gamma, \alpha_1, \ldots, \alpha_{i-1}, (v, w){:}{-}y\delta, \alpha_{i+1}, \ldots, \alpha_k]_c}{[(p, q){:}\gamma, \alpha_1, \ldots, \alpha_{i-1}, (v, w){:}\delta, \alpha_{i+1}, \ldots, \alpha_k]_c} \quad \text{Move-2}$$

For all rules the following holds: $0 \le p, q, v, w \le n$; $0 \le i, k, l \le licensees$; $t, t_1, t_2 \in \{s, c\}$; $\delta \neq \emptyset$; $=x \in select$; $x \in base$; $+y \in licensors$; and $-y \in licensees$. The rules Merge-3 and Move-2 come with an additional condition on their application, reflecting the Shortest Movement Constraint mentioned in section 2: if the left-most feature of δ is $-z \in licensees$, then none of the left-most features of $\alpha_1, \ldots, \alpha_k, \iota_1, \ldots, \iota_l$ (Merge-3) or $\alpha_1, \ldots, \alpha_{i-1}, \alpha_{i+1}, \ldots, \alpha_k$ (Move-2) is $-z$. In this way we achieve that that $m \le |licensees|$ for every item $[\alpha_0, \alpha_1, \ldots, \alpha_m]_t$, $t \in \{s, c\}$, produced by the recognizer, i.e., no item represents a tree that violates the Shortest Movement Constraint.

Example 2 The derivation of a goal item for the sentence *Titus praise s Lavinia* given the Minimalist Grammar from example 1 is represented by the derivation tree in 1. The leaves of this tree are axioms of the deductive system. An item labeling a binary branching node in the tree is produced by applying one of the rules of inference Merge-1, Merge-2, or Merge-3 to the items labeling its daughters; an item labeling a non-branching node is produced by applying one of the rules of inference Move-1 or Move-2 to the item labeling its daughter. The item labeling the root of the derivation tree, $[(0, 4):c]_c$, is a goal item.[8]

1

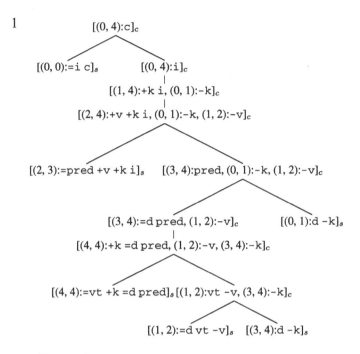

4.   Correctness

Since Shieber et al. (1995) proved that the deductive procedure is sound and complete, establishing the correctness of the recognizer entails showing that the deductive system defined above is sound and complete relative to the intended interpretation of the items. This will be done in the next two sections.

4.1   Proof of Soundness

The following two lemmas will be helpful for establishing soundness of the deductive system.

Lemma 1a. *If* τ, τ' *and* v, v' *are trees such that* merge$(\tau, v) = [_<\tau', v']$ *or* merge$(\tau, v) = [_>v', \tau']$, *then* $Y_n(\tau') = Y_n(\tau)$ *and* $Y_n(v') = Y_n(v)$.

Proof. According to the definition of *merge*, τ' and τ are identical except for the labels of their heads in both cases. Hence, it follows immediately from the definition of narrow yield that $Y_n(\tau') = Y_n(\tau)$. Analogously, $Y_n(v') = Y_n(v)$. □

Lemma 1b. *If* τ, τ' *and* τ_0, τ_0' *are trees such that* move$(\tau) = [_>\tau_0', \tau']$ *and* τ_0 *is the maximal subtree of* τ *that moves, then* $Y_n(\tau') = Y_n(\tau)$ *and* $Y_n(\tau_0') = Y_n(\tau_0)$.

Proof. According to the definition of *move*, τ' is like τ except that feature $+y$ is deleted and subtree τ_0 has been replaced by a single node with no features. The yield of τ_0 is excluded from $Y_n(\tau)$ because τ_0 has a feature $-y \in$ *licensees*. The yield of τ_0 is also excluded from $Y_n(\tau')$ because τ_0 is not a subtree of τ'. Since trees τ and τ' are otherwise the same, $Y_n(\tau') = Y_n(\tau)$. Concerning τ_0' and τ_0, these trees differ only with regard to the labels of their heads. Hence, $Y_n(\tau_0') = Y_n(\tau_0)$. □

Proving soundness of the recognizer amounts to showing that the axioms and the rules of inference of the deductive system are sound. Then it will follow that every derivable item in the deductive system will represent a true grammatical statement under the intended interpretation.

4.1.1 Soundness of the Axioms. According to the interpretation given in section 3.2, an axiom $[(i, j){:}\gamma]_s$ asserts the existence of a tree $\tau \in$ CL(G) with the following properties: τ is a simple tree, the head of τ is labeled by $\gamma\pi\iota$ for some $\pi \in$ P* and $\iota \in$ I*, and the narrow yield of τ is $w_{i+1}\ldots w_j$. Obviously, the lexical item in Lex which occasioned the axiom $[(i, j){:}\gamma]_s$ has exactly these properties. By definition this lexical item is in $CL^0(G) \subseteq$ CL(G).

4.1.2 Soundness of the Rules of Inference. There are five rules of inference. Their soundness will be established below.[9]

Merge-1: the items $[(p, q){:=}x\gamma]_s$ and $[(q, v){:}x, \alpha_1, \ldots, \alpha_k]_t$ of the antecedent of Merge-1 assert the existence of trees $\tau, \upsilon \in$ CL(G), whose heads are labeled $=x\gamma$ and x, respectively. Hence, τ and υ are in the domain of the function *merge*. This function will apply to τ and υ and produce a complex tree $\phi = [_<\tau', \upsilon'] \in$ CL(G), where τ', υ' are trees according to the definition of *merge*. The head of ϕ is labeled γ. Furthermore, $Y_n(\phi) = Y_n(\tau'){\cdot}Y_n(\upsilon')$. By lemma 1a, $Y_n(\tau'){\cdot}Y_n(\upsilon') = Y_n(\tau){\cdot}Y_n(\upsilon) = w_{p+1}\ldots w_q{\cdot}w_{q+1}\ldots w_v = w_{p+1}\ldots w_v$.[10] Also, all maximal subtrees properly contained in υ will be included in ϕ with their head labels and narrow yields unchanged, since *merge* does not touch any proper subtrees of υ. As is easy to check, the item $[(p, v){:}\gamma, \alpha_1, \ldots, \alpha_k]_c$ in the consequent of the rule Merge-1 claims the existence of a tree in CL(G) with the properties of ϕ. Thus Merge-1 is sound.

Merge-2: the argument follows the pattern of Merge-1.

Merge-3: the items $[(p, q){:=}x\gamma, \alpha_1, \ldots, \alpha_k]_{t_1}$ and $[(v, w){:}x\delta, \iota_1, \ldots, \iota_l]_{t_2}$ of the antecedent of Merge-3 imply the existence of trees $\tau, \upsilon \in$ CL(G) which will produce another tree $\phi = merge(\tau, \upsilon) = [_<\tau', \upsilon'] \in$ CL(G), where τ', υ' are trees according to the definition of *merge*. As a result of our assumptions about the syntactic features labeling lexical items, the left-most feature of δ, which labels the head of υ', must be a feature $-y \in$ *licensees*. Therefore, by lemma 1a, $Y_n(\phi) = Y_n(\tau') = Y_n(\tau) = w_{p+1}\ldots w_q$. The narrow yield of the maximal subtree projected by the node in ϕ labeled δ is $Y_n(\upsilon')$, and by lemma

1a, $Y_n(v') = Y_n(v) = w_{v+1} \ldots w_w$. Now it is easy to see that the grammatical claim made by the item in the consequent of the rule Merge-3 is justified by tree ϕ.

Move-1: the item $[(p, q):+y\gamma, \alpha_1, \ldots, \alpha_{i-1}, (v, p):-y, \alpha_{i+1}, \ldots, \alpha_k]_c$ of the antecedent of Move-1 guarantees the existence of a complex tree $\tau \in$ CL(G) whose head is labeled $+y\gamma$, containing a maximal subtree τ_0 that has feature $-y \in$ *licensees*. It follows from the conditions on Merge-3 and Move-2 that τ contains only one such maximal subtree. Hence, τ is in the domain of the function *move*. Its result is a complex tree $\phi = [_>\tau_0', \tau'] \in$ CL(G), with trees τ_0', τ' as in the definition of *move*. The head of ϕ is labeled γ. Moreover, $Y_n(\phi) = Y_n(\tau_0') \cdot Y_n(\tau') = Y_n(\tau_0) \cdot Y_n(\tau)$, by lemma 1b. Since $Y_n(\tau_0) = w_{v+1} \ldots w_p$ and $Y_n(\tau) = w_{p+1} \ldots w_q$, $Y_n(\phi) = w_{v+1} \ldots w_q$. The function *move* does not affect the labels or narrow yields of any of the maximal subtrees properly contained in τ, except for τ_0. Now it is easily verified that the item in the consequent of Move-1 actually describes $\phi \in$ CL(G).

Move-2: the argument follows the pattern of Move-1. As in the case of Merge-3, the left-most feature of δ is some $-y \in$ *licensees*.

4.2   Proof of Completeness

This section presents a completeness proof for the recognizer. A recognizer is complete if for every string that is in the language defined by the grammar, there is a derivation of a goal item from the axioms.

First, the following two useful lemmas will be proved.

Lemma 2a. *If ϕ, τ, and v are trees such that $\phi =$ merge(τ, v), then for every maximal subtree σ of τ or v there is a maximal subtree σ' of ϕ such that $Y_n(\sigma)$ is a substring of $Y_n(\sigma')$.*

Proof. Either $\phi = [_<\tau', v']$ or $\phi = [_>v', \tau']$, where τ' and v' are as specified in the definition of *merge*. First, assume $\sigma = \tau$. Then, by lemma 1a, $Y_n(\sigma) = Y_n(\tau) = Y_n(\tau')$. Let $\sigma' = \phi$. Trivially, σ' is a maximal subtree of ϕ, and, by the definition of narrow yield, $Y_n(\sigma)$ is a substring of $Y_n(\sigma')$. Secondly, assume $\sigma = v$. Then, by lemma 1a, $Y_n(\sigma) = Y_n(v) = Y_n(v')$. Let $\sigma' = v'$. Obviously, v' is a maximal subtree of ϕ, and, trivially, $Y_n(\sigma)$ is a substring of $Y_n(\sigma')$. Thirdly, assume σ is a maximal subtree properly contained in τ. Since τ' is like τ except that some feature $=x \in$ *select* is deleted from its head, σ is a maximal subtree properly contained in τ'. Let $\sigma' = \sigma$. Obviously, σ' is a maximal subtree of ϕ, and, trivially, $Y_n(\sigma)$ is a substring of $Y_n(\sigma')$. Finally, assume σ is a maximal subtree properly contained in v. This case is similar to the previous case $\quad\square$

Lemma 2b. *If ϕ and τ are trees such that $\phi =$ move(τ), then for every maximal subtree σ of τ there is a maximal subtree σ' of ϕ such that $Y_n(\sigma)$ is a substring of $Y_n(\sigma')$.*

Proof. $\phi = [_>\tau'_0, \tau']$, with τ', τ'_0, and τ_0 as in the definition of *move*. First, assume $\sigma = \tau$. This case is similar to the first case of lemma 2a. Secondly, assume σ is a maximal subtree properly contained in τ and and τ_0 is a proper subtree of σ. Then, by the definition of *move*, τ' will contain a tree σ' which is like σ, except that subtree τ_0 is replaced by a single node without features. Obviously, σ' is a maximal subtree of ϕ. Moreover, $Y_n(\sigma) = Y_n(\sigma')$, since the yield of τ_0 is excluded from $Y_n(\sigma)$ because of its feature $-y \in$ *licensees*, and the yield of τ_0 is excluded from $Y_n(\sigma')$ because τ_0 is not a subtree of σ'. Hence, trivially, $Y_n(\sigma)$ is a substring of $Y_n(\sigma')$. Thirdly, assume $\sigma = \tau_0$. Then, by lemma 1b, $Y_n(\sigma) = Y_n(\tau_0) = Y_n(\tau'_0)$. Let $\sigma' = \tau'_0$. Obviously, σ' is a maximal subtree of ϕ, and, trivially, $Y_n(\sigma)$ is a substring of $Y_n(\sigma')$. Finally, assume σ' is a maximal subtree of τ_0. This case is similar to the third case of lemma 2b. $\square$

Lemma 3. *If ϕ and τ are trees such that ϕ is a complete tree derived from τ by one or more applications of the structure building functions* merge *and* move, *then $Y_n(\tau)$ is a substring of $Y(\phi)$.*

Proof. By repeated application of lemmas 2a and 2b, ϕ contains a maximal subtree σ' such that $Y_n(\tau)$ is a substring of $Y_n(\sigma')$. Since ϕ is a complete tree, $Y_n(\sigma')$ is a substring of $Y_n(\phi) = Y(\phi)$. Consequently, $Y_n(\tau)$ is a substring of $Y(\phi)$. $\square$

Completeness of the recognizer now follows as a corollary of lemma 4 below. If $w \in L(G)$ for some Minimalist Grammar G, then there is a complete tree $\phi \in CL(G)$ such that $Y(\phi) = w$. Since $\phi \in CL(G)$, there must be a $k \in \mathbb{N}$ such that $\phi \in CL^k(G)$. Since ϕ is a complete tree, lemma 4 guarantees that an item corresponding to ϕ will be generated. This item will be a goal item, for ϕ is complete and $Y(\phi) = w$.

Lemma 4. *For a Minimalist Grammar G, if $\phi \in CL^k(G)$ for some $k \in \mathbb{N}$, and ϕ is a complete tree or a complete tree can be derived from ϕ via applications of the structure building functions* merge *and* move, *then an item $[\alpha_0, \alpha_1 \ldots, \alpha_m]_t$ corresponding to ϕ will be generated.*

Proof. The proof will be by induction on $k \in \mathbb{N}$.[11]

Base case: $k = 0$. Then $\phi \in CL^0(G) = Lex$, and ϕ is covered by one of the axioms.

Recursive case: assume the items corresponding to $\phi \in CL^k(G)$, ϕ a complete tree or involved in the derivation of a complete tree, are generated for a particular $k \in \mathbb{N}$. To show: for any $\phi \in CL^{k+1}(G)$, ϕ a complete tree or involved in the derivation of a complete tree, a corresponding item will be generated.

Pick an arbitrary $\phi \in CL^{k+1}(G)$. Three cases are distinguished: $\phi \in CL^k(G)$, $\phi \in \{merge(\tau, v) \mid (\tau, v) \in \text{Dom}(merge) \cap CL^k(G) \times CL^k(G)\}$, and $\phi \in \{move(\tau) \mid \tau \in \text{Dom}(move) \cap CL^k(G)\}$.

In the first case, the claim follows immediately from the induction hypothesis.

In the second case, there are trees τ, $v \in CL^k(G)$ such that $\phi = merge(\tau, v)$. Since ϕ is involved in the derivation of a complete tree or ϕ is a complete tree itself, τ is involved in the derivation of a complete tree,[12] and v is a complete tree itself or involved in the derivation of a complete tree. Hence, by the induction hypothesis, there are items corresponding to τ and v. Since $(\tau, v) \in$ Dom($merge$), the heads of τ and v are labeled $=x\gamma$ and $x\delta$ respectively, for some $=x \in licensees$, $x \in base$, and γ, $\delta \in Cat^*$. Tree τ is either simple or complex. With regard to v, $\delta = \emptyset$ or $\delta \neq \emptyset$. Hence, there are four cases to be dealt with. If τ is a simple tree and $\delta = \emptyset$, then $\phi = [<\tau', v']$, and $Y_n(\phi) = Y_n(\tau') \cdot Y_n(v')$. By lemma 1a, $Y_n(\phi) = Y_n(\tau) \cdot Y_n(v)$. Suppose ϕ participates in a successful derivation of a complete tree whose yield is the string $w_1 \ldots w_n$.[13] Then, by lemma 3, $Y_n(\tau) \cdot Y_n(v)$ is a substring of $w_1 \ldots w_n$, that is, there are p, q, and v such that $Y_n(\tau) = w_{p+1} \ldots w_q$ and $Y_n(v) = w_{q+1} \ldots w_v$, $0 \leq p \leq q \leq v \leq n$. Hence, the items corresponding to τ and v will match the antecedents of rule Merge-1. Alternatively, ϕ is a complete tree itself. Assume $Y_n(\phi) = Y(\phi) = w_1 \ldots w_n$. Then it follows immediately that there is a q such that $Y_n(\tau) = w_1 \ldots w_q$ and $Y_n(v) = w_{q+1} \ldots w_n$, $1 \leq q \leq n$. Again, the items corresponding to τ and v will match the antecedents of rule Merge-1. In both cases, application of Merge-1 will generate the item corresponding to ϕ. In a similar way it is established that the trees τ and v for the other three cases will correspond to items that match the antecedents of the rules Merge-2 (τ is complex, $\delta = \emptyset$) and Merge-3 (τ is simple or complex, $\delta \neq \emptyset$). Application of these rules will produce an item corresponding to tree ϕ.[14]

In the third case, $\phi \in \{move(\tau) \mid \tau \in$ Dom($move$) $\cap CL^k(G)\}$. In a way similar to the previous case it can be shown that the item for tree τ triggers one of the rules Move-1 or Move-2, producing an item corresponding to ϕ. $\square$

5. Complexity Results

For a Minimalist Grammar $G = (V, Lex, Cat, \mathcal{F})$ and input string of length n, the number of items is polynomially bounded by the length of the input string. All items are of the form $[(x_0, y_0):\gamma_0, (x_1, y_1):\gamma_1, \ldots, (x_m, y_m):\gamma_m]_t$, as defined in section 3.2. Each part $(x_i, y_i):\gamma_i$ of an item, $0 \leq i \leq m$, has $O(n^2)$ possible instantiations, as both x_i and y_i range between 0 and n, 0 and n included. The possible choices of γ_i do not depend on the length of the input string. The number of choices is bounded, however, because the labels occurring in any tree in $CL(G)$ are substrings of the labels of the expressions in Lex. This follows immediately from the the definition of the structure building functions $merge$ and $move$. Moreover, Lex is a finite set and the labels assigned by $Label$ are finite sequences. Thus, the set of possible labels is bounded by the grammar, and, since the recognizer is sound, the number of possible γ_i's is bounded by the grammar, too. Since an item has at most $k + 1$ parts (x_i, y_i):γ_i, where $k = |licensees|$, the number of items in the chart is bounded by $O(n^{2k+2})$.

As regards the time complexity of the recognizer, step 2(b) of the deduction procedure specified in section 3.1 requires every item on the agenda to be compared with the items already in the chart. Since the number of items in the chart is $O(n^{2k+2})$, this step will take $O(n^{2k+2})$ per item on the agenda. For any item on the agenda but not already in the chart, step 2(c) of the deduction procedure checks whether any rule of inference will apply. Checking applicability of the Merge rules involves looking through all the items in the chart, since all Merge rules have two antecedents. Given an item on the agenda and an item from the chart, actually verifying whether any of the Merge rules applies to these items takes constant time. Thus, the time cost is $O(n^{2k+2})$ per item on the agenda. In order to determine whether one of the two Move rules will apply, the label γ_0 in an item has to be inspected and compared to the other labels γ_i, $1 \leq i \leq m$ in the same item. Since m is bounded by $k = |licensees|$, there is no dependency on the length of the input string. Since steps 2(b) and 2(c) are performed in sequence, the time cost of both steps is bounded by $O(n^{2k+2})$ per item on the agenda, ignoring without loss of generality the fact that step 2(c) is not performed for all items on the agenda. Steps 1 and 3 of the deduction procedure do not exceed this bound. The number of items that will be put on the agenda while recognizing a string is $O(n^{2k+2})$. This is the upper bound on the number of possible items. There will be duplicates in the agenda, but their number is finite and does not depend on n, essentially because the number of axioms and the number of inference rules is finite and all items in the chart are unique. Thus, the overall time complexity of the recognizer is $O(n^{4k+4})$.

6. Conclusions and Future Work

In this chapter we have provided a formal definition of a recognizer for Minimalist Grammars, together with proofs of completeness and soundness and an analysis of its space and time complexity. The recognizer can be turned into a parser by extending items with a field for recording their immediate ancestors, and using this field to retrieve (derivation) trees or forests from the chart of items produced by the algorithm. The practical efficiency of the recognizer can be improved by imposing some order on the chart. In the current recognizer, the entire chart is searched in order to determine whether any one of the Merge rules will apply. The definitions of the Merge rules suggest that grouping the items in the chart according to the left-most feature feature of their 'head labels' will allow for a more efficient search.

The current recognizer operates in a bottom-up manner: no constituent is recognized until all substrings that make up its yield have been encountered. Applying the rules of inference discussed in section 3.2.3 in reverse will produce a top-down recognizer for languages generated by Minimalist Grammars. Using the rules of inference in reverse and adding a mechanism to record the progress of the recognizer through a rule will give an Earley-style recognizer. However, as illustrated by the tree in 1, a depth-first, left-to-right traversal of a derivation tree (or any other fixed order of traversal) will in general not visit the axioms at the leaves of the tree in the order in which their words appear in the sentence to be recognized. Thus, additional machinery is needed to obtain top-down and Earley-style recognizers that go through the input sentence from left to right. For the same reason, recording the progress through a rule requires a more elaborate book-keeping scheme than the dotted rules used for Context-Free Grammars – see (Harkema, 2001b) for discussion and solutions.

When the bottom-up recognizer described in this chapter is confronted with a choice regarding what axiom to use for a word in the input sentence or what rule of inference to apply to an item, it will simply pursue all possibilities and store the results in the chart. Some of these choices will produce items that are not involved in the derivation of a goal item. These dead-ends may be avoided by looking at the words that follow in a sentence. It is still an open question whether there is a useful way to characterize Minimalist Grammars that generate languages such that k words of look-ahead suffice to make bottom-up recognition deterministic, i.e. for any input sentence the number of choices facing the recognizer at each choice point is at most one.

Finally, we note that the deductive system of the bottom-up recognizer presented in this chapter provides a succinct reformulation of Minimalist Grammars that does not depend on trees. Just as the recognizer can ignore most of the structure of a tree, so can the grammar. Simple expressions, in particular: the items from section 3.2.1 with strings rather than position vectors, suffice to generate any and all languages generated by the original Minimalist Grammars, without any effect on the structure assigned to sentences. A complete definition of reformulated Minimalist Grammars can be found in (Stabler and Keenan, 2001), for example.

Notes

1. The Minimalist Grammars defined in (Stabler, 1997) also allow for head movement and covert phrasal movement. We will not discuss these kinds of movement in this chapter, but the recognizer presented in section 3 can be adapted to deal with grammars including these kinds of movement, e.g. see (Stabler, 2001) for head movement. Note also that Minimalist Grammars with and without head movement and covert phrasal movement are weakly equivalent (Harkema, 2001a; Michaelis, 2001).

2. If tree τ has more than one maximal subtree that has feature $-y \in \textit{licensees}$, all of these subtrees will want to move to the same position, but moving any one of these subtrees will deprive the others of their "shortest move".

3. In particular, as shown in Harkema (2001a) and Michaelis (2001), Minimalist Grammars are weakly equivalent to Multiple Context-Free Grammars (Seki et al., 1991), Linear Context-Free Rewriting Systems (Vijay-Shanker et al., 1987), Simple Positive Range Concatenation Grammars (Boullier, 1998), and Multi-Component Tree-Adjoining Grammars (Weir, 1988).

4. Extending the recognizer presented in section 3 to handle grammars with complex trees in their lexicon is a straightforward exercise.

5. Some important notational issues: ϵ denotes an empty sequence of phonetic features and $\emptyset$ denotes a node in a tree without any features. The expression $[_< \tau_0, \tau_1]$ is written as a tree in the following way: the root of the tree is labeled $<$, its daughters are the trees for τ_0 and τ_1; similarly for $[_> \tau_0, \tau_1]$. Semantic features will be ignored in this example.

6. Note that successful applications of Move-1 and Move-2 as defined in section 3.2.3 do not involve any items from the chart.

7. For any pair of strings s and t, $s \cdot t$ denotes their concatenation in the obvious order.

8. In this example, book-keeping issues involving the chart and the agenda of the deductive procedure are ignored. Note also that the recognizer, being a recognizer rather than a parser, delivers a chart of items which are not organized into derivation trees.

9. Since applicability of the structure building functions and the rules of inference does not depend on non-syntactic features, their presence in trees will be ignored in the discussion to follow. Thus, the statement 'the head of tree ϕ is labeled γ', for example, means: 'the head of tree ϕ is labeled $\gamma \pi \iota$, for some $\pi \iota \in$ P*I*'.

10. Note that the maximal projection of the head of a tree is the tree itself.

11. As in the discussion of the soundness proof, the presence of non-syntactic features in trees will be ignored.

12. Since τ is the first argument of *merge*, τ cannot be a complete tree.

13. Reference to the yield of a complete tree derived from ϕ precludes a general proof of completeness, i.e. a proof that for all $\phi \in CL^k(G)$, $k \in \mathbb{N}$, a corresponding item $[\alpha_0, \alpha_1 \ldots, \alpha_m]_t$ will be generated.

14. As ϕ is either a complete tree or involved in the derivation of one, ϕ does not violate the Shortest Movement Constraint. Hence, Merge-3 will always apply to the items corresponding to τ and v.

References

Boullier, P. (1998). Proposal for a Natural Language Processing Syntactic Backbone. *Research Report N° 3342*, INRIA-Rocquencourt, France.

Chomsky, N. (1995). *The Minimalist Program*. MIT Press.

Harkema, H. (2001a). A Characterization of Minimalist Grammars. In: *Logical Aspects of Computational Linguistics*. P. de Groote, G.F. Morrill, and C. Retoré (eds.). Lecture Notes in Artificial Intelligence, 2099. Springer Verlag.

Harkema, H. (2001b). *Parsing Minimalist Languages*. Ph.D. dissertation, University of California, Los Angeles.

Michaelis, J. (1998). Derivational Minimalism is Mildly Context-Sensitive. In: *Logical Aspects of Computational Linguistics*. M. Moortgat (ed.). Lecture Notes in Artificial Intelligence 2014. Springer Verlag.

Michaelis, J. (2001). Transforming Linear Context-Free Rewriting Systems into Minimalist Grammars. P. de Groote, G.F. Morrill, and C. Retoré (eds.). Lecture Notes in Artificial Intelligence, 2099. Springer Verlag.

Seki, H., T. Matsumura, M. Fujii and T. Kasami. (1991). On Multiple Context-Free Grammars. In: *Theoretical Computer Science*, 88.

Shieber, S.M., Y. Shabes and F.C.N. Pereira. (1995). Principles and Implementation of Deductive Parsing. In: *Journal of Logic Programming*, 24.

Stabler, E.P. (1997). Derivational Minimalism. In: *Logical Aspects of Computational Linguistics*. C. Retoré (ed.). Lecture Notes in Artificial Intelligence 1328. Springer Verlag.

Stabler, E.P. (1999). Remnant Movement and Complexity. In: *Constraints and Resources in Natural Language Syntax and Semantics*. G. Bouma, E. Hinrichs, G.-J. Kruijff, D. Oerhle (eds.). CSLI.

Stabler, E.P. (2001). Recognizing Head Movement. In: *Logical Aspects of Computational Linguistics*. P. de Groote, G.F. Morrill, and C. Retoré (eds.). Lecture Notes in Artificial Intelligence, 2099. Springer Verlag.

Stabler, E.P., and E.L. Keenan. (2000). Structural Similarity. In: *Algebraic Methods in Language Processing, AMiLP 2000*. A. Nijholt and G. Scollo (eds.). University of Iowa.

Vijay-Shanker, K., D.J. Weir and A.K. Joshi. (1987). Descriptions Produced by Various Grammatical Formalisms. In: *Proceedings of the 25th Annual Meeting of the Association for Computational Linguistics*.

Weir, D.J. (1988). *Characterizing Mildly Context-Sensitive Grammar Formalisms*. Ph.D. dissertation, University of Pennsylvania.

Younger, D.H. (1967). Recognition and Parsing of Context-Free Languages in n^3. In: *Information and Control*, 10(2).

Chapter 13

RANGE CONCATENATION GRAMMARS

Pierre Boullier

INRIA, Domaine de Voluceau, Rocquencourt, BP 105
78153 Le Chesnay Cedex, France
Pierre.Boullier@inria.fr

Abstract   We present Range Concatenation Grammars, a syntactic formalism which possesses many attractive features, among which we emphasize here generative capacity and closure properties. For example, Range Concatenation Grammars have stronger generative capacity than Linear Context-Free Rewriting Systems, although this power is not to the detriment of efficiency, since the generated languages can always be parsed in polynomial time. Range Concatenation Languages are closed under both intersection and complementation, and these closure properties suggest novel ways to describe some linguistic phenomena. We also present a parsing algorithm which is the basis for our current prototype implementation.

1.   Introduction

The fact that current natural language (NL) processing is based on a large number of syntactic formalisms may be interpreted in two ways: on the one hand it shows that the research field is very active, but on the other hand it shows that there is no consensus for a single formalism, and that one with the *right* properties is still to be discovered. What properties should such an ideal formalism have? Of course, it must allow the description of features that have been identified so far in various NLs, while staying computationally tractable. We know that, due to their lack of expressiveness, context-free grammars (CFGs) cannot play this role (see Shieber, 1985). Context sensitive grammars are powerful enough but are too greedy in computer time. A first answer is given by the notion of mild context-sensitivity. This notion is an attempt to express the formal power needed to define NLs (see Joshi, 1985, and Weir, 1988). However, there are some language phenomena such as large Chinese numbers (Radzinski, 1991) and word scrambling (Becker, Rambow,

H. Bunt et al. (eds.), New Technologies in Parsing Technology, 269-289.

and Niv, 1992) that are outside the power of mildly context-sensitive (MCS) formalisms. In this chapter, we present an alternative: Range Concatenation Grammars (RCGs). RCG is a syntactic formalism which is a variant of the simple version of literal movement grammar (LMG), described in (Groenink, 1997), and which is also related to the framework of LFP developed in (Rounds, 1988). In fact RCGs may be considered to lie halfway between the *string* and *integer* versions of the above formalisms: RCGs retain from the string version of LMGs or LFPs the notion of concatenation, applying it to *ranges* (pairs of integers which denote occurrences of substrings in a source text) rather than strings; also, RCGs retain from the integer version of LMGs or LFPs the ability to handle only (part of) the source text – this feature being the key to computational tractability. The rewrite rules of RCGs, called *clauses*, apply to composite objects named *predicates* which can be seen as nonterminal symbols with arguments. Boullier (1998) shows that the positive version of RCGs, in common with simple LMGs and integer indexing LFPs, exactly defines the class *PTIME* of all languages recognizable in deterministic polynomial time (see Bertsch and Nederhof, 2001 for a direct proof). Since the composition operations of RCGs are not restricted to be linear and non-erasing, its languages (RCLs) are not semi-linear. Therefore, RCGs are *not* MCS and they have a stronger generative capacity than linear context-free rewriting systems (LCFRS; Vijay-Shanker, Weir, and Joshi, 1987),[1] while staying computationally tractable: their sentences can be parsed in polynomial time. However, the formalism shares with LCFRS the fact that derivations are context-free (CF), i.e., the choice of the operation performed at each step depends only on the object being derived from. As in the CF case, derived trees can be packed into polynomial sized parse forests. Besides its generative power and efficiency, the formalism possesses many other attractive properties. We emphasize in this introduction the fact that RCLs are both closed under intersection and complementation, and, like CFGs, RCGs can act as syntactic backbones that decorations from other domains (such as probabilities, logical terms, or feature structures) can be grafted on.

This chapter studies the full class of RCGs and presents a polynomial time parsing algorithm.

2. Positive Range Concatenation Grammars

In this section we introduce the positive version of RCGs and, by a rewriting mechanism, we define their languages.

Definition 1 *A positive range concatenation grammar* (PRCG) $G = (N, T, V, P, S)$ *is a 5-tuple where N is a non-empty finite set of* predicate names, *T and V are finite, disjoint sets of* terminal symbols *and* variable symbols *respec-*

tively, $S \in N$ is the start *predicate name, and P is a finite set of* clauses *of the form*

$$\psi_0 \to \psi_1 \cdots \psi_m$$

where $m \geq 0$ and each of $\psi_0, \psi_1, \ldots, \psi_m$ is a predicate *of the form*

$$A(\alpha_1, \ldots, \alpha_p)$$

where $p \geq 1$ is its arity, *$A \in N$ and each $\alpha_i \in (T \cup V)^*$, $1 \leq i \leq p$, is an* argument.

Each occurrence of a predicate in the right-hand side of a clause is a predicate *call*, and each occurrence on the left-hand side is called a predicate *definition*. Clauses that define a predicate A are called A-clauses. This definition assigns a fixed arity to each predicate name $A \in N$ with value $arity(A)$. By definition, $arity(S)$, the arity of the start predicate name, is one. The *arity* of a grammar is the maximum arity of its predicates. A PRCG of arity k is called a k-PRCG.

2.1 Ranges and Bindings

If we consider a derivation in a CFG, headed by the start symbol and leading to some sentence, each nonterminal occurrence is responsible for the generation of the substring lying between two indices, say i and j. For a given input string $w = a_1 \cdots a_n$, the pair (i, j) is called a *range*. We know that in CFG theory, ranges play a central role. For example the (unbounded number of) parse trees associated with some input string w can be represented by a CFG, called a *shared forest* (Lang, 1994). Its nonterminal symbols have the form (A, i, j), where A is a nonterminal of the initial grammar and (i, j) is a range in w. In an analogous way, ranges are the core of our formalism.

We use the convention that terminal symbols in T are denoted by early occurring lower case letters such as $a, b, c, \ldots$, while variables in V are denoted by late occurring upper case letters such as X, Y, Z. If $w \in T^*$, $|w| = n$, its set of ranges is $\mathcal{R}_w = \{\rho \mid \rho = (i, j), 0 \leq i \leq j \leq n\}$. We shall sometimes use vectors to denote elements of cartesian products. For example elements in $\mathcal{R}_w^k$ (i.e., tuples of ranges with k components) may be denoted by $\vec{\rho}$ and clauses by $A_0(\vec{\alpha_0}) \to A_1(\vec{\alpha_1}) \cdots A_m(\vec{\alpha_m})$, $\vec{\alpha_i} \in ((T \cup V)^*)^{k_i}$, $k_i = arity(A_i)$.

We shall use several equivalent denotations for ranges in $\mathcal{R}_w$. If $w = w_1 w_2 w_3$ with $w_1 = a_1 \cdots a_i$, $w_2 = a_{i+1} \cdots a_j$ and $w_3 = a_{j+1} \cdots a_n$, the range (i, j) can be denoted either by an explicit dotted term $w_1 \bullet w_2 \bullet w_3$, or by $\langle i..j \rangle_w$, or even by $\langle i..j \rangle$ when w is understood or of no importance. Given a range $\langle i..j \rangle$, the integer i is its *lower bound*, j is its *upper bound* and $j - i$ is its *size*. A range such that $i = j$ is an *empty* range. The range $\bullet w \bullet = \langle 0..|w| \rangle_w$ is the *initial* range. The three substrings w_1, w_2 and w_3 associated with $\langle i..j \rangle$ are denoted by $w^{\langle 0..i \rangle}$, $w^{\langle i..j \rangle}$ and $w^{\langle j..n \rangle}$ respectively. Therefore we have $w^{\langle j..j \rangle} = \varepsilon$, $w^{\langle j-1..j \rangle} = a_j$ and $w^{\langle 0..n \rangle} = w$. If $\vec{\rho} = \rho_1, \ldots, \rho_i, \ldots, \rho_p$ is a vector of ranges, by definition $w^{\vec{\rho}}$ denotes the tuple of strings $w^{\rho_1}, \ldots, w^{\rho_i}, \ldots, w^{\rho_p}$.

In any PRCG, terminals, variables and arguments in a clause are supposed to be bound to ranges by a substitution mechanism. Any pair (X, ρ) is called a *variable binding* and is denoted by X/ρ, where ρ is the *range instantiation* of X and w^ρ is its *string instantiation*. A set $\sigma = \{X_1/\rho_1, \ldots, X_p/\rho_p\}$ of variable bindings is a *variable substitution* if and only if $X_i/\rho_i \neq X_j/\rho_j \Rightarrow X_i \neq X_j$. A pair (a, ρ) is a *terminal binding*, denoted by a/ρ, if and only if $\rho = \langle j - 1..j \rangle$ and $a = a_j$.

The *concatenation of ranges* is a partial (associative) binary operation on $\mathcal{R}_w$ defined by $\langle i_1..j_1 \rangle_w \langle i_2..j_2 \rangle_w = \langle i_1..j_2 \rangle_w$ if and only if $j_1 = i_2$. If we consider a string $w \in T^*$, a string $\alpha = u_1 \cdots u_i \cdots u_p \in (T \cup V)^*$, a variable substitution σ and a range $\rho \in \mathcal{R}_w$, the pair (α, ρ) is a *string binding* for σ, denoted α/ρ if and only if:

- for each u_i there exists a range ρ_i such that

  - if $u_i \in V$, $u_i/\rho_i \in \sigma$,
  - if $u_i \in T$, u_i/ρ_i is such that $u_i = w^{\rho_i}$; *and*

- $\rho_1 \cdots \rho_i \cdots \rho_p = \rho$

For a given variable substitution σ, a set $\omega = \{\alpha_1/\rho_1, \ldots, \alpha_p/\rho_p\}$ is called a *string substitution* (for $\{\alpha_1, \ldots, \alpha_p\}$) if and only if each α_i/ρ_i is a string binding for σ. A clause c is *instantiable* by ω if and only if there is a string substitution ω for the set of arguments of its predicates. If a clause is instantiable by ω, and if each of its arguments α is replaced by the range ρ such that $\alpha/\rho \in \omega$, we get a *positive instantiated clause* whose components are *positive instantiated predicates*.

As an example, the expression $A(\langle g..h \rangle, \langle i..j \rangle, \langle k..l \rangle) \rightarrow B(\langle g + 1..h \rangle, \langle i + 1..j - 1 \rangle, \langle k..l - 1 \rangle)$ is a positive instantiation of the clause $A(aX, bYc, Zd) \rightarrow B(X, Y, Z)$ if the source text $a_1 \cdots a_n$ satisfies $a_{g+1} = a, a_{i+1} = b, a_j = c$ and $a_l = d$. In this case, the variables X, Y and Z are bound to $\langle g + 1..h \rangle$, $\langle i + 1..j - 1 \rangle$ and $\langle k..l - 1 \rangle$, respectively.[2]

For a PRCG $G = (N, T, V, P, S)$ and a string $w \in T^*$, we define the set of *positive instantiated predicates* $IP_{G,w}^+$ by

$$IP_{G,w}^+ = \{A(\vec{\rho}) \mid A \in N, \vec{\rho} \in \mathcal{R}_w^h, h = arity(A)\}$$

We denote as $IC^+_{G,w}$ the set of *positive instantiated clauses*. By definition, any element $A_0(\vec{\rho_0}) \rightarrow \phi_1 \cdots \phi_m$ of $IC^+_{G,w}$ is the positive instantiation of some clause $A_0(\vec{\alpha_0}) \rightarrow \psi_1 \cdots \psi_m$ for some string substitution.

2.2 Derivation, Language, Derived Tree and Shared Forest

For a PRCG $G = (N, T, V, P, S)$ and a source text w, we define a binary relation $\underset{G,w}{+\Rightarrow}$, called *positive derive*, on strings of positive instantiated predicates. If Γ_1 and Γ_2 are strings in $(IP^+_{G,w})^*$, we have

$$\Gamma_1 \, A_0(\vec{\rho_0}) \, \Gamma_2 \quad \underset{G,w}{+\Rightarrow} \quad \Gamma_1 \, A_1(\vec{\rho_1}) \cdots A_m(\vec{\rho_m}) \, \Gamma_2$$

if and only if $A_0(\vec{\rho_0}) \rightarrow A_1(\vec{\rho_1}) \cdots A_m(\vec{\rho_m}) \in IC^+_{G,w}$.

A sequence of strings of positive instantiated predicates $\Gamma_0, \ldots, \Gamma_{i-1}, \Gamma_i, \ldots, \Gamma_l$ such that $\forall i, 1 \leq i \leq l : \Gamma_{i-1} \underset{G,w}{+\Rightarrow} \Gamma_i$ is called a *derivation*, or more precisely a Γ_0-*derivation* or even a Γ_0/Γ_l-*derivation*. A *complete* derivation is a $S(\bullet w \bullet)/\varepsilon$-derivation. Each consecutive pair of strings (Γ_{i-1}, Γ_i) is a *derivation step*. We say that a PRCG is *cyclic for w* if, for the input string w, there exists a complete $S(\bullet w \bullet)/\varepsilon$-derivation of unbounded length. We say that a PRCG G is *cyclic* if G is cyclic for some fixed string w.[3]

Definition 2 *The* (string) language *of a PRCG* $G = (N, T, V, P, S)$ *is the set*

$$\mathcal{L}(G) \;=\; \{w \mid S(\bullet w \bullet) \underset{G,w}{\overset{+}{\Rightarrow}} \varepsilon\}$$

An input string $w \in T^*$, $|w| = n$, is a *sentence* if and only if the empty string (of positive instantiated predicates) can be derived from $S(\langle 0..n \rangle)$, the positive instantiation of the start predicate on the whole source text.

More generally, we define the string language of a nonterminal A by

$$\mathcal{L}(A) \;=\; \bigcup_{w \in T^*} \mathcal{L}(A, w)$$

where

$$\mathcal{L}(A, w) \;=\; \{w^{\vec{\rho}} \mid \vec{\rho} \in \mathcal{R}^h_w, h = arity(A), A(\vec{\rho}) \underset{G,w}{\overset{+}{\Rightarrow}} \varepsilon\}$$

Unfortunately, the language $\mathcal{L}(G)$ defined by a PRCG G is not the language $\mathcal{L}(S)$ defined by its start predicate name S. For example, consider the grammar G such that

$$
\begin{aligned}
S(X) &\rightarrow A(Xa) \\
A(X) &\rightarrow \varepsilon
\end{aligned}
$$

On the one hand we have $\mathcal{L}(G) = \emptyset$, since for any input string w the first clause cannot be instantiated: X always denotes the initial range $\bullet w \bullet$ and thus the argument $X a$ cannot denote a range in $\mathcal{R}_w$. On the other hand, for every $w = u_1 u_2 a v, u_1 u_2 v \in T^*$ we have $S(u_1 \bullet u_2 \bullet av) \underset{G,w}{+\Rightarrow} (u_1 \bullet u_2 a \bullet v) \underset{G,w}{+\Rightarrow} \varepsilon$ and thus $\mathcal{L}(S) = T^* a T^*$. In fact, we have $\mathcal{L}(G) \subset \mathcal{L}(S)$, and the equality is reached for non-increasing grammars.[4]

As in the CF case, if we consider a derivation as a rewriting process, at each step the choice of the (instantiated) predicate to be derived does not depend on its neighbors (the derivation process is context-free). All possible derivation strategies can be captured in a single canonical tree structure which abstracts all possible orders and which is called a *derived tree* (or *parse tree*). For any given $A(\vec{\rho})$-derivation, we can associate a single derived tree whose root is labeled $A(\vec{\rho})$. Conversely, if we consider a derived tree, there may be associated derivations which depend on the way the tree is traversed (for example a top-down left-to-right traversal leads to a leftmost derivation). Note that from a derivation step (Γ, Γ'), it is not always possible to determine which predicate occurrence in Γ has been derived. Moreover, even if this occurrence is known, the clause used cannot be determined in the general case. This is due to the fact that $A_0(\vec{\rho_0}) \to A_1(\vec{\rho_1}) \cdots A_m(\vec{\rho_m})$ may be an instantiation of different clauses. But, of course, each of these interpretations is a valid one.

Consider a k-PRCG $G = (N, T, V, P, S)$, a terminal string w and the set $\mathcal{D}_w$ of all complete derivations. If $N_i = \{A \mid arity(A) = i\}$ is the subset of N whose arity is i, we define a terminal-free CFG $G_w = (\cup_{1 \leq i \leq k} N_i \times \mathcal{R}_w^i, \emptyset, P_w, S(\bullet w \bullet))$ whose set of rules P_w is formed by all the instantiated clauses $A_0(\vec{\rho_0}) \to A_1(\vec{\rho_1}) \cdots A_m(\vec{\rho_m})$ used in the derivation steps in $\mathcal{D}_w$. This CFG is called the *shared forest* for w with respect to G. Note that, if $\mathcal{D}_w$ is not empty, the language of a shared forest for w is not $\{w\}$, as in the CF case, but is $\{\varepsilon\}$.

Moreover, this shared forest has polynomial size with respect to the input string length and may be viewed as an exact packed representation of all the (unbounded number of) derived (parse) trees in G for w: the set of parse trees for G for the input w and the set of parse trees of its associated CF shared forest G_w (for the input ε), are identical.

The arguments of a given predicate may denote discontinuous or even overlapping ranges. Fundamentally, a predicate name A defines a notion (property, structure, dependency, ...) between its arguments, whose associated ranges can be arbitrarily scattered over the source text. PRCGs are therefore well suited to describing long distance dependencies. Overlapping ranges arise as a consequence of the non-linearity of the formalism. For example, the same variable (denoting the same range) may occur in different arguments in the right-hand side of some clause, expressing different views (properties) of the same portion of the source text.

Note that the order of predicate calls in the right-hand side of a clause is of no importance (in fact, right-hand sides of clauses may be seen as sets of predicate calls rather than lists).

Example 1. *As an example of a PRCG, the following set of clauses describes the three-copy language* $\{www \mid w \in \{a, b\}^*\}$ *which is not a context-free language (CFL) and even lies beyond the formal power of tree adjoining grammars (TAGs).*

$$
\begin{aligned}
S(XYZ) &\rightarrow A(X, Y, Z) \\
A(aX, aY, aZ) &\rightarrow A(X, Y, Z) \\
A(bX, bY, bZ) &\rightarrow A(X, Y, Z) \\
A(\varepsilon, \varepsilon, \varepsilon) &\rightarrow \varepsilon
\end{aligned}
$$

Below, we check that the input string $w = a_1 b_2 a_3 b_4 a_5 b_6$ *is a sentence. Of course, indices are not part of the input letters, they are used to improve readability of ranges: for each pair* (letter, index), *we know where* letter *occurs in the source text. At each derivation step, we show both the clause and the variable substitution used.*

$$
S(a_1 b_2 a_3 b_4 a_5 b_6) \quad
\begin{array}{c}
\{X/a_1 b_2, Y/a_3 b_4, Z/a_5 b_6\} \\
S(XYZ) \rightarrow A(X,Y,Z) \\
\overset{+}{\underset{G,w}{\Longrightarrow}}
\end{array}
\quad A(a_1 b_2, a_3 b_4, a_5 b_6)
$$

$$
\begin{array}{c}
\{X/b_2, Y/b_4, Z/b_6\} \\
A(aX,aY,aZ) \rightarrow A(X,Y,Z) \\
\overset{+}{\underset{G,w}{\Longrightarrow}}
\end{array}
\quad A(b_2, b_4, b_6)
$$

$$
\begin{array}{c}
\{X/\langle 2..2\rangle, Y/\langle 4..4\rangle, Z/\langle 6..6\rangle\} \\
A(bX,bY,bZ) \rightarrow A(X,Y,Z) \\
\overset{+}{\underset{G,w}{\Longrightarrow}}
\end{array}
\quad A(\varepsilon, \varepsilon, \varepsilon)
$$

$$
\begin{array}{c}
\emptyset \\
A(\varepsilon,\varepsilon,\varepsilon) \rightarrow \varepsilon \\
\overset{+}{\underset{G,w}{\Longrightarrow}}
\end{array}
\quad \varepsilon
$$

Example 2. *Another way to define the three-copy language is with the following set of clauses:*

$$
\begin{aligned}
S(XYZ) &\rightarrow L(X)\, eq(X, Y)\, eq(X, Z) \\
L(\varepsilon) &\rightarrow \varepsilon \\
L(Xa) &\rightarrow L(X) \\
L(Xb) &\rightarrow L(X) \\
L(Xc) &\rightarrow L(X)
\end{aligned}
$$

where the equality predicate *eq is defined by*

$$eq(Xt, Yt) \rightarrow eq(X, Y)$$
$$eq(\varepsilon, \varepsilon) \rightarrow \varepsilon$$

in which the first clause is a schema over all terminals $t \in T$.

Example 3. *The power of this formalism is shown by the following grammar that defines the non semi-linear language $\mathcal{L} = \{a^{2^p} \mid p \geq 0\}$*

$$S(XY) \rightarrow S(X) \, eq(X, Y)$$
$$S(a) \rightarrow \varepsilon$$

3. Negative Range Concatenation Grammars

In this section we present another subclass of RCGs, obtained as the negative version of PRCG. Though this subclass does not add any generative power to PRCGs, it allows complement languages to be defined easily.

By definition, a term of the form $\overline{A(\vec{\alpha})}$ is called a *negative predicate*. A *negative clause* is like a non-empty clause, except that at least one of its right-hand side members is a negative predicate.

Definition 3 *A negative range concatenation grammar (NRCG) $G = (N, T, V, P, S)$ is a 5-tuple, like a PRCG, except that at least one element of P is a negative clause.*

Definition 4 *A range concatenation grammar (RCG) is a PRCG or a NRCG.*

The term PRCG (NRCG) will be used to emphasize the absence (respectively, presence) of negative predicate calls.

The intended meaning of a negative predicate call $\overline{A(\alpha_1, \ldots, \alpha_p)}$ is to define the complement language (with respect to $(T^*)^p$) of its positive counterpart $A(\alpha_1, \ldots, \alpha_p)$: an instantiated negative predicate succeeds if and only if its positive counterpart (always) fails. This definition is based on a "negation by failure" rule.

More formally, let $G = (N, T, V, P, S)$ be a RCG, and let w be a string in T^*. The set of *negative instantiated predicates* $IP_{G,w}^-$ is defined by $IP_{G,w}^- = \{\overline{A(\vec{\rho})} \mid A(\vec{\rho}) \in IP_{G,w}^+\}$,[5] and the set of *instantiated predicates* $IP_{G,w}$ is defined by $IP_{G,w} = IP_{G,w}^+ \cup IP_{G,w}^-$. We denote as $IC_{G,w}^-$ the set of *negative instantiated clauses*. By definition, any element $A_0(\vec{\rho_0}) \rightarrow \phi_1 \cdots \phi_m$ of $IC_{G,w}^-$ is the instantiation of some negative clause $A_0(\vec{\alpha_0}) \rightarrow \psi_1 \cdots \psi_m$ for some string substitution. The set of *instantiated clauses* $IC_{G,w}$ is defined by $IC_{G,w} = IC_{G,w}^+ \cup IC_{G,w}^-$.

For RCGs, we redefine the *positive derive* relation $\underset{G,w}{+\Rightarrow}$ in the following way. If Γ_1 and Γ_2 are strings in $(IP_{G,w})^*$, we have

$$\Gamma_1 \, A_0(\vec{\rho_0}) \, \Gamma_2 \;\; \underset{G,w}{\overset{+}{\Rightarrow}} \;\; \Gamma_1 \, \phi_1 \cdots \phi_m \, \Gamma_2$$

if and only if $A_0(\vec{\rho_0}) \to \phi_1 \cdots \phi_m \in IC_{G,w}$. Let ω be the string substitution such that $A_0(\vec{\rho_0}) \to \phi_1 \cdots \phi_m$ is the instantiation of the clause $A_0(\vec{\alpha_0}) \to \psi_1 \cdots \psi_m$ in P. If $\vec{\alpha_i}/\vec{\rho_i} \in \omega,$[6] $1 \le i \le m$, then we have $\phi_i = A_i(\vec{\rho_i})$ in case $\psi_i = A_i(\vec{\alpha_i})$, and we have $\phi_i = \overline{A_i(\vec{\rho_i})}$ in case $\psi_i = \overline{A_i(\vec{\alpha_i})}$.

Note that negative instantiated predicates cannot be further derived by positive derive relations.

We also define on strings of instantiated predicates a *negative derive* relation, denoted by $\underset{G,w}{-\!\!\Rightarrow}$. If Γ_1 and Γ_2 are strings in $(IP_{G,w})^*$, we have

$$\Gamma_1 \, \overline{A(\vec{\rho})} \, \Gamma_2 \;\; \underset{G,w}{-\!\!\Rightarrow} \;\; \Gamma_1 \Gamma_2$$

if and only if $\overline{A(\vec{\rho})}$ is a negative instantiated predicate such that $(A(\vec{\rho}), \varepsilon) \notin \underset{G,w}{\overset{+}{\Rightarrow}}$.

Therefore, when a derivation step of $\underset{G,w}{-\!\!\Rightarrow}$ applies to any $\overline{A(\vec{\rho})}$, this negative instantiated predicate is rewritten into the empty string. As a consequence of this definition, the structure (parse tree) associated with a negative derivation step is void, and, more generally, the structure of the (complement) language associated with a negative predicate call is void. In other words, within the RCG formalism, we cannot define any structure between a negative predicate call and the parts of an input string that it selects.

Let $\underset{G,w}{-\!\!-\!\!\Rightarrow}$ be some subset of $\underset{G,w}{-\!\!\Rightarrow}$. We define a *positive/negative derive* relation $\underset{G,w}{\pm\!\!\Rightarrow}$ by

$$\underset{G,w}{\pm\!\!\Rightarrow} \;\; = \;\; \underset{G,w}{\overset{+}{\Rightarrow}} \;\cup\; \underset{G,w}{-\!\!-\!\!\Rightarrow}$$

We say that $\underset{G,w}{\pm\!\!\Rightarrow}$ is *consistent* if and only if for each $A(\vec{\rho}) \in IP_{G,w}^+$ we have either $A(\vec{\rho}) \underset{G,w}{\overset{+}{\Rightarrow}} \varepsilon$ or $\overline{A(\vec{\rho})} \underset{G,w}{\pm\!\!\Rightarrow} \varepsilon$, but not both. In all other cases we say that $\underset{G,w}{\pm\!\!\Rightarrow}$ is *inconsistent*. Note that the existence of both such derivations would mean that the tuple of strings $w^{\vec{\rho}}$ simultaneously belongs to the language of A and to its complement! We say that a grammar G is *consistent* if for every $w \in T^*$, there exists a unique consistent relation among all relations $\underset{G,w}{\pm\!\!\Rightarrow}$ resulting from possible choices for $\underset{G,w}{-\!\!-\!\!\Rightarrow}$. In all other cases we say that G is *inconsistent*. If G is consistent, the unique consistent positive/negative derive relation is simply called *derive* and is notated $\underset{G,w}{\Rightarrow}$.

Note that PRCGs are always consistent. In some cases, however, a RCG may be inconsistent, since there may not exist a unique consistent derive relation. Consider the RCG G_1 whose set of clauses is the pair

$$
\begin{aligned}
S(X) &\rightarrow \overline{A(X)} \\
A(X) &\rightarrow \overline{S(X)}
\end{aligned}
$$

By definition, for any $w \in T^*$ and for any $\rho \in \mathcal{R}_w$, we have

$$
\{(S(\rho), \overline{A(\rho)}), (A(\rho), \overline{S(\rho)})\} \subset \underset{G_1,w}{\overset{+}{\Longrightarrow}}
$$

and

$$
\{(\overline{S(\rho)}, \varepsilon), (\overline{A(\rho)}, \varepsilon)\} \subset \underset{G_1,w}{\overset{-}{\Longrightarrow}}
$$

Among the various possibilities for $\underset{G_1,w}{\overset{-}{\dashrightarrow}}$, two lead to two different consistent positive/negative derive relations. The first of these is $(\overline{S(\rho)}, \varepsilon) \in \underset{G_1,w}{\overset{-}{\dashrightarrow}}$ and $(\overline{A(\rho)}, \varepsilon) \notin \underset{G_1,w}{\overset{-}{\dashrightarrow}}$ while the second is $(\overline{A(\rho)}, \varepsilon) \in \underset{G_1,w}{\overset{-}{\dashrightarrow}}$ and $(\overline{S(\rho)}, \varepsilon) \notin \underset{G_1,w}{\overset{-}{\dashrightarrow}}$. Both lead to a consistent positive/negative derive relation for G_1 which therefore is not unique.

Now, consider the RCG G_2 whose set of clauses is the singleton $\{S(X) \rightarrow \overline{S(X)}\}$. By definition, for any $w \in T^*$ and for any $\rho \in \mathcal{R}_w$, we have

$$
\{(S(\rho), \overline{S(\rho)})\} \subset \underset{G_2,w}{\overset{+}{\Longrightarrow}}
$$

and

$$
\{(\overline{S(\rho)}, \varepsilon)\} \subset \underset{G_2,w}{\overset{-}{\Longrightarrow}}
$$

There are two possibilities for $\underset{G_2,w}{\overset{-}{\dashrightarrow}}$. In the first case, the pair $(\overline{S(\rho)}, \varepsilon)$ does not belong to $\underset{G_2,w}{\overset{-}{\dashrightarrow}}$. Then $\underset{G_2,w}{\overset{\pm}{\Longrightarrow}}$ is inconsistent, since we have both $(S(\rho), \varepsilon) \notin \underset{G_2,w}{\overset{+}{\Longrightarrow}}$ and $(\overline{S(\rho)}, \varepsilon) \notin \underset{G_2,w}{\overset{\pm}{\Longrightarrow}}$. In the second case, the pair $(\overline{S(\rho)}, \varepsilon)$ belongs to $\underset{G_2,w}{\overset{-}{\dashrightarrow}}$. Then $\underset{G_2,w}{\overset{\pm}{\Longrightarrow}}$ is also inconsistent, since $(S(\rho), \varepsilon)$ and $(\overline{S(\rho)}, \varepsilon)$ are both in $\underset{G_2,w}{\overset{+}{\Longrightarrow}}$. Thus there is no consistent positive/negative derive relation for G_2.

We say that a consistent RCG G is *cyclic for w* if, for the input string w, there exists a complete $S(\bullet w \bullet)/\varepsilon$-derivation (w.r.t. $\underset{G,w}{\Longrightarrow}$) of unbounded length. We say that a consistent RCG G is *cyclic* if G is cyclic for some fixed string w.

Below, we present a subclass of NRCGs which is consistent. We introduce a binary relation on $IP_{G,w}$, called *depend* and denoted by $\underset{G,w}{\mapsto}$, defined as

$$\underset{G,w}{\mapsto} \ = \ \{(\overline{A(\vec{\rho})}, A(\vec{\rho})) \mid A(\vec{\rho}) \in IP_{G,w}^{+}\} \cup$$

$$\bigcup_{A_0(\vec{\rho_0}) \to \phi_1 \cdots \phi_m \in IC_{G,w}} \{(A_0(\vec{\rho_0}), \phi_i) \mid 1 \le i \le m\}$$

In other words we say that any negative instantiated predicate depends on its positive counterpart and that a (positive) left-hand side instantiated predicate depends on each of its (positive or negative) right-hand side instantiated predicates.[7]

We say that a NRCG G is *strongly sound for w* if, for the input string w, there is no recursive dependency through negation. We say that a NRCG G is *strongly sound* if it is strongly sound for any w. In strongly sound NRCGs we thus prohibit dependencies of the kind $A(\vec{\rho}) \underset{G,w}{\overset{+}{\mapsto}} \overline{A'(\vec{\rho'})} \underset{G,w}{\overset{+}{\mapsto}} A(\vec{\rho})$. This restriction is a necessary condition for a positive instantiated predicate $A(\vec{\rho})$ not to depend on its own complement. In other words, this guarantees that we reject grammars in which a tuple of strings $w^{\vec{\rho}}$ simultaneously belongs to the language of some A and to its complement.

We will show how, under the assumption that G is strongly sound, it is possible to build a (unique consistent) derive relation. Intuitively, the idea is the following. Starting from two empty sets $\mathcal{P}_{G,w}$ and $\mathcal{N}_{G,w}$, we will evaluate (in a way defined below) all the instantiated predicates. Any instantiated predicate will evaluate either to true or to false. If a positive instantiated predicate evaluates to true, it will be put in $\mathcal{P}_{G,w}$. Similarly, if a negative instantiated predicate evaluates to true, it will be put in $\mathcal{N}_{G,w}$. Since the grammar is strongly sound, we will show that there exists an evaluation order allowing the evaluation of all the instantiated predicates. This evaluation order induces on $IP_{G,w}$ a directed acyclic graph (DAG) structure. The leaves of this DAG are first evaluated, a mother node is evaluated when all its daughters are evaluated and, eventually, all the root nodes are evaluated. Thus, at the end of the evaluation process, the sets $\mathcal{P}_{G,w}$ and $\mathcal{N}_{G,w}$ will partition $IP_{G,w}$.

Let Γ be a string in $(IP_{G,w})^*$. We associate with Γ a subset of $IP_{G,w}$, denoted δ_Γ, defined by

$$\delta_\Gamma \ = \ \{\phi \mid \phi \in IP_{G,w}, \ \Gamma = \Gamma_1 \phi \Gamma_2\}$$

A set δ_Γ, $\Gamma \in (IP_{G,w})^*$, is called a *δ-set*.

Now, considering the set of all positive $A(\vec{\rho})$-derivations, we define $\Delta_{A(\vec{\rho})}$, a subset of $2^{IP_{G,w}}$, by

$$\Delta_{A(\vec{\rho})} \ = \ \{\delta_\Gamma \mid A(\vec{\rho}) \underset{G,w}{\overset{+}{\Rightarrow}} \Gamma\}$$

and its *reduced* form, the subset $\Delta_{A(\vec{\rho})}^{\mathsf{C}}$ whose elements are the δ-set elements of $\Delta_{A(\vec{\rho})}$ which do not contain any positive instantiated predicate $A'(\vec{\rho'})$ depending on $A(\vec{\rho})$. In other words, we exclude from $\Delta_{A(\vec{\rho})}^{\mathsf{C}}$ the δ-sets which exhibit cyclic dependencies with respect to $A(\vec{\rho})$. Formally, we have

$$\Delta_{A(\vec{\rho})}^{\mathsf{C}} = \{\delta \mid \delta \in \Delta_{A(\vec{\rho})}, \forall A'(\vec{\rho'}) \in \delta, (A'(\vec{\rho'}), A(\vec{\rho})) \notin \overset{*}{\underset{G,w}{\mapsto}}\}$$

We say that a positive instantiated predicate $A(\vec{\rho}) \in IP_{G,w}^{+}$ is *evaluated* either if $A(\vec{\rho}) \in \mathcal{P}_{G,w}$ or its negative counterpart $\overline{A(\vec{\rho})}$ is in $\mathcal{N}_{G,w}$. A negative instantiated predicate $\overline{A(\vec{\rho})} \in IP_{G,w}^{-}$ is *evaluated* either if $\overline{A(\vec{\rho})} \in \mathcal{N}_{G,w}$ or its positive counterpart $A(\vec{\rho})$ is in $\mathcal{P}_{G,w}$. We say that a δ-set δ can be evaluated if and only if all its elements are evaluated. Moreover, the value of δ is true either if δ is the empty set or if, $\forall \phi \in \delta$, we have $\phi \in \mathcal{P}_{G,w} \cup \mathcal{N}_{G,w}$; otherwise the value of δ is false.

We say that a set $\Delta_{A(\vec{\rho})}$ can be evaluated if and only if all the elements of its reduced associated set $\Delta_{A(\vec{\rho})}^{\mathsf{C}}$ can be evaluated. If one of its elements is true, the value of $\Delta_{A(\vec{\rho})}$ is true, otherwise its value is false (this covers the case where $\Delta_{A(\vec{\rho})}^{\mathsf{C}}$ is the empty set). If $\Delta_{A(\vec{\rho})}$ evaluates to true, we put $A(\vec{\rho})$ in $\mathcal{P}_{G,w}$, otherwise we put $\overline{A(\vec{\rho})}$ in $\mathcal{N}_{G,w}$.

We also define $\underset{G,w}{\succ}$, a subset of $\overset{+}{\underset{G,w}{\mapsto}}$, as the *evaluate after* relation, by

$$\underset{G,w}{\succ} = \{(\overline{A(\vec{\rho})}, A(\vec{\rho})) \mid A(\vec{\rho}) \in IP_{G,w}^{+}\} \cup$$
$$\bigcup_{A(\vec{\rho}) \in IP_{G,w}^{+}} \{(A(\vec{\rho}), \phi) \mid \phi \in \delta, \delta \in \Delta_{A(\vec{\rho})}^{\mathsf{C}}\}$$

By construction, in $\underset{G,w}{\succ}$, there is no cyclic positive dependency around any positive instantiated predicate. Since the grammar is strongly sound, there is also no dependency between any positive instantiated predicate and its negative counterpart. Therefore, the relation $\underset{G,w}{\succ}$ induces on $IP_{G,w}$ a DAG structure $\mathcal{D}_{G,w}$ which defines a bottom-up evaluation strategy. The smallest elements (i.e., the leaves of $\mathcal{D}_{G,w}$) are first evaluated. These leaves are positive instantiated predicates $A(\vec{\rho})$. Two cases happen. If $A(\vec{\rho}) \overset{+}{\underset{G,w}{\mapsto}} \varepsilon$, we have $\varepsilon \in \Delta_{A(\vec{\rho})}^{\mathsf{C}}$ and $A(\vec{\rho})$ is put in $\mathcal{P}_{G,w}$. Otherwise, $A(\vec{\rho})$ is not the left-hand side of any instantiated clause, thus $\Delta_{A(\vec{\rho})} = \Delta_{A(\vec{\rho})}^{\mathsf{C}} = \emptyset$, and $\overline{A(\vec{\rho})}$ is put in $\mathcal{N}_{G,w}$.

As described above, we evaluate a non-leaf node when all its daughters are evaluated. As a result, we put either $A(\vec{\rho})$ in $\mathcal{P}_{G,w}$ or $\overline{A(\vec{\rho})}$ in $\mathcal{N}_{G,w}$. This process stops when all the connected components of the DAG are evaluated (a connected component of a DAG is evaluated when all its roots are evaluated).

At that time, all the instantiated predicates of $IP_{G,w}$ are evaluated and $\mathcal{P}_{G,w}$ and $\mathcal{N}_{G,w}$ partition $IP_{G,w}$. In other words, any tuple of strings belongs either to some language or to its complement.

We then define the $\underset{G,w}{--\Rightarrow}$ relation, only using the elements of $\mathcal{N}_{G,w}$ that is

$$\underset{G,w}{--\Rightarrow} \quad = \quad \{(\Gamma_1 \, \overline{A(\vec{\rho})} \, \Gamma_2, \Gamma_1 \, \Gamma_2) \mid \overline{A(\vec{\rho})} \in \mathcal{N}_{G,w}\}$$

This choice defines a unique consistent positive/negative derive relation which is the derive relation (we have $\underset{G,w}{\pm\Rightarrow} = \underset{G,w}{\Rightarrow}$). Therefore, every strongly sound grammar is consistent. From this point onwards we shall only consider strongly sound RCGs.

Definition 5 *The (string) language of a (strongly sound) RCG $G = (N, T, V, P, S)$ is the set*

$$\mathcal{L}(G) \quad = \quad \{w \mid S(\bullet w \bullet) \underset{G,w}{\overset{+}{\Rightarrow}} \varepsilon\}$$

In the following sections, without loss of generality, we will both prohibit clauses whose right-hand side contains arguments that are in T^*, and assume that no argument has more than one instance of any variable.

4. A Parsing Algorithm for RCGs

Figure 13.1 gives a pseudo-code specification of a recognition algorithm for non-cyclic PRCGs.[8] Let $G = (N, T, V, P, S)$ be a non-cyclic k-PRCG and $w \in T^*$ a fixed input string. In this algorithm, the function *pred-call* is memoized: its returned value is kept in a global $(k + 1)$-dimensional matrix Π which is indexed by elements in $N \times \mathcal{R}_w^k$. We assume that its elements are initialized to **unset**. The matrix Π is also used (see the assignment of $\Pi[A_0, \vec{\rho_0}]$ to **false** at line 4) to block identical recursive calls. The statement at line 10 is executed for each instantiated predicate in the right-hand side of each instantiated A_0-clause. The only constraint is that the left-hand side arguments of these instantiated A_0-clauses are bound to $\vec{\rho_0}$. We assume that the function *pred-call* is called with *pred-call*$(S, \bullet w \bullet)$. It is not difficult to see that the sequence of instantiated predicate calls exactly follows a leftmost derivation strategy and thus, we have designed a top-down recognizer.

To turn this recognizer into a parser, we add between lines 10 and 11 the statement

if *local-val* **then output** $(A_0(\vec{\rho_0}) \to A_1(\vec{\rho_1}) \cdots A_m(\vec{\rho_m}))$ **end if**

In order to handle non-cyclic strongly sound NRCGs, we have to change line 10 to

(1)   **function** *pred-call* $(A_0, \vec{\rho_0})$ **return boolean**
(2)   **if** $(ret\text{-}val := \Pi[A_0, \vec{\rho_0}]) \neq$ **unset then**
(3)   **return** *ret-val*
      end if
(4) $\Pi[A_0, \vec{\rho_0}] :=$ **false** /* for recursion detection */
(5)   *ret-val* := **false**
(6)   **foreach** $A_0(\vec{\alpha_0}) \rightarrow \psi_1 \cdots \psi_m \in P$ **do**
(7)   **foreach** $A_0(\vec{\rho_0}) \rightarrow \phi_1 \cdots \phi_m$ **do**
(8)   *local-val* := **true** /* empty right-hand sides */
(9)   **for** $j := 1$ **to** m **do**
(10)   *local-val* := *pred-call* $(A_j, \vec{\rho_j})$ /* $\phi_j = A_j(\vec{\rho_j})$ */
(11)   **if not** *local-val* **then**
          break
        end if
        end for
(12)   *ret-val* := *ret-val* $\vee$ *local-val*
      end foreach
      end foreach
(13)   **return** $\Pi[A_0, \vec{\rho_0}] :=$ *ret-val*
    end function

Figure 13.1.   A Recognition Algorithm for non-cyclic PRCGs.

(10')   **if** $\phi_j \in IP^+_{G,w}$
        then *local-val* := *pred-call* $(A_j, \vec{\rho_j})$ /* $\phi_j = A_j(\vec{\rho_j})$ */
        else *local-val* := **not** *pred-call* $(A_j, \vec{\rho_j})$ /* $\phi_j = \overline{A_j(\vec{\rho_j})}$ */
      end if

Cyclic strongly sound NRCGs can be handled as well. Without entering too much into details, we can say that the processing of cyclic grammars for a given input string w is strongly related to the computation of (a subset of) the *depend* relation and to the detection of cycles in its transitive closure. Moreover, the check that a grammar is not strongly sound for w simply results in the detection of negative instantiated predicates into those cycles.

Note that in the corresponding shared forest, *negative nodes* of the form $\overline{A_j(\vec{\rho_j})}$ must be considered either as leaves or, equivalently, we must add in the parser a statement such as **output** $(\overline{A_j(\vec{\rho_j})} \rightarrow \varepsilon)$.

4.1   Parse Time Complexity

The parse time complexity of the previous algorithm is proportional to the number of times the body of the most internal loop is executed. Since this body is the statement at line 10, the parse time complexity is proportional to the number of calls to the *pred-call* function.

For a fixed k-RCG G and a fixed input string $w \in T^*$, $|w| = n$, the number of instantiations of a given clause $\vec{P}[i] = \psi_0 \to \psi_1 \cdots \psi_{l_i}$ is smaller than or equal to $n^{2k(l_i+1)}$. Thus, for a given clause, thanks to the memoization mechanism, the total number of calls of the form *pred-call* $(A_j, \vec{\rho_j})$ at line 10 is less than or equal to $l_i n^{2k(1+l_i)} \leq l_i n^{2k(1+l)}$, where l is the number of predicate calls in the longest clause. Thus, for all possible clauses this upper bound becomes $\sum_{i=1}^{|P|} l_i n^{2k(1+l)} = |G| n^{2k(1+l)}$, where $|G| = \sum_{i=1}^{|P|} l_i$ is the *size* of the grammar. Thus, the time complexity of this algorithm is $\mathcal{O}(|G| n^{2k(1+l)})$.[9] Its space complexity is $\mathcal{O}(|N| n^{2k})$, since the size of the memoization matrix Π is $|N| n^{2k}$ and there are at most $|N| n^{2k}$ activation frames of *pred-call* in the run-time stack.

Let us define the *typology* of a RCG G as the pair (k, l) formed by k, the arity of G, and l, the number of predicate calls in the longest clause of G. It is important to note that, for RCGs of fixed typology, the time upper bound $\mathcal{O}(|G| n^{2k(1+l)})$ expresses a linear dependency with respect to the grammar size $|G|$, and a polynomial dependency with respect to the length of the input string n. The degree of such polynomial only depends on the typology of the grammar itself.

In the above evaluation, we have assumed that arguments in a clause are all independent; this is rarely the case. If we consider a predicate argument $\alpha = u_1 \cdots u_p \in (V \cup T)^*$ and the string binding α/ρ for some variable substitution σ, each position $0, 1, \ldots, p$ in α is mapped onto a *source index* (a position in the source text) $i_0, i_1, \ldots, i_p$ such that $i_0 \leq i_1 \leq \cdots \leq i_p$ and $\rho = \langle i_0..i_p \rangle$. These source indices are not necessarily independent (free). In particular, if for example $u_j \in T$, we have $i_j = i_{j-1} + 1$. Moreover, variables in a clause may have multiple occurrences. This means that, in a clause instantiation, the lower source indices and the upper source indices associated with all the occurrences of the same variable are always the same, and thus are not free. In fact, the degree d of the polynomial which expresses the maximum parse time complexity associated with a clause is equal to the number of free bounds in that clause. For any RCG G, if d is its maximum number of free bounds, the parse time for an input string of length n is at worst $\mathcal{O}(|G| n^d)$.

If we consider a bottom-up non-erasing[10] k-RCG G, by definition there is no free bound in its right-hand side. Thus, in this case, the number of free bounds is less than or equal to $d = \max_{\vec{P}[i]} (k_i + v_i)$, where k_i and v_i are the arity and the number of (different) variables in the left-hand side predicate of $\vec{P}[i]$ respectively.

However, if we work with grammars with a fixed typology, we emphasize the fact that a linear dependency on the grammar size is extremely important, especially in NL processing where we handle huge grammars and small sentences. For example, it is possible to transform any TAG into an equivalent PRCG such that $d = 6$ (see Boullier, 1999b). Thus, in that case, we get a parse time which is linear in grammar size.

In example 2 above, we defined a predicate named *eq* which may be useful in many grammars; therefore, in our prototype implementation we decided to predefine it, together with some others, among which we give here *len*, *eqlen* and *eq*:

$len(l, X)$**:** checks that the size of the range denoted by the variable X is the integer l;

$eqlen(X, Y)$**:** checks that the sizes of X and Y are equal;

$eq(X, Y)$**:** checks that the substrings X and Y are equal.

It should be noted that these predefined predicates do not increase the formal power of RCGs insofar as each of them can be defined by a pure RCG. Their introduction is justified by the fact that they are more efficiently implemented than their RCG-defined counterpart and, more significantly, because they convey static information which can be used to decrease the number of free bounds and may thus lead to an improved parse time.

Consider again example 2. The grammar is bottom-up non-erasing, and the most complex clause is the first one. Its number of free bounds is four (one argument and three variables), and so its parse time complexity is at worst $\mathcal{O}(n^4)$. In fact, neither the left bound nor the right bound of the argument XYZ is free, since their associated source index values are always 0 and n, respectively, thus this complexity is at worst quadratic (two free bounds). Note that, in each of the four last clauses which define the unary predicate name L, the left bound of the unique argument of L is not free either, since its value is always the source index zero. The parse time complexity of this grammar further decreases to linear if *eq* is predefined, because in that case we statically know that the sizes of X, Y and Z must be equal (there is no longer a free bound within the first clause, so it is executable in constant time). The linear time comes from the right bound of the left-hand side argument in the last three clauses. We can also check that the actual parse time complexity of example 3 is logarithmic in the length of the source text!

Boullier (2003) presents some applications in which RCGs are used as counting devices.

5.　　Closure Properties and Modularity

We shall show below that RCLs are closed under union, concatenation, Kleene iteration, intersection and complementation.

Let $G_1 = (N_1, T_1, V_1, P_1, S_2)$ and $G_2 = (N_2, T_2, V_2, P_2, S_2)$ be two RCGs defining the languages L_1 and L_2 respectively. Without loss of generality, we assume that $N_1 \cap N_2 = \emptyset$ and that S is a unary predicate name not in $N_1 \cup N_2$. Consider two RCGs $G' = (N_1 \cup \{S\}, T_1, V_1 \cup \{X\}, P_1 \cup P', S)$ and $G'' = (N_1 \cup N_2 \cup \{S\}, T_1 \cup T_2, V_1 \cup V_2 \cup \{X\}, P_1 \cup P_2 \cup P'', S)$ defining the languages L' and L'' respectively. By careful definition of the additional sets of clauses P' and P'', we can get $L'' = L_1 \cup L_2$, $L'' = L_1 L_2$ or $L'' = L_1 \cap L_2$ and $L' = L_1^*$ or $L' = \overline{L_1}$.

Union: $P'' = \{S(X) \rightarrow S_1(X), S(X) \rightarrow S_2(X)\}$

Concatenation: $P'' = \{S(XY) \rightarrow S_1(X) \ S_2(Y)\}$

Intersection: $P'' = \{S(X) \rightarrow S_1(X) \ S_2(X)\}$

Kleene iteration: $P' = \{S(\varepsilon) \rightarrow \varepsilon, S(XY) \rightarrow S_1(X) \ S(Y)\}$

Complementation: $P' = \{S(X) \rightarrow \overline{S_1(X)}\}$

Boullier (1999d) shows that the emptiness problem for RCLs is undecidable and that RCLs are not closed under homomorphism. In fact, we have shown that a polynomial parse time formalism that extends CFGs cannot be closed both under homomorphism and intersection and we advocate that, for a formalism describing NL, it is preferable to have the property of closure under intersection rather than the propery of closure under homomorphism. This is specially true when this closure property is reached without changing the component grammars.

Let G_1 and G_2 be two grammars in some rewriting formalism $\mathcal{F}$ defining the languages L_1 and L_2 respectively, and let their sets of (rewrite) rules be P_1 and P_2. We say that $\mathcal{F}$ is *modular* with respect to some binary (set theoretic) operation f if $\mathcal{F}$ is closed under f, i.e., the language $L = f(L_1, L_2)$ can be generated by a grammar G in $\mathcal{F}$, and if P, the set of rules of G, is such that $P_1 \cup P_2 \subset P$. The idea behind this definition is of course to be able to (re)use any sub-grammar as such, without any modification (up to some renaming). In that sense, we can say that CFGs are modular with respect to the union operation since CFGs have, on the one hand, the formal property of being closed under union and, on the other hand, this union is described without changing the component grammars G_1 and G_2 (we simply have to add the two rules $S \rightarrow S_1$ and $S \rightarrow S_2$). Conversely, CFGs are not modular with respect to intersection or complementation since we know that CFLs are not closed under intersection or complementation.

Now, if we consider regular languages, we know that they possess the formal property of being closed under intersection and complementation; however we cannot say that left or right linear CFGs (which define regular languages) are modular with respect to these operations. For example, let us take a right-linear CFG G, defining the language L. We know that it is possible to construct a right-linear CFG $\overline{G}$ generating its complement language $\overline{L}$, but the set of rules of $\overline{G}$ seems hardly related to the set of rules of G.

Following our definition, we see that RCLs are modular with respect to union, concatenation, Kleene iteration, intersection and complementation. We emphasize that it is of considerable benefit for a formalism to be modular with respect to intersection and complementation.

Modularity with respect to intersection allows one to directly define a language with the property $P_1 \wedge P_2$, assuming that we have two grammars G_1 and G_2 describing properties P_1 and P_2, respectively, without changing either G_1 or G_2.

Modularity with respect to complementation (or set difference) allows one to model the paradigm "general rule with exceptions", for example. Assume that we have a property P defined by a general rule R with some exceptions E to this general rule. Thus, formally we have $P = R - E = R \cap \overline{E}$. Within the RCG formalism, we simply have to add a clause of the form

$$P(X) \quad \rightarrow \quad R(X)\, \overline{E(X)}$$

assuming that P, R and E are unary predicate names. If, moreover, these exceptions are described by some rules, say D, we simply have to add the clause

$$P(X) \quad \rightarrow \quad D(X)$$

6. Conclusion

In (Boullier, 1999d) we showed that the 1-RCG subclass of RCGs with a single argument is already a powerful extension of CFGs which can be parsed in cubic time and which contains both the intersection and the complement of CFLs. In (Boullier, 1999b) and (Boullier, 1999c) we showed that unrestricted TAGs and set-local multi-component TAGs can be translated into equivalent PRCGs. Moreover, these transformations do not result in any overhead. For example we have a linear parse time for regular CFGs, a cubic parse time for CFGs and a $\mathcal{O}(n^6)$ parse time for TAGs.

In this chapter we have presented the full class of RCGs which we can use to express several NL phenomena outside the formal power of MCS formalisms, while staying computationally tractable. The associated parsers work in time polynomial with the size of the input string and in time linear with the size of the grammar for a fixed typology. Moreover, in a given grammar, only complicated (many arguments, many variables) clauses produce higher parse times whereas simpler clauses induce lower times.

For a given input string, the output of a RCG parser may be an exponential or even unbounded set of derived trees but it can be represented in a compact structure, the shared forest, which is a CFG of polynomial size and from which each individual derived tree can be extracted in time linear in its own size.

As CFGs, RCGs may themselves be considered a syntactic backbone on which other formalisms such as Herbrand's domain or feature structures can be grafted.

And lastly, we have seen that RCGs are modular. We could therefore imagine libraries of generic linguistic modules which any grammar writer could pick up at will in order to specify a particular phenomena.

All of these properties seem to suggest that RCGs have the right level of formal power needed for NL processing.

Notes

1. In (Boullier, 1999a) we argue that this extra power can be used in NL processing.

2. Often, for a variable binding X/ρ, instead of saying ρ is the range which is bound to X or denoted by X, we shall simply say *the range X*, or even for w^ρ, instead of saying *the string whose occurrence is denoted by the range which is bound to X*, we shall simply say *the string X*.

3. This definition is borrowed from Bertsch and Nederhof (2001).

4. A grammar is *non-increasing* if and only if, for every instantiated clause and for each argument binding α'/ρ' in its right-hand side with $\rho' = \langle j..k \rangle$, there exists in its left-hand side an argument binding α/ρ with $\rho = \langle i..l \rangle$ such that $i \le j \le k \le l$. Non-increasing grammars represent an important and fairly large subclass of RCGs.

5. The previous definition of $IP^+_{G,w}$ still holds for (N)RCGs.

6. $\vec{\alpha_i}/\vec{\rho_i}$ is a shorthand notation for $\{\alpha_{i1}/\rho_{i1}, \ldots, \alpha_{ip_i}/\rho_{ip_i}\}$ if $\vec{\alpha_i} = \alpha_{i1}, \ldots, \alpha_{ip_i}$ and $\vec{\rho_i} = \rho_{i1}, \ldots, \rho_{ip_i}$.

7. When a grammar is cyclic, we can note that relation $\overset{+}{\underset{G,w}{\mapsto}}$, the transitive closure of the relation *depend*, is itself cyclic.

8. In our prototype system, we have implemented a PRCG parser which also works for cyclic grammars.

9. In fact we have $\mathcal{O}(|G|n^{2r})$ where r is the maximum number of arguments in a clause.

10. A RCG is *bottom-up non-erasing* if, for each clause, all variables that occur in the right-hand side also occur in the left-hand side.

References

Becker T., Rambow O., and Niv M. (1992). The Derivational Generative Power of Formal Systems or Scrambling is Beyond LCFRS. In *Technical Report*, IRCS-92-38, Institute for Research in Cognitive Science, University of Pennsylvania, Philadelphia, PA.

Bertsch E. and Nederhof M.-J. (2001). On the Complexity of Some Extensions of RCG Parsing. In *Proceedings of the Seventh International Workshop on Parsing Technologies (IWPT-2001)*, Beijing, China, pages 66–77.

Boullier P. (1998). Proposal for a Natural Language Processing Syntactic Backbone. In *Research Report*, RR-3342, at http://www.inria.fr/RRRT/RR-3342.html, INRIA-Rocquencourt, France, 41 pages.

Boullier P. (1999a). Chinese Numbers, MIX, Scrambling, and Range Concatenation Grammars. In *Proceedings of the 9th Conference of the European Chapter of the Association for Computational Linguistics (EACL'99)*, Bergen, Norway, pages 53–60.
See also *Research Report No 3614* at http:// www.inria.fr/RRRT/RR-3614.html, INRIA-Rocquencourt, France, Jan. 1999, 14 pages.

Boullier P. (1999b). On TAG Parsing. In 6ème *conférence annuelle sur le Traitement Automatique des Langues Naturelles (TALN'99)*, Cargèse, Corsica, France, pages 75–84. Also in *Traitement Automatique des Langues*, Vol. 41, No. 3 (2000), pages 759–793. See also *Research Report No 3668* at http:// www.inria.fr/RRRT/RR-3668.html, INRIA-Rocquencourt, France, Apr. 1999, 39 pages.

Boullier P. (1999c). On Multicomponent TAG Parsing. In 6ème *conférence annuelle sur le Traitement Automatique des Langues Naturelles (TALN'99)*, Cargèse, Corse, France, pages 321–326. See also *Research Report No 3668* at http://www.inria.fr/RRRT/RR-3668.html, INRIA-Rocquencourt, France, Apr. 1999, 39 pages.

Boullier P. (1999d). A Cubic Time Extension of Context-Free Grammars. In *Sixth Meeting on Mathematics of Language (MOL6)*, University of Central Florida, Orlando, Florida, USA, pages 37–50. Also in *Grammars*, Vol. 3, Nos. 2–3 (2000), pages 111–131. See also *Research Report No 3611* at http://www.inria.fr/RRRT/RR-3611.html, INRIA-Rocquencourt, France, Jan. 1999, 28 pages.

Boullier P. (2003). Counting with Range Concatenation Grammars. In *Theoretical Computer Science*, Vol. 293, No. 2, pages 391–416, Elsevier Science Publishers, Amsterdam.

Groenink A. (1997). Surface without Structure Word Order and Tractability in Natural Language Analysis. PhD thesis, Utrecht University, The Netherlands.

Joshi A. (1985). How Much Context-Sensitivity is Necessary for Characterizing Structural Descriptions – Tree Adjoining Grammars. In *Natural Language Parsing – Theoretical, Computational and Psychological Perspective*, pages 206–250, D. Dowty, L. Karttunen, and A. Zwicky, editors, Cambridge University Press, New-York, NY.

Lang B. (1994). Recognition Can Be Harder Than Parsing. In *Computational Intelligence*, Vol. 10, No. 4, pages 486–494.

Radzinski D. (1991). Chinese Number-Names, Tree Adjoining Languages, and Mild Context-Sensitivity. In *Computational Linguistics*, Vol. 17, No. 3, pages 277–299.

Rounds W. (1988). LFP: A Logic for Linguistic Descriptions and an Analysis of its Complexity. In *Computational Linguistics*, Vol. 14, No. 4, pages 1–9.

Shieber S. (1985). Evidence Against the Context-Freeness of Natural Language. In *Linguistics and Philosophy*, Vol. 8, pages 333–343.

Vijay-Shanker K., Weir D. and Joshi A. (1987). Characterizing Structural Descriptions Produced by Various Grammatical Formalisms. In *Proceedings of the 25th Meeting of the Association for Computational Linguistics*, Stanford University, CA, pages 104–111.

Weir D. (1988). Characterizing Mildly Context-Sensitive Grammar Formalisms. PhD thesis, University of Pennsylvania, Philadelphia, PA.

Chapter 14

GRAMMAR INDUCTION BY MDL-BASED DISTRIBUTIONAL CLASSIFICATION

Yikun Guo

Computer Science Department, Fudan University
Shanghai, China 200433
ykguo2000@yahoo.com

Fuliang Weng

Research and Technology Center, Robert Bosch Corporation
4009 Miranda Avenue, Palo Alto, CA 94304
fuliang.weng@rtc.bosch.com

Lide Wu

Computer Science Department, Fudan University
Shanghai, China 200433
ldwu@fudan.edu.cn

Abstract   This chapter describes our grammar induction work using the Minimum Description Length (MDL) principle. We start with a diagnostic comparison between a basic best-first MDL induction algorithm and a pseudo induction process, which reveals problems associated with the existing MDL-based grammar induction approach. Based on this, we present a novel two-stage grammar induction algorithm which overcomes a local-minimum problem in the basic algorithm by clustering the left hand sides of the induced grammar rules with a seed grammar. Preliminary experimental results show that the resulting induction curve significantly outperforms traditional MDL-based grammar induction, and in a diagnostic comparison is very close to the ideal case. In addition, the new algorithm induces grammar rules with high precision. Finally, we discuss our future research directions to improve both the recall and precision of the algorithm.

H. Bunt et al. (eds.), New Technologies in Parsing Technology, 291-306.

1.   Introduction

With the increasing demand for high quality natural language processing in various applications, such as automatic speech recognition and dialog systems, the acquisition of large amount of high quality grammar rules becomes more and more important. The availability of manually annotated corpora, such as Penn Treebank, alleviates the knowledge-engineering bottleneck. However, parsers trained on these corpora could run into the problem of overfitting, and therefore may not scale well to other domains. To parse sentences from a new domain, one would then try to obtain a new set of grammar rules from that domain, which often would require a huge amount of expensive manual work for the new domain. Past experience shows that manual annotation of a large corpus is both a labor-intensive and a time-consuming task. Therefore, it would be very desirable to automatically derive grammar rules from raw text data of a particular domain with a minimal manual effort.

In this chapter, we report our ongoing research work in automatic grammar acquisition using the minimal description length principle (Rissanen, 1978; Rissanen, 1989) with contextual distributional classification. In particular, we want to answer the following questions:

1 What problems do existing MDL-based grammar induction approaches have?

2 Is there any measurable gold standard or an approximation to a standard for any MDL-based grammar induction?

3 Are there any new approaches that can lead to performance close to a gold standard?

To answer these questions, we start with a diagnostic comparison between a basic best-first MDL induction algorithm and a pseudo induction process. The pseudo induction process and its relaxed variants assume that the grammar rules and/or their order of application are known. Since there is no easy way to obtain a measurable gold standard for grammar induction, the pseudo grammar induction process serves as a good approximation. The diagnostic results show that the basic MDL algorithm alone induces reasonable phrase grammar rules at the beginning, but it leads to a local minimum quickly. In addition, most of induced rules are not adequate. On the other hand, applying the rules from the Treebank in bottom-up order together with the MDL principle results in a monotonic and sharp decrease of the MDL value. Based on this, we present a novel two-stage grammar induction algorithm that overcomes the key local-minimum problem in the basic algorithms by clustering the left hand sides of the induced grammar rules with a classifier trained with a seed grammar. Preliminary experimental results show that the resulting induction curve significantly outperforms the traditional MDL-based grammar induction, and is very close to the ideal case in a diagnostic comparison. In addition, we found the new algorithm induces grammar rules with high precision. Finally, we will discuss our future research directions to improve both recall and precision of the algorithm.

The rest of this chapter is organized as follows: section 2 presents the MDL principle with an emphasis on description length gain (DLG). Section 3 presents two grammar induction strategies and their corresponding experimental results in a diagnostic evaluation. Based on these results, section 4 gives a new induction algorithm and encouraging evaluation results. The final section reviews previous MDL-based research on grammar learning and gives our conclusions.

2. Grammar Induction with the MDL Principle

Grammar induction can be viewed as a process that searches for the best grammar in a predefined grammar (or hypothesis) space, where permissible rules or rule formats, e.g., context-free grammar (CFG) rules, are given. Essentially, there are two sub-tasks in obtaining a CFG rule. One is to decide what the right-hand terminals or non-terminals should be, and the other is to decide the left-hand side (LHS) symbol. When a set of rules are given, it becomes practical to use the Baum-Welch (or forward-backward) algorithm and its extension, the inside-outside algorithm (Baker, 1979; Lari and Young, 1990), to estimate the probabilistic parameters for these grammars. In this section, we briefly review MDL as it relates to search in a grammar space.

2.1 The MDL Principle

Researchers have proposed various techniques and criteria to constrain the grammar space and to conduct an efficient and effective search process, such as genetic algorithms (Holland, 1975) and simulated annealing (Kirkpatrick et al., 1983). Since the objective function used in the search decides which grammar rule to select, it is very important to find the right function. Among others, the minimal description length principle (Shannon and Weaver, 1949; Solomonoff, 1964; Kolmogorov, 1965; Rissanen, 1978; Rissanen, 1989; Cover and Thomas, 1991) has received wide attention as an objective function.

When we pick the *best* candidate from multiple accountable theories for a data set, Occam's razor says the simplest is the best. The MDL principle is a quantitative translation of the principle. Intuitively, there are two aspects associated with the MDL principle (Rissanen, 1978). One is the complexity with which a theory describes the data, and the other is the complexity for the description of the theory itself. There is a trade-off between these two aspects.

Formally, given a data set D, the theory T should be selected that minimizes the formula

$$L(D \mid T) + L(T) \tag{14.1}$$

where $L(D \mid T)$ is the number of bits needed to minimally encode data D using theory T, and $L(T)$ is the number of bits needed to minimally encode theory T. From information theory (Shannon and Weaver, 1949), we know that given a countable set of items X with a probability distribution of $P(x)$, to send a message identifying $x \in X$ requires approximately $L(x) = -\log_2 P(x)$ bits. In other words,

$$P(x) = 2^{-L(x)} \tag{14.2}$$

This enables us to interpret the MDL principle in a Bayesian framework. From the equation, it is obvious that minimizing $L(D \mid T) + L(T)$ corresponds to maximizing $P(D \mid T) * P(T)$ and hence $P(T \mid D)$. This means that searching for the most likely theory for a given set of data in a Bayesian modeling framework is equivalent to searching for a model with the minimal description length. It should be noted that the MDL principle enables us to assign prior probabilities to items in a meaningful way when not enough prior knowledge is available. In other words, we can always assume minimal length encoding for items as the prior knowledge.

2.2   Description Length Gain

The application of MDL is independent of the encoding scheme (Rissanen, 1989). To calculate the description length $L(D \mid T) + L(T)$, an ideal encoding scheme, instead of a real compression program, is needed. The empirical description length DL can be formulated in terms of token counts in the corpus (see also Kit, 1998):

$$DL(X) = n\hat{H}(X) = -n \sum_{x \in V} \hat{p}(x) \log \hat{p}(x) = - \sum_{x \in V} c(x) \log \frac{c(x)}{|X|} \tag{14.3}$$

where V is the set of distinct tokens (i.e., the vocabulary) in corpus X, $c(x)$ is the count of token x in X, n is the sum of the counts for all the tokens in V, and $\hat{H}$ is the empirically computed entropy. Accordingly, the description length gain of selecting the substring of tokens $x_i x_{i+1} \cdots x_j$, $i < j$, henceforth denoted as $x_{i..j}$, as the right-hand side (RHS) of a candidate rule in corpus X is defined as:

$$DLG(x_{i..j} \in X) = DL(X) - DL(X[r \to x_{i..j}] \bigotimes x_{i..j}) \tag{14.4}$$

where $DL(X[r \rightarrow x_{i..j}])$ represents a new corpus obtained by replacing all instances of $x_{i..j}$ with r throughout corpus X, r is a randomly selected symbol that is not previously used, and $\otimes$ denotes a string concatenation operation that inserts a delimiter between its two operands, in this case, the new corpus and the learned phrase $x_{i..j}$. Henceforth we use $\in$ very loosely in $x \in X$ to mean that string x occurs in corpus X. We also remark that the vocabulary is updated with new token r, in order to compute $DL(X[r \rightarrow x_{i..j}])$.

It is worth noting that we can find the substring with the maximum DLG value at each iteration without carrying out any actual string substitutions in the original corpus. The calculation can be solely based on the token count changes involved in the substitution to derive the counts for the new corpus. After a substring with the maximum DLG is found, we can then replace all the occurrences of the substring in the original corpus with the randomly selected symbol r. The counts for the new instances after the replacement correspond to the number of occurrences of the replaced substring (i.e., RHS of the rule) in the original corpus. This is important for efficient search of the best candidates during the various induction processes presented in the subsequent sections.

Another task is the computation of the counts for all the possible substrings x (in this case, n-grams) to obtain a set of good candidates. Because long rules normally occur less frequent than short rules, the MDL principle prefers short grammar rules over long grammar rules. Consequently, longer grammar rules have fewer chances to be selected in the induction. In addition, it is too computationally expensive to consider each possible n-gram at every point in the search. For a clear understanding of the induction and to make it computationally feasible, we use only bi-grams and tri-grams in our induction experiments. To obtain a fair comparison, we use the same constraints on the sizes of the RHS strings for both automatic induction and manually annotated rules.

3.   Induction Strategies

In the following subsections, we will describe three grammar induction algorithms, two for the diagnostic comparison, and the other for the improved one.

3.1   Basic Induction Algorithm

The basic MDL-based induction algorithm that uses best first search and description length as the criterion is illustrated in Fig. 14.1. Given an utterance $U = t_0 t_1 \cdots t_n$ as the input string of linguistic tokens, e.g., part-of-speech tags, the unsupervised grammar induction first looks for the substring with the maximum description length decrease, i.e., maximum DLG, at each iteration. Then, it replaces the n-gram (i.e., bi-grams or tri-grams in this case) in the

1 Set $k = 0$ and extract all bi-grams and tri-grams in X_k with their counts.

2 If for all n-grams $x_{i..j} \in X_k$ with $2 \leq j - i \leq 3$ relation $DL(X_k[r_k \to x_{i..j}]) \geq DL(X_k)$ holds, then exit.

3 $rhs_k = argmax_{x_{i..j} \in V_k} DLG(x_{i..j} \in X_k)$.

4 $X_{k+1} = X_k[r_k \to rhs_k]$, output $r_k \to rhs_k$, set $k = k + 1$.

5 Go to step 2.

Figure 14.1.   The basic MDL induction algorithm.

whole corpus with a random symbol not previously used. In the meantime, it outputs the learned rules in this iteration. This process loops until the description length value does not decrease, which means DLG has a zero or negative value.

3.2   Pseudo Grammar Learning with the MDL Principle

It is evident that the learning algorithm may not reach the real shortest description length for the data, since it is a best first strategy that may stop at any local minimum. To get a good estimation of the limit of the MDL-based algorithms, we implement a pseudo grammar induction algorithm that assumes knowledge of the manually annotated rules in Penn Treebank as well as the rule application order. Figure 14.2 outlines this pseudo induction algorithm.

In the algorithm, all human created rules from the corpus and the rule application order are predetermined based on the parse trees. The MDL principle is only used to pick a rule in the current step so as to maximize the description length gain. In the pseudo-learning process, when all the child rules are selected and applied, their parent rules may subsequently be considered. Thus, these manually annotated rules are applied roughly in bottom-up parsing order, guided by the MDL criterion. The experimental results from this algorithm tell us that when the rules and their application order are known, how much it differs from the basic induction algorithm. In addition, the results provide an approximation to the gold standard for MDL-based grammar induction.

3.3   Results for Basic and Pseudo Grammar Induction Algorithms

We first conducted two experiments using the two algorithms described above. Both of the experiments use as input 2,500 sentences randomly se-

1 Extract all hand-annotated grammar rules from Penn Treebank, sort those rules in the bottom-up parsing order. Initially, mark all the leaf rules as *visible* and all the other rules as *hidden*, and place *visible* rules in a rule pool.

2 For all rules in the rule pool, at each iteration, apply step 2, 3 and 4 of the basic induction algorithm in Fig. 14.1, and select the rule with the maximum *DLG*.

3 When all the children of a grammar rule are *visible*, mark the grammar rule as *visible* and place it in the rule pool.

4 Go to step 2 if there are remaining rules in the rule pool.

Figure 14.2. The pseudo grammar induction algorithm.

lected from Penn Treebank with manually labeled part-of-speech (POS) tags. The use of POS tags is necessary, due to the sparse data problem.

3.3.1 Experiments with Basic MDL Grammar Induction. The first experiment induces a grammar using the basic MDL principle. The test corpus contains 2,500 sentences and the vocabulary contains 32 POS tags, a subset of the 47 POS tags used in Penn Treebank. The grammar space consists of CFG rules whose RHS strings are either bi-grams or tri-grams. The first thirty of the induced rules are given in appendix A. From the appendix, we can see that most of the learned grammar rules are reasonable, such as [NNP NNP], [TO VB] and [MD VB]. However, other rules seem to be quite "flat", i.e., lack internal structure. Rule [PRP RB VBD], for instance, should be broken down into [PRP [RB VBD]]. The MDL value curve is plotted in Fig. 14.3, showing the tendency of the DL to decrease as the search proceeds. It is clear from this figure that having induced about a hundred rules, the basic MDL induction algorithm quickly becomes flat.

3.3.2 Experiments with Pseudo Induction Algorithm. In this experiment, we use the same search strategy but with rules directly extracted from the Penn Treebank. The rules are organized so that only after all child rules are applied does a rule become applicable. The task of the search process is to choose the rule with the maximum description length decrease from the partially ordered rule set. The DL value curve is shown in Fig. 14.3, together with the curve using the basic MDL induction algorithm.

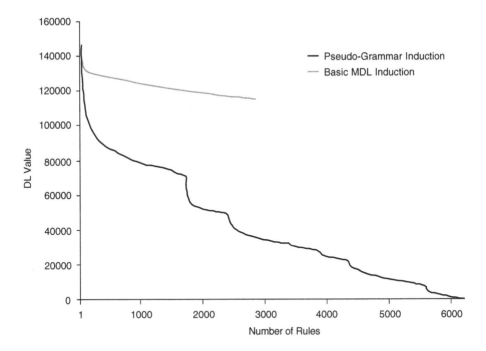

Figure 14.3.   The two grammar induction curves (basic MDL vs. pseudo-grammar).

From this figure we see that although the two curves are very close in the beginning, they soon diverge. On one hand, the general MDL value trend for the pseudo induction algorithm heads down quite consistently with the increase of the number of applied rules. On the other hand, for the basic MDL induction algorithm, the curve quickly becomes flat and has to be terminated because it is computationally too expensive to infer new rules. The reason for such a large computational cost is because the large number of randomly selected LHS of the induced rules leads to a large number of candidate rules that must be considered by the algorithm. For example, when a new LHS symbol r is introduced, five new rule patterns need to be considered for the tri-gram case, i.e., x_2x_1r, x_2rx_1, rx_2x_1, xr, and rx.

Furthermore, for the pseudo grammar induction algorithm, the curve decreases irregularly, that is, a few "critical" rules decrease the description length much more dramatically than the other rules. We suspect that this is because certain rules may occur more frequently than others, and when they are applied, a larger decrease in the DL value takes place.

To verify whether the result curve of the pseudo grammar induction is just a special case for the particular data set, we performed two more experiments

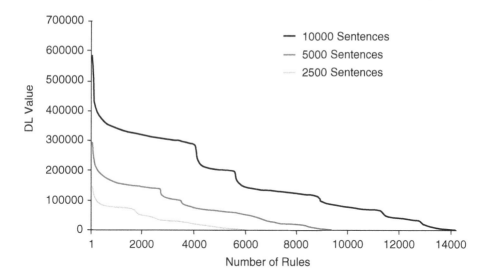

Figure 14.4.   Different data sets in the pseudo grammar induction experiment.

on different sets of sentences. The results are shown in Fig. 14.4. The three curves are obtained by applying the same pseudo grammar induction algorithm on three sets of sentences extracted from Penn Treebank, with the smaller sets being included in the larger ones. Their sizes are 2,500, 5,000, and 10,000 sentences. The results show a remarkable consistency for the three different sentence sets.

4.   MDL Induction by Dynamic Distributional Classification (DCC)

From the above experimental results, we discover that the basic MDL induction algorithm alone does infer reasonable phrasal grammar rules at the beginning, but it quickly reaches a local-minimum and most of the induced rules are not adequate. We suspect that this may be due to the random labeling of LHS symbols for those induced rules. This is because if all the LHS symbols of the induced rules are different, the repetition of certain patterns becomes less likely, and therefore their MDL value decreases less drastically. Based on this observation, we propose a new algorithm that integrates some linguistic information into the search strategy. The information is used to classify the LHS symbols of the induced rules, using distributional analysis, to help the search process to infer more syntactically plausible rules.

The algorithm has two stages: one is the context vector training stage; the other is the improved MDL induction process. The context vector training algorithm is based on the following assumption. While rules with the same LHS category tend to occur in similar contexts, the contexts of the rules of the "VP" category, for instance, differ greatly from those of the "NP" rules. If the context is restricted to a fixed sliding window, then we can define the context distribution for all rules of a syntactic category. For our experiments, we define as the context window the three part-of-speech tags on both sides of the rules. The context distribution of a category can then be estimated from the observed contexts of sample sentences in the same category. Note that a rule may occur at a high level in the parse tree. In that case, the left and right strings next to the region the rule covers are taken as the context.

In the next MDL induction stage, we use the Kullback-Leibler (KL) distance function to measure the similarity of each MDL induced rule to the center of context vectors of each syntactic category. The induced rule is assigned the LHS symbol whose context vector center has the shortest distance from the induced rule. At each iteration, we also dynamically update the contexts and the context vector centers of the induced rules for every syntactic category.

For simplicity, in our experiment, the syntactic categories are limited to five non-terminals, i.e., "NP", "VP", "S", "ADJP", and "PP", which are main syntactic components in syntactic parsing. We take as a *seed grammar* a set of most frequently used grammar rules for each of the five syntactic categories and analyze their contexts for each of those rules in the training corpus. A context of a category is defined as its three left POS tags and its three right POS tags. The thirty seed rules used in the algorithm are given in Table 14.1. Note that we not only use the base grammar rules, i.e., the rules at the leaf levels of the parse trees, but also the ones at the upper levels, since exploiting the context of these rules on-the-fly will make the search process more robust. Another important issue in the selection of seed grammar rules is to decide the distribution of the numbers of rules for different categories. We adopt the same ratio for these five categories in the seed grammar as the ratio in which they occur in the training corpus. For example, "NP" rules alone account for two thirds of all rules in the Penn Treebank and they overwhelm other rules especially in the lower levels of the parse trees. Therefore, we choose the corresponding ratio for "NP" seed rules.

4.1 Experimental Results with MDL-Based DCC Induction

In this section, we give experimental results for the two-stage induction algorithm described above. A classifier for determining the context vector centers of the 5 syntactic categories is first trained on 1,000 POS tagged sentences

Table 14.1.   The set of seed grammar rules.

NP → DT JJ NN	NP → DT JJ NNS	NP → DT NN
NP → DT NNS	NP → PRP	NP → JJ NNS
NP → JJ NN	NP → NNP POS	NP → DT NN POS
NP → JJ JJ NN	NP → JJ JJ NNS	NP → DT NN NN
NP → DT CD NNS	NP → NP NP	NP → NP CC NP
ADJP → RB JJ	ADJP → RB JJR	ADJP → RB JJS
ADJP → RBS JJ	ADJP → RBR JJ	VP → VB NP
VP → TO VP	VP → MD VP	VP → VBD NP
VP → VBZ NP	PP → IN NP	PP → TO NP
PP → IN S	S → NP VP	S → PP NP VP

These rules are organized based on their LHS symbols. For rules with the same LHS symbol, their order is decided by the corresponding frequencies in the Penn Treebank corpus in decreasing order.

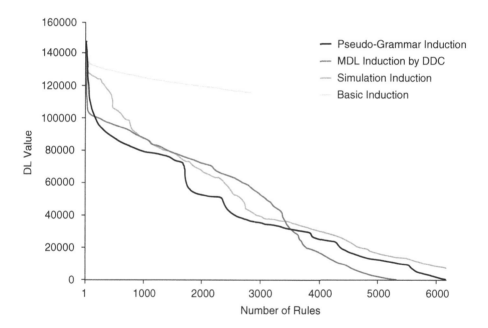

Figure 14.5.   The MDL curves for all the algorithms.

using the seed grammar rules. Then, we construct the induction sets using another set of 2,500 sentences, the same sentence set as the one used in the previous experiments. The curve labeled with "MDL Induction by DDC" in Fig. 14.5 summarizes the results.

Table 14.2.   Precision and recall for DCC induced rules.

# of Induced rules	100	200	500	1000
Precision	0.92	0.89	0.82	0.74
Recall	0.13	0.16	0.18	0.22

From the chart, we see that the MDL value curve decreases monotonically, and it does not flatten out as in the basic MDL induction algorithm. Instead, the curve is very close to the pseudo grammar induction case, i.e., the ideal gold standard case. In addition, this algorithm learns not only the right-hand sequences of terminals/non-terminals, but also their LHS syntactic categories.

In addition, we also calculate the precision and recall for those induced rules, in contrast with the hand-annotated grammar rules extracted from the same set of 2,500 sentences. The results are given in Table 14.2, where the first 100 induced rules have a high precision of 92%, but a low recall of 13%, with respect to the manual rules from the 2,500 sentences. The low recall is understandable given the denominator is the total number of rules in the 2,500 sentences. When more rules are induced, the precision goes down but the recall goes up.

Examining the results, we obtained the following findings. Many induced grammar rules that reduce the description length dramatically are not syntactically plausible, and are not found in the manual rule set. However, the algorithm assigns a syntactic category for them and updates the center of the context vector for that category in the search process. This, in turn, has a negative impact on the classification in the subsequent induction process. Although we include several high-level grammar rules in our seed grammar and explore their context in the induction process to compensate for this effect, how to improve the robustness needs further investigation. Another major factor contributing to these results is the overly restricted number of syntactic categories and the overly short length limit of the RHS strings used in our experiment. That is, there are only five categories in the experiment and only bi-grams and tri-grams are used for the RHS strings, while there are more than fifteen categories in the Treebank and many "flat" grammar rules are found in Treebank (Gaizauskas, 1995).

To better understand the effect of these constraints in our new algorithm, we conducted another experiment, assuming that the LHS syntactic category of every induced rule is correctly identifiable using extra knowledge, and also assuming that the induced rules are a subset of the grammar rules found in the manually annotated Treebank corpus.

We designed the experiment as follows. At each iteration of the induction process described in section 4, we sort the candidate rules by their DLGs in a descending order, choose the first induced rule in the candidate list that matches a manual rule in the Penn Treebank, and replace all the occurrences of the RHS sequence with the corresponding LHS in the corpus.

There are two consequences of this change. Firstly, we make sure that the LHS for any induced rule is always correct if there is no ambiguity. Therefore, this procedure does not perform any classification, and it reduces the negative impact of earlier induced rules on rules induced later. Secondly, all rules learned are syntactically plausible, since they are a subset of the manual-annotated grammar rules. The remaining differences between the induced rule set and the manual rule set are due to two factors: the number of the right-hand symbols and the syntactic category of the left-hand symbol when there is an ambiguity.

The result of the experiment is illustrated in Fig. 14.5, labeled "Simulated Induction". As shown in Fig. 14.5, compared with the "Pseudo Grammar Induction" curve, the different number of n-grams and the syntactic categories does affect the results, especially in the later stages of the search process. A second finding is that, compared with "Grammar Induction by DDC" curve, the classifier is really distracted by previously induced "bad" grammar rules. In addition, a better DL value also does not imply a better set of induced rules, especially in the later stages of the induction. These issues warrant further investigation.

5.　　Comparison and Conclusion

The difficulty of grammar induction depends greatly on the amount of supervision provided. One extreme example is shown by Charniak (1996), where grammar rules are easily constructed when the examples are fully labeled parse trees. However, if the examples consist of only raw sentences with no extra structural information, grammar induction is very difficult, even theoretically impossible (Gold, 1975). Our work explores an intermediate case, where the categories of learned rules are decided by a supervised learning algorithm.

A second important issue in grammar induction is the objective function for the search. In addition to the MDL principle (for instance Kit, 1998), other objective functions have also been investigated. Cook et al. (1976) explore a hill-climbing search for a grammar with a smaller weighted sum of the grammar complexity and the discrepancy between the grammar and corpus; Brill et al. (1990) derive phrase structures from a bracket corpus using an approach based on generalized mutual information. Brill and Marcus (1992) attempt to induce binary branching phrase structure by distributional analysis using the information-theoretic divergence measure. De Marken in his PhD thesis (de Marken, 1995) gives an in-depth discussion of the kind of issues involved in pure distributional analysis and of the disadvantages of the inside-outside algorithm for grammar induction. Following Cook's work, Stolcke (1994) revealed the relationship between MDL and the Bayesian modeling framework. Furthermore, Chen (1996) uses the universal prior probability $p(G) = 2^{l(G)}$ for grammar induction. These research efforts report good results only on small to medium size artificial corpora. However, to our knowledge, no one has tried to induce all levels of syntactic grammar rules on large scale real corpora before.

In this chapter, we have presented and compared four MDL-based grammar induction algorithms. The basic MDL algorithm uses only MDL as the objective function in a best-first search. The pseudo grammar induction algorithm uses MDL as the objective function and assumes that the rule set and the rule application order are known. The DCC induction algorithm uses MDL as the objective function and a seed grammar for finding the LHS symbols based on a distributional analysis. The simulation induction algorithm is based on the DCC algorithm with additional oracle information. Among the four, the pseudo-grammar induction algorithm is used to find an approximation to a gold standard while the simulation induction algorithm is used to find potential improvements for the DCC algorithm.

Experimental results on Penn Treebank corpus are encouraging. These results also reveal promising directions for the DCC algorithm, including the addition of constituent-internal features to the classifier, relaxation of the number of the LHS categories and the length of the RHS symbols, and features used in the description for MDL.

References

Baker, J. K. (1979). Trainable grammars for speech recognition. In Wolf, J. J. and Klatt, D. H., editors, *Speech Communication Papers for the 97th Meeting of the Acoustical Society of America*, pages 547–550, Cambridge, Mass.

Brill, E., Magerman, D., Marcus, M., and Santorini, B. (1990). Deducing linguistic structure from the statistics of large corpora. In *Proceedings of the Speech and Natural Language Workshop*, pages 275–282, Hidden Valley, PA.

Brill, E. and Marcus, M. (1992). Automatically acquiring phrase structure using distributional analysis. In *Proceedings of the Speech and Natural Language Workshop*, pages 155–159, Harriman, N.Y.

Charniak, E. (1996). Tree-bank grammars. In *Proceedings of the National Conference on Artificial Intelligence*, pages 1031–1036. AAAI Press/MIT Press.

Chen, S. F. (1996). *Building Probabilistic Models for Natural Language*. PhD thesis, Harvard University, Cambridge, Mass.

Cook, C., Rosenfeld, A., and Aronson, A. R. (1976). Grammatical inference by hill climbing. *Information Sciences*, 10:59–80.

Cover, T. and Thomas, J. (1991). *Elements of Information Theory*. John Wiley & Sons, New York, N.Y.

de Marken, C. (1995). The unsupervised acquisition of a lexicon from continuous speech. Technical Report A.I. Memo No. 1558, AI Lab., MIT, Cambridge, M.A.

Gaizauskas, R. (1995). Investigations into the grammar underlying the penn treebank II. Technical Report CS-95-25, University of Sheffield, Sheffield, England.

Gold, E. M. (1975). Language identification in the limit. *Information and Control*, 10:447–474.

Holland, J. (1975). *Adaptation in Natural and Artificial Systems*. MIT Press, Cambridge, Mass.

Kirkpatrick, S., Gelatt, C., and Vecchi, M. (1983). Optimisation by simulated annealing. *Science*, 220:671–680.

Kit, C. (1998). A goodness measure for phrase learning via compression with the MDL principle. In Kruijff-Korbayova, I., editor, *The ESSLLI-98 Student Session*, chapter 13, pages 175–187.

Kolmogorov, A. N. (1965). Three approaches for defining the concept of information quantity. *Problems of Information Transmission*, 1:4–7.

Lari, K. and Young, S. J. (1990). The estimation of stochastic context-free grammars using the inside-outside algorithm. *Computer Speech and Language*, 4:35–56.

Rissanen, J. (1978). Modeling by shortest data description. *Automatica*, 14:465–471.

Rissanen, J. (1989). *Stochastic Complexity in Statistical Inquiry*. World Scientific Publishing Company, Singapore.

Shannon, C. and Weaver, W. (1949). *The Mathematical Theory of Communication*. University of Illinois Press.

Solomonoff, R. J. (1964). A formal theory of inductive inference. *Information and Control*, 7:1–22.

Stolcke, A. (1994). *Bayesian Learning of Probabilistic Language Models*. PhD thesis, University of California, Berkeley, Berkeley, California.

Appendix

The first 30 grammar rules learned by the basic MDL grammar induction algorithm from 2,500 sentences in the Treebank corpus are given in Table 14.A.1. Rules are flagged by human evaluators as true (t), false (f) or unsure (u). The four columns in Table 14.A.1 are rule identifier, the current description length with model and data combined when the grammar rule is acquired, the RHS of the rule, and the evaluation flag. Rules with brackets indicate that the bracketed parts were induced in preceding steps, and the randomly selected symbols for the LHS of the bracketed sequences are removed for clarity.

Table 14.A.1.   Basic MDL induced rules.

rule id	curr. desc length	RHS of rule	correctness
1	146186	NNP NNP	t
2	144823	TO VB	t
3	142641	MD VB	t
4	141748	MD RB VB	t
5	141411	DT JJ NN	t
6	140245	IN DT NN	t
7	138981	PRP VBP	u
8	138625	PRP VBD	u
9	138119	PRP VBZ	u
10	137703	PRP [MD VB]	t
11	137471	NNS VBP	t
12	136989	NNS WDT VBP	f
13	136834	WDT VBZ	t
14	136681	NNS WP VBP	f
15	136567	RB VB	t
16	136398	NNP NNPS	t
17	136274	TO CD CD	t
18	136128	NNP POS	t
19	135916	EX VBZ	u
20	135839	WDT [MD VB]	t
21	135762	WDT VBD	t
22	135666	PRP RB VBD	u
23	135569	PRP [MD RB VB]	t
24	135508	EX VBZ	u
25	135456	WP VBZ	t
26	135369	JJR IN CD	f
27	135271	TO DT NN	t
28	135082	PRP RB VBP	u
29	135023	NNS RB VBP	f
30	134936	[NNP NNP] POS	t

CD: Cardinal number   PRP: Personal pronoun
DT: Determiner   MD: Modal
JJ: Adjective   RB: Adverb
JJS: Adjective, superlative   TO: "to"
IN: Preposition or subordinating conjunction   VBD: Verb, past tense
POS: Possessive ending   VBN: Verb, past participle
VB: Verb, base form   VBZ: Verb, 3rd person singular present
NNP: Noun, singular form   NN: Noun, base form

Chapter 15

OPTIMAL AMBIGUITY PACKING
IN CONTEXT-FREE PARSERS
WITH INTERLEAVED UNIFICATION

Alon Lavie
Language Technologies Institute, Carnegie Mellon University
5000 Forbes Avenue, Pittsburgh, PA 15213
alavie@cs.cmu.edu

Carolyn Penstein Rosé
Learning Research and Development Center, University of Pittsburgh
3939 O'Hare Street, Pittsburgh, PA 15260
rosecp@pitt.edu

Abstract   Ambiguity packing is a well known technique for enhancing the efficiency of context-free parsers. However, in the case of unification-augmented context-free parsers where parsing is interleaved with feature unification, the propagation of feature structures imposes difficulties on the ability of the parser to effectively perform ambiguity packing. We demonstrate that a clever heuristic for prioritizing the execution order of grammar rules and parsing actions can achieve a high level of ambiguity packing that is provably optimal. We present empirical evaluations of the proposed technique, performed with both a Generalized LR parser and a chart parser, that demonstrate its effectiveness.

1.   Introduction

Efficient parsing algorithms for purely context-free grammars have long been known. Most natural language applications, however, require a far more linguistically detailed level of analysis that cannot be supported in a natural way by pure context-free grammars. Unification-based grammar formalisms (such as HPSG), on the other hand, are linguistically well founded, but are

H. Bunt et al. (eds.), New Technologies in Parsing Technology, 307-321.

difficult to parse efficiently. Unification-augmented context-free grammar formalisms have thus become popular approaches where parsing can be based on an efficient context-free algorithm enhanced to produce linguistically rich representations. Whereas in some formalisms, such as the ANLT grammar formalism (Briscoe and Carroll, 1993; Carroll, 1993) a context-free "backbone" is compiled from a pure unification grammar, in other formalisms (Tomita, 1990) the grammar itself is written as a collection of context-free phrase structure rules augmented with unification constraints that apply to feature structures that are associated with the grammar constituents. When parsing with such grammar formalisms, the goal of the parser is to produce both a *c-structure* – a constituent phrase structure that satisfies the context-free grammar – and an *f-structure* – a feature structure that satisfies the functional unification constraints associated with phrasal constituents.

Regardless of the specific context-free parsing algorithm used, the most common computational approach to performing the dual task of deriving both c-structure and f-structure is an interleaved method, where the unification functional constraints associated with a context-free rule are applied whenever the parser completes a constituent according to the rule. If a "bottom-up" parsing approach is used, this process usually involves applying the unification constraints that augment a grammar rule at the point where the right-hand side (RHS) constituents of the rule have all been identified and are then reduced to the left-hand side (LHS) constituent in the rule. The functional unification constraints are applied to the already existing feature structures of the RHS constituents, resulting in a new feature structure that is associated with the LHS constituent. In the case that any of the specified functional constraints cannot be satisfied, unification fails, and the completed left-hand side (LHS) constituent of the rule is pruned out from further consideration.

The computational cost involved in the construction and manipulation of f-structures during parsing can be substantial. In fact, in some unification-augmented formalisms, parsing is no longer guaranteed to be polynomial time, and in certain cases may even not terminate (when infinitely many f-structures can be associated by the grammar with a given substring of the input (Shieber, 1986). Additionally, as pointed out by Maxwell and Kaplan (1993), interleaved pruning is not the only possible computational strategy for applying the two types of constraints. However, not only is interleaved pruning the most common approach used, but certain grammars, in which the context-free backbone in itself is cyclic, actually rely on interleaved f-structure computation to "break" the cycle and ensure termination. Thus, in this paper, we only consider parsers that use the interleaved method of computation.

Ambiguity packing is a well known technique for enhancing the efficiency of context-free parsers. However, as noted by Briscoe and Carroll (Briscoe and Carroll, 1993; Carroll, 1993), when parsing with unification-augmented CFGs, the propagation of feature structures imposes difficulties on the ability of the parser to effectively perform ambiguity packing. In this paper, we demonstrate that a clever heuristic for prioritizing the execution order of grammar rules and parser actions can significantly reduce the problem and achieve high levels of ambiguity packing. We prove that our ordering strategy is in fact optimal in the sense that no other ordering strategy that is based only on the context-free backbone of the grammar can achieve better ambiguity packing. We then present empirical evaluations of the proposed technique, implemented for both a chart parser and a generalized LR parser, which demonstrate the effectiveness of our rule prioritization technique. Finally, our conclusions and future directions are discussed in Section 5.

2. Ambiguity Packing in Context Free Parsing

2.1 Ambiguity Packing

Many grammars developed for parsing natural language are highly ambiguous. It is often the case that the number of different parses allowed by a grammar increases rapidly as a function of the length (number of words) of the input, in some cases even exponentially. In order to maintain feasible runtime complexity (usually cubic in the length of the input), many context-free parsing algorithms use a shared parse node representation and rely on performing *Local Ambiguity Packing*. A local ambiguity is a case in which a portion of the input sentence can be parsed and reduced to a particular grammar category (non-terminal) in multiple ways. Local ambiguity packing allows storing these multiple sub-parses in a single common data structure, indexed by a *single* pointer. Any constituents further up in the parse tree can then refer to the set of sub-parses via this single pointer, instead of referring to each of the sub-analyses individually. As a result, an exponential number of parse trees can be succinctly represented, and parsing can still be performed in polynomial time.

Obviously, in order to achieve optimal parsing efficiency, the parsing algorithm must identify all possible local ambiguities and pack them together. Certain context-free parsing algorithms are inherently better at this task than others. Tabular parsing algorithms such as CKY (Younger, 1967) by design synchronize processing in a way that supports easy identification of local ambiguities. On the other hand, as has been pointed out by Billot and Lang (1989), the Generalized LR (GLR) Parsing algorithm (Tomita, 1987) is not capable of performing full ambiguity packing, due to the fact that stacks that end in different states must be kept distinct. There has been some debate in the parsing community regarding the relative efficiency of GLR and chart parsers, with conflicting evidence in both directions (Schabes, 1991; van Noord, 1997; Briscoe and Carroll, 1993; Nederhof and Satta, 1996). The relative effectiveness of performing ambiguity packing has not received full attention in this debate, and may in fact account for some of the conflicting evidence[1].

2.2   The Problem: Ambiguity Packing in CFG Parsing with Interleaved Unification

Most context-free parsing algorithms, including GLR and chart parsing, are under-specified with respect to the order in which various parsing actions must be performed. In particular, when pursuing multiple ambiguous analyses, the parsing actions for different analyses may be arbitrarily interleaved. In a chart parser, for example, this non-determinism is manifested via the choice of which key (or inactive edge) among the set of keys waiting in the agenda should next be used for extending active edges. In the case of a GLR parser the non-determinism appears in the choice of which among a set of possible rule reductions should be picked next.

The particular order in which parsing actions are performed determines when exactly alternative analyses of local ambiguities are created and detected. With certain orderings, a new local ambiguity for a constituent may be detected after the constituent has already been further processed (and incorporated into constituents higher up in the parse tree). When parsing with a pure CFG, this does not affect the ability of the parser to perform local ambiguity packing. When a new local ambiguity is detected, it can simply be packed into the previously created node. Any pointers to the packed node will now also point to the new sub-analysis packed with the node. However, when parsing with unification-augmented CFGs, this is often not the case. Since feature structures corresponding to the various analyses are propagated up the parse tree to parent nodes, a new local ambiguity requires the creation of a new feature structure that must then be propagated up to any existing parent nodes in the parse tree. In effect, this requires re-executing any parsing actions in which the packed node was involved. With certain "pure" unification grammar formalisms such as GPSG (Gazdar *et al.,* 1985; Alshawi, 1992; Carroll, 1993), feature structure subsumption provides a solution to this problem. Other unification-augmented CFG grammar formalisms, however, require a full encoding of the ambiguous feature structures. In many implementations – for example, the Generalized LR parser/compiler (Tomita, 1990) and the CLE, (Alshawi, 1992) – to avoid the rather complex task of re-calculating the feature structures, ambiguity packing is not performed if it is determined that the previous parse node has already been further processed. Instead, the parser creates a new parse node for the newly discovered local ambiguity and processes the new node separately. As a result, the parser's overall local ambiguity packing is less than optimal, with a significant effect on the performance of the parser.

It should be noted that effective local ambiguity packing when parsing with unification-augmented CFGs requires not only a compact representation for the packed constituent (c-structure) nodes, but also an effective representation of the associated feature structures (f-structures). The issue of how to effectively pack ambiguous f-structures has received quite a bit of attention in the literature over the last decade (Eisele and Dorre, 1998; Maxwell and Kaplan, 1991; Maxwell and Kaplan, 1993; Miyao, 1999; Kiefer *et al.*, 1999). Particularly noteworthy is Placeway's recent work (Placeway, 2002) on how to improve overall parser efficiency using a two-pass feature structure computation method. While the issues of c-structure and f-structure packing are related, we focus here on how to achieve optimal packing of c-structures, so that unification operations do not have to be re-executed due to the later detection of an additional local ambiguity. While there is much to be gained from improved packing on the f-structure level, one should note that effective ambiguity packing on the c-structure level is a necessary pre-condition for efficient parsing, regardless of how well f-structures are packed.

3. The Rule Prioritization Heuristic

In order to ensure effective ambiguity packing in unification-augmented context-free parsers, the situation in which a new local ambiguity is detected after the previous ambiguity has already been further processed must be avoided as much as possible. Ideally, we would like to further process a constituent only after all local ambiguities for the constituent have been detected and packed together into the appropriate node. Our goal was thus to find a computationally inexpensive heuristic that can determine the optimal ordering, or at least closely approximate it. The heuristic that we describe in this section uses only the context-free backbone of the grammar and the spans of constituents in determining what grammar rule (or parsing action) should be "fired" next. Later in the section we prove that this heuristic does in fact achieve the best amount of packing possible, given the information available. In practice, it is easy and fast to compute, and it results in very substantial parser efficiency improvements, as demonstrated by the evaluations presented in the following section. The heuristic was initially developed for the GLR parser, parsing with a unification-augmented CFG. It was then modified to handle the corresponding ordering problem in a chart parser.

3.1 The GLR Ordering Heuristic

In the context of the GLR parser, the heuristic is activated at the point where a decision has to be made between multiple applicable grammar rule reductions. The following example demonstrates the problem and how we would like to address it. Let us assume we have just executed a rule reduction by `[rule0:`   `A --> B C]` that created a parse node for a constituent A that spans words $4-7$ of the input. Assume we now have to choose between the following possible rule reductions:

1. Reduce by `[rule1:`   `D --> A]` that would create a constituent D spanning words $4-7$ (using the previously just created constituent A).

2. Reduce by `[rule2:`   `A --> E F]` that would create a constituent A spanning words $4-7$.

3. Reduce by `[rule3:`   `G --> B A]` that would create a constituent G spanning words $3-7$ (using the previously just created constituent A).

Which rule reduction should be picked next? Since the last rule reduction created a constituent A spanning $4-7$, by picking `[rule2]` we can create another constituent A spanning $4-7$, that can then potentially be packed with the previous A. If we pick `[rule1]` on the other hand, we would further process the previously created constituent A. When `[rule2]` is then executed later, the new A can no longer be packed with the previous A. Thus, it is best to choose to perform the `[rule2]` reduction first.

The first criterion we can use in a heuristic aimed at selecting the desired rule is the span of the constituent that would result from applying the rule. Obviously, we wish to delay applying rules such as `[rule3]` which process the first A until all other possible A's of the same span have been found and packed. Ignoring for the moment the complications arising from unary rules (such as `[rule1:`   `D --> A]` above) and epsilon rules (which consume no input), selecting a rule that is "rightmost" - creating a constituent with the greatest possible starting position, will in fact achieve this goal. This is due to the fact that in the absence of unary and epsilon rules, every constituent must cover some substring of the input, and thus every RHS constituent in a grammar rule must start at a different input position. Thus, the "rightmost" criterion supports the goal of delaying the construction of constituents that extend "further to the left" until all ambiguities of the previous span have been processed, and all potential local ambiguities have been packed.

In the presence of unary grammar rules, however, the "rightmost" criterion is insufficient. Looking again at our example above, both `[rule1]` and `[rule2]` are "rightmost", since both create a constituent that starts in position 4. However, `[rule1]` would further process the existing A constituent before `[rule2]` detects a local ambiguity. The problem here is that the application of unary rules does not consume an additional input token. We therefore require a more sophisticated measure that can model the dependencies between constituents in the presence of unary rules. To do this, we use the context-free backbone of the grammar, and define the following partial-order relation "$\geq$" between constituent non-terminals:

Input: A set of applicable grammar rule reductions.

Output: A selected grammar rule reduction to be performed next.

Selection Heuristic:

(1) For each potential grammar rule reduction, determine the span (start and end positions) and category of the constituent that would result from the rule reduction.

(2) Select the rule reduction that is rightmost - has the largest start position.

(3) If there is more than one rightmost rule reduction, pick a rule reduction that results in a category that is "least" according to the "$> *$" partial-order.

Figure 15.1. Rule Reduction Selection Heuristic for GLR Parser

- For every unary rule A $-->$ B in the grammar G, $A \geq B$.
- We compute "$\geq^*$" - the transitive closure of "$\geq$"

We can now extend our heuristic to use the partial-order information. The idea is not to perform a unary reduction resulting in a constituent B when there is an alternative "rightmost" reduction that produces a constituent A where $B \geq^* A$. The resulting GLR parser heuristic can be seen in Figure 15.1.

The partial-order "$\geq^*$" can easily be pre-compiled from the grammar. Note that it is theoretically possible that for particular non-terminals A and B, both $A \geq^* B$ and $B \geq^* A$. This implies that the context-free backbone of the grammar contains a cycle. With unification-augmented CFGs, this is indeed possible, since the unification equations augmenting the grammar rules may resolve the cycle. In such cases, the above heuristic may encounter situations where there is no unique rule that is minimal according to the partial-order. If this occurs, we pick one of the "least" categories randomly. This may result in sub-optimal packing, but only full execution of the unification operations can in fact correctly decide which rule should be picked in such cases. In practice, the computational cost of such a test would most likely far exceed its benefits.

3.2   Handling Epsilon Rules

The case that the grammar contains epsilon rules requires some additional attention. In this case, the premise that every RHS constituent of a grammar rule starts at a different position (i.e. consumes input) no longer holds. Consequently, the "rightmost" criterion no longer ensures that a rule that includes a constituent A on the RHS will not fire until all possible local ambiguities of A have been processed and packed. It is useful to note, however, that the problem is in fact similar to that of unary rules, and can be treated quite similarly as well. We first find all "nullable" non-terminals in the grammar G - the set of all non-terminals that can derive the empty string. A well known algorithm for detecting nullable non-terminals can be found in Hopcroft and Ullman (1979). We denote by $A \in EP(G)$ that A is nullable. We now modify the partial-order relation defined above to handle the case of nullable categories. We define "$\geq_\epsilon^*$" as follows:

1 if $A \geq^* B$ then $A \geq_\epsilon^* B$

2 for every rule $A \rightarrow B_1 \ B_2 \ \cdots B_k$ in G, check if $B_i \in EP(G)$ (for $1 \leq i \leq k$). If all $B_i \in EP(G)$, then for all $1 \leq i \leq k$, $A \geq_\epsilon^* B_i$. Otherwise, if the rule is such that only *one* $B_i \notin EP(G)$, then $A \geq_\epsilon^* B_i$.

3 we compute the transitive closure of $\geq_\epsilon^*$

We then replace the "$\geq^*$" relation in our ordering heuristic with the extended "$\geq_\epsilon^*$" relation. Intuitively, the idea is to identify grammar rules $A \rightarrow B_1 \ B_2 \ \cdots B_k$ that are not unary, but where when "fired", the LHS constituent A may have a span identical to that of one (or more) of the B_i RHS constituents. This is the case whenever all the RHS constituents (and thus also the LHS constituent) derive the empty string, or else all but one of the RHS constituents (B_i) derive the empty string. In the first case, we want to ensure that all empty derivations of the B_i are selected before the rule reducing to A is applied. In the second case, we want to ensure that all derivations of the non-nullable B_i are selected before the rule reducing to A. We thus extend the partial-order so that the appropriate RHS constituents in such rules are "lesser" in the order than the LHS constituent. This ensures that such rules will not be selected until all local ambiguities of the RHS constituents have been processed and packed.

3.3   Proof of Optimality

We now argue that the complete ordering heuristic that uses the "rightmost" and "least" criteria as defined above is in fact optimal in the sense that it achieves the maximal ambiguity packing possible given only the context-free backbone of the grammar as available information. Let us assume to the contrary that the heuristic does not result in optimal packing. This implies that a constituent A_1 of span (i, j) was created, that a rule in which A_1 serves as a RHS constituent was then selected by the heuristic, executed, and created a LHS constituent B_1, and that subsequently, another rule with a LHS of A was executed, creating a new A_2 of span (i, j) that can no longer be packed with the previous A_1. B_1 must also be of span (i, j), since otherwise it could not have been chosen due to the "rightmost" criterion. At the time the rule creating B_1 was selected by the heuristic, B must have satisfied the "least" criterion. If the A_2 is created as a result of processing A_1 via a series of rule applications, then the grammar is in fact cyclic. As mentioned earlier, while our heuristic is not guaranteed to be optimal in such cases, any better heuristic would require using f-structure unification information. So we assume that A_2 was created via a series of rule applications that did not involve A_1. We look at the sequence of constituents $X_1, X_2, \cdots A$ created in the series of rule applications that resulted in A_2 after A_1 had already been created. All must have span (i, j), since otherwise A_2 cannot have a span of (i, j). At least one of these rule applications must have been a possible candidate at the point in time that the rule using A_1 and creating B_1 was chosen and executed. However, by the definition of $\geq_\epsilon^*$, for each of the X_i, $A \geq_\epsilon^* X_i$, and since B_1 is created by applying a rule that uses A_1, we also have that $B \geq_\epsilon^* A$. By the transitive closure property of $\geq_\epsilon^*$ we thus have that for all of the X_i, $B \geq_\epsilon^* X_i$. Thus, at the point in time where the rule creating B_1 was fired, either B was *not* minimal according to the "least" criterion, and we derive a contradiction, or else both B and some X_i were minimal, requiring a random choice between the two. In the latter case, as mentioned earlier, the grammar contains a cycle, and only full execution of the unification operations could correctly decide which of the two rules should be picked first for execution. This case excluded, we can thus conclude that the heuristic is in fact optimal.

3.4 The Chart Parser Ordering Heuristic

In order to achieve effective ambiguity packing in the case of the chart parser, we require that the parser process the input strictly left-to-right, in order to synchronize the creation and processing of constituents with similar spans. While chart parsers in general do not require such ordered processing, many chart-based parsers are in fact left-to-right, and this is usually not a burdensome restriction. Our rule reordering heuristic can then be added to the parsing algorithm in a straightforward way. In the case of the chart parser, rather than directly reordering reductions, the reordering heuristic modifies the order in which active edges are extended. The idea is that the most efficient way to extend active edges is to ensure that active edges like $[A \rightarrow \ldots \bullet C \ldots]$ are not extended over inactive edges of category C until all possible inactive edges of category C starting in the appropriate position in the chart have been inserted and packed. The same criteria of "rightmost" and "least" are applied in deciding which active edge should be selected next for extension.

4. Empirical Evaluations and Discussion

To evaluate the effectiveness of our rule selection heuristic we conducted empirical test runs with both a GLR parser and a chart parser. Both parsers are designed to support the same LFG style unification grammar framework. The two parsers and the grammar formalism are briefly described below. Both parsers also have robust versions that are designed to overcome input that is not completely grammatical due to disfluencies or lack of grammar coverage. The robust parsers can skip over words or segments of the input that cannot

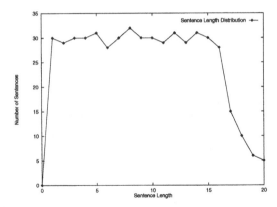

Figure 15.2.   Distribution of evaluation set sentence lengths

be incorporated into a grammatical structure. When operated in robust mode, the skipping of words and segments introduces a significantly greater level of local ambiguity. In many cases, a portion of the input sentence may be reduced to a non-terminal symbol in many different ways, when considering different subsets of the input that may be skipped. Thus, efficient runtime performance of the robust versions of the parsers is even more dependent on effective local ambiguity packing. We therefore conducted evaluations with the two parsers in both robust and non-robust modes, in order to quantify the effect of the rule selection heuristic under both scenarios.

All of the described experiments were conducted on a common test set of 520 sentences from the JANUS English Scheduling Task (Lavie et al., 1996), using a general English syntactic grammar developed at Carnegie Mellon University. The grammar has 412 rules and 71 non-terminals, and produces a full predicate-argument structure analysis in the form of a feature structure. For the GLR parser, the grammar compiles into an SLR parsing table with 628 states and 8822 parsing actions. Figure 15.2 shows the distribution of sentence lengths in the evaluation set.

4.1   The GLR Parser

The Generalized LR Parser/Compiler (Tomita, 1990) is a unification based practical natural language analysis system that was designed around the GLR parsing algorithm at the Center for Machine Translation at Carnegie Mellon University. The system supports grammatical specification in an LFG framework, that consists of context-free grammar rules augmented with feature bundles that are associated with the non-terminals of the rules. Feature structure computation is, for the most part, specified and implemented via unification operations. This allows the grammar to constrain the applicability of context-free rules. A reduction by a context-free rule succeeds only if the associated feature structure unification is successful as well. The Generalized LR Parser/Compiler is implemented in Common Lisp, and has been used as the analysis component of several different projects at the Center for Machine Translation at CMU in the course of the last decade.

GLR* (Lavie, 1994; 1996b; 1996a), the robust version of the parser, was constructed as an extended version of the unification-based Generalized LR Parser/Compiler. The parser skips parts of the utterance that it cannot incorporate into a well-formed sentence structure. Thus it is well-suited to domains in which non-grammaticality is common. The parser conducts a search for the maximal subset of the original input that is covered by the grammar. This is done using a beam search heuristic that limits the combinations of skipped words considered by the parser, and ensures that it operates within feasible time and space bounds. The GLR* parser also includes several tools designed to address the particular difficulties of parsing spontaneous speech. These include a statistical disambiguation module and a collection of parse evaluation measures which are combined into an integrated heuristic for evaluating and ranking the parses produced by the parser.

4.2 The LCFLEX Parser

The LCFLEX parser (Rosé and Lavie, 2001) is a recently developed robust left corner chart parser designed to incorporate the flexibility of GLR* within a more efficient parsing architecture. Its left corner chart parsing algorithm is similar to that described in (Carroll, 1993). Thus, it makes use both of bottom-up predictions based on newly created inactive edges as well as top-down predictions based on active edges bordering on those edges. It utilizes the same grammar formalism used in GLR*, described above. The context- free backbone within the GLR grammar formalism allows for efficient left corner predictions using a pre-compiled left corner prediction table, such as that described by Van Noord (1997). It incorporates similar statistical disambiguation and scoring techniques to those used in GLR*, as described by Lavie (1996a).

4.3 Evaluation Results

We first ran both the GLR and the LC parsers in non-robust mode (with no word skipping allowed), once without the rule reordering heuristic and once with the heuristic. Figure 15.3 (left) shows a plot of the average number of created parse nodes as a function of sentence length. For both parsers, the total number of nodes created when rule reordering is applied significantly decreases, especially with longer sentences. This is a direct result of the increased level of ambiguity packing performed by the parsers when rule reordering is applied. For the LC parser, the savings are quite dramatic. For example, for

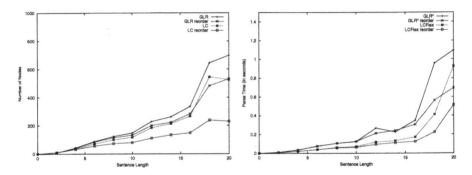

Figure 15.3. Non-robust parsers: number of parse nodes and parse time as a function of sentence length

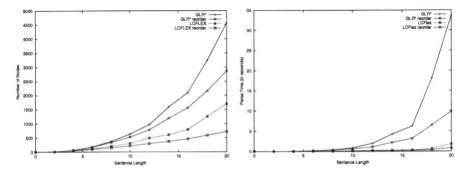

Figure 15.4. Robust parsers: number of parse nodes and parse time as a function of sentence length

sentences of length 12, the average relative reduction in number of parse nodes with reordering was about 12% for the GLR parser and about 40% for the LC parser. As can be expected, this relative reduction rate appears to grow as a function of sentence length, due to increasing levels of ambiguity. Figure 15.3 (right) shows a plot of the average parse times as a function of sentence length. As can be seen, the LC parser is for the most part faster than the GLR parser, regardless of whether or not rule reordering is applied. However, for both parsers, the improved ambiguity packing with rule reordering results in a significant reduction in parsing time which increases with sentence length, due to increasing levels of ambiguity. For sentences of length 12, the time savings were about 21% for both parsers.

We then re-ran the experiment with the robust versions of the two parsers. The GLR* parser was run with a search beam of 30, which was determined in various previous experiments to be a reasonable setting for achieving good parsing results within feasible parsing times. The LCFLEX parser was then run in a way that simulated the same skipping behavior of GLR* (i.e. the exact same word skipping possibilities were considered by the parser). Figure 15.4 (left) shows a plot of the average number of created parse nodes as a function of sentence length. Once again, the total number of nodes created when rule reordering is applied significantly decreased. For GLR*, the reduction in number of nodes was more significant than the non-robust case, while for LCFLEX it appears to be about the same. For example, for sentences of length 12, the average relative reduction in number of parse nodes with reordering was about 19% for the GLR* parser and about 39% for the LCFLEX parser. Figure 15.4 (right) shows a plot of the average parse times as a function of sentence length. As can be seen, in robust mode, the LCFLEX parser is much faster than GLR*. As expected, runtimes when rule reordering is applied significantly decreased. For GLR*, the decrease is more pronounced than in the non-robust experiment, while for LCFLEX, it was about the same. For sentences of length 12, the time savings were about 44% for GLR* and about 21% for LCFLEX.

5. Conclusions and Future Directions

The efficiency of context-free parsers for parsing natural languages crucially depends on effective ambiguity packing. As demonstrated by our experimental results presented in this paper, when parsing with CFGs with interleaved unification, it is vital to execute parsing actions in an order that allows detecting local ambiguities in a synchronous way, before their constituents are further processed. Our grammar rule prioritization heuristic orders the parsing actions in a way that achieves the best possible ambiguity packing using only the context-free backbone of the grammar and the constituent spans as input to the heuristic. Our evaluations demonstrated that this indeed results in a very substantial improvement in parser efficiency, particularly so when incorporated into robust versions of the parsers, where local ambiguities abound.

The focus of most of our current and planned future research is on efficient parsing within the context of the robust LCFLEX parser. In particular, we are interested in investigating the interdependence between the parser's robustness capabilities, its search strategy, and its disambiguation and parse selection heuristics. Effective ambiguity packing will continue to be an important factor in this investigation. We plan to further explore strategies other than interleaved pruning for efficiently applying both phrasal and functional constraints, while using the existing grammar framework and broad-coverage grammars that are at our disposal.

Notes

1. For example, van Noord (van Noord, 1997) compares left corner and chart parsers that do apply ambiguity packing with a GLR parser without ambiguity packing.

References

Alshawi, H., editor (1992). *The Core Language Engine.* ACL-MIT Series in Natural Language Processing. MIT Press, Cambridge, MA.

Billot, S. and Lang, B. (1989). The Structure of Shared Forests in Ambiguous Parsing. In *Proceedings of the 27th Annual Meeting of the Association for Computational Linguistics (ACL'89)*, Vancouver, BC, Canada, pages 143–151.

Briscoe, T. and Carroll, J. (1993). Generalized Probabilistic LR Parsing of Natural Language (Corpora) with Unification-Based Grammars. *Computational Linguistics*, 19(1):25–59.

Carroll, J. (1993). *Practical Unification-Based Parsing of Natural Language.* PhD thesis, University of Cambridge, Cambridge, UK. Computer Laboratory Technical Report 314.

Eisele, A. and Dorre, J. (1988). Unification of Disjunctive Feature Descriptions. In *Proceedings of the 26th Annual Meeting of the ACL (ACL-88)*, Buffalo, NY, pages 286–294.

Gazdar, G., Klein, E., Pullum, G., and Sag, I. (1985). *Generalized Phrase Structure Grammar.* Harvard University Press, Cambridge, MA.

Hopcroft, J. E. and Ullman, J. D. (1979). *Introduction to Automata Theory, Languages and Computation*, chapter 4.4, page 90. Addison-Wesley.

Kiefer, B., Krieger, H.-U., Carroll, J., and Malouf, R. (1999). A Bag of Useful Techniques for Efficient and Robust Parsing. In *Proceedings of the 37th Annual Meeting of the Association for Computational Linguistics (ACL'99)*, pages 473–480, College Park, MD.

Lavie, A. (1994). An Integrated Heuristic Scheme for Partial Parse Evaluation. In *Proceedings of the 32nd Annual Meeting of the Association for Computational Linguistics (ACL-94)*, pages 316–318, Las Cruces, New Mexico.

Lavie, A. (1996a). *GLR*: A Robust Grammar-Focused parser for Spontaneously Spoken Language.* PhD thesis, School of Computer Science, Carnegie Mellon University. Technical Report CMU-CS-96-126.

Lavie, A. (1996b). GLR*: A Robust Parser for Spontaneously Spoken Language. In *Proceedings of ESSLLI-96 Workshop on Robust Parsing*.

Lavie, A., Gates, D., Gavalda, M., Mayfield, L., Waibel, A., and Levin, L. (1996). Multi-lingual Translation of Spontaneously Spoken Language in a Limited Domain. In *Proceedings of International Conference on Computational Linguistics (COLING'96)*, pages 442–447, Copenhagen, Denmark.

Maxwell, J. T. and Kaplan, R. M. (1991). A Method for Disjunctive Constraint Satisfaction. In Tomita, M., editor, *Current Issues in Parsing Technology.* Kluwer Academic Press.

Maxwell, J. T. and Kaplan, R. M. (1993). The Interface between Phrasal and Functional Constraints. *Computational Linguistics,* 19(4):571–590.

Miyao, Y. (1999). Packing of Feature Structures for Efficient Unification of Disjunctive Feature Structures. In *Proceedings of the 37th Annual Meeting of the Association for Computational Linguistics (ACL'99),* pages 579–584, College Park, MD.

Nederhof, M.-J. and Satta, G. (1996). Efficient Tabular LR Parsing. In *Proceedings of the 34th Annual Meeting of the Association for Computational Linguistics (ACL'96),* pagex 239–246.

Placeway, P. (2002). *High-Performance Multi-Pass Unification Parsing.* PhD thesis, Carnegie Mellon University, Pittsburgh, PA. Technical Report CMU-LTI-02-172.

Rosé, C. P. and Lavie, A. (2001). Balancing Robustness and Efficiency in Unification-augmented Context-Free Parsers for Large Practical Applications. In van Noord and Junqua, editors, *Robustness in Language and Speech Technology,* ELSNET. Kluwer Academic Press.

Schabes, Y. (1991). Polynomial Time and Space Shift-Reduce Parsing of Arbitrary Context-free Grammars. In *Proceedings of the 29th Annual Meeting of the Association for Computational Linguistics (ACL'91),* pages 106–113.

Shieber, S. M. (1986). *An Introduction to Unification-based Approaches to Grammar.* Number 4 in CSLI Lecture Notes. CSLI Stanford Univerity, Stanford, CA.

Tomita, M. (1987). An Efficient Augmented Context-free Parsing Algorithm. *Computational Linguistics,* 13(1-2):31–46.

Tomita, M. (1990). The Generalized LR Parser/Compiler - Version 8.4. In *Proceedings of International Conference on Computational Linguistics (COLING'90),* pages 59–63, Helsinki, Finland.

van Noord, G. (1997). An Efficient Implementation of the Head-Corner Parser. *Computational Linguistics,* 23(3):425–456.

Younger, D. (1967). Recognition and Parsing of Context-Free Languages in Time n^3. *Information and Control,* 10(2):189–208.

Chapter 16

ROBUST DATA ORIENTED
SPOKEN LANGUAGE UNDERSTANDING

Khalil Sima'an

Computational Linguistics, University of Amsterdam
Nieuwe Achtergracht 166, Amsterdam, The Netherlands
khalil.simaan@hum.uva.nl

Abstract Spoken utterances do not always abide by linguistically motivated grammatical rules. These utterances exhibit various phenomena considered outside the realm of theoretically-oriented linguistic research. For a language model that extends linguistically motivated grammars with probabilistic reasoning, the problem is how to feature the robustness that is necessary for speech understanding. This paper addresses the issue of the robustness of the Data Oriented Parsing (DOP) model within a Dutch speech-based dialogue system. It presents an extension of the DOP model into a head-driven variant, which allows for Markovian generation of parse trees. It is shown empirically that the new variant improves over the original DOP model on two tasks: the formal understanding of speech utterances, and the extraction of semantic concepts from word lattices output by a speech recognizer.

1.   Introduction

Speech understanding is a challenging task for probabilistic parsing models. The problem with speech utterances is that they do not always abide by linguistic grammar rules. Speech utterances exhibit phenomena such as repairs, repetitions and hesitations, all of which are considered problems outside the domain of linguistic research. The challenge for a parsing model is to deal with such phenomena. A greater challenge is set by real speech understanding tasks in noisy environments, such as speech over the telephone. In such cases, the speech recognizer's accuracy degrades and language models might be of some use in recovering some of the lost accuracy.

In this paper we address the problem of robustness in speech understanding using the DOP model when applied within the Dutch Travel-Information Di-

H. Bunt et al. (eds.), New Technologies in Parsing Technology, 323-338.

alogue System (OVIS). We present a new version of the DOP model which is more suitable for the processing of spoken language utterances than the original DOP model. Robustness in this new version, called the Tree-gram model, is the result of integrating into DOP the Markovian approach for grammar-rule generation, as in some existing models, e.g., (Charniak, 1999). We exhibit significant empirical improvements, over the DOP model, in the major OVIS tasks: (1) the formal understanding of spoken utterances and (2) the extraction of the best semantic content from an ambiguous word lattice (also called word-graph), output by a speech recognizer.

The structure of this paper is as follows. Section 2 provides a short overview of the OVIS system, the OVIS tree-bank and the experience with applying DOP within OVIS. Section 3 provides a review of the DOP model and presents the new version: the Tree-gram model. Section 4 exhibits the results of experiments in applying DOP and the Tree-gram model to speech understanding within the OVIS domain. Finally, section 5 concludes the paper.

2.   Brief Overview of OVIS

OVIS is a prototype, Dutch language, speech-based dialogue system which is aimed at providing users with railway time-table information (Openbaar Vervoer Informatie Systeem - OVIS). The system interacts (over the telephone) with a human user that is assumed to seek travel information. It consists of a number of modules including a Dialogue Manager, a Speech Recognizer, a Natural Language Processing (NLP) module, and a Language Generation module. Within speech understanding, we focus on the role of the NLP module which constitutes the interface between the speech recognizer and the dialogue manager. The output of the speech recognizer is processed by the NLP module, and the semantic content of the user's spoken utterance is extracted and supplied to the dialogue manager. The latter incorporates this information into its information state and then decides on the next step (e.g., ask the user one more question, or supply the travel information that the user seeks).

The OVIS system provides an interesting problem for language modeling because it addresses a real application of the processing of spoken language in a noisy environment. Furthermore, the task of language understanding in OVIS has been formalized in terms of *domain-dependent semantic criteria* making the evaluation of language models more linked to the actual task.

In the OVIS demonstrator system, the communication with the human user takes place over the telephone through a spoken-language dialogue aiming at providing the user with travel information. The dialogue manager in OVIS maintains an information state to keep track of the information extracted from the user's answers to questions posed by the system. This information state consists of a small number of slots that are typical of train travel information, e.g., origin, destination, date, time. The semantic content of a user's utterance is used for updating the slots in the information state. Hence, the output of the natural language processing module is exactly an *update expression* specifying what slots must be updated and with what values. In OVIS, these update expressions are terms in a formal language of update semantics developed by (Veldhuijzen van Zanten, 1996). This update language provides ways for expressing various updates including speech-act information such as denials and corrections. Here, we are merely interested in the fact that the update language has been expressed in terms of a formally specified hierarchy of the slots: for example, the slots "place" and "time" provide more specific information over the slot "destination".

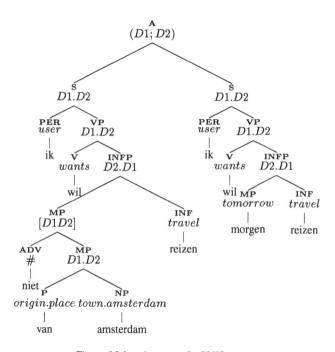

Figure 16.1. An example OVIS parse tree.

The OVIS tree-bank (Scha et al., 1996) contains 10000 utterances annotated syntactically and semantically. The interesting part of the OVIS tree-bank is that the semantics is largely compositional (Bonnema et al., 1997): the semantics of a non-terminal node is expressed in terms of the semantics of its child-nodes; this is expressed as a simplified form of Lambda expressions, e.g., "(D1;D3)" where Di refers to the i-th child. The part-of-speech (POS) tag labeled nodes are annotated with ground semantic expressions, e.g., "(PPN-amsterdam amsterdam)" or "(PP-origin.place naar)". In (Bonnema et al., 1997) a method is also described for transforming the semantic expressions at every node into a label using the semantic hierarchy of (Veldhuijzen van Zanten, 1996): roughly speaking, the semantic expressions are categorized according to the kind of slots which they aim at filling, e.g., place expressions specify a category while time expressions specify another, different category. Crucially, this semantic categorization aims at labeling the grammar rules in the tree-bank trees in such a way that it is possible to retain the exact semantics of the tree-bank trees unambiguously. In this work we employ the OVIS tree-bank enriched with this categorization scheme.

Figure 16.1 exhibits an OVIS parse tree with the compositional semantics shown under the label of every node. The update expression of the whole utterance is computed compositionally in a bottom-up fashion, substituting for Di the update expression of the i-th child. The English equivalent of the given utterance is *"I do not want to travel from Amsterdam I want to travel tomorrow"*. The update expression for this parse tree is: *(user.wants. travel.[#origin.place.town.amsterdam]; user.wants.travel.tomorrow)*, where the operator "[#A]" denotes the denial of A, "A;B" denotes the concatenation of update expressions A and B and "A.B" denotes that B is a more specific slot than A or that B is the update value for slot A.

The present paper addresses the problem of applying the Data Oriented Parsing (DOP) model (Scha, 1990; Bod, 1995) to the understanding of utterances and word-graphs that are output by a speech recognizer (Oerder and Ney, 1993) in the OVIS domain. In earlier experiments (Veldhuijzen van Zanten et al., 1999; van Noord et al., 1999), the DOP model scored significantly worse than a complex hybrid system which combines a broad coverage grammar for Dutch, a word trigram model and a smart concept spotting strategy (van Noord et al., 1999). Our research revealed three sources of problems with DOP: *lack of robustness, weak lexicalization and a biased probability-estimation method*. Among these three problems, the focus here is on robustness. Next we present the Tree-gram model by contrasting it to DOP. We subsequently test it on the same OVIS tasks.

3.   DOP vs. Tree-Gram

A probabilistic model assigns a probability to every parse tree given an input sentence S, thereby distinguishing one parse

$$\begin{aligned} T^* &= argmax_T \ P(T|S) \\ &= argmax_T \ \frac{P(T,S)}{P(S)} = argmax_T \ P(T,S). \end{aligned}$$

The probability $P(T, S)$ is usually estimated from co-occurrence statistics of linguistic phenomena extracted from a given tree-bank. In generative models, the tree T is generated through top-down derivations that rewrite the start symbol TOP into the sentence S. Each rewrite-step involves a "rewrite-event" together with its estimated probability of application. Here we compare two generative models, DOP and the Tree-grams, to one another. But first we provide an overview of both.

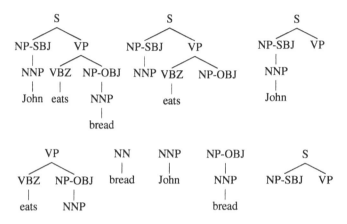

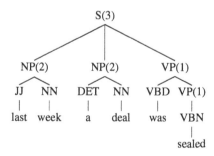

Figure 16.2. Some subtrees: DOP decomposition.

Figure 16.3. An example parse tree. Between brackets head-child numbers.

3.1 The DOP Model

In Data-Oriented Parsing (DOP) e.g., (Bod, 1995), the rewrite-events are *subtrees* of the tree-bank trees: a subtree of a given parse tree is a *multi-node connected subgraph* in which every node either dominates all its children or it dominates none of them. If we view the tree-bank trees as generated by derivations of some linguistic Context-Free Grammar (CFG; Aho and Ullman, 1972), then a DOP subtree consists of one or more connected CFG rules that co-occur in a tree-bank tree. Hence, the parse trees and sentences which a DOP model recognizes are exactly those which the original linguistic CFG does. Figure 16.2 shows some DOP subtrees extracted from the parse tree that is identical to the subtree in the top-left corner of the same figure.

Let $root(t)$ denote the root label of the root of any subtree t, and let $freq(x)$ denote the frequency count of subtree x in the tree-bank. The probability of a subtree t is estimated by the formula:

$$P(t|root(t)) = \frac{freq(t)}{\sum_{x:root(x)=root(t)} freq(x)}$$

The probability of a derivation d, involving subtrees $t_1, \ldots, t_n$, is estimated as follows

$$P(d) = \prod_{1 \leq i \leq n} P(t_i|root(t_i)).$$

The probability of a parse tree T and a sentence S, generated respectively by the sets of derivations $D(T, S)$ and $D(S)$, are estimated by $P(T, S) = \sum_{d \in D(T,S)} P(d)$, and by $P(S) = \sum_{d \in D(S)} P(d)$. In (Sima'an, 1996; 2002) it is shown that the problems of disambiguation under the DOP model, concerning the computation of the Most Probable Parse (MPP) (and the Most Probable Sentence (MPS) in a word-graph) are NP-complete. Here we suggest to approximate the probabilities of a parse tree T and a sentence S by:

$$P(T, S) \approx argmax_{d \in D(T,S)} P(d)$$
$$P(S) \approx argmax_{d \in D(S)} P(d)$$

This formulation has the advantage of being efficiently solvable by a deterministic polynomial-time algorithm, similar to the well known Viterbi-algorithm (Viterbi, 1967). The negative side, however, is that it still contains some of the bias that the original DOP definition had (Bonnema et al., 1999) and that it under-estimates the probabilities. However, we think that this underestimation in itself is not harmful since the exact values are not important as much as the relative ordering between the parses (and sentences).

3.2   The Tree-Gram Model

In the Tree-gram model, the set of "rewrite-rules" subsumes the CFG rules and the connected combinations thereof (i.e., DOP subtrees). We refer to these rewrite-events with the term *Tree-grams* (abbreviated T-grams). A T-gram extracted from a parse tree in the training tree-bank is a *multi-node connected subgraph* of that parse tree. Crucially, this definition implies that when extracting a T-gram from some node μ in a tree-bank parse tree, not necessarily all children of μ are included into the T-gram. In the current implementation, however, we demand that the children of μ that are included in the T-gram are direct sisters to one another, e.g., we do not allow including the first and the fifth child if any of the second, third and fourth are not included also. This tends to simplify the parsing algorithms.

T-grams are inspired by Markov Grammars (Collins, 1997; Charniak, 1999): in fact T-grams provide a direct general form both for Markov Grammar rules (called bilexical dependencies) as well as DOP subtrees. Next we describe in short how T-grams are employed in the Tree-gram model. Further detail can be found in (Sima'an, 2000).

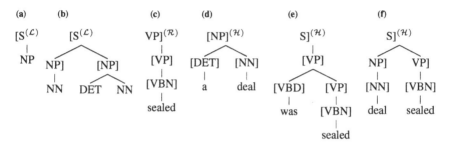

Figure 16.4. Some T-grams extracted from the tree in figure 16.3. Note that in this figure the superscript on the root label specifies the *T-gram role*, e.g., the left-most T-gram is in the LEFT role. Non-leaf nodes are marked with "[" (left-STOP) and "]" (right-STOP) to specify whether they are complete from the left/right or both (the other non-complete nodes, i.e., from both sides, are not marked at all).

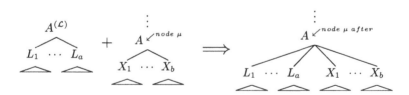

Figure 16.5. A T-gram is generated by attachment at μ in a partial parse tree. The T-gram being generated is marked with $\mathcal{L}$ (or $\mathcal{R}$) to denote its role. We show a LEFT T-gram being generated.

We assume that for every non-leaf node μ in the training tree-bank trees, one of its child nodes is specified as being the "head child": the child that dominates the head word of μ. The T-grams acquired from the tree-bank trees are partitioned into three subsets, called *roles*, according to the kind of children that the root of a T-gram dominates. When a T-gram's root dominates its head child (and possibly other children), the T-gram is in the "Head" role; when it dominates only children which are originally found (in the tree-bank tree from which the T-gram was extracted) to the left (right) of the head child (e.g., left modifiers of the head child), it is in the LEFT (RIGHT) role. In essence, these roles express information about the nature of the T-gram with respect to the context from which it was extracted. Some example T-grams are shown in figure 16.4.

In contrast with DOP subtrees, T-grams allow also for a "horizontal" expansion of the parse trees as depicted in figure 16.5. This horizontal expansion of parse trees takes place by combining T-grams labeled with the same root node in a "Markovian fashion". Formally speaking, the horizontal combination of T-grams must have a probability of terminating. Therefore, the horizontal combination of T-grams is governed by a formal definition of when a node "terminates". The termination process is "inherited" from the tree-bank trees: the sequence of children of every node in a tree-bank tree is explicitly marked as terminated from the left and from the right by a special symbol "STOP". To the left of the sequence of children, the STOP is denoted by "[" and to the right it is denoted by "]". When a T-gram is extracted from a tree in the tree-bank, the STOP symbols ("[" and "]") might either be included or they might not be included with the non-leaf nodes of the T-gram. For any non-leaf node in a T-gram, if both STOP symbols are included along with its children, the node is called *complete*. When STOP is absent from either the left or right hand sides of a node (or both), the node is incomplete. In the latter case, the partial parse trees that the node dominates may be extended with additional T-grams as described next (hence, non-terminal leaf nodes are always incomplete allowing substitution as in DOP). See figure 16.4 for examples.

Tree-gram rewrite processes, i.e., derivations, start from the start symbol TOP, which is an incomplete non-terminal. At each rewrite-step, an incomplete node μ is selected and rewritten by a suitable T-gram as follows:

Head-step: When μ is a leaf node labeled with a non-terminal A, it is rewritten by a HEAD T-gram with a root labeled A (much like rewriting takes place in DOP, i.e., "vertical expansion").

Modify-step: When a non-leaf node μ is labeled with a non-terminal A and it is incomplete, it may be rewritten with LEFT and RIGHT T-grams that have roots also labeled A. This rewriting allows for *horizontal* expansion of the parse tree at node μ (see figure 16.5).

The rewrite process terminates when the resulting parse tree consists entirely of complete nodes and the leaf nodes are labeled with terminal symbols. Figure 16.6 shows an example derivation.

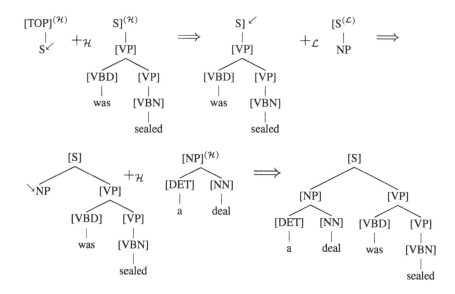

Figure 16.6. A T-gram derivation using T-grams from figure 16.4: the rewriting of TOP is not shown. An arrow marks the node where rewriting takes place. Following the arrows: 1. HEAD T-gram (e) is generated at the leaf node labeled S (under TOP). 2. LEFT T-gram (a) with root $[S$ is generated at node $S]$: S is complete. 3. HEAD T-gram (d) is generated at node NP: all nodes are either complete or labeled with terminals.

With every T-gram that is extracted from the tree-bank, the model associates a conditional probability $P(t|root(t), h_t)$. The conditioning context (or history) h_t consists of the role of t (i.e., HEAD, LEFT or RIGHT) and the following information depending on the role of t:

HEAD: the POS tag of the head word of the root node of t.

LEFT (RIGHT): (1) the label of the head sister of its root node, and (2) the label of the sister to the right (resp. left) of the root node in the original tree-bank tree (thereby yielding a 1-st order *Markov process* generating sister nodes).

Our conditioning context is similar to those used in e.g., (Charniak, 1999). Just like in DOP, the probability of a T-gram derivation d involving the sequence of T-grams $t_1, \ldots, t_n$ is estimated by

$$P(d) = \prod_{i=1}^{n} P(t_i|root(t_i), h_{t_i})$$

As we argued for DOP earlier, we approximate the probabilities of a parse tree and a sentence as the highest probability of any of their derivations.

3.3 A Theoretical Comparison

Formally speaking, the DOP and the Tree-gram models assign probabilities to Context-Free languages. As Bod shows (Bod, 1995), the probability distribution assigned to the members of the set of parse trees generated by a DOP model cannot always be generated by a Probabilistic Context-Free Grammar (PCFG) (Jelinek et al., 1990). The crucial point lies in the way each of the models generalizes over the finite sample of training tree-bank trees: T-grams generalize over DOP subtrees to allow for an extra dimension of freedom in the generation of parse trees and sentences. In fact, one may simulate the Tree-gram model by first transforming the CFG rules in the training tree-bank trees into linearized trees, and then acquiring a DOP model from the resulting tree-bank. We will not discuss this here any further.

For a given tree-bank, the set of sentences accepted (or generated) by the Tree-gram model acquired from that tree-bank is a superset of (or equal to) the set accepted by the DOP model acquired from the same tree-bank. The same relation applies between the respective sets of parse trees generated by both models. Hence, the Tree-gram model, just like Markov-grammars, generates sentences and parse trees that cannot be generated by the DOP model or by the linguistic CFG that underlies the annotation of the tree-bank. This is an important facility in the various cases of deviating input, as in spoken utterances and the noise-prone speech recognizer's output.

The next question is of course: how do the distributions over derivations, parse trees and sentences generated by both models compare to one another? The empirical estimation of probabilities from a tree-bank makes this comparison complicated due to problems of bias in the current method of probability estimation which both models suffer from (Bonnema et al., 1999). However, if we assume an unbiased estimate then[1] both models will assign a "similar" relative ordering to the derivations that they generate. This can be seen by the fact that all subtrees of the DOP model are included as HEAD T-grams in the Tree-gram model with the same relative frequency (up to a finer conditioning context in T-gram probabilities). In any case, the Tree-gram model, at least theoretically, allows for a more "subtle" model than the DOP model. But then, does this subtlety translate into more robust processing for speech understanding?

4. Application to the OVIS Domain

Before applying the Tree-gram model to OVIS, it is necessary to specify how we identify the head children in the tree-bank trees. We note that with a few exceptions, every CFG rule has a semantic formula associated with it. This formula expresses how the semantics of the node is composed from the semantics of its children using a small set of operators, e.g., concatenation

"D1;D2", correction "[!D2]", denial "[#D3]". Some of these operators take a single argument, others take two arguments. We decided to specify the head children using these formulae through a few rules of thumb, (e.g., take the first child specified in the formula, except for a few specific situations). This specifies the head children for all tree-bank nodes unambiguously. Our choice for "semantically identified heads" over syntactic heads is motivated by the intuition that our system's output is a semantic expression. We feel that this has two advantages: (1) the probabilities are conditioned on semantic content, and (2) the "most influential" semantic argument is *always* generated first by the Markovian T-gram derivations, and all other arguments are conditioned on it. For interpreting "newly generated" CFG-rules we simply concatenate the semantics of all children. In most cases this results in well-formed semantic expressions, but in a few cases this results in ill-formed expressions, which we correct automatically using a few heuristic rules.[2]

4.1 Experiment Setting

We trained a DOP model (with subtree-depth upper bound 4) and a Tree-gram model (with T-gram depth upper bound 5) on the same training tree-bank of 10000 utterances.[3] We compare the models on a held-out set of 1000 utterances, which was used for similar experiments in (Veldhuijzen van Zanten et al., 1999). We also report preliminary results on a set of 500 speech recognizer's word-graphs. We use the same parser for the DOP model as well as the Tree-gram model (Sima'an, 1999). This is a CYK (Younger, 1967) based algorithm using an optimized version of the Viterbi-algorithm with a simple pruning technique. The parser is applicable to utterances as well as word-graphs (for the latter extension see van Noord, 1997 and Sima'an, 1999). For the disambiguation of word-graphs the probabilities of the speech recognizer (given on the transitions in the word-graphs) are integrated with the probabilities of the language model (DOP or Tree-gram). The integration is based on the noisy channel model[4]

$$P(A,U) = P(A|U)P(U)$$

where U is an utterance and A is the acoustic signal (hence, $P(U)$ is the language model and probability $P(A|U)$ is the channel model, output by the speech recognizer).

4.2 Smoothing

We apply the Katz backoff smoothing technique (Katz, 1987; Chen and Goodman, 1998) to the T-gram probabilities. The sister generation 1-st order Markov process (for LEFT and RIGHT T-grams) is backed off to the 0-th order: this is applied only to the T-grams of depth 1. Furthermore, we allow backoff on the stop symbols "[" and "]" on the root node of a T-gram of depth 1 in one of two ways: (1) we add a stop symbol "[" to the left ("]" to the right) of the node with a suitable backoff probability, or (2) we remove these symbols, if they are there, with a suitable backoff probability. The resulting backoff T-grams are included in the model together with the original ones. For semantic interpretation, all new rules generated by the Tree-gram model are assigned a heuristic formula depending on the parse tree in which they occur; the heuristic semantics of a new rule depends on the label of the parent node and on the types of the semantics of the child-nodes, and aims at combining these types in acceptable ways (with respect to the OVIS update language).

4.3   Evaluation Criteria

The semantic evaluation criteria were developed by (van Noord, 1997) following similar criteria suggested in (Boros et al., 1996). A semantic expression is translated into a set of "semantic units"; each semantic unit addresses a specific OVIS slot. Given this view on semantic expressions, now we can compare the semantic expression U output by a given system to the gold-standard expression G in the same way as in Labeled Recall and Precision in syntactic parsing (Black et al., 1991): (1) semantic exact match is the average test-set utterances for which $U \equiv G$, (2) semantic recall (precision) is the average, over the test-set utterances, of $\frac{|U \cap G|}{|G|}$ (respectively, $\frac{|U \cap G|}{|U|}$ — when $|U| = 0$, this is by definition zero). For word-graph parsing we also use the word-accuracy (*WA*) and sentence-accuracy (*SA*) measures to compare the proposed utterance P to the gold G: $WA = 1 - \frac{d}{n}$, where n is the length of the G, and d is the Levenshtein distance between G and P, and SA is the proportion of cases in which P and G are exactly the same. Further details can be found in (Veldhuijzen van Zanten et al., 1999).

4.4   Empirical Results

Table 16.1 shows the results of the Tree-gram model, the DOP model and the Dutch broad-coverage grammar (DBCG) on utterances. Clearly, the Dutch broad-coverage system is still producing the best results, however the Tree-gram model has narrowed the gap on utterances for recall from 3.9% (DOP) to 0.8% (T-gram). For word-graphs, our results (table 16.2) cannot be compared to those of the DBCG-based system (although we suspect that the DBCG improves over the Tree-gram results) because this preliminary experiment is on a different set than the final test-set. However, the Tree-gram model improves over DOP by at least 7% on *WA* and semantic recall and 4.2% on semantic match.

Our explanation of the improvements on DOP's results is that on utterances the Tree-gram model is capable of producing parses which DOP cannot pro-

	% Match	% Prec.	% Recall
DOP	93.0	94.0	92.5
T-gram	**94.5**	**95.0**	**95.6**
DBCG	95.7	95.7	96.4

Table 16.1. Results on 1000 utterances: update-expression match, recall and precision

	WA	% SA	% Match	% Prec.	% Recall
DOP	72.2	71.8	77.2	82.0	77.3
T-gram	**79.6**	**74.0**	**81.4**	**85.2**	**84.3**
T-gram−DOP	+7.4	+2.2	+4.2	+3.2	+7.0

Table 16.2. Results on 500 word-graphs: word- and sentence-accuracies and update-expression measures

duce; on about 2.2% of the utterances, DOP does not produce any parse and these utterances are usually some of the longer ones. Then, in a few more cases, it seems that DOP produces only a less useful parse than the Tree-gram model. When we inspected some of the cases it turned out that DOP tends to assign the special label "ERROR" (used to mark repetitions and corrections in the OVIS tree-bank) to various constituents for which it could not find an approximate label.

We can think of various reasons why the Tree-gram's results are still behind those of the DBCG results: (1) the DBCG grammar has been developed manually, incrementally inspecting how the system behaves on a large collection of over 100000 utterances from the OVIS domain; our models are trained only on a tree-bank containing 10000 trees, (2) the model probabilities are not conditioned on lexical information, and (3) in contrast to the DBCG module, we did not try to optimize the heuristic rules which correct "informative", yet formally ill-formed semantic formulae output by the parser. We only devised four such rules.

5. Conclusions

We have shown how the DOP model can be extended in a useful way for better parsing of speech utterances. We are encouraged by the fact that the Tree-gram model has narrowed the gap with the Dutch Broad-Coverage Grammar system: our system is automatically acquired from a tree-bank, while the grammar took more than three years to develop. It is unclear how fast each of the systems can be adapted to a new domain of language use.

Our preliminary results on word graphs improve considerably over DOP's results. Again this is due to the more robust nature of the new model in comparison with the original DOP model. However, on first inspection of some of the problems, we find that the model still suffers from the weak lexicalization, just like DOP. The gain is solely due to the fact that the Tree-gram model could parse many more of the word-graph paths than DOP did, thereby having more paths to choose from. We suspect that the fact that our word accuracy and sentence accuracy are still lagging behind simpler models (e.g., a trigram model) implies that our current models are not sensitive enough to the lexical influence.

One problem which should be pointed out here is the fact that taking the most probable derivation from an input word word graph suffers from weak lexicalization (as it only considers one way for generating the utterance generated by that derivation). However, extracting the most probable path/ sentence/ semantics from an input word graph implies at least two problems: (1) another probability estimation model must be used since the current model suffers from bias towards larger subtrees/T-grams (Bonnema et al., 1999), and (2) more efficient algorithms must be designed to deal with the huge space needs and the exponential ambiguity (as these problems are NP-complete). Whether the DOP and Tree-gram models then would result in better accuracies than simpler models to justify the effort, is a question to be addressed in future work.

Another possibility for improving the lexical sensitivity of the models, is to condition the probabilities of these models on lexical information in a similar fashion to the bilexical dependency models. This too demands much attention as it is not obvious how to do so in a workable manner.

Acknowledgments

This work is funded by a project of the Netherlands Organization for Scientific Research (NWO). I am grateful to Remko Scha, Remko Bonnema, and Walter Daelemans for discussions and support. Some software packages, which were used for evaluation of the models, were developed by Gertjan van Noord and Remko Bonnema.

Notes

1. In our experiments we marginalize the bias of the estimate by restricting the subtrees and T-grams that are acquired from the tree-bank by setting upper bounds on e.g., depth or width of a subtree/T-gram – see section 4.

2. Based on the OVIS semantic hierarchy, it is possible to devise a set of heuristic rules for the correction of such "informative" formulae (e.g., by guessing the identity of the operator from the kind of available arguments).

3. We choose to employ depth 4 as it performed best for a DOP model, while depth 5 was chosen for the Tree-gram model to fit the physical limitations (available RAM) of the machine.

4. We apply a common scaling heuristic to the likelihoods that are found on the transitions in the word-graphs and then combine the resulting weights (numbers in the region $(0, 1]$) with the probabilities of the parser.

References

Aho, A. and Ullman, J. (1972). *The Theory of Parsing, Translation and Compiling*, volume I, II. Prentice-Hall Series in Automatic Computation.

Black et al., E. (1991). A procedure for Quantitatively Comparing the Syntactic Coverage of English Grammars. In *Proceedings of the February 1991 DARPA Speech and Natural Language Workshop*.

Bod, R. (1995). *Enriching Linguistics with Statistics: Performance models of Natural Language*. PhD thesis, ILLC-dissertation series 1995-14, University of Amsterdam.

Bonnema, R., Bod, R., and Scha, R. (1997). A DOP Model for Semantic Interpretation. In *Proceedings of ACL-97*, Madrid, Spain.

Bonnema, R., Buying, P., and Scha, R. (1999). A new probability model for data oriented parsing. In Dekker, P. and Kerdiles, G., editors, *Proceedings of the 12th Amsterdam Colloquium*, Amsterdam, The Netherlands. Institute for Logic, Language and Computation, Department of Philosophy.

Boros, M., Eckert, W., Gallwitz, F., Gorz, G., Hanrieder, G., and Niemann, H. (1996). Towards understanding spontaneous speech: Word accuracy vs. concept accuracy. In *Proceedings of the Fourth International Conference on Spokenm Language Processing (ICSLP 96)*, Philadelphia.

Charniak, E. (1999). A maximum-entropy-inspired parser. In *Report CS-99-12*, Providence, Rhode Island.

Chen, S. and Goodman, J. (1998). An empirical study of smoothing techniques for language modeling. In *Technical report TR-10-98*, Harvard University.

Collins, M. (1997). Three generative, lexicalized models for statistical parsing. In *Proceedings of the 35th Annual Meeting of the ACL and the 8th Conference of the EACL*, pages 16–23, Madrid, Spain.

Jelinek, F., Lafferty, J., and Mercer, R. (1990). *Basic Methods of Probabilistic Context Free Grammars, Technical Report IBM RC 16374 (#72684)*. Yorktown Heights.

Katz, S. (1987). Estimation of probabilities from sparse data for the language model component of a speech recognizer. *IEEE Transactions on Acoustics, Speech and Signal Processing*, 35(3).

Oerder, M. and Ney, H. (1993). Word graphs: An efficient interface between continuous-speech recognition and language understanding. In *ICASSP Volume 2*, pages 119–122.

Scha, R. (1990). Language Theory and Language Technology; Competence and Performance. In de Kort, Q. and Leerdam, G., editors, *Computertoepassingen in de Neerlandistiek*, Almere: LVVN-jaarboek. www.hum.uva.nl /computerlinguistiek/scha/IAAA/rs/cv.html

Scha, R., Bonnema, R., Bod, R., and Sima'an, K. (1996). *Disambiguation and Interpretation of Wordgraphs using Data Oriented Parsing.* Probabilistic Natural Language Processing in the NWO priority Programme on Language and Speech Technology, Amsterdam.

Sima'an, K. (1996). Computational Complexity of Probabilistic Disambiguation by means of Tree Grammars. In *Proceedings of COLING'96*, volume 2, pages 1175–1180, Copenhagen, Denmark.

Sima'an, K. (1999). *Learning Efficient Disambiguation.* A PhD dissertation. ILLC dissertation series 1999-02 (Utrecht University / University of Amsterdam), Amsterdam.

Sima'an, K. (2000). Tree-gram Parsing: Lexical Dependencies and Structual Relations. In *Proceedings of the 38th Annual Meeting of the Association for Computational Linguistics (ACL'00)*, pages 53–60, Hong Kong, China.

Sima'an, K. (2002). Computational Ccomplexity of Prababilistic Disambiguation. NP-compleneness Results for Parsing Problems That Arise in Speech and Language Processing Applications. *Grammars* 5(2): 125–151.

van Noord, G. (1995). The intersection of finite state automata and definite clause grammars. In *Proceedings of ACL-95*.

van Noord, G. (1997). Evaluation of OVIS2 NLP components. In *Technical Report #46, NWO Priority Programme Language and Speech Technology*.

van Noord, G., Bouma, G., Koeling, R., and Nederhof, M. (1999). Robust Grammatical Analysis for spoken dialogue systems. *Journal of Natural Language Engineering*, 5 (1):45–93.

Veldhuijzen van Zanten, G. (1996). *Semantics of update expressions*. Technical report 24, NWO Priority Programme Language and Speech Technology, $http://odur.let.rug.nl:4321/$.

Veldhuijzen van Zanten, G., Bouma, G., Sima'an, K., van Noord, G., and Bonnema, R. (1999). Evaluation of the NLP Components of the OVIS2 Spoken Dialogue System. In F. van Einde, I. S. and Schelkens, N., editors, *Proceedings of* Computational Linguistics In the Netherlands 1998.

Viterbi, A. (1967). Error bounds for convolutional codes and an asymptotically optimum decoding algorithm. *IEEE Trans. Information Theory*, IT-13:260–269.

Younger, D. (1967). Recognition and parsing of context-free languages in time n^3. *Inf.Control*, 10(2):189–208.

Chapter 17

SOUP: A PARSER FOR REAL-WORLD SPONTANEOUS SPEECH

Marsal Gavaldà

Interactive Systems, Carnegie Mellon University
5000 Forbes Ave., Pittsburgh, PA 15213, U.S.A.
marsal@alumni.carnegiemellon.edu

Abstract   This chapter describes the key features of SOUP, a stochastic, chart-based, top-down parser, especially engineered for real-time analysis of spoken language with very large, multi-domain semantic grammars. SOUP achieves *flexibility* by encoding context-free grammars, specified for example in the Java Speech Grammar Format, as probabilistic recursive transition networks, and *robustness* by allowing skipping of input words at any position and producing ranked interpretations that may consist of multiple parse trees. Moreover, SOUP is very efficient, which allows for practically instantaneous backend response.

1.   Introduction

Parsing can be defined as the assignment of structure to an utterance according to a grammar, i.e., the mapping of a sequence of words (utterance) into a parse tree (structured representation). Because of the ambiguity of natural language, the same utterance can sometimes be mapped into more than one parse tree; statistical parsing attempts to resolve ambiguities by preferring most likely parses. Also, spontaneous speech is intrinsically different from written text (see for example Lavie, 1996), therefore when attempting to analyze spoken language, one must take a different parsing approach. For instance one must allow for an utterance to be parsed as a *sequence* of parse trees (which cover non-overlapping segments of the input utterance), rather than expect a single tree to cover the entire utterance and fail otherwise.

The SOUP parser herein described, inspired by Ward's PHOENIX parser (Ward, 1990), incorporates a variety of techniques in order to achieve both *flexibility* and *robustness* in the analysis of spoken language: flexibility is given by the lightweight formalism it supports, which allows for rapid grammar devel-

H. Bunt et al. (eds.), New Technologies in Parsing Technology, 339-350.

opment, dynamic modification of the grammar at run-time, and high parsing speed; robustness is achieved by its ability to find multiple-tree interpretations and to skip words at any point, thereby recovering in a graceful manner not only from false starts, hesitations, and other speech disfluencies but also from insertions unforeseen by the grammar. SOUP is currently the main parsing engine of the JANUS speech-to-speech translation system (Levin *et al.,* 2000; Woszczyna *et al.,* 1998).

Section 2 briefly describes the grammar representation, section 3 outlines the parsing process, section 4 presents some performance results, section 5 emphasizes the key features of SOUP, and section 6 concludes this chapter.

2.   Grammar Representation

The grammar formalism supported by SOUP is purely context-free. Each nonterminal (whose value is simply a label), has a set of alternative rewrite rules, which consist of possibly optional, possibly repeatable terminals and nonterminals. We have found over the years (Mayfield *et al.,* 1995; Woszczyna *et al.,* 1998) that, at least for task-oriented semantic grammars used in speech translation systems, the advantages in parsing speed and ease of grammar construction of such a formalism outweigh the lack of the more expressive power offered by richer formalisms (cf., for example, the Verbmobil Semantic Formalism, see Bos et al., 1994).

SOUP represents a context-free grammar (CFG) as a set of probabilistic recursive transition networks (PRTNs), where the nodes are marked as initial, regular or final, and the directed arcs are annotated with (*i*) an arc type (namely, specific-terminal (which matches and consumes a particular word), any-terminal (which matches and consumes any out-of-vocabulary word or any word present in a given list), nonterminal (which recursively matches a subnet and, in the parsing process, spawns a subsearch episode) or lambda – the empty transition, which can always occur, (*ii*) an ID to specify which terminal or nonterminal the arc has to match (if arc type is specific-terminal or nonterminal), and (*iii*) a probability (so that all outgoing arcs from the same node sum to unity). For example, the right-hand side *good +bye (where * indicates optionality and + repeatability and therefore matches *good bye, bye, bye bye* – and also *good bye bye,* etc) is represented as the PRTN in Figure 17.1.

SOUP also directly accepts grammars written in the Java Speech Grammar Format (see section 5.5).

Grammar arc probabilities are initialized to the uniform distribution but can be perturbed by a training corpus of desired (but achievable) parses. Given the direct correspondence between parse trees and grammar arc paths, training the PRTNs is very fast (see section 4).

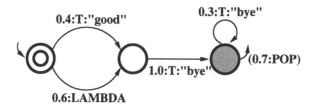

Figure 17.1. Representation of right-hand side *good +bye as a probabilistic recursive transition network (PRTN). A PRTN has a unique initial node (double circle) and possibly many final nodes (painted gray). A pop arc leaving each final node is implicit.

There are two main usages of this stochastic framework of probabilities at the grammar arc level: one is to incorporate the probabilities into the function that scores partial parse lattices, so that more likely ones are preferred; the other is to generate synthetic data, from which, for instance, a language model can be computed.

The PRTNs are constructed dynamically as the grammar file is read; this allows for eventual on-line modifications of the grammar (see section 5.4). Also, strict grammar source file consistency is enforced, e.g., all referenced nonterminals must be defined, warnings for nonterminal redefinitions are issued, and a variety of grammar statistics are provided. Multiple grammar files representing different semantic domains as well as a library of shared rules are supported, as described by Woszczyna *et al.* (1998).

The lexicon is also generated as the grammar file is being read, for it is simply a hash table of grammar terminals.

3. Sketch of the Parsing Algorithm

Parsing is a particular case of search. In SOUP, parsing proceeds in the following steps:

1 *Construction of the input vector*: Given an utterance to be parsed, it is converted into a vector of terminal IDs. Special terminals <s> and </s> are added at the beginning and end of an utterance, respectively, so that certain rules only match at those positions. Also, user-defined global search-and-replace string pairs are applied, e.g., to expand contractions (as in *I'd like → I would like*) or to remove punctuation marks. Other settings allow the determination whether out-of-vocabulary words should be removed, or whether the input utterances are case-sensitive.

2 *Population of the chart*: The first search populates the chart (a two-dimensional table indexed by input-word position and nonterminal ID) with parse lattices. (A parse lattice is a compact representation of a set

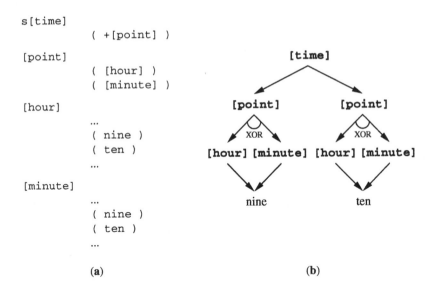

```
s[time]
            ( +[point] )

[point]
            ( [hour] )
            ( [minute] )

[hour]
            ...
            ( nine )
            ( ten )
            ...

[minute]
            ...
            ( nine )
            ( ten )
            ...

           (a)
```

Figure 17.2.   (**a**) Grammar fragment to illustrate ambiguity packing. The s indicates that non-terminal [time] is a starting symbol of the grammar. (**b**) Parse lattice for input *nine ten* according to the grammar fragment. It can give rise to four different parse trees, but some will be more likely than others.

of parse trees (similar to Tomita's shared-packed forest; Tomita, 1987; see Figure 17.2 for an example).

This beam search involves the top-down, recursive matching of PRTNs against the input vector. All top-level nonterminals starting at all input vector positions are attempted. The advantage of the chart is that it stores, in an efficient way, all subparse lattices found so far, so that subsequent subsearch episodes can reuse existing subparse lattices.

To increase the efficiency of the top-down search, the set of allowed terminals with which a nonterminal can start is precomputed (i.e., the FIRST set), so that many attempts to match a particular nonterminal at a particular input vector position can be preëmpted by the lack of the corresponding terminal in the FIRST set. This bottom-up filtering technique typically results in a threefold speedup.

The beam serves to restrict the number of possible subparse lattices under a certain nonterminal and starting at a certain input position, e.g., by only keeping those subparse lattices whose score is at least 30% of the best score. The score function is such that (*i*) coverage (number of words parsed) and (*ii*) sum of arc probabilities are maximized, whereas (*iii*) parse lattice complexity (approximated by number of nonterminals) and (*iv*) usages of the wildcard (approximated by maximal number of **any-terminal** arcs along the parse lattice) are minimized. Also, pruning of structurally-equal parse lattices is performed, thereby eliminating the redundancy that arises from several right-hand sides matching the same input vector span under the same nonterminal.

3 *Finding the best interpretations*: Once the chart is populated, a second beam search finds the best N interpretations, i.e., the best N sequences of top-level, non-overlapping parse lattices that cover the input vector. Scoring of interpretations adds, to the above scoring function, a fifth factor, namely the minimization of parse fragmentation (number of parse trees per utterance). This search problem can be divided into subproblems (divide and conquer strategy) since both unparsed words and words parsed by a single parse lattice offer a natural boundary to the general problem. A beam search is conducted for each subproblem. In this case, the beam limits the number of active sequences of top-level, non-overlapping parse lattices that form a partial interpretation. Since the single best interpretation is simply the concatenation of the best sequence of each subproblem, even when asked to compute the top N interpretations ($N > 1$), the best interpretation is always computed separately and output immediately so that backend processing can begin without delay. The final result is a ranked list of N interpretations, where the parse lattices have been expanded into parse trees.

Figure 17.3 shows a sample interpretation in a travel domain.

4.   Performance

SOUP has been coded in C++ and Java and compiled for a variety of platforms including Windows (95, 98, NT) and Unix (HP-UX, OSF/1, Solaris, Linux). The upper portion of Table 17.1 lists some parameters that characterize the complexity of two grammars, one for a scheduling domain and the other for a scheduling plus travel domain; the lower portion lists performance results of parsing a subset of transcriptions from the English Spontaneous Speech Scheduling corpus (briefly described by Waibel *et al.*, 1996).

Parsing time increases substantially from a grammar with 600 nonterminals and 2,880 rules to a 6,963-nonterminal, 25,746-rule grammar but it is still well under real-time. Also, as depicted in Figure 17.4, although worst-case complexity for chart parsing is cubic in the number of words, SOUP's parse time appears to increase only linearly. Such behavior, similar to the findings reported by Slocum (1981), is due, in part, to SOUP's ability to segment the input utterance in parsable chunks (i.e., finding multiple-tree interpretations) during the search process.

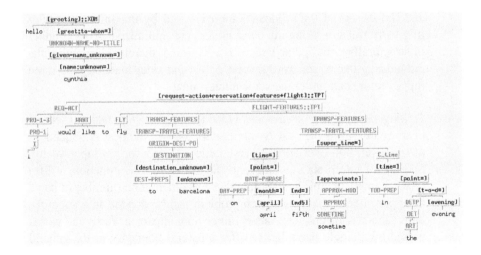

Figure 17.3. Parse of *Hello Cynthia I'd like to fly to Barcelona on April fifth sometime in the evening.* Upper case nonterminals such as PRO-1-3 denote auxiliary nonterminals and are typically removed from the parse trees before backend processing. Note the ability to combine rules from different task domains (XDM for cross-domain, TPT for transportation) and to parse out-of-vocabulary words (*Cynthia, Barcelona*).

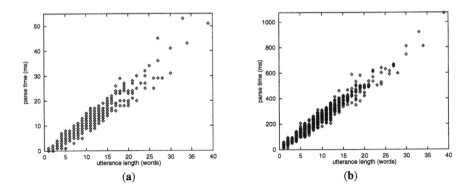

Figure 17.4. Utterance length vs. parse time for **(a)** scheduling grammar and **(b)** scheduling plus travel grammar. Same test and machine as in Table 17.1. Parse time appears to increase only linearly with regard to utterance length.

Therefore, even though comparisons of parsers using different grammar formalisms are not well-defined, SOUP appears to be faster than other "fast parsers" described in the literature (cf., for example, Rayner and Carter, 1996 or Kiefer and Krieger, 1998).

	Scheduling	Scheduling + Travel
Nonterminals	600	6,963
Top-level nonterminals	21	480
Terminals	831	9,640
Rules	2,880	25,746
Nodes	9,853	91,264
Arcs	9,866	97,807
Avg. cardinality of FIRST sets	44.48	240.31
Grammar creation time	143 ms	3,731 ms
Training time for 1000 trees	452 ms	765 ms
Memory	2 MB	14 MB
Avg. parse time	10.09 ms/utt	228.99 ms/utt
Max. parse time	53 ms	1070 ms
Avg. coverage	85.52%	88.64%
Avg. fragmentation	1.53 trees/utt	1.97 trees/utt

Table 17.1. Grammar measurements and performance results of parsing 606 naturally-occurring scheduling domain utterances (average length of 9.08 words) with scheduling grammar and scheduling plus travel grammar on a 266-MHz Pentium II running Linux.

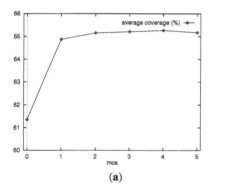
    (a)

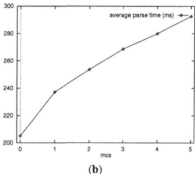
    (b)

Figure 17.5. (a) Average coverage and (b) parse times for different values of mcs (maximal number of contiguous words that can be skipped within a nonterminal). Same test set and machine as in Table 17.1 but with travel grammar only.

5. Key Features

The following are some of the most interesting features of SOUP.

5.1 Skipping

Given the nature of spoken speech it is not realistic to assume that the given grammar is complete (in the sense of covering all possible surface forms). In

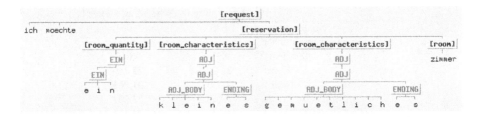

Figure 17.6. Parse of German *Ich möchte gern ein kleines gemütliches Zimmer* to exemplify character-level nonterminals and skipping. Repeated nonterminals (as in EIN with daughter EIN) indicate the joint between word-level and character-level parse trees. Also note the intra-concept skipping of *gern* (an adverb with practically zero information content).

fact it turns out that a substantial portion of parse errors comes from unexpected insertions, e.g., adverbs that can appear almost anywhere.

SOUP is able to skip words both between top-level nonterminals (inter-concept skipping) and inside any nonterminal (intra-concept skipping). Inter-concept skipping is achieved by the second search step described in section 3 (the search that finds the best interpretation as a sequence of non-overlapping parse lattices), since an interpretation may naturally contain gaps between top-level parse lattices. Intra-concept skipping, on the other hand, occurs during the first search step, by allowing, with a penalty, insertions of input words at any point in the matching of a net. The resulting exponential growth of parse lattices is contained by the beam search. A word-dependent penalty (e.g. one based on word saliency for the task at hand) can be provided but the experiments reported here use a uniform penalty together with a list of non-skippable words (typically containing, for example, the highly informative adverb *not*). The parameter mcs regulates the maximal number of contiguous words that can be skipped within a nonterminal. Figure 17.5 plots coverage and parse times for different values of mcs. These results are encouraging as they demonstrate that coverage lost by skipping words is offset (up to mcs = 4) by the ability to match longer sequences of words.

5.2   Character-level Parsing

To facilitate the development of grammars for languages with a rich morphology, SOUP allows for nonterminals that operate at the character-level (see Figure 17.6 for an example). Character-level parsing is achieved using the same functions that parse at the word level. In fact it is during word-level parsing that character-level parses are spawned by exploding the current word into characters and recursively calling the parse functions. The only difference is that, in a character-level parse, the desired root nonterminal is already known and no skipping or multiple-tree interpretations are allowed.

```
#JSGF V1.0 ISO8859-1 en;
grammar Toy;
public <get> =   <polite>* (get | obtain | request) <obj>+;
    <polite> =   please;
       <obj> =   apple | pear | orange;
```

Figure 17.7. Toy JSGF grammar used in Figures 17.8 and 17.9. In this case * indicates the Kleene star (i.e., optionality and repeatability), + repeatability, and | separates alternatives.

5.3   Multiple-tree Interpretations

SOUP is designed to support a modular grammar architecture and, as we have seen, performs segmentation of the input utterance into parse trees as part of the parsing process itself. Different interpretations of the same utterance may have different segmentations and the most likely one will be ranked first. Knowledge of the grammar module (which usually corresponds to a task domain) that a nonterminal is from is used in the computation (see Woszczyna *et al.* (1998) for details on the statistical model employed).

5.4   Dynamic Modifications

Encoding the grammar as a set of PRTNs gives SOUP the flexibility to activate/deactivate nonterminals and right-hand sides at run-time. For example, grammar nonterminals can be marked as belonging only to a specific speaker side (say, agent vs. client); then, at run-time and for each utterance, nonterminals not belonging to the current speaker are deactivated. Also, in the case of a multi-domain grammar, one could have a topic-detector that deactivates all non-terminals not belonging to the current topic, or at least lowers their probability.

More generally, nonterminals and right-hand sides can be created, modified and destroyed at run-time, which allows for the kind of interactive grammar learning reported by Gavaldà and Waibel (1998).

5.5   Parsing JSGF Grammars

SOUP has been extended to natively support grammars written according to the specifications of the Java Speech Grammar Format JSGF (1998). The JSGF is part of the Java Speech Application Programming Interface JSAPI (1998) and is likely to become a standard formalism for specifying semantic grammars, at least in the industrial environment.

SOUP is able to represent a `RuleGrammar` as defined by JSGF with the same underlying PRTNs. This is accomplished by the usage of **lambda** arcs to encode the JSGF `Rule` source, so that, out of a parse tree, the corresponding `RuleParse` (the result of a parse as specified by the JSAPI), can

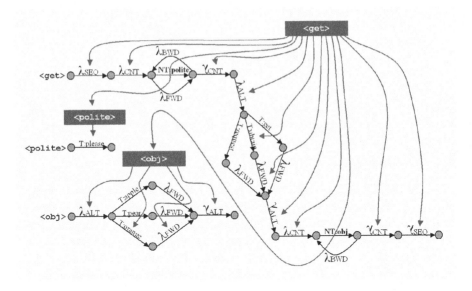

Figure 17.8. PRTNs for the grammar in Figure 17.7 and schematic parse of *Please obtain orange*. Upside-down lambdas mark end of JSGF `Rule` scope.

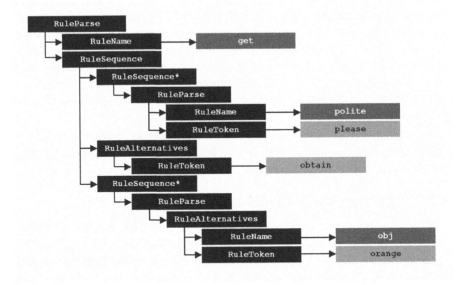

Figure 17.9. Resulting JSGF `RuleParse` constructed from the parse in Figure 17.8. Note that `RuleCounts` become `RuleSequences` as specified by the JSAPI (marked with *).

be constructed. In more detail, for each JSGF `RuleSequence`, `RuleAl-ternatives`, `RuleCount` and `RuleTag`, a corresponding **lambda-SEQ**, **lambda-ALT**, **lambda-CNT** or **lambda-TAG** arc is built in the PRTNs, as well as a closing **lambda** arc (pictured upside-down) to indicate the end of scope of the current JSGF `Rule`.

Figure 17.7 shows a toy grammar in the JSGF formalism. Figure 17.8 depicts the corresponding PRTNs as well as a schematic sample parse tree. Figure 17.9 shows the resulting `RuleParse` object constructed from such a parse.

6. Conclusion

We have presented SOUP, a parser designed to analyze spoken language under real-world conditions, in which analysis grammars are very large, input utterances contain disfluencies and never entirely match the expectations of the grammar, and yet backend processing must begin with minimal delay. Given its robustness to ill-formed utterances, general efficiency and support for emerging industry standards such as the JSAPI, SOUP has the potential to become widely used.

Acknowledgments

Laura Mayfield Tomokiyo wrote the Scheduling grammar, Donna Gates and Dorcas Wallace wrote the Travel grammar; Detlef Koll programmed the methods that read in a JSGF `RuleGrammar`. Klaus Zechner, Matthias Denecke and three anonymous reviewers gave helpful comments to earlier versions of this chapter.

References

Bos, J., E. Mastenbroek, S. McGlashan, S. Millies and M. Pinkal (1994) The Verbmobil Semantic Formalism. Verbmobil Report 6. Universität des Saarlandes. http://www.dfki.uni-sb.de/cgi-bin/verbmobil/htbin/doc-access.cgi

Gavaldà, M. and Waibel, A. (1998) Growing Semantic Grammars. In *Proceedings of COLING/ACL-1998*.

Java^{TM} Speech API, version 1.0 (1998) http://java.sun.com/products/java-media/speech/

Java^{TM} Speech Grammar Format, version 1.0 (1998) http://java.sun.com/products/java-media/speech/forDevelopers/JSGF/

Kiefer, B. and Krieger, H.-U. 1998. A Bag of Useful Techniques for Efficient and Robust Parsing. DFKI Research Report 98-04.

Levin, L., Lavie, A., Woszczyna, M., Gates, D., Gavaldà, M., Koll, D. and Waibel, A.. 2000. The JANUS-III Translation System. To appear in *Machine Translation*.

Lavie, A. (1996) *GLR*: A Robust Grammar-Focused Parser for Spontaneously Spoken Language*. PhD Thesis, School of Computer Science, Carnegie Mellon University.

Mayfield, L, Gavaldà, M., Ward, W. and Waibel, A. (1995) Concept-Based Speech Translation. In *Proceedings of ICASSP-1995*.

Rayner, M. and Carter, D. (1996) Fast Parsing using Pruning and Grammar Specialization. In *Proceedings of ACL-1996*.

Slocum, J. (1981) A Practical Comparison of Parsing Strategies. In *Proceedings of ACL-1981*.

Tomita, M. (1987) An Efficient Augmented-Context-Free Parsing Algorithm. In *Computational Linguistics*, Volume 13, Number 1-2, 31–46.

Waibel, A., Finke, M., Gates, D., Gavaldà, M., Kemp, T., Lavie, A., Levin, L., Maier, M., Mayfield, L., McNair, A., Rogina, I., Shima, K., Sloboda, T., Woszczyna, M., Zeppenfeld, T. and Puming Zhan (1996) JANUS-II: Translation of Spontaneous Conversational Speech. In *Proceedings of ICASSP-1996*.

Ward, W. (1990) The CMU Air Travel Information Service: Understanding spontaneous speech. In *Proceedings of the DARPA Speech and Language Workshop*.

Woszczyna, M., Broadhead, M., Gates, D., Gavaldà, M., Lavie, A., Levin, L. and Waibel, A. (1998) A Modular Approach to Spoken Language Translation for Large Domain. In *Proceedings of AMTA-1998*.

Chapter 18

PARSING AND HYPERGRAPHS

Dan Klein

Department of Computer Science, Stanford University
klein@cs.stanford.edu

Christopher D. Manning

Departments of Computer Science and Linguistics, Stanford University
manning@cs.stanford.edu

Abstract   While symbolic parsers can be viewed as deduction systems, this view is less natural for probabilistic parsers. We present a view of parsing as directed hypergraph analysis, which naturally covers both symbolic and probabilistic parsing. We illustrate the approach by showing how a dynamic extension of Dijkstra's algorithm can be used to construct a probabilistic chart parser with an $O(n^3)$ time bound for arbitrary PCFGs, while preserving as much of the flexibility of symbolic chart parsers as is allowed by the inherent ordering of probabilistic dependencies.

1.   Introduction

An influential view of parsing is as a process of logical deduction, in which a parser is presented as a set of parsing schemata. The grammar rules are the logical axioms, and the question of whether or not a certain category can be constructed over a certain span becomes the question of whether that category can be derived over that span, treating the initial words as starting assumptions (Pereira and Warren 1983; Shieber et al. 1995; Sikkel and Nijholt 1997). But such a viewpoint is less natural when we turn to probabilistic parsers, since probabilities, or, generalizing, scores, are not an organic part of logical systems.[1]

In addition to the fundamental connection between logic and parsing, there is also a deep connection between logic, in particular propositional satisfiability, and directed hypergraph analysis (Gallo et al. 1993). In this chapter,

351

H. Bunt et al. (eds.), New Technologies in Parsing Technology, 351-372.
© 2004 *Kluwer Academic Publishers. Printed in the Netherlands.*

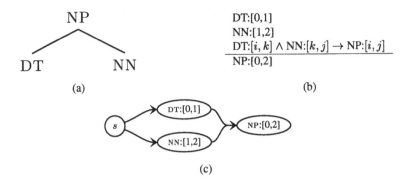

Figure 18.1. Three views of parsing: (a) tree construction, (b) logical deduction, and (c) hypergraph exploration.

we develop and exploit the third side of this triangle, connecting parsing with directed hypergraph algorithms. The advantage of doing this is that scored arcs *are* a central and well-studied concept of graph theory, and we can exploit existing graph algorithms for parsing. We illustrate this approach by developing a concrete hypergraph-based parsing algorithm, which does probabilistic Viterbi chart parsing over word lattices. Our algorithm offers the same modular flexibility with respect to exploration strategies and grammar encodings as a categorical chart parser, in the same cubic time bound.

2.   Hypergraphs and Parsing

First, we introduce directed hypergraphs, and illustrate how general-purpose hypergraph algorithms can be applied to parsing problems.

The basic idea underlying all of this work is rather simple, and is illustrated in figure 18.1. There is intuitively very little difference between (a) combining subtrees to form a tree, (b) combining hypotheses to form a conclusion, and (c) visiting all tail nodes of a hyperarc before traversing to a head node. We will be building hypergraphs which encode a grammar and an input, and in which paths correspond to parses of that input.

2.1   Directed Hypergraph Basics

We give some preliminary definitions about directed hypergraphs, objects like in figure 18.2, weaving in a correspondence to propositional satisfiability as we go. For a more detailed treatment, see Gallo et al. (1993).

Directed hypergraphs are much like standard directed graphs. However, while standard arcs connect a single tail node to a single head node, hyperarcs connect a set of tail nodes to a set of head nodes. Often, as in the present work,

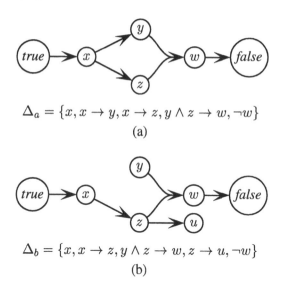

$$\Delta_a = \{x, x \to y, x \to z, y \wedge z \to w, \neg w\}$$
(a)

$$\Delta_b = \{x, x \to z, y \wedge z \to w, z \to u, \neg w\}$$
(b)

Figure 18.2. Two hypergraphs. Graph (a) is a B-path from *true* to *false*, while (b) is not. Also shown are propositional rule sets to which these graphs correspond. Δ_b is satisfiable, while Δ_a is not.

multiplicity is needed only in the tail. When the head contains exactly one node, we call the hyperarc a *B-arc*.

Definition 1 *A* directed hypergraph **G** *is a pair* (N, A) *where N is a set of nodes and A is a set of directed hyperarcs. A* directed hyperarc *is a pair* (T, H) *where the tail T and head H are subsets of N.*

Definition 2 *A* B-arc *is a directed hyperarc for which H is a singleton set. A* B-graph *is a directed hypergraph where the hyperarcs are B-arcs.*

It is easy to sketch the construction which provides the link to satisfiability. Nodes correspond to propositions, and directed hyperarcs $\{t_1, \ldots, t_m\} \Rightarrow \{h_1, \ldots, h_n\}$ correspond to rules $t_1 \wedge \cdots \wedge t_m \to h_1 \vee \cdots \vee h_n$. In the case of B-arcs, the corresponding rules are Horn clauses. The construction also requires two special nodes, *true* and *false*. Figure 18.2 shows two sets of clauses, along with their induced hypergraphs. For the Horn clause case, it turns out that the satisfiability of a set of clauses is equivalent to the non-existence of a certain kind of path, which we describe below, from *true* to *false* in the induced hypergraph.

With the notion of arc generalized, there are multiple kinds of paths. The simplest is the kind inherited from standard graphs, in which a path can enter a hyperarc at any tail node and leave from any head node.

Definition 3 *A* simple path $p = s \rightsquigarrow t$ *is a sequence* $(s = v_0, a_1, v_1, \ldots, a_n,$ $v_n = t)$ *of alternating nodes and hyperarcs where: (1) each hyperarc* a_i *is distinct, (2)* $\forall i \in \{0, \ldots, n-1\}, v_i \in tail(a_{i+1})$, *and (3)* $\forall i \in \{1, \ldots, n\}, v_i \in$ $head(a_i)$ *A node t is* simply reachable *from a node s if a simple path exists from s to t.*

In the more important kind of path, all of an arc's tail nodes must be reachable before that arc is traversable.

Definition 4 *A* B-path P *in a* B-graph **G** *from a node s to a node t is a minimal subgraph*[2] $(N_P, A_P) < \mathbf{G}$ *in which: (1)* $s, t \in N_P$, *and (2)* $\forall v \in N_P, \exists p =$ $s \rightsquigarrow v$, p *a simple path in* P. *A node t is* B-reachable *from a node s if a B-path exists from s to t.*

This fits well with the logical rule interpretation: each hypothesis must be true before a conclusion is implied. It is perhaps not surprising, then, that B-paths from *true* to *false* are what correspond to non-satisfiability.

As an example, the B-graph in figure 18.2(a) is a valid B-path from *true* to *false*. However, the one in figure 18.2(b) is not a B-path, for two reasons. First, not all nodes are simply reachable from s (y is not). Second, even if we added a B-arc $\{x\} \Rightarrow y$, the graph would not be minimal (the B-arc $\{z\} \Rightarrow u$ could be removed). Correspondingly, there is no satisfying assignment to the rule sets in figure 18.2(a), while $\{x = true, y = false, z = true, w = false, u = true\}$ is a satisfying assignment for figure 18.2(b).

For the remainder of this chapter, we will often drop the "B-" when it is clear from context what kind of graph, arc, path, or reachability is meant.

2.2   Symbolic Parsing and Reachability

We now show how reachability in a certain hypergraph corresponds to parse existence.

In chart parsing terminology, the core declarative object is the *edge*, which is a labeled span. For example, NP:[0,2] represents an NP spanning position 0 to 2. Parsing requires a grammar and an input. Here, we take the input to be a *lattice*, which is a collection of edges stating which words can occur over which spans. The grammar is a set of context-free productions of the form $C \rightarrow X_1 \ldots X_n$. These productions state that adjacent edges with labels X_i can be combined to form an edge with label C. When a production is instantiated with specific edges, it is called a *traversal*. Traversals state a particular way an edge can be constructed; for example, the production S→NP VP might be instantiated as the traversal S:[0,8]→NP:[0,2] VP:[2,8], representing the composition of NP:[0,2] and VP:[2,8] into S:[0,8].

There is an unfortunate clash between chart parsing and hypergraph terminology. A chart is typically seen as an undirected graph with input positions as nodes and edges as arcs, as shown in figure 18.3(c). Traversals, which record how an edge was constructed, are not part of the graph, but are stored in an auxiliary data structure, if at all. However, in the hypergraph context, the input positions are not represented graphically (their relative structure is self-evident), edges are nodes in the hypergraph, and traversals are B-arcs, as in figure 18.3(b). For this chapter, we use "edge" to refer only to labeled spans, and "arc" when we mean a (hyper)graph connection.

Given a grammar G and a lattice L, we wish to construct a hypergraph in which node reachability corresponds to edge parsability. This graph, which we call the *induced B-graph of G and L*, is given as follows. For each instantiation of category C in G as an edge $C{:}[i,j]$, create a node. For each instantiation of a production $C \rightarrow X_1 \ldots X_n$ in G as a traversal $C{:}[i,j] \rightarrow X_1{:}[i,k_1]\, X_2{:}[k_1,k_2] \ldots X_n{:}[k_{n-1},j]$, create a B-arc $\{X_1{:}[i,k_1],\, X_2{:}[k_1,k_2], \ldots, X_n{:}[k_{n-1},j]\} \Rightarrow C{:}[i,j]$. This much of the construction represents the connectivity of the grammar. To represent the data, create a special source edge s, and add arcs of the form $\{s\} \Rightarrow C{:}[i,j]$ for each word edge $C{:}[i,j]$ and $\{s\} \Rightarrow C{:}[i,i]$ for each category C with an empty production.

Similarly, we define a mapping π which takes a parse tree T to a B-graph $\pi(T)$, where the nodes of $\pi(T)$ are the edges of T (along with s), and the B-arcs in $\pi(T)$ are the traversals of T (along with s arcs to terminals in T). For example, figure 18.1(c) is the image of figure 18.1(a). For any tree T, $\pi(T)$ is not only a B-graph, but a B-path from s to the root edge of T.

For a given G and L, this mapping is onto the set of B-paths in the induced graph with source s: any B-path from s is $\pi(T)$ for some tree T which can be constructed over L using G. It is not necessarily one-to-one, because of cyclic same-span constructions.[3] However, this does not matter for determining parse *existence*; it is enough that the inverse image of a B-path be non-empty.

The reduction between parse existence and hypergraph reachability is expressed by the following theorem.

Theorem 1 *For a grammar G and a lattice L, a node e in the induced B-graph is B-reachable from s iff a parse of the edge e exists. Each parse T of e corresponds to a particular B-path $\pi(T)$ from s to e, and for each B-path P, there is a unique canonical tree $\pi^{-1}(P)$ in which no edge dominates itself.*

For instance, in figure 18.3(b), the NP node is B-reachable, but the PP node is not (because IN:[0,1] is not). Thus, over the span [0,2], an NP can be parsed, while a PP cannot.

Therefore, if we wish to know if some edge e can be parsed over L, we can construct the induced graph and use any B-reachability algorithm to ask whether e is reachable from s. For example, Gallo et al. (1993) describe an algorithm which generalizes depth-first search, and which runs in time linear in

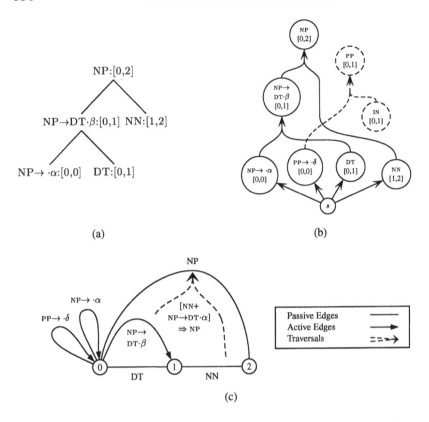

Figure 18.3. Various representations of a parse: (a) a binary tree of chart edges, (b) a path in an induced hypergraph, and (c) a collection of edges and traversals entered into a standard chart.

the size of the graph. Moreover, since π is easy to invert, any B-path produced can be turned into a concrete parse of e.

2.3   Viterbi Parsing and Shortest Paths

A more complex problem than parse existence is the problem of discovering a best, or Viterbi, parse for an edge e, where "best" is given by some scoring function over trees. For the present work, we assume that the scoring function takes a particular form. Namely, for the proofs to go through, it must be that combining trees (1) cannot yield a score better than the best scored sub-tree, and (2) replacing a subtree with a lower scoring subtree will worsen the score of any containing tree. These assumptions are true, for example, if trees are scored by the product of their production probabilities, with high probabilities being better. The assumptions are also satisfied if trees are scored by the number of non-terminal nodes they contain, with fewer nodes being better.

A useful sufficient condition on scoring functions is that each production is associated with an element σ of a $\preceq_S$-ordered c-semiring[4] (Bistarelli et al. 1997), and a tree's score is the semiring product of its production scores. Such semirings are 5-tuples $\langle A, \oplus, \otimes, 0, 1 \rangle$ where $\oplus$ is idempotent and $1 \oplus x = 1$ for all x. The order $\preceq_S$ required is that $a \preceq_S b$ iff $a \oplus b = b$. The semiring which corresponds to multiplied production probabilities is $\langle [0, 1], \max, \times, 0, 1 \rangle$, and little is lost if this special case is used for concrete intuition.

In the case of such scoring functions, the same induced graph used for parse existence can be used for finding a best parse. If we score each arc a with the (atomic) score $\sigma(a)$ of the local tree to which it corresponds, and score each node with the multiplicative identity 1, then parse scores will correspond to B-path scores.

The score $\sigma(P)$ of a B-path P from s to t is defined as the score $\sigma(t, P)$ of its target. The score of a node in a B-path is defined recursively:

$$\sigma(v, P) = \bigotimes_{a \in P: v = head(a)} \left[\sigma(a) \bigotimes_{v' \in tail(a)} \sigma(v', P) \right]$$

The outermost product is over exactly one arc for any non-source node (because of B-path minimality), and the recursion bottoms out at the source s, which has no incoming arcs (and is therefore scored as the multiplicative identity 1). This recursion is parallel to a recursive definition of tree scores in which the score of a tree is the score of its root production combined with the scores of the root's child trees. In particular, the score of a B-path P is the score of at least one concrete parse tree which maps to P. Furthermore, the canonical parse mentioned in theorem 1 for that B-path is a best parse and has the same score as its B-graph.

Thus, any algorithm for finding shortest (or, more generally, best) paths in B-graphs can be used to find best parses, using the construction and mapping above. For example, Gallo et al. (1993) describe an extension of Dijkstra's algorithm to B-graphs, which runs in time linear in the size of the graph.[5]

2.4   Practical Issues

At this point, one might wonder what is left to be done. We have a reduction which, given a grammar G and a lattice L, allows us to build and score the induced graph. From this graph, we can use reachability algorithms to decide parse existence, and we can use shortest-path algorithms to find best parses. Furthermore, this view can be extended to other problems of parsing. For example, A* search methods can be generalized to improve search speed (see

Klein and Manning 2002) and path-summing algorithms can be adapted to calculate inside probabilities (see Klein and Manning 2001a).

However, there are two primary issues which are specific to parsing and justify the presentation of a slightly more specialized algorithm. First, there is the issue of asymptotic efficiency. Reachability and shortest-path algorithms, such as those cited above, generally run in time linear in the size of the induced graph. However, the size of the induced graph, while polynomial in the size of the lattice L, is exponential in the arity of the grammar G, having a term of $|L|^{arity(G)+1}$ in its size. The grammar binarization done by chart parsers, either explicitly or implicitly, is responsible for their cubic bounds, and we would like to preserve this bound for our Viterbi parser.

Second, one does not, in general, wish to construct the entire induced graph in advance, or even at all. Rather, one would like to dynamically create only the portions which are needed, as they are needed. Various factors which can affect what regions of the graph are built at what times include:

- Structural search strategies, such as bottom-up, top-down, left-corner, and so on (Moore 2000).

- Lattice scanning strategies, such as scanning the lattice from left to right, or in whatever order it becomes available from previous processing.

- Rule encodings. Within large systems, grammars are often encoded in a variety of ways, such as tries or fully minimized DFSAs (Klein and Manning 2001b), rather than simply as linear rewrite rules as in theoretical presentations.

Therefore, in section 3, we present a chart parser for arbitrary PCFGs which can be seen as dynamically constructing reachable regions of an induced graph and doing a Dijkstra's-algorithm-style shortest-path computation over it. This parser preserves the time bounds of categorical chart parsers and allows a variety of introduction strategies and rule encodings. We discuss the kinds of subtle errors that can arise in a naive implementation and present simple conditions that ensure the correctness of various parsing strategies.

2.5   Relation to Other Work

We would like to stress that the primary advantage of the hypergraph view is conceptual. There is no real magic in the reduction; the linear reachability algorithm for parsability is essentially a recasting of a standard chart parser. Furthermore, the only operational differences between the shortest-path parser which we present here and a more standard bottom-up, best-first parser are (1) the tree-score agenda policy gives a stronger correctness guarantee and affords a simpler implementation than existing best-first parsers (see section 3 for details), and (2) our parser, like classical categorical chart parsers, operates with a variety of rule introduction strategies, scanning strategies, and rule encodings without sacrificing that correctness. However, we have found the hypergraph view to have conceptual benefit as well; it allows both efficient algorithm extension and clear reasoning about algorithm correctness conditions.

There are certainly other ways to view the parsing problem, beyond the logical and hypergraph views. Knuth (1977) introduces a formalism of *superior grammars*, where the terminals are superior functions, which calculate a score for a rule as a function of the scores of nonterminals on the righthand side. The formalism is closely related to the above hypergraph formalism, and can also be seen as a generalization of PCFGs. He also presents another, related generalization of Dijkstra's algorithm for the problem of finding the best cost string in the language defined by such a grammar (there is no concept of comparing parses for a single string). Rather than constructing B-graphs, we could cast the present work in terms of superior grammars, building a large grammar isomorphic to our B-graph, with a non-terminal for each edge and a terminal for each lattice element. Knuth's superiority criterion would then be used in place of the $\preceq_S$-ordered c-semiring property.[6] When the superior functions are uniform across productions, superior grammars reduce to c-semiring scored B-graphs. The choice of which formalism to base our work on is thus more aesthetic than substantive, but we believe that the hypergraph presentation allows easier access to a greater variety of algorithmic tools, and presents a clearer, more visually appealing intuition. At any rate, the practical issues described above, and their solutions, would be the same under either framework.

3. Viterbi Parsing Algorithm

Agenda-based active chart parsing (Kay 1980; Pereira and Shieber, 1987) is an attractive presentation of the central ideas of tabular methods for CFG parsing. Earley (1970)-style dotted items combine via deduction steps ("the fundamental rule") in an order-independent manner, such that the same basic algorithm supports top-down, bottom-up, and left-corner parsing, and the parser deals naturally and correctly with the difficult cases of left-recursive rules, empty elements, and unary rules.

However, while $O(n^3)$ methods for parsing PCFGs are well known (Baker 1979; Jelinek et al. 1992; Stolcke 1995), an $O(n^3)$ probabilistic parser corresponding to active chart parsing for categorical CFGs, has not yet been provided. Producing a probabilistic version of an agenda-driven chart parser is not trivial. A central idea of such parsers is that the algorithm is correct and complete regardless of the order in which items on the agenda are processed. Achieving this is straightforward for categorical parsers, but problematic for probabilistic parsers. For example, consider extending an active edge VP→V.NP PP:$[1,2]$ with an NP:$[2,5]$ to form an edge VP→V NP.PP over [1,5]. In a categorical chart parser (CP), we can assert the *parsability* of this edge as soon as both component edges are built. Any NP edge will do; it need not be a best NP over that span. However, if we wish to score edges as we go along, there is a problem. In a Viterbi chart parser, if we later find a better way to form the NP, we will have to update not only the score of that NP, but also the score of any edge whose current score depends on that NP's score. This can potentially lead to an extremely inefficient upward propagation of scores every time a new traversal is explored.[7]

Most exhaustive PCFG parsers have used the bottom-up CKY algorithm (Kasami 1965; Younger 1967) with Chomsky Normal Form (CNF) Grammars (Baker 1979; Jelinek et al. 1992) or extended CKY parsers that work with n-ary branching grammars, but still not with empty constituents (Kupiec 1991; Chappelier and Rajman 1998). Such bottom-up parsers straightforwardly avoid the above problem, by always building all edges over shorter spans before building edges over longer spans which make use of them. However, such methods do not allow top-down grammar filtering, and often do not handle empty elements, cyclic unary productions, or n-ary rules. Stolcke (1995) presents a top-down parser for arbitrary PCFGs, which incorporates elements of the control strategies of Earley's (1970) parser and Graham et al.'s (1980) parser. Stolcke provides a correct and efficient solution for parsing arbitrary PCFGs, avoiding the problem of left-recursive predictions and unary rule completions through the use of precomputed matrices giving values for the closure of these operations. However, the add-ons for grammars with such rules make the resulting parser rather complex, and again we have a method only for a single parsing regimen, rather than a general tabular parsing framework.

In the current hypergraphical context, we can interpret these effects as follows. A CP is performing a single-source reachability search. Any path from the source is as good as any other for reachability, and the various processing orders all eventually explore the entire region of the graph which is accessible given the rule introduction strategy (and goal). However, once scores are introduced, one cannot simply explore traversals in an arbitrary order, just as how, in relaxation-based shortest path algorithms, one cannot relax arcs in an arbitrary order. CKY parsers ensure a correct exploration order by exploring an entire tier of the graph before moving on to the next. For CNF grammars, all parses of the same string have the same number of productions in them, and so this tiering strategy works. However, in general, we will have to follow the insight behind Dijkstra's algorithm: always explore the current best candidate, leaving the others on a queue until later.

3.1   The Algorithm

Our algorithm has many of the same data structures of a standard CP. The fundamental data structure is the *chart*, which is composed of numbered *vertices* (positions between words), edges, and traversals (see figure 18.3(c)). Unlike in the general presentation above, there are two kinds of edges, active and passive. *Passive edges* are identified by a span and a category, such as NP:[2,5], and represent that there is some parse of that category over the span. *Active edges* are identified by a span and a grammar state, such as VP→V.NP PP:[1,2], and indicate that the grammar state is reachable over that span. In the case where grammar rules are encoded as lists, this state is simply an Earley-style dotted rule, and reachability means that one can parse the sequence of categories to the left of the dot over the span. However, grammar rules can be compacted in various ways, and so the label of the active edges for this parser is in general a deterministic finite state automaton (DFSA) state. List rules denote particularly simple, linear DFSAs, whereas trie DFSAs are equivalent to left-factoring the grammar (Moore 2000). The "fundamental rule" states that new edges are produced by combining active edges with compatible passive edges, advancing the dot of the active edge. For example, the two edges described above can combine to form the active edge VP→V NP.PP:[1,5]. This information is recorded in a traversal, which, due to the active/passive binarization, is simply an (active edge, passive edge, result edge) triple.[8] As each edge can potentially be formed by many different traversals, this distinction between an edge and a traversal of an edge is crucial to parsing efficiently (but often lost in pedagogical presentations: e.g., Gazdar and Mellish (1989)).

The core cycle of a CP is to process traversals into edges and to combine new edges with existing edges to create new traversals. Edges which are not formed from other edges via traversals (for example, the terminal edges in figure 18.3(a)) are *introduction edges*. *Passive introduction edges* are words from the lattice and are often all introduced during initialization. *Active introduction edges* are the initial states of rules and are introduced in accordance with the grammar strategy (top-down, bottom-up, etc.). To hold the traversals or edges which have not yet been processed, a CP has a data structure called an *agenda*, which holds both traversals and introduction edges. Items from this agenda can be processed in any order whatsoever, even arbitrarily or randomly, without affecting the final chart contents.

In our probabilistic chart parser (PCP), the central data structures are augmented with scores. Grammar rules, which were previously encoded as symbolic DFSAs are scored DFSAs, as in Mohri (1997), with a score for entering the initial state, a score on each transition, and, for each accepting state, a score for accepting in that state. Each edge e is also scored at all times. This value, $score(e)$ (or $score(e, t)$ at a time t), is the best estimate to date of that edge's

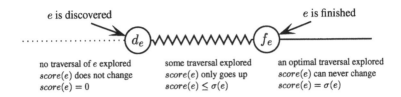

e is discovered   e is finished

no traversal of e explored   some traversal explored   an optimal traversal explored
$score(e)$ does not change $score(e)$ only goes up $score(e)$ can never change
$score(e) = 0$ $score(e) \leq \sigma(e)$ $score(e) = \sigma(e)$

Figure 18.4. The life cycle of an edge e

true best score, $\sigma(e)$. In our algorithm, the estimate will always be conservative: $score(e)$ will always be worse than or equal to $\sigma(e)$.

The full algorithm is shown in pseudocode in the appendix. It is broadly similar to a standard categorical chart parsing algorithm. However, in order to solve the problem of entering edges into the chart before their correct score is known, we have a more articulated edge life cycle (shown in figure 18.4).[9] We crucially distinguish edge *discovery* from edge *finishing*. A non-introduction edge is discovered the first time we explore a traversal which forms that edge (in exploreTraversal). An introduction edge is discovered at a time which depends on our parsing strategy (during initialize or another edge's finishEdge). Discovery is the point when we know that the edge *can* be parsed. An edge is finished when it is inserted into the chart and acted upon (in finishEdge). The primary significance of an edge's finishing time is that, as we will show, our algorithm maintains the Dijkstra's algorithm property that when an edge is finished, it is correctly scored, i.e., $score(e) = \sigma(e)$.

A CP stores all outstanding computation tasks in a single agenda, whether the tasks are unexplored traversals or uninserted introduction edges. We have two agendas and stronger typing. To store edges which have been discovered but not yet finished, we have a *finishing agenda*. To store traversals which have been generated but not explored, we have an *exploration agenda*.

The algorithm works as follows. During initialization, all passive introduction edges (one per word in the lattice) are discovered, along with any initial active edges (for example, all $s \rightarrow .\alpha:[0,0]$ edges if we are using a top-down strategy and $s:[0,n]$ is the goal edge).[10] Passive introduction edges get their initial scores from the lattice, while active introduction edges get their initial scores from the grammar (often all are simply given the maximum score, i.e., 1). Introduction edges are correctly scored at discovery and their scores never change afterwards.

The core loop of the algorithm is shown in figure 18.5. If there are any traversals to explore, a traversal t is removed from the exploration agenda and processed with exploreTraversal. Any removal order is allowed. In explore-Traversal, t's result edge e is calculated. If e is an undiscovered edge, then it becomes discovered (and is given the minimum score). In any case, e's score is

Explored traversals cause edges to be discovered and possibly improve
their score estimates, advancing them in the finishing agenda.

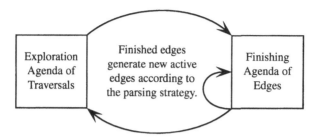

Finished edges generate traversals which
are inserted into the exploration agenda.

Figure 18.5.   The core loop of the parser

checked against t (relaxEdge). If t forms e with a better score than previously
known for e, e's score (and best traversal) is updated.

If the exploration agenda is empty, the finishing agenda is checked. If it is
non-empty, the edge with the best current score estimate is finished – removed
and processed with finishEdge. This is the point at which the fundamental
rule is applied (doFundamentalRule) and new active edges are introduced (in
accordance with the active edge introduction strategy).[11]

4.   Analysis

We outline the completeness of the algorithm: that it will discover and finish
all edges and traversals which the grammar, goal, and words present allow. Then
we argue correctness: that every edge e which is finished is, at its finishing time,
assigned the correct score. Finally, we give tight worst-case bounds on the time
and memory usage of the algorithm.

4.1   Completeness

For space reasons, we simply sketch a proof of the reduction of the completeness of our PCP to the known completeness of a CP. We state this reduction
rather than prove completeness directly in order to stress the parallelism between the two parser types. To argue completeness for a variety of word and
rule introduction strategies, it is important to have a concrete notion of what such
strategies are. Constraints on the word introduction strategy are only needed for
correctness, and so we defer discussion until then. Let E be the set of edges, P

the set of passive introduction edges (i.e., word edges), and A the set of active introduction edges (i.e., rule introductions).

Definition 5 *An* edge-driven *rule introduction strategy is a mapping* $R: E \rightarrow 2^A$ *which takes an edge e to a set A_e of active introduction edges which are to be immediately discovered when e is finished.*

The standard top-down and bottom-up strategies are both edge-driven.[12]

Theorem 2 *For any edge-driven active edge introduction strategy R, any DFSA grammar G and input lattice L, and goal edge g, there exists some agenda selection function S for which the sequence of edge insertions I made by a categorical chart parser and the sequence of edge finishings F made by our probabilistic chart parser are the same.*

The proof is by simulation. We run the two parsers in parallel, showing by induction over corresponding points in their execution that $I = F$ and that every edge in the PCP's finishing agenda is backed by some edge or traversal from the CP's agenda. The selection function is chosen to make the CP process agenda items which will cause the insertion of whichever edge the PCP will next select from its finishing agenda.

The completeness reduction means that the edges found (i.e., *finished*) by both parsers will be the same. From the known completeness of a CP under weaker conditions (Kay 1980), this means that the PCP will find every edge which has a parse allowed by the grammar, words, and goal, *not* that it will score them correctly.

4.2   Correctness

We now show that any edge which is finished is correctly scored when it is finished.

First, we need some terminology about traversal trees. A traversal tree T is a binary tree of edge tokens, as in figure 18.3(a). A leaf in this tree is a token of an introduction edge, either a word (if passive) or a rule introduction (if active). A non-leaf x is a token of a non-introduction edge and has two children, a and p, which are tokens of an active edge and a passive edge, respectively, forming a traversal token (a, p, x). The reason we must make a type/token distinction is that a given edge or traversal may appear more than once in a traversal tree. For example, consider empty words which may be used several times over the same zero-span, or an introduction active edge for a left-recursive rule. We use $type(x)$ to denote the type of an edge token x.

The basic idea is to avoid finishing incorrectly scored edges by always finishing the highest-scored edge available. This will cause us to work in an inside-outwards fashion when necessary to ensure that score propagation is never needed. The chief difficulties therefore occur when what should have been a high-scoring edge is unavailable for some reason. A subtle way this can occur is if an introduction edge is discovered too late. If this happens, we may have already mistakenly finished some other edge, assigning it the best score that it could have had *without* that introduction edge's presence in the grammar or input. Therefore, we need tighter constraints on word and rule introduction strategies to prove correctness than those needed for completeness.

The condition on word introduction is simple.

Definition 6 *The* Word Introduction Condition *(or "no internal insertion"): Whenever an edge e with span S is finished at time f_e, all words (passive introduction edges) contained in S must have been discovered at f_e.*

This is satisfied by any reasonable lattice scanning algorithm and any sentence scanning algorithm whatsoever. The only disallowed strategy is to insert words from a lattice into a span which has already had some covering set of words discovered and parsed. It should be fairly clear that this kind of internal-insertion strategy will lead to problems.

Now we supply some theoretical machinery for a condition on rule introductions.

Definition 7 *A (possibly partial) ordering $\prec_T$ of nodes (edge tokens) in a traversal tree T allows descent if whenever a node x dominates a set of children C, for any $c \in C$, $c \preceq_T x$.*

Definition 8 *The* Rule Introduction Condition *(or "no rule blocking"): In any parse T of an edge e, there is some ordering $\prec_T$ of nodes which allows descent and such that for any active introduction edge $a \in T$,* EITHER

(1) there is some edge x with a token x' in T which does not dominate any token a' of a and whose finishing will cause the introduction of a (i.e., $a \in R(x)$) and $x' \prec_T a'$, OR

(2) any parse of e will contain either a or an edge b whose discovery would be simultaneous with that of a.

This is wordy, but the key idea is that active introduction edges must "depend" on some other edge in the parse in such a way that if an active introduction edge is undiscovered, we can track back to find another edge earlier in the parse which must also be undiscovered.

The last constraint we need is one on the scores of the DFSA rules. If a prefix of a rule is bad, its continuations must be as bad or worse. Otherwise, we may incorrectly delay extending a low scoring prefix.

Definition 9 *The* Grammar Scoring Condition *(or "no score gain"): The grammar DFSAs are scored by assigning an element of a $\preceq_S$-ordered c-semiring to*

each initial state, transition, and accepting state. The score of a trajectory (sequence of DFSA states) is the semiring product of the scores of the initial state and the transitions, along with the accepting cost (for complete trajectories).

If this is met, then the score of a traversal tree is then simply a product of scores for each introduction edge token and traversal token. Therefore, the score of an entire traversal tree is no better than the score of any subtree, and monotonically increasing under substitution of a better scored subtree.

A subtle concrete implication of this condition is that, for example, if grammar productions are going to be compressed into a DFSA which transduces rule RHSs to sums of log-probabilities, not only must the log-probabilities of the full productions all be non-positive, but so must each starting cost, transition, and accepting cost.[13] Otherwise, the scoring of the underlying n-ary grammar trees might have the property that adding structure reduces the score, but the scoring of the traversal trees will not.

Now we are ready to state the completeness theorem.

Theorem 3 *Given any DFSA grammar G, lattice L, and introduction strategies obeying the conditions above, any edge e which is finished by the algorithm at some time f_e has the property that $score(e, f_e) = \sigma(e)$.*

The proof is by contradiction. Take the first edge e which is selected from the finishing agenda and finished with an incorrect score estimate, so at e's finishing time f_e, $score(e, f_e) \neq \sigma(e)$.

Perhaps $score(e, f_e) > \sigma(e)$, contrary to our earlier claim that scoring was always conservative (see figure 18.4). For e to ever be scored incorrectly, e must be a non-introduction edge. Its current incorrect score was then either set at discovery (when it was initialized to the minimum score, which is not greater than $\sigma(e)$ or anything else, a contradiction) or by relaxing a traversal (a, p, e). But such a traversal cannot be created until both a and p are already finished. By choice of e, a and p were correctly scored at their finishing. Consider the traversal tree T formed by taking best parses of a and p, and joining them under a root token of e. After relaxation, we had $score(e) = \sigma(T)$.[14] But, since T is a parse of e, $\sigma(T) \leq \sigma(e)$. Since that relaxation gave e the score it still has at f_e, we have $score(e, f_e) \leq \sigma(e)$, again a contradiction.

Therefore, $score(e, f_e) < \sigma(e)$. Since e has a parse (by completeness), it has at least one best parse. Choose one and call it B. By virtue of being a best parse, $\sigma(B) = \sigma(e)$. We claim that there is some edge x in B which, at f_e, has been discovered, is correctly scored, yet has not been finished. Assume such an x exists. Since x is discovered but not finished at f_e, it was in the finishing agenda with its current score just before e was chosen to be finished. But e was chosen from the finishing agenda, not x, so it must be that $score(x, f_e) \leq score(e, f_e)$.

On the other hand, since x is contained in B, some best parse P of x is a subtree of B. But then by "no score gain" it must be that $\sigma(e) = \sigma(B) \leq \sigma(P) =$

$\sigma(x)$. Thus, if we find such an edge x, then $\sigma(e) \leq \sigma(x) = score(x, f_e) \leq score(e, f_e) < \sigma(e)$, a contradiction.

The rest of the proof involves showing the existence of such an x. Consider the nodes in B. Since e is unfinished, there is a non-empty set of unfinished nodes, call it U. We want some $u \in U$ which both has no unfinished children and which is minimal by $\prec_T$. Clearly some elements are minimal since U is non-empty and finite. Call the set of minimal elements M. For any $u \in M$ which has an unfinished child, that child must also be minimal since $\prec_T$ allows descent. Therefore, removing all elements from M which have an unfinished child leaves a non-empty set. Choose any u from this set.

If u dominates two finished children (call them a and p), then since e is the first incorrectly finished edge, $type(a)$ and $type(p)$ had their correct scores at their finishing times. Whenever the later of $type(a)$ and $type(p)$ was finished, the traversal $t = (type(a), type(p), type(u))$ was generated. And before anything else could have been finished, t was explored. Thus, $type(u)$ has been discovered and has been relaxed by t, say at time r_t. Therefore, at r_t, and therefore still at f_e, $score(type(u))$ can be no worse than its score in B, which of course means its score has been correct since r_t, so $type(u)$ is correctly scored at f_e. But recall that $type(u)$ is unfinished, so we are done.

If u dominates no finished nodes, then it is a leaf. If $type(u)$ is a passive introduction edge, then by "no internal insertion" $type(u)$ has been discovered. Since passive introduction edges are correctly scored at discovery, we are done. If $type(u)$ is an active introduction edge, then we need only show that it has been discovered, since these are also correctly scored on discovery. To be sure it has been discovered, we must appeal to "no rule blocking." It is possible that any parse of e contains an edge whose discovery would be simultaneous with that of $type(u)$. If so, since there is some finished parse of e, $type(u)$ must be discovered, and we are done. If not, then let x be an edge from clause (2) whose finishing would guarantee $type(u)$'s discovery. If x is unfinished, then some instance of x is $\prec_T u$ and unfinished, contradicting u's minimality. Thus we are done.

We have now proven the correctness of the algorithm for strategies meeting the given criteria. The traditional bottom-up, top-down, and left-corner strategies satisfy the Rule Introduction Condition. We prove this for only the top-down strategy here; the other proofs are similar.

Theorem 4 *The top-down rule introduction strategy satisfies the Rule Introduction Condition.*

Order the nodes in T by the order in which they would be built in a top-down stack parse of T. Since no node is completed before its children in such a parse, this allows descent. In a top-down parse, for every active introduction token a' except for the leftmost node in the tree, there is another (active) node x' which is a left sibling of a node dominating a' and for which $type(x')$'s finishing will introduce $type(a')$. For any active introduction edge a, let a' be its leftmost token in T. Because it is leftmost, its x' will not dominate any token of a. Therefore, (1) holds unless a' is the leftmost node. Assume it is leftmost. Since T is a parse of some edge e either of category C or with a label with LHS C, a has a label with LHS C. Thus, if any parse S of e whatsoever is found, its leftmost leaf is a token of some active introduction edge b with a label with LHS C. But then, whenever b was discovered, so was a, since the top-down introduction strategy always simultaneously introduces the initial states of all rules with the same LHS.

4.3   Asymptotic Bounds and Performance

We briefly motivate and state the complexity bounds. Let n be the number of nodes in the input lattice, C the number of categories in the grammar, and S the number of states in the grammar. $C \leq S$ since each category's encoding contains at least one state. The maximum number of edges E is $O(Sn^2)$, and the maximum number of traversals T is $O(SCn^3)$. Time is dominated by the work per traversal, which can be made amortized $O(1)$ (with a Fibonacci heap-backed priority queue), so the total time is $O(T) = O(SCn^3)$. For memory, there are several $O(E)$ data structures holding edges. The concern is the exploration agenda which holds traversals. But everything on this agenda at any one time resulted from a single call to doFundamentalRule, and so its size is also $O(E)$. Therefore, the total memory is $O(E) = O(Sn^2)$. This is not necessarily true for a standard CP, which can require $O(T)$ space for its agenda. It is also not true for an update-percolating parser (Caraballo and Charniak 1998) which will require cubic space to record which edges' updates effect which other edges.

We have implemented the parser in Java, and tested it with various rule encodings on parsing of Penn Treebank Wall Street Journal sentences. With efficient rule encodings, sentences of up to 100 words can be parsed in 1 Gb of memory. Graphs of runtime performance can be found in (Klein and Manning 2001b).

5.   Conclusion

We have pointed out a deep connection between parsing and hypergraphs, and described how parse existence and Viterbi parsing can be reduced to hypergraph reachability and shortest-path computations. Using that connection, we have presented an agenda-based probabilistic chart parser which naturally handles arbitrary PCFG grammars and works with a variety of word and rule introduction strategies, while maintaining the same cubic time bounds as a categorical chart parser.

Acknowledgments

We would like to thank participants at the 2001 Brown Conference on Stochastic and Deterministic Approaches in Vision, Language, and Cognition for comments, particularly Mark Johnson. Thanks also to the anonymous reviewers for valuable comments on this work, and in particular for bringing Knuth (1977) to our attention. This chapter is based on work supported in part by the National Science Foundation under Grant No. IIS-0085896, and by an NSF Graduate Fellowship.

Appendix: Pseudocode for the Probabilistic Chart Parser

parse(Lattice sentence, Edge goal)
  initialize(sentence, goal)
  while finishingAgenda is non-empty
    while explorationAgenda is non-empty
      get a traversal t from the explorationAgenda
      exploreTraversal(t)
    get a best edge e from the finishingAgenda
    finishEdge(e)

initialize(Lattice sentence, Edge goal)
  create a new chart and new agendas
  for each word w:[start,end] in the sentence
    discoverEdge(w:[start,end])
  for each vertex x in the sentence
    if allow-empties
      discoverEdge(empty:[x,x])
  doRuleInitialization(goal)

exploreTraversal(Traversal t)
  $e = t$.result
  if notYetDiscovered(e)
    discoverEdge(e)
  relaxEdge(e, t)

relaxEdge(Edge e, Traversal t)
  t.score = combineScores(t)
  if (t.score is better than e.score)
    e.score = t.score
    e.bestTraversal = t

discoverEdge(Edge e)
  add e to the finishingAgenda

finishEdge(Edge e)
  add e to the chart
  doFundamentalRule(e)
  doRuleIntroduction(e)

doFundamentalRule(Edge e)
  if e is passive

    for all active edges a which end at e.start
      for active and/or passive result edges r
        create the traversal $t = (a, e, r)$
        add t to the explorationAgenda
if e is active
    for all passive edges p which start at e.end
      for active and/or passive result edges r
        create the traversal $t = (e, p, r)$
        add t to the explorationAgenda

doRuleIntroduction(Edge e)
    if top-down and e is active
      for all categories c that can follow e.label
        for all intro active edges a at e.end with LHS c
          if notDiscovered(a) then discoverEdge(a)
    if bottom-up and e is passive
      for all categories c with a RHS beginning with e.label
        $a = c$:[e.start, e.start]
        if notDiscovered(a) then discoverEdge(a)

doRuleInitialization(Edge goal)
    if top-down
      for all intro active edges a at goal.start with LHS goal.label
      discoverEdge(a)

Notes

1. This is not to say that scores cannot be incorporated into a deductive framework, for example by reifying probabilities.

2. An important point to note is that one cannot choose only part of a hyperarc to include in a subgraph; once the arc is included, all nodes in its head and tail must also be included.

3. It will be one-to-one if the grammar contains neither empty nor unary productions; not much is lost if this case is used for intuition.

4. These semirings have been used in work on soft constraint satisfaction, hence the "c-" prefix.

5. The choice of algorithm may impact the permitted generality of the scoring function. The algorithm in (Gallo et al. 1993) actually does work for all $\preceq_S$-ordered c-semiring scoring functions, though their presentation does not state this; one must also note that their score addition corresponds to the semiring multiplication. In any case, the algorithm in section 3 is entirely self-contained.

6. This has the theoretical – but not clearly useful – advantage of allowing the score combination function to vary per production.

7. Goodman (1998) provides an insightful presentation unifying many categorical and probabilistic parsing algorithms in terms of the problem's semiring structure, but he merely notes this problem (p. 172), and on this basis puts probabilistic agenda-based chart parsers aside. The agenda-based chart parser of Caraballo and Charniak (1998) (used for determining inside probabilities) suffers from exactly this problem: In Appendix A (p. 293), they note that such updates "can be quite expensive in terms of CPU time", but merely suggest a method of thresholding which delays probability propagation until the amount of unpropagated probability mass has become significant, and suggest that this thresholding allows them to keep the performance of the parser "as $O(n^3)$ empirically." We do not present an inside probability algorithm here, but the hypergraphical view of parsing can be developed to give an inside parsing algorithm, as discussed in (Klein and Manning 2001a).

8. The result edge is primarily to simplify proofs and pseudocode; it need not ever be stored in a traversal's coded representation.

9. Note that the comments in the figure apply only to non-introduction edges, but the timeline applies to all edges.

10. Other word introduction strategies are possible, such as scanning the words incrementally in an outer loop from left-to-right whenever the finishing agenda is empty. A sufficient constraint on scanning strategies is presented in section 4.

11. In the application of the fundamental rule, an (active, passive) pair can potentially create two traversals. In categorical DFSA chart parsing, edges may be active, passive, or both. However, the passive and active versions of what would have been a single active/passive edge in a categorical parser will not in general have the same score, because the passive one is assessed an acceptance cost, and so the algorithm introduces separate edges.

12. An example of a non-edge-driven strategy would be if we introduced an arbitrary undiscovered edge from A into an arbitrary zero-span whenever the finishing agenda was empty. It appears very difficult to state a criterion for non-edge-driven strategies which guarantees both their completeness and correctness.

13. The condition implies this because positive elements are not in the relevant semiring: $\langle [-\infty, 0], \max, +, -\infty, 0 \rangle$.

14. We define the score function σ for a traversal tree T to be the score of that specific parse.

References

Baker, J. K. (1979). Trainable grammars for speech recognition. In D. H. Klatt and J. J. Wolf (Eds.), *Speech Communication Papers for the 97th Meeting of the Acoustical Society of America*, 547–550.

Bistarelli, S., U. Montanari, and F. Rossi (1997). Semiring-based constraint satisfaction and optimization. *Journal of the ACM* 44(2):201–236.

Caraballo, S. A., and E. Charniak (1998). New figures of merit for best-first probabilistic chart parsing. *Computational Linguistics* 24:275–298.

Chappelier, J.-C., and M. Rajman (1998). A generalized CYK algorithm for parsing stochastic CFG. In *First Workshop on Tabulation in Parsing and Deduction (TAPD98)*, 133–137, Paris.

Earley, J. (1970). An efficient context-free parsing algorithm. *Communications of the ACM* 6(8):451–455.

Gallo, G., G. Longo, S. Pallottino, and S. Nguyen. (1993). Directed hypergraphs and applications. *Discrete Applied Mathematics* 42:177–201.

Gazdar, G., and C. Mellish (1989). *Natural Language Processing in Prolog*. Wokingham, England: Addison-Wesley.

Goodman, J. (1998). *Parsing inside-out*. PhD thesis, Harvard University.

Graham, S. L., M. A. Harrison, and W. L. Ruzzo. (1980). An improved context-free recognizer. *ACM Transactions on Programming Languages and Systems* 2(3):415–462.

Jelinek, F., J. D. Lafferty, and R. L. Mercer (1992). Basic methods of probabilistic context free grammars. In P. Laface and R. De Mori (Eds.), *Speech Recognition and Understanding: Recent Advances, Trends, and Applications*, Vol. 75 of *Series F: Computer and Systems Sciences*. Springer Verlag.

Kasami, T. (1965). An efficient recognition and syntax analysis algorithm for context-free languages. Technical Report AFCRL-65-758, Air Force Cambridge Research Laboratory, Bedford, MA.

Kay, M. (1980). Algorithm schemata and data structures in syntactic processing. Technical Report CSL-80-12, Xerox PARC, Palo Alto, CA.

Klein, D., and C. D. Manning (2001a). An $O(n^3)$ agenda-based chart parser for arbitrary probabilistic context-free grammars. Technical Report dbpubs/2001-16, Stanford University, Stanford, CA.

Klein, D., and C. D. Manning (2001b). Parsing with treebank grammars: Empirical bounds, theoretical models, and the structure of the Penn treebank. In *ACL 39/EACL 10*, 330–337.

Klein, D., and C. D. Manning (2002). A* parsing: Fast exact Viterbi parse selection. Technical Report dbpubs/2002-16, Stanford University.

Knuth, D. E. (1977). A generalization of Dijkstra's algorithm. *Information Processing Letters* 6(1):1–5.

Kupiec, J. (1991). A trellis-based algorithm for estimating the parameters of a hidden stochastic context-free grammar. In *Proceedings of the Speech and Natural Language Workshop*, 241–246. DARPA.

Mohri, M. (1997). Finite-state transducers in language and speech processing. *Computational Linguistics* 23(4):269–311.

Moore, R. C. (2000). Improved left-corner chart parsing for large context-free grammars. In *Proceedings of the Sixth International Workshop on Parsing Technologies*.

Pereira, F., and S. M. Shieber (1987). *Prolog and Natural-Language Analysis*. Stanford, CA: CSLI Publications.

Pereira, F. C., and D. H. Warren (1983). Parsing as deduction. In *ACL 21*, 137–144.

Shieber, S., Y. Schabes, and F. Pereira (1995). Principles and implementation of deductive parsing. *Journal of Logic Programming* 24:3–36.

Sikkel, K., and A. Nijholt (1997). Parsing of Context-Free languages. In G. Rozenberg and A. Salomaa (Eds.), *Handbook of Formal Languages*, Vol. 2: Linear Modelling: Background and Application, 61–100. Berlin: Springer.

Stolcke, A. (1995). An efficient probabilistic context-free parsing algorithm that computes prefix probabilities. *Computational Linguistics* 21:165–202.

Younger, D. H. (1967). Recognition and parsing of context free languages in time n^3. *Information and Control* 10:189–208.

Chapter 19

MEASURE FOR MEASURE: TOWARDS INCREASED COMPONENT COMPARABILITY AND EXCHANGE

Stephan Oepen

Center for the Study of Language and Information
Stanford University, Stanford, CA 94305 (USA)
oe@csli.stanford.edu

Ulrich Callmeier

Department of Computational Linguistics
Saarland University
66041 Saarbrücken (Germany)
uc@coli.uni-sb.de

Abstract   Over the past few years, significant progress has been made in efficient processing with wide-coverage HPSG grammars. HPSG-based parsing systems are now available that can process medium-complexity sentences (of ten to twenty words, say) in average parse times equivalent to real (i.e. human reading) time. A large number of engineering improvements in current HPSG systems have been achieved through collaboration of multiple research centers and mutual exchange of experience, encoding techniques, algorithms, and even pieces of software. This article presents an approach to grammar and system engineering, termed *competence & performance profiling*, that makes systematic experimentation and the precise empirical study of system properties a focal point in development. Adapting the profiling metaphor familiar from software engineering to constraint-based grammars and parsers enables developers to maintain an accurate record of system evolution, identify grammar and system deficiencies quickly, and compare to earlier versions or between different systems. We discuss a number of example problems that motivate the experimental approach, and apply the empirical methodology in a fairly detailed discussion of progress made during a development period of three years.

H. Bunt et al. (eds.), New Technologies in Parsing Technology, 373-395.

Dramatis Personæ

> *Let there be some more test made of my metal,*
> *Before so noble and so great a figure*
> *Be stamp'd upon it.*
> (Shakespeare, 1623)

> [...] *we view the discovery of parsing strategies as a largely exper-*
> *imental process of incremental optimization.* (Erbach, 1991a)

> [...] *the study and optimisation of unification-based parsing must*
> *rely on empirical data until complexity theory can more accurately*
> *predict the practical behaviour of such parsers.* (Carroll, 1994)

Early in 1994, research groups at Saarbrücken[1] (Uszkoreit et al., 1994) and CSLI Stanford[2] (Copestake, 1992; Flickinger and Sag, 1998) started to collaborate on the development of large-scale HPSG grammars, suitable grammar engineering platforms, and efficient processors. While both sites had worked on HPSG implementation before, the joint effort has greatly increased productivity, resulted in a mutual exchange of knowledge and technology, and helped build a collection of grammar development environments, several highly engineered parsers (Kiefer et al., 1999) and an efficient generator (Carroll et al., 1999). Around 1998, the grammar formalisms and parsing group at Tokyo University[3] (Torisawa and Tsujii, 1996) made an entrance on stage and now supplies additional expertise on (abstract-machine-based) compilation of typed feature structures, Japanese HPSG, and grammar approximation techniques. More recently, people from Cambridge, Edinburgh, and Sussex Universities (UK) and from the Norwegian University of Science and Technology (in Trondheim) have also joined the cast.

Although their individual systems often supply extra functionality, the groups have converged on a common descriptive formalism – a conservative blend of Carpenter (1992), Copestake (1992), and Krieger and Schäfer (1994) – that allows grammars[4] to be processed by (at least) five different platforms. The LinGO grammar, a multi-purpose, broad-coverage grammar of English developed at CSLI and among the largest HPSG implementations currently available, serves as a common reference for all three groups (while of course the sites continue development of additional grammars for English, German, and Japanese). With one hundred thousand lines of source, roughly eight thousand types, an average feature structure size of some three hundred nodes, twenty seven lexical and thirty seven phrase structure rules, and some six thousand lexical (stem) entries, the LinGO grammar presents a difficult challenge for processing systems. While scaling the systems to this rich set of constraints and improving processing and constraint resolution algorithms, the groups have regularly exchanged benchmarking results, in particular at the level of individual components, and discussed benefits and disadvantages of particular encodings and algorithms. Precise comparison has been found essential in this process and has facilitated a degree of cross-fertilization that has proved beneficial for all participants.

Act 1 below introduces the profiling methodology, supporting tools, and the sets of common reference data and benchmarking metrics that were used among the groups. By way of example, the profiling metaphor is then applied in Act 2 to a choice of engineering issues that (currently) can only be approached empirically. Act 3 introduces the PET platform (Callmeier, 2000) as another actor in the experimental setup: PET synthesizes a variety of techniques from the individual systems in a fresh, modular, and highly parameterizable re-implementation. On the basis of empirical data obtained with PET, Act 4 provides a detailed comparison of competence and performance profiles obtained in October 1996 with the development status three years later. Finally, Act 5 applies some of the metrics introduced earlier to a multi-dimensional, cross-grammar *and* cross-platform comparison.

1.   Competence & Performance Profiling

In system development and optimization, subtle algorithmic and implementational decisions often have a significant impact on system performance, so monitoring system evolution very closely is crucial. Developers should be enabled to obtain a precise record of the status of the system at any given point; also, comparison with earlier results, between various parameter settings, and across platforms should be automated and integrated with the regular development cycle. System performance, however, cannot be adequately characterized merely by measurements of overall processing time (and perhaps memory usage). Properties of (i) individual modules (in a classical setup, especially the unifier, type system, and parser), (ii) the grammar being used, and (iii) the input presented to the system all interact in complex ways. In order to obtain an analytical understanding of strengths and weaknesses of a particular configuration, finer-grained records are required. By the same token, developer intuition and isolated case studies are often insufficient, since in practice, people who have worked on a particular system or grammar for years still find that an intuitive prediction of system behaviour can be incomplete or plainly wrong.

Although most grammar development environments have facilities to batch-process a test corpus and record the results produced by the system, these are typically restricted to processing a flat, unstructured input file (listing test sentences, one per line) and outputting a small number of processing results into a log file.[5] In sum, we note a striking methodological and technological

Table 19.1.   Some of the parameters making up a competence & performance profile.

readings	number of complete analyses obtained (when applicable, after unpacking)
filter	percentage of parser actions predicted to fail (rule filter plus 'quick check')
etasks	number of attempts to instantiate an argument position in a rule
stasks	number of successful instantiations of argument positions in rules
aedges	number of active edges built by the parser (where appropriate)
pedges	number of passive edges built by the parser (typically in all-paths search)
unifications	number of top-level calls into the feature structure unification routine
copies	number of top-level feature structure copies made
tcpu	amount of cpu time (in milliseconds) spent in processing
space	amount of dynamic memory allocated during processing (in bytes)

deficit in the area of precise and systematic, let alone comparable, assessment of grammar and system behaviour.

Oepen and Flickinger (1998) propose a methodology, termed *grammar profiling*, that builds on structured and annotated collections of test and reference data (traditionally known as *test suites*). The *competence & performance profiling* approach we advocate in this play can be viewed as a generalization of this methodology, in line with the experimental paradigm suggested by, among others, Erbach (1991a) and Carroll (1994). A *competence & performance profile* is defined as a rich, precise, and structured snapshot of system behaviour at a given development point. The production, maintenance, and inspection of profiles is supported by a specialized software package (called [incr tsdb()][6]) that supplies a uniform data model, an application program interface to the grammar-based processing components, and graphical facilities for profile analysis and comparison. Profiles are stored in a relational database which accumulates a precise record of system evolution, and which serves as the basis for flexible report generation, visualization, and data analysis via basic descriptive statistics. All tables and figures used in this play were generated using [incr tsdb()].

The profiling environment defines a common set of descriptive metrics which aim both for in-depth precision and also for sufficient generality across a variety of processing systems. Most parameters are optional, though analysis potential may be restricted for partial profiles. Roughly, profile contents can be classified into information on (i) the processing *environment* (grammar, platform, versions, parameter settings and others), (ii) grammatical *coverage* (number of analyses, derivation and parse trees per reading, corresponding semantic formulae), (iii) *ambiguity* measures (lexical items retrieved, number of active and passive edges, where applicable, both globally and per result), (iv) *resource consumption* (various timings, memory allocation), and indicators of (v) *parser*

Table 19.2. Reference data sets used in comparison and benchmarking with the LinGO grammar.

1	2	3	4	5	6	7	8	9
Set	Aggregate	total items ♯	word string φ	lexical entries φ	total results ♯	parser analyses φ	passive edges φ	fs size φ
'tsnlp'	wellformed	1574	4·96	13·8	945	2·00	86	273
	illformed	2775	4·50	11·5	409	1·83	39	257
'csli'	wellformed	918	6·45	15·3	732	2·16	115	302
	illformed	375	6·11	14·9	85	2·31	84	298
'aged'	wellformed	96	8·41	23·1	72	7·00	292	315
'blend'	wellformed	1910	11·13	32·1	1008	51·39	1181	336
	illformed	142	11·05	34·2	24	20·33	611	317

and *unifier* throughput. Excluding relations and attributes that encode annotations on the input data, the current *competence & performance* database schema includes some one hundred attributes in five relations. Table 19.1 summarizes some of the profiling parameters as they are relevant to the drama to come.

While the current [incr tsdb()] data model has already been successfully adapted to six or so different parsing systems (with more underway; see Act 6), it remains to be seen how well it scales to the description of a larger variety of processing regimes. And although absolute numbers must be viewed with a grain of salt, the common metric has greatly increased comparability and data exchange among the groups mentioned above, and has in some cases also helped to identify unexpected sources of performance variation. For example, we have found that two Sun UltraSparc servers (at different sites) with identical hardware configuration (down to the level of cpu revision) and OS release reproducibly exhibit a performance difference of around ten per cent. This appears to be caused by different installed sets of vendor-supplied operating system patches. Also, average cpu load and availability of main memory have been observed to have a noticeable effect on cpu time measurements; therefore, all data reported in this play was collected in an (artificial, in some sense) environment in which sufficient cpu and memory resources were guaranteed throughout each complete test run.

The [incr tsdb()] package includes a number of test suites and development corpora for English, German, and French (and has facilities for user-level import of additional test data). For benchmarking purposes with the LinGO grammar four test sets were chosen: (i) the English TSNLP test suite (Oepen et al., 1997), (ii) the CSLI test suite derived from the original Hewlett-Packard data (Flickinger et al., 1987), (iii) a small collection of transcribed scheduling dialogue utterances collected in the Verb*mobil* context (Wahlster, 2000), and (iv) a larger extract from later Verb*mobil* corpora that was selected pseudo-randomly to achieve a balanced distribution of one hundred samples for each input length below twenty words. Some salient properties of these test sets are summarized in Table 19.2.[7] Looking at the degrees of lexical (i.e. the ratio between columns five and four), global (column seven), and local (approximated in column eight by the number of passive edges created in pure bottom-up parsing) ambiguity, the three test sets range from very short and unambiguous to mildly long and highly ambiguous. The '*blend*' test set is a good indicator of maximal input complexity that the available parsers can currently process (in plausible amounts of time and memory). Contrasting columns six and three (i.e. items accepted by the grammar vs. total numbers of well- or ill-formed items) provides a measure of grammatical coverage and overgeneration, respectively.

2. Strong Empiricism: A Few Examples

A fundamental measure in comparing two different versions or configurations of one system as well as for contrasting two distinct systems is correctness and equivalence of results. No matter what unification algorithm or parsing strategy is chosen, parameters like the numbers of lexical items retrieved per input word, total analyses found, passive edges derived (in non-predictive bottom-up parsing, at least) and others should only vary when the grammar itself is changed. Therefore, regular regression testing is required. In debugging and experimentation practice, we have found that minor divergences in results are often hard to identify; using an experimental parsing strategy, for example, over- and undergeneration can even out for the number of readings and even the accounting of passive edges. Hence, assuring an exact match in results (for a given test set) is a non-trivial task.

The [incr tsdb()] package eases comparison of results on a per-item basis, using an approach similar to the Unix diff (1) command, but generalized for structured data sets. By selection of a set of parameters for intersection (and optionally a comparison predicate), the user interface allows one to browse the subset of items that fail to match in the selected properties. One dimension that we found especially useful in intersecting profiles is on the derivation trees (a bracketed structure labeled with rule names and identifiers of lexical items) associated with each parser analysis. Once a set of missing or extra derivations (representing under- or overgeneration, respectively) between two profiles is identified, they can be fed back into the defective parser as a request to try and reconstruct each derivation. Reconstruction of derivation trees, in a sense, amounts to fully deterministic parsing, and enables the processor to record where the failure occurs that caused undergeneration in the first place; conversely, when dealing with overgeneration, reconstruction in the correct parser can be requested to identify the missing constraint(s). While these techniques illustrate basic debugging facilities that the profiling and experimentation environment provides, the following two scenes discuss algorithmic issues in parser design and tuning that can only be addressed empirically.

2.1   Hyper-Active Parsing

The two oldest development platforms within the consortium, the LKB (CSLI Stanford) and PAGE (DFKI Saarbrücken) systems, have undergone homogenization of approaches and even individual modules for quite a while (the conjunctive PAGE unifier, for instance, was developed by Rob Malouf at CSLI Stanford).[8] Until recently, however, the parsing regimes deployed in the two systems were significantly different. Both parsers use quasi-destructive unification, are purely bottom-up, chart-based, perform no ambiguity packing, and can be operated in exhaustive (all paths) or agenda-driven best-first search modes. Before any unification is attempted, both parsers apply the same set of pre-unification filters, viz. a test against a rule compatibility table (Kiefer et al., 1999), and the 'quick check' partial unification test (Malouf et al., 2000). The LKB passive chart parser (in exhaustive mode) uses a breadth-first CKY-like algorithm; it processes the input string strictly from left to right, constructing all admissible complete constituents whose right vertex is at the current input position before moving on to the next lexical item. Attempts at rule application are made from right to left. All and only complete constituents found (passive edges) are entered in the chart. The active PAGE parser, on the other hand, uses a variant of the algorithm described by Erbach (1991b). It operates bidirectionally, both in processing the input string and instantiating rules; crucially, the *key* daughter (see Scene 2.2 below) of each rule is analyzed first, before the other daughter(s) are instantiated.

But while the LKB and the PAGE developers both assumed the strategy chosen in their own system was the best-suited for parsing with large feature structures (as exemplified by the LinGO grammar), the choices are motivated by conflicting desiderata. Not storing active edges (as in the passive LKB parser) reduces the amount of feature structure copying but requires frequent recomputation of partially instantiated rules, in that the unification of a daughter constituent with the rightmost argument position of a rule is performed as many times as the rule is applied to left-adjacent sequences of candidate chart edges. Creating active edges that add partial results to the chart, on the other hand, requires that more feature structure copies are made, which in turn avoids the necessity of redoing unifications. Given the effectiveness of the pre-unification filters it is likely that for some active edges no attempts to extend them with adjacent inactive edges will ever be executed, so that the copy associated with the active edge was wasted effort. Profiling the two parsers individually showed that overall performance is roughly equivalent (with a minimal lead for the passive LKB parser in both time and space). While the passive parser executes far more parser tasks (i.e. unifications), it creates significantly fewer copies – as should be expected from what is known about the differences in parsing strategy. Hence, from a superficial comparison of parser throughput one could conclude that the passive parser successfully trades unifications for copies, and that both basic parsing regimes perform equally well with respect to the LinGO grammar.

To obtain fully comparable results, the algorithm used in PAGE was imported into the LKB, which serves as the (single) experimentation environment for the remainder of this scene. The direct comparison is shown in Table 19.3 for three of the standard test sets. The re-implementation of the active parser in the LKB, in fact, performs slightly better than the passive version and does not allocate very much more space. On the *'aged'* test set, the active parser even achieves a modest reduction in memory consumption which most likely reflects the larger proportion of extra unifications compared to the savings in copies (columns five and six) for this test set. Having profiled the two traditional parsing strategies and dissected each empirically, it now seems natural to synthesize a new algorithm that combines the advantages of both strategies (i.e. reduced unification *and* reduced copying). The following algorithm, termed 'hyper-active' by Oepen and Carroll (2000), achieves this goal:

- use the bottom-up, bidirectional, key-driven control strategy of the active parser;

- when an 'active' edge is derived, store this partial analysis in the chart but do *not* copy the associated feature structure;[9]

- when an 'active' edge is extended (combined with a passive edge), re-compute the intermediate feature structure from the original rule and already-instantiated daughter(s);

- only copy feature structures for complete passive edges; partial analyses are represented in the chart but the unification(s) that derived each partial analysis are redone on-demand.

Essentially, storing 'active' (or, in a sense, hyper-active) edges without creating expensive feature structure copies enables the parser to perform a key-driven search effectively, and at the same time avoids over-copying for partial analyses; additional unifications are traded for the copies that were avoided only where hyper-active edges are actually extended in later processing.[10]

Table 19.3. Contrasting parser performance: passive, active, and hyper-active in the LKB.

Set	Parser	filter %	etasks ϕ	stasks ϕ	unifs ϕ	copies ϕ	tcpu ϕ (s)	space ϕ (kb)
	passive	94·2	658	555	663	114	0·38	2329
'csli'	active	95·8	283	180	288	180	0·31	2432
	hyper-active	95·8	283	180	354	114	0·28	1686
	passive	94·2	1843	1604	1845	293	1·14	5692
'aged'	active	96·1	716	452	718	452	0·93	5449
	hyper-active	96·1	716	452	928	293	0·71	3830
	passive	93·6	9209	7968	9214	1074	5·87	16757
'blend'	active	96·0	2849	1580	2853	1580	3·42	13767
	hyper-active	96·0	2849	1580	4156	1074	3·31	10393

(generated by [incr tsdb()] at 3-nov-1999 (19:08 h)

Table 19.3 confirms that hyper-active parsing combines the desirable properties of both basic algorithms: the number of copies made is exactly the same as for the passive parser, while the number of unifications is only moderately higher than for the active parser (due to on-demand recomputation of intermediate structures). Accordingly, average parse times are reduced by twenty six ('*csli*') and thirty seven ('*aged*') per cent, while memory consumption drops by twenty seven and thirty two per cent, respectively. Applying the three parsers to the much more challenging '*blend*' test set reveals that the greater search space poses a severe problem for the passive parser, and limits the relative advantages of the hyper-active over the plain active strategy somewhat: while in the latter comparison the amount of copying is reduced by one third in hyper-active parsing, the number of unifications increases by thirty per cent at the same time (but see the discussion of rule instantiation below). Still, the hyper-active algorithm greatly reduces memory consumption, which by virtue of lower garbage collection times (not included in *tcpu* values) results in a significant overall speed-up. Compared to the original LKB passive parser, hyper-active parsing achieves a time and space reduction of forty three and thirty eight per cent, respectively. Thorough profiling and eclectic engineering have resulted in an improved parsing algorithm that is now used standardly in both the LKB and PAGE; for the German and Japanese Verb*mobil* grammars in PAGE, the observed benefits of hyper-active parsing were broadly confirmed.

2.2 Rule Instantiation Strategies

Head-driven approaches to parsing have been explored successfully with lexicalized grammars like HPSG (see van Noord, 1997 for an overview) be-

Figure 19.1.　Effects of head- vs. key-driven rule instantiation on parser work load (*'blend'*).

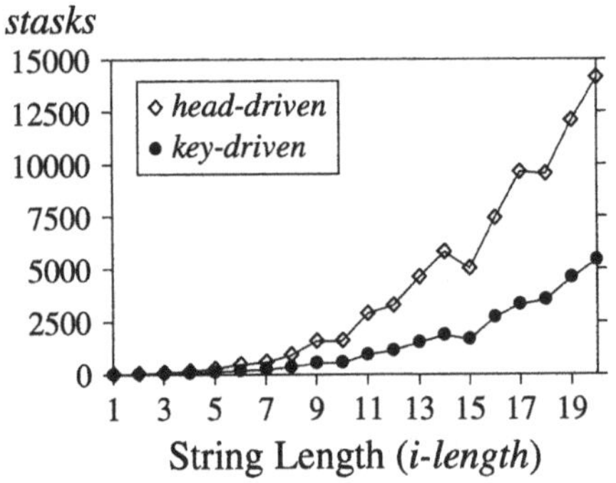

stasks

PET	head-driven	key-driven	Δ
filter (%)	93·2	95·5	—
etasks (ϕ)	8441	2995	64·5 %
stasks (ϕ)	4170	1465	64·9 %
tcpu (s)	1·47	0·64	56·4 %
space (kb)	7861	6472	17·7 %

cause, basically, they can avoid proliferation of partial rule instantiations (i.e. active edges in a chart parser) with rules that contain very unspecific argument positions. Many authors either implicitly (Kay, 1989) or explicitly (Bouma and van Noord, 1993) assume the *linguistic head* to be the argument position that the parser should instantiate first. However, the right choice of argument position in each rule, such that it best constrains rule applicability (with respect to all categories derived by the grammar), cannot be determined analytically. Though the selection is likely to be related to the amount and specificity of information encoded for each argument, for some rules a single feature value (e.g. the [WH +] constraint on the non-head daughter in one of the instantiations of the filler-head schema used in LinGO) can be the most important. For terminological clarity, PAGE has coined the term *key* daughter to refer to the argument position in each rule that is the best discriminator with respect to other categories that the grammar derives; at the same time, the notion of *key-driven* parsing emphasizes the observation that for individual rules in a particular grammar a non-(linguistic)head daughter may be a better candidate.

Figure 19.1 compares parser performance (using the PET parser; see below) for a rule instantiation strategy that always fills the (linguistic) head daughter first (labelled *'head-driven'*) with a variant that uses an idiosyncratically chosen key daughter for each rule (termed *'key-driven'*; see below for key selection). The data shows that the number of executed (*etasks*) as well as the number of successful (*stasks*) parser actions increase far more drastically with respect to input length in the head-driven setup (on the *'blend'* test suite, truncated above 20 words due to sparse data). Since parser tasks are directly correlated to overall parser performance, the key-driven strategy on average reduces parsing time by more than a factor of two. Clearly, for the LinGO grammar at least, linguistic headedness is not a good indicator for rule instantiation. Thus, the choice of good parsing keys for a particular grammar is an entirely empirical issue. Key

Table 19.4.   Head and key positions and distribution of active vs. passive edges for selected rules.

Rule Name	head	key	aedges left → right	aedges right → left	pedges	ratio
head-complement	left	left	84,396	1,404,652	264,137	3·13
specifier-head	right	right	582,736	108,450	14,849	0·14
subject-head	right	left	48,464	364,846	300,561	6·20
head-marker	left	left	1,494	1,404,652	106,349	71·18
head-adjunct (*scopal*)	left	right	856,419	12,946	73,975	5·71
adjunct-head (*intersective*)	right	left	34,482	1,260,660	37,343	1·08
adjunct-head (*scopal*)	right	left	11,177	1,260,660	119,513	10·69
filler-head (*wh, subj*)	right	left	162	147,636	546	3·37

daughters, in the current setup, are stipulated by the grammar engineer(s) as annotations to grammar rules; in choosing the key positions, the grammarian builds on knowledge about the grammar and observations from parsing test data. The [incr tsdb()] performance profiling tools can help in this choice since they allow the accounting of active and passive edges to be broken down by individual grammar rules (as they were instantiated in building edges). Inspecting the ratio of edges built per rule, for any given choice of parsing keys, can then help to identify rules that generate an unnecessary number of active edges. Thus, in the experimental approach to grammar and system optimization the effects of different key selections can be analyzed precisely and compared to earlier results.[11] Table 19.4 shows the head and key positions together with the differences in the number of active edges derived (in strict left to right vs. right to left rule instantiation modes) for a subset of binary grammar rules in LinGO. For the majority of head-argument structures (with the notable exception of the subject-head rule) the linguistic head corresponds to the key daughter, whereas in adjunction and (most) filler-head constructions we see the reverse; for some rules, choosing the head daughter as the key can result in an increase of active edges close to two orders of magnitude.

Inspecting edge proliferation by individual rules reveals another property of the particular grammar: the ratio of passive to active edges (column seven in Table 19.4, using the key-driven values for *aedges*) varies drastically. The specifier-head rule, for example, licenses a large number of active edges but, on average, only one out of seven active edges can be completed to yield a passive edge. The head-marker rule, on the other hand, generates on average seventy one passive edges from just one active edge. While the former should certainly benefit from hyper-active parsing, this seems very unlikely for the latter; Scene 2.1 above suggests that no more than three unifications should be traded for one copy in the LKB. Therefore, it seems plausible to apply the hyper-active parsing regime selectively to rules with a *pedges* to *aedges* ratio below a certain threshold.

3. PET – Synthesizing Current Best Practice

PET is a platform for building processing systems based on the descriptive formalism represented by the LinGO grammar. It aims to make experimentation with constraint-based parsers easy, including comparison of existing techniques and evaluating new approaches. Thus, flexibility and extendibility are primary design objectives. Both desiderata are achieved by a tool box approach: PET provides an extendible set of configurable building blocks that can be combined and configured in different ways to instantiate a concrete processing system. The set of building blocks includes objects like *chart*, *agenda*, *grammar*, *type hierarchy*, and *typed feature structure*. Using the available objects, a simple bottom-up chart parser, for instance, can be realized in a few lines of code.

Alternative implementations of a certain object may be available to allow comparison of different approaches to one aspect of processing in a common context. For example, the current PET environment provides a choice of destructive, semi-destructive, and quasi-destructive implementations of the *typed feature structure* object – viz. the algorithms proposed by Wroblewski (1987), Ciortuz (2001), Tomabechi (1991), and Malouf et al. (2000). In this setup properties of various graph unification algorithms and feature structure representations can be compared among each other and in interaction with different processing regimes.

In a parser called **cheap**, PET implements all relevant techniques from Kiefer et al. (1999) (i.e. conjunctive-only unification, rule filters, quick-check, restrictors), as well as techniques originally developed in other systems (e.g. key-driven parsing from PAGE, caching type unification and hyper-active parsing from the LKB, and partial expansion from DFKI CHIC). Re-implementation and strict modularization often resulted in improved representations and algorithmic refinements; since individual modules can be specialized for a particular task, the overhead often found in monolithic implementations (like slots in internal data structures, say, that are only required in a certain configuration) could be reduced.

Efficient memory management and minimizing memory consumption was another important consideration in the development of PET. Experience with Lisp-based systems suggests that memory throughput is one of the main bottlenecks when processing large grammars. In fact, one observes a close correlation between the amount of dynamically allocated memory and processing time, indicating much time is spent moving data, rather than in actual computation. Using builtin C++ memory management, allocation and release of feature structure nodes can account for up to forty per cent of total run time. As in the Warren Abstract Machine (Aït-Kaci, 1991), a general memory allocation scheme allowing arbitrary order of allocation and release of structures is not necessary in this context. Within a larger unit of computation – the application of a rule, say – the parser typically builds up structure monotonically; memory is only released in the case of a top-level unification failure when all partial structure built during this unification is freed. Therefore, PET employs a simple stack-based memory management strategy, acquiring memory from the operating system in large chunks which are then sub-allocated. A *mark-release* mechanism allows saving the current allocation state (the current stack position) and returning to that saved state at a later point. Thus, releasing a chunk of objects amounts to a single pointer assignment.

Also, feature structure representations are maximally compact.[12] In combination with other memory-reducing techniques (e.g. partial expansion and shrinking, substructure sharing, hyper-active parsing) this results in very attractive memory consumption characteristics for the **cheap** parser, allowing it to process the *'blend'* test set with a process size of around one hundred megabytes (where Lisp- or Prolog-based implementations easily grow beyond half a gigabyte). To maximize compactness and efficiency, PET is implemented in ANSI C++, but uses traditional C representations (rather than C++ objects) for some central objects where minimal overhead is required (e.g. the basic feature structure elements).

4. Quantifying Progress

The preceding acts have exemplified the benefits of competence and performance profiling applied to isolated properties of various parsing algorithms. In this penultimate act we take a slightly wider perspective and use the profiling approach to give an impression of overall progress made in processing the LinGO grammar over a development period of three years. The oldest available profiles (for the *'tsnlp'* and *'aged'* test sets) were obtained with PAGE (version 2.0 released in May 1997) and the October 1996 version of the grammar; the current best parsing performance, to our best knowledge, is achieved in the **cheap** parser of PET. All data was sampled on the same Sun UltraSparc server (dual 300 megahertz; 1.2 gigabytes memory; mildly patched Solaris 2.6) at Saarbrücken.

The evolution of grammatical coverage is depicted in Table 19.5, contrasting salient properties from the individual competence profiles (see Table 19.2) side by side; to illustrate the use of annotations on the test data, the table is further

Table 19.5. Development of LinGO grammatical coverage and overgeneration over three years.

Test Set	test items ♯	October 1996				August 1999			
		lexical ϕ	parser ϕ	in %	out %	lexical ϕ	parser ϕ	in %	out %
'tsnlp' test set	**4463**	**2·32**	**1·75**	**65·3**	**26·7**	**2·67**	**2·21**	**76·7**	**26·5**
S_Types	174	2·70	2·16	78·7	40·0	3·37	1·24	96·0	51·6
C_Agreement	123	2·59	1·33	58·8	10·0	2·27	1·28	77·9	10·0
C_Complementation	1010	2·45	2·19	62·2	12·1	2·99	1·67	83·1	10·5
C_Diathesis-Passive	220	3·58	2·87	25·3	8·1	3·52	3·52	50·5	6·3
NP_Agreement	1196	1·56	1·06	47·8	14·8	1·70	1·21	62·2	15·9
Other	1740	2·28	1·72	73·2	54·9	2·70	2·66	79·9	53·3
'aged' test set	**95**	**2·11**	**2·55**	**65·8**	—	**2·74**	**7·00**	**75·0**	—

(generated by [incr tsdb()] at 5-nov-1999 (17:11 h))

broken down by selected syntactic phenomena for the TSNLP data (Oepen et al., 1997, give details of the phenomenon classification). Comparison of the *lexical* and *parser* averages shows a modest increase in lexical but a dramatic increase in global ambiguity (by close to a factor of three for *'aged'*). Columns labeled *in* and *out* indicate coverage of items marked wellformed and overgeneration for ill-formed items, respectively. While the *'aged'* test set does not include negative test items, it confirms that coverage within the Verb*mobil* domain has improved. However, the TSNLP test suite is far better suited to gauge development of grammatical coverage, since it was designed to systematically exercise different modules of the grammar. In fact, a net increase in coverage (from sixty five to seventy seven per cent) in conjunction with slightly reduced overgeneration confirms that the LinGO grammar engineers have steadily improved the overall quality of the linguistic resource.

The assessment of parser performance shows a more dramatic development. Average parsing times per test item (on identical hardware) have dropped by more than two orders of magnitude (a factor of two hundred and seventy on the *'aged'* data), while memory consumption has reduced to about two per cent of the original values. Because in the early PAGE data the 'quick-check' pre-unification filter was not available, current filter rates for PET (and the other systems alike) are much better and result in a reduction of parser tasks that are actually executed. At the same time, comparing the number of passive edges licensed by the two versions of the grammar provides a good estimate on the size of the search space processed by the two parsers. Although for the (nearly) ambiguity-free TSNLP test suite the *pedges* averages are almost stable, the *'aged'* data shows an increase by a factor of three. Assuming that the average

Table 19.6. Development of salient performance parameters (PAGE vs. PET) over three years.

Version	Platform	Test Set	filter %	etasks ϕ	pedges ϕ	tcpu ϕ (s)	space ϕ (kb)
October 1996	PAGE	'tsnlp'	49·9	656	44	3·69	19016
		'aged'	51·3	1763	97	36·69	79093
August 1999	PET	'tsnlp'	93·9	170	55	0·03	333
		'aged'	95·1	753	292	0·14	1435
		'blend'	95·5	3084	1140	0·65	10589

(generated by [incr tsdb()] at 5-nov-1999 (21:23 h))

number of passive edges is a direct measure of input complexity (with respect to a particular grammar), we extrapolate the overall speed-up in processing the LinGO grammar as a factor of roughly eight hundred (again, *tcpu* values in Table 19.6 do *not* include garbage collection for PAGE which in turn is avoided in PET; hence, the net speed-up is more than three orders of magnitude). Finally, Table 19.6 includes PET results on the currently most challenging *'blend'* test set (see above). Despite of greatly increased search space and ambiguity, the cheap parser achieves an average parse time of 650 milliseconds and processes almost ninety per cent of the test items in less than one second.[13]

5. Multi-Dimensional Performance Profiling

The preceding acts have demonstrated how the [incr tsdb()] profiling approach enables comparison over time and across platforms, using the same grammar and reference input in both cases. In this final application of the framework, we draw the curtain wide open and attempt a contrastive study along several dimensions simultaneously. The basic theme of the exercise is the search for a reliable point of comparison across two distinct (though, of course, abstractly similar) systems, using different grammars (of different languages) and unrelated test data.

Table 19.7 summarizes a number of performance metrics for four different configurations that result from the cross product of applying two distinct processing environments (the LKB and PET) to two distinct grammars (the LinGO grammar and the Japanese HPSG developed within Verb*mobil*; see Siegel, 2000). While of course within each row the results for both platforms were profiled against the same data set (viz. a sample of one thousand sentences randomly extracted from English and Japanese Verb*mobil* corpora, respectively), the exact details of the two test corpora will not matter for the present exercise; besides asserting a general, if rough similarity in origin and average length, nothing in the following paragraphs will hinge on inherent properties of the

Table 19.7.   The matrix: simultaneous cross-grammar, cross-platform comparison.

	LKB		PET		Speed-Up
English	aedges pedges etasks stasks tcpu space	854 1850 5946 2695 2.96 s 16894 kb	aedges pedges etasks stasks tcpu space	854 1850 6541 2661 0.56 s 3436 kb	~ 5.34
Japanese	aedges pedges etasks stasks tcpu space	153 725 950 851 0.56 s 4053 kb	aedges pedges etasks stasks tcpu space	153 725 893 851 0.07 s 604 kb	~ 8.40
Speed-Up	~ 5.29		~ 8.10		

test data. As both systems implement the same common typed feature structure formalism and obey the [incr tsdb()] application program interface, the matrix is complete and for each corresponding pair it has been confirmed that the results across systems yield an exact match (the minor diversions in task accounting are due to slightly different sets of 'quick check' paths and to a technical difference in how inflectional rules are applied by PET). Therefore, the complete symmetric matrix allows contrastive analyses both across grammars (vertically comparing within a column) and across platforms (horizontally comparing within a row). Before looking at the diagonals of the matrix – comparing across grammars and platforms simultaneously – we will use the available data to observe a number of relevant differences in the two grammars and parsing systems, respectively.

Comparing the two grammars, it seems to be the case that the Japanese grammar presents a smaller challenge to the processing system than is posed by the English grammar: while the absolute differences in the total numbers of passive edges (as a measure of global ambiguity, say) and overall parse times could in principle be a property of different test corpora (i.e. suggest that the Japanese sample on average was significantly less ambiguous and therefore easier to analyze than the English data), putting the two metrics into proportion reveals a genuine difference between the two grammars. Assuming that the average cost to build a single passive edge is relatively independent of the input data, the ratio of passive edges built per second is 625 (English) to 1295 (Japanese) for the LKB and 3304 to 10357, respectively, for PET. Further looking at the average size of a passive edge – i.e. relating the average amount of dynamically allocated memory during parsing (*space*) to the total number of passive edges built – suggests an explanation for the higher cost per edge in the English grammar: the ratio of *space* per passive edge is 9·3 kb (English) to 5·6 kb (Japanese) for the LKB (i.e. a ratio of 1·66) and 1·9 kb to 0·8 kb, respectively, for PET (i.e. a ratio of 2·38). Ignoring the somewhat surprising mismatch in exactly how much less memory is allocated per edge for the Japanese grammar in the two platforms for a moment, parsing with the Japanese grammar clearly seems to take both less time and memory.[14] The difference in average allocation per passive edge (the ratios of $\frac{9\cdot3}{5\cdot6} = 1\cdot66$ for the LKB constrasted with $\frac{1\cdot9}{0\cdot8}$ = 2·38 for PET, on the other hand, points to another differences between the grammars that, in turn, makes an asymmetry between the two platforms surface. Unlike the LKB, the PET grammar preprocessor deploys a technique known as *unfilling* (Götz, 1993; Gerdemann, 1995; Callmeier, 2000) – essentially a recursive elimination of information in feature structures that is implicit in the type of the structure – to reduce feature structure size at run-time. While the English LinGO grammar has been hand-tuned to achieve an effect similar to unfilling through an increased use of types (Flickinger, 2000), such a manual optimization has not been applied to the Japanese grammar. Accordingly, PET obtains a bigger boost from the unfilling operation for structures of the Japanese grammar than it does for English (while the LKB in both cases uses the complete structures). The unfilling advantage on the Japanese grammar also explains the observed difference in the ratios of average cost per passive edge (measured as *pedges* per second: $\frac{1295}{625} = 2\cdot07$ for the LKB vs. $\frac{10357}{3304} = 3\cdot13$ for PET); again, the comparatively better performance of PET on the Japanese grammar almost exactly equals the relative ratio in edge size ($\frac{2\cdot07}{3\cdot13} = 0\cdot66$ vs. $\frac{1\cdot66}{2\cdot38} = 0\cdot69$). We can therefore conclude that the overall vertical speed-up across the two grammars (5·29 for the LKB and 8·10 for PET) accumulates three factors: (i) reduced processing complexity (partly due to smaller feature structures) for the Japanese grammar, (ii) reduced test corpus complexity (to account for the additional speed-up over the factor-of-two decrease in cost per edge observed in the LKB), and (iii) increased unfilling efficiency (explaining why PET performs relatively better on the Japanese than on the English grammar).

Finally, what if we pretended that the comparison matrix was only partially available, say providing one profile of the LKB applied to the English grammar and another sample of PET processing the Japanese grammar? At first, it seems nothing much can be concluded from the observation that PET takes 0·07 seconds to solve one problem while the LKB requires 2·96 seconds to solve a different problem. Without knowledge about the complexity of the actual problem, relating raw processing times must be completely uninformative. To arrive at a comparative assessment of relative performance for the two systems, instead, would require a derived measure of generalized (or inherent) complexity, a metric that with sufficient confidence can be expected to provide a stable predictor of processing cost independent of the grammar and type of test data. From some of the observations reviewed in the previous paragraphs, it follows that the rate of passive (or active) edges per (cpu) second will not be a good measure because the proportion of successful vs. failing unifications may vary drastically across grammars (and indeed does for the data in Table 19.7), where only succeeding unifications will be reflected as an edge in the chart. By the same token, looking at *stasks* per second would suffer from the same potential for skewing.

But what about the ratio of executed parser actions (*etasks*) per second of total parsing time? Applying this metric to the problem at hand, we obtain $\frac{12757}{2009} = 6.35$ and $\frac{11680}{1520} = 7.68$ for the lower right to upper left and upper right to lower left diagonals of Table 19.7, respectively. If executed tasks per second was a suitably independent metric, the diagonal comparison would thus predict that PET is between a factor of 6.35 and 7.68 more efficient than the LKB. Looking at the actual values (speed-ups of 5.34 and 8.40 on the English and Japanese grammars, respectively) the prediction is reasonably accurate; it would indeed seem that the average cost of executing a single parser task is a relatively stable indicator of overall system efficiency, at least for two platforms that despite all their technical differences share a large number of basic assumptions and design. At this point, however, we can only speculate about why *etasks* per seconds appears to be a surprisingly good metric of (abstract) efficiency for the two systems considered. Firstly, total parsing times are dominated by feature structure manipulation, that is calls to the unification and copy routines; executing a parser task is the fundamental operation that (in most cases) requires exactly one unification and, for some subset of tasks, also a subsequent copy. Independent of the unification to copy cost and the unification failure to success ratios, all constraint solver activity somehow originates in a task execution. Secondly, even with moderate-size and mildly ambiguous test data, the number of executed tasks will be very large and therefore the ratio of *etasks* per cpu second has been found to be quite stable across varying test data or grammars. Thirdly, where two (closely related) systems incorporate similar approaches to parsing and reducing search, the number of parser tasks that come to be executed will correlate in some informal sense to the size of the search space (or problem complexity) that has been explored; therefore relating it to the time that a system takes to solve that problem yields a measure of efficiency. Obviously, these conclusions are necessarily preliminary and, given remaining noise in the cost per parser task across platforms and grammars, the metric proposed can only approximate relative efficiency; indeed, looking at another broad-coverage HPSG – viz. the German Verb*mobil* grammar – we found the general prediction confirmed but the variance of diagonal comparison slightly larger than with the English-Japanese pairing.

6.   Conclusion – Recent Developments

Precise, in-depth comparison has enabled a large, multi-national group of developers to quantify and exchange algorithmic knowledge and benefit from each others' experience. The [incr tsdb()] profiling package has been integrated with some six processing environments for (HPSG-type) unification grammars and has thus facilitated a previously unmatched degree of cross-fertilization. Many of the parameters of variation in system design and optimization – including the choice of parsing strategy, feature structure encoding, and unification scheme – require detailed knowledge about the relative contributions of sub-tasks (feature structure unification vs. copying, for example) to the overall problem size as well as a fine-grained, accurate understanding of which aspects of the problem (as defined by the grammar and input data) are especially hard on the processor. Our integrated competence and performance profiling approach aims to make appropriate data and suitable analysis techniques available to grammar and system engineers.

The modular PET platform provides an experimentation tool box that allows developers to combine various encoding and processing techniques and rapidly assess both their strong and weak points. The attractive practical performance of the cheap parser has made it the preferred run-time system for test set processing in the development of several large-scale HPSG grammars. PET has also been successfully deployed in commercial products.

As this play was first brought to stage early in 2000, obviously there have been a number of recent developments not reflected here. Beyond what was shown in Acts 3 through 5, the range of experimental choices in PET has been increased significantly, particularly in the areas of fixed-arity feature structure encodings (in the tradition of Prolog compilation) and ambiguity packing (from the LKB). Callmeier (2002) presents an empirical study comparing the benefits of various feature structure encoding techniques. A teichoscopic view of collaborative activities among the groups has been produced by Oepen et al. (2002).

Acknowledgments

This play builds heavily on results obtained through collaboration between a largish group of people at several sites. The peripeteia achieved in this period of close collaboration between sites over several years would not have been possible without the main characters, researchers, engineers, grammarians, and managers at Saarbrücken, Stanford, Tokyo, and Sussex University. To name a few, John Carroll, Liviu Ciortuz, Ann Copestake, Dan Flickinger, Bernd Kiefer, Hans-Ulrich Krieger, Takaki Makino, Rob Malouf, Yusuke Miyao, Stefan Müller, Mark-Jan Nederhof, Günter Neumann, Takashi Ninomiya, Kenji Nishida, Ivan Sag, Kentaro Torisawa, Jun-ichi Tsujii, and Hans Uszkoreit have all greatly contributed to the development of efficient HPSG processors as described above. Many of the individual achievements and results are reflected in the bibliographic references given throughout the play.

Notes

1. See 'http://www.dfki.de/lt/' and 'http://www.coli.uni-sb.de/' for information on the DFKI Language Technology Laboratory and the Computational Linguistics Department at Saarland University, respectively.

2. The 'http://lingo.stanford.edu/' web pages list HPSG-related projects and people involved at CSLI, and also provide an on-line demonstration of the LKB system and LinGO grammar.

3. Information on the Tokyo Laboratory, founded and managed by Professor Jun-ichi Tsujii, can be found at 'http://www.is.s.u-tokyo.ac.uk/'.

4. In the HPSG universe (and accordingly our present play) the term 'grammar' is typically used holistically, referring to the linguistic system comprised of (at least) the type hierarchy, lexicon, and rule apparatus.

5. (Meta-)Systems like PLEUK (Calder, 1993) and Hdrug (van Noord and Bouma, 1997) that facilitate the exploration of multiple descriptive formalisms and processing strategies come with slightly more sophisticated benchmarking facilities and visualization tools. However, they still largely operate on monolithic, unannotated input data sets, restrict accounting of system results to a small number of parameters (e.g. number of analyses, overall processing time, memory consumption, possibly the total number of chart edges), and only offer a limited, predefined choice of analysis views.

6. See 'http://www.coli.uni-sb.de/itsdb/' for the (draft) [incr tsdb()] user manual, pronunciation rules, and instructions on obtaining and installing the package.

7. While wellformedness and item length are properties of the test data proper, the indicators for average ambiguity and feature structure (fs) size were obtained using the release version of the LinGO grammar, frozen in August 1999. Here and in the tables to come the symbol '♯' indicates absolute numbers, while 'φ' denotes arithmetic mean values. Coverage on the '*blend*' corpus is comparatively low, as it includes Verb*mobil* data (specifically vocabulary) that became available only after the grammar had been frozen for our experiments.

8. Still, the two systems are by no means merely two instantiations of the same concept, and continue to focus on different application contexts. While the LKB is primarily used for grammar development, education, and generation (in an AAC basic research project), PAGE develoment since 1997 has emphasized robust parsing methods with speech recognizer output (in application to Verb*mobil*).

9. Although the intermediate feature structure is not copied, it is used to compute the 'quick-check' vector for the next argument position to be filled; as mentioned above, this information is sufficient to filter the majority (up to ninety five per cent) of subsequent operations on the 'active' edge.

10. There is an additional element (termed 'excursion') to the algorithm proposed in Oepen and Carroll (2000) that aims to take advantage of the feature structure associated with an active edge while it is still valid (i.e. within the same unification generation). Put simply, the hyper-active parser is allowed to deviate slightly from the control strategy governed by the agenda, to try and combine the active edge with a single suitable passive edge immediately.

11. For a given test corpus, the optimal set of key daughters can be determined (semi- or fully automatically) by comparing results for unidirectional left to right to pure right to left rule instantiation; the optimal key position for each rule is the one that generates the smallest number of active items.

12. The size of one dag node in the PET implementation of the unification algorithm of Tomabechi (1991) is only twenty four bytes, compared to, for example, fifty six in the Lisp-based LKB system.

13. To obtain the results on the '*blend*' test set shown in Table 19.6, an upper limit on the number of passive edges was imposed in the cheap parser; with a permissible maximum of twenty thousand edges, around fifty (in a sense pathological) items from the '*blend*' set cannot be processed within the limit and, accordingly, are excluded in the overall assessment. Maximal parsing times for the remaining test items range up to around fourteen seconds for input strings that approximate twenty thousand edges and derive a very large number of readings.

14. The calculation of average allocation cost per passive edge is, of course, only an approximation, in that other computation (primarily dag and arc allocations during failed unification attempts and the edge structures themselves) also contributes to overall memory consumption. However, both platforms utilize a hyper-active chart parser, so active edges do not have a feature structure associated with them; likewise, a high filter efficiency reduces the number of failed unifications, such that (the feature structures associated with) passive edges certainly account for the bulk of dynamic allocation.

References

Aït-Kaci, H. (1991). *Warren's Abstract Machine: A Tutorial Reconstruction.* MIT Press, Cambridge, MA.

Bouma, G. and van Noord, G. (1993). Head-driven parsing for lexicalist grammars. Experimental results. In *Proceedings of the 6th Conference of the European Chapter of the ACL*, pages 71–80, Utrecht, The Netherlands.

Callmeier, U. (2000). PET — A platform for experimentation with efficient HPSG processing techniques. *Natural Language Engineering*, 6 (1) (Special Issue on Efficient Processing with HPSG):99–108.

Calder, J. (1993). Graphical interaction with constraint-based grammars. In *Proceedings of the 3rd Pacific Rim Conference on Computational Linguistics*, pages 160–169, Vancouver, BC, Canada.

Callmeier, U. (2002). Preprocessing and encoding techniques in PET. In Oepen, S., Flickinger, D., Tsujii, J., and Uszkoreit, H., editors, *Collaborative Language Engineering. A Case Study in Efficient Grammar-based Processing*. CSLI Publications, Stanford, CA.

Carpenter, B. (1992). *The Logic of Typed Feature Structures*. Cambridge University Press, Cambridge, UK.

Carroll, J. (1994). Relating complexity to practical performance in parsing with wide-coverage unification grammars. In *Proceedings of the 32nd Meeting of the Association for Computational Linguistics*, pages 287–294, Las Cruces, NM.

Carroll, J., Copestake, A., Flickinger, D., and Poznanski, V. (1999). An efficient chart generator for (semi-)lexicalist grammars. In *Proceedings of the 7th European Workshop on Natural Language Generation*, pages 86–95, Toulouse, France.

Ciortuz, L. (2001). LIGHT. A feature constraint language applied to parsing with large-scale HPSG grammars. Unpublished DFKI research report, Deutsches Forschungszentrum für Künstliche Intelligenz, Saarbrücken, Germany.

Copestake, A. (1992). The ACQUILEX LKB. Representation issues in semi-automatic acquisition of large lexicons. In *Proceedings of the 3rd ACL Conference on Applied Natural Language Processing*, pages 88–96, Trento, Italy.

Erbach, G. (1991a). An environment for experimenting with parsing strategies. In Mylopoulos, J. and Reiter, R., editors, *Proceedings of the 12th Interna-*

tional Joint Conference on Artificial Intelligence, pages 931–937, San Mateo, CA. Morgan Kaufmann Publishers.

Erbach, G. (1991b). A flexible parser for a linguistic development environment. In Herzog, O. and Rollinger, C.-R., editors, *Text Understanding in LILOG*, pages 74–87. Springer, Berlin, Germany.

Flickinger, D. (2000). On building a more efficient grammar by exploiting types. *Natural Language Engineering*, 6 (1) (Special Issue on Efficient Processing with HPSG):15–28.

Flickinger, D., Nerbonne, J., Sag, I. A., and Wasow, T. (1987). Toward evaluation of NLP systems. Technical report, Hewlett-Packard Laboratories. Distributed at the 24th Annual Meeting of the Association for Computational Linguistics.

Flickinger, D. P. and Sag, I. A. (1998). Linguistic Grammars Online. A multi-purpose broad-coverage computational grammar of English. In *CSLI Bulletin 1999*, pages 64–68, Stanford, CA. CSLI Publications.

Gerdemann, D. (1995). Term encoding of typed feature structures. In *Proceedings of the 4th International Workshop on Parsing Technologies*, pages 89–97, Prague, Czech Republic.

Götz, T. (1993). A normal form for typed feature structures. Magisterarbeit, Universität Tübingen, Tübingen, Germany.

Kay, M. (1989). Head-driven parsing. In *Proceedings of the 1st International Workshop on Parsing Technologies*, pages 52–62, Pittsburgh, PA.

Kiefer, B., Krieger, H.-U., Carroll, J., and Malouf, R. (1999). A bag of useful techniques for efficient and robust parsing. In *Proceedings of the 37th Meeting of the Association for Computational Linguistics*, pages 473–480, College Park, MD.

Krieger, H.-U. and Schäfer, U. (1994). *TDL* — A type description language for constraint-based grammars. In *Proceedings of the 15th International Conference on Computational Linguistics*, pages 893–899, Kyoto, Japan.

Malouf, R., Carroll, J., and Copestake, A. (2000). Efficient feature structure operations without compilation. *Natural Language Engineering*, 6 (1) (Special Issue on Efficient Processing with HPSG):29–46.

van Noord, G. (1997). An efficient implementation of the head-corner parser. *Computational Linguistics*, 23 (3):425–456.

van Noord, G. and Bouma, G. (1997). HDRUG: A flexible and extendible development environment for natural language processing. In *Proceedings of the EACL/ACL workshop ENVGRAM,* Madrid, Spain.

Oepen, S. and Carroll, J. (2000). Performance profiling for parser engineering. *Natural Language Engineering*, 6 (1) (Special Issue on Efficient Processing with HPSG):81–97.

Oepen, S., Flickinger, D., Tsujii, J., and Uszkoreit, H., editors (2002). *Collaborative Language Engineering. A Case Study in Efficient Grammar-based Processing*. CSLI Publications, Stanford, CA.

Oepen, S. and Flickinger, D. P. (1998). Towards systematic grammar profiling. Test suite technology ten years after. *Journal of Computer Speech and Language*, 12 (4) (Special Issue on Evaluation):411–436.

Oepen, S., Netter, K., and Klein, J. (1997). TSNLP — Test Suites for Natural Language Processing. In Nerbonne, J., editor, *Linguistic Databases*, pages 13–36. CSLI Publications, Stanford, CA.

Shakespeare, W. (1623). *Measure for Measure*. I. Iaggard and E. Blount, London, UK, first folio edition.

Siegel, M. (2000). HPSG analysis of Japanese. In Wahlster, W., editor, *Verbmobil. Foundations of Speech-to-Speech Translation*, pages 265–280. Springer, Berlin, Germany.

Tomabechi, H. (1991). Quasi-destructive graph unification. In *Proceedings of the 29th Meeting of the Association for Computational Linguistics*, pages 315–322, Berkeley, CA.

Torisawa, K. and Tsujii, J. (1996). Computing phrasal signs in HPSG prior to parsing. In *Proceedings of the 16th International Conference on Computational Linguistics*, pages 949–955, Copenhagen, Denmark.

Uszkoreit, H., Backofen, R., Busemann, S., Diagne, A. K., Hinkelman, E. A., Kasper, W., Kiefer, B., Krieger, H.-U., Netter, K., Neumann, G., Oepen, S., and Spackman, S. P. (1994). DISCO — an HPSG-based NLP system and its application for appointment scheduling. In *Proceedings of the 15th International Conference on Computational Linguistics*, Kyoto, Japan.

Wahlster, W., editor (2000). *Verbmobil. Foundations of Speech-to-Speech Translation*. Springer, Berlin, Germany.

Wroblewski, D. A. (1987). Non-destructive graph unification. In *Proceedings of the 6th National Conference on Artificial Intelligence*, pages 582–587, Seattle, WA.

Index

accept, 137, 141
acquiring subcategorisation frames, 62
active edge, 376, 379–380, 382–383, 390, 392
adjacency sequence, 94–95
adjunction, 127, 130, 155, 159, 161
  null (NA), 127, 133, 142
  obligatory (OA), 127, 133, 142
algorithm, 299–304
alpha-reduce (α-reduce), 137, 141, 148
ambiguity packing, 307–320
  local, 309
anchor node, 126
anchor, 75
ANLT grammar formalism, 308
approximation
  as fixpoint construction, 231–234, 240–242
  as least fixpoint construction, 233
  of Context-Free Grammar, 229–248
argument table, 76
ATIS grammar, 74, 187–188, 193, 197–198
auxiliary tree, 75, 127, 154
  modifier, 77

Bayesian modeling, 294
best-parse parsing, 125–126
beta-reduce (β-reduce), 137, 140–141, 148
bidirectional parsing, 178–180
bidirectional rule instantiation, 379–380
bilexical dependencies, 329
BNC (British National Corpus), 59
boosting algorithms, 42–46
bottom-up
  filtering, 190, 193
  prefix merging, 192, 194, 197
  recognition, 251
bpack, 134, 137–139, 141, 148–149, 151–152
British National Corpus, 59
BUP parser, 189–190

c-structure, 308, 311
captions
  table, 300, 302, 305
CFG *see* Context-Free Grammar
character-level parsing, 346

chart parser, 2, 91, 309–310, 315
chart parser
  agenda-based
    for DPSG, 92, 95,–98
    for DPSGchart parser, 351
  for DPSG, 92, 95–101
  for Probabilistic DPSG, 98–101
  probabilistic, 351, 361
    correctness of grammar scoring condition, 365
    correctness of rule introduction condition, 365
    correctness of word introduction condition, 365
    correctness proof, 366
    pseudocode, 369
    Viterbi, 360
chart parsing, 185–199, 315–316, 341, 354, 359
  left-corner, 185–199, 317–318
CHEAP parser, 384–387, 391
chunk parsing, 58
CKY parser (*see also* CYK parser), 2, 23, 162, 186–187, 189, 197–199, 309, 319, 360, 379
CLE (Core Language Engine), 229, 242, 249
closure, 135, 284–286
cochain, 241
Cocke-Schwartz filtering, 192–194
CommandTalk system, 187
complement adjunct table, 76
completeness, 257, 262
  of a probabilistic chart parser, 363–364, 366
    edge-driven rule introduction condition, 364, 367–368
    proof, 364
complexity, 343
  space, 264
  time, 264, 282–284
compositional semantics, 326
context daughter, 93–102, 105
context vector, 299–300
  center, 300
  distribution, 299
Context-Free Grammar, 91–92, 98, 101, 103, 125–126, 128, 135, 183–184, 270–271, 274, 285–287, 293, 328
  approximation of, 229–248

Lexicalized Probabilistic, 59
Multiple, 252, 257, 267
Probabilistic, 20–28, 65, 98–100, 102–103, 105, 107–108, 117–123, 247–248, 332, 351, 359
Weighted, 22
context-freeness
    of Linear Indexed Grammar, 160
    of natural language, 2
convergence bounds
    uniform, 30, 34
Core Language Engine (CLE), 190, 229, 242, 249
correct prefix property (*see also* valid prefix property), 171–178
correctness
    of a probabilistic chart parser, 364–365
        grammar scoring condition, 365–366
        rule introduction condition, 365
        word introduction condition, 365
        proof, 366
crossing branches, 91–92
crown, 241
cutoff grammar, 80, 83–84
cyclic restrictor, 245
CYK parser, *see also* CKY parser, 162, 167, 251, 323

Data-Oriented Parsing (DOP), 10, 323, 326–328, 332–334, 336
DCC (dynamic distributional classification) *see* induction algorithm, 299
debugging facility, 379
deduction step, 160
dependency parsing, 58
derivation tree, 127, 378
derived tree, 127, 273–276, 286–287
description length, 294
    empirical, 294
    gain, 294–295
        calculation, 294–295
        maximum, 295
    value curve, 297–298, 301, 303
    see also minimal description length (MDL), 293–294
discontinuous constituents, 91–92, 95, 101, 104
Discontinuous Phrase Structure Grammar, 6, 91–92, 95, 101, 103
    parsing, 91–105
    Probabilistic, 6, 98–105
        parsing, 98–105
    restricted, 104
discontinuous tree, 92–99, 101–104
discotree, 92–98, 101–102
distribution-free methods
    19–52 distributional analysis, 299
distributional analysis
    distance measure, 300
document retrieval, 3
dominance, 93, 105

immediate, 240
DOP *see* Data-Oriented Parsing
DPSG parsing, 91–105
DPSG *see also* Discontinuous Phrase Structure Grammar, 91–92
dynamic
    distributional classification (DCC) *see also* induction algorithm, 299
    grammars, 347
    programming, 65, 189

Earley parsing, 184, 189, 194, 197, 360
Earley's algorithm, 2, 166–169, 171–178, 196–199
edge, 354
    active, 376, 379–380, 382–383, 390, 392
    passive, 376, 378–380, 383, 386–388, 390, 392
edge-based best-first chart parsing, 104
edge-driven rule introduction strategy, 364
elementary tree, 75, 158
empirical risk minimization, 29, 32, 35
empty categories, 184, 192–193, 197
encode
    data, 294
    theory, 294
entropy, 104, 294
    maximum-entropy model, 19–20, 23, 46–49, 110
epsilon rules, 314–315
ERM, *see* empirical risk minimization
estimating probabilities, 109–110
expected governors, 58, 65
extended extracted grammar, 84

f-structure (feature structure), 308, 311
FACILE project, 4
feature structure
    copying, 379
    encoding, 391
    expansion, 216
    sharing, 385
    unfilling, 216, 389
    unification, 203–204, 206, 213–214, 216–217, 220, 222, 224
filtering
    bottom-up, 190, 193
    Cocke-Schwartz, 192–194
    left-corner, 192–194, 197
    top-down, 188, 190, 192, 197
finite-state parsing, 58
fixed-arity encoding, 391
foot node, 75, 126, 154
free word order, 91

Gemini grammar, 243–244
generalized LR parsing, 307, 309
generalized reduction, 203–214, 216–225
    evaluation, 220, 222

GR-paths, 204, 224
GR-vectors, 223
incremental GR algorithm, 218
non-incremental GR algorithm, 217
generative models, 327
GHR (Graham-Harrison-Ruzzo) parsing, 2, 186,
    189, 194, 197–199, 360
GLR
    algorithm, 10, 309, 317, 319
    parser, 197–199, 309–311, 313, 316–317
    parsing, 2, 184, 190, 197
Gorn address, 127, 142, 152
goto transition, 129–142
GR, *see* generalized reduction
grammar approximation, 229–248
    probabilistic, 247–248
    regular, 230
grammar binarization, 358
grammar induction, 291–306
    objective function, 293
    search, 293–295, 297, 299
    space, 293
grammar modularity, 285–287
grammar scoring condition, 365
grammatical relations, 58, 60
    consistent sets of, 67
    weight threshold, 63
    weighted, 60

Hdrug environment, 392
head percolation table, 75
head-dependent relations, 57
Head-driven Phrase Structure Grammar, 201,
    215–216, 373–374, 381, 387, 390–392
Hidden Markov Models, 58, 82, 109
Hoare order, 241
HPSG *see also* Head-driven Phrase Structure
    Grammar, 201, 215, 373, 381
hyper-active parsing, 208, 379–381
hypergraphs, 352–371
    B-graphs, 353–354
    directed hypergraphs, 352
    hyperarcs, 353
        B-arcs, 353
    hypergraphs and satisfiability, 353
    induced B-graphs, 355
    paths, 353
        B-paths, 354
        simple paths, 353
hyperplane classifiers, 26, 34–40, 42, 45
hypothesis, 160

immediate dominance, 240
induced B-graphs, 355
induction algorithm
    basic MDL, 295–296
    DCC, 299–304

gold standard, 297
    pseudo, 296
    simulated, 302
information extraction, 4
information retrieval, 3
    cross-lingual, 4
initial tree, 75, 127, 158
interleaved unification
    307–320 item, 160
item
    axiom, 258
    dotted, 134, 359
    goal item, 258
    final item, 160

JSGF (Java Speech Grammar Format), 339–340,
    347–349

kernel, 149–150
KXDC project, 4

Lancaster-Leeds treebank, 119
language models, 323
LCFlex parser, 4, 10, 317–318, 320
LCFRS (Linear Context-Free Rewriting System),
    270
left factoring, 194–197
left-corner
    chart parsing, 185–199
    filtering, 192–194, 197
    parsing, 185–186, 188–195, 197–198, 317–319
left-to-right parsing, 126
leftmost daughter, 93
lexicon restrictor, 230
LFG (Lexical Functional Grammar), 201, 203
LIG *see* Linear Indexed Grammar
LIGHT system, 203–204, 206–208, 214, 220–221,
    224–225
LiLFeS system, 215
Linear Indexed Grammar, 7, 157–158, 160–162,
    166–169, 180–182
    context-freeness property, 160
    dependent child, 158
    dependent descendent, 158
    dependent successor, 158
    derivation relation, 158
    mother, 158
    parsing, 157–182
linear models, 20–23
linear precedence, 93
LinGO grammar, 8, 205–206, 212, 214–215, 217,
    219–224, 245–248, 374, 377, 379–380,
    382–384, 386–387, 389, 392
LIQUID project, 3
LKB system, 206–207, 214, 379–381, 384,
    387–392
LMG (Literal Movement Grammar), 270

local ambiguity packing, 309
log-linear probability model, 110
long distance dependencies, 75–76, 80
look-ahead, 266
LR parsing, 2, 10, 125–126, 128, 149
  "true" LR parser, 126, 149
  "early reduction", 130–132, 151–152
  degenerate models for TAG, 126, 129–133
  for CFGs, 129, 148
LR parsing
  for TAG
    closure, 135
    congruence relation, 134, 149
    driver, 140–141
    general case, 142
    implementation, 142
    minimization, 149
    NA/OA case, 133, 142
    Nederhof's model, 131–132, 151–152
    properties, 148
    proposed model, 133–140, 150
    table generation, 136
  generalized, 307
  lookahead, 152
  Nederhof's model for TAG, 131–132, 151–152
  probabilistic, 59
LTAG (Lexicalized Tree-Adjoining Grammar), 6,
    74–75, 78–81, 86–88

machine translation, 2–5
margin bounds for parsing, 38–39
margins on training examples, 35
Markov Grammars, 329
Markov random fields (MRFs), 23, 47–49
maximum entropy model, 19–20, 23, 46–49, 110
maximum entropy, 104
MCS (mildly context-sensitive) grammars, 270,
    286, 293–295
MDL see Minimal Description Length Principle
memory consumption, 375, 380–381, 384, 386
memory management, 384
metrics, 376, 387
  aedges, 383–384
  etasks, 382, 390
  filter, 382
  lexical, 386
  out, 386
  parser, 386
  pedges, 384, 386, 389
  space, 382, 389
  stasks, 382, 390
  tcpu, 381–382, 387
  [incr tsdb()], 376–378, 383, 387–388,
    391–392
mildly context-sensitive (see also MCS), 254
Minimal Description Length principle see also
    description length, 9, 291
Minimalist Grammar, 9, 251–256, 260, 266–267

feature, 251, 253
parsing, 265
recognition, 251
Minimalist Program, 9, 251
modifier auxiliary tree, 77
Most Probable Parse, 91–92, 101, 113
MRF (see also Markov random field), 48
multi-layered perceptron, 109
Multiple Context-Free Grammar, 252
multiple-tree interpretations, 347

narrow yield, 257
Negative Range Concatenation Grammar
    276–281 NEGRA corpus, 6
NEGRA corpus, 91–92, 101, 104
neural networks, 107–109, 120
null adjunction (NA), 127, 133, 142

obligatory adjunction (OA), 127, 133, 142
Occam's razor, 293
optical character recognition, 4
OSF logic, 215
  atomic OSF constraints, 215
over copying, 380
OVIS
  system, 323–326
  treebank, 324–326

PAGE system, 206–207, 214, 379–382, 384,
    386–387, 392
parametric models, 19–20, 27
parse existence, 354
parse forest, 65
parser tasks, 382, 390
PARSEVAL, 62
parsing schemata, 160
parsing
  best-parse, 125–126
  bidirectional, 176
  chart, 2, 185–199, 315–316, 354, 359
    left-corner, 318, 317
  chunk, 58
  CKY, 2, 184–185, 197, 319
  dependency, 58
  Earley, 184, 190, 194, 197
  finite-state, 58
  GHR, 2, 184, 189, 194, 197
  GLR, 2, 184, 190, 197, 309–311, 316–317
  head-driven, 381
  hyper-active, 380, 384–385
  key-driven, 380, 382
  left-corner, 185–199
  left-to-right, 126
  LR, 10, 125–126, 128, 149
    for TAG: closure, 135
    for TAG: congruence relation, 134, 149

for TAG: degenerate models, 126, 129–133
for TAG: driver, 140–141
for TAG: general case, 142
for TAG: implementation, 142
for TAG: minimization, 149
for TAG: NA/OA case, 133, 142
for TAG: Nederhof's model for TAG, 131–132, 151–152
for TAG: properties, 148
for TAG: proposed model for TAG, 150
for TAG: proposed model, 133–140
for TAG: table generation, 136,
for TAG, 136
lookahead, 152
probabilistic, 59
"true" LR parser, 126, 149
"early reduction", 130–132, 151–152
for CFG, 129, 148
generalized, 307
neural network, 107–123
probabilistic, 59, 323, 361, 369
of DPSG, 91, 104
statistical *see also* statistical parsing, 19–35, 37–52, 57, 117
strategy, 378–380, 382, 391
Viterbi, 328, 333, 356–357, 360
passive edge, 376, 378–380, 383, 386–388, 390, 392
PATR-II grammar, 203, 229, 231, 242–243, 245–246
PCFG *see* Probabilistic Context-Free Grammar
PDPSG *see* Probabilistic Discontinuous Prase Structure Grammar
Penn Treebank, 74, 118–119, 123, 125, 150, 183, 185, 187–188, 197, 296–297, 299–300, 368
perceptron
algorithm, 34, 38–40, 44–47, 49–50
multi-layered, 109
performance profiling, 373, 376, 386, 391
PET system, 204, 206, 214, 375, 382, 384–392
PHOENIX parser, 4, 10, 339
PLEUK environment, 392
polynomial parse time, 270, 283, 285–286
polynomial time parsing, 270
Positive Range Concatenation Grammar, 270
PP attachment, 68
PRCG (Positive Range Concatenation Grammar) 267
270–276 pre-unification filter, 379
pre-unification filter, 380
precision
weighted, 62
predicative auxiliary tree, 79
probabilistic
chart parser, 361
pseudocode, 369
Probabilistic

Context-Free Grammar (PCFG), 20–28, 98–100, 102–103, 105, 117–123, 247–248, 332, 351, 359
Discontinuous Prase Structure Grammar (PDPSG), 6, 98–105
probabilistic
DPSG parsing, 98–105
LR parsing, 59
parsing, 323
probability estimation, 109–110
profiling environment, 376
PRTN (probabilistic recursive transition network), 340–342, 347–349

question answering, 3
quick check, 203–225, 235–237, 379
compilation of, 209
computation of QC-vectors, 212
filter, 204–207, 384, 386, 392
main idea, 206
pre-computation of QC-vectors, 210
QC-paths, 204, 223–224
QC-vectors, 206–213, 223, 236–237
technique, 235
two-stage computation of, 207
quick check
vector (*see also* quick check QC-vector), 236

Range Concatenation Grammar (RCG), 9, 369–387
range, 270
recall
weighted, 62
recognizer
bottom-up, 251
deterministic, 266
Earley, 265
top-down, 265
recursive restrictor, 246
reduction, 128–134, 138, 141, 148–149
generalized, 203–225
evaluation, 220, 222
GR-paths, 204, 224
GR-vectors, 223
incremental GR algorithm, 218
non-incremental GR algorithm, 217
regression testing, 378
regular grammar approximation, 230
restrictor
cyclic, 246
lexicon, 230
recursive, 246
rule, 230
risk minimization
empirical, 29, 32, 35
structural, 32–34
robustness, 323
rule filter, 235

rule instantiation, 381–382
  bidirectional, 379–380
rule introduction condition, 365
rule restrictor, 230

satisfiability
  hypergraphs and satisfiability, 353
seed grammar, 300
  category ratio, 300
semirings, 357
  $\preceq_S$-ordered c-semiring, 357
shared forest, 271, 274, 282, 287
shift, 141, 149
Shortest Movement Constraint, 254, 259, 267
shortest paths, 356
Simple Recurrent Network, 108–109
Simple Synchrony Network
  107–123 skipping, 345
soundness, 257, 260
Soup parser, 4, 10
sparse data, 108, 117–118
speech translation, 5
spine, 75,
spoken language understanding
  323–337 SSN parser
    7, 26
statistical learning theory, 27–29
statistical parsing, 19–35, 37–52, 57, 117
  semi-lexicalized, 59, 68
structural risk minimization, 32–34
structure building function
  merge, 253
  move, 253
subcategorisation frame
  acquisition, 62
subdiscotree, 93–95, 105
substitution node, 75, 126
substitution operation, 127
summarization, 4
supertagging, 82
support vector machine, 34, 36, 39–42, 50
SUSANNE corpus, 59, 118–119, 123

TAG see Tree-Adjoining Grammar
tagset table, 77
TDL formalism, 206, 394
Temporal Synchrony Variable Binding, 108
terminology extraction, 3
test corpus, 375
test suite, 376–377
text alignment, 4
top-down filtering, 188, 190, 192, 197
traversal, 354–355, 361–362
tree extraction procedure, 74
tree family, 84
tree frame, 80
tree, 252

auxiliary, 75, 127, 158
complete, 254
complex, 253
derivation, 127, 378
derived, 127, 273–276, 286–287
discontinuous, 92–99, 101–104
elementary, 75, 158
head, 253
initial, 75, 127, 158
maximal, 253
modifier auxiliary, 77
narrow yield, 257
simple, 253
yield, 254
Tree-Adjoining Grammar, 125–126, 135, 158,
    160–162
  Lexicalized (LTAG), 6, 74–75, 78–81, 86–88
  adjunction, 127, 130, 159, 161
  auxiliary tree, 158
  derivation relation, 157
  elementary tree, 158
  foot node, 158
  initial tree, 158
  linguistic relevance, 128
  LR parsing, 125–153
  normal form, 127, 133, 142, 145
  OA/NA, 142
    decomposition, 143
  parsing see also LR parsing, 133, 142, 148
  shorthand notation, 127, 142–143
  tabular parsing, 157–182
Tree-gram model
  324
    326–336 Tree-Insertion Grammar (TIG), 86
Tree-Insertion Grammar (TIG), 152
Tree-Insertion Grammar, 86, 152
  Lexicalized (LTIG), 86–87
treebank, 57, 327
  Lancaster-Leeds, 119
  NEGRA, 6, 91–92, 101, 104
  OVIS, 324–326
  Penn, 74, 125, 150, 183, 187
trunk, 75
TSNLP test suite, 377, 386

unification
  interleaved, 307–320
  unification-based grammar, 59, 65, 203–225,
    228–248
uniform convergence bounds, 30, 34
unsupervised learning, 62
update expression, 325
update semantics, 325

valid prefix property, 132, 136, 145, 149, 152
  see also correct prefix property, 169
Verbmobil system, 5, 9, 378, 381, 386–387, 390,
    392

Viterbi
  algorithm, 328, 333
  chart parser, 360
  parsing, 356–357

weak tabular interpretation, 180
weighted context-free grammar, 21–23
word introduction condition, 365

XTAG grammar, 74, 79, 84–85, 87, 125–126, 150

Text, Speech and Language Technology

1. H. Bunt and M. Tomita (eds.): *Recent Advances in Parsing Technology.* 1996
    ISBN 0-7923-4152-X
2. S. Young and G. Bloothooft (eds.): *Corpus-Based Methods in Language and Speech Processing.* 1997 ISBN 0-7923-4463-4
3. T. Dutoit: *An Introduction to Text-to-Speech Synthesis.* 1997 ISBN 0-7923-4498-7
4. L. Lebart, A. Salem and L. Berry: *Exploring Textual Data.* 1998
    ISBN 0-7923-4840-0
5. J. Carson-Berndsen, *Time Map Phonology.* 1998 ISBN 0-7923-4883-4
6. P. Saint-Dizier (ed.): *Predicative Forms in Natural Language and in Lexical Knowledge Bases.* 1999 ISBN 0-7923-5499-0
7. T. Strzalkowski (ed.): *Natural Language Information Retrieval.* 1999
    ISBN 0-7923-5685-3
8. J. Harrington and S. Cassiday: *Techniques in Speech Acoustics.* 1999
    ISBN 0-7923-5731-0
9. H. van Halteren (ed.): *Syntactic Wordclass Tagging.* 1999 ISBN 0-7923-5896-1
10. E. Viegas (ed.): *Breadth and Depth of Semantic Lexicons.* 1999 ISBN 0-7923-6039-7
11. S. Armstrong, K. Church, P. Isabelle, S. Nanzi, E. Tzoukermann and D. Yarowsky (eds.): *Natural Language Processing Using Very Large Corpora.* 1999
    ISBN 0-7923-6055-9
12. F. Van Eynde and D. Gibbon (eds.): *Lexicon Development for Speech and Language Processing.* 2000 ISBN 0-7923-6368-X; Pb: 07923-6369-8
13. J. Véronis (ed.): *Parallel Text Processing.* Alignment and Use of Translation Corpora. 2000 ISBN 0-7923-6546-1
14. M. Horne (ed.): *Prosody: Theory and Experiment.* Studies Presented to Gösta Bruce. 2000 ISBN 0-7923-6579-8
15. A. Botinis (ed.): *Intonation.* Analysis, Modelling and Technology. 2000
    ISBN 0-7923-6605-0
16. H. Bunt and A. Nijholt (eds.): *Advances in Probabilistic and Other Parsing Technologies.* 2000 ISBN 0-7923-6616-6
17. J.-C. Junqua and G. van Noord (eds.): *Robustness in Languages and Speech Technology.* 2001 ISBN 0-7923-6790-1
18. R.H. Baayen: *Word Frequency Distributions.* 2001 ISBN 0-7923-7017-1
19. B. Granström, D. House and. I. Karlsson (eds.): *Multimodality in Language and Speech Systems.* 2002 ISBN 1-4020-0635-7
20. M. Carl and A. Way (eds.): *Recent Advances in Example-Based Machine Translation.* 2003 ISBN 1-4020-1400-7; Pb 1-4020-1401-5
21. A. Abeillé: *Treebanks.* Building and Using Parsed Corpora. 2003
    ISBN 1-4020-1334-5; pb 1-4020-1335-3
22. J. van Kuppevelt and R.W. Smith (ed.): *Current and New Directions in Discourse and Dialogue.* 2003 ISBN 1-4020-1614-X; pb 1-4020-1615-8
23. H. Bunt, J. Carroll and G. Satta (eds.): *New Developments in Parsing Technology.* 2004 ISBN 1-4020-2293-X; pb 1-4020-2294-8

KLUWER ACADEMIC PUBLISHERS – DORDRECHT / BOSTON / LONDON